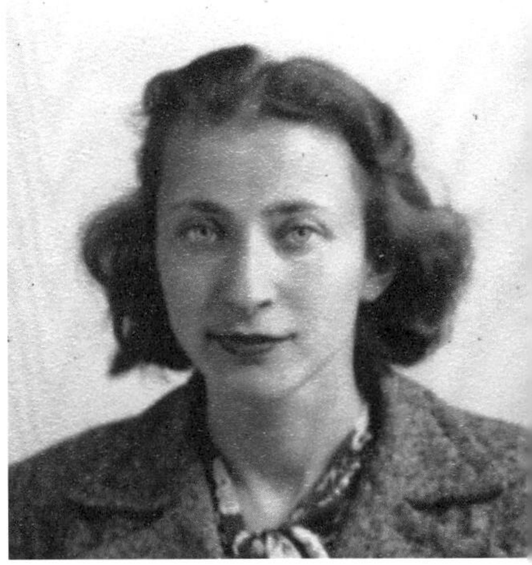

Unposted Letters

edited by
Jasia Reichardt

with a coda by
Nick Wadley

Unposted Letters
correspondence, diaries, drawings, documents
1940–1942

Franciszka Themerson
& Stefan Themerson

Gaberbocchus & De Harmonie
Amsterdam

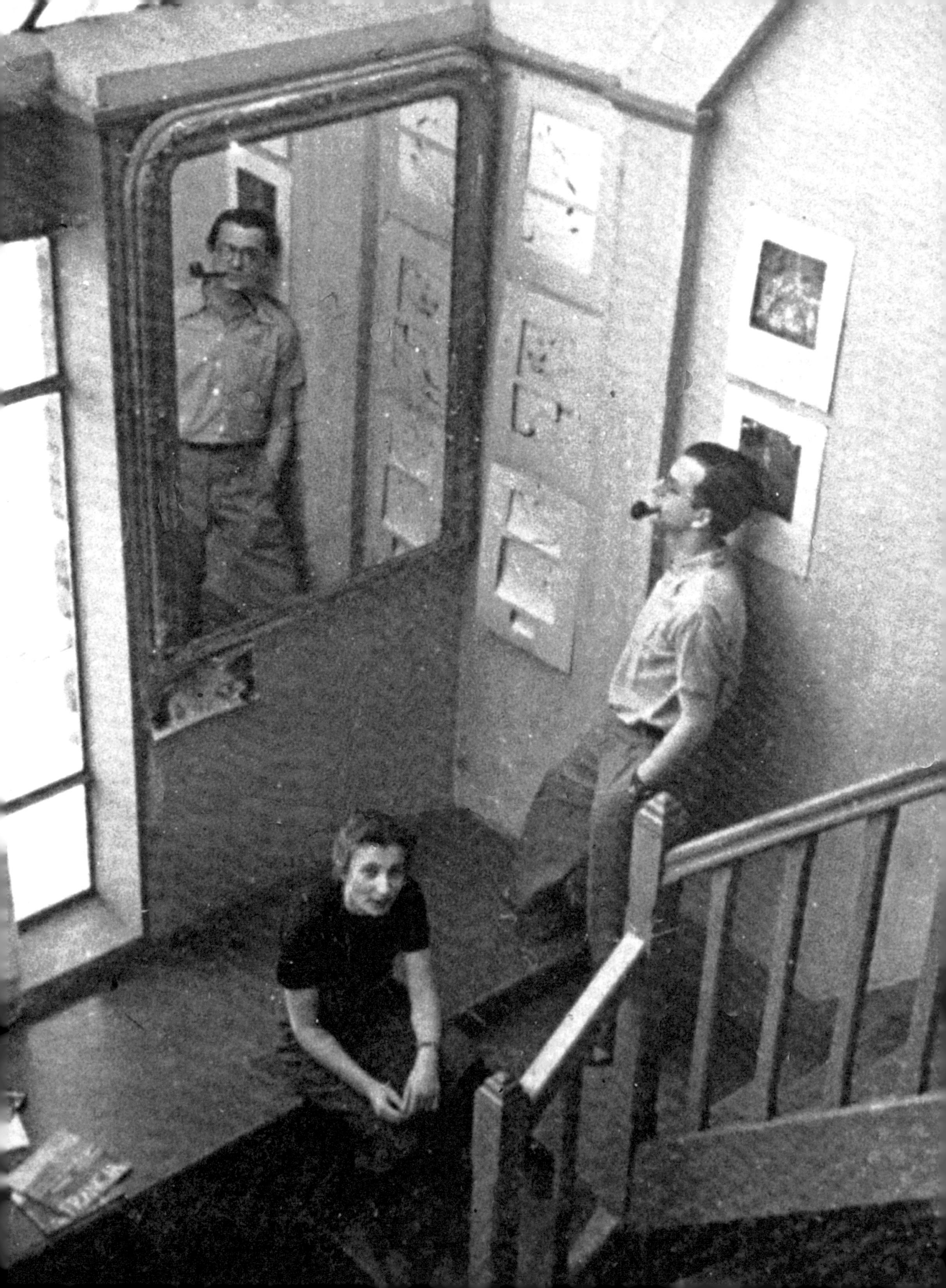

Contents

facing page: Franciszka and Stefan
in their studio in Paris, 1938

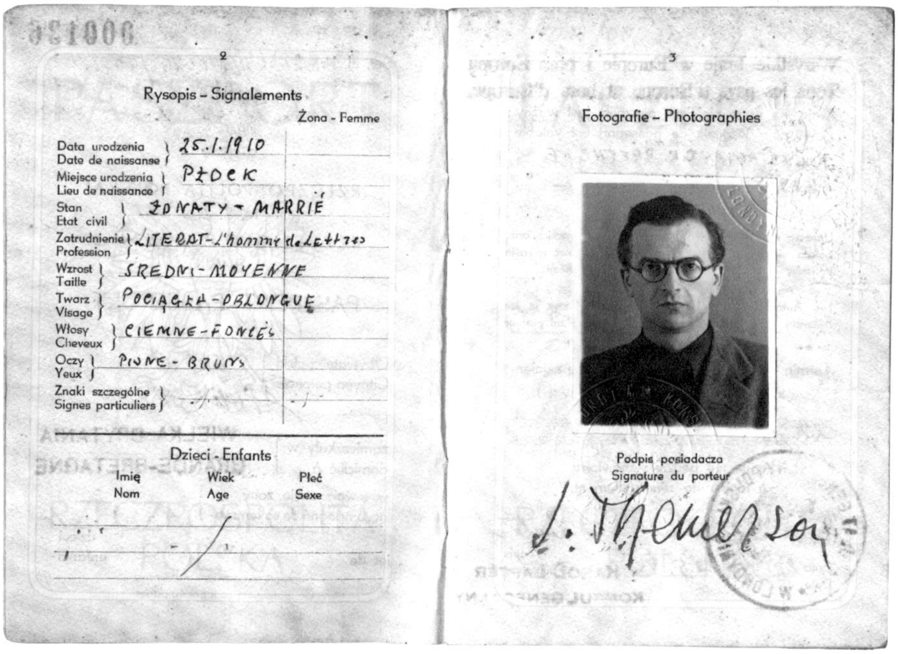

2

Rysopis – Signalements

Żona - Femme

Data urodzenia / Date de naissance: 25.1.1910

Miejsce urodzenia / Lieu de naissance: PŁOCK

Stan / Etat civil: ŻONATY - MARRIÉ

Zatrudnienie / Profession: LITERAT - L'homme de Lettres

Wzrost / Taille: ŚREDNI - MOYENNE

Twarz / Visage: POCIĄGŁA - OBLONGUE

Włosy / Cheveux: CIEMNE - FONCÉS

Oczy / Yeux: PIWNE - BRUNS

Znaki szczególne / Signes particuliers

Dzieci - Enfants

Imię / Nom — Wiek / Age — Płeć / Sexe

3

Fotografie – Photographies

Podpis posiadacza / Signature du porteur

S. Themerson

Stefan's passport, issued in London in 1946, based on his 1941 passport issued in Lisbon

2

CARTE

VALABLE

Délivrée par Mr le Préfet

Le Préfet

Signature du titulaire

Timbre

5

Visas en cas de changement de domicile

Vu au départ de Paris

à destination Varsovie

le 7 Juillet 1938

Timbre

Vu à l'arrivée à Paris

(adresse) 203 Bd Raspail

le 26 Août 1938

Timbre

6

Visas en cas de changement de domicile

Vu au départ de Paris 14e

à destination de 45 av Richaud à Arcueil

Timbre

Vu à l'arrivée à Arcueil

(adresse)

le

24 JANV 1939

Timbre

3 MAI 1939

10 November 1939
Franciszka's *Carte d'identité*

Franciszka gives the date of birth of her father, Jakub as 1869 and of her mother, Łucja Kaufman, as 1879. Perhaps the original document acts as visa for a visit to Poland from 7 July 1938 to 26 August 1938 [when she returns to 203 boulevard Raspail]. Subsequently, her addresses in France are: 19 January 1939 : 45 avenue Richaud in Arcueil, Paris 14; 24th January 1939 : 1a rue Jeanne d'Arc. Paris; 10 November 1939 : 11 rue Victor Cousin, Paris 5; 16 April [1940] : 37 Quai des Grands-Augustins, Paris 5; 21 June 1940 : 4 avenue de la Ribire, Lourdes. Controlée au passage à Angers le 31 mai 1940, par le service de la Sûreté – Le Commissaire de Police

This book is a record of the lives of a young couple, Franciszka and Stefan Themerson, between 1939 and 1942, when they were separated by the events of World War II – he in France and she in England.

Their wartime story starts in August 1939, in Paris. They have been there for over a year. Why are they in Paris? Stefan is asked this question time and again. Did they emigrate? Did they leave Poland to escape anti-Semitism? Neither was the case. Stefan explains:

> At the time, Paris was the world's centre of the arts and one need not search for any other motives. If one wrote, painted or made films, one had to be in Paris. So, in the end we went to Paris, and there the war found us.

When the war breaks out, Franciszka wants to return to Warsaw to be with her family. Stefan refuses to go, and so they stay.

Two days after the declaration of war, the Themersons volunteer for the Polish Army in France. Franciszka is assigned to the Polish Government-in-Exile as cartographer and illustrator, and eventually ends up in England. Stefan becomes a soldier and stays in France.

150 of their letters survive, as do 150 telegrams, Stefan's nine diaries, 70 official documents and Franciszka's many drawings. It is from these sources that their story is told. I provide the interjections which relate some background events and identify some of the other participants in the story.

Letters are difficult to decipher, diaries are often illegible, and so there is some guesswork and some gaps not only in the story but also in completing available information. For instance, we may have a first name of someone close to Stefan but not the surname; we may have a record of an event but not of precisely where it took place. But the story has a beginning, a middle and an end. We can read it because Stefan and Franciszka were unable to talk to each other and so wrote down their thoughts and experiences instead. It articulates the inner life of two remarkable individuals who are borne along, like all of Europe at the time, by an erratic and unstable course of events over which they have next to no control.

The story is called Unposted Letters because this is what Franciszka called her drawings. They are never sent and end up in her drawer. Some of her letters, long soliloquies like Stefan's diaries, meet the same fate.

Jasia Reichardt

1 Polish Government-in-Exile, i.e. the Government of the Republic of Poland in Exile, was established in Paris on 2 October 1939 under the leadership of General Władysław Sikorski. Considering the possibility of a German invasion of Paris, the office moves to Angers on 10 June 1940.

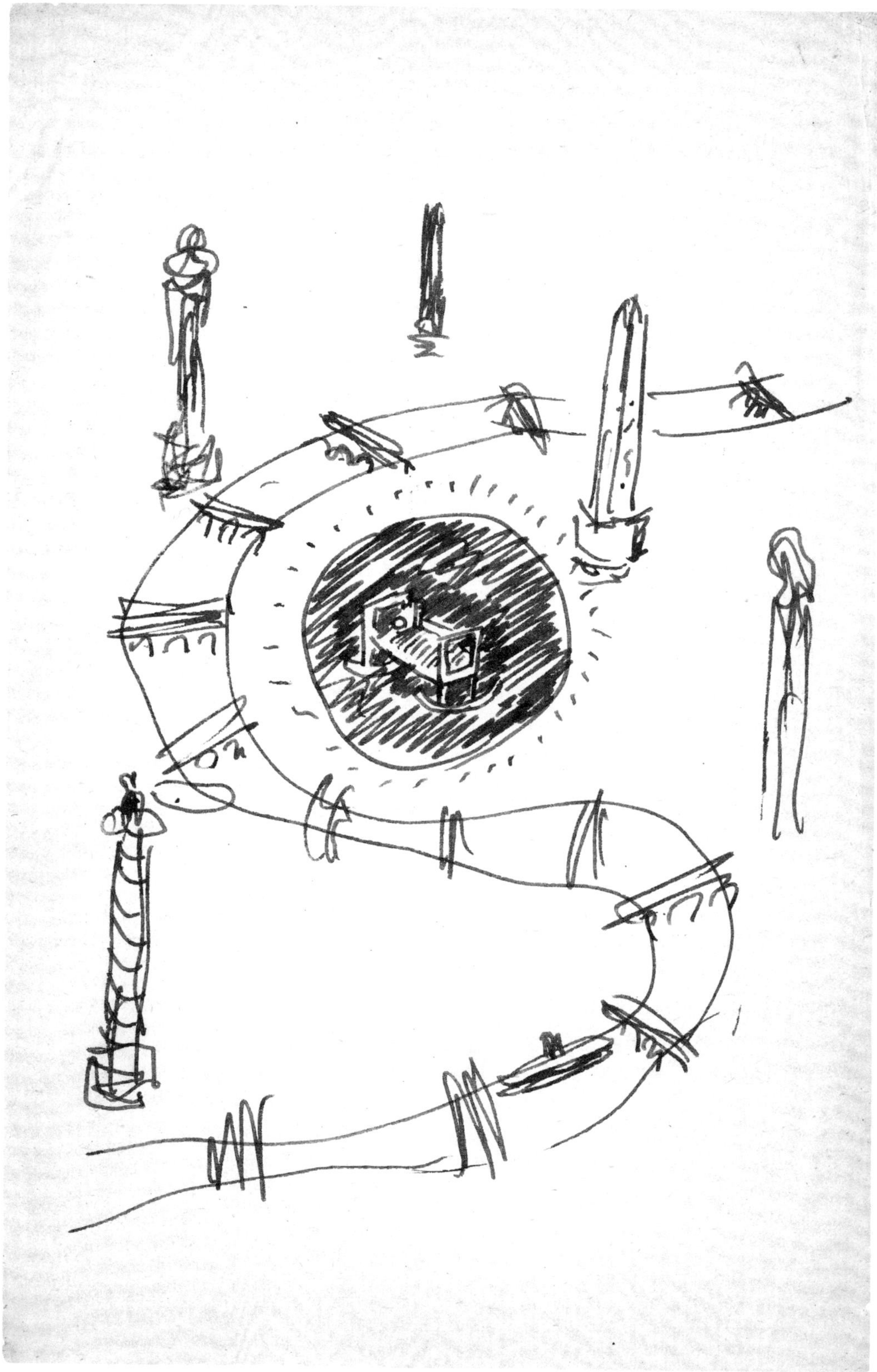

Two of Stefan's pen and ink sketches for a film about Paris, 1938/1939, unrealised.

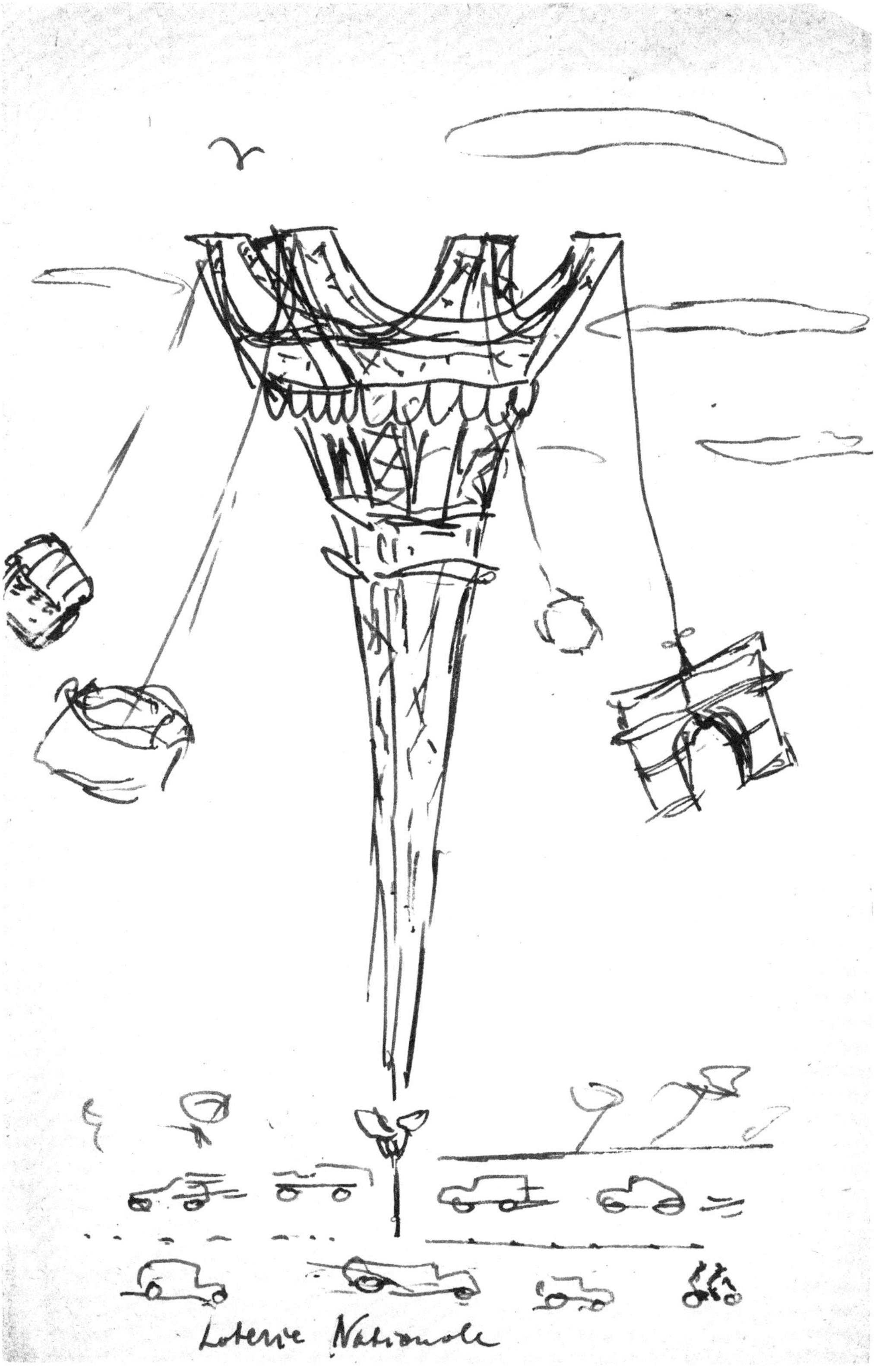
Loterie Nationale

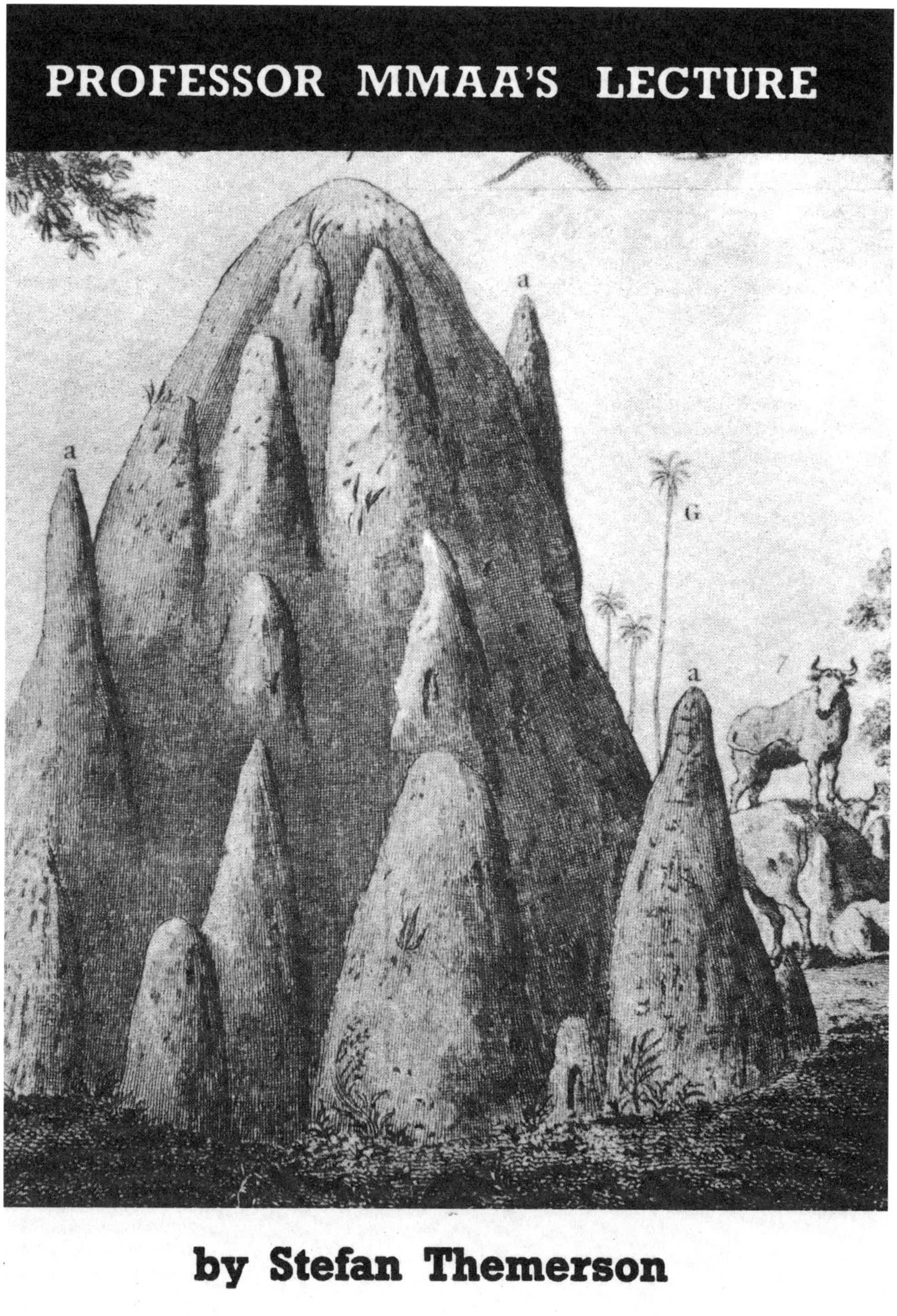

Professor Mmaa's Lecture, London, Gaberbocchus, 1953, preface by Bertrand Russell, illustrated by Franciszka Themerson.

The book had a long gestation period. Stefan started writing it in Voiron in 1941 and sending it page by page to Franciszka in London, who started working on the illustrations. He continued writing it, while in the army in Scotland in 1942, and later in London. The first extracts, subtitled 'fragment of a novel' were published in *Nowa Polska* in 1943.

The Themersons moved to Paris early in 1938 and are living there at the outbreak of World War II. Franciszka paints, and illustrates books for children for Flammarion, and for *Moja Gazeta* [My Newspaper], the children's supplement of *Głos Polski* [The Voice of Poland], of which Stefan is the editor and the main contributor. Stefan is also writing a novel which is later lost, and makes plans for a film about Paris.

In September 1939, they volunteer for the Polish Army in France. From March 1940, Franciszka is assigned to the Polish Ministry of Information and Documentation, as a cartographer and illustrator, and is involved in the production of their official publications. On 10 June, in anticipation of the German invasion, General Sikorski transfers the headquarters of the Polish Government-in-Exile from Paris to Angers. On 22 June 1940, together with other colleagues from the Ministry, Franciszka escapes from Bayonne on a ship to England, and arrives in London.

Stefan, drafted into the army, is sent to Coëtquidan, the military academy in Brittany where the Polish Army in France is organised. The story of Polish soldiers in Stefan's regiment is farce from start to finish. They never actually go to war. One night in June 1940, during one of the most bizarre events of the war, the commandants flee 'towards the ports and hope'. The general escapes in a fishing boat. Soldiers remain. The regiment disintegrates near Saint-Nazaire and the 'Sauve qui peut' strategy results in men dispersing throughout the countryside. It takes Stefan six weeks to get back to what is by then the 'new' Paris. His diaries relate some details of this journey: picking beetroots, working in the fields, dreaming of food. Once he gets to Paris, the diary entries list many different places where he spends the night, carefully avoiding staying anywhere too long. In due course he travels to Vichy France, contacts the Polish Red Cross and is assigned to a shelter in Voiron, where he spends most of the following two years. From time to time, he tries to get away from this Polish colony. Its inmates construct their own hierarchies and tribunals, and enact social rituals imbued with the prejudices and mores of pre-war Polish society. The inhabitants tell their stories and Stefan notes them down. There is heroism and there is tragedy. Taken away from their normal lives, the men talk. Among them are artists, dancers, soldiers, teachers, ambassadors, and even a future president of the Polish People's Republic. Stefan makes countless attempts to leave, to get visas, money, permits, invitations. In the meantime his writings accumulate: essays, poems and chapters of his *chef d'oeuvre*, *Professor Mmaa's Lecture*, a satire in which all the characters are termites.

Once she reaches London, Franciszka tries to trace Stefan and eventually learns that he is alive and well through friends in America. When she has Stefan's address, she sends him money through various means, letters and telegrams. She tries to help him obtain an exit visa via Spain and Portugal, either to go to America or to come to London. Telegrams are the most convenient means of keeping in touch. Letters sometimes arrive and sometimes don't. Some letters are written but not sent. Franciszka is reluctant to let Stefan know her true feelings of despair. These letters remain in her drawer. Sometimes she announces in the first line that this will be a letter that will not be sent. There are other 'letters' that are not posted either. These are the drawings, over 100 of them. Some are responses to the texts and poems that Stefan sends her and some are imaginary scenes from his life: his landscape, his room, his view out of the window. Some are allegories. Others are caricatures of the people she works with. The Themersons try to protect each other from the reality of their situations.

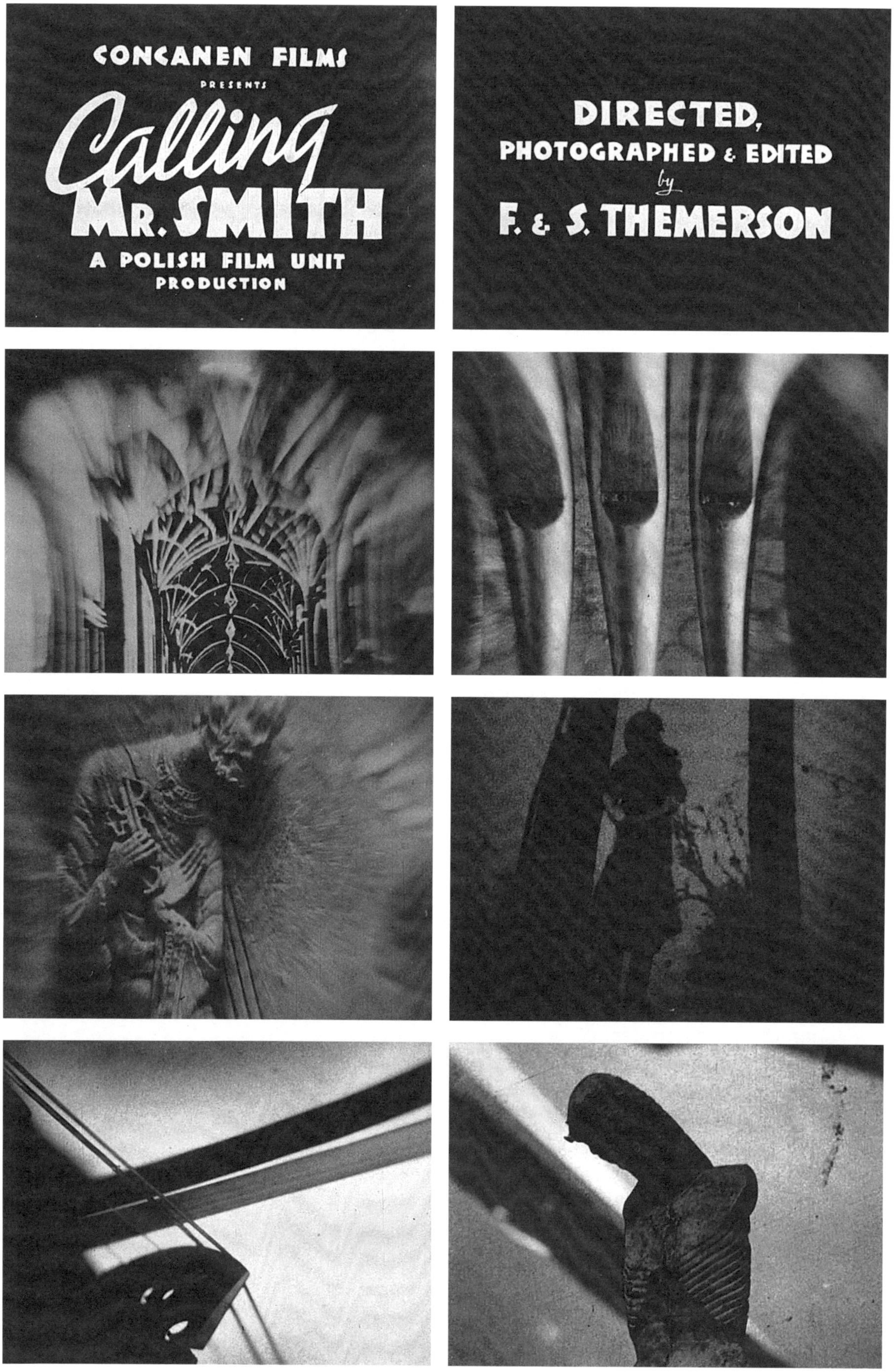

From *Calling Mr. Smith*, 1943

They receive intermittent news, from and about their families in Poland, via a relative in Romania. To begin with these are from Franciszka's mother and sister Maryla from the old address in Warsaw and afterwards from the ghetto. Around the ghetto is an 8-foot-high wall and by November 1940, the ghetto is closed. Supplies of food are stopped. Franciszka sends money which does not arrive and food parcels, some of which do. Eventually she learns that it is her food parcels that are responsible for keeping them alive. When the Foreign Office forbids her to send parcels to enemy territory, Franciszka is called for an interview [see page 131]. She acquiesces, but her friends in Lisbon and America continue to help. News is repeated time and again in all correspondence during the war, since nobody could be sure what, if anything, would arrive. Cryptic phrases and metaphors are used and names are changed.

In their letters Stefan and Franciszka try to persuade one another that each is coping, doing some work and not feeling too sad. Powerlessness consumes Franciszka. She can do nothing for her family in Poland, she moves heaven and earth to get Stefan out of France. Their correspondence concentrates on work, projects and the hopes of collaboration in some distant future. The documents necessary to bring Stefan to England sometimes seem within their grasp but then recede. They hardly dare ask about what is happening at home in Poland. Then in August 1942, Stefan arrives in England and rejoins the Polish Army.

In 1943 the Themersons make an experimental anti-war film commissioned by the Polish Ministry of Information, *Calling Mr Smith*. The ten-minute film is a collage in Dufaycolour, drawing the attention of the British public to the effects of Nazi occupation in Poland. The British Board of Film Censors refuses to give it a certificate unless the Themersons remove an image of a figure hanging from the gallows. The Themersons stand firm and, at the time, the film cannot be shown publicly.

1943–1945. Franciszka publishes an edition of 25 numbered copies of *Forty Drawings for Friends London 1940–42*, hors commerce. (This is a selection from the 'unposted letters'.) She starts to paint again. In 1944 the Themersons move to the Maida Vale district of London, where they live and work for the rest of their lives.

The Themersons resume their creative lives. In 1948, they start an independent publishing company, Gaberbocchus Press, whose name is taken from the Latin rendering of Lewis Carroll's Jabberwocky (from *Through the Looking-Glass*). The company starts with a hand press in their home in Maida Vale.

During the next 31 years, 60 titles are published. The many exceptional volumes include the first translation of Jarry's *Ubu Roi*; the drawings of Jankel Adler and the calligrammes of Apollinaire; the English writings of Kurt Schwitters and Raoul Hausmann; the first translation of Raymond Queneau's 'untranslatable' *Exercises in Style*; Dietrich Grabbe; Anatol Stern's Polish surrealist poem and the then completely unknown Pol-Dives, apostle of holy poverty, who several years before had sheltered Stefan in Paris. They also publish their own works.

The following pages relate the story of the Themersons during 1940–1942 through the documents and letters which have survived.

1940

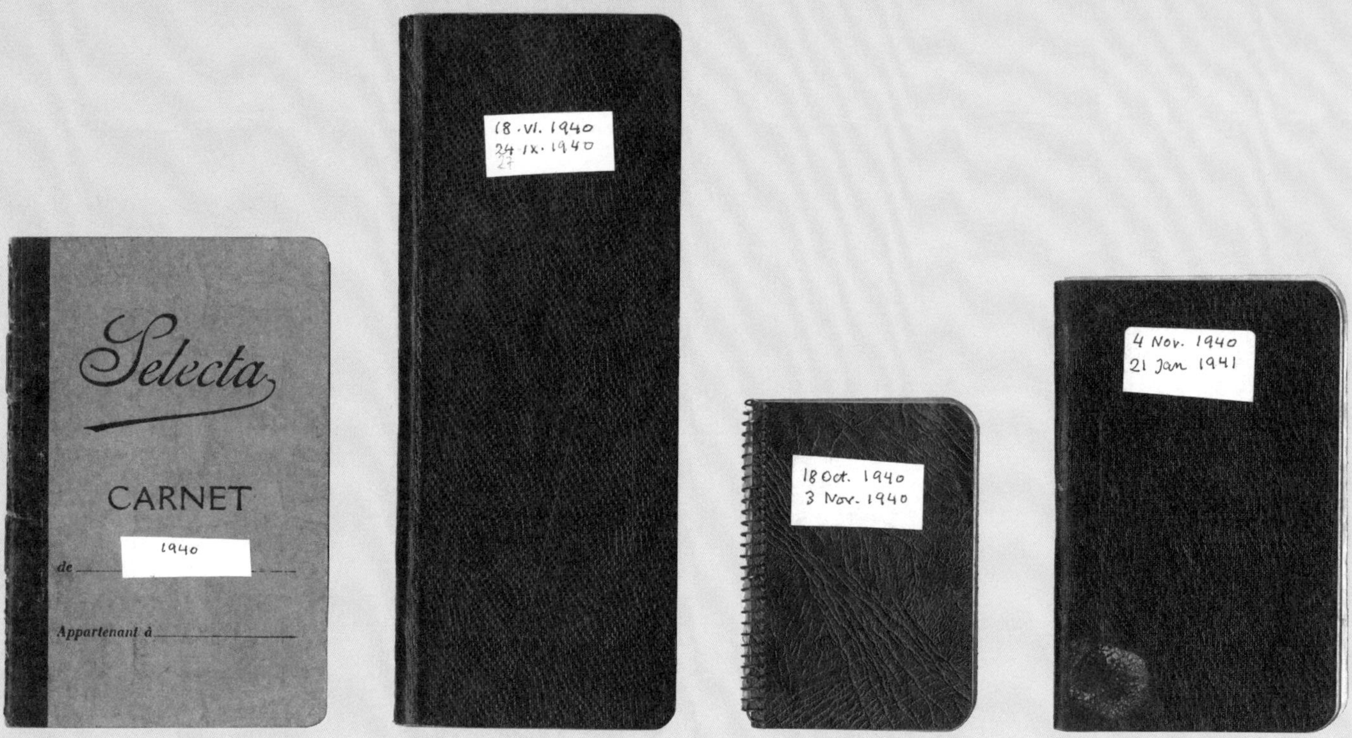

For 1940, there are entries from the first two of Stefan's diaries. In the first (lilac) diary entries are minimal, just a word or two, or a few names of the places where he stops and a few dates, and yet these entries cover the first four months from the time that he joins his regiment. There are longer entries in the second (black) diary, in which he mentions people he meets, what he is doing, what he eats or doesn't eat and how hungry he feels during the journey. There are also some loose pages with longer entries. But it is the first lilac diary that provides the skeleton of Stefan's journeys.

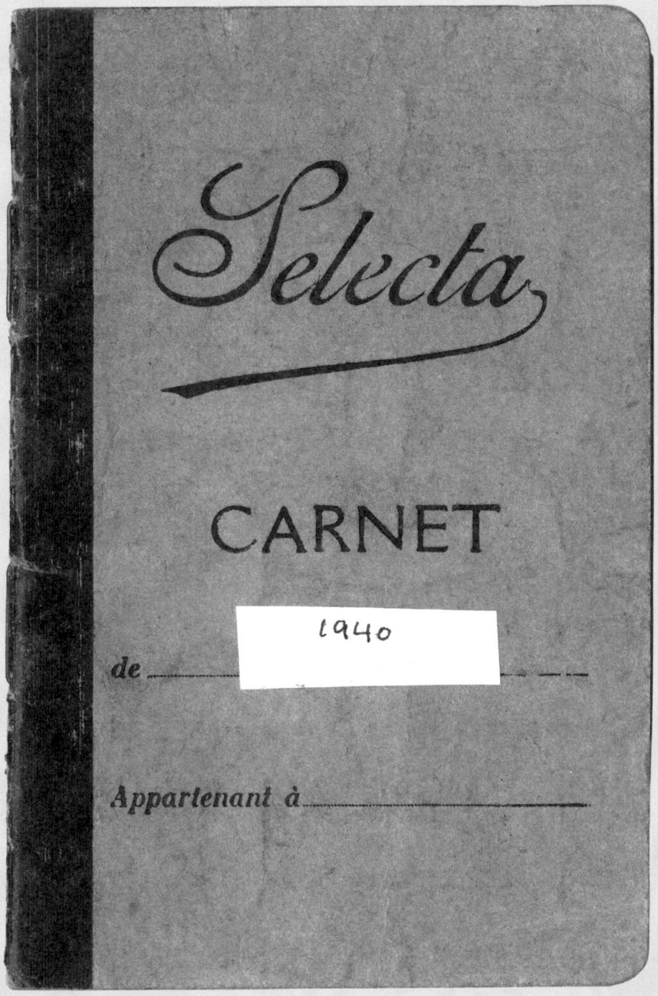

The 50 entries in the lilac diary, listing the places where Stefan spends his nights, start in quai des Grands-Augustins and end in Vichy France. The entries are minimal, often a single word. It is likely that he made them in retrospect because the character of the writing is the same throughout and the occasional question mark suggests that some detail has been forgotten.

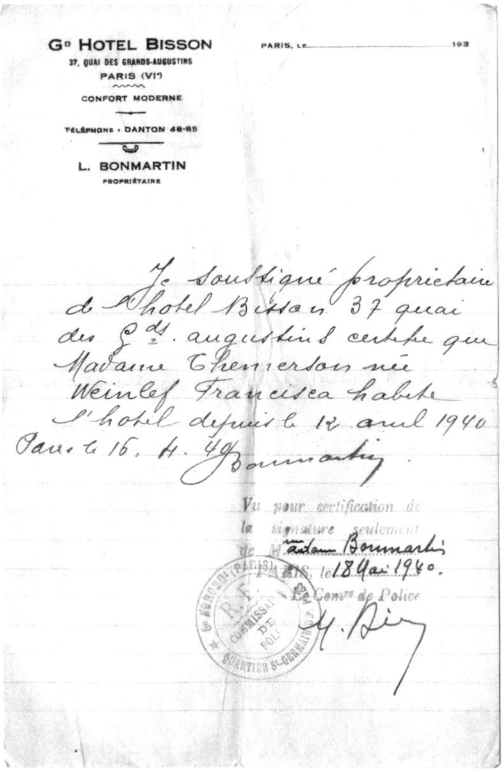

Gᴰ HOTEL BISSON
37, QUAI DES GRANDS-AUGUSTINS
PARIS (VIᵉ)
CONFORT MODERNE
TÉLÉPHONE : DANTON 48-85
L. BONMARTIN
PROPRIÉTAIRE

PARIS, LE 193

Je soussigné propriétaire de l'hotel Bisson 37 quai des Gds. augustins certifie que Madame Chemerson née Weinlef Francisca habite l'hotel depuis le 12 avril 1940
Paris le 16. 4. 40
Bonmartin

Vu pour certification de la signature seulement de Madame Bonmartin
Paris, le 18 Mai 1940.
Le Comre de Police

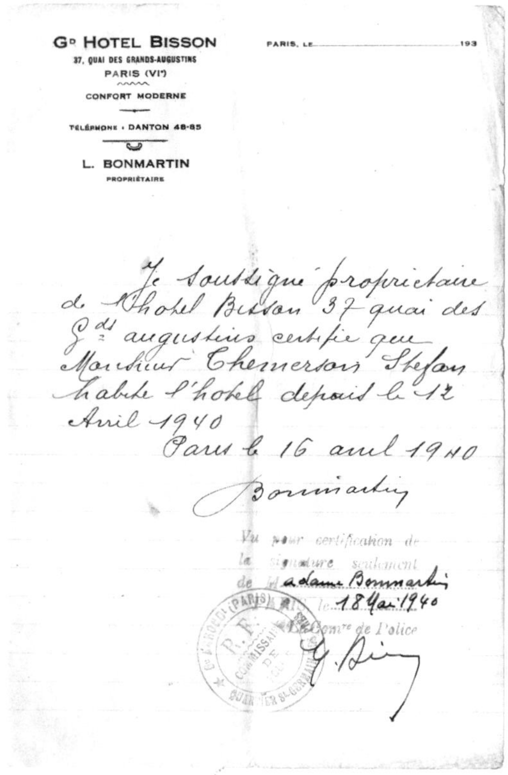

Gᴰ HOTEL BISSON
37, QUAI DES GRANDS-AUGUSTINS
PARIS (VIᵉ)
CONFORT MODERNE
TÉLÉPHONE : DANTON 48-85
L. BONMARTIN
PROPRIÉTAIRE

PARIS, LE 193

Je soussigné propriétaire de l'hotel Bisson 37 quai des Gds. augustins certifie que Monsieur Chemerson Stefan habite l'hotel depuis le 12 Avril 1940
Paris le 16 avril 1940
Bonmartin

Vu pour certification de la signature seulement de Madame Bonmartin
le 18 Mai 1940
Le Comre de Police

16 April 1940
Letters from Gd Hotel Bisson, 37 quai des Grands-Augustins, Paris VI, signed by Police, 18 May 1940, certifying that Stefan and Franciszka stayed there from 12 April 1940

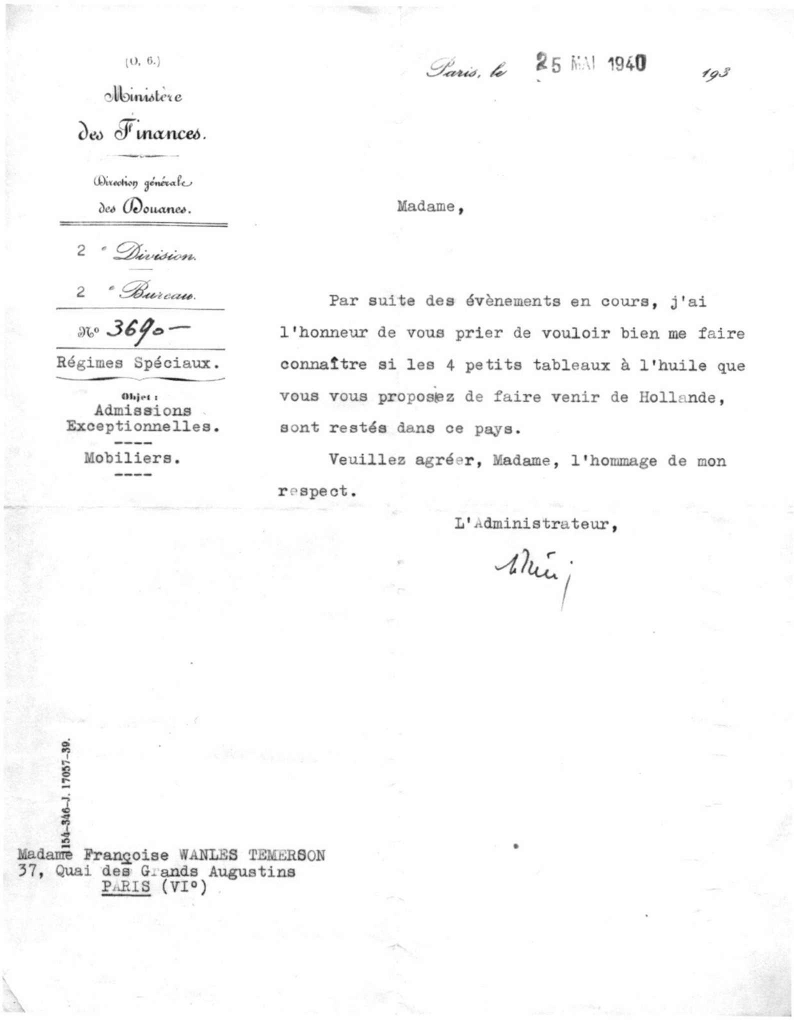

(O. 6.)
Ministère des Finances.
Direction générale des Douanes.
2 e Division.
2 e Bureau.
Nº 3690—
Régimes Spéciaux.
Objet : Admissions Exceptionnelles.

Mobiliers.

Paris, le 25 MAI 1940 193

Madame,

Par suite des évènements en cours, j'ai l'honneur de vous prier de vouloir bien me faire connaître si les 4 petits tableaux à l'huile que vous vous proposez de faire venir de Hollande, sont restés dans ce pays.

Veuillez agréer, Madame, l'hommage de mon respect.

L'Administrateur,

154-346-J. 17057-39.

Madame Françoise WANLES TEMERSON
37, Quai des Grands Augustins
PARIS (VI°)

25 May 1940
Letter from the *Ministère des Finances* to Françoise Weinles Temerson, 37 quai des Grands-Augustins, Paris VI

Madame, Par suite des événements en cours, j'ai l'honneur de vous prier de vouloir bien me faire savoir si les 4 petits tableaux à l'huile que vous vous proposez de faire venir de Hollande, sont restés dans ce pays.

Veuillez agréer, Madame, l'hommage de mon respect.

L'Administrateur

According to a certificate of residence, Stefan and Franciszka stayed at Hotel Bisson, 37 Quai des Grands-Augustins, Paris 6 from 12 April, Stefan till 28 May 1940, and perhaps Franciszka too.

During 1939, Franciszka is registered at four different addresses in Paris. The Polish Government-in-Exile for which she will work for the next three years is formed in Paris on the 30 September 1939, ten days after the arrival of the vice premier, Professor Stanisław Stroński, Franciszka's future boss. Initially the seat of the government is in Paris at 10 rue de Bassaud. On 5 October the new Polish Government is officially installed in rue de Rivoli in Paris, and then after 22 November, General Sikorski, Prime Minister and Commander in Chief, transfers the headquarters of the Polish Government-in-Exile to the Château Pignerolle in Angers, 300 kilometres west of Paris. The city, with the blessing of the Angevins, becomes the capital of Poland. Franciszka starts work for the government in March 1940, but initially stays in Paris. According to Franciszka's close friend, Hanna Segal (then Hanka Poznańska), they both leave Paris early in June 1940 mainly on foot and only once taking a train.

By the time the Germans enter Paris on 14 June, Franciszka is in Angers as a 'fonctionnaire temp. du Gouvernement Polonais'. Soon the Government-in-Exile has to move to Lourdes, but on the 19th, at the invitation of the British Government, it officially moves to London. In the evening of 22 June, Franciszka's wedding anniversary and the day that France capitulates, she is in the port of St-Jean-de-Luz, Bayonne. She is taken on board the *Batory*, a liner in service as a troop ship, which takes on some of the Polish officials and members of the Polish Army. The last transport ship to leave France for England is on 25 June. Not all will reach their destination, but the *Batory* crosses safely and Franciszka finds herself in London.

Stefan leaves the quai des Grands-Augustins on 28 May 1940 and joins the recruits in the 3rd Division of foot soldiers [according to the Ministry of Defence, 8 Infantry Regiment] of the 16th Battalion of Dragoons who arrive at Rennes to attend the regimental barracks in Coëtquidan, (Ille-et-Vilaine), one of the two main camps that the French authorities have put at General Sikorski's disposal. The site of the old French military academy is now the headquarters of the Polish Army. According to one of the Polish soldiers this is a 'gloomy place – flimsy wooden barracks built during the last war by the American Army'.
The Polish Army numbers 84,000 men, of whom 45,000 Polish conscripts were already living in France, the rest reached France from Poland. Stefan's division consists of more than 9,000 men, most of them new, untrained recruits. New arrivals appear daily. The volunteers are given French 'horizon blue' uniforms (from World War I) with oversize navy-blue berets and boots that don't always fit. They have a motley collection of firearms, which appear obsolete even to the raw recruits. There are several soldiers to each rifle, minimal amounts of ammunition, and there is a shortage of billeting facilities. Target practice takes place once a week. No means of communication are provided. There are four divisions and two infantry brigades. Only two divisions are equipped. Stefan's division isn't even trained to the minimum level of preparedness. The soldiers start training on 5 June. While the trained soldiers leave for the front, Stefan's division is not allowed to take part in combat. Some may have dreamed of going to war in tanks but they are just foot soldiers. Stefan does not speak of the details except for endless

marching, but three months later, in Paris, he writes a poem about it: 'Fragment Poematu' (Fragment of a Poem). How many barracks there are we don't know, but during his stay there Stefan mentions three where he sleeps: numbers 76, 78 and 80. Nor do we know precisely how long Stefan stays at Coëtquidan (it was probably from his arrival after 28 May until 17 June). On 11 June Paris is declared an 'open city'. Stefan's division is supposed to leave Coëtquidan for Saintes from where it would have been possible for the soldiers to board troop ships for England, but because of disagreements between General Louis Faury and his colonels, the division stays behind. Evacuation orders for 14 to 16 June were supposed to be given by the Deputy War Minister, General Marian Kukiel, but in the prevailing chaos nothing could happen until the disappearance of General Faury from the scene.

The Polish Government stays in Angers a mere month before Sikorski orders it to move to Toulouse. The French Government meanwhile leaves Paris for Tours in anticipation of the German invasion.

On June 14 the German Army enters Paris.

14 June Telegram from Franciszka to Stefan

PARTONS TOULOUSE SOIS TRANQUILLE ÉCRIS POSTE RESTANTE ET CONSULAT DE POLOGNE TENDRESSES FRANKA THEMERSON

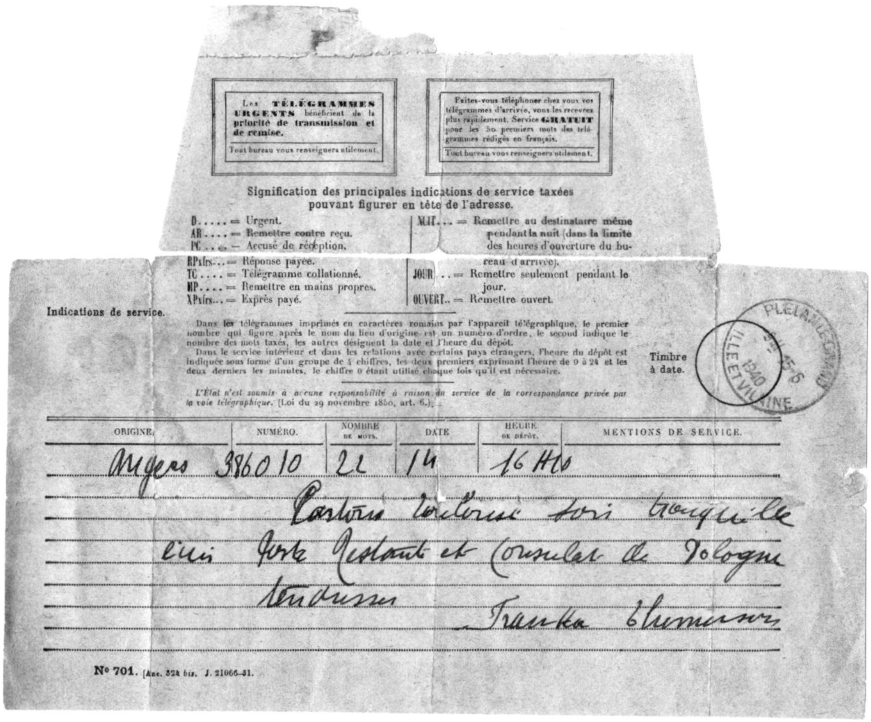

Les TÉLÉGRAMMES URGENTS bénéficient de la priorité de transmission et de remise.
Tout bureau vous renseignera utilement.

Faites-vous téléphoner chez vous vos télégrammes d'arrivée, vous les recevrez plus rapidement. Service GRATUIT pour les 50 premiers mots des télégrammes rédigés en français.
Tout bureau vous renseignera utilement.

Signification des principales indications de service taxées pouvant figurer en tête de l'adresse.

D..... = Urgent.
AR.... = Remettre contre reçu.
PC.... = Accusé de réception.
RPxfrs... = Réponse payée.
TC.... = Télégramme collationné.
MP.... = Remettre en mains propres.
XPxfrs... = Exprès payé.
NUIT... = Remettre au destinataire même pendant la nuit (dans la limite des heures d'ouverture du bureau d'arrivée).
JOUR.. = Remettre seulement pendant le jour.
OUVERT.. = Remettre ouvert.

Indications de service.

Dans les télégrammes imprimés en caractères romains par l'appareil télégraphique, le premier nombre qui figure après le nom du lieu d'origine est un numéro d'ordre, le second indique le nombre des mots taxés, les autres désignent la date et l'heure du dépôt.
Dans le service intérieur et dans les relations avec certains pays étrangers, l'heure du dépôt est indiquée sous forme d'un groupe de 4 chiffres, les deux premiers exprimant l'heure de 0 à 24 et les deux derniers les minutes, le chiffre 0 étant utilisé chaque fois qu'il est nécessaire.

L'État n'est soumis à aucune responsabilité à raison du service de la correspondance privée par la voie télégraphique. (Loi du 29 novembre 1850, art. 6.)

Timbre à date.

ORIGINE.	NUMÉRO.	NOMBRE DE MOTS.	DATE	HEURE DE DÉPÔT.	MENTIONS DE SERVICE.
Angers	386010	22	14	16H10	

Partons Toulouse sois tranquille
écris Poste Restante et Consulat de Pologne
tendresses Franka Themerson

N° 701. [Ann. 324 bis. J. 21066-31.]

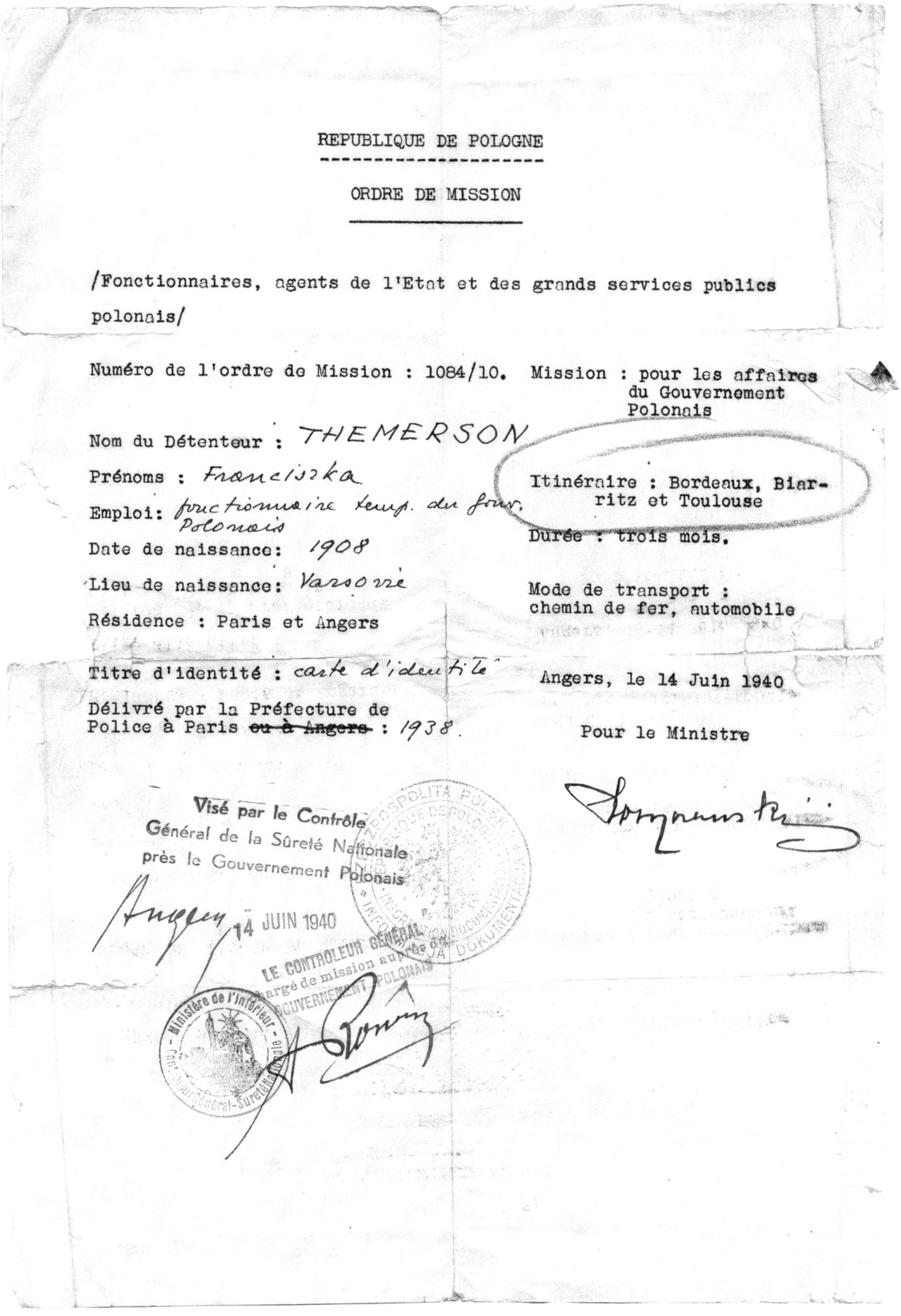

REPUBLIQUE DE POLOGNE

ORDRE DE MISSION

/Fonctionnaires, agents de l'Etat et des grands services publics polonais/

Numéro de l'ordre de Mission : 1084/10.

Nom du Détenteur : THEMERSON

Prénoms : Franciszka

Emploi: fonctionnaire temp. du Gouv. Polonais

Date de naissance: 1908

Lieu de naissance: Varsovie

Résidence : Paris et Angers

Titre d'identité : carte d'identité

Délivré par la Préfecture de Police à Paris ~~ou à Angers~~ : 1938.

Mission : pour les affaires du Gouvernement Polonais

Itinéraire : Bordeaux, Biarritz et Toulouse

Durée : trois mois.

Mode de transport : chemin de fer, automobile

Angers, le 14 Juin 1940

Pour le Ministre

Visé par le Contrôle Général de la Sûreté Nationale près le Gouvernement Polonais

Angers 14 JUIN 1940

LE CONTROLEUR GÉNÉRAL chargé de mission auprès du GOUVERNEMENT POLONAIS

14 June 1940
République de Pologne
– Ordre de Mission

Note from Stefan to Franciszka

Darling, how was the journey? How are you? I'm OK. Don't worry about anything and above all don't be anxious about the lack of letters from me. I am still at the same address.

It is not out of the question that I will see Gienek Złotowski. I embrace you so lovingly and kiss you so much.

PS: Please write if by any chance you have some news of [Stefania] Bender. My colleague, Jortner, is very anxious about her. Her address in Paris is 22 rue Saint-Sulpice, Paris 6.

I kiss you, darling, I don't have time to write at length, because nothing is settled yet. What do you think about Gienek? Will you be staying long in Toulouse? Write more. Love, Stefan

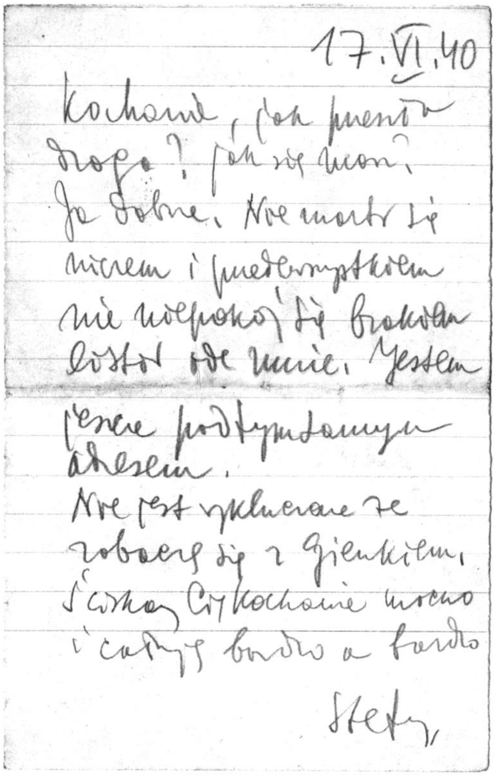

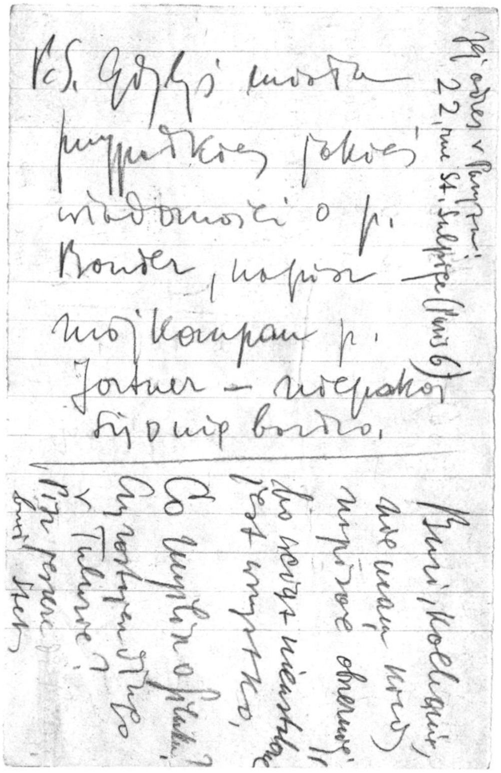

On 17 June, Pétain requests armistice terms from Germany and Italy, declares the cessation of hostilities against the Germans and the end of combat. However, Sikorski, who leaves for London by air the following day, is opposed to this and the Polish Government refuses to give up arms. Stefan's division will disperse soon after this, but first there is a forced march towards Nantes, after recruits at Coëtquidan receive orders to evacuate the camp.[1] They march 120 kilometres in three days and by the time they get there, Nantes, having fallen on the 19th, is an open city. There are 1,000 soldiers, Stefan among them. This battalion is unlucky not to have been sent to Saint-Nazaire, Verdon-sur-Mer or Saint-Jean-de-Luz, from where other Polish soldiers were evacuated between 19 and 25 June, and reached England by sea. According to Colonel Łakiński, General Faury deliberately

1 Beskid.com, La Pologne Online: L'Armée polonaise durant la Bataille de France

made it impossible for Stefan's division to reach the British ships. The events leading to the 'sauve-qui-peut' situation are difficult to imagine. General Faury did not accept the solution proposed to him by the colonels in charge of dissolving the division. He ordered them to stay with the division and to negotiate surrender to the Germans. At the time he was issuing this order, at 2 am on 19 June, he himself was departing from La Turballe in a fishing boat. The colonels refused to comply or to stay with the men, who for want of a better solution were given 'freedom of action', and the liquidation of the 3rd Division was announced.

Stefan is on the road immediately, not sure whether to head for Toulouse, where the Polish Consulate becomes the centre of demobilisation, or for Paris. He has no money so wherever he is to get to will have to be on foot. Of course, he is not the only Polish soldier on the road. Hundreds of them are on the move in different directions, and their groups diminish as each individual goes his own way. It is hot, and Stefan recalls that when the soldiers stop to ask local farmers for a drink of water, they are asked to pay. Stefan looks for work and sleeps in a field.

On June 22 France capitulates. Stefan's journey, to what is now occupied Paris, will take almost six weeks.

The first place Stefan walks to is Plélan-le-Grand some 13 kilometres from Coëtquidan. He stops for a rest at the roadside, goes to the town hall, probably to exchange his regimental identification for demobilisation papers and a laissez-passer, but learns that this has to be done in a larger town, Plessé. He reaches Plessé on 19 or 20 June at noon and this will be the centre to which he keeps returning. He finds an attic to sleep in and looks for work. The next day he is in Fégréac and sleeps in a meadow, returning to Plessé the following day. He gets work in fields, stacking hay, transporting vegetables on a cart, digging beetroots. He mentions the names of people he meets and of those who work with him. Jobs are not always easy to find and the people who employ him don't always pay. During the following days, apart from Fégréac, he is in Le Coudray, Guenrouet, Les Saints-Bois, Le Dresny, Plume Chat Huant, Puceul, Nort-sur-Erdre, and Les Touches, all of them small towns or villages which he reaches either on foot or by getting a lift.

Card from Stefan in Plélan-le-Grand to Franciszka in Angers

Darling, I still don't have a letter from you. How are you? How are you managing? I am well. I kiss you with so much love. Stefan.

Is Tymon Terlecki still in Paris?

By this time Franciszka is already in England, having arrived on the *Batory* with other employees of the Polish Government-in-Exile and hundreds of Polish soldiers. In all some 20,000 Polish troops are evacuated to the UK, i.e. one quarter of all the Polish soldiers on French soil in June 1940.

On the ship, Franciszka travels together with Hanka Poznańska and her father, Czesław Poznański and Zosia Wojciechowska. On arrival in London, they are offered a house in Royal Avenue, Chelsea, by the International Federation of University Women, round the corner from Logan Pearsall-Smith and his sister, Alys Russell, who was instrumental in making these arrangements.

June 1940

Stefan's black diary which gives most of the information about his travels and travails during the first few months opens with quotations from Corneille:

Le Cid

'Et j'allumai leurs feux pour éteindre les miens'
'Ma plus douce espérance est de perdre l'espoir'
(L'Infante) Acte I, Scene II
'Remplir les bons d'amour, et les méchants d'effroi'
(Le Comte) Acte I, Scene III
'Passe (l'épée) pour me venger, en de meilleures mains'
(D. Diègue) Acte I, Scene IV
'Avec tous vos lauriers, craignez encore le foudre'
(Don Arias) Acte II, Scene I

Stefan doesn't know that Franciszka is about to leave France, and during the journey continues to send cards to places where he knows that there is an office of the Polish Red Cross or where he supposes she still might be. He expects to hear from her since he sends his poste restante addresses, but his letters don't reach her and she, in London, has no idea where he is.

21 June A Nazi injunction orders Jews in the 'occupied zone' to declare themselves at the police stations. A day later France concludes armistice with Germany.

Franciszka doesn't keep a diary, but we know what happened to her that June because she relates her story a year later in a letter to Nadia and Léon Temerson dated 29 April 1941.

Most of Stefan's diary entries during his journey to Paris are brief: names of places, names of people, prices of food. Many things are unclear. Words act as pointers. There are facts and descriptions but we don't and can't always know what they mean. Some of the characters whose names are given appear throughout the diaries, and they are identified. Others belong to an episode in a place through which Stefan passes, so there is little to be said about them.

24 June **Diary Entry**

Plume Chat Huant
Stanislas Gautier

25 June **Diary Entry**

Plume Chat Huant (Le Dresny) Jalousie
Day of mourning for the blacksmith.
Landlady's present.

27 June **Diary Entry**

on foot to Plessé
laundress in the castle
sending cards
lunch – market

18 · VI. 1940
24 · IX · 1940
27

27 June 1940

brother Stanislas – Pierre Gautier
bread, onion, buttermilk,
come back with a two-wheel cart
Alfred at the tree

28 June Diary Entry

Plume Chat Huant
beetroots

29 June Diary Entry

Plume Chat Huant
Edek in Plessé
demob commission

30 June Diary Entry

Plume Chat Huant, Sunday

Stefan receives two laissez-passer documents from the Mairie de Plessé. One allowing him to rejoin his family in Toulouse – the one below, and the other to return to his work in Paris via Nantes, where he can find out about available transport.

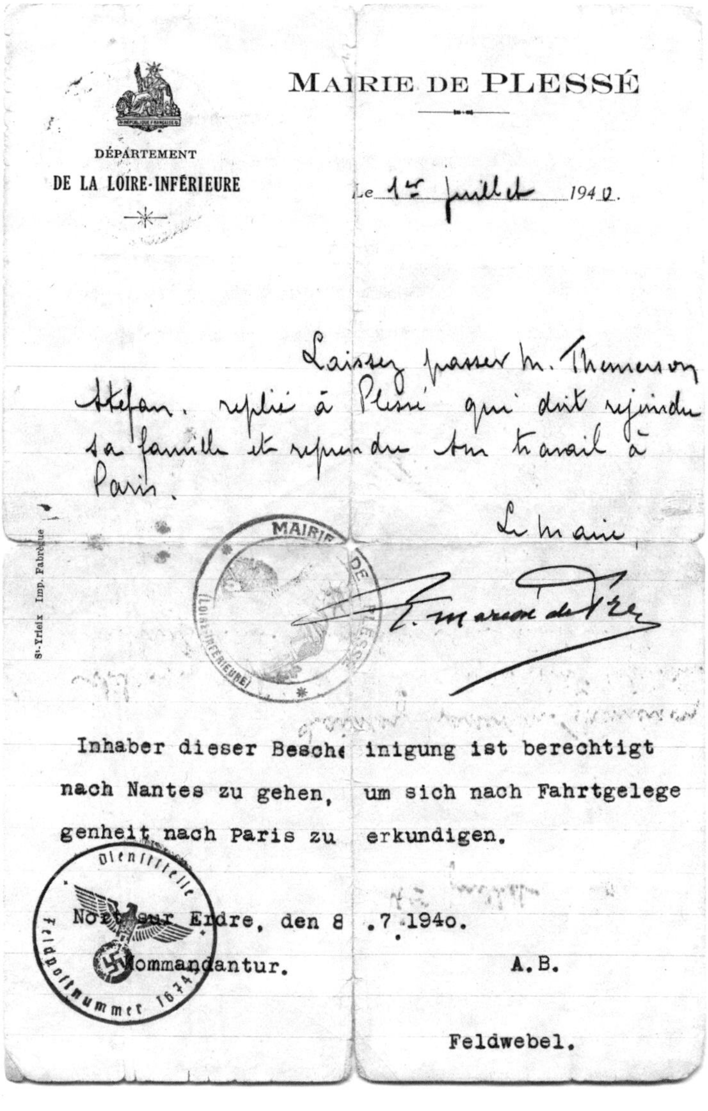

MAIRIE DE PLESSÉ

DÉPARTEMENT
DE LA LOIRE-INFÉRIEURE

Le 1er juillet 1940.

Laissez passer M. Themerson Stefan. replié à Plessé qui doit rejoindre sa famille et reprendre son travail à Paris.

Le Maire,

Inhaber dieser Bescheinigung ist berechtigt nach Nantes zu gehen, um sich nach Fahrtgelegenheit nach Paris zu erkundigen.

Nort sur Erdre, den 8 .7.1940.
Kommandantur.

A.B.

Feldwebel.

1 July 1940
Stefan's laissez-passer
from Mairie de Plessé

The holder of this document is permitted to proceed to Nantes to find out about available transport to Paris.

1 July 1940

Diary Entry

Goodbyes cider distillery
le Roux – Pierre Gautier
Albert is drunk
new clothes for three[2]

2 July Diary Entry

Plessé – le Roux – le Coudray
goodbyes
supper
sleeping in the rectory
Theatre hall

3 July Diary Entry

Goodbyes
a path through the woods
le Coudray – Vay (Étienne Malo)
a priest on a motorcycle
Pucuel
Nort-sur-Erdre
Belgian café
mayor – teacher with a beard
old man (selling grapes?)
Hahanses[3]
strange house
street

4 July Diary Entry

cars
town hall
male and female secretaries
command post 12 o'clock
German officer – on foot
where do I want to go?
on the way – to where?
farm, a miller,
emigrant – there's no work
farm at the cross roads
farm Baron
('too early to sleep')
Les Touches
town hall, cafés,
rectory, attic
emigrant family
1m = 20 frs

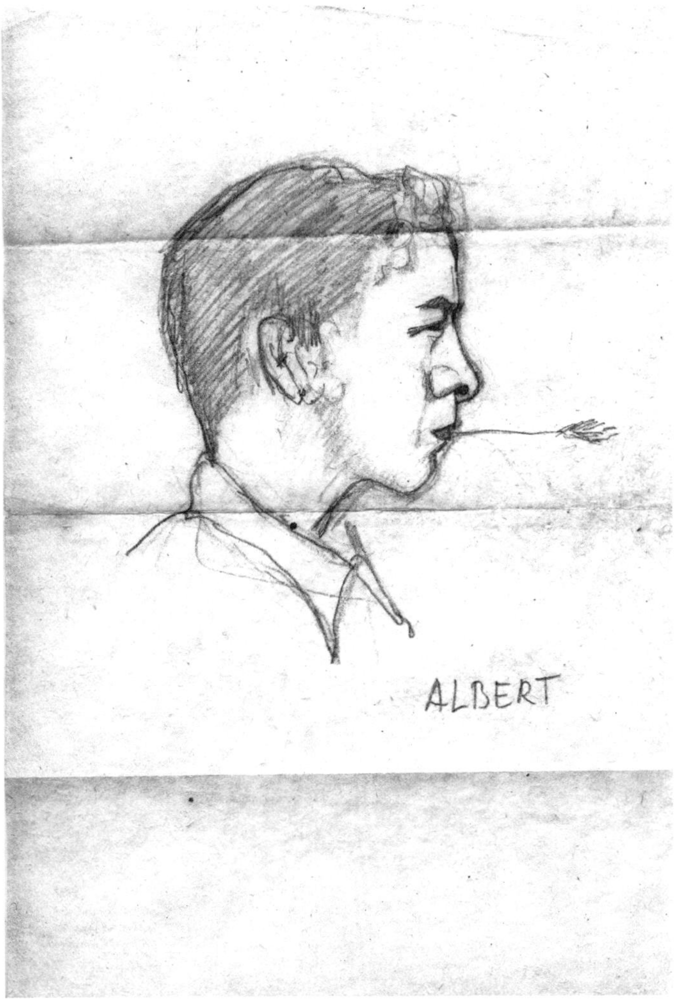

Stefan's drawing of Albert on a piece of toilet paper inserted in the July 1940 diary

5 July

Vichy France breaks off diplomatic relations with Britain.

2 Presumably for Albert, Pierre and Stefan – all going to Le Roux.
3 Germans?

5 July 1940

'Where do I want to go?' – But anyway, there is still not enough money for a ticket, and the question 'where do I want to go?' Stefan will ask himself many times during the following months.

The roads are full of men walking, many of them from disbanded regiments, looking for work, looking for places to spend the night, for food, for lost contacts and friends. This is why Stefan's diary contains many names of casual acquaintances, farmers, landladies, tramps. Conditions are appalling; by now whatever footwear anyone had is falling apart.

Stefan is holding his head above the water – just. For the moment he has some confidence that he will get to Paris, and that he will be able to contact his friends and cousins there.

Nearly every day, he writes letters, postcards, telegrams to friends, acquaintances, Polish Government offices, looking for Franciszka and trying to find information about his family in Poland.

Stefan's own words set the flat mood of the diaries.

Diary Entry

letters
menu
5 frs
Mme Pachulska, Maurice, Sara, Albert
old man with spectacles
his daughter and son-in-law
Charles Bydkowski and Maurice Prossover
also Jean

6 July **Diary Entry**

Charles and Maurice want to go North
'Les amis', M and Mme Alfard from Hungary
Mme Binenstock
father
Jean is learning to bargain
garçon
Schwarz from Romania
Madeleine, Simon
5 frs

7 July **Diary Entry**

rien
5 frs
réparation de pantalon

Concerning language: I speak French well enough, but when it comes down to it they communicate better. Because they know how to express their thoughts. And I don't have any thoughts.

8 July **Diary Entry**

Charles and Maurice depart for Nantes
Moi à Nort pour viser mon laissez-passer
M and Mme Odé
bibliothèque: Corneille
Fenélon
France
5 frs

8 July 1940

En cherchant du travail
Non, non, non…
Aux mines à Ronoz? – non
Mme du petit Château – non merci
& Mme Odé. Colette (15 ans)

On 8 July, at Nort-sur-Erdre, Stefan collects his laissez-passer document. Still looking for work. The most frequent answer on that day is 'No', but for the following day there will be work picking beetroots, however by 10 July work with cabbages and beetroots is over. 'Nous avons changé de travail' says Mme Odé, so there is no pay and no breakfast. The next job will be spraying grapes.

9 July Diary Entry

8am café Château du Soleil
café de betterave
12pm un verre de whisky, un morceau de pain, une pomme
déjeuner – lapin, pommes frites, salade,
confiture, café
old man asks for a menu
Albert's eyes are popping out
2–3pm picking beetroots
3pm le repos
4–10pm fou (group) picking cabbages

10 July Diary Entry

fireplace and weeds in the wardrobe
after the rain – blue clouds in the north
déjeuner – jambon purée, pommes frites, salade, café
dîner – la soupe

les choux, les betteraves sont presque finis. 'Demandez en passant demain'
trousers have split again. Worried about the boots

11 July Diary Entry

no breakfast
Mme Odé is doing the laundry with Colette.
'Nous avons changé de travail'
They didn't pay 5 frs
lunch – (soup with noodles, a bit of scrambled egg)
supper – (milk with noodles, lettuce)
mending trousers
burnt cakes
Colette works for nothing – farm's tenants
dominoes with the old man
daughter goes to get newspaper
feeding the dog with burnt cakes

12 July Diary Entry

pas de lettres
spraying the grapes – fine weather!
5 frs

12 July 1944

1) coffee, bread
2) soup, carrots (tinned peas!)
library
Post Office – card to Franka
still not enough for a ticket
letter from Paris for Mme Pachulska
from Maurice's family –
pawnshop in French?

13 July Diary Entry

never any letters
Albert cuts off snail's horns
apples
conversation with Mme Pachulska and Mme Odé
Jean – garçon de bistro près du Boulevard Magenta
teacher, her husband is in the army 15 days after the wedding
son of a doctor
washing – Maurice's comments on the subject of the penis

14 July Diary Entry

no post 10 frs
emptiness (stomach)

Stefan makes lists of the people he writes to and checks the post every day. On 15 July the news comes that on 17 June Franciszka was in Lourdes. He writes a card to Lourdes which is returned nine days later.

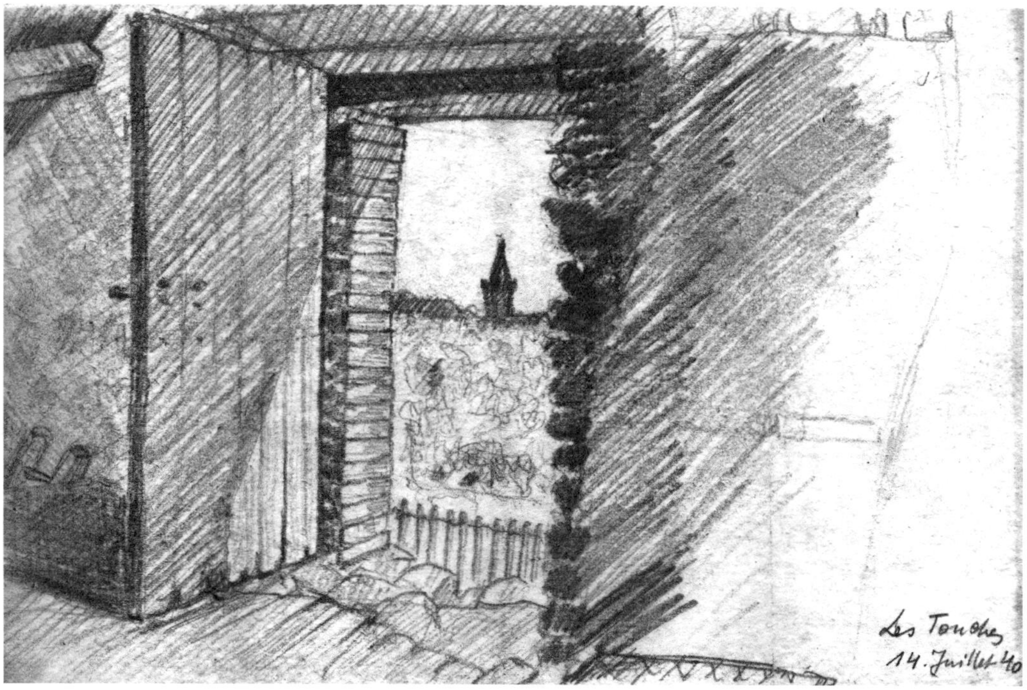

Inserted in the diary are two drawings on toilet paper, this one of Les Touches, a boarding house, and the other of Albert [page 29]. Later on [14 July 1940], there is also a drawing in the diary itself [page 34].

15 July 1940

Diary Entry

Enfin deux lettres

1. Dragignan
2. Ministry says that Franka is in Lourdes (was 17.VI.40)

permanent hunger
journées sans tabac
little Maurice broke his leg
why does he scream? because he broke his leg?
I am hungry but I sit quietly

16 July Diary Entry

no letters
allocation à la mairie[4]
doctor visits Maurice
Alphin, autocars, tomorrow 7.30
1 Gauloise – first cigarette
1 elegante
Mme Alphin makes a proposition.
5 frs
petit Nosenholc (fou)

Problems of survival loom large every day. Stefan often notes that he has to mend his trousers, that he is worried that his boots will fall apart. That he doesn't really know what to do next or how to get money for a train ticket, and that he's permanently hungry, and there's no tobacco. Today, at last, he receives unemployment benefit at the town hall and smokes his first cigarette, a Gauloise. The following day he is ready to leave Plessé. There are meat balls for the journey. He makes a drawing of the local bistro and is soon ready to leave for Nantes. From Nantes he will be able to get to Paris.

17 July Diary Entry

no letters
meat balls for the journey
Mme Bịnenstry wine 20 frs
6 km/h
In front of Coress, a lady with a suitcase.
Mme Perier?
from the prefecture. Nantes. Tramway
centre ville.
Beau Séjour
supper. And perhaps 5 frs per day?

Sleeping in my clothes. Children

Once in Nantes [where he arrives on 17 July], he meets other people, some like him en route for the capital. He moves in, listens to their stories: 'Chaqu'un sa petite histoire'. The most frequent diary entry is that there are no letters and no news from or about Franciszka, although there are occasional letters from people he has met on his journey. Stefan has a bath, goes to the laundry, visits the library, and plays dominoes. He makes more drawings, one with the caption: *monologue, I, the neighbour from Normandy* [see overleaf].

18 July Diary Entry

breakfast, and once again lunch, supper
Lepanowski (1 finger on his hand)

4 Unemployment benefit

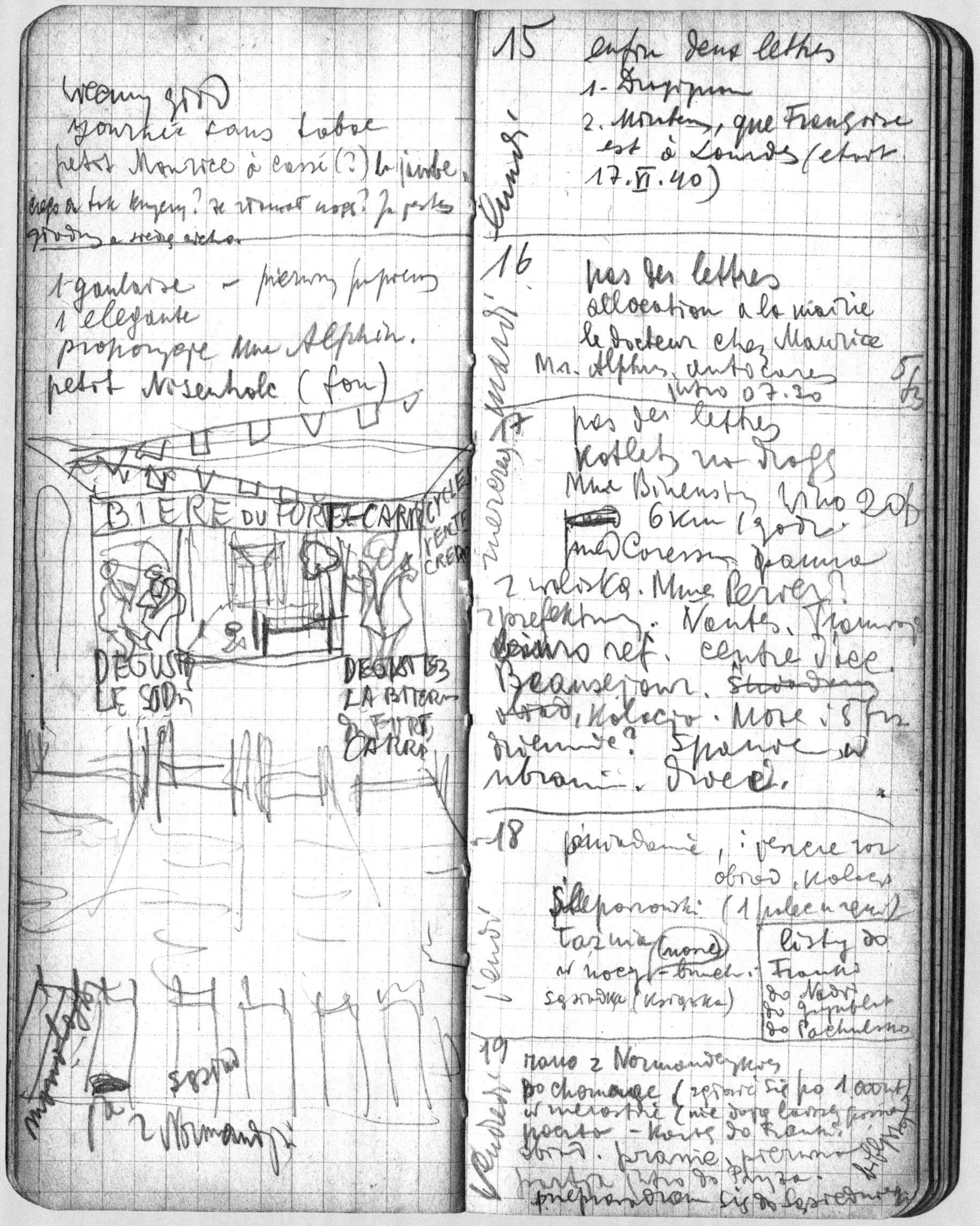

Stefan's diary, 15–19 July 1940

18 July 1940

bath house
in the night a stretcher – stomach
female neighbour – a book
letters to Franka, Nadia, Grynblat, Pachulska

19 July Diary Entry

morning with a man from Normandy
to get unemployment benefit (to apply for 1,000nt) [sic]
in the town hall they don't give laissez-passer
Post Office – card to Franka
lunch, laundry
the first group leaves tomorrow for Paris
library
I move in with my neighbours –
Chaqu'un sa petite histoire
Les visions (dreams)
surnames
bread and pomegranates
7 princes
dominoes with an old gentleman, born 1873
Beau Séjour
Grown-up conversations
Olga
Dives

20 July Diary Entry

no letters
2 lunches.
The first group has gone to Paris: Jan Kamieniarz, Ludwik Ślepecki,
the young one from Lyon, the one with black hair and a little moustache,
the one-eyed Yugoslav, the fat stepmother with husband and children,
the 62-year-old woman singer.

21 July Diary Entry

Card from Pachulska
no letters
nurse, chef, M Luret, landlady, conversation
grandfather is going to Belgium
carpenter, wife, hunchbacked daughter

22 July Diary Entry

letters from Pachulska, from Kramsztyk and from Gruszczyńska
Voltaire: Choix de Lettres
no post
rain, espèce de bruyère

23 July 1940

Meanwhile, 23 July, Franciszka sends telegram to Aleksander Żyw at the Polish Consulate in Toulouse asking him to look for Stefan, only to hear two weeks later that they have no news.

Telegram from Franciszka to Aleksander Żyw

CHERCHEZ MARI SI POSSIBLE TÉLÉGRAPHIEZ 9 ROYAL AVENUE
LONDON SW3 AMITIÉS – FRANKA THEMERSON

Diary Entry

Post Office in the morning – nothing
I read: *Choix de Lettres*
nurse: answer tomorrow afternoon
a Pole in a beret, cigarettes

24 July Diary Entry

no post. nurse didn't come
Frenchman from Paris

25 July Diary Entry

tomorrow last train to Paris.
The fat woman's birthday, wine
town hall, prefecture
During the night some people arrived from Bordeaux

26 July Diary Entry

I get up at 7. Card sent back from Lourdes
letter from Edek and Ludwik
40 frs unemployment
To Paris (René Clair, Anka)
the journey via Lille

Some groups had already gone to Paris, Stefan takes the last train on 26 July. Paris is the same as he remembers it and different at the same time. Most importantly, he is not safe, and it is not wise for him to stay at any address for too long. He spends the first night in Paris with Ludwik Lille, and the next one with his old friend Mietek Bibrowski.

27 July Telegram from Hania Kawa in Bucharest to Franciszka in London

NO NEWS ABOUT STEFEK STOP MARYLA FAMILY[5] ALRIGHT ASK
GILDESGAME WHERE MARYSIA SZYMEK STOP ARON ALRIGHT
= HANIA KAWA

Diary Entry

Paris
mairie

rue Monsieur le Prince
bistrot coffee
Ludwik
Rozenblat
Lamander

5 Maryla Family refers to Maryla, Franciszka's sister; Łucja, her mother; Jasia, her daughter; and Stefan's family: his mother; sister Irena; her husband, Stefan Miller; cousin Anka.

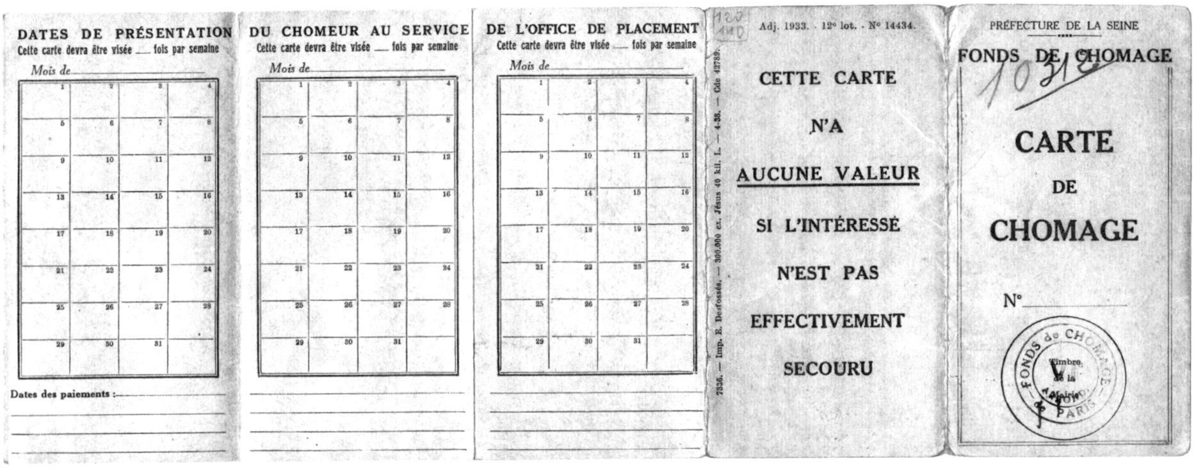

DATES DE PRÉSENTATION DU CHOMEUR AU SERVICE DE L'OFFICE DE PLACEMENT

Cette carte devra être visée ___ fois par semaine

Mois de ___

Dates des paiements :

Adj. 1933. - 12e lot. - No 14434.

CETTE CARTE N'A AUCUNE VALEUR SI L'INTÉRESSÉ N'EST PAS EFFECTIVEMENT SECOURU

PRÉFECTURE DE LA SEINE

FONDS DE CHOMAGE

CARTE DE CHOMAGE

N°

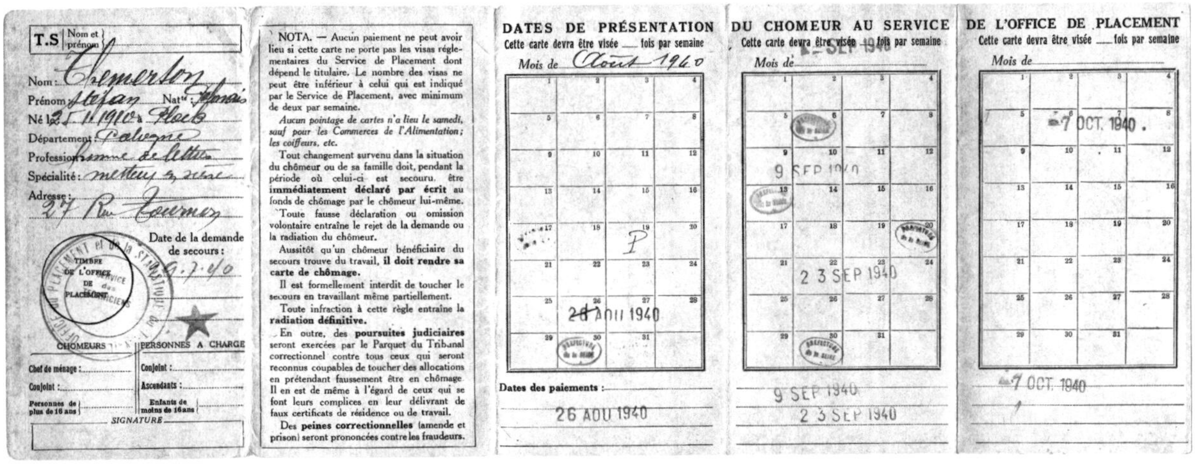

T.S | Nom et prénom

Nom : Themerson

Prénom : Stefan Natté : Polonais

Né le 25 II 1910 à Plock

Département : Pologne

Profession : homme de lettres

Spécialité : metteur en scène

Adresse : 27 Rue Tournon

Date de la demande de secours : 29.7.40

CHOMEURS | PERSONNES A CHARGE

NOTA. — Aucun paiement ne peut avoir lieu si cette carte ne porte pas les visas réglementaires du Service de Placement dont dépend le titulaire. Le nombre des visas ne peut être inférieur à celui qui est indiqué par le Service de Placement, avec minimum de deux par semaine.

Aucun pointage de cartes n'a lieu le samedi, sauf pour les Commerces de l'Alimentation; les coiffeurs, etc.

Tout changement survenu dans la situation du chômeur ou de sa famille doit, pendant la période où celui-ci est secouru, être **immédiatement déclaré par écrit** au fonds de chômage par le chômeur lui-même.

Toute fausse déclaration ou omission volontaire entraîne le rejet de la demande ou la radiation du chômeur.

Aussitôt qu'un chômeur bénéficiaire du secours trouve du travail, **il doit rendre sa carte de chômage.**

Il est formellement interdit de toucher le secours en travaillant même partiellement.

Toute infraction à cette règle entraîne la **radiation définitive.**

En outre, des **poursuites judiciaires** seront exercées par le Parquet du Tribunal correctionnel contre tous ceux qui seront reconnus coupables de toucher des allocations en prétendant faussement être en chômage. Il en est de même à l'égard de ceux qui se font leurs complices en leur délivrant de faux certificats de résidence ou de travail.

Des **peines correctionnelles** (amende et prison) seront prononcées contre les fraudeurs.

DATES DE PRÉSENTATION DU CHOMEUR AU SERVICE DE L'OFFICE DE PLACEMENT

Mois de Août 1940

26 AOU 1940 — 9 SEP 1940 — 23 SEP 1940 — 7 OCT. 1940

Stefan's *Carte de chômage*,
L'Office de Placement in Paris,
applied for 29 July 1940,
covering August, September,
last date 7 October 1940

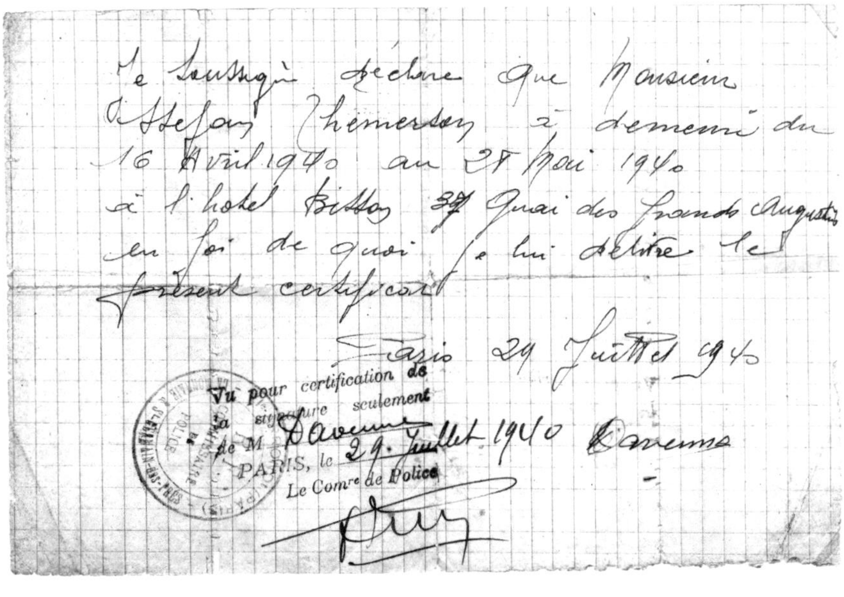

Je soussigné déclare que Monsieur Stefan Themerson a demeuré du 16 Avril 1940 au 28 Mai 1940 à l'hotel Bisson 37 Quai des Grands Augustins en foi de quoi je lui délivre le présent certificat

Paris 29 Juillet 1940

Vu pour certification de signature seulement de M. Davenne

PARIS, le 29 Juillet 1940 Davenne

Le Comre de Police

29 July 1940
Handwritten document from the
Police, Saint-Germain-des-Prés,
Paris

Je soussigné déclare que
Monsieur Stefan Themerson
a demeuré du 16 avril au 28 mai
1940 à l'Hotel Bisson, 37 quai
des Grands-Augustins en foi
de quoi je lui delivre le present
certificat.

signed: M. Davenne,
Le Commissaire de Police

28 July 1940

Diary Entry
Bibrowski is in Paris

29 July **Diary Entry**
Pol-Dives. Sleep at Bibrowski's

Stefan's first night in Paris, 57 bd Saint-Jacques, Paris 14. He receives Certificat de Domicile for Paris at the town hall and 30 francs.

One of the people who offer him shelter is Pol-Dives, the master of the magic lantern, whom Stefan had befriended and written about.

30 July **Diary Entry**
railway station
Grenelle, rue des Eaux, Olga
Ludwik, Pol-Dives – Hangar
bed
Bibrowski – supper with X

31 July **Diary Entry**
lunch at the 'Bund'
Polish bookshop

1 August **Diary Entry**
soupe populaire

4 August **Diary Entry**
lunch at Mme Pachulska's
letters returned
hotel landlord/or/landlady

5 August

Britain signs an agreement with the Polish Government in London, and two days later with the Free French under Charles de Gaulle.

Telegram from Polconsul in Toulouse to Franciszka
CHERCHONS MARI COMMUNIQUERONS ADRESSE = POLCONSUL

Diary Entry
town hall
morning Zber
supper at Kaliszers
money from Sacha

6 August **Telegram from Polconsul in Toulouse to Franciszka**
MARI INCONNU

Telegram from Polmission État Vichy to Franciszka
ADRESSEZ DEMANDE CROIX ROUGE POLONAISE TOULOUSE QUI
RECHERCHE STEFAN THEMERSON RÉFÉRENCE 645 = POLMISSION

6 August 1940

Cable from Mira Złotowska in Casablanca to Franciszka

STEFEK SAIN ET SAUF EN FRANCE STOP AVISEZ TENNENBAUM TEMPEL AVEC NOUS = ZŁOTOWSCY 156 BOULEVARD ANFA CHEZ LAREDO

Only on 6 August does FT receive news from Mira and Ignacy Złotowski in Casablanca that Stefan is alive and well in France. That he is in contact with Zosia Kramsztyk and she can pass her address to Stefan so that he can write to her direct.

Later, Mira advises Franciszka that Stefan is in the Occupied Zone. They have no further details for the moment although they are trying to find out more from Sophie [i.e. Zosia].

Diary Entry

Edek – breakfast in Parc Monceau on a bench
town hall – refusal

evening at Sacha's
soap, margarine ASTRA

Recensement des étrangers motif de séjour:

> Je veux, pour composer chastement mes églogues,
> Coucher auprès du ciel, comme les astrologues,
> Et, voisin des clochers, écouter en rêvant
> Leurs hymnes solennels emportés par le vent.
> Les deux mains au menton, du haut de ma mansarde,
> Je verrai l'atelier qui chante et qui bavarde;
> Les tuyaux, les clochers, ces mâts de la cité,
> Et les grands ciels qui font rêver d'éternité.

from 'Paysage' (Tableaux Parisiens), *Les Fleurs du Mal* by Baudelaire.

Stefan's dream: holes, vermin
meat next to the bugs
Irka to clean out the holes with a key
I – a sublimator
NapoLéon's soldiers…

– Zber is knocking at the door. Meat.
Edek, gardien de nuit, in Hôtel Univers, rue Monsieur le Prince

7 August **Diary Entry**

soap
lunch at home
 pea soup
 slice of tomato
 onion, carrot
 steamed potatoes
 carrots with sugar
 tea
Mietek to town hall

8 August 1940

Diary Entry

moving from Sacha [Bronstein] – possibility of finding out something about Franka
Hangar[6]
rue La Rochefoucauld, lunch in Civiale[7]
cousin – 50 frs
jar of jam
barber – haircut
supper

Stefan has to keep on the move. Strict measures against the Jews and immigrants come into force at the beginning of August 1940. On 8 August, he finds shelter with Pol-Dives, in his hangar, at 12 rue Berryer. Pol-Dives advises him not to open the door should anyone knock. Stefan met Pol-Dives originally when Teresa Żarnower, an artist of great originality whom he admired, introduced him to his magic lantern performances. There is a note from Pol-Dives and another one later.

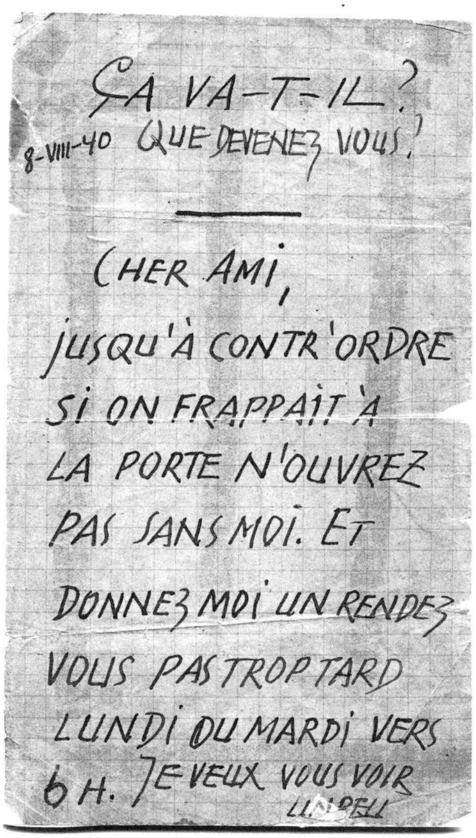
ÇA VA-T-IL?
8-VIII-40 QUE DEVENEZ VOUS?

CHER AMI,
JUSQU'À CONTR'ORDRE
SI ON FRAPPAIT À
LA PORTE N'OUVREZ
PAS SANS MOI. ET
DONNEZ MOI UN RENDEZ-
VOUS PAS TROP TARD
LUNDI OU MARDI VERS
6 H. JE VEUX VOUS VOIR

Another note

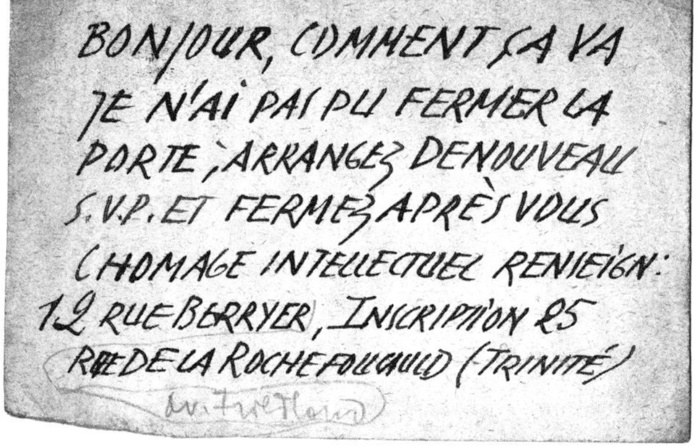
BONJOUR, COMMENT ÇA VA
JE N'AI PAS PU FERMER LA
PORTE; ARRANGEZ DE NOUVEAU
S.V.P. ET FERMEZ APRÈS VOUS
CHOMAGE INTELLECTUEL RENSEIGN:
12 RUE BERRYER, INSCRIPTION 25
RUE DE LA ROCHEFOUCAULD (TRINITÉ)

6 The hangar belongs to Pol-Dives who offers it to Stefan for the night.

7 Civiale is the home of Andrée and Tema Temerson, and Marcel, 3 rue Civiale, Paris 10.

8 August 1940

On the back of the card of *Les Amis de la Lanterne Magique*, on which Pol-Dives writes his message, Stefan drew a map showing rue Berryer, and wrote this poem:

Apart from this moment
there's nothing anywhere to recall

No one will put crumbs of hope
into your extended palm
I am a republic of people,
cuddle up to me
You will go when you want to
and you will be free
not to go
If you don't need anything
you won't want anything.
Wanderer, you must not rest
wind covered you with the illusion of
warmth
Like Andersen's Little Match Girl
Christmas Eve frost will anaesthetise you
if you fall asleep.

Look ahead, already behind me
are traces of those footsteps
get up and follow them,
to the sound of rubber soles
Get up
and go

Oprócz obecnej chwili
nic nie masz nigdzie wspominać

Nikt ci w dłoń wyciagniętą
nie złoży jałmużnej nadziei
Jam jest rzecz pospolita ludzi,
przytul się do mnie
Iść będziesz mógł kiedy zechcesz
i będzie ci wolno
nie iść
Jeśli ci nic już nie trzeba
więc ci nie zbywa na niczem.
Wędrowcze, nie wolno ci spocząć
Złudzeniem ciepła wiatr cię owinął
jak Andersena dziewczynkę z zapałkami
uśpi cię mróz wigilijny
jeżeli zaśniesz.

Spójrz naprzód, już po mnie kroczą
Ślady tych stóp
wstań podąż niemi
gumowych podeszew mlaskiem
Wstań
naprzód idź

9 August **Telegram from the Złotowskis in Casablanca to Franciszka**

STEFEK EN CONTACT AVEC SOPHIA KRAMSTYK TRANSMIS TON ADDRESSE IL ÉCRIRA DIRECTEMENT OÙ EST LEYBERG MILLE BAISERS = ZŁOTOWSCY

Diary Entry

Rochefoucauld
Polish bookshop[8]
supper at Sacha's
letter to Franka via [Józef] Wittlin

10 August **Diary Entry**

Polish bookshop
telephone conversation with [Szymon] Konarski
lunch in Civiale
provisions for home
invitation to the country

8 Polish bookshop in Saint-Germain-des-Prés.

10 August 1940

work for a week
pile de poche
supper
lettuce, sugar, semolina, tea, cofee-chicory, paté, macaroni

Marcel, the barber, asks if I have work and says 'we'll leave payment for later!'

On 10 August Stefan loses the Memento Magnitudinis, which Franka gave him before they parted. He leaves it behind in the town hall. Stefan often mentions it later in his letters to Franka, but by that time he can't remember when and where it was lost.

Although it is never described, we can assume that it is a drawing on paper – perhaps there are some words or a quotation apart from the title.

12 August **Diary Entry**

[Szymon] Laks. Rochefoucauld

13 August **Diary Entry**

Rochefoucauld no

14 August **Diary Entry**

mayor's office

16 August **Diary Entry**

Hotel Bisson (son-in-law is dead)
bare head
(printer of works by Władysław Broniewski and Bruno Jasieński)

18 August **Telegram from Mira Złotowska in Casablanca to Franciszka**

STEFEK ZONE OCCUPÉE CONTACT ROMPU TÉLÉGRAPHIERONS DÈS QU AURONS NOUVELLES SOIS TRANQUILLE AMITIÉS = ZŁOTOWSKA

20 August **Telegram from Polish Consulate in Toulouse to Franciszka**

AUCUNE NOUVELLE DE STEFAN THEMERSON = POLCONSUL

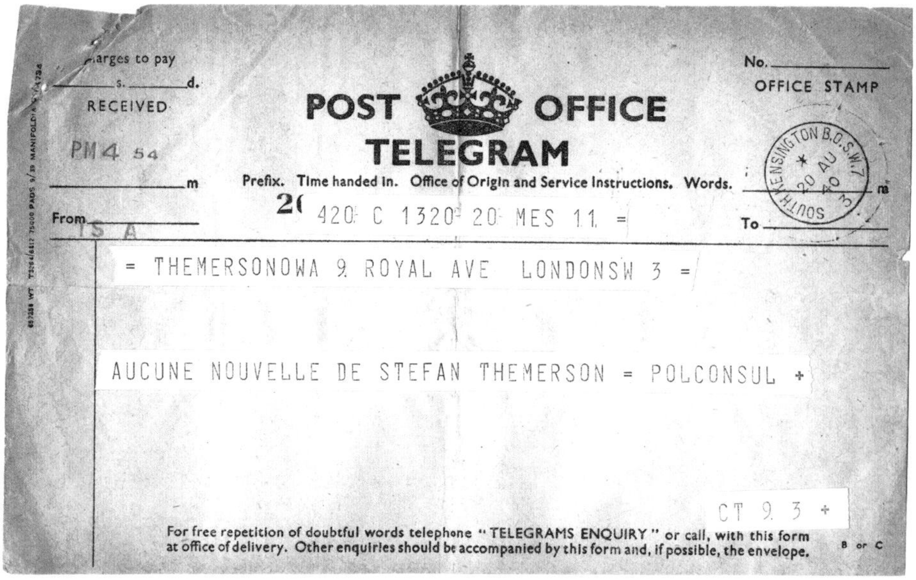

Charges to pay ___s. ___d.
RECEIVED
PM 4 54

POST OFFICE TELEGRAM

No.
OFFICE STAMP

Prefix. Time handed in. Office of Origin and Service Instructions. Words.

From TS A

2(420 C 1320 20 MES 11 =

To

= THEMERSONOWA 9 ROYAL AVE LONDONSW 3 =

AUCUNE NOUVELLE DE STEFAN THEMERSON = POLCONSUL +

CT 9 3 +

For free repetition of doubtful words telephone "TELEGRAMS ENQUIRY" or call, with this form at office of delivery. Other enquiries should be accompanied by this form and, if possible, the envelope.

B or C

23 August 1940

On 23 August, Józef Wittlin, in Nice, writes to Stefan, advising him to find a place at one of the Polish Red Cross hostels in Vichy France, which are filling up quickly.

24 August **Telegram from Ignacy Złotowski in Casablanca to Franciszka**

JAMAIS EU ADRESSE NI DETAILS ESPÉRONS OBTENIR BIENTÔT PAR INTERMÉDIAIRE SOPHIE TRANSMETTRONS IMMÉDIATEMENT AMITIÉS
= ZŁOTOWSKI

31 August **Diary Entry**

M. ceases trading

The Polish Consulates in Lyon, Marseille and Toulouse close at the end of August. After the Polish Embassy in France closes in September 1940, Poles in France can receive assistance from the offices of the Polish Red Cross, the so-called Bureaux Polonais. From 12 June 1941, and officially from 1 September 1941, Groupement d'Assistances aux Polonais en France (GAPF) offered assistance under the auspices of the French Ministry of the Interior and the Ministry of Labour.

6 September **Diary Entry**

Kama C[lavel].

7 September

The worst bombing of the London Blitz begins, although heavy bombing had already started a week before. These very heavy raids will continue into mid-October.

Diary Entry

arrival of Mme Bibrowska
meeting with Kama C.
I am moving

8 September **Diary Entry**

cleaning
soup
Le Misanthrope – Comédie-Française
meeting with trader 'Wy'

matches - .50; coffee - 1.0; theatre 3.25; coffee 0.75; bread 1.60;

Do some people imagine that Molière wrote poems in order to break the metre of the poem, to recite in 'literary fashion' what belongs to poetry, to art?

As far as lines of poetry are concerned. The lines of poetry could be a theatrical convention just as arias are a convention of the opera, and I don't see any reason why they should be made 'naturalistic'.

9 September **Diary Entry**

Kama with [Bronisław] Horowicz to lunch on rue Tournon 9
unemployment money
cigarettes 7.00; lighter fuel – 4.00; wine 2.00; lunch 2.75; bread 1.60.

8 September 1940

Stefan finds work for a week but does not say what it is. He continues to write down what he eats, spends, borrows, pays back. He goes to see *Le Misanthrope* at the Comédie-Française, *Tartuffe* at the Odéon; visits the Polish bookshop, goes to Hotel Bisson, where he'd stayed earlier. He reads and translates Molière.

10 September **Diary Entry**

cinema
Kama. Supper

11 September **Diary Entry**

news about a money transfer [from Franciszka in London]
accommodation at the Clavels
Kama's husband
fountain pen

13 September **Diary Entry**

checking in on Mietek
lunch on St Honoré
dîner chez Chonchon [Sacha Bronstein]
Bergson's *Le Rire*

20 September **Diary Entry**

dropping in on Civiale and lunch

21 September **Diary Entry**

Lille in the morning, soup
evening at the café de Flore
Could there be letters in Toulouse?

24 September **Diary Entry**

Lolleum quotes a poem

25 September **Diary Entry**

pre. Odéon *Tartuffe*.

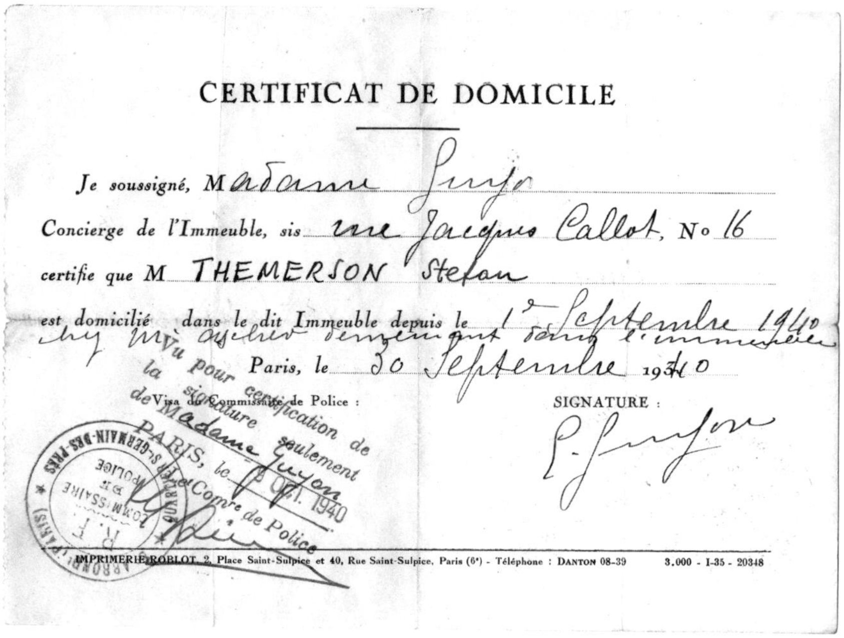

CERTIFICAT DE DOMICILE

Je soussigné, M adame Guyon
Concierge de l'Immeuble, sis rue Jacques Callot, No 16
certifie que M THEMERSON Stefan
est domicilié dans le dit Immeuble depuis le 1er Septembre 1940

Paris, le 30 Septembre 1940

Visa du Commissaire de Police :

Vu pour certification de la signature de Madame Guyon seulement
Paris, le 9 Oct. 1940
Le Comre de Police

SIGNATURE :

IMPRIMERIE ROBLOT, 2, Place Saint-Sulpice et 40, Rue Saint-Sulpice, Paris (6e) - Téléphone : DANTON 08-39 3.000 - 1-35 - 20348

30 September 1940
Certificat de Domicile
Certified by police 9 October 1940

Certificate from the concierge, Mme Guyon, of 16 rue Jacques-Callot, Paris, certifying that Stefan has stayed there from 1 September 1940

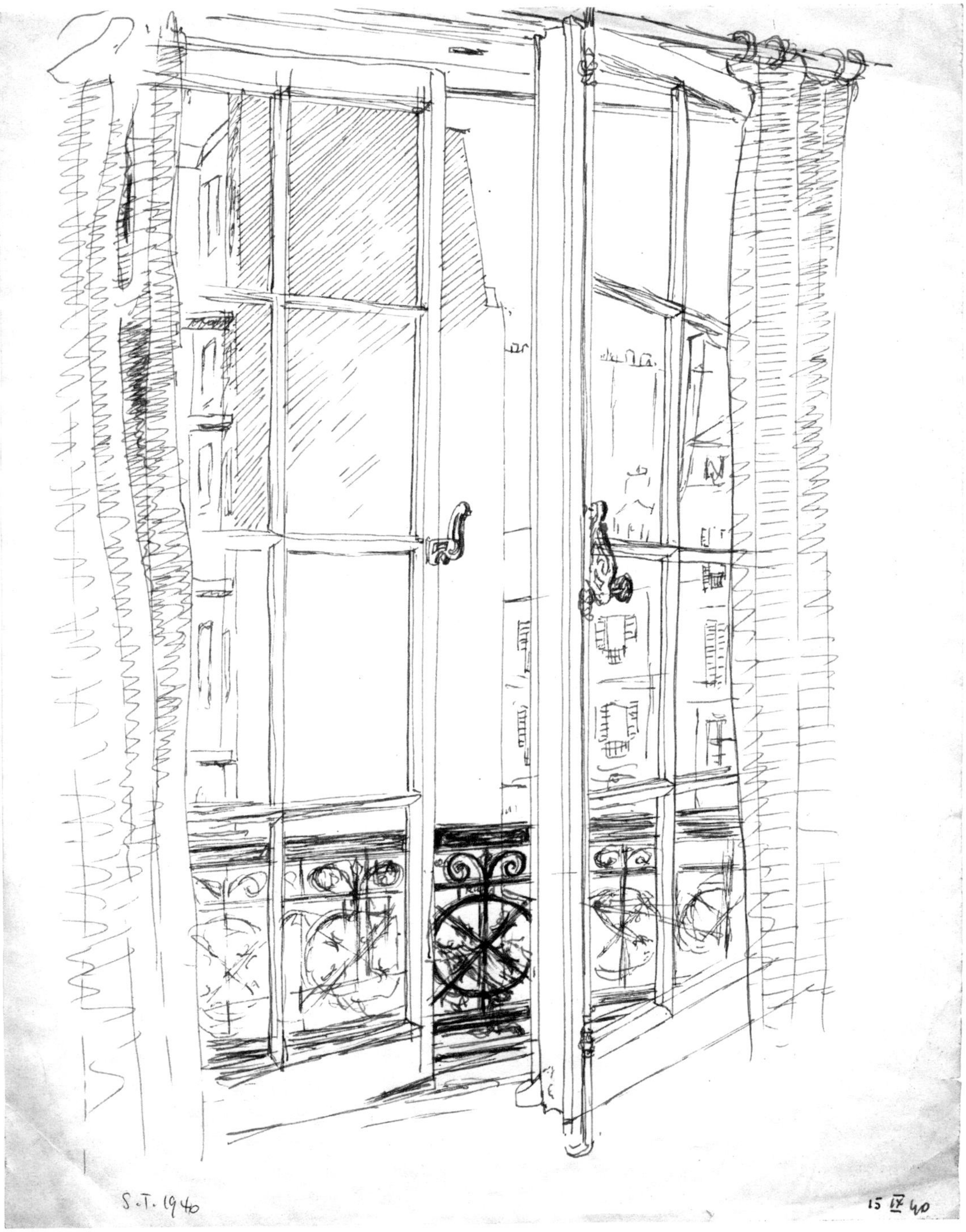

Stefan's drawing of french windows in the flat of the Bronsteins at 4bis rue des Eaux in Paris

At the end of the diary, he writes two poems: 'Mademoiselle Jeanette...' and 'Och, kurwa mać, panowie...', but what he is really thinking of is making a film, in colour. And there are few words in capitals in different colours on the end paper of the diary: FILM EN COULEUR SCENARIO.

26 September 1940

Entries from here up to and including 13 October 1940 were written on unattached dated pages, loose inside the diaries

Diary Entry

Matinée at the Odéon. *Tartuffe*. I intended to spend 3.50 frs but it turned out to be 15. A monstrous sum, but I didn't leave the ticket office. And instead of finding myself in the gods, in a Galician way, with the swallows (how much they resemble bats in flight. I was familiar with bats from pictures, but after staying in Plume Chat Huant and afterwards in the attic in Les Touches, I shall always confuse them with myself. 'Elle est belle, l'hirondelle, – il est beau aussi le roi des souris'). I found myself in the fourth row of the stalls. Next to me – a German sailor. The sailor had been in Paris 20 years before. He had been looking for materials for his work on the 16th century in the Bibliothèque Nationale. He was at any rate a literary critic, or theatre critic 'chez nous'. All this emerged from a conversation he initiated with his neighbour on the left. The neighbour on the right didn't participate in this polite exchange – perhaps because he spoke French worse than the sailor. In the third row, also a bespectacled uniform. A young chap, who blushed scarlet, when after a series of misunderstandings the usherette explained to him that 'they don't pay her here' and that it was the audience that had to pay her. 'Triumph' – some polite Frenchman called out. In the second row Erik von Stroheim was in uniform and with a monocle – but looking as if he had been through a mangle. It is a pity that the monocle fell from his eye only during the Molière one-act play, *Les précieuses ridicules*, in the course of a clownish burlesque.

I prefer to look at 'these gentlemen' as the French call them here or in Comédie-Française. (I saw one at *Le Misanthrope* about ten days ago – a thin bespectacled youngster, 'an intellectual', who after prolonged attempts, got leave, as it happens, to Paris. 'À Paris…' I remember that – record, at a showing of SAF[9], and later at Anka's. 'À Paris… a, a; a, a!') then in the metro going to Place Pigalle.

Rome conquered Greece, but Greece subjugated Rome. It's possible that this is what it will now look like from point of view of history. But should an ordinary mortal insert into his eye-socket the glass eye of history? If everybody thought about it as history, it would stop happening, simply because it is built from the testimony of endless living eyes, glinting with hatred and winking slyly, or screwed up penetratingly, or misted over lustfully, or bright and blunt, blurred and 'bloodthirsty', stupified and mad – one could go on and on. But, on the other hand – what does it mean, this 'if everyone did it'? These words are meaningless. And why should we try to behave like everyone else? Or even as everyone else tries to behave? Nonsense.

People don't think much about Tartuffe himself. There's only great amazement that he wanted to expend so much energy and inventiveness – just in order to gain a million francs – the value of a house and a cash box entrusted to him for safekeeping by the landlord. If, through his hypocrisy, he had really wanted to gain his landlord's friendship – the disproportion of the means to the goal would have in it all the characteristics of the tragic. But still – it is we who more readily want to be cheated than Tartuffe wants to cheat. Unnoticed by us, neglected by Molière, what is simultaneously taking place is the tragedy of the landlord.

9 Spółdzielnia Autorów Filmowych (SAF) – Co-operative of Art Film Authors – a vital, avant-garde film-making co-operative, co-founded by the Themersons in Warsaw in 1935.

– Not only did he realise that he had been cheated, but his faith in the ideal that he had held on to was shattered. Also, it was not Molière who developed that theme, but Shakespeare. I don't suppose that I would behave like Molière's landlord if I assume at this moment, that it would not be Molière but Shakespeare who would have to take to his writer's desk this sailor, sitting next to me in the stalls – if, after leaving the theatre, he were to have to take part in some act of destruction, for instance, of the Bibliothèque Nationale, where he worked. People make their lives easier by simplifying and generalising (in that way, they discard things that raise the cost of certainty), because they want, at any price, to be unflawed heroes, just as the heroes of the theatre. Hamlet doesn't belong here – no, really only this 'strange' Hamlet is the most normal, the most straight-from-the-mould-human – the most filled out character. If we discarded from Hamlet one after another, each time a different 99 percent of his character, one will get 100 uniform heroes – because uniformity is achieved by rejecting – ergo (as the Gravedigger said in Act 5) – by impoverishing oneself. I remember the words of Monsieur P. in the café Deux Magots and elsewhere, often repeated – how one has to slaughter, burn, and not forgive. Not so long ago, M Ch. said that he would be less moved by the sight of a slaughtered child than a slain puppy. It is the same M Ch. who pronounced the sentence – not without sense – that the French spirit was expressed by Frenchmen not willing to fight. But what do these few words connected one to another according to the logic of syntax really mean? One would have to describe the entire life of M Ch. for them to assume weight and form. Because in these matters there are no truths that are abstract and absolute. These are all truths pronounced by people, they are all individual truths – they cannot be proved or disproved by any physicist or by any mystic. Today, one can only describe them, just as physics and astronomy were only descriptive at their beginnings. And, if science is to encompass EVERYTHING, and not only what can be measured directly with a physical instrument, then the novelist fulfils the role of an investigator – a describer, a dramaturg tries to create a synthesis, and a poet… a poet?

Sent five cards today.

27 September

An edict against the Jews is announced in Paris and a census of the Jewish population in France is ordered.

On 29 August, Mira Złotowska writes from Laredo to Franciszka to tell her that she heard from Zosia Kramsztyk that Stefan has been found and is alright. By now this letter should have reached her.

29 September Diary Entry

On Friday, Tema had the last oral exam. I waited for her in the hall of the Sorbonne. From somewhere I remember that smell of the Ciechocinek[10] baths, but from where? The smell of wet marble? The hall is lined not with wallpaper but with plaques showing the names of donors (sums in millions of francs and dollars), the Rockefellers, the Carnegies, the Rothschilds, and other *minorum pecuniarum*. Looking at the names of departments, chairs, lectures – there are none that I would not like to attend. (Maybe this is why I didn't complete any

10 Ciechocinek – spa and holiday resort in Poland.

course of study.) But I would not like to attend any single one, not any one by itself. Oh, how frightened I feel of these specialisms, and how I should not like to get to the state of these people who look at the world from the point of view of history, or point of view of physics, point of view of religion, point of view of economics, point of view of art. Studies in any one discipline seem to me just like choosing one of many possible lenses through which to look at the world. I am reminded of Carrell's appeal to the young; *L'Homme, cet inconnu*,[11] to produce from their ranks such a boy, who would wish to devote 20 years to higher studies, in order to make it possible to have, at least on the earth, a man who would be au courant of all studies. It seems to me rather naïve and perhaps it would even fulfil one of Bergson's recipes for the ridiculous.

Synthesis of studies, that's something else. One will have to find out what is this institution, L'Histoire des Sciences?

Hypertrophy of one field of knowledge seems to me to be not so different from atrophy. In order to penetrate their field, specialists leap onto all sorts of radiating paths. But to widen the horizon, to see the whole better, one has to climb always onto some sentry tower, to look around and observe what the specialists have learned and their fates. Unfortunately, at the Sorbonne, there are all sorts of lecture theatres in different departments, but I could not see a tower. Unless it is that of L'Histoire des Sciences.

Tema passed her exam. It made me very glad. She entered knowing very little French. In one year she did a two-year course, while working – sewing – and now is a teacher of French as a foreign language. Leaving the Sorbonne, she remembered a Gypsy, who came to visit them at home in Płock. Tema was 8 at the time. 'The young lady will learn in great schools' – the Gypsy predicted from her hand. And now Tema weaves further plans, she wants to continue to study, write a thesis, etc.

On the way back, I dropped in at the Bibrowskis. They reminded me that it was the anniversary, simultaneously, of the occupation of Warsaw and the death of his father. It was black in the streets when I was returning home.

Today, I sent 3 cards.

Yesterday, M K. came to see me. He brought four enormous Canadian apples. I gave him supper – rollmops, tomato salad, spaghetti with tomato sauce, bread, butter!, tea with sugar, biscuits, grapes. My bouts of hunger have started again. I eat twice as much as before the war, but despite that there's never a moment when I've had enough. I can eat everything in any quantities, at any time of day or night. Hunger does not go away. One day, I didn't eat at all, but instead had two glasses of cognac – it proved to be a good remedy. I didn't feel hunger, didn't think about food and advanced the poem a good way forward. M K. is very nice but I still don't see him clearly. I wouldn't be able to write his psychological portrait yet.

We walked for quite a long time into the night. He likes Saint-Sulpice and all the time refers to Huysmans. He suggests that I still prefer Gothic. Still? Because

11 Alexis Carrell (1873-1944) French surgeon and biologist, *L'Homme, cet inconnu,* 1935.

young people prefer Gothic, afterwards they discover Romanesque, and afterwards the bulk of the Renaissance. He is planning two works in the area of psychology-mythology-history of art. But talks about them very timidly and calls them – 'trifles'. I have decided on the plan of the poem. 7 parts.

Lille
filter of Teresa
friendship
poem
apples
hunger – biscuits, grapes, bread, lunch
brother lawyer, story of the lawyer, who defended a thief – children, did he really steal?
he wants to paint the angels – is it possible now? To write.

This first preprinted card Stefan sends to Franciszka from 3 rue Civiale, Paris X is dated 27 September. He sends it to Bureau des Recherches des Réfugiés Polonais, 72 bld de Strasbourg, Toulouse. A similar card follows three days later.

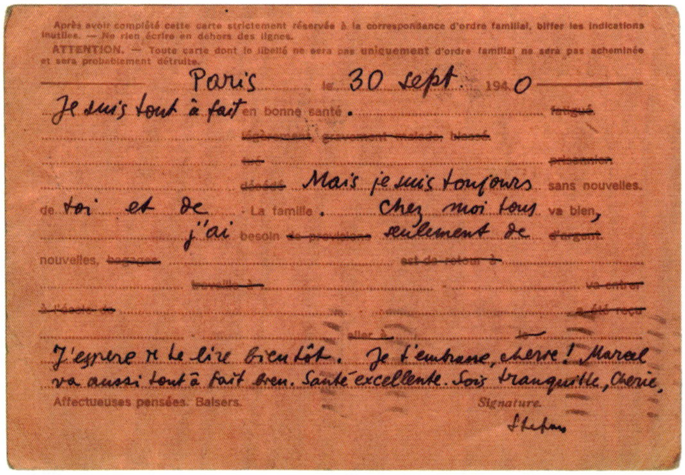

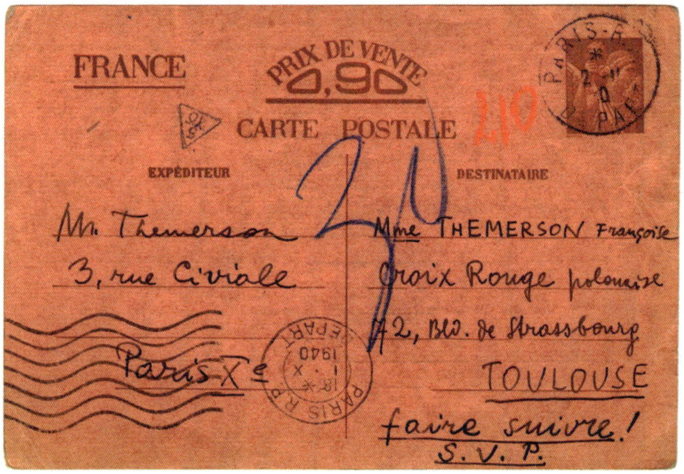

30 September 1940
Preprinted card from Stefan to Franciszka

Je suis tout à fait en bonne santé. Mais je suis toujours sans nouvelles de toi et de La famille. Chez moi tout va bien, j'ai besoin seulement de nouvelles.
J'espère de te lire bientôt. Je t'embrasse, Chérie! Marcel[12] va aussi va tout à fait bien. Santé excellente. Sois tranquille, Chérie. Stefan

Diary Entry

Yesterday Ludwik woke me up. It was already 11.30. That beautiful time of early rising had gone. In truth, I don't go to sleep before 2 or 3 am, I read. I write. Ludwik suggested writing a play. Together. This is already the second 'proposal'. The first came from Mietek. At that time when I still lived at his place. The theme of that one was to be an American gangster, who arrives in Paris to introduce Chicago's methods, but sees that the chief gangster who beats him to it by a head is an even bigger criminal. Broken, he feels that he has lost, returns to America. I withdrew. Mietek was going to write it himself but I don't think he is bothering. He started [some] 'systematic' studies and perhaps this killed his project. Ludwik was promising to come with a completed scenario. But what he brought had neither meat nor bone. 'Freedom'– His definition of freedom: that everyone should be able to choose the regime to suit him. For God's sake – so freedom is to exist, in other words, in the sort of political system in which everyone can choose the political system he prefers. This is a false recipe and not a definition. A Stalinist-communist is free in the Soviet Union; a Nazi is free in the German Reich, and a rich man is free in a democratic country. Freedom is the opposite of captivity. But we are enslaved not only by the political system, but also by the laws of nature, and trapped by our past, which determines what we are (this adds up to our lives). He finally proposed a screenplay like this: a lawyer, who became disgusted by lies, abandons everything, wife and family, and moves to another town. Works as a labourer. A new slavery of the daily grind. He associates with a woman who abandons him.

Ludwik stayed with me until the evening. We left together. Cold already grabs you. I dropped in at the Ludwiks' and stayed with them for supper. Of course, the menu is important enough to note: chicken soup, tomato salad, sweet pasta. The little one is very funny. Speaks slowly and seriously, through his nose. He turns around to look at women, very self-possessed, assessing them expertly and asking himself in his heart of hearts, why actually this one is supposed to be more terrific than that one? Tomorrow he goes to school for the first time this year.

On the boulevard – 'Viens mon chéri'. Willingly in principle, but it's already late (hour of the curfew), it's cold, dark, a matter of money, maybe even a worrying sexual inertia.

A brisk walk home. The saga of devouring. I ate a slice of bread, the rest of the butter, the rest of the bœuf fumé and decide to repeat tomorrow the strategy with cognac on empty stomach. There is nothing that I can do. I go to bed and read. Still Huxley – (The country of conditioned reflexes) in *Le Meilleur des mondes* [Brave New World], and I find a chapter about freedom, which is a lesser or greater degree of slavery.

Menu Grèze – prima Stroganoff
sewing
tomorrow a rentier's speech
sugar

This morning, about 11 am to the Bureau de Placement, to have my unemployment card stamped. Usually, I go on Friday, but that last time I waited for Tema, who left me a note saying she will come. Telephone Sacha. I told him that I've been advised that there might be some letters for me. On Thursday I sent the cards (pre-printed cards), there could even be an answer. We dropped in at a milk-bar, where he usually eats lunch. And, of course, instead of cognac, beef and yoghurt. Everyone pays for himself.

I was at Hotel Bisson. Took the canvases that were decaying there and one suitcase with warm clothes. A coat.

The sight and touch of things releases feelings. One can prove this quite objectively, investigating for instance the dampness of the eye. A concrete biological phenomenon. And now I would ask the gentlemen-physicists to describe this phenomenon quantitatively, that is 'scientifically'. Or, I would ask the gentlemen-physicists to put on the table a porcelain plate, to weigh it and examine it under a microscope, or in any other way, and then to tell me – how much time has elapsed between the moment when this bit of porcelain was fired and today? M K. weights such a thing in his hand, closing his eyes. He strokes it with a fingertip, looks at it from a distance and replies à peu près.

Supper at Tema's. Metro both ways. One more hour at the table. Useless. The poem doesn't budge. Nothing goes. I force myself to write these few notes. It is already 2.15 am I am lying down. I shall read a bit. And then to sleep. Where do you sleep now, darling?

Tema: asked about a suitcase, if she can leave it with me, and wanted to bring provisions.

2 October **Diary Entry**

The clock chimed 1.30. Today I sleep somewhere else. On the first floor of that Galerie d'Art, on the corner of rue des Beaux Arts and rue de Seine. Among a crowd of sculptures, figurines, masks. This happened unexpectedly, but even 5 minutes now is enough time for me to move from one place to another.

On Tuesday, early evening, I rushed out of the house. My work isn't getting anywhere, even my reading isn't, with the idea that I shall meet M K. He was going to Saint-Sulpice with Zber. Zber was in a hurry to meet his girlfriend, the one with a stye in her eye, and we went to my place for tea. There we found both the Clavels – they say they are sorry, they sold their things and already it's Wednesday and they have to sleep in rue Jacques-Callot, and that I can sleep in rooms above the shop. I had thought of going to a hotel (today I even found a cheap hotel in Passage des Princes for 10 frs per day), but these figurines here tempted me and the books. Yesterday evening I rushed out again, just to walk, just to walk around the streets. Coming back I suddenly overheard a sentence. The speaker was a chap carrying a child and just coming out of a bistro. To the woman inside, [he said] 'la guerre est finie'. And suddenly, even though I knew that he was not talking about the war that's still going on, but about the one that has really ended, long ago, – [it was] as if these words blinded me [momentarily]. After all this would mean that I would get letters, that our separation would end.

2 October 1940

I ate the rest of the food, so as not to have to take it with me somewhere else. – Stock cube with noodles, bread, remainder of the grapes (that M K. brought today) and the last of the apples. I read Huxley again till late at night. Today at noon I dropped in at the Clavels' 'home' (18 rue de Seine). Immediately, first question: have I read the papers? – No! – and suddenly I see yesterday's chap, who is leaving the bistro – is that really possible? – But it was about something else: a list of Jews. And it is already known who is a Jew: anyone who has, or had, more than 2 grandparents of 'Jewish' faith. Zber called on me. He arrived at the moment when I was tidying up the flat. He said he had already had a desire to work – the news deprived him of it completely.

In the evening, supper at Tema's. With the Rusaks and Marcel. They reminisce about the year 1936, 'people smiled at everybody in the street', 'I arrived in France, as if into honey', 'two days per week, free' (that was Marcel). In the gallery I arrange a bed for myself on the sofa and take from the shelves a few books, for sleep. Baudelaire's *Paradis Artificiels*; *Henri Rousseau* by Adolf Basler – reproductions. *Étoiles et Atomes* by Oddington; *Les Caves du Vatican* by Gide; Lucien's *Dialogues des Courtisanes*. I read this last one. I put it back. I force myself to make a note of that page – clock strikes 2.15.

4 October Diary Entry

Projects to note:

1. Film – from the 'play' *Yadwighe* by Douanier Rousseau. Great visual possibilities. Fragments of his paintings and those that he never painted. Then where there are whole unwritten acts marked with dots, these sections are to be played slowly in a purely free filmic treatment.

2. Reworking of the texts of Hamlet and Othello to bring them up to date for staging.

3. Life in someone else's apartment. Getting to know the previous tenant. The effect of established psychological routines on the new tenant. (Something similar, but fundamentally 'different', it seems, was the case with Emerson, or even with Poe.)

Still no letters. No replies to the cards sent over a week ago.

With a new fragment, I completed the second part of the poem.

The Clavels dropped in and pressed me to join them for a cake. And, I them for a cognac. On an empty stomach because I get up at 12 and I didn't tell anyone. In the evening to Sacha. Also cognac. He offered a box of camembert. Yesterday I visited M K. – tomorrow I am to go again – about a new place to stay. This will be the fifth since my return. At Lille's in a sleeping bag on the floor. At Tournon, in one bed with Bibrowski. At Jacques-Callot in an apartment with a bathroom, library, Greek head on a column, an Etruscan vase, African coffer, etc. here – on Friday above the gallery – among books (a complete Balzac on a shelf in the loo) and a thousand bits of ancient carved stone – and now? I wouldn't like to settle in too much. To be able, at any moment, to say goodbye – and to leave. To where? (midnight)

4 October

The Vichy Government publishes a new Jewish Statute depriving Jewish refugees of their civil rights. Not one of these declarations is mentioned in Stefan's diaries, but he is obviously aware of the danger and keeps moving from place to place.

5 October Diary Entry

Soup on Saint-Honoré.
Accommodation – tomorrow, Anjou [pear wine] Chez Florian in the park.
'Will exchange Aryan grandmother for a bicycle'.
I will help M Florian (?). He will be there on Monday. Clavels low morale. In the evening I drop in on Edek. Lili is there. Supper. Conversations, plans. Edek – duty in the hotel. Confessions of Lili – the story of three sisters.

Stenia [Bender], Zber's wife. Death of her first fiancé. Arrival of Lili. Widow and 'Bacchante'. Fur from a market. Edek (on foot, flowers, hunchbacked garçon brings cigarettes, borrows 200 frs). She came for herself and not for her sister: letter that she can leave home. She forgets the anniversary of her sister's fiancé's death. She finds a note at home: probably your scholarship is finished, perhaps you need money. She runs, to say 'no', that she has money. Cold. Yes… no… Zber. Genka, the younger sister, reports later that Zber said: 'if only she were as nice as she is pretty'. – Sorbonne – 'Me too'. The motive is envy.

A gaffe: Stenia is lying in bed (she is really ill with that heart, but she draws it to everyone's notice). 'You don't even ask why I am in bed' 'Because you are lazy'. It just came out without thinking. She is sorry. –

Motive: unfulfilled ambitions. Putting oneself in the forefront. The means – illness. Emotional blackmail. Lili cannot bear this emotional blackmail in the family. Here, the sister wants to replace the family for her.

Father. Rich merchant. Taken advantage of by his wife and three daughters – all takers. Lili didn't want to – but now she understands that father would prefer her to take money from him. For this, he worked. And wanted to pay with a fur coat for a word or a smile – he is unsure of himself.

The mother is a despot. Commotion. Something has to be happening all the time in the family. She apologises so that she can offend again.

In Warsaw she had her own room. Not for the family. (Only Boy! [Tadeusz Boy-Żeleński] used to visit). Stenia was the only one in the family who wrote from Paris: now she can see why Lili wanted to be 'independent'. But now in Paris herself, she won't accept it.

5 October 1940

(Janusz Korczak orphanage, music lessons, Stefa's sadism towards Sara. 'She is studying hard because she is vain', she wants to play because she is vain, she thinks that she will be a performer. The ladies of the committee, 25 years of service, etc.)

She wanted to get to know us better, so we had 'an open house', (to reconsider all that happened since we met at Aronson's reception – i.e. the conversation with Słonimski (he translated the play); Stefan K(onorski)'s erotic dream; the surrealists; the reading aloud of Apollinaire; Mietek Bibrowski's reflections after our meeting at Lille's.

(confrontation with a page from her diary) (12-1, after midnight)

To express this thought more clearly. NB, even if someone is not in conflict like Hamlet, this has nothing to do with judgments that people hold about him, but with unfolding psychological experiences. But in her case, what is concerned is actually the sum of judgments about her.

Stefan stays at the gallery another night.

6 October Diary Entry

Sunday Mass in the church on Saint-Honoré.[13] RC Communion. Offerings. Sermon about suffering. Suffering as a school in life's wisdom. The Cross as a school leading to human improvement. (The parable about a servant, whose debt was forgiven by his master, but who did not forgive the debt of his debtor).[14] (*Saecula sæculorum* – revealed truths, truisms which depend on the inner man – the power of the Catholic church. Revealed truth ultimately offers standards in the everyday world, in contrast to the materialist idea, where the end justifies the means and for this reason leaves nonbelievers helpless, without moral support in everyday life).

A parable about an artist who destroyed his Crucifixion twice, because it did not match the image that he had within him. Only after many years, after the loss of his wife and children, after going through the school of suffering did he make a work of art that was 'appropriate'. So from an art depicting suffering there comes a school of excellence. (The influence of Paris!)

A parable of a saint who on his deathbed asked for a book. He pushed away the Bible. They gave him others, which he also pushed away. He accepted the Cross, the book of life's wisdom.

A parable about St Paul, who said: 'I am glad of my weaknesses'.[15] Apparent contradictions of the Gospel: 1. the Church counsels the avoidance of temptation, 2. St Paul rejoices in his weakness. The church looks differently on suffering. Holding a grudge against God, for not removing our unnecessary suffering in his omnipotence: suffering is an instrument with whose help God wants to illuminate more perfect values, the same applies not only to individuals, but societies and nations. 'God save Poland...'[16]

Go home with K. Talk about the immediate future. I shall miss Paris. Tomorrow, I have to find somewhere to live.

13 Église Saint-Roch
14 The Parable of the Wicked Servant: Matthew 18:21-35.
15 'I glory in my infirmities', 2 Corinthians 12.10.
16 Patriotic Catholic hymn: 'Boże coś Polskę przez tak liczne wieki...' (1863)

Edek nothing new. Doubts. Continued conversation about the immediate future.

Bibrowski. Apartment of a rentier 'uncle', for 30 years not redecorated (his parents' flat), he is 67, looks 50, like one of van Gogh's models, black moustache, 1½ litres of wine for lunch, litre of wine for supper). Wallpaper. Garden – chestnut trees. Figurines on sideboards, landscapes. Rather kitsch attempts at modernism. Attempts at resolving colours in forms (gouache), that shouldn't have been hung at all.

Library – philosophy – art. Braque, Matisse, etc. The Impressionists. 'A.M.' (NB to look through: *Revue de l'Art et d'Esthétique* I–II, June 1935 – 23 rue de Constantinople, Paris 8), article 'L'idée de l'art pur' – Étienne Souriau among others, graphic interpretation of music, a fragment of Chopin's *Nocturne*, refers to the logarithmic pattern in *Revue Psychologique* (?)

The story of the cat. Cat Nunon, will eat only one kind of fish (is 15 years old). In the queue for hake; it has to be cooked in a special way. Uncle detests the cat. The cat stops him doing what he wants, impedes his right to his French freedom. The cat blackmails him with its animal helplessness. The cat goes on strike. The cat does not understand the situation and couldn't care less. The cat jumps onto his lap and goes to sleep. It moults. The cat doesn't miaow. The cat makes its demands in silence and is resentful. The cat is master in the house. 'Chat bourgeois' – says uncle's friend. Uncle's friend wonders what to do. The uncle wonders what to do. Mme B., M B. Principles – says the friend. Self interest – says B. This time we don't pay with our blood, but he gets black marks against his name, says uncle. One agrees with the other, one doesn't contradict the other – there's general agreement.

I go to Civiale. Touching and warm – as usual. Supper. Marcel goes to work. Andrée still has no letter from her husband. No longer works at her mother-in-law's (she had taken on an employee – hats). Tema is completely exhausted from this exam. She is very brave, intelligent and sensible. She knows and can do many things. If only she could use what she knows when she is with Hanka. *Cum grano salis*. Less dogmatically. *Ex cathedra*. With an injection of a little welcome doubt. Random books as a contrast to the school syllabus. Anxiety, abstract, internal struggle, the search for one's own version of truth – something analogous – *mutatis mutandis* – with moral benefit gained through suffering talked about in the sermon. The role of a writer – the role of a priest, and professions that I wanted to choose up to the age of 5: horse carriage [driver] (but only as long as I was controlling the reins); a priest (but only while conducting a funeral procession); actor (but only the image of being on stage); after the age of 9: detective (on the trail); a soldier (at the time of the victory march); inventor (at the moment of making the invention); scientist (in the laboratory); traveller (during the journey); writer (at the moment of writing – never an image of a completed book); actor (on the stage, reciting, miming – never at the time of applause); stage director (at the time of directing the performance); physicist (at the time of 'creating' a philosophical theory); engineer (at the time of making a machine – never during the daily work of the engineer in a factory); architect (rather at the time of creating projects and closer to the sphere of pure art than that applied to building) – these psychoanalytical reminiscences à propos one moment from a story about two brothers related by Tema.

This story should be related to the history of 3 sisters, which is in some ways the continuation of this one, and completed with a psychological portrait of the cat, Nunon.

There is Albert and I. I. is older. The sister never had a chance. 2½ years with a wet nurse. Tied to a stool. Not properly fed. Weak legs. Hardly talked at all. Tema visited Dolczowa's daughter and reported what she saw. Change of diet. Irradiation with a quartz lamp. Fed some concoction to accelerate circulation to those parts of the brain that are functioning sluggishly. Came back after a year. The boy developed, became talkative, rowdy. After a year of tests, as a 4-year-old, he was perfectly normal for his age. At the same time – the younger Albert was 6 months old when Tema arrived. She threw away the nappies and bandages. The whole family had warm feelings towards Albert. Albert never cries – always smiling. Doesn't complain if he's in pain, (dislocated leg, teeth, 40° fever). I. suffers from jealousy, beats A., sticking his hand through the rails of the cot. In need of affection (first at the wet nurse, and later at home wants to be better liked when he comes back home, in the presence of his newly born brother) – the only person who likes him is the mother-in-law Andrée – he calls her 'ma petite chérie', he gets flowers from all the flower beds, effusive devotion, etc., sexus? – on the beach interested in the girls, chases a little English girl, who runs away frightened that he wants to fight with her – but he catches up, and kisses her. He looks at Tema in bed – says you have lovely eyes, you have a pretty hand, etc. – But on the dark side, he throws things, spoons etc. out through the window. Once (when he was 4), the whole dinner service of plates went over the balcony into the street. (Why? – revenge?) He is always noisy, can't keep still, meddling with the saucepans; the story of flowers – on Mother's Day... He took artificial flowers from school, brought them to his mother – they were standing on the chest of drawers (back to the same motive – need for affection, the need to occupy 'a social position' in the family), was proud the whole week. He planted the flowers in soil in the garden at night, so that they would grow. It just rained on them – bitter disappointment.

(Other aspects of the motive is a desire for 'social position' in the family, concerning money) – his mother is selling a bag, the buyer can't decide, says that she will come back. I.: 'You should take it now, because by next week it won't be there.' Then the matter of the bicycle: I. wants a bicycle. The son of the owner of the house has a bicycle. Mother – I don't have money. And he? – His father has money. When I have some, I'll buy it for you. After a month A. sees: the mother is counting money. You have some now, buy it for me now. I have it, but I have to give it away. To whom? To the owner of the house, for the rent. But how is that so? He has money; his son has a bicycle; I haven't got one; and still you give the money to him? – He can't understand it. – There are two possible resolutions: 1) the injustice of it all, which one must change, 2) the lack of enough money to have everything that he never had at the wet nurse's and in his family. He will choose to deal with the second. He wants to be an engineer. Why not a doctor? Because an engineer builds cars and a doctor buys from the engineer, so the engineer has more money.

Albert doesn't understand the value of money. A's needs aren't the kind that money could satisfy. A. gets everyone's love, but above all Tema's. A. doesn't feel wronged.

A. feels indebted. X gives 1 fr each to I. and A. I. grabs it and rushes to town, ice cream, cakes, returns – there is no sign of ice cream, cakes, or any change. A. doesn't want 1 fr. A. wants 25 centimes. A. is given both 1 fr and 25 centimes. He gives 1 fr to Tema and keeps 25 centimes.

I return home on the metro loaded with a sausage ring and a bar of chocolate and 5 m. I don't need money. And I feel pained, when I think of how many blouses Tema had to make while preparing for the exam, to earn that 5 m. But she gives it in such a direct way and making refusal so impossible, that I recognise I could only cause more pain if I didn't take it.

I telephoned today my 'good friend Mr Edv. K.' to enquire, if by any chance he had any news. It was the first time that I had telephoned since I came back, already 2 months ago. Then he boasted about having stayed. He was afraid that I might need something. He conducted the conversation in a masterly fashion so that he found out that I have friends and acquaintances, that I haven't yet disappeared – he still hadn't asked for the address, but already suggested, or rather promised that when I telephone for the third time, then we might make a date to meet somewhere. À propos his art collection, of which the authenticity is questionable, I learned that he deals in art. When it's a question of how he gets by – apparently he is in it for the money, what's more all his books are anthologies. Conclusion – an assimilated, Frenchified brat.

8 October **Diary Entry**

Temerson Andrée at Tema's, 3 rue Civiale, (10e)
L'Histoire d'Anie Boleux

13 October **Diary Entry**

Already nearly a whole week. Yesterday, I was in Civiale. 'Why haven't you been for so long?' asked Marcel. 'J'étais bien emmerdé'. On Friday I had the chance but couldn't take advantage of it. I still have no news. That brat couldn't tell me anything. And I myself don't know what to do next. Tomorrow anyway, I am moving to rue Euler. Tonight I shall sleep in Edek's hotel. The Clavels took the key and didn't leave it for me. They must have felt terrible about this. Let's return to the story of Anie Boleux (trois lettres suffisent pour faire mon nom), or rather to the story that I consider relevant to myself.

> Tu es fou, chéri, mais comme tu es fou. Je ne suis pas comme les autres. J'étais bien élevée. J'étais à l'école. Après je me suis mariée. J'avais vingt ans. J'ai quitté l'école pour me marier. Mais c'était un brute. Alors, après je me suis divorcée. J'étais en Bretagne, à Rennes. Après je suis venue à Paris. Et après. Et c'est tout.

One can't describe one's past more concisely, and what's more, as the sort of past one would have wanted to have.

> 'Mais pourquoi tu me regarde toujours comme ça? Mais pourquoi tu me regarde? Chéri', 'Mon pauvre chéri', 'Je te demande une chose quand tu vas au Métro, ou quelque part, dans la rue, que

tu te rappelles de moi de temps en temps? Veux tu? Si c'est possible, je te le demande bien, chéri.' J'ai menti, je n'habite pas Montparnasse. J'habite rue Saint-Sulpice. J'ai la chance de tomber toujours sur le "13". Je suis née le 13, j'habite le no.13, et la chambre 13.' 'Écoute, chéri, quand tu as le cafard, viens me voir. Tu peux laisser un mot là bas.' 'Tu est un peu fou, chéri, ça ce voit, et je peux t'aimer pour ça.'

I telephoned Rzewska and Jaworska. They are both in Paris. They returned. I met them. The Wittlins are in Nice. I wrote him a card – a card-form. To all previous ones, not a single answer.

15 October **Telegram from Zofia Kramsztyk in Nice to Franciszka**

MARI COMMUNIQUE VA BIEN PARIS 9 BIS RUE DES EAUX CHEZ BRONSTEIN COMMUNIQUERAI VOTRE ADRESSE = KRAMSZTYK

16 October **Letter from Franciszka to Zofia Kramsztyk**

Dear Zosia! Thank you so much for the news! I am so happy that at last I know something about Stefan. Please write and tell him that I am well and he shouldn't worry about me from any point of view.

Somehow things are going so very smoothly for me that sometimes it's even distressing. I have work and I earn. If not for the anxiety about family and friends, what more could anyone wish for (at present).

I sent two letters to Stefan, but they will probably take a long time to get there. This is why I am asking you to send him news. I also had news from our families – they are well. Mira and Ignacy are in touch with me. Perhaps I will see them here, but truthfully it is more than difficult to persuade them.

With kindest regards, yours sincerely. Franciszka Themerson

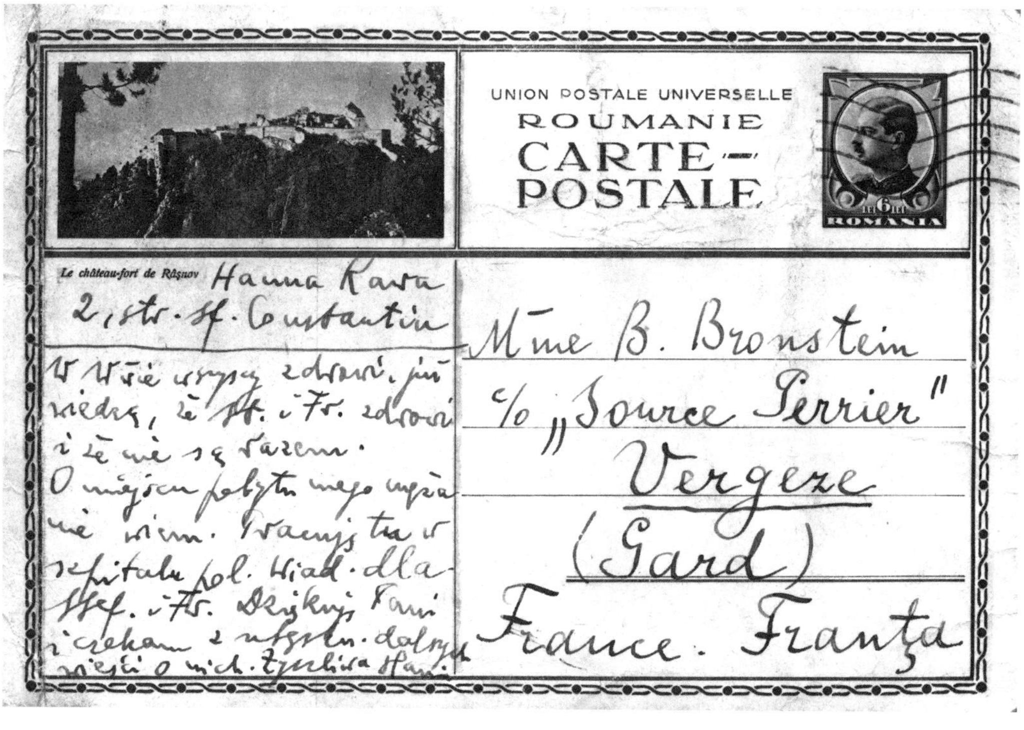

Card from Hania Kawa to Blanche Bronstein [see facing page]

17 October 1940

Card from Hania Kawa in Bucharest to Blanche Bronstein in Vergèze

Dear Mme Bronstein

I received your card of 10 October today and hasten to let you know that I had several telegrams from Franciszka and from Cękalski asking for Stefan's address, but they know anyway that he is well. The most recent telegram from Franka in London, arrived today, saying that Stefan is in the army. Is that true? Her address is SW3, Royal Avenue 9. I keep writing to her and to Stefek by various routes but it seems that nothing arrives. I sent a telegram to Franka to say that I haven't got Stefek's address. I am in touch with both the families of Franka and Stefek, also with Sewek [Seweryn Chaykin], who wrote to me on 27 September. I've had bad news from my family in London. The factory no longer exists, my sister and sister-in-law have been sent out of town, not a word about my brother-in-law. No answer to my telegram.

In Warsaw everybody is well. They already know that Stefek and Franka are not together. I don't know the whereabouts of my husband. I work in a Polish hospital here. Information for Stefek and Franka. I want to thank you very much, and long for further news about them.

Sincerely Hania

Letter from Franciszka to Stefan

Dearest Stefciu! I give you such a big hug. I received today at last your address from Zosia. Oh, it made me so happy! I was anxious and missed you so much, so terribly much.

Treasure, write and tell me what you are doing? How are you all managing? Hug Blanche and Sacha for me. I am so glad that you are with them. Have they received a letter from me? I wrote to them a long time ago.

Darling, I walk around town and all the time am reminded of our old walks here. You so much wanted to live here darling. Greetings from Genek [Cękalski] and Feliks [Topolski] also, and Tymon [Terlecki]. and Tola [Korian], Stefan [Konorski], Adam [Pragier] and Stefanja [Zahorska]. There are so, so many friends here. And I miss you so much Stefciu! I want to know everything, everything, how you are, what you are doing and all about you.

I am working as before, I earn far more and manage extremely well. Don't worry about me in any respect. I am so happy today after receiving news about you. Oh, how wonderful! Have you written to our family? Hania [Kawa] let me know that they are well.

I hug you with so much love. Franka

Write to Teresa [Żarnower]. She lives not far away. Lisbon, 105 Amoreiras.
Kisses, Franka

Also a note from Ernst Freyd

I am taking advantage of the empty space in this letter to send you kind regards and to ask you whether you have received 1300 frs. – Best regards. Ernst Freyd

Stefan is planning his departure and writes down names of places or hotels to stay:

Saint-Jacques, [unreadable], Petit Noüielle, La Cumbrian in Marseille

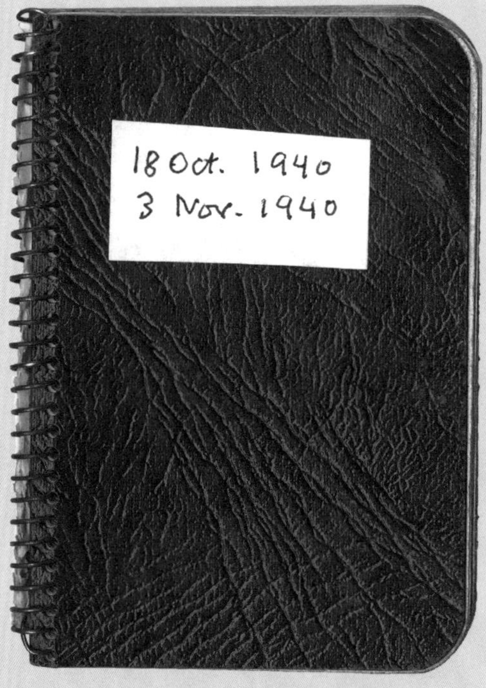
18 Oct. 1940
3 Nov. 1940

18 October 1940

Diary Entry

R. MacIsaac, Detachement W, Saint-Hippolyte-du-Fort, Gard (Henri)

20.40 Gare de Lyon

Stefan leaves Paris for Vichy France.

Tema sees me off – cash
on the platform Edek and Lili
3 changes 6 am
Montceau-les-Mines

Polish Red Cross [Polski Czerwony Krzyż] had several hostels in the so-called Free Zone that looked after the Polish soldiers who had escaped from Poland to join the Polish Army in France and were left behind when most of their colleagues were evacuated to England. It also cared for others, including children who had lost their homes. In 1941, there were probably 10,000 people in the care of PCK [Polski Czerwony Krzyż], which had its main office in Lille.

19 October **Diary Entry**

Polish priest
A squint. If it wasn't for the squint he wouldn't be a clergyman
Mass, washing, breakfast
to Rychlik
Hospice St-Marie

Sister, plaiting a chair
Ma mère, ma soeur, little wood, Rychlik, bicycle
Rychlik today cannot lunch,
nap in the refectory, supper
for the night to the miners

Stefan sleeps in an attic.

20 October **Diary Entry**

Son – bicycle. Brother has already gone.
Woman on the road.
Run
Car
mud – Hallelujah
boards. (like blackboards)
Bus – Mâcon –
~~cartes lunch~~
train 2.45 – Monday
through Tarascon
4 am Toulouse

21 October **Diary Entry**

Walk, then Fukusiewicz
waiting for dawn in a restaurant Red Cross – letters to Vichy?
white coffee – saccharine

21 October 1940

Toulouse
Mlle Ginsberg
trams, canal
Mme Blum Benda
Sleeping in rue du Coq d'Inde

22 October **Diary Entry**

telegrams – Blanche, Wittlin, Vichy, Teresa, Polish Embassy in England
letters: Wittlin, Blanche, Fira, Kaczor, Tema
visits: Jean T. (swine), Katz, Red Cross

supper 12 frs
return to rue Coq d'Inde, sleeping in the kitchen

Polish Red Cross, Vichy, Hôtel Beau-Site
depart Allier, arrive Briand
visit to Winowska and Julia
telegram to Franka

The following paragraph was crossed out

Fira Vinceum's uncle doesn't have work. Lucien sent application to the Sorbonne. Bela visited Zber, but he can do very little for Lucien. May, Lidka and Lorrage are well, they work. Parcels to Fira and Tadzik. Letters from Lucien arrive, but they take a long time. He is very well. Teaches French in the family. Changed address, everything is the same, only Stalag B

22 October **Registered Letter from Polish Red Cross Search Division to Stefan**

Dear Sir, in response to your telegram and following our telegram in response, we are sending you herewith the whole correspondence that we have had here in your name.
Search Office PCK in France.

4 enclosures

Telegram from Wittlin to Stefan

ON M'A DIT FRANÇOISE PARTIE AVEC PRAGIER STÉPHANIE
TÉLÉGRAPHIEZ GRYDZEWSKI 36 GREAT RUSSELL STREET LONDON
HEUREUX VOUS SAVOIR RETROUVÉ MILLE TENDRESSES = WITTLIN

23 October **Cable from Croix Rouge Polonaise to Polish Embassy in London**

PRIÈRE ENVOYER ADRESSE DE FRANÇOISE THEMERSON SON MARI
BONNE SANTÉ = CROIX ROUGE POLONAISE

Telegram from Blanche Bronstein to Stefan

PARTEZ PAS SANS M'ÉCRIRE LAISSEZ INDICATION POSSIBILITÉ
VOUS REJOINDRE ENSUITE STOP AI VU A VICHY TÉLÉGRAMME DE
FRANÇOISE DE JUILLET AVEC ADRESSE 3 AVENUE ROYALE STOP
LETTRE SUIT AMITIÉS = BLANCHE BRONSTEIN

POLSKI CZERWONY KRZYŻ
DZIAŁ POSZUKIWAŃ

Nr 2195/40/B.P.

Vichy, dn.22 października 1940
Hôtel Beau Site

Polecony

WPan
THEMERSON Stefan
Poste-Restante
Toulouse
(H-te Gar.)

Szanowny Panie,

W załatwieniu Pana depeszy i w ślad za naszą telegraficzną odpowiedzią przesyłamy przy niniejszym całą korespondencję, jaką mieliśmy u siebie na nazwisko Pana.

Za BIURO POSZUKIWAŃ P.C.K.
we Francji

4 zał.

CABLE AND WIRELESS
LIMITED.

PASSED BY CENSOR No. 2401

CABLE AND WIRELESS LIMITED 23 OCT 40 CENTRAL STATION

FXG FYEJBR59 MB 149

435 TOULOUSE 16 22 1935

POLISH AMBASSY LDN

PRIERE ENVOYER ADRESSE DE FRANCOISE THEMERSON SON MARIE BONNE SANTE
CROIX ROUGE POLONAISE +

NO ENQUIRY RESPECTING THIS TELEGRAM CAN BE ATTENDED TO WITHOUT PRODUCTION OF THIS COPY. REPLIES SHOULD BE HANDED IN AT ONE OF THE COMPANY'S OFFICES.

---

87 NICE 80900 26 22 1555 CLE

ON M A DIT FRANCOISE PARTIE AVEC PRAGIER STEPHANIE TELEGRAPHIEZ GRYDZEWSKI 36 GREAT RUSSEL STREET LONDON- HEUREUX VOUS SAVOIR RETROUVE MILLE TENDRESSES = WITTLIN

ADMIS 36

72 VERGEZE 113 37 22 1800 = CLE

PARTEE PAS SANS M ECRIRE LAISSEZ INDICATION POSSIBILITE VOUS REJOINDRE ENSUITE STOP AI VU A VICHY TELEGRAMME DE FRANCOISE DE JUILLET AVEC ADRESSE 3 AVENUE ROYALE STOP LETTRE SUIT AMITIES =
BLANCHE BRAESTEIN = =

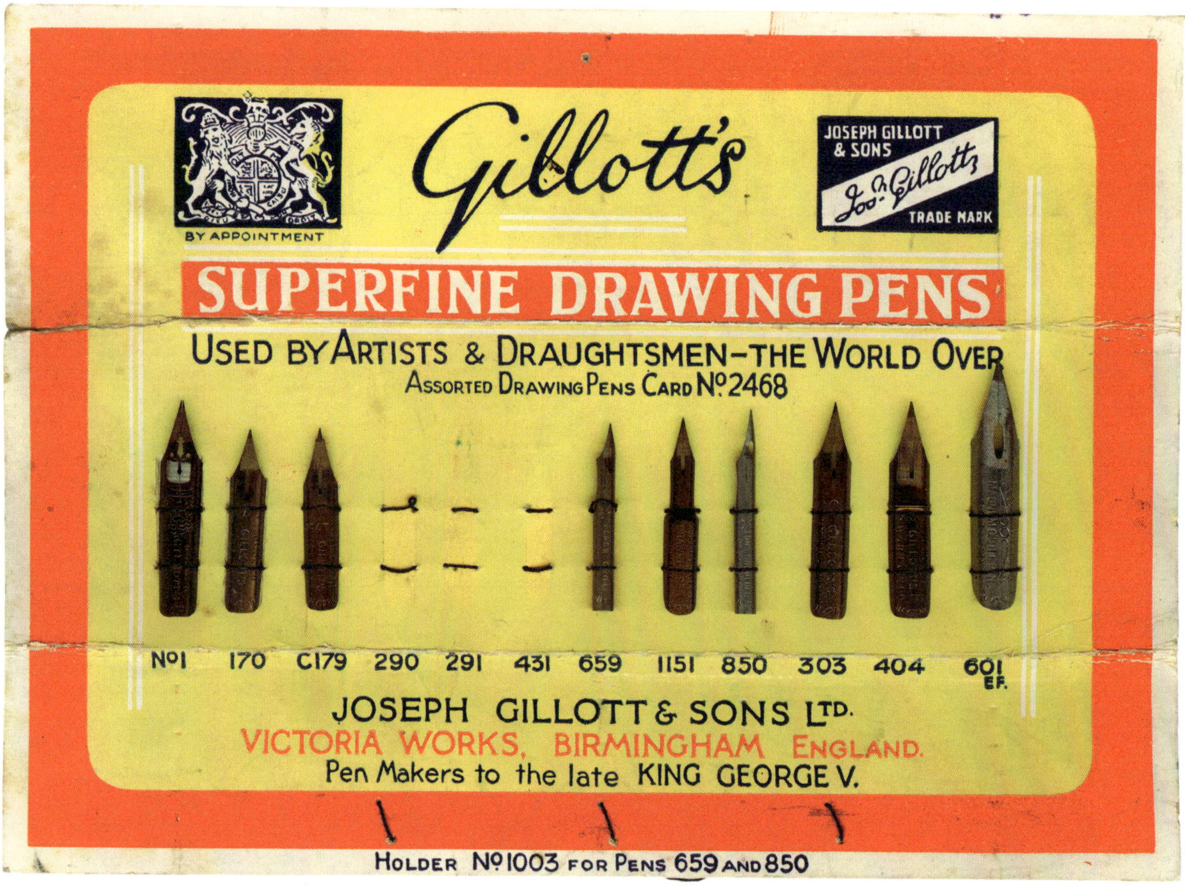

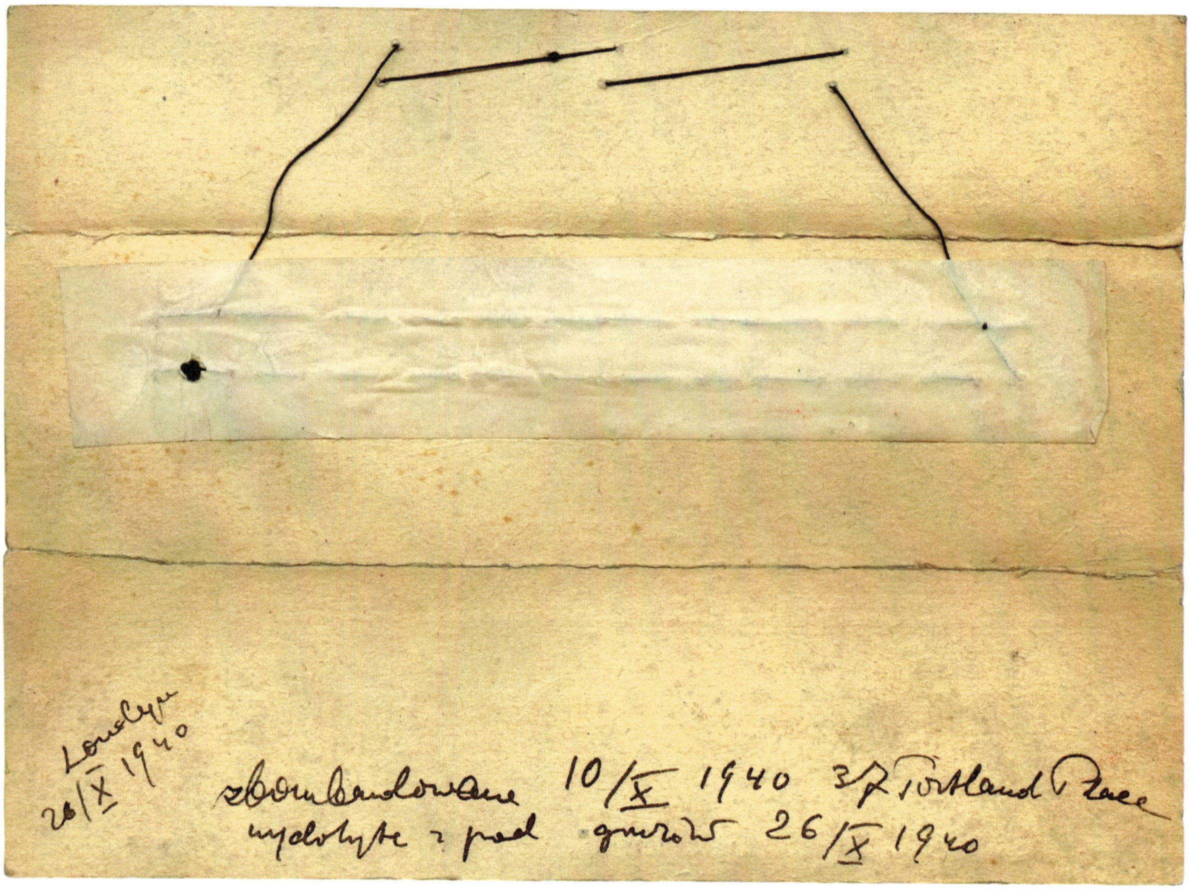

Franciszka finds a packet with drawing pen nibs in the ruins of 37 Portland Place, bombed on 10 October 1940

23 October 1940

Diary Entry

telegram from Vichy – letter sent, post
Red Cross
sleeping at Pierre Bernos
Halina Bl[it]
driver
letters
Two neighbours
Conversations in the dark
Archimerde…

24 October **Diary Entry**

6 am raid, police station, camp
return at 1.30
visit to Helen and Julia
5 pm cleaning, sleeping, neighbour, supper

the story of a colonel and his wife – she married him to get French nationality,
son born in Lourdes hospice of St Maria
Type: Julia
colonel – grandfather's Napoleon
woolly Jewish philosophy – Spinoza isn't woolly. More woolly than the others.
But everything together.
Type [Kazimierz] Borkowski? mister! hey mister!
Benda at place Wilson!

25 October **Diary Entry**

summons to Toulouse with things/luggage
Hel. is coming to Grenoble
at the Post Office letters, telegram with Franka's address
Molle, Winowska
evening at Julia's
sleeping at the Indian Coq

26 October **Diary Entry**

letter from Wittlin
visit to [Maria] Winowska and to Julia
coffee bread
telegram to Franka

apples 2.25
sausage without wine 1.75

(rendez-vous with chap fixé for Sunday at noon)
sleeping in the dining room

27 October

In London, General de Gaulle proclaims the Free French Government.

27 October 1940

Diary Entry
Little Berthe – soup
Café on Place Wilson
Doctor Henri and his pregnant wife
M Molle

28 October

France introduces anti-Semitic legislation.

Diary Entry
A chap at home at Coq d'Inde
evening at Julia's
letter from Stefan Konorski
Sleeping behind a curtain

29 October **Diary Entry**
visit to Mme Julia
nephew studying mathematics
English university
with progress – nothing

Telegram from Croix Rouge Polonaise to Stefan
TÉLÉGRAMME AVEC ADRESSE VOTRE FEMME EXPÉDIONS LETTRE RECOMMANDÉE = CROIX ROUGE POLONAISE

Telegram from Stefan Ginsberg in Toulouse to Franciszka
HEUREUX T'AVOIR RETROUVÉE SOIS TRANQUILLE PATIENCE SANTÉ EXCELLENTE = STEFAN GINSBERG 3 RUE MALETACHE TOULOUSE

30 October **Telegram from Franciszka to Stefan Ginsberg**
TELLEMENT HEUREUSE AVOIR NOUVELLES STEFEK EST IL TOULOUSE PRIÈRE TÉLÉGRAPHIER QUELS BESOINS PEUT AIDER TENDRESSES = THEMERSONOWA

Diary Entry
breakfast bonne marmite 8.50 + 1 = 9.50
raid on Boulevard Strasbourg
landlords took 12 frs per day = 60 frs
telegram to Franka

31 October **Diary Entry**
visit to Fukusiewicz
meeting with Budzyński
visit to Orleans
either today to Blanche, or tomorrow to Caylus[17]
evening at Julia's
J's talk about Konopnicka, about war for ideals
Julia walks me back to the railway station
night in the train

17 Medieval town in Midi-Pyrénées.

Card from Hanna Kawa to Stefan

Dearest Stefek, I have just received your very short letter of 25 October. Darling, I am so happy! I am writing at once to Warsaw (only yesterday I wrote to Maryla [Chaykin] about you, and Franka and Sewek). Stay in contact with me for as long as possible, ignore all the present circumstances, and keep me informed about you. If, however, you had reason to suppose that I am not here, write to Mme Renée Autoli, str. Plevuli 18, pour H[anna] K[awa]. She is the manageress of the branch Post Office in the neighbourhood, she is well disposed towards me and will forward it. I can't find the address of Blanche, is that Mme Bronstein? But I wrote twice to Mme Brunet.

Marysia Bryn is again in Grenoble, 26 Colonel Bougautt, and my brother in Belgium with his wife and two children in Sete (Herault), rue Mistral 5. These are addresses just in case. My very good friend, Sonia Grynblat is 85 km from Marysia Bryn, her address is Mégisserie du Blanchissage, Bêdarieux (Herault). Write what happened to you. My family is well. From your mother, Irka, Stefan, Aneczka, Ginia and Władek, I have good news.

I kiss you on behalf of them all. Hania

Mietek in Wilno, hasn't written since 28 April

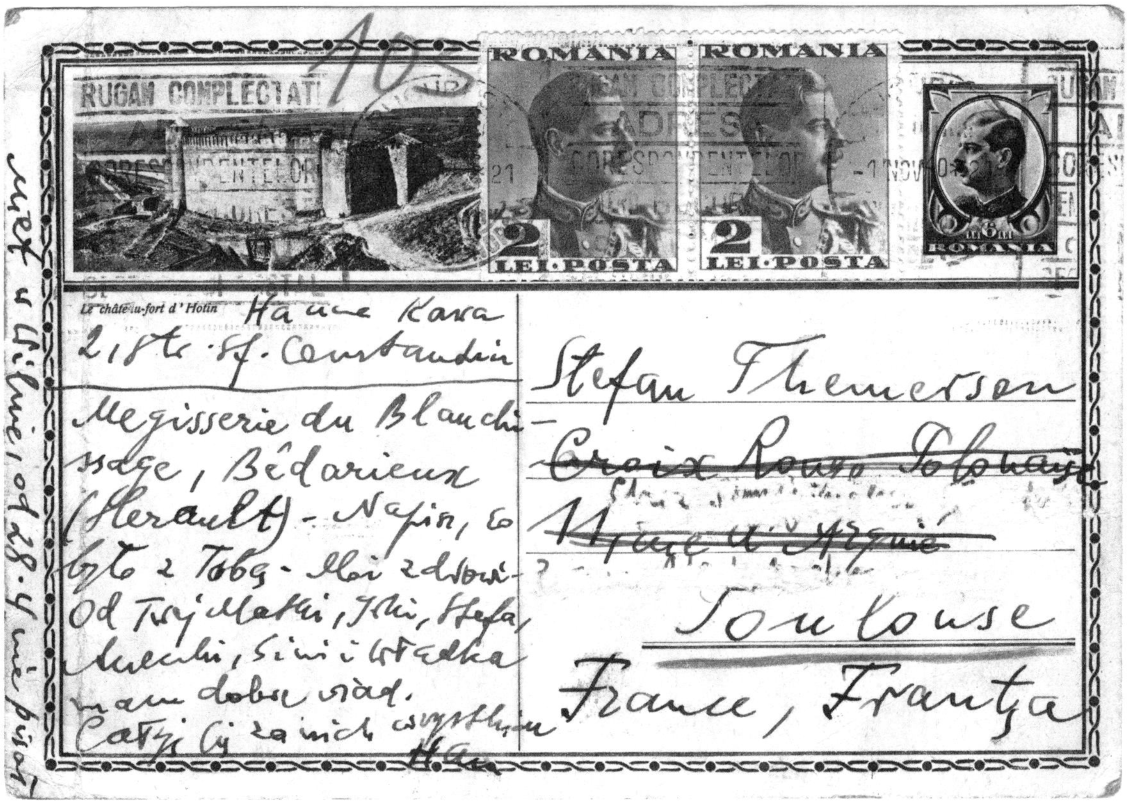

1 November 1940

Car to Vergèze, where Stefan visits Blanche Bronstein who works for Source Perrier mineral water company.

Diary Entry

Friday morning 1 November 1940
arrival in Nîmes
road – sunrise –
apple, bread, pickled cucumbers
the road there and back
Blanche and Władek [Vinaver]
night with Władek

2 November **Diary Entry**

4.30 car to Montpellier
meeting – café Grillon
night – Hôtel Verdun

In Montpellier
lawyer Lieutenant Sev.
Dyma – oil engineer
Rattner and his grievances
telegram to Franka
to go or to stay
room 12 frs

Montpellier hotel room 12 frs
'Verdun'?

3 November **Diary Entry**

Montpellier
sleeping – Hôtel Helvetia
washing legs/feet

16 h. Mont Dôre 1.25 113 francs, 14.57 Terescos? 17.50

1) rue Pierre Brunnière, 2) courtyard on the left, 1st floor

To Poland
my forwarding address:
S.T. Tolochenaz (Vaud), Schweiz
Mlle H. Lübke, 3, Joliette, Lausanne, Suisse
letter to Julia

telephone Halina
time of departure to Grenoble
Montpellier
telegram to Franka

3 November 1940

Léon Katz, chez Mme David, 25 rue de la Colombette, Toulouse
Russak.
She can't do anything with the flat. Papers from the faculty can be transferred to another town so she can finish there. She will try to apply through the faculty so that she could come here.

To go or to stay

Draft of Telegram

Prière télégraphier si êtes possession lettres télégrammes pour moi quelle provenance. Prière les expédier recommandé Stefan Themerson poste restante Toulouse

Je suis venu Toulouse mais je sens ne pas rester longtemps ça va chez vous Sacha va bien pas de nouvelles de Franka. T

tel. 22 October. PCK, Vichy, Hôtel Beau-Site, dep. Allier arrondissement, Briand provenance – telegram through Julia, 26 October

4 November **Diary Entry**

I sleep to 10 or 11. Write letters in a small bistro where coffee and sandwiches turn out to be no cheaper than lunch. Letters to Halina B., Julia, Blanche, Léon Temerson, Hades, Cz. Kri. and Hanka's letter to Bobrowski.

At 9 in the evening just as I was about to go to bed, Dyma dropped in. Władek and Rattner waited downstairs. Chess players' café.

A Chesterton type, specialist in foreigners, stammers and also has a blue squint. Game of draughts with Rattner. Return to the hotel.

Thousands of pens and pencils, hundreds of typewriters, cover sheets of paper.

Berlewi tells Koczorowski that this calms him, especially the tapping of the machine. Julia advises the Australian woman. Difficult construction of the novel, actions. You give it a title. Diaries or – recollections.

The topography of Sebastian [18]
people as towns

Approaching a camouflaged town, detectors sensitive to infrared start to function. You feel the approach of a man with whom you will, in a moment, engage in conversation. Author, let's suggest the existence of some waves.

No, science hasn't proved anything like this so far. Literature is science, descriptive homology. It can extract things that haven't been proved.

There is also pure, theoretical literature – nobody wants to understand it. (Utilitarian literature)

18 Sebastian becomes the protagonist in Stefan's *Croquis dans les Ténèbres*.

4 Nov. 1940
21 Jan 1941

4 November 1940

(Telescope – man). It is only an assembly of astronomical instruments. But the description usually ends with the window.

5 November Diary Entry

Bibliothèque Municipale, Montpellier
Jeans – *Les nouvelles bases philosophiques de la science* (1935)[19]
Eddington – *Sur le problème du déterminisme* (1934)[20]
Carnap – *La science et la métaphysique devant l'analyse logique du langage* (1935)[21]
Enriques F. – *Signification de l'histoire de la pensée scientifique* (1934)[22]
Frank – *Théorie de la connaissance et physique moderne* (1934)[23]
Schlick – *Les énoncés scientifiques et la réalité du monde extérieur* (1934)[24]

> Nous continuons examen des découvertes de la science moderne, sans oublier qu'elles decrivent, non pas la nature, mais les questions posées par l'homme à la nature.[25]

Hélène Konczewska[26]
L'unité de la matière et le problème des transmutations (1939)

6 November Cable from Blanche Bronstein to Franciszka

STEFAN VENU ME VOIR SOURCE PERRIER VERGÈZE GARD PENSE RESTER PROXIMITÉ ATTENDANT POUVOIR REJOINDRE FRANÇOISE EMBRASSONS = BLANCHE BRONSTEIN

Diary Entry

To sleep more economically till 12, walk, university, student's bistro (Chez Jules): radio, cards. Man, the nicer looking (literally prettier) the uglier. But male youth can be the nicer looking.

One approaches people like towns, in an overture, in expressionist perspective, in hope, in raincoats – in travel clothes.
Unexpected discoveries, premonition of disappointments.
One leaves people, as one leaves towns, villages, neighbourhoods

Bibliothèque, Montpellier
Aldous Huxley – *L'Ange et la Bête*[27]

L'Ange et la Bête 'Unité et Diversité' not to neglect the project – of Hamlet and Faust.

> Il est bien des sortes de dieux. C'est pourquoi il est bien des sortes d'hommes. Car les hommes font les dieux à leur image. (...) "...quelque chose qui n'est pas nous-mêmes, et qui conduit à la justice." (Matthew Arnold) des modernistes cultivés. (...)

19 Sir James Jeans (1877–1946) physicist and mathematician, *The New Background to Science*, 1933
20 Sir Arthur Eddington (1882–1944) astrophysicist, 'The Decline of Determinism', 1932
21 Rudolf Carnap (1891–1970) philosopher, *Überwindung der Metaphysik durch logische Analyse der Sprache*, 1932
22 Federigo Enriques (1871–1946) mathematician, *Storia del pensiero scientifico*, 1932
23 Philipp Frank (1884–1966) physicist, 'Was bedeuten die gegenwärtigen physikalischen Theorien für die allgemeine Erkenntnistheorie?', 1930
24 Moritz Schlick (1882–1936) philosopher, 'Die Wende der Philosophie', 1930
25 Sir James Jeans, *Les nouvelles bases philosophiques de la science*, 1935, p.78
26 Philosopher (1887 –1959)
27 French translation by Jules Castier of *Do what you will*, 1929

> "Il n'y a jamais eu, et il n'aura jamais, un homme qui possède une connaissance certaine de dieux et de toutes les choses dont je parle. Car même s'il lui arrive de dire toute la vérité, lui-même n'en sait rien, mais il est loisible à tous d'avoir leur fantaisie." Ainsi écrivit Xénophane il y a quelque deux mille cinq cents ans. Et malgré cela, les hommes continuent encore à pousser leurs fantaisies au rang de Vérités universelles et absolues, ils s'imaginent encore qu'ils savent quelque chose sur l'objet en soi. Mais l'objet en soi est inconnaissable, et "il est loisible à tous" de le voir "à leur fantaisie". La science n'est pas plus "vraie" que le sens-commun ou la folie, que l'art ou la religion. (...) L'art, par exemple, traite de bien plus d'aspects de cette réalité intérieure que ne le fait la science, qui se borne délibérément et par convention à l'étude d'une classe fort limité d'expériences – les expériences des sens. (...) L'Apparence – pour employer la phraséologie de Platon – est elle intrinsèquement et absolument, moins vraie que l'Idée? Platon lui-même eût répondue par l'affirmative. Les Apparences sont illusoires; les Idées (nos abstractions à partir d'apparences dont nous nous souvenons) son vraies. Mais... il n'y a pas plus de raison pour qu'une abstraction effectuée d'après le fait soit plus proche de la chose en soi qu'une sensation immédiate. C'est uniquement pour certaines fins strictement humaines, que l'Idée peut être considérée comme plus vraie que l'Apparence.

I am doing all sorts of things – letters, conversations – so that it will not be noticed that I'm not really here at all.

> Mais les hommes sont libres de ne pas poursuivre une fin utilitaire. Ils peuvent parfois être artistes, par example. (...) Pour des gens de cette sorte, la sensation immédiate, ou "Apparence", sera plus vraie que l'abstraction ou "Idée".

[in art – in film, appearances were called a false abstraction]

> En tous cas, le critère du vrai et du faux doit toujours demeurer intérieur, psychologique. Parler de la verité comme d'un rapport entre les notions humaines et les choses en elles-mêmes, est une absurdité.

To break up time, the chronology of a novel – relationships and sequences out of time.

> De la Nature Humaine et de la Nature Divine.
> Presque toutes les discussions historiques, il faut le remarquer, sont des discussions de goûts personnels.[28]

28 This quotation from the chapter 'Du Progrès en Mythologie.'

Diary Entry

In the morning to Władek – he is not there
the post – letter from Léon, the park, aqueducts. Chez Jules – wine.
Midday – practice alarm, first time since May. Then running to the wood.

It seemed that it was for real. Tedium.
Make use of action from end to the beginning.

(Władek left for Vergèze – he had a telephone call from Blanche)

Make another version of Sebastian – perhaps as an introduction to what will have to be done.

Sketch from nature

Wandering through little streets, leaves blow in the wind

Casse-croûte Chez Roche

Stefan paints a portrait in words of the scene in front of him. The scene may take an hour, but it's a picture, or perhaps an animation. It is like an image in greys and black. Here it is:

½ litre of wine, radio, Wurlitzer organ, pot-pourri.
tabby cat, a customer throws a ball of bread at him, the cat shakes himself and licks himself.

In the corner, after the evening rain, sits a fellow in a beret, a cigarette.

The landlord, a pale queer or a spy plays dice. Zeus with a beard, in a cap, old, looking like a tramp, apparence à l'idée – Zeus – vide yesterday's Huxley – wine at the bar, trousers in brown 'velvet' – shaggy grey – radio plays *Petrushka*, like the one in René Clair's *Entr'acte* in Warsaw – what is happening with Haltrecht? – Zeus knows that wine for 2 francs allows one to forget about lunch for 12. – Landlord turned off the radio – a moment of incredible silence – c'est pas joli – young woman switched it on – tact won the day. Zeus is looking around and understands everything – Radio – tutti and speaker – and now burlaks – Zeus doesn't hear anything, for Zeus always burlaks, downs half a glass of red wine – at the table those that order prix fixe talk and talk and they also know what they know and s'amusent burlaks crescendo – landlord switches off – the young woman c'est pas joli ça – mes oreilles n'aiment pas cette musique – silence – those at the table: 100 km or 400 km respondez moi – ! Zeus stands and already understands everything – so far drank half a glass, filled it up, in the bottle there is still a third, Zeus doesn't drink yet, looks at the watch – 'dix francs km?' – St. François 1er a depasse dix francs cents km. Zeus downs half a glass – Soixante km. 'Parlez italien?' 'Cento km'. 'Trois millions par an. Trois cents par jour, et tu a fait trois francs km.' Zeus observes from under the peak of his cap. Customers at the table smoke cigars. Zeus emptied the bottle. He is searching in the pocket of his waistcoat. Looks in his hand, jangles, counts. 20 sous drop from his hand – merci bien Monsieur – two young women leave – landlord, vous avez oublié – oh! ce truc – ha ha ha – guests to the other room – 200 km – il n'y a pas que cinq – Zeus drank a bit from the glass – young women are drinking liqueurs – jour sans alcool – Zeus looks in front of him at a wall of bottles – already 5 past 2. Young women leave, the cat runs through – landlord is clearing up – Zeus pulls out a cigarette, Zeus has fingers like my grandfather during winter – lights up the match – the face of Zeus lit up by the flame – au revoir says Zeus – he goes out, shambling, like Herman. Customers return from the other room – combien ça fait là? – cinquante voilà soixante frs. Girl with an open mouth shows the white chewed food on her tongue. Silence. Landlord is counting.

Stefan is acutely aware how the fat people with money who are eating must appear to Zeus. He observes Zeus because he too is not eating and we learn that for the time being and for the next 18 months, Stefan will always be hungry. What else? There are notes about letters or lack of them, usually the latter. But in one sense the Themersons are not completely alone. There are people who are concerned about them: the Złotowskis, Józef Wittlin, Teresa Żarnower, Tema Kaliszer, the Bronsteins.

Hallo! Rosette!

Philosophical life – gospel
Brick from Grabinoulor[29] develop psychologically

Volume by volume prospectus of man with drawings, explanation of action – in answers to questions. Dear sir, we have the honour of sending you the prospectus of a man who would ask you for the hand of your daughter.

Library – Huxley

Prospectus. Introduction – antiquity: analyses – raised blood pressure, only with the lowering of the blood pressure to a minimum
It showed up once in the nasal membrane
What equals Mount Everest in height?
Examination of reflexes
sexus
Individual characteristics, etc

Letter to Blanche, letter to Halina

Stefan checks train times to Lyon. Grenoble, where he is going, is on the way. In the morning there are more familiar faces in the hotel. Rattner arrives, also WT, and eventually Władek Vinaver who brings him 100 frs. There will be no train till 6.35 but Stefan proceeds to the station. He will wait there for Saturday to arrive. When it does Stefan is on the train sitting by the window looking at the sun on the snow covered mountains and notices a patch of sun that has penetrated through the glass into the interior of his carriage. Halina meets him at the station and they proceed to a hotel to meet Bolesław Miciński, 'the only man in the free zone with whom one can communicate'. Bobrowski is also there. At last Stefan learns that now he will stay at Voiron. He will have an address: 'I shall have an address and will send a telegram… a telegram…!' But there are still four days to go and now there is still a room to be found. And then when a Red Cross ambulance appears he feels the jolt of an unpleasant memory of Toulouse, but this time it's not a raid. 'Joy' writes Stefan, that it is only a sick man on a stretcher. And now Stefan will spend the night in the 13th hotel since he started the journey. 'Bread. Hotel dinner for 13 frs. Sleep.'

29 Character in the book of that title by Pierre Albert-Birot, 1919

8 November 1940

Diary Entry

Trains Lyon 6,35
[notes about train times]

morning – 4th man in the hotel – Rattner, WT will arrive Saturday, Monday
railway station
more train times
viens samedi 10.52, remerciements, amitiés. WT
Louis XIV. Władek arrives. He is looking for a room (or I am looking for a room?). Walk out of town. Bread, cheese, wine. At his place – quarter of an hour.
Finally a word: 'I am sick of life'. (100 frs from Władek)
post – nothing
at 10 to the station
until 12 in the buffet
until 3.30 in the salle d'attente

9 November **Diary Entry**

Journey. Window. Sun outside the window – patch of sun inside and a map
Mountains – snow
Halina at the station
Gren. Hotel
Paczkowski (manner in which he hurried to lunch)
Mrs Micińska and the journey to Bolek Miciński
at Bol. Micińskis'
conversation
The only man in the free zone with whom one can have an understanding.
Gren. Hotel – Bobrowski
'I am very glad'
To Voiron – on the 13th. To the 13th hotel from tomorrow.
Departure. Joy – I shall have an address and will send a telegram… a telegram…
Search for a room.
Collecting my things. Red Cross ambulance. Police. Memory of Toulouse. 'Joy' that it is a sick man on a stretcher and not a raid. – Bread. Hotel Dinner for 13 frs.
Sleep.

10 November

Stefan meets more people who will be accommodated at Voiron. He will be one of three among the permanent quota. There is a performance at The Academy: following the director's speech, a poetry reading, then Chopin, then the 1937 film *Hearts Aflame*, and finally the hymn 'Rejoice, Oh Mother Poland'. At the end, a dead silence, no applause.

They sleep three to a room. Stefan shares a room with Rozenblat and Jahl. Snoring keeps him awake until 3.30.

Diary Entry

A teacher should be a hypocrite.
'What actually is the truth? – storm of electrons – the content of an atom and quantity of light.'
That's a question for Hamlet.
16.45
Mrs Gubrynowiczowa
recommended by the Micińskis

3000 frs approximate price
c. 50 frs per person depending on how long they stay
Mrs Budkiewicz and I act as permanent quota for Voiron
until 6 in the Terminus
possibly telephone and Morawski

The Academy
director's speech
Słonimski's 'Alarm' – Minszajn – Andrzej Chmurny
Chopin
'Passionate Heart'
'Gaude Mater Polonia'
dead silence, lack of applause
(Andrzej Chmurny – Minszajn)
Rozenblat, Jahl, engineer Wolf from Clairefontaine. Sleeping three in a room
Snoring
I don't sleep until 3.30

Dream: I am being taken to an exhibition of paintings. We are on our way. Private studio in a flat, on the floor stains of white, more dirt and signs of destitution than pictures (conversation in the evening with Jahl about Lille and about a meeting with Aronson in Toulouse. Description of the flat = a pauper's description (and a pauper that's somebody). Someone says that it's cheek to ask people to such a studio. I said something in response that I can't remember, but there was in it a lot of pain and sarcasm. But also unnecessary, like the note which sounded yesterday on the lips of the lady (at the next table during supper) who offended her neighbour during a discussion about language (Rej – Żeromski – introduction of new words). She turned to her neighbour: 'You should pay attention because you might learn something.' Conflicting feelings, I go to another room – knock on the door, Bugajska wakes me up – it's 8 in the morning.

11 November

Paraphrasing Stefan's own diary entries, this is what the following three days look like. On Monday, 11 November, instead of Mass, Stefan goes to the Post Office, sends telegrams to Franka and Blanche. Then breakfast and an application to be completed. He longs to be left alone, to have some space to think and to work but the circumstances don't allow it. He writes: 'The only quiet place to work is the lavatory, but one can't sit there for ever.'

Diary Entry

Instead of going to Mass, I go to the Post Office. Telegram to Franka, telegram to Vergèze.
Breakfast. Application.
The only quiet corner for work is the lavatory but one can't sit here for ever.

The lady so inclined to instruct is called Golińska and is the friend of the Gloomy Minszajn. I sit with him at same table at lunchtime. Conversation with the former chauffeur of the ministerial circle, about communism, peasantry, etc. Deadly bore.

Draft of a Letter

Dearest Blanche, I am in Voiron since yesterday – and I still can't accept the fact that this is the end of this wandering. B. was in Grenoble and thanks to your letter he received me with open arms. For the time being there are three of us here. After the 14th I am to move to another room – and there will be two of us. Unfortunately only a ghost of a chance of being alone, about which I long since dream. Maybe because of this, I feel that I won't be here for long.

Voiron is a little town, half an hour by train from Grenoble. We live in a hotel. There is little to recommend either the countryside or the town. I snatched a quarter of an hour of peace to write this letter – how to steal 24 hours to even begin to think about work seems impossible, and this is the only prospect that I can see ahead of me.

Materially, it is very good here, one can live and eat, etc. But these are things I really couldn't care less about. I should very much like to receive a reply from you whether a telegram has arrived from Franka. I took 100 frs from Władek (I don't even write borrowed) – that helped me here considerably, because I was cleaned out after the stay in Montpellier and the journey, and I had to stay for one day in Grenoble at my own expense and also today I sent a telegram to Franka. Apart from that it seems that here they will also be handing out some initial financial payments. Please forgive me – I realise that, driven from place to place, I live as if on another plane, often recoiling from reality. Vergèze and Montpellier. Words are inadequate – glances miss one another in the wind.

Well, but one would have to eat an entire barrel of salt[30] – and for this there was no time.

I embrace you and ask you to remember me. St.

Anatole France: *Le livre de mon ami*, chapter v

> Ne souriez pas à ce que je dis là, ou n'y souriez que par amitié et songez-y; quiconque vit, fût-il petit chien, est au milieu des choses.

Telegram from Blanka [Blanche], i.e. 1300 frs from Franka
The promised room

12 November Diary Entry

Corridor duty. Sweeping. Lunch. 30 frs. Anatole France
Lipski and his wife

Christened – actors: it will be frowned upon if his wife spends time with a Jewish woman

Anatole France: *Le livre de mon ami* (113)

> Je n'ai jamais été veritable observateur; car if faut à l'observation un système qui la dirige, et je n'ai point de système. L'observateur conduit sa vue; le spectateur se laisse prendre par les yeux.

second lieutenant – a miner
conversation about Poles – three for wine (with R…?)

13 November Diary Entry

Breakfast – engineer Wolf (reminiscence of Clarefond)
Leftist. Promoting Russia
Bobrowski. Cafard

30 There is a saying that before you make a friend, you have to eat a barrel of salt with him.

Diary Entry

Breakfast. Laundry. Conversation. Toccata, Chaconne
Evening – talks by Bych and Okoński. Bych in Silesia. Okoński in the Subcarpathian Ruthenia (Ruś Podkarpacka)
Bych – grenades through the Olza river, guerrilla warfare.
'I didn't understand what it was all about.' Innocent people in service. The skirmish started at 1 o'clock at night – 4 at an arranged meeting place. 6 arrived 1 was missing. At 6 they went to look, moans. R. wounded – was dying. Abdomen, chest, head smashed, eye invisible, ear in shreds, blood. They had to carry him 3 km through the frontier to the Polish side and leave him there. The cross of independence. 'I am sorry for the Czechs, but these Krauts, I'd burn on a slow fire.'

Okoński worked in a factory that made mines.

They took him at once, he couldn't even go home. They told his wife that he went skiing. Guerrilla warfare. They revenged themselves on Ukrainian chauvinists. They spoke good Ukrainian. They were marching together – 7 to 4. Suddenly into those 4 – puf! – They left them behind.

They made the uprising in Hungary. They were told to repaint signboards in Hungarian. No Hungarian could read it.

In a hut. A tree stump in front of the hut. Snow crunching underfoot. From the bushes shots. They hide behind a tree stump, only rucksacks are sticking out. Bang, over the rucksacks. After two hours, they come out and go behind a single tree, one behind the other. And then the others – as anyone leans out – Bang from revolvers. 2 hours. Until frontier guards moved in from the side!

They bashed up one of them – the others fled. I didn't know what it was all about, they ordered so one went. I am sorry for the Czechs. I carried over a child in a rucksack. The woman went on foot over 50 cm of snow. He on skis. What was it all for? He went back home. Nobody asked him about anything. Back at midday.

Bych in Preszów. In a hut. He saw through the window, 15 soldiers in the barn, officer, lieutenant commander.

Suddenly one German soldier on a motorbike. He stopped – 'die Hände hoch!' As if hypnotised they all raised their hands. One after another weapons and belts on the ground. Afterwards he drove them in front of him. Bych would never have believed it if somebody had told him about it.

He must have got an Iron Cross for sure.

Okoński: 'If someone told me that I would kill a man, I would think, that it was terrible, that I won't be able to sleep, and guilt, nightmares. The first shot cost me the most. I was running behind a platoon with a revolver in my fist. Germans escaped, but a non-commissioned officer tore a gun with a bayonet from a soldier and stayed behind. He skewered one at once. He ran up to another and then started a fencing match. A real fencing match. Everyone was standing around looking to see who would win. And nobody helped, nobody intervened.

OK buddy! We all looked. I too. It was a fencing match. They had guns. I didn't. Only a revolver. Anyway I was running behind the platoon. But they fought together, just like in a [public] square. At last, the German hit our man with a butt on the jaw, he then staggered and then the bayonets came into action. Bayonet gets stuck between the bones, doesn't want to come out, he pushes the soldier with his leg until he falls off the bayonet. And then to me. He is running. I look how he is running towards me with a red bayonet – and I stand completely paralysed. I am holding the revolver in my hand and can't shoot. Finally, when he was nearly on top of me and the bayonet touched my chest – I heard a shot. It wasn't me that was shooting, although smoke was coming out of my gun barrel. So he got it – through the jaw, brain, skull, even made a hole in his helmet. But I was wet afterwards, Mister, covered in sweat.

Bych: 'For bayonets – there is nothing like Polish soldiers.'
Okoński: '(Mister) if you saw the French, how they fought!'
Bych: 'They fought, what are you talking about?'
Okoński: 'I was there with the 11th division that held the retreat. Bombers, one French plane (shot down dropped half of the bombs) and to the other. That one under the cover of the bridge, but he fell, and then 4 gunners went for the French plane.'

'The Czech met the gunners on the road. Landed. Pale. So nervous. His jaw quivers. 180 holes in the body of the plane, not counting the wings. Rubber on the wheels in shreds. Got hit from the back. All the instruments in smithereens. Seat. Mascot. But he, nothing.'

15 November **Diary Entry**

Conversation with Władysław Jahl, the anarchist, (Rosa Bailly, sent him a letter with an invented refusal). Not a hope. What to do? He explains why he doesn't paint in the open air. In 1914 a crowd nearly tore him to bits. Behind the wood that he painted was a strategic railway. The Public Prosecutor, a friend of [Antoine] Pevsner recognised him and freed him after 14 days in prison.

Social meeting, in the evening, radio with Wolf, readings (inspection of the premises).

Telegram from Franciszka to Stefan

CHÉRI VAIS PARFAITEMENT BIEN LETTRE SUIT TENDRESSES
BAISERS = THEMERSON

16 November

The Warsaw ghetto is sealed off from the outside world.

Diary Entry

Jahl – hernia, reminiscence of the Wittlins, in the evening a bath.
Tedium.

17 November 1940

Stefan visits Jahl and is given a drawing. Meets the young Wolf [son of the engineer] and makes a list of people to write to. Dyboski and Dzieniowski are his table companions at lunch, and again in the evening. There is poetry and there are speeches which Stefan notes down very carefully.

Diary Entry

Letters from Toulouse
Must write to:
~~Léon Temerson~~, Julia, ~~Blanche~~, Brunet, Casablanca [i.e. Mira Złotowska], Vita Asch, ~~Edek~~, Ludwik, Mietek, Tema, ~~Kaczorowski~~, ~~Marysia Bryn~~, Zosia K[ramsztyk], Hania, Janowski, Rzewska, Miciński, ~~Grynblat~~

evening – a speech, 2 poems
at lunch
Dyboski at the table, and Dzieniowski
(to describe in biblical style)
Bych's story

1. Magistrate in Kraśnik. To get petrol. Bombing. Young woman wounded in the leg, and a colleague crushed. Hysteria. Little river. Grey

2. Cart, ditch, train to Warsaw. Stops before Brześć. Two days. They come out. Seven. Revolvers. Hens. Return. Clearing in the forest. Cavalry officer, boots, Ukrainians at the rear. Hands up! They do it. They undress. Hen clucks. To escape. Running. In Brześć. Convoy 150 in front are escaping. Shots. Soldiers forward. Then he at the back. To a hut. On the left a room, on the right a room, in front stairs. Onto the stairs and covers himself with a frock. One minute or hours. Door slams. Fear of bayonets. Where to?

Stefan is in many ways appalled by the chaos of chatter, confessions, speeches and the general social interaction, and yet he is fascinated by much of what he sees and hears. Some of the talks, which usually deal with the speaker's war experiences, he notes in a telegraphic style. Other descriptions are longer. In due course, he will crystallise some of the events in a story: 'The Investigation'. [pp. 375–392]

18 – 19 November

Monday and Tuesday. These two days merge into one. There are more conversations, more contacts. Stefan's discomfort is private. He does not realise to what extent his presence, his comments, his determination to overcome the pettiness of his environment and the tragedy of the times, and to work despite everything, become enormously important to some of his co-inhabitants of the Hôtel de la Poste. This is revealed in the post-war correspondence with some of them.

Diary Entry

I can't remember at all what happened yesterday. Just as one can't remember sums, except yes, I was at the Post Office. It gave me an unpleasant turn that Blanche deducted 100 frs. I received 1200. I wrote letters. Talked to young Wolf, Jahl. All sorts of things happened but without any sense. Today, the move.
At the moment I am alone. The suitcase of Szeryng. Bag with things, a lion rug. I thought, if I were a child that would be the most important thing. Who dictates our hierarchies: our impressions, judgments, etc. Engineer Wolf administers accommodation (Wolf's past – Spain. Second wife, son born 10 days before the war. He comes from Sosnowiec. Imagine him, this young man in that role, as together with the landlady downstairs, he organises the register of the Hôtel de

la Poste, (and Puget – [illegible] looks on from the side with his dark searching eyes) 'For Themerson, lion on the rug.'

First course of French, conversation. Budnay Chugur […] Mon Dieu, he does not know how to contradict anyone, or correct mistakes. He smiles. Supper. Return with Mme Szeryng to La Chaumière (assigned theme [for an essay] – The Situation of the Poles in Paris.[31])

Stefan's story is not about Poles but about a Monsieur Durand who leaves his suburban home, travels to the centre of Paris, visits a department store in the rue de Rivoli, travels up and down on the escalator and buys various things he needs. The sun is shining and the bouquinistes as usual line the right bank of the Seine. Durand then takes the Métro to return home and as he opens the door, the telephone is ringing. He rushes to the phone and has a pleasant conversation with a colleague from the army of the First World War. 'You know', says M Durand, 'I've just been to town, and I saw soldiers marching. I recognised the weapons of course, but why have our soldiers been given different uniforms?'

For the following three days, Stefan's sole entry consists of three words: 'nothing and nothing'. This is a refrain. Another few days pass: drinking wine in the evening, drifting, lessons between lunch and supper. Stefan feels that his sensibility has been blunted.

There are people whom God did not create, but man – Don Quixote, Pickwick. T.

19 November **Letter from Franciszka to Blanche Bronstein**

Blanche, darling! Finally I have regained some balance and can write to you. How are you, are you working? From your address I gather that you are. I suppose that you are together with Sacha, not like us blockheads. It will be difficult to write just like that, how and what happened, and how it is now. I am so happy that finally I know what is happening with Stefek. I am terribly grateful to you for the telegram and for everything, because I have no doubt that you took care of Stefek a bit. Here, one could say, one lives quietly. I have always liked classical music, and since childhood I would go to sleep while the piano was being played. The city, just like a city, you know, it is ugly. But fantastically hospitable. From the first moment we were fed and housed. Anyway, I continue to work. I have money. *À propos*, I sent some money for Stefek to your address. I don't know what it will amount to, but at any rate a few thousand francs. I have his new address, but anyway I expect that you will be in contact with him and your address is more permanent.

Michał and Ada send their best regards. I shall go to visit them next Sunday. There are lots of friends here. As far as your family is concerned, Władek M. and his wife are in Stockholm. They are planning to go to America. Perhaps I will see them here on their way there.

My dear, I so much miss here our intimate friends. Although things here may create that impression, it is not so. Apart from that I am extremely well physically. Complete *prosperité*. So much so that one could cry. How does Stefek look? Tell me everything, how are you physically and mentally? Do you have news from your parents and brother?

I embrace you my very dear Blanche, please hug Sacha for me. Please write to Teresa's address.[32]

Bye! Franka

The letter passes through the hands of Teresa Żarnower, who adds 2 paragraphs:

Dear Monsieur and Madame Bronstein

I am so happy to learn where you are and everything. Since recently I have been living in Lisbon, a very pleasant city. I should be very glad if you would

31 There is a small manuscript by Stefan Themerson with that title.

32 The address is crossed out, although it is possible to see that it is the Polish Legation in Lisbon.

add a fcw words to me. Please don't delay with the reply – I shall also respond immediately. Best wishes and a warm handshake. Teresa Żarnowerówna.

PS: Franka made a mistake. I have nothing to do with the address she gave you. Please write to Poste-Restante-Lisbona. I will forward the letter to Franka as soon as I receive an answer.

20 – 22 Nov. **Diary Entry**

Wednesday, Thursday, Friday – Nothing and nothing

20 November **Letter from Franciszka to Stefan – Unposted**

Darling, look, I've gone quite insane. I know that I won't send this letter, because how could I? I must write to you not to go completely mad. Dear child, how I miss you! Why, why aren't we, can't we be together? What are you doing, how are you managing? It was so terribly difficult – so long before I had any news! And it's still difficult even now, because I miss you so terribly. In the letters that I sent, only a few stupid words were possible. But what to do with all that I feel, that grips my heart with anxiety and brings tears to the eyes from tenderness.

They were so good your telegrams – I know that you wouldn't write me anything else, you wouldn't complain or ask for help; I know that the quiet and sincere tone of the telegrams is no proof that you are well, but I couldn't, and probably subconsciously didn't want to recognise this, and it was better for me not to. I could almost feel good, so long as the joy of receiving them was still fresh in me. Now, again, days pass and again I know nothing. Oh darling, if I imagine for a moment, even though it's so difficult, that somehow you are managing (but how?), and that you have money (but from where?) and perhaps, perhaps you are trying to work – oh, you can imagine how my head spins. I so believe in your work and I love it so much. How sad I am if I think that perhaps I could be helpful, but I am not there with you. I don't know, maybe it's better like this, so often I feel guilty about so many things. – You know, but it's probably always like that, when you're suddenly so far apart, and so helpless.

My darling, when will I see you? And I am so frightened of it all for you. I was so happy to get the news from Voiron, I felt so aware of the whole of you in that. Even though you didn't get to the south, but are suddenly in the mountains – and you like mountains so much, little one – just to think that outside the window of Hôtel de la Poste, you have perhaps a stream and in the distance, mountains, just as once at that cobbler's in Zakopane. That perhaps, perhaps… things are well with you. But I am so frightened that these images are simply dictated by my instinct of self-preservation. Whereas in fact you probably have to go around Polish and other offices, to get a few francs, listen to unpleasant things from boring people – my dearest pet, how I should like to cuddle up close to you.

My dearest sunshine, I so want to get on with my work, and to do that for you – really, only for you. Alone, I break down completely. Already a long time ago I bought a small drawing pad that would fit in the pocket, to bring it to you, wherever that may be, just as I carry with me your poems that you copied for me before leaving, before that unnecessary departure.

And then nothing – I drew a few pages, worthless, I threw them out, or gave them to whoever was around. Perhaps something will come out in due course. But everything is worthless and too superficial to show you, darling.

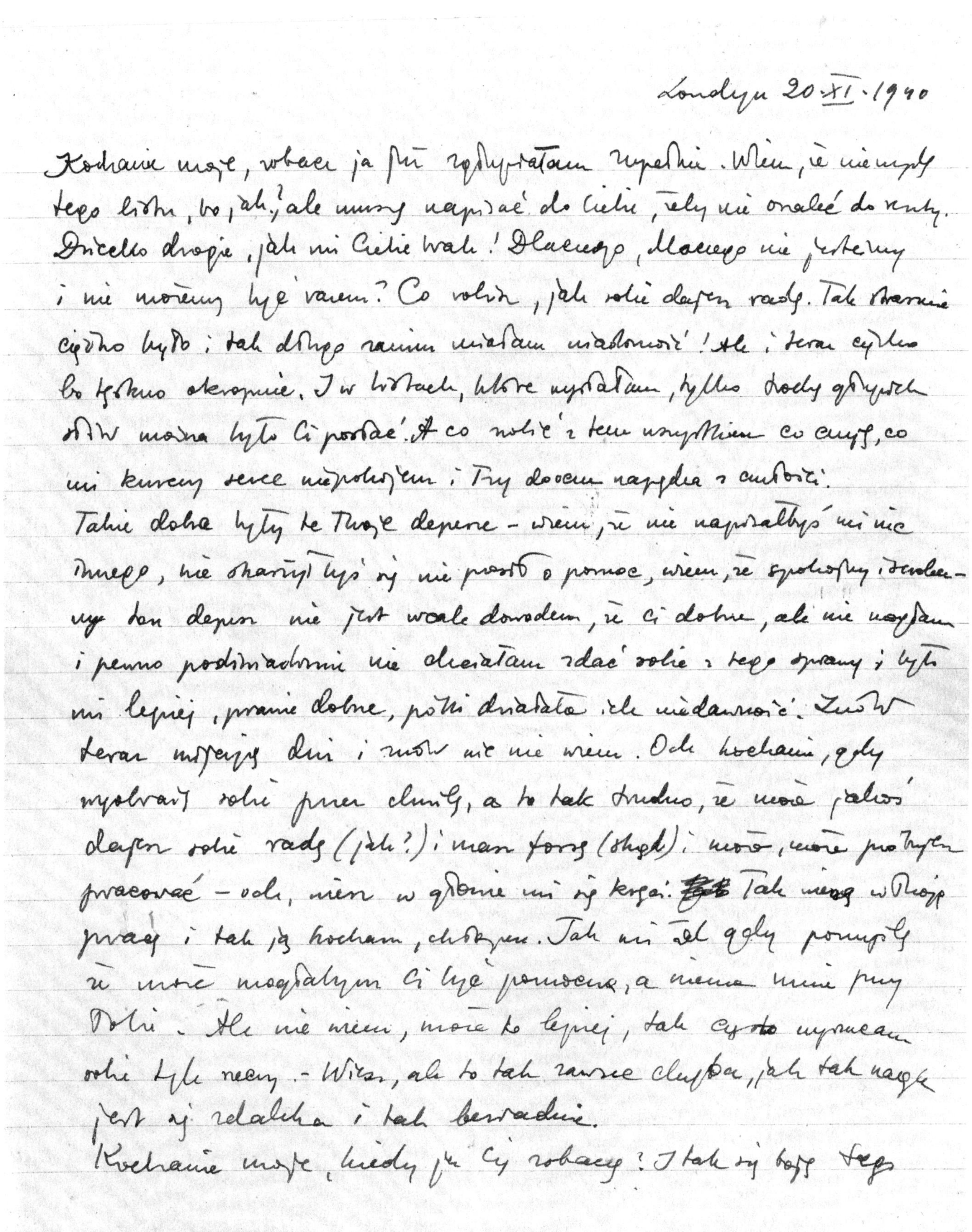

Londyn 20.XI.1940

Kochanie moje, właściwie już zgłupiałam zupełnie. Wiem, że nie wyślę tego listu, bo jak?, ale muszę napisać do Ciebie, żeby nie oszaleć do reszty. Dziecko drogie, jak mi Ciebie brak! Dlaczego, dlaczego nie jesteśmy i nie możemy być razem? Co robisz, jak sobie dajesz radę. Tak strasznie często było i tak długo razem miałam wiadomość! Ale i teraz często bo tęsknię okropnie. I w listach, które wysłałam, tylko kiedy gdzieś słów można było Ci posłać. A co robić z tym wszystkim co czuję, co mi kurczy serce nieopisanie i Twój dosyć nagła z czułości.
Takie dobre były te Twoje depesze – wiem, że nie napisałbyś mi nic innego, nie skarżyłbyś się nie prosił o pomoc, wiem, że spokojny i zadowolony ten depesz nie jest wcale dowodem, że Ci dobrze, ale nie wyczułam i pewno podświadomie nie chciałam zdać sobie z tego sprawy i było mi lepiej, prawie dobrze, potem działała ich wiadomość. Znów teraz mroczniejsze dni i znów nic nie wiem. Och kochanie, gdy wyobrażasz sobie przez chwilę, a to tak trudno, że może jakoś dajesz sobie radę (jak?) i masz forsę (skąd), może, może nawet pracować – och, wiem w głowie mi się kręci. Tak wierzę w Twoją pracę i tak ją kocham, chłopcze. Tak mi żal gdy pomyślę że może mogłabym Ci być pomocną, a nie ma mnie przy Tobie. Ale nie wiem, może to lepiej, tak często wyrzucam sobie tyle rzeczy. – Wiesz, ale to tak zawsze chodziło, jak tak nagle jest się zdalnika i tak bezradnie.
Kochanie moje, kiedy już Cię zobaczę? I tak się boję tego

Unposted letter from Franciszka to Stefan, 20 November 1940; pages 1 & 2 (overleaf) of six.

wszystkiego dla Ciebie. Tak się ucieszyłam tym uświadomieniem i Verzon, tak poczułam w tem całego Ciebie. Właśnie wczoraj nie na południu, właśnie nagle w górach – tak lubisz góry, mały – gdy nagle pomyślę, że za oknem „Hotel de la Porte" mam morze słoneczne i zdaleka góry, tak jak kiedyś u tego szewca w Zakopanem. Że morze, morze... jest Ci dobrze.
Ale tak się boję, że te obrazy dyktuje mi po prostu mój instynkt samoobrony. Że muszę właśnie chodzić po jakichś nowych i dziwnych urzędach, starać się o jakiś parę papierków, słuchać rzeczy przykrych od nudnych ludzi – malutko, jak chciałabym przytulić się do Ciebie.
Słonko moje, chcę tak pracować, i to dla Ciebie, naprawdę, tylko dla Ciebie. Sama zadziwiłam się już wczoraj, ale dawno już kupiłam taki mały szkicownik, żeby zmieścił się w kieszeni i żeby go donieść do Ciebie, gdziekolwiek to będzie, tak jak noszę wszędzie przy sobie Twoje wiersze które mi przepisałeś przed wyjazdem, przed tym niepotrzebnym wyjazdem.
I nic, – parę stron zrobiłam, nic nie warte, wyrzuciłam, albo dałam jakimś niepotrzebnym ludziom. Może dalej coś wyjdzie. Ale wszystko jest za złe i za powierzchowne dla Ciebie kochanie. Trudno mi się wziąć do kupy.
Jak trudno jest być samej, kiedy się jest przyzwyczajonym do stałej podpory serdeczności i czułości. Jak trudno jest

How difficult it is to be alone, when what you're used to is a constant flow of warmth and tenderness. How difficult to be simply *alone*, and so consciously alone. With how many people and in how many situations I got swept along on the way. And always when they did something hurtful to me (some small superficial thing, unimportant) I thought of you. Do you feel that, too – no-one close enough to feel sincere and real concern for you?

Do you remember, once, when things were very bad for us, you didn't want to cuddle up to me, to calm down and to forget, because, you said, that it is like valerian, that it just anæsthetises. Look how I console myself with the thought, that you know how to, perhaps want to and are able to contain the storm by yourself during that lonely difficult period. Perhaps you have enough strength to do without valerian. Oh dear child! If only it were like this – that you know how to cope with everything alone, that you don't pine as cruelly as I do.

I so need your wise eyes here, so much, my pet. Not just as an intoxicant, quite the contrary. I need you here to give me back some strength of purpose – so that we can both believe in being alive in these dreadful times and get our teeth into something worthwhile again, and know that it matters. I need to feel some grounding in normality under my feet, to hold back all the terror and baseness that's everywhere around.

I sometimes remind myself of the last phase of our work together, a few years ago, that strange time of trials and hopes, as if we were spreading our wings, but inside a net, and how difficult it was to stay positive, creating enough belief in ourselves and in what we were doing. Looking back it feels as though when we faced up to the problem of transplanting ourselves, we already had some premonition of what was coming. And what an unfortunate choice we made. Thinking of my 33 years fills me with terror. Shall I ever be able to do something again? Where? How? And for what?

Stefciu, there's no 'metaphysical' dimension to my world, let alone any creative impulse. Somewhere, in the previous apartment, I found a book, an old English book with silly limericks, and full of beautiful nonsensical drawings.[33] That was an experience. I felt electrified, like someone who can suddenly feel the ground alive under her feet again. I cried like a fool looking at these wonderful drawings. When I was leaving I asked if I could borrow the book for a while. And when the old battleaxe abruptly reminded me 'not to forget to give it back' I felt so deeply wounded that though it was no more than tactlessness on her part, I closed the book without another glance and gave it back. From my next apartment, I 'borrowed' El Greco's Madonna and it is now hanging here, at my place, on the wall. Again it will be hurtful for me to give it back. I am becoming a morbid thief of metaphysical excitements. My pet, you see how I miss you!

I have also become a kleptomaniac when it comes to warmth and friendship, I simply freeze in this organised loneliness. I have developed a friendship with Jaś Leyberg 'through correspondence'. This friendship of hopelessly lost people comes from our friendship with the Złotowskis and of theirs with him so there is some direct connection, even if it's arbitrary. Mira and Ignacy went to America. This makes me very sad because I was really attached to them. We went through a lot together, even though in such a short and seemingly uneventful time. It's becoming empty all around and so very lonely. And so you see, dearest, how could I send you such a sad letter? Perhaps, perhaps when you are in Lisbon. – Oh

33 *A Book of Nonsense* by Edward Lear

darling! I am very frightened for you, and I have already written this so many times in this letter which is not for posting.

And probably you are worried about me too, from what you read of what is happening here in London. It's true that it is really horrible, but surely not as bad as they write about conditions where you are. And English people react with such fantastic, almost terrifying composure. I have learned not to care, as well. After the first few days, I got used to it simply physically. And you know, during the worst air raids they tend to steep themselves in problems about the nature of art. I dream that the cooking pot in the shape of my head was not as empty as it seems. My pet!

Perhaps something will come out of all this. Perhaps it will turn out that, suddenly, I shall be able to do something. And perhaps it will be something that isn't so silly and/or bad? I cuddle close to you, darling, even though you are so far away. Look after yourself, look after yourself my dearest. Bye! F.

23 November Cable from Emanuel Freyd to Franciszka

INFORMEZ THEMERSON MARI BIEN INSTALLÉ MAISON ACCUEIL ARTISTES HÔTEL POSTE VOIRON ISÈRE ARGENT TRANSMIS = EMANUEL FREYD

23 – 25 Nov. Diary Entry

In the evening drinking wine, drifting, lessons between lunch and supper, blunted sensibility.

There are people who live for the moment that has just passed. There are people that live for the moment that is about to come. To live for a second the moment that exists, that is a revelation, inspiration, foray into an unknown dimension. T.

24 November Cable from Stefan to Franciszka

CHÉRIE MERCI SUIS PARFAITEMENT BIEN ESPÈRE TOUJOURS TE REVOIR MAIS OÙ ET QUAND CELA SERA POSSIBLE COMMENT VAS TU QUELS SONT TES PROJETS REPONDS EXPLICITEMENT JE T'EMBRASSE CHÉRIE BAISERS = THEMERSON

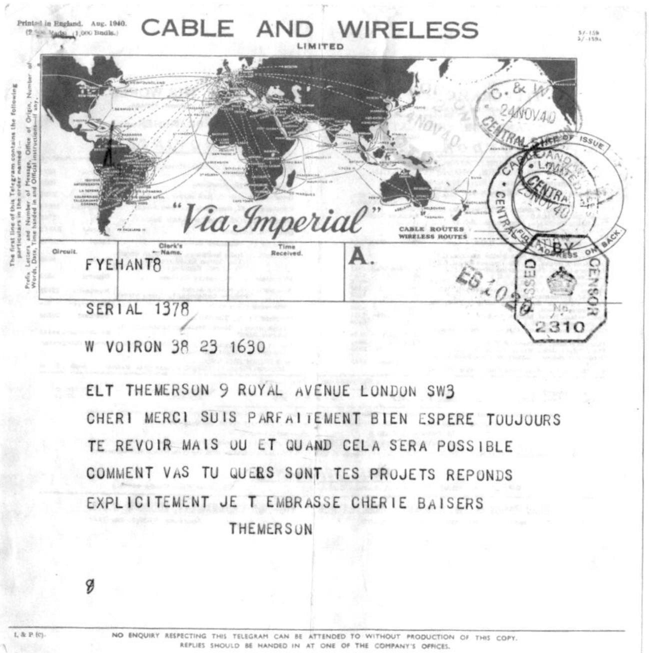

Printed in England. Aug. 1940.
CABLE AND WIRELESS LIMITED
"Via Imperial"
CABLE ROUTES
WIRELESS ROUTES
C. & W. 24NOV40 CENTRAL
PASSED BY CENSOR No. 2310

Circuit.	Clerk's Name.	Time Received.	A.
FYEHANT8			

SERIAL 1378

W VOIRON 38 23 1630

ELT THEMERSON 9 ROYAL AVENUE LONDON SW3
CHERI MERCI SUIS PARFAITEMENT BIEN ESPERE TOUJOURS
TE REVOIR MAIS OU ET QUAND CELA SERA POSSIBLE
COMMENT VAS TU QUERS SONT TES PROJETS REPONDS
EXPLICITEMENT JE T EMBRASSE CHERIE BAISERS
THEMERSON

NO ENQUIRY RESPECTING THIS TELEGRAM CAN BE ATTENDED TO WITHOUT PRODUCTION OF THIS COPY. REPLIES SHOULD BE HANDED IN AT ONE OF THE COMPANY'S OFFICES.

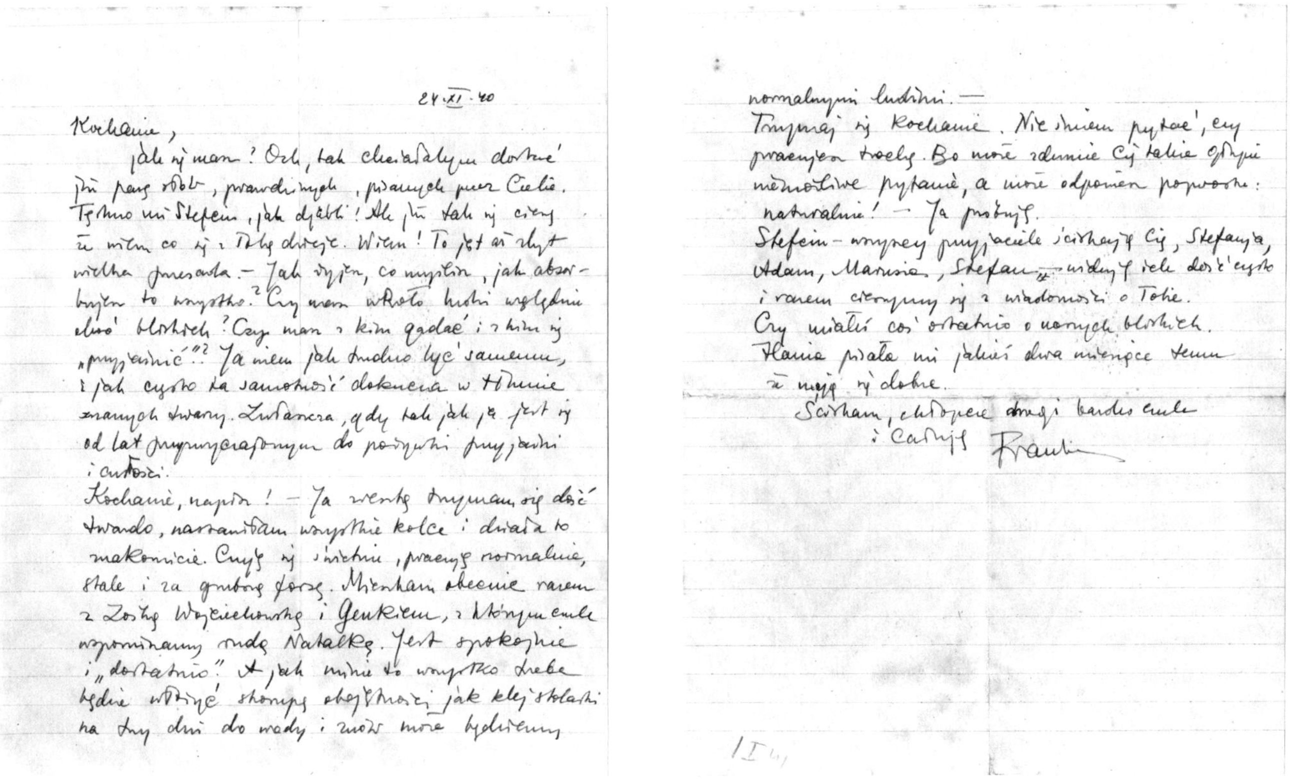

24.XI.40

Kochanie,

jak się masz? Och, tak chciałabym dostać już parę słów, prawdziwych, pisanych przez Ciebie. Tęskno mi Stefciu, jak diabli! Ale już tak się cieszę że wiem co się z Tobą dzieje. Wiem! To jest aż zbyt wielka przesada. — Jak żyjesz, co myślisz, jak absorbujesz to wszystko? Czy masz wkoło ludzi względnie bliskich? Czy masz z kim gadać i z kim się „przyjaźnić"? Ja wiem jak trudno być samemu, i jak często ta samotność dokucza w tłumie znanych twarzy. Zwłaszcza, gdy tak jak ja, jest się od lat przyzwyczajonym do podniety przyjaźni i czułości.

Kochanie, napisz! — Ja zewnątrz trzymam się dość twardo, nastawiłam wszystkie kolce i działa to znakomicie. Czuję się świetnie, pracuję normalnie, stale i za grubą forsę. Mieszkam obecnie razem z Zośką Wojciechowską i Genkiem, z którym czule wspominamy rudą Natalkę. Jest spokojnie i „dostatnio". A jak minie to wszystko trzeba będzie włożyć skorupę obojętności, jak klej stolarski na trzy dni do wody i znów może będziemy normalnymi ludźmi. —

Trzymaj się Kochanie. Nie śmiem pytać, czy pracujesz trochę. Bo może zdumieć Cię takie głupie niemożliwe pytanie, a może odpowiesz po prostu: naturalnie! — Ja próbuję.

Stefciu — wszyscy przyjaciele ściskają Cię, Stefanja, Adam, Marusia, Stefan K. — widzę ich dość często i razem cieszymy się z wiadomości o Tobie.

Czy miałeś coś ostatnio o naszych bliskich. Hania pisała mi jakieś dwa miesiące temu że mają się dobrze.

Ściskam, chłopcze drogi bardzo czule i całuję

Franka

Letter from Franciszka to Stefan

Darling, how are you? Oh, I should so much like to receive a few words now, real ones, written by you. I miss you, Stefciu, like hell! But I am already so happy to know what is happening with you. At last I know! Is that too great an exaggeration? How do you live, what are you thinking, how are you able to absorb everything? Do you have around people that you can feel relatively close to? Do you have someone to talk to and be friendly with? I know how difficult it is to be alone, and what a problem that loneliness can aggravate among a crowd of familiar faces. Especially if, like me, for years one has been used to the sustenance of friendship and tenderness.

Write, darling! – I somehow maintain a hardened exterior, bristling with spikes and this works extremely well. I feel very well, I work normally, full time and for a lot of money. I live now with Zośka Wojciechowska and Genek [Cękalski], with whom we fondly remember Natalka with red hair. It is quiet and 'adequate'. And when it is all over, we shall have to don a shell of indifference, like carpentry glue setting for three days in water, and then perhaps we shall become normal people again.

Look after yourself. I daren't ask if you work a little. Because perhaps you will be troubled by such a stupid impossible question, or perhaps you will answer quite simply: naturally! – I am trying.

Stefciu – all our friends send their love, Stefanja [Zahorska], Adam [Pragier], Marusia [Lebenhaft], Stefan [Konorski] – I see them fairly often and we are all glad to have your news. Have you had anything recently about our nearest and dearest? Hania [Kawa] wrote to me some two months ago that they are well.

I embrace and kiss you very tenderly

Franka

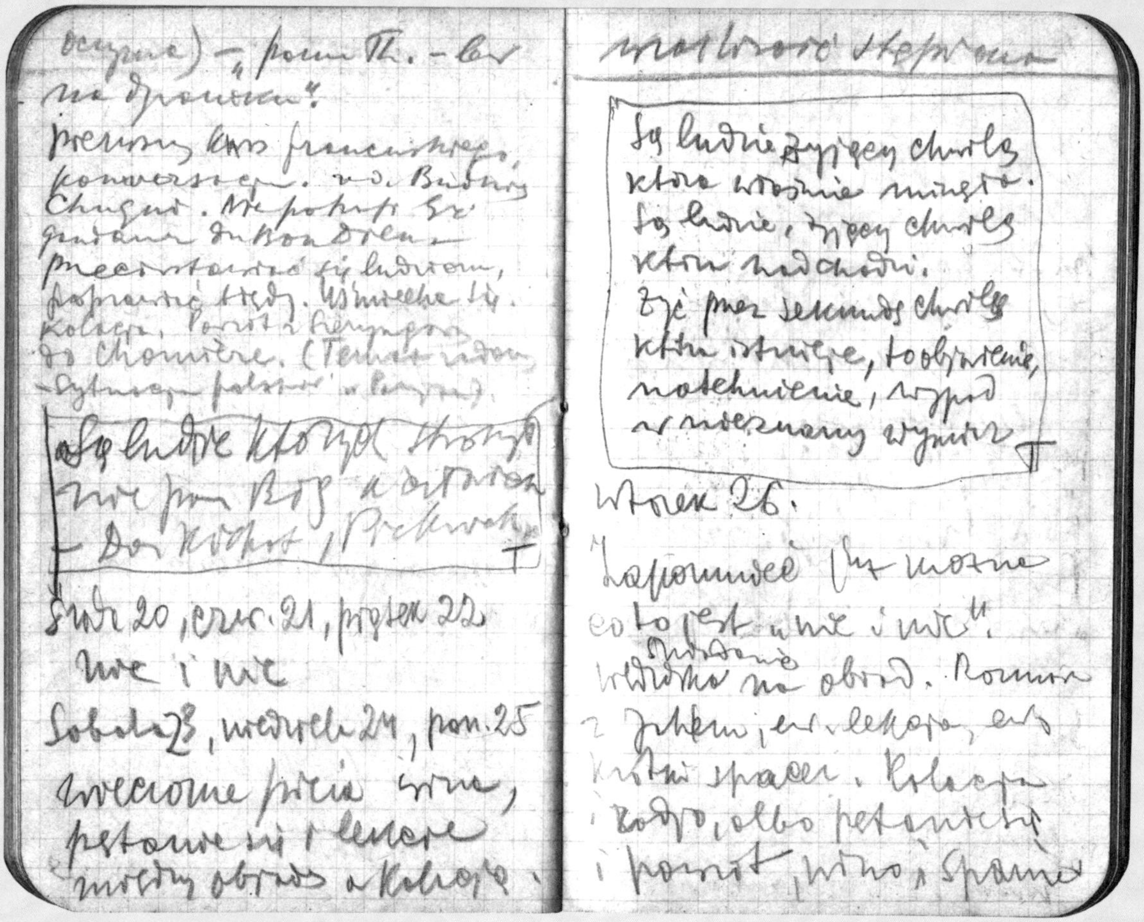

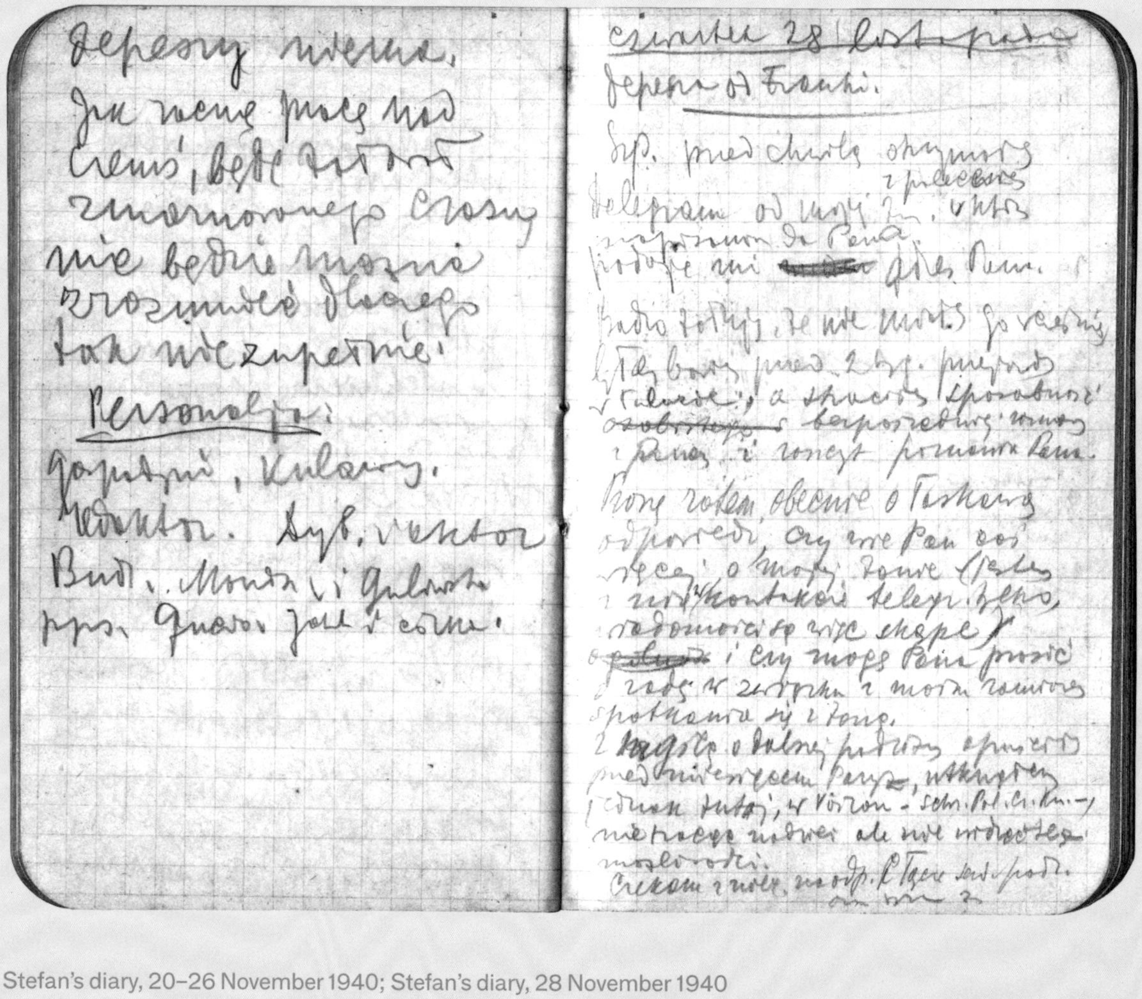

from top: Stefan's diary, 20–26 November 1940; Stefan's diary, 28 November 1940

24 November 1940

Letter from Stefan to Andrzej Ruszkowski [?]

Dear Sir,
Only today I received your address from Mme Blanche Bronstein. Thank you very much for forwarding the money to me.

Are you in correspondence with my wife? I send her telegrams and have already received a telegram from her but it is difficult to find out very much by these means.

After six weeks tramping through the countryside and two months' stay in the new Paris, I made my way here with the thought of reaching Franka, but it proved to be already too late.

If you could write me a few words about what can be done, I should be very grateful!

At the moment, I am in Voiron (Isère), 'Hôtel de la Poste', used by the Polish Red Cross. Material conditions are excellent, better than anywhere else – and if I stay here longer, whether of my own free will or not, I don't suppose I will spend the sum I received during the whole year.

Would you be so kind as to send Franka these few bits of news about me? Will you stay long in Lisbon? I hope that your wife and daughter are with you.

Did you receive any news from my wife?

With warmest thanks and kindest regards
Stefan Themerson

I have just received a letter from my wife written to Zosia Kramsztyk on 16 October 1940. It is her first letter for almost half a year.

26 November **Diary Entry**

One can finally forget what it is 'nothing and nothing'. Breakfast, expedition to lunch. Conversation with Jahl, possibly a lesson, possibly a short walk. Supper and radio, or drifting and return, wine and sleep. There is no telegram. When I start work on something, I shall regret the wasted time and it won't then be possible to understand why it all seemed so hopeless.

Stefan lists the characters around him: the landlady. a cripple. an editor. Dyboski, and the playwright and actor, Wiktor Budzyński, Mondszejn and Gulińska, messrs Gucio and Jahl and daughter. Some of them will appear in Stefan's 6-part poem, *Croquis dans les Ténèbres*.

28 November **Telegram from Franciszka to Stefan**

MON PETIT CONCRETS PROJETS DIFFICILES JE NE PEUX PARTIR PRIE D'ÉCRIRE STANISŁAW ZATORSKI TOULOUSE 21 RUE ORLÉANS PROMIT T'AIDER DONNER CONSEIL DONNERA ARGENT CHERCHE POSSIBILITÉS RAISONNABLES REJOINDRE FRANÇOISE JE NE PREVOIS POSSIBILITÉS NOUS ÊTRE AVEC MIRA DOIS JE LES CHERCHER ZŁOTOWSKI PARTIS AMÉRIQUE MOI SUIS PARFAITEMENT BIEN TRAVAILLE COMME AVANT NE T'INQUIÈTE DU TOUT PATIENCE CHÉRI EMBRASSE TENDREMENT BAISERS = THEMERSON

After receiving the above telegram from Franciszka, Stefan immediately drafts a letter to Zatorski [he refers to it in his letter to her of 11 January 1941.] This letter remains unposted [see overleaf].

28 November 1940

Draft of a Letter from Stefan to Stanisław Zatorski

Dear Sir, a moment ago, I received a telegram from my wife with your address and the suggestion that I write to you. I am very sorry that I did not receive it earlier, I was perhaps two weeks ago on my way through Toulouse, and missed the chance of a direct conversation with you and the honour of meeting you. I should be grateful for your kind answer, if you know something more about my wife (I am in contact with her only through telegrams, so news is meagre) could I ask you for advice in connection with my intention to meet my wife.

With a thought of a further journey, I left Paris over a month ago, and got stuck here, in Voiron – hostel of the Polish Red Cross, without losing hope but also without seeing any possibility…

I await your answer with impatience. Kind regards.

Diary Entry

1.30 bus to Grenoble
[Illegible]. Halina Blit, the Micińskis
He didn't touch the child
conversation with M. (a Japanese, vitromagie)
Father Jakubisiak? – to say hello after arrival in Warsaw. Word about Tarnowski, needing help – let's take a taxi

Hôtel du Globe
Nothing is happening?, there are only Micińskis, Themersons, Tarnowskis. The school of Kotarbiński – they ransack their brains and think that they will find a thought. Lunch at Grydzewski's. Cock's comb in the soup. Calf's head with an eye intact. Emotions generate judgments. Freudianism.

29 November **Diary Entry**

Meeting with Halina in Grand Hôtel.
But in the silence of the streets of dead days in despair Paris was drowning
Kalamos[34] fixation – Kalamos.
To end a few chords from Miss M. Rozenblat

Now a gap in the diary of over 2 weeks

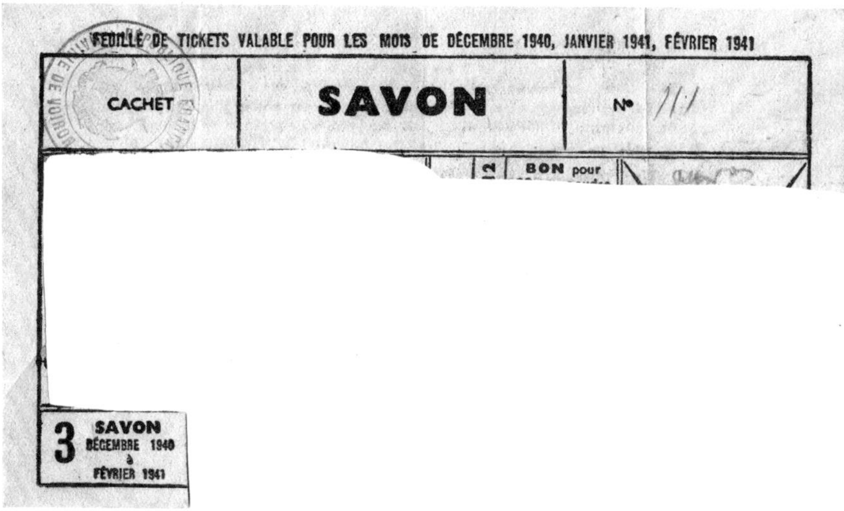

December 1940 – February 1941
Soap ration card

34 A Greek myth about a swimming contest between Karpos and Kalamos in the Meander River, during which Karpos drowned. In his grief, Kalamos allowed himself to drown also.

Letter from Franciszka to Stefan – unposed

Darling, what are you doing now, where are you, who do you talk to? It's very hard for me, and so I must write to you again and again. On the left side of the writing pad are blue envelopes. Again, I can't put this letter in the envelope and send it, so many people will read it on the way. I feel idiotic. And if it reached you, you would only feel sad to know how much I miss you and that there is nothing to be done about it. I would so much like you to be able to have some quiet life there, I am so frightened that you will break out one day over the mountains[35] or something. I thought for a long time, what to answer to your long darling telegram. I waited two nights to stop myself writing stupidities to you, and I still don't know if I did the right thing to give you the address of that man who may not even be in Toulouse yet, and you might think that it has more significance than it has. And what I wrote about America. But perhaps, that is what you prefer, my love? For me they're equally good. And anyway, it probably won't work out in the end. Because, how could it? And if you sent me an answer now, then what happens? My darling!

Will these times leave us some memories? Will this modest temporary state one day find form as some paintings, words, emotions and scents? Such a nothing is happening with me, I try with all my strength to compress inside myself everything that could leave any trace. Quietly, quietly. This has to pass, it will pass. Only not to think of what will be, how it will be then.

I should like to be a child now, absorbing a whole range of impressions, things that are already inaccessible to old cows like me, to be able to store something that might change itself one day into energy. Idiocy! But there are moments when I regret (I!!) that I don't have a child, yours and mine, for whom this English apartment would be a whole world, and not four rooms for four guineas. For whom London fog and the red ball of the sun would be more than a landscape that momentarily clutches at my throat, in a choking memory of visual sensations. For whom the environment would still remain to be discovered, absorbed and cultivated. To whom one could explain how awful it is what is happening now, and to whom that wouldn't be boringly obvious, but a revelation. And perhaps one would have to say how it should be in the world. And this perhaps would be a signpost.

But the way it is, it's a matter of gritted teeth and eyes closed. Behind my burning, moist eyelids, it's impossible to disentangle all the confusion of recent events from the turmoil of childhood memories that churn around in my head and torment me.

These times won't leave any treasured memories: there is no fragrance in the air today to linger pleasantly in my mind; no people whose way of life would be a dear or moving thing to recall. There is nothing.

I can't imagine that I shall be able to work again, I don't believe that I can ever 'start from the beginning'. I don't believe in anything. I can imagine only one thing – to work with you – back in Poland. And I know, of course, that this is impossible and that we shall never go back there. That's terribly hard to accept. What are our mothers doing there, darling? It's not possible just to abandon them there. And don't say that one can do nothing, nothing at all about it. Is this where our brave new ideas of citizens of the world have got us? It is all so difficult, so very difficult.

35 Attempt to dash across the border.

1 December 1940

Can one swim if the water you're in just comes up to your ankles? But that's the only thing that saves us from drowning.

In three weeks Christmas. In one month a new year – 1941

Give me a hug darling.

2 December **Telegram from Hania Kawa to Franciszka**

EVERYBODY FAMILY ALRIGHT = HANIA

5 December **Card from Hania Kawa to Stefan**

Dearest Stefek. You don't know how much of my time is spent with you both, with you and Franka. Above all I abide in the hearts of your relatives, secondly, in my room are your books that I bought before your departure, in Franka's presence at the Mortkowicz's [bookshop]. I pass on the originals of all your letters, and I copy them and send them, I also copy the telegrams. I inform Sewek [Chaykin] about everything too. I am glad that you will see our Marcelina and Szymek, and that I envy you. We have no visas, even though we talked about them all the time and all our acquaintances have them. Now it's too late, because we would go empty-handed, nothing can be accomplished. I kiss you, please kiss my family. Your Hania

12 December **Telegram from Ruszkowski to Stefan**

LETTRE REÇUE RÉPONSE SUIT = RUSZKOWSKI

16 December **Diary Entry**

I am sending letters to: Freyd, Hania and my family, Ruszkowski, Red Cross in Lourdes, Red Cross in Lyon; two to Teresa, Blanche

Their vitality of reaction depends on the fact that their most urgent private concern is in public activity, the weaknesses of these people – their closest private concern is in the advance of industry.

20 December **Cable from Stefan to Franciszka**

CHÉRIE REÇU LETTRE FREYD MERCI ZATORSKI PAS REPONDU SUIS PARFAITEMENT BIEN TOUJOURS VOIRON MAIS AVEC ESPOIR QUAND MÊME COMMENT VAS TU SUIS INQUIET TRAVAILLES TU POUR TOI AUSSI AMITIÉS CORDIALES TOUS NOS AMIS MEILLEURS VOEUX EMBRASSE CHÉRIE SI TENDREMENT BAISERS = THEMERSON

22 December **Stefan's draft letter to an unidentified recipient**

Dear Sir

I have never dared to trouble you with my problems, seeing that there are thousands of matters that you have to deal with all the time. But this morning I woke up, looked at my hands and saw that they had become mouldy. I tried to get hold of a pen – but it fell from my fingers. The only thing that my fingers can still hold onto is a glass of acrid wine. It fills me with a sense of dread and this is why I am writing.

Service in the army, unsuccessful march to the port, dispersal, 6 weeks (dragging myself through the country…) work in the fields, 2 months in occupied

22 December 1940

Paris, getting through to 'free' France, desire to reach England, lack of information about my wife, Angers, Toulouse, telegram from wife in England, raid, camp in [unreadable], illness, escape, Grenoble, Voiron – in short, one of a thousand petty little histories known to you.

I see two roads before me: the first, simplest and most direct, is to try once more, or ten times, to struggle to reach America. But for this, one has to be near a place where there happen to be such opportunities and this is why I would ask you to move me to a shelter in Marseille.

Second – well, that is to give up further travel, to 'settle down' and work.

It is because of this, that I am not treating and, 'good God' don't want to treat the excellent conditions in Voiron like a pension – it is because of this, that I want to defend myself against it with all my strength, that I should like to ask you to move me to Grenoble (Library!) into the most modest four walls with my own table on which to spread my papers, my own table, close to a library – that is my workshop. And for that workshop I ask you, if you consider Marseille impossible.

I am sure that you will forgive me the length of this letter and that you will feel in it reasons that are ordinary, simple and human, that direct me. I take advantage of this occasion to convey to you best wishes for a good Christmas and a happy New Year.

Yours faithfully
and please forgive me for my directness – with deepest respect. ST

Diary Entry

going further away
Marseille,
library
just because
not a pension

Les Djinns XCIV (*Préliminaires à l'Esthétique* Alain)

Mur, ville
Et port
Asile
De mort
Merguise
Oùbrise
La brise
Tout dort

On doute
La nuit
J'écoute
Tout finît
Tout passe
L'espace
Efface
Le bruît

25 December **Telegram from Franciszka to Stefan**

CHÉRI BEAUCOUP DE TENDRESSES POUR NOUVELLE ANNÉE BAISERS = THEMERSON

27 December **Diary Entry**

I buy a beret with Spisak. Wolf has all sorts of projects, also for publishing.

28 December 1940

Diary Entry

Formalities at the police station, why yellow stains on the card. Need application for sauf-conduit to Lyon. They extend the permit for 10 months

Talko's lecture on wartime poetry. A girl – flower in a field, where they do military training and fighting. There is no poetry of jokes, there is poetry of sadness, that grows high like ivy, high wall of ivy, that will cover the new building of the government even while it is being built. What an idiot. In the end mentions [Waldemar] Bakalarski and Mondszejn.

For a whole week there are no diary entries of any sort.
Is Stefan in Lyon?

31 December **Card from Hania Kawa to Stefan**

Dearest Stefek, Today's date closes the balance sheet of this bloodbath year – for me it is also the last day of my mother's life that ended in the morning of 1 January. We live through such a saturation of impressions, and especially me (working and running around incessantly), that I don't remember whether I've replied to your letter of 15 December. I sent the section intended for your family par avion, the rest to Ala Brynowa; she sees them all. By these means, letters from me take a maximum of 5 days. Did you see Marysia Bryn in Grenoble? Write to me about them both. We don't know her husband. They got married on 20th January 1940. For your birthday on the 26th [sic], I am already sending you my best wishes. I sent a letter to Franka through Jasio, a friend of Marysia Bryn. He hasn't written to me. It's been over a month since Warsaw stopped any outgoing letters. My sister warned me that such a stoppage would occur. I always send all your and Franka's letters to Warsaw. Are you writing? I wish for you to be together with Franka. I kiss you Hania

Be careful that we don't lose each other again.

1941

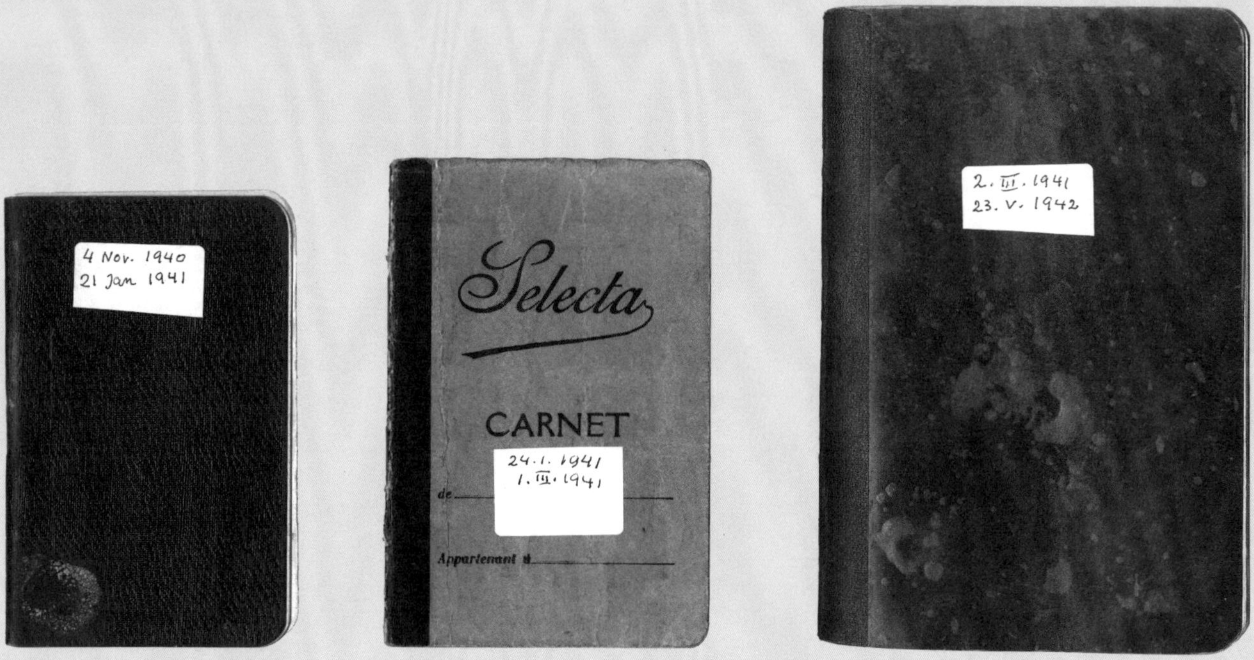

The three diaries Stefan used in 1941

3 January 1941

Cable from Stefan to Franciszka

INQUIETS BAISERS = THEMERSON

4 January **Letter from Franciszka to Stefan**

Darling, at last, I have received a few words from you, really written by you – letter to Teresa. How are you, my pet? How do you live? I still know nothing. I don't even know if and when this letter will reach you, but I will send it anyway. – Often, when 'I can't bear it any longer', I write to you and throw the letter in the drawer. It is difficult to write when you know how many people will read it on the way. We haven't yet unlearned our embarrassment about tenderness. It is about time.

It's increasingly difficult to keep the avalanche of events at bay – and still, for me, the quiet surface of the river is more interesting and fecund. But it isn't easy to look at it for long.

Are you working darling, for yourself? With the same anxiety I ask you the same question that you asked me in your telegram. I know how important it is. And meanwhile, when one manages to grasp some mental equilibrium – and those moments happen more often now – the effect is the same as a good sleep.

Every so often I manage to exorcise my mental storms in drawings – they are a charming blend of humour and the macabre.

Write, darling, please – even if it arrives after two months, it will give me such enormous pleasure! Darling!

I live here in shameless *prosperité*. I earn a lot of money and emotionally fall to pieces among friends who are well, even very well, disposed towards me.

I work regularly all day, but this is not tiring and I can arrange the hours to suit myself.

I live now with Genek [Cękalski], Zośka Wojciechowska, and Genek's charming girlfriend [Urszula Lubelska]. At this moment also staying with us is Stefan [Konorski], who arrived in the last few days to stay here for good and is looking for a room. We live in a beautiful flat on the ground floor of a modern building. It is quiet and peaceful. In front of the fire the conversations of us compatriots continue well into the night. I expect you can imagine them perfectly well yourself. Oh, how I should love to cuddle up to you by that same fireplace!

Freyd is returning within a few days. That worries me because I counted on him to help Marceljanek[1] with his visa to Ignacy and his wife.[2] It seems that he must have it anyway to be able to leave, even if not to go to them [i.e. either to America or England]. I only hope that Freyd has sent him money for the second time, so that he won't be so dependent on his environment which may not always be such a good thing.

Darling, we drank your health on New Year's Eve with incredible quantities of alcohol. I still experience almost physically the happiness of knowing where you are and at least from time to time having a word from you. For so long, so very long, there was nothing.

I had two letters from Maryla. I have told you about the first one. The second one I got for the New Year. It is more than sad. They are in the ghetto. Śliska 7 m 10. Write to them c/o Teresa's address. They live together with Henieks[3] family. Sewek[4] hasn't returned. They are keeping a pregnant rabbit so that there will be meat for Jasia[5]. The house committee is buying a goat so that there will be milk for the children. Maryla writes that in the next generation there won't be a

1 Marceljanek is a character in the Themersons' book, *Przygody Marceljanka Majster Klepki*. Franciszka is using the name as a code name for Stefan

2 Ignacy and Mira Złotowski

3 The Haller-Sobieralskis

4 Sewek, [Seweryn Chaykin], Maryla's husband

5 Jasia Chaykin/Reichardt

single architect. All the children have a complex about bricks and walls. The letter is from 4 December. It is very hard to bear and one can't do anything to help. I sent two food parcels to the old address. These couldn't have arrived. I shall find out if it is possible to do so now and will send parcels again.

Stefan continues to work in Zofiówka[6]. Irka[7] also. Stefan's Mother[8] is with them and is well. Anka [Poznańska] lives and works in town, but travels there frequently. Granny died in July.

Darling, write about yourself – do you have friends around you? New ones, or old ones? I had a letter from Blanche [Bronstein]. Letters arrive, so do write. What are you doing, what are you thinking? Do you have mountains near you? Darling, I know by heart all your poems which you copied for me before leaving and I always have them with me. I am embarrassed that this tenderness might sound like sentimentality. But it only comes out like that when I write it down.

Darling, I kiss you so very warmly. Franka

Give my warm regards to friends

The address of Ignacy and Mira is C/o Dr Paxton, New York City, NY, 150 Claremont Avenue, USA Do make a note of it.

The letter passes through the hands of Stefan Konorski, who adds:

Dear Stefek, an affectionate hug. Make contact by letter should you need anything from my good friend, Ludwik Śliwiński, 'Les Floralies' Beaulieu-sur-Mer, A.M. When shall I see you? Your Stefan

5 January Diary Entry

First Sunday of January.

Today, there's a service in the kitchen

> Le geste dessine l'action, mais n'est point l'action. Sous la forme de la danse, il rassemble à la musique en ce qu'il se continue en s'imitant lui même…[9]

Why is it that gestures in opera and ballet seem so artificial to us, so hypocritical? – it's either because we have not adopted the convention, or because we have abandoned it. We became so accustomed to the 'truth' of realism that we lost touch with convention. In realism the gesture doesn't represent an action, but *is* an action, or pretends to be. How else can we identify what it is that distinguishes realism?

We have got used to using real bricks to build the houses of fiction. But in ballet or the opera, we depict fictitious bricks and build an edifice of fable, an edifice of epic poetry, an edifice of romance.

Realism from realism does not make Art. The public turns its back on fiction made from fiction. What is left is fiction from reality – the discovery of Russian cinema – after Eisenstein, Pudovkin, detective novels, and reality of fiction – ballet, opera, certain novels for women.

6 Hospital for nervous diseases directed by Dr Stefan and Dr Irena Miller, Stefan Themerson's sister and brother-in-law, in Otwock.

7 Irka [Irena Miller].

8 The reference here is to Stefan Themerson's mother

9 Alain. *Préliminaires à l'Esthétique*. Le Potier 157, 14 April 1923

La Musique n'exprime pas les passions, elle les efface [10]

Stefan also notes on that day that at the end of a 3-day battle, the English took Bardiah in Libya, enabling the Allied forces to continue to advance.

There are more forms to be filled in. Under the heading 'Qualifications/profession', Stefan writes: film operator.

He wonders what sort of exemptions or qualifications are required to enter Spain. He will need a passport and demobilisation papers. He must phone Michał Spisak who has obtained an extension to his passport.

6 January Letter from Stefan to Franciszka

Darling, I now have your real letter, written to me in your own hand. For so long I had no idea what really happened to you – I could only guess until I arrived in Toulouse, at the end of October, when I managed to get your telegram to Żyw. I'd already assumed [that you had left for London] and wanted to do the same but it was all delayed – beyond my control – and that delay affected everything that followed.

How are you managing darling? I worry so much sometimes, but I'm very glad to know that you have friends around you. They couldn't imagine how warmly I think of them and send them fond regards – Stefanja [Zahorska] and Adam [Pragier] and Stefan [Konorski] and Genek [Cękalski] and Marusia [Lebenhaft] and all of them [11]. I saw a few old news reports and they are very depressing. Here it is much the same but on a very reduced scale. Don't worry about me at all. I had been able to manage everywhere throughout my solitary wanderings, and by the Seine, and even here.

One needs to have so much patience, darling, but we shall persevere, of course. I am so happy that you are painting. All the time I thought and thought about it. I tried to work a bit during my stay in Paris, but here, in the atmosphere of hypocrisy that we know so well, it is very difficult, one has to detach oneself from the stupid daily details. And all the time I recall the card you gave me for the journey with its inscription: Memento Magnitudinis. I have it in my memory, because it stayed behind with other things, somewhere, sometime.

I embrace you darling and kiss you so passionately. Stefan

PS: A moment ago, I received a card from Hania, it says: 'I haven't had any news for over a month, somehow a pause, which my sister warned me would happen.'

7 January Letter from Ernest Freyd in Lisbon to Stefan in Voiron

Dear Stefan Themerson

I deluded myself until recently that we would see each other and have a chat face to face about all sorts of concerns of the here and beyond.

Meanwhile, 'man goes about his business, God his' and nothing came of my visit to Voiron, and nothing will.

So I write.

About Franciszka, please don't worry. She has a well-paid job and from material point of view she doesn't lack anything. However, she is literally going mad from missing you, about which – even knowing you only casually as I do – it is difficult to be surprised.

She gave me millions of messages for this visit that did not come off. Of these I can only fulfill the first part, as follows:

1. You will receive from her some financial assistance of 3000 francs

10 Alain, *Dessin et Peinture* LXXXI

11 Here Stefan refers to the other friends and colleagues who arrived in London with Franciszka.

2. I asked Jurkowski in Vichy by letter to take care of you and to help you in every possible way
3. St[anisław] Schimitzek in Lisbon (at the same address as me) has been asked by me as well as Jaś, to advise and help. In view of my imminent departure, please communicate with him [Schimitzek]. You can also write to me always at this address, but I must warn you to put 'faire suivre' in case.

Of course, together with Franciszka, we shall be thinking about you and do everything to make it possible for you to re-unite and start your life together again.

A few days ago, good news arrived from Franciszka's family. '*Tout va aussi bien que possible dans cette époque lugubre*'.

Since you were kind enough to take interest in my family, I wanted to let you know, that alas, we are not together. But I have news that they survive somehow and, so far, courageously deal with the events.

My warm greetings, and wishing you a positive frame of mind in the New Year.

Ernst Freyd

9 January

The following day Stefan must catch a train early and sets his alarm clock. Where is he going? To Marseille. At the station the colonel's wife asks: 'Do they give us money for the journey?' (unlikely, he thinks) The train arrives. Then a tram ride. Ruszkowski is also there. Conversations of those waiting. Lunch on the Sully. The dining room has painted walls. Stefan is introduced to a man with a small cross. They are all waiting for the captain, who doesn't turn up. Once more they go to Ruszkowski's. Then Stefan walks around the town and returns to the Sully. Talko from the Vichy Polish Office is in Marseille, also Stefan Wentland and Captain Kamiński, and an acquaintance, a stuttering junior policeman. There is a job on offer – 840 francs per month, clearing snow 4 hours per day. Stefan buys a volume of Shelley's poems in French and English. There is a list of train times for Voiron, about every two hours. Stefan decides to stay for the night. He has supper at the Tête d'Or, and stays at the Hôtel des Voyageurs.

10 January Telegram from Franciszka to Stefan

MON PETIT MERCI NE T'INQUIÈTE DU TOUT. J'HABITE TRANQUILLEMENT PARFAITEMENT BIEN ESSAYE TRAVAILLER POUR MOI AUSSI. ZATORSKI RÉPONDRA AUSSITÔT ARRIVÉ. REÇU LETTRE MARYLA FAMILLE BONNE SANTÉ T'EMBRASSE STEFAN TRAVAILLE ZOFIÓWKA ADRESSE MARIA TYWONEK PIUSA 25 M12 TENDRESSES CHÉRI THEMERSON

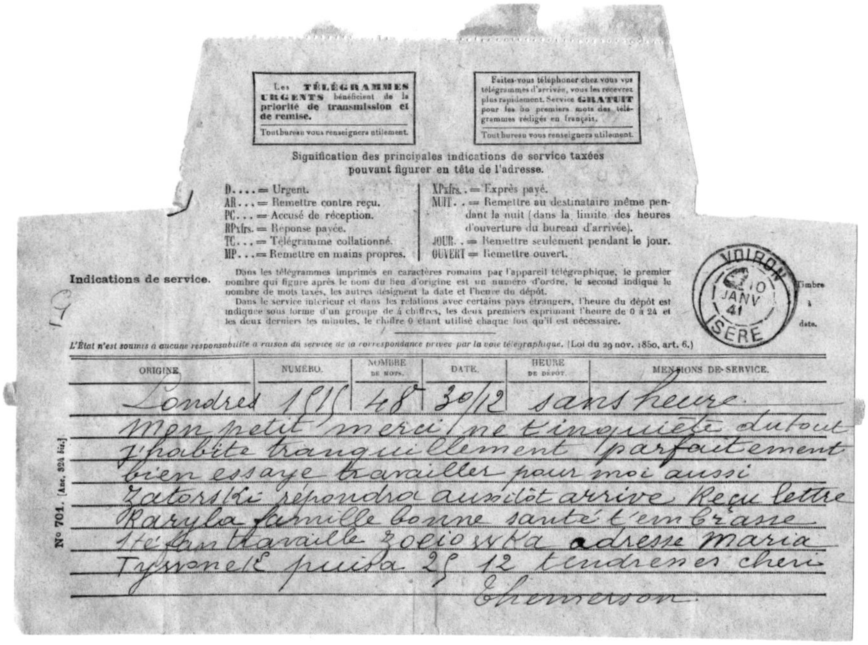

Londres 1811 48 30/12 sans heure
Mon petit merci ne t'inquiète du tout
j'habite tranquillement parfaitement
bien essaye travailler pour moi aussi
Zatorski répondra aussitôt arrivé Reçu lettre
Maryla famille bonne santé t'embrasse
Stefan travaille Zofiowka adresse Maria
Tywonek piusa 25 12 tendresses chéri
Themerson

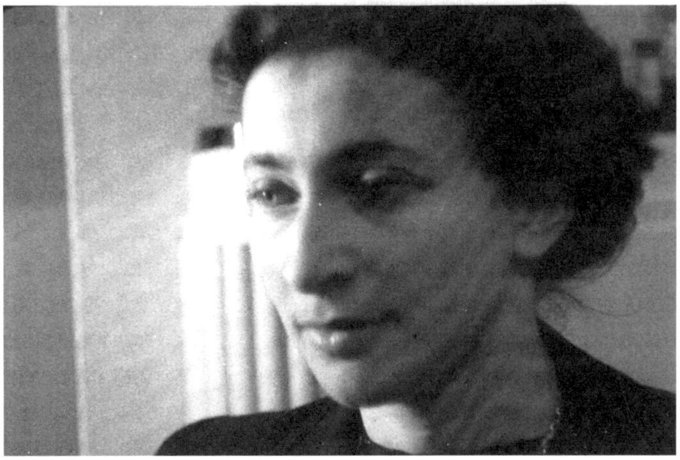

Franciszka, 1941

10 January **Letter from Franciszka to Stefan**

Stefulku, darling,

perhaps, perhaps it will work out, that you will get this letter on the 25th. I kiss you so much my pet – I miss you maddeningly.

Teresa forwarded to me the letter you wrote to her. At last a few words written by you. Write to me, darling, a lot and as soon as you can. Teresa will send it on. Or, address it simply to Lisboa Central, Caixa 512 in my name.

I would so much like to know at last how you really are. Is there anyone of our friends near you? Remember me to them, darling, to all those around you.

A few days ago, I sent you a long letter. And today I just want to kiss you.

I am quite well, darling. In truth, even too well.

Don't worry about me at all, at all. I live quietly and peacefully, I work, – and do what I can so as not to become stupid. If you received some of my letters, I was probably repeating this every time – to tell the truth, that's what most concerns me. Oh, dearest, how I should like to cuddle close to you. Are you working a bit? What are you thinking about? How do you live?

Masses, masses of love and whole mountains of tendresses
My darling
Franka

Stefan and Irka continue to work in Zofiówka. Mother is with them. Sends lots of kisses and asks for a letter. Maryla's address is Śliska 7 m 10.

Love Franka

Stefan goes to the cinema for a programme of shorts, and at 16.30 catches the train back. And once more he is in Voiron until he can escape from it again.

11 January **Diary Entry** – draft letter to Zatorski

Dear Sir,

I take the liberty of writing to you now, even though my previous letter was returned with the notice – address unknown. I suppose that you were not in Toulouse at that time. It is with great impatience that I await a few words from you, expecting among them news of my wife, and maybe some messages from her.

Please accept in advance my heartfelt thanks (as well as expressions of my deep respect)

12 January 1941

Stefan describes another Sunday evening at the Hôtel de la Poste, when the incumbents recite, read aloud, play music, discuss.

Diary Entry

Józef Żmigrodzki reads a fragment from his diary. The first time he killed someone. He analyses it with precision and sincerity. But in conclusion he quotes something that could easily have been said by one of his subordinates: 'When force is used, with force respond and wrath' ('Ode to youth')[12]. Whereas then he lacked courage of his own convictions, whatever they were, today, he says, he would shoot at once without getting involved in all those issues that concerned him before. This goes to prove that he wasn't sure what they were anyway. As a last resort he protects himself with the authority of this or that quotation. A pity, because his analysis was genuinely felt.

Franciszka makes the following notes. These were made separately, but Franciszka keeps an address book in which many of the people mentioned in the correspondence are listed with their addresses.

Diary Entry FT

Gildesgame, Flat 4, 95 Greencroft Gardens, NW6 CLE 3846
Stefan PRI 4024

Ordyński, 149-157 East 67th Street
Grodzicki, 47 Putney Hill
Goldstein, 62 Leicester Road, Hinckley, Nr Leicester
Egmont Colerus *Vom Punkt zur vierten Dimension*, 1935

Zalewski, Bobrowski, Bobrowska, Paczkowska, Halina, Micińska and Miciński

10, rue Bayard (place Nôtre Dame)
II p. Coop. des Et.
12.30-13.30

M le Directeur: Varian M. Fry, Secretaire: Daniel Bénédite

14 January **Telegram from Franciszka to Stefan**

CHÉRI JE VAIS PARFAITEMENT BIEN. EMBRASSE SI TENDREMENT. BAISERS THEMERSON, ONE REDCLIFFE, OLD BROMPTON ROAD, LONDON SW5

Letter from Franciszka to Stefan

Stefciu, darling,

I wrote to you several letters during the past few days. Did you get them? Darling, how are you? Still not a single word from you apart from telegrams.

I am fine, but I miss you so madly that it's frightening.

Write and tell me what you are doing, how you are, who is there together with you?

I saw Freyd yesterday. We nattered for a long time and today I sent various cables concerning Marceljanek. Among others to the old, irritable film-maker,

12 From 'Oda do młodości' by Adam Mickiewicz (tr. by Jarek Zawadzki).

for whom he once acted as secretary, for about three quarters of an hour. That was to facilitate his meeting with Ignacy, or if not with Ignacy at least with Teresa. Stefan is also running about in connection with all this like a dog onto a scent. Perhaps something will work out at last.

Darling, I so much want to send you a lot, a lot of tenderness in the letter, but sometimes it is even easier in a telegram. You can read it yourself. Each comma is a 'kiss', and the full stops are all '*tendresses*'.

For the past two days I am working at home because there are builders in the office. I don't have to look around at those stupid faces. And at home there is a fire-place and a black cat. We warm ourselves in the evenings, with the cat and the other lodgers, and natter about all the pains we share, each of us hiding our private pains.

Darling, are you working a bit? I so much need a letter from you!

Zatorski is living with Teresa and doesn't want to leave her. He should write to you. Darling, greet fondly all the friends. What about Ludka and Kazik? Are they with you? And Zber?

I kiss you as much as possible.

Franka

PS: Note down the address of Ordyn. New York 24 East 10th Street, c/o A. Hays

15 January **Letter from Franciszka to Stefan**

Darling, only yesterday I posted a letter to you, but again – if only a few words.

Today I received your letter written to Freyd, 24.11. But to me still nothing, absolutely nothing.

Stefulku, so you too only had a first communication from me at the end of November?

It is so very difficult all this, but we've got to hang on, little one, after all we shall see each other in the end.

I lead a life that is quite routine and quiet. Far more so than you can imagine. Only in my head various things come to the boil and all the time I am waiting for a real letter from you.

Above my table is hanging, as always, El Greco. And *The Adventures of Marceljanek* and *Pan Tom* are on the shelf in the bookcase. That really is all that I brought with me. Also a few books and drawings in the Złotowski[13] rucksack.

Dearest love, how are you?

I would so much want you to go and live with Teresa. Maybe Ignacy will be able to help and perhaps you could also see Mira.

I sent many letters to friends, and to friends of friends. I wrote to you about it already yesterday and now only repeat it.

Genek sends you a hug. We live together and reminisce with tears about Natalia. The husband of Zośka Wojciechowska (from whom I hadn't been separated for 7 months), lives in Grenoble, Hôtel Terminus, chez Jurgielewicz. Write a few words to him and send best regards from me and from his wife. I don't know if he is still there, but if he is, I am sure that you will get on. He is a nice fellow. He plans to go to Złotowskis. Oh, darling, it's already the end of this sheet of paper, so only masses and masses of kisses. Franka

13 The rucksack that belonged to Mira Złotowska and her husband.

Letter from Franciszka to Stefan – unposted

My darling, another letter that I won't send.

Times are bad here, the atmosphere unbearably stifling. It's as if we were up to our waist in mud – but not as a cure for arthritis. Endless discussion, with all those around, on and on. It's not real politics – more like a primitive, early form of politics. We can't do anything; we don't quite know either what we want or what we're capable of. We are at the same time too wise and too stupid, as usual. We see the political situation only from a distance, and then only superficially. We experience things, without understanding them. We're borne along on some opportunistic spirit. It's disgusting.

The people around me are all small-minded and mean, with brain tumours, toothpicks buried in their intellect, and feathers stuck up their arse. They need to have the simplest, most basic and natural values explained to them – and who's going to do that? When the time comes to settle the accounts will the few relatively intelligent people be able to stick together? Do you remember what happened to the 'unity' of SAF?

Whether our talk is of Russia, fascism, democracy or Genek's famous 'anarcho-communism', it's all talk of nothing leading to nothing. And in the morning, those same bums again in the office.

Will you blame me for not doing anything 'for myself'? How can I?

It was simpler before, even during the Blitz. Because then the emotions were 100% egocentric, one had only to translate them. The fear of the bombs and the will to work for oneself are two sides of my self-preservation instinct. I'm no more complicated than that.

The last discussion was long, and this time I didn't leave feeling that all but me were idiots (this is a very humbling experience). The resolution (as you might guess, it was my proposal – a familiar fault) was passed unanimously. It proposed that all that remains is to teach the children: to raise a new generation of adults, with open minds. I was led there this time by a rather interesting mental process – simply that all of our ideas that might seem obvious to a person on a certain level, remain totally incomprehensible to this bunch of blockheads that we're surrounded by. It struck me that these ideas would appear fresh and fertile only from the point of view of the young, whose minds and characters were still developing. Many, many of our old projects (those to do with art history, for instance) could create exciting work now, by being filtered through real events and 'ripened' through our experiences.

But my pet – don't you get tired? Don't you want, as I often do, to 'switch off' like a lamp or some other electrical device, to stop functioning, or to just function 'for oneself'. I am so frightened that the issues that have always nourished us might have been resolved in our absence by others. That *there won't be anywhere left* to function for oneself. That it won't be possible, and that there will be no reason to do it.

Does it mean we're really finished? What kind of psychological changes have you suffered? How have you coped with all that? After all, in Paris you were clearly in the ascendant, with growing power and greater impetus. – Have you found a way to hold on to all that?

Do you still believe that we can be citizens of the world? And I don't mean because we teach the children of the world, but because we are working 'for ourselves' and not for the whole world. These are truisms I know – but they still,

still have for me freshness and meaning. Even though I've been overtaken by cynicism. Intellectually, I always end up thinking that it is better to have one good poem that will last, than spend 50 years creating illusions that end in catastrophe.

And I can't. There's no way I can deceive myself that I shall 'survive'. Perhaps I simply don't know how to any more, and that's that. Darling, I miss you so much.

What egocentricity, oh my Lord! – rambling on about all these things! What is this – creeping paralysis?

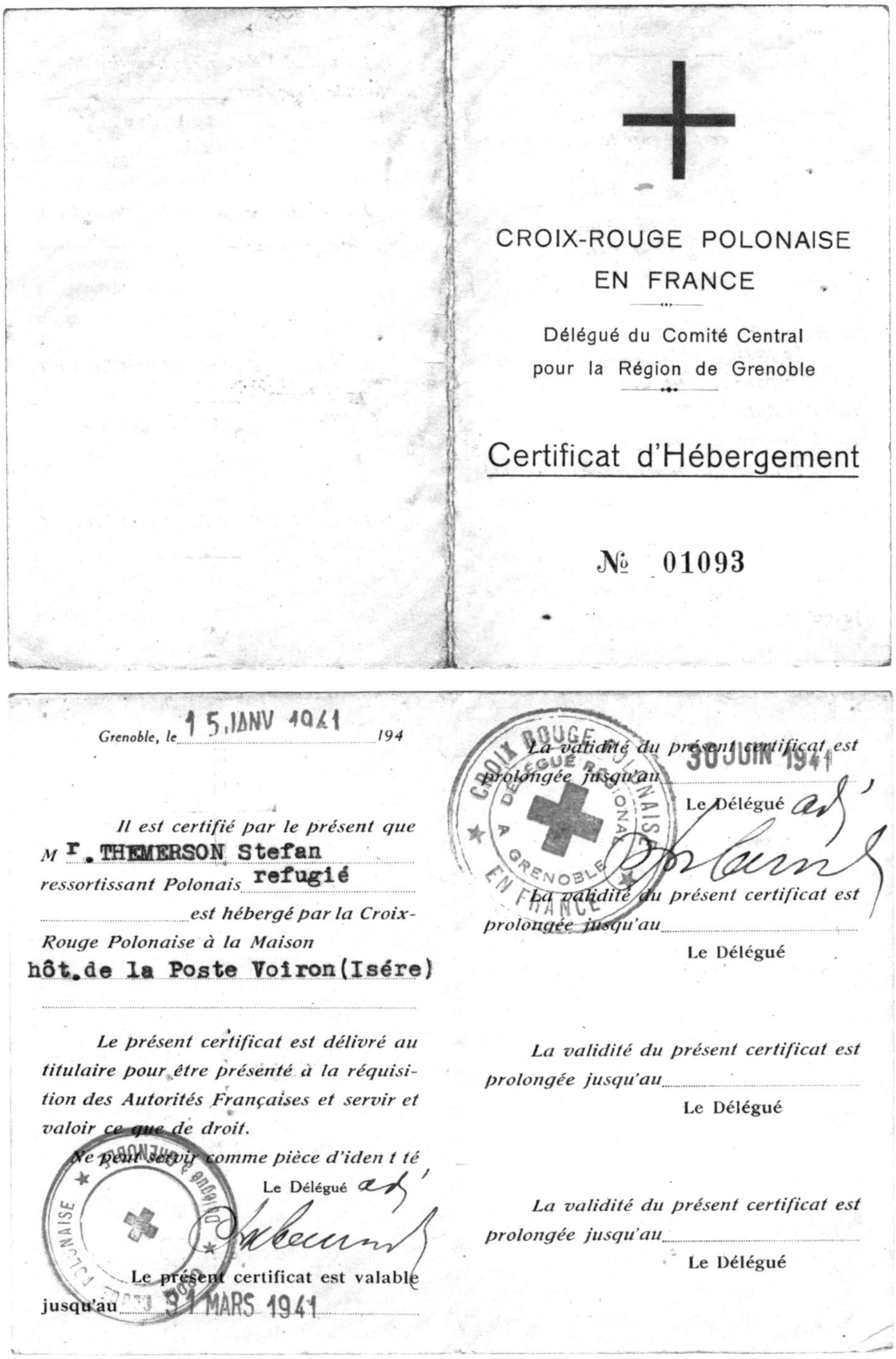

CROIX-ROUGE POLONAISE
EN FRANCE

Délégué du Comité Central
pour la Région de Grenoble

Certificat d'Hébergement

№ 01093

Grenoble, le 15 JANV 1941 194

Il est certifié par le présent que
M r. THEMERSON Stefan
ressortissant Polonais refugié
est hébergé par la Croix-Rouge Polonaise à la Maison
hôt.de la Poste Voiron(Isére)

Le présent certificat est délivré au titulaire pour être présenté à la réquisition des Autorités Françaises et servir et valoir ce que de droit.
Ne peut servir comme pièce d'identité

Le Délégué

Le présent certificat est valable jusqu'au 31 MARS 1941

La validité du présent certificat est prolongée jusqu'au 30 JUIN 1941
Le Délégué

La validité du présent certificat est prolongée jusqu'au
Le Délégué

La validité du présent certificat est prolongée jusqu'au
Le Délégué

La validité du présent certificat est prolongée jusqu'au
Le Délégué

15 January 1941
Polish Red Cross in France
Lodgings certificate

Il est certifié par le présent que Themerson Stefan ressortissant Polonais refugié est hébergé par la Croix Rouge Polonaise à la Maison hôtel de la Poste Voiron (Isère).

Le présent certificat est valable jusqu'au 31 mars 1941 et prolongé jusqu'au 30 juin 1941

17 January 1941

Diary Entry

Despite everything, I am going to Grenoble. Snow.

Earlier on, a conversation with Lipska about the possibilities of departure. About her husband – that he was in a hurry to get to school; that he is sensitive. About a Brazilian visa, Aryan section, swearing that he is not a Jew and with seven photographs to choose from. Grenoble. Maria Anna Brysz Jakubowicz. Supper. Uncle Léon and uncle René. A year after the wedding. Hôtel Mont Blanc

Stefan makes a note of Varian Fry's address: Centre Américain de Secours, 60 rue Grignan in Marseille, where one could possibly get an American visa.

He also notes that at Les Eyzies, Montignac, there are the caves with prehistoric drawings.

18 January **Diary Entry**

In the tabac I see *Cochon aérodynamique* [book for children illustrated by Franciszka and published by Flammarion]. It wasn't to be found anywhere, not in Lyon, not in Toulouse, not in Montpellier, and here in Grenoble, I buy it for myself as a present. Black coffee. One must shave and then to Bobrowska.

Bobrowska is not there – only at 3 o'clock, so by tram to Halina. She's left for Marseille. – However, there is Danuta [Seweryńska]. Gave me the address of the Centre Américain. A room – I borrow Freud's *Nouvelles Conférences sur la Psychanalyse* [1936][14] and Zuckerman's *La vie sexuelle et sociale des singes* [1937].[15] Cakes, coffee. We arrange to meet at 7 in front of the charcuterie. Visit to Bobrowska – meeting in the corridor with monsieur S. Br. and a fellow from Toulouse. Mme B. (tick). – Poem. Duplicator. Get me over to Grenoble. Still 2 ½ hours left. Café. Journals. Illustrations – the above-mentioned caves. 'Those who lend their voice'.

Rain with snow. I buy 400 gr bread. Break it, and into the pocket. At 7 she arrives. Before supper. She eats. And afterwards into a bistro for mulled wine. Tomorrow morning skiing. And the building closes at 9.30. As if that uninterrupted meeting went on for too long. Talks about Mietek. Earlier, still at home, she showed me photographs taken in his atelier on Skorupki[16]. About Wistusia: that she knows everybody and knows how to swim. She became a teacher of Polish in Montpellier. That she joined the association of Catholic women students, but that she is not a believer. Danuta couldn't do that. I am reminded of a conversation with Wirti. About the inner strength, which runs through us. Reminds me of Miciński. Everywhere the shadow of Jakubisiak. It is life made easy. Association with predictions. – He reminds me of a first lieutenant who asked me for a translation of Johannes[17]. And afterwards I shall read in a brothel a chapter from Freud about the occult sciences – a weapon against science. But meanwhile, Danuta mentions Mietek. She is curious how he has changed again. She relates how with Olek [?] they were terrified by the change in Mietek after his return from the West. I remember how he came to see us in Paris. Danuta [says], that Wirti (it's a she) had a K.St. [Catholic Students'] grant, but Mietek couldn't get one, because he would not sign up for the Student Catholic Organisation. And of course, Mietek, idealistic social dictator – but he deserved it. And further: that actually Mietek was finished. After all, he hadn't actually done anything.

14 Sigmund Freud, *Neue Folge der Vorlesungen zur Einfürung in die Psychoanalyse*, 1931.

15 Solly Zuckerman, *The Social Life of Monkeys and Apes*, 1932.

16 Street in Warsaw

17 Johannes – Gospel/Apocalypse of St John.

I remember a detail from the department of architecture. That he has an idea, but won't say what it is – until ten years later. That was 12 years ago. I don't actually remember how many years, he said. When I remembered for the first time, I thought it was something like 20. But that's not important, not at all. I am reminded only of the conversation with Kulski and Czechowicz in 1938 in the Café Club.

Józef [Czechowicz) was talking about a Gypsy, who predicted his fortune: a woman, and something about death. I told myself that I would remember but I forgot. I remembered only when Mietek told me about the death of Czechowicz in La Régence. And I felt, and even now feel, a search for some connection with the prediction. If he hadn't controlled himself, if he had not thought of himself with detachment and lack of confidence, he could have very well believed that the Gypsy told him the truth.

In the life of the psyche, one cannot *post factum* slip a coin into a column of coins of memories and get away with it.

But meanwhile, Danuta talks about Mietek. That he is finished. That, after all, he is 30 or 31. And suddenly I remember that I am 31. And that I haven't yet done my life's work.

I escort Danuta back to La Trouche and then return along the bank of the Isère. And it seems to me, that if now some passers-by wanted to throw me into the river, the first action would be to take the bread out of my pocket, so that it wouldn't drown – to give them what's valuable so that it wouldn't perish. And I think how difficult it is to explain this. And there is no Christianity in this. No posturing. At this moment, a Freudian insinuation comes into my mind. Being subconsciously frightened of darkness, I remember a little fairy tale about a saint, who turned back and gave to the bandits one more coin that he had found, and they – moved – repented and gave everything back to him. And I am defenceless because this fairy tale fits very well. I walked for a long time through streets and alleys, I didn't want to return to the Hôtel Mont Blanc. I rented a room in a brothel on rue Jean-Jacques Rousseau for 12 frs. Signboard opened onto the street. On the table, cards from a calendar. 'Jeudi matin gare, soirée J. Jan café. Vendredi', and a list of films that were showing at one of the cinemas. That must have been written by someone in the brothel, because further along, in crooked letters, their name, surname and the address of the secteur postal. Next door, drinking till 3 am I think about a poem. And the idea of Faust comes back to me. 'Viens faire l'amour, profitons des jours' – a choir sings in the wings.

I see a fragment of a poem, based on that 'thesis' and 'antithesis' emerging from a conversation with Danuta, about Mietek and his 30 years. And I can't remember it now, I feel how it vanished from my memory a moment ago, the sense and form of that fragment.

And already it is *Sunday*.

18 January 1941

I get up at 10 and go to the station. It appears that the train is at 12.45. I counted the coins. I ate a bite of bread from my pocket and I shall sit here over coffee. It is 11.50. And now what?

20 January **Cable from Ordyński in New York to Franciszka**

MATTER VERY DIFFICULT BUT AM DOING MY BEST STOP FOR YOU DOUBTFUL BUT PLEASE MAIL ALL DATA 347 58 STREET CORDIALLY = ORDYŃSKI

21 January **Draft of a Telegram by Franciszka to Gildesgame, Hotel Dorset, in New York**

Please secure Affidavits soonest possible and post respective addresses Stefan Themerson 25 January 1910 Płock residing at present Hôtel Delaposte Voiron Isère unoccupied France also for his unhappy wife Franciszka Temerson without H after Tee 28 June 1907 Warszawa residing One Redcliffe Old Brompton Road London SW5 stop affidavits will enable Stefan travel Lisbon Franciszka to join him eventually sail together stop Themersons assert able earn living as film producers special features also as book illustrators will be no burden anyone STOP Franciszka has good job Polish Government will defray all expenses STOP do utmost cable sponsors name
Gildesgame and Themersonowa

Telegram from Franciszka to Stefan

CHÉRI MILLE BAISERS COMMENT VAS-TU REPONDS. ESPÈRE REUSSIR POUR MARCELJANEK POSSIBILITÉ REJOINDRE THÉRÈSE, FRANÇOISE OU ENSEMBLE IGNACE STOP. LÉON, FRÈRE HANIA ENVERRA AFFIDAVIT EMBRASSE SI TENDREMENT MON PETIT MEILLEURS SOUHAITS THEMERSONOWA

Diary Entry

Tuesday. there was a warm wind all night. As if it were spring that propels you on.

Duty in the kitchen.

Dentist

Letters to write: Blanche, Julia, Teresa, Jurkiewicz, Léon T., Halina Bl., Danuta, Bibrowski, Hania, Grynblat, Morawski – passport

Grand Hôtel
Rue de la République

Faulkner

La Trouche p.6; 5 before 4; 8, Chemin de l'Église

There are also notes of the train timetable between Voiron and Grenoble and lists of his expenses. Then some notes about French grammar; train and bus timetable between Voiron and Grenoble; and list of expenses: food, hotel, etc, 3-7 November 1940

[inserted in the Lilac diary which starts on 21 January 1941: a notice of a concert with Lélia Gousseau and André Remond, on Sunday, 16 February, at Au Splendid-Hôtel, with ST's notes on verso]

Diary Entry

Conversation with Jahl at dusk. He is afraid of death. 'Oh, Stefan, how I don't want to die!' And for sure after death, you continue to live for a certain period of time, the brain still functions and one knows everything for a few hours, or days, and that is horrible. I tell him that even with a silly fainting fit, when the blood leaves the brain one doesn't know anything. Yes, you are right, it is a valid argument. But the hernia is terrible, what will happen if he starts shouting in the street? What will happen if in a camp or with lice – do I realise that lice can get under a truss! And about art – that it is simplicity and elegance. I say this is a matter of his taste and not of value.

Jahl: that a tree, an ordinary tree in a landscape. Manifestation of disinterestedness. (In poetry if he were a tree – that would be an event.)

I say that the author must express less than he knows, because he must encompass more than he sees, the field of vision must be greater than the object. In the example of the tree we choose an object smaller than our field of vision. But there are objects that are greater and more valuable – but to express them one would have to expand one's field of vision, and for this, one needs months, years of experience, learning, resolution. Jahl in his ink drawings catches a certain sort of light like nobody else. It is a small thing, but you would like it to stay, not to disappear, and yet nobody wants to take and frame his drawings. It is worth doing what nobody has done. But to do it, one has to know everything that everybody else has ever done (it reminded me of Haltrecht). It doesn't seem fair to me. One does what one wants to do and if one has individuality it will be something worthwhile and unrepeatable. Jahl – but who among us knows that he has [this sort of] individuality? – If he hasn't got it then the desire to do what nobody has ever done will not help at all. And often just the opposite – (we correct ourselves according to the vision of what we would like it to be, according to ourselves 'moved one centimetre to the side') – we correct our works. Painter creates a figure, sculpts himself by means of his paintings but the meaning of a painter's life is not the paintings, but the figure. Such conclusion comes to my mind and Jahl seizes it eagerly, but I can see that it could happen like that or it could happen differently. A new lodger – a priest. Spisak's project – a shitty five-minute opera: a priest, a whore, a poet, a homosexual.

Conversation with Żmigrodzki who insists that Polish art is among the greatest in the world and quotes the names: Grottger, Matejko, Chełmoński. Painting especially has failed to become known in the West for lack of publicity. Was that because of the partitions? – on the contrary: Polish art was introduced to Europe through emigrés. Which was, of course, the consequence of the partitions. But there is a lack of universal qualities in [Polish] art itself because of the 'elephant and the Polish question' approach. The purpose was not creating masterpieces but saving the masterpiece - Poland. The West was not interested in the means of saving Poland but would have been interested in masterpieces. 'Greatness' is not an issue but 'universality' is. Neither Żeromski, nor the great poets: Mickiewicz, Słowacki, Krasiński are known, but *Quo vadis* by Sienkiewicz, as well as books by Ossendowski and Marczyński, have gained international popularity.

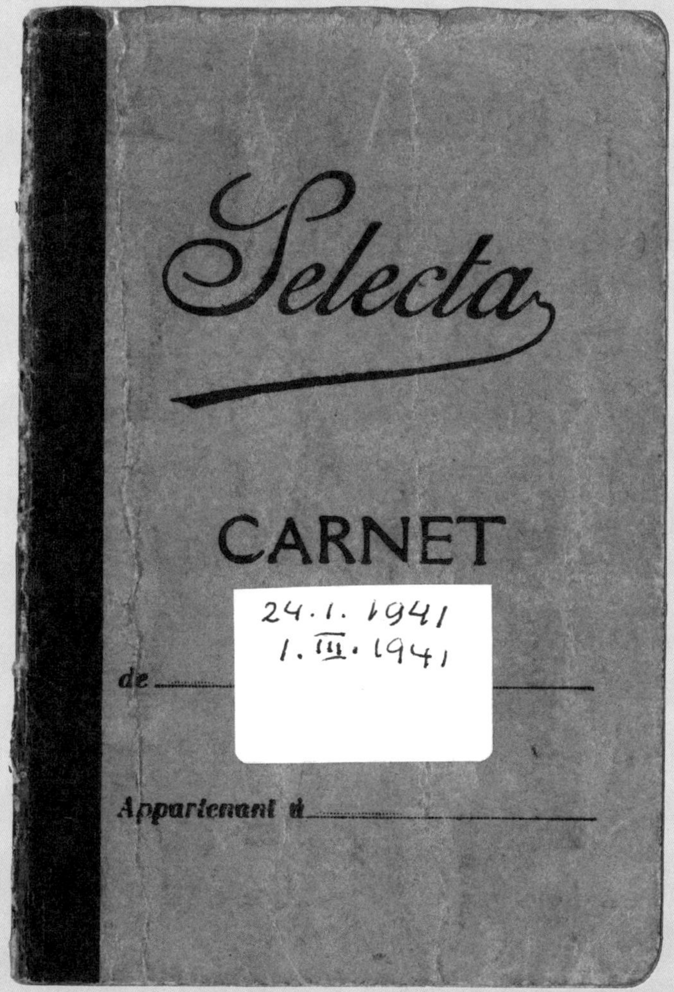
Selecta
CARNET
24.1.1941
1.III.1941
de
Appartenant à

Shakespeare's Hamlet is about, not an English, but a Danish prince. But in Poland that prince would have to be Kordian, Konrad, or Gustaw [heroes of great Polish Romantic dramas by Słowacki and Mickiewicz] so involved in the intricacies of Polish history that no commentaries could help decipher them.

In the world of the individual there is nothing apart from music, painting, poetry and science.

In the world of community economic processes are paramount.

We are not attracted by an individual who lives by economic issues alone.

And we cannot imagine a community living, for instance, on art.

Yet the community is the means of achieving an individual life.

25 January **Diary Entry** – Stefan's birthday

I am already thirty-one. Yesterday, I asked my landlady for a small branch from a cherry tree. It stood all night in water, in a glass. And already two little buds are sprouting green. I shall put a red pencil behind the glass and will have a picture by van Gogh when they bloom.

Wolf – supper
(parcel)
Post Office –

Drafts in Stefan's diary

Telegram to Franka

Themerson one Redcliffe Old Brompton Road, London SW5
Chérie merci suis parfaitement bien reçu trois mille francs ~~pense aller Marseille~~
Faut-il attendre nouvelles Léon ici STOP Embrasse si tendrement baisers
Themerson

Telegram to Lisbon

Comité Amoreiras, 102 Lisboa
Reçu trois mille francs, merci Themerson

100 frs

Letter to Blanche

Dearest Blanche
In a few days I shall go

Letter to Teresa

Dearest Teresa,
I have just received the money you mentioned in the last letter. 3000 francs. It will help me greatly to move around. I shall probably go to Marseille. I shall write again before I go and after my arrival, en es-tu tout à fait sûr?

Police station – sauf-conduit

Lipski } Jabłoński
Dejeuner }

Lyon

Visiting card
Dr. A. Syngałowski, Hôtel de la Poste, Marseille telephone number 05-82
jeudi 5 mardi après midi

Letter from Franciszka to Stefan

Allou petit,

Je t'ai écrit quelques lettres dans les dernières semaines. En as-tu reçu quelques-unes?

Moi, je n'ai toujours, que des télégrammes. Écris moi, chéri!

C'est ton anniversaire aujourd'hui! Je t'embrasse si tendrement mon petit! C'est pour la première fois que nous ne soyons pas ensemble ce jour-ci.

J'ai demandé à Léon [Gildesgame], frère de Hania [Kawa], qui est maintenant a New York (Hotel Dorset) de te procurer un affidavit pour USA. Pour moi aussi. J'espère qu'il réussira un au moins. Enfin, tu pourras voir Thérèse en tout cas. J'ai toujours dans ma valise ton passeport polonais, que tu m'as laissé par mégarde. Je l'ai pris en partant et maintenant je crois qu'il faudra te l'envoyer pour que tu n'aies pas des embêtements en sollicitant les visas.

La demande d'affidavit prendra sûrement quelques semaines. L'argent, comment ça va? avec argent? Je t'ai envoyé quelques fois des différentes sommes. Tu as confirmé seulement la première. Je voudrais bien savoir si tu en a reçu encore?

Mira et Ignace sont à New York. Leur adresse: C/o Paxton, 150 Claremont Avenue, New York City, NY

Peut-être tu passeras maintenant à la ville où ils habitaient quelque mois avant de partir en Amérique. Quelle ironie! Chéri, je t'embrasse mille fois, tendresses, tendresses Franka

Letter from Franciszka to Stefan

My very own darling! Today is your birthday. I wrote to you a moment ago in French and [it's all] so silly. And now I send you so very many kisses darling. I bought you a pipe darling, I so want to touch you! Look, somehow things have been falling into place these last few days that already, already I hope that we will see each other soon. But I know that it can still take time, endless time.

Do you want to go to America? Do you want to come here? I still haven't had a single word from you. Why?

Will it be possible to set everything in motion, everything that came together during the last few days so as to really and quickly help you to move? My darling! I so distrust this whole menagerie.

I was interrupted because Urszulka called me to supper. And again you were not there. And then we wrote silly limericks and I made idiotic drawings. It's tremendously pleasant. And even the hand moves just as ever. What rotten nerves I have, that I do nothing. – I cannot concentrate at all. And I am pursued constantly by such trivial problems. Probably I demand too much of myself. (i.e. I can't do enough.)

In our French bar in Oxford [Street] we were throwing darts at a dartboard. I only threw once and hit a bull's eye having put my entire trust in the instinctive movement of the hand. – In reality it is better like this. My upper right limb is wiser than the head. Why do I write these stupidities, my pet?

Child, I shall probably even start to pray, so that something may work out and so that we'll be together. I am so terribly anxious. I send each telegram in a state of fear. And to organise the journey for you, such a difficult journey – it is almost beyond my strength. I am frightened for you, darling.

Do you know how terribly alone I feel?

And yet I have friends around me and they are really attached to me, I don't even know how it happened. I have never had such ease in attracting people. But the only creature with whom I had a common language – Hanka [Poznańska] – went to Manchester. Of course I am surrounded by conversation in Polish, but in truth I feel a more painful lack of common language than when I speak in English. I may always be the strongest voice in this company, but what the hell use is that when there's nothing here for me to exercise my moral or intellectual muscle on?

Darling, I shall burst into tears of happiness, when once again I'll be able to sit down next to you and without even saying a word. 'The pleasure of such a possibility'.

I could actually send you this silly letter, but I just don't know what you're doing and whether these letters arrive and altogether. Is that why you also don't write? I am sad my treasure. This is the first time we have ever been apart for your birthday.

I kiss you my dearest, so much. Franka

26 January **Letter from Franciszka to Blanche in Vergèze**

Blanche, chérie!

Comment vas-tu? Demeures-tu toujours à Vergèze? Ecris-moi, je t'en prie à Lisbonne Caixa 512.

J'ai reçu ta lettre écrite à Freyd, et je crois que tu es toujours avec Władek. Je vous salue tous les deux de tout mon coeur. As-tu des nouvelles de Sacha?

Chérie, j'ai envoyé quelquefois l'argent pour Stefek à Vergèze. As-tu reçu quelque chose encore après les premiers 1300?

Je fais des efforts pour obtenir le visa USA pour lui. J'espère réussir. Je le sollicite aussi pour moi. S'il sera pas possible de partir le visa doit lui faciliter de me rejoindre. Et c'est pour ça que je veux savoir est-ce qu'il a une somme suffisante pour partir tout de suite après avoir reçu les visas.

Télégraphie moi, je t'en prie si tu reçois quelque chose, bon?

En tout cas, écris-moi, je t'en prie. Je voudrais tellement savoir comment vous allez.

Stephane K[onorski] est ici. Il vous salue. J'ai visité ces jours tes amis Michel et Ada. Ils vont très bien et te saluent aussi.

Quant à moi, je travaille régulièrement et vais parfaitement bien. En tout cas je tiens ma bonne humeur par les cheveux vu les circonstances. Je te salue cordialement et t'embrasse mille fois. Franka

29 January 1941

Telegram from Franciszka to Blanche

AS TU REÇU AIDE POUR STEFEK ET COMBIEN STOP RESTES-TU VERGÈZE RÉPONDS EMBRASSE – FRANKA THEMERSON ONE REDCLIFFE OLD BROMPTON ROAD LONDON SW5

30 January **Telegram from Blanche to Franciszka**

REÇU NOVEMBRE FREYD MILLE TROIS CENTS FRANCS STEFAN REÇU LETTRE THÉRÈSE ANNONÇANT AIDE JURKIEVICZ RESTERAI VERGÈZE TENDRESSES BRONSTEIN

1 February **Letter from Franciszka to Stefan** – unposted

My darling, what to do? It seems now that I shall really get you out of France. And then what? Here? To America? Alone, without money – where, how? And when shall I see you? Will I anyway get out of here? I must, I must be with you somewhere! And here, whether home or to that job without any sense or purpose. After all there are only these two possibilities, also for you. But we would be together – Stefek, once more together! How can I decide anything? But it seems – I don't know if it is so – that so much now depends on me! Advise me, darling! What do you want – I don't know anything. Do you have the strength and courage to go to New York alone? My heart contracts at the thought that you will go there, so far away, so terribly far – and I am here and still without a word from you. Now not even a telegram. I am so anxious!

Now that I have at last the possibility (if indeed it is real) to do something so that you could move from there, now I don't even have a word.

My dearest, how terribly difficult it is for me. Maybe I shall stop writing these letters that are not to be sent. Today, the whole evening I am drawing – actually these are also letters (or a diary?) to you. I can't cope any longer! I have to do something that reminds me that I am human. I have come to my senses – but for how long? And anyhow I must, must work just in order to be able to live! Help! This is the only word that I should really write.[18]

I could bear it, even that you would go so far away, if I knew to what. But there you will drown again in the stinking mire of emigration. And who will help you?

But perhaps it would be better – perhaps you will manage and we shall truly meet there to do better work – real work – My boy, now I really feel the burden of such terrible responsibility. What to do?

Ah, to cuddle up, to cuddle close to you at last! Dearest boy, I am frightened for you, so very frightened – I got drunk today – forgive. Fr

I suppose I shall start drawing. F.

Draft of a cable from Franciszka to Mira [Złotowska]

Stefan's cousin L.T. 91 Central Park West promised affidavit, this month please ask him to do it urgently affidavit being the only way for Stefan to leave France and join me. Staying there most dangerous. Permanent address for correspondence: Blanche Bronstein, pour Themerson, Source Perrier, Vergèze, Gard. Temporary address: Themerson pour Stephane, 283 rue Endoume, Marseille.

4 February **Telegram from Franciszka to Blanche**

MERCI NOUVELLES INQUIÈTE STEFEK NE RÉPOND PAS ESPÈRE RÉUSSIR QU'IL VOIE THÉRÈSE BIENTÔT STOP RECEVRA NOUVELLES PRIÈRE TENIR AU COURANT TOUT CHANGEMENT D'ADRESSE RÉPONDS TENDRESSE = THEMERSON

18 See Franciszka's drawing on page 194 (XIV)

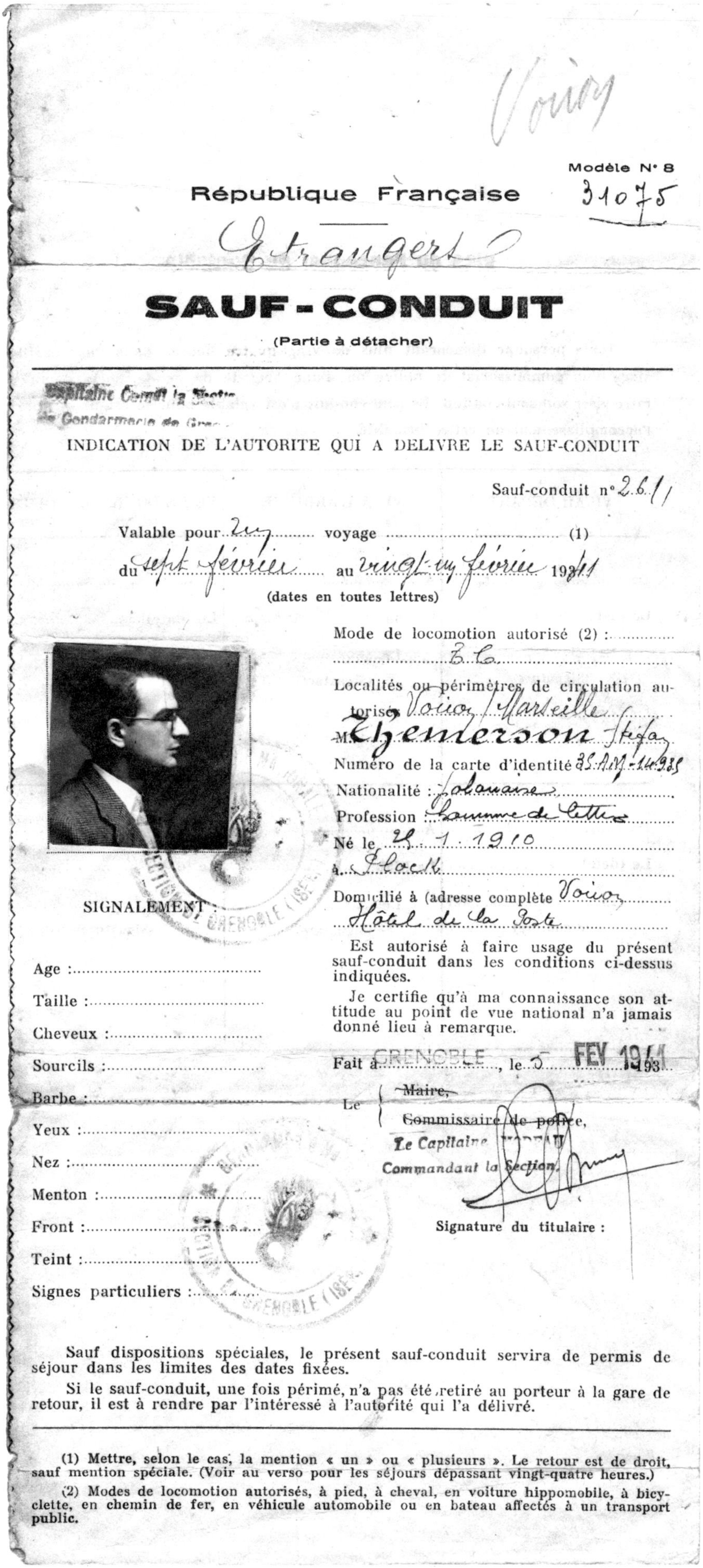

Voiron

Modèle N° 8

République Française 31075

Etrangers

SAUF-CONDUIT

(Partie à détacher)

Capitaine Cmdt la Section
de Gendarmerie de Gre...

INDICATION DE L'AUTORITE QUI A DELIVRE LE SAUF-CONDUIT

Sauf-conduit n° 2611

Valable pour un voyage (1)

du sept février au vingt-un février 1941

(dates en toutes lettres)

Mode de locomotion autorisé (2) : .... E.C.

Localités ou périmètres de circulation autorisés Voiron / Marseille

M. Themerson Stefan

Numéro de la carte d'identité 35 A.M. 14938

Nationalité : Polonaise

Profession homme de lettres

Né le 25 1 1910

à Plock

Domicilié à (adresse complète Voiron Hôtel de la Poste

SIGNALEMENT :

Age : ....

Taille : ....

Cheveux : ....

Sourcils : ....

Barbe : ....

Yeux : ....

Nez : ....

Menton : ....

Front : ....

Teint : ....

Signes particuliers : ....

Est autorisé à faire usage du présent sauf-conduit dans les conditions ci-dessus indiquées.

Je certifie qu'à ma connaissance son attitude au point de vue national n'a jamais donné lieu à remarque.

Fait à GRENOBLE, le 5 FEV 1941

Le ~~Maire,~~ ~~Commissaire de police,~~ Le Capitaine ... Commandant la Section.

Signature du titulaire :

Sauf dispositions spéciales, le présent sauf-conduit servira de permis de séjour dans les limites des dates fixées.

Si le sauf-conduit, une fois périmé, n'a pas été retiré au porteur à la gare de retour, il est à rendre par l'intéressé à l'autorité qui l'a délivré.

(1) Mettre, selon le cas, la mention « un » ou « plusieurs ». Le retour est de droit, sauf mention spéciale. (Voir au verso pour les séjours dépassant vingt-quatre heures.)

(2) Modes de locomotion autorisés, à pied, à cheval, en voiture hippomobile, à bicyclette, en chemin de fer, en véhicule automobile ou en bateau affectés à un transport public.

5 February 1941
Sauf-conduit No.2611
Grenoble

Sauf-conduit for Stefan to travel from Voiron to Marseille. He arrives in Marseille on 19 February. His address is given as Hôtel de la Poste, Voiron

4 February 1941

Diary Entry

telegrams	40.00
cigarettes	4.50
Vial [bistro]	13.00
letters	+ 5.00
	63.00

Żmigrodzki 100 (15)

5 February **Diary Entry**

cigarettes	4.50
cigarettes	5.25
debt Plesons	143.00
Vial	+ 9.75
	162.50

paper 3.50

	225.50
	+ 3.90
	229.40 = 230 frs

Mainssieux
chez Mlle Dubouchet, bd de la République, au 1er étage, au dessus du Café Chrisolome, sitôt après le viaduc

alto
partie alto Mozart
archet et Valnie [?]

Dreams:
Michał's dream: he introduces me to Nadia Boulanger and I, instead of holding out my hand, I hold out a button.
Madzia Turpin's dream: Mainssieux is dying. She sneaks into his studio to steal a Renoir. Fright. Will they notice? She steals four bars of toilet soap and runs away.

Telegram from Blanche to Franciszka

STEFAN BIEN ATTEND ARGENT POUR DÉMÉNAGER MARSEILLE OÙ SERA PRES THÉRÈSE SACHA PARIS VLADEK MONTPELLIER TENDRESSES = BRONSTEIN

6 February **Diary Entry**

tobacco	4.50
Vial	9.75
cinema	+ 21.00
	35.25
	+ 230.00
	265.00 + 100 with Żmigr

6 February 1941

Wolf's case. They didn't allow him to speak about the press. Imbirowicz intercedes with the manager, he is a representative of 'the Polish People'. First Bobrowski, then cinema.

7 February **Telegram from Stefan to Franciszka**

CHÉRIE MERCI SUIS PARFAITEMENT BIEN REÇU TROIS MILLE FRANCS FAUT IL ATTENDRE NOUVELLES LÉON ICI STOP PENSE ALLER MARSEILLE COMMENT VAS TU EMBRASSE SI TENDREMENT BAISERS = THEMERSON

Draft of a Telegram by Franciszka to Gildesgame in New York

Did you receive telegram 21 January. Matter affidavits. Stefan's new address Bronstein pour Themerson, Source Perrier, Vergèze, Unoccupied France. Urgent expect reply, Themersonowa, 1 Radcliffe, Old Brompton Road

8 February **Diary Entry**

vodka	31.50
cigarettes	4.50
matches	5.00
coffee	2.50
Gillette	1.50
Marc	25.00

An invitation to Jahl – Menu.
Major Brzozowski
Major Laskowski
English hospital

from Poland?
Amelja Sedlok
Wysocki
Strzałkowski
vis-à-vis hospital, a narrow door
tramway 70 from the arch
Chem Madlagne 416 (426?)
(Colade)
Lieutenant Kamionka
(Chciuk was talking)

Voiron –	Grenoble –	Valence –	Marseille
6.49			
9.22			
11.39			
14.35			
18.02			
19.21			
22.15	22.56	0.48	
		1.16	6.13

telephone Halina
ration cards
letter to Tema
Chciuk – brother's address
[get document stamped for departure]
books, Lipska

Grenoble:
Bobrowski – letter, telegram
Puget – passport
Lipski – Africa
Halina – Genek's father got a summons
3.91 Bobrowski
Garrigues (dep. Gard) par Nîmes
headquarters of Polish camp
Caylus
Sevrier
Geneva Red Cross
Philadelphia office
prix de passage
payer avant

Is it enough to get an American visa?
Uncle
Marseille (Garrick Rogowski on Uncle's behalf)

Stefan continues to make notes: where to go, whom to see, what to write

Marseille, Mat. Moszkowska, 120 rue de la Canebière, hotel No.6 Léon Alter (Halina, Mira)
Hicem[19], 51 rue de Breteuil, Marseille
29 bd d'Athènes

The Quakers – the person whom they promised to help has academic references, University of Baltimore, applies for a fellowship, financial affidavit, not of a relative, affidavit of a professor fiancé, moral affidavit of another professor of mathematics. Will it be enough to get an American visa?
Hôtel des Deux Mondes, 46 cours Belsunce, Marseille
Żmigrodzki telegram, letter? Mandate
Chéri conseille rester à Voiron. Blanche recevra dans quelque semaines toutes nouvelles concernant visas. tendresses mon petit. Them

13 February **Telegram from Stefan to Franciszka**

MON PETIT CHÉRI ENFIN CONSULAT LYON A TÉLÉGRAPHIÉ POLINTERNACION CETTE DEMANDE NUMERO 161 STOP JE L'AI TÉLÉGRAPHIÉ DÉJÀ POLMISSION STOP MERCI MON PETIT JE T'EMBRASSE LE PLUS TENDREMENT TON VIEUX STEPHAN = THEMERSON

19 Hebrew Immigrant Aid Society, organisation established in 1927 to help European Jews to emigrate. 80 Rua do Arsenal, Lisbon; 51 rue Breteuil, Marseille.

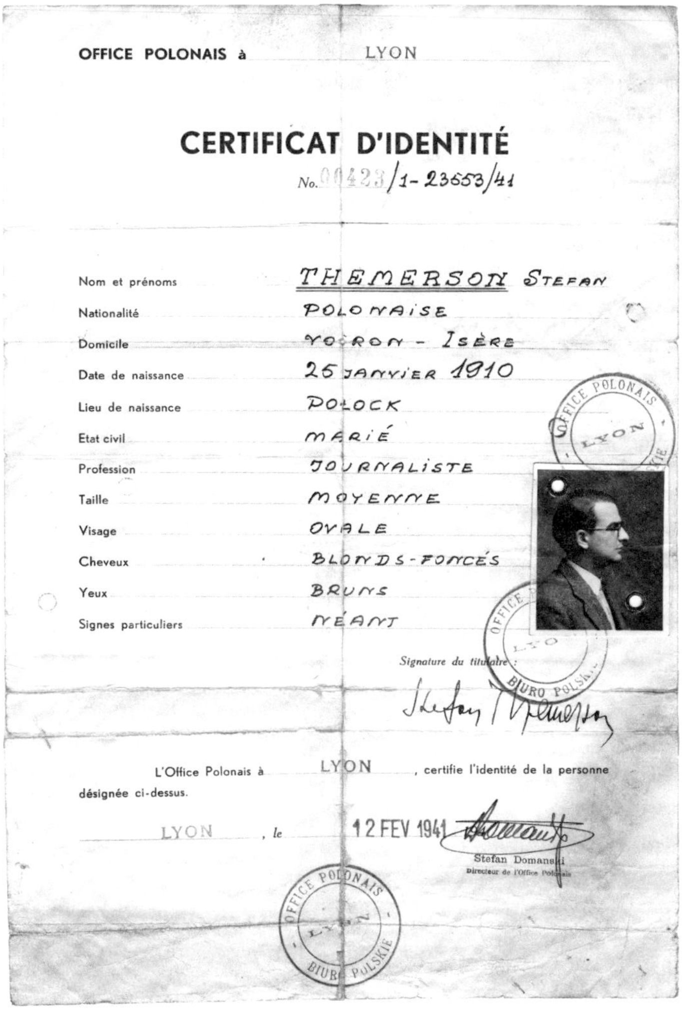

OFFICE POLONAIS à LYON

CERTIFICAT D'IDENTITÉ

No. 00423/1-23553/41

Nom et prénoms	THEMERSON Stefan
Nationalité	POLONAISE
Domicile	VOIRON - ISÈRE
Date de naissance	25 JANVIER 1910
Lieu de naissance	POLOCK
Etat civil	MARIÉ
Profession	JOURNALISTE
Taille	MOYENNE
Visage	OVALE
Cheveux	BLONDS-FONCÉS
Yeux	BRUNS
Signes particuliers	NÉANT

Signature du titulaire :

L'Office Polonais à LYON, certifie l'identité de la personne désignée ci-dessus.

LYON, le 12 FEV 1941

Stefan Domanski
Directeur de l'Office Polonais

12 February 1941
Stefan's Certificat D'Identité
no. 00423/1-23553/41
issued by Office Polonais à Lyon

On verso:
Visé à la Préfecture de l'Isère pour se rendre à New York. Sortie de France par Cerbère, visa valable jusqu'au 15 Sept. 1941. Motifs du Voyage: Rejoint sa femme, Grenoble 15 July 1941. Le Chef de Cabinet

17 February **Letter from Franciszka to Stefan**

Stefciu, my darling,

At last, at last, I too have a letter from you. Darling, I miss you so much. It is after all the first letter since how many months!

How are you darling? Are you working a bit? Do you have there with you any of our old friends? And new ones? And here one has to pull oneself up by the hair, and others even.

Since last month I am working, quite intensely even. It turned out that evenings are long and one can do a lot, though sometimes the eyes just close, eyelids stick together. I miss you very, very much, darling, and feel so anxious about you sometimes.

Will you still [be there to] get this letter?

Actually I dream of you being already on the way. Léon [Temerson] cabled me from New York that he hopes to be able to send you an affidavit during next month. People squander months so easily. But perhaps one can do it without him.

I give everybody Blanche's address for letters to you. So if you change your address, please stay in touch with her.

Darling, I think, that at last, at last, I'll be able to cuddle up to you. All our friends send you their very warmest regards. Stefan [Konorski] almost jumps for joy when there is news from you. Stefanja [Zahorska] still talks about you and altogether everyone misses you.

You probably had a letter from Mira [Michałowska]. She wrote to you. Ignacy got a job at the university in Minneapolis and she is in New York and writes very sad letters.

Darling, you can write as before to Freyd's address. They give him the letters immediately and he, at once, brings them to me.

I embrace you my darling so very much and send you masses and masses of kisses. Franka

Draft telegram to Franciszka

FW Themerson, One Redcliffe, Old Brompton Road, London SW5
Ma petite chérie tous très bien Toujours inquiet… reçu encore 6400 frs. en sûreté… j'ai assez d'argent réponse adresse Nadia Léon 283 rue Endoume jc t'aime embrasse. Them

The Quakers
Dr A. Syngałowski (lady clerk from Witkiewicz)

18 February

Franciszka writes to Józef Wittlin in New York:

'All day I am fiddling with maps and at night make macabre drawings – the eye fades – just to feel that I am, despite it all, a human being.'

Telegram from Stefan in Marseille to Franciszka

```
MA PETITE CHÉRIE TOUJOURS INQUIET DE TOI SUIS TRÈS BIEN
REÇU ENCORE 6400 FRS RÉPONSE ADRESSE NADIA LÉON 283 RUE
ENDOUME JE T'AIME BAISERS = THEMERSON
```

Diary Entry

Hicem – meeting with Dyma and Gurnfinkel

Brasil bateau
Portugal bateau
Alcina
avances pour les bateaux brasiliens
Maroc – Algérie 11 300

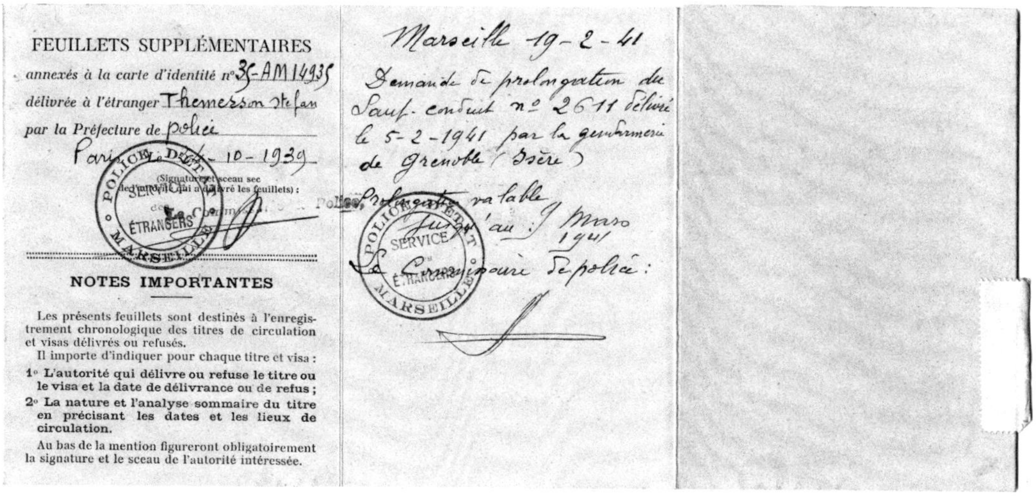

FEUILLETS SUPPLÉMENTAIRES
annexés à la carte d'identité n° 3C-AM 14935
délivrée à l'étranger Themerson Stefan
par la Préfecture de police
Paris le 4-10-1939
(Signature et sceau sec de l'autorité qui a délivré les feuillets) :

NOTES IMPORTANTES

Les présents feuillets sont destinés à l'enregistrement chronologique des titres de circulation et visas délivrés ou refusés.
Il importe d'indiquer pour chaque titre et visa :
1° **L'autorité qui délivre ou refuse le titre ou le visa et la date de délivrance ou de refus ;**
2° **La nature et l'analyse sommaire du titre en précisant les dates et les lieux de circulation.**
Au bas de la mention figureront obligatoirement la signature et le sceau de l'autorité intéressée.

Marseille 19-2-41
Demande de prolongation du Sauf-conduit n° 2611 délivré le 5-2-1941 par la gendarmerie de Grenoble (Isère)
Prolongation valable jusqu'au : 9 Mars 1941
Le Commissaire de police :

19 February 1941
Additional document to Stefan's identity card

Marseille, 19-2-1941
Demande de prolongation du sauf-conduit no 2611 délivré le 5-2-1941 par la gendarmerie de Grenoble (Isère). Prolongation valable jusqu'au: 9 mars 1941
Le Commissaire de Police

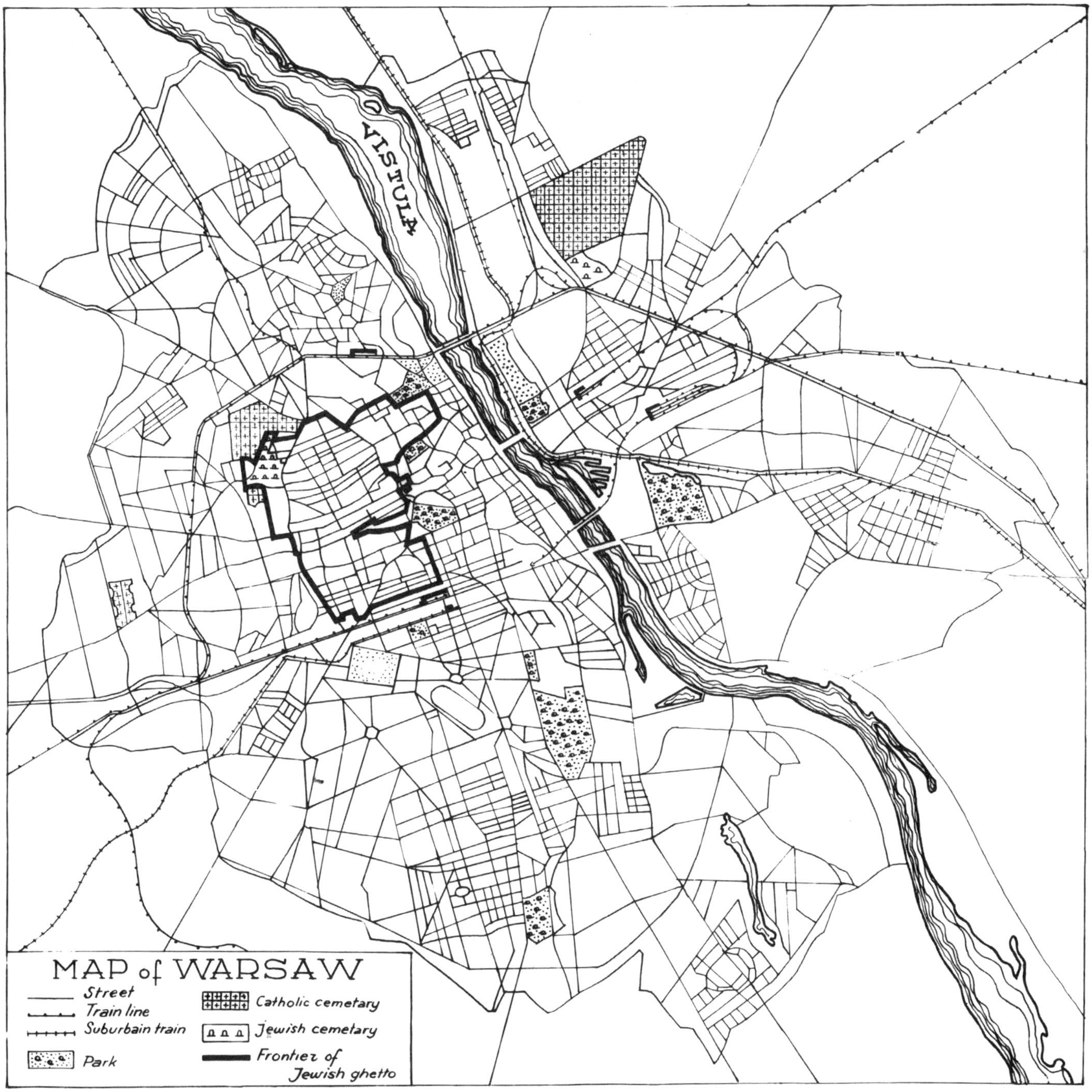

One of the maps of Warsaw drawn by Franciszka while working as cartographer for the Polish Ministry of Information and Documentation

Telegram from Franciszka to Stefan

CHÉRI VAIS PARFAITEMENT BIEN TOUS AMIS T EMBRASSENT AMITIÉS SINCÈRES POUR NADIA LÉON STOP TOUTE CORRESPONDANCE DIRIGERAI BLANCHE TENDRESSE = THEMERSON

Stefan is still in Marseille; his sauf-conduit will be renewed.

Diary Entry

6 pm at Syngałowski's

1 pm
Café at the corner of rue Canalière with a view on the old harbour.
I am waiting for Dyma.

Sketch from nature:
'Moment psychologique', says the man next to me – a grey hat (here they wear berets in good weather), yellow leather watch strap. Sun is streaming through the windows and warming the back of my neck. In the harbour, opposite the window, a ship – French flag. And it's docking. But at the steps an armed soldier stands guard, red pompom on his cap – and I start remembering a film, perhaps even with the Marx brothers, and lottery posters – toucher pompon rouge. The man next to me has green eyes. Dyma walks in. Photomontage. Visit to the police station to extend sauf-conduit. Post Office, letters from Franka, Mira, and Lipski. Bakeries closed. Cheese and lemons. Syngałowski's lecture in one hour. Supper 8 francs. Meeting with Syngałowski. Fifty-seven people die in camp every day. Café Vézelise – mugs from Le Dôme.

Zofia Kramsztyk, Hôtel Floride, 52 bd de Cimiez, Nice
D. Bronsztejn, 2 rue Martin Chaissy, Montpellier (Hérault)

Letter from Franciszka to Stefan

Stefciu, my darling,

Today I received your telegram from Marseille. Darling, I kiss you so much and so tenderly.

What are you doing? Where do you live? Are you together with Nadia and Léon? I am so happy that you have the money. Have you anything at all to wear, darling?

All letters from me and from friends will be addressed to Blanche.

I communicate with her from time to time. I presume that you let her know your change of address, is that right?

We are all becoming terribly sentimental here. I would like to send Blanche a photograph of Marceljanek with Teresa's signature. I shall probably do it, but it's frightening how long letters now take to reach their destination. One simply can't bear having to wait. Do write to me a lot and as soon as possible. You absolutely cannot imagine what it means to me to have just these few words from you. Hug Nadia and Léon for me.

I kiss you darling – masses and masses of times. Franka

20 February 1941 **Diary Entry**
evening
The Moszkowskis

21 February **Diary Entry**
café at 11
at 6.30 pm tel. NO582 Syngałowski
at Léon's in the evening
doctor's certificate
Morocco
after Monday
Mazur (Polish Office)
Lipski's visa
Fry, 18 Garibaldi

Yesterday, what was yesterday? When was yesterday?

Obralski, Jankowski, former combatants – they got rid of me beautifully, I even thanked them. And then the Post Office, a letter from Tema's friend Obrębski and then supper and worms in the soup, and then a visit to Moszkowska and meeting with Sawicz and the doctor at Claridge and a cinema and streets and Dickens and sleep. And what happened during sleep? I woke up at 11.

At 11 am meeting with Dyma in the café on the corner. He returns to Montpellier. He has already left for the station.

The same place as the day before yesterday. To continue the sketch from nature. Outside the window today, a propaganda ship. The man next to me no longer has green eyes. He is somewhat bald, with curly hair, and wears thick black-rimmed glasses. He is silent. And the other one is saying: 'Non!' and explains something fast, very fast. And then another one barges in, with a leather brief-case in his hand. He disappears and emerges again somewhere in the distance behind a pillar. He glances from above at the tables and there he is, wearing a white apron and a white lace cap on his head, far from here, under the mirror, where the restaurant is, and he wipes his nose, and then runs with a tray, as somebody motions to him. Mam'selle.

And today the port is covered with furrows of the waves, and seaside walks, Château d'If – 6 francs... Every few moments trams cut off the distant view of the sea. The man with glasses reveals his crooked finger, discovers America and says: voilà. But the other is wiser. He explains something persistently – and suddenly, in your memory, you see – from yesterday – a dog, and you hear yelping, yelping, in front of the prefecture, yelping, when you were buying the book by Dickens in a secondhand bookshop, the dog yelped three times, behind chippings under the street lamp and died yelping, and it was the first corpse you saw during this war.

22 February **Diary Entry**
Moszkowska, Claridge
The doctor didn't find out anything

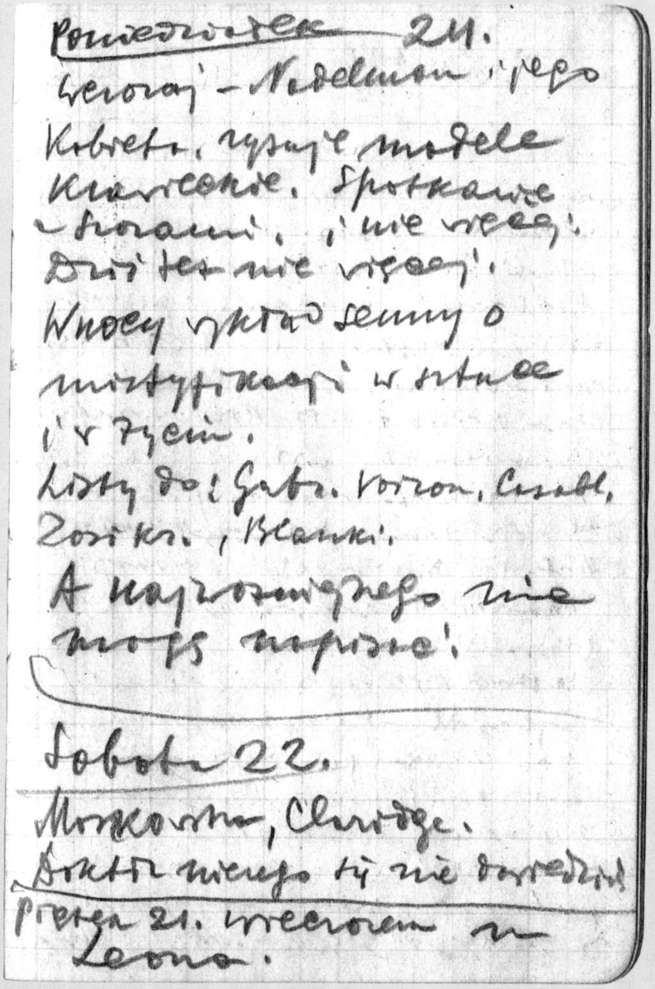

Stefan's diary, 24 February 1941

24 February 1941

Diary Entry

Yesterday – Nadelman and his woman. He draws tailoring patterns.
Meeting with the Szors, and nothing else. Today, also, nothing else.
At night, a dream-lecture about mystification in art and life.
Letters to: Gabr., Voiron, Casablanca [Mira Złotowska], Zosia Kr[amsztyk], Blanche [Bronstein].

And the most important one I cannot write.

In the office, conversation with Mazur and then with Mme Zajączkowska. Negresco. Meeting Mme Rotsztejn. Sister of the man with moustache, about Martinique. Tomorrow at 1.30. Today she witnessed a brawl there. 'What language are you speaking?' 'English'. A mug of beer in the face. Police. I collected the sauf-conduit, extended till March 5. I drop in at the hospital but don't find Henri [Temerson]. Venereal ward for the army. No post. I buy a sausage. There is no bread, so sandwich, apples and back home. Chciuk has gone. And then around the streets and cinema. A story about false diamonds and Accord frivole. Orchestra, Beethoven. A small beer and back home. And I so much want to sleep.

Marie-Louise Verrier, *Les yeux et la vision* [1938].

I do not know if I shall succeed in making the egg of Columbus stand up [20] or perhaps I shall return to Voiron to continue my vigil.

Dear

Thanks for your postscript. Meanness goes on. It is difficult to have a room for oneself and it is sultry.

Only the sense of humour saves your soul.

Hugs for your daughter. I would feel like writing in French to her, but I would have to wake up and I want to sleep all the time, all the time in a dream.

I hope to see you in Voiron soon. St.Th.

Draft letter to Franciszka, dated 25 February follows [below], and other draft letters, as well as a list of people he is writing to inserted in his diary, 24 January 1941 to 1 March 1941

25 February **Draft Letter from Stefan to Franciszka**

Darling, all the time, all the time in my thoughts, I am writing a huge enormous letter to you. And all the time I pick up the pen and hold it, and the ink on the nib dries, I sit for hours in front of a sheet of paper, and cannot find the letters to form what I think and feel. Darling, it's already so many months! And how many still to live through to meet you at last somewhere in this wide world?

I sit here now, but where shall I be when you get this letter? Perhaps back again in my Voiron shelter.

And you? I am so worried about you. I received recently a letter from Mira. Would you not like to be together with her? I already feel quite safe here and there is nothing absolutely nothing to aggravate me. Don't wait for me darling, if you have some possibilities. Darling, I kiss you lots and lots. For so long I looked for your traces all over the world. There is nothing that I want except to cuddle up to you and to be together on some desert island.

Love, darling, Stefan

20 The egg of Columbus refers to a brilliant idea or discovery that seems simple after the fact. The expression refers to a popular story of how Christopher Columbus, having been told that discovering the Americas was no great accomplishment, challenged his critics to make an egg stand on its tip; and after they gave up, he did it himself by tapping the egg on the table so as to flatten its tip.

25 February 1941

Diary Entry

Au Brûleur de Loups[21]

26 February **Diary Entry**

9–12, Centre Américain de Secours
Thursday, 5 pm Syngałowski
Yesterday, the library.
Moszkowska
The Szors.
Dr. Foata, 68 bd Notre Dâme, 2 – 4 Monday, pour 17. privt [?]
~~Dr Benoit Gambetta, Marseille~~

27 February **Diary Entry**

A letter from Blanche, card from Wundheilen, lunch on Quai Juliette.
Syngałowski – Monday
Laundrywoman. Supper at Léon's: the Ortamberts, Henri with wife. Léon and Henri
Received letters – that they won't renew their contracts.

28 February **Diary Entry**

Bath, Dr Foata, examination.

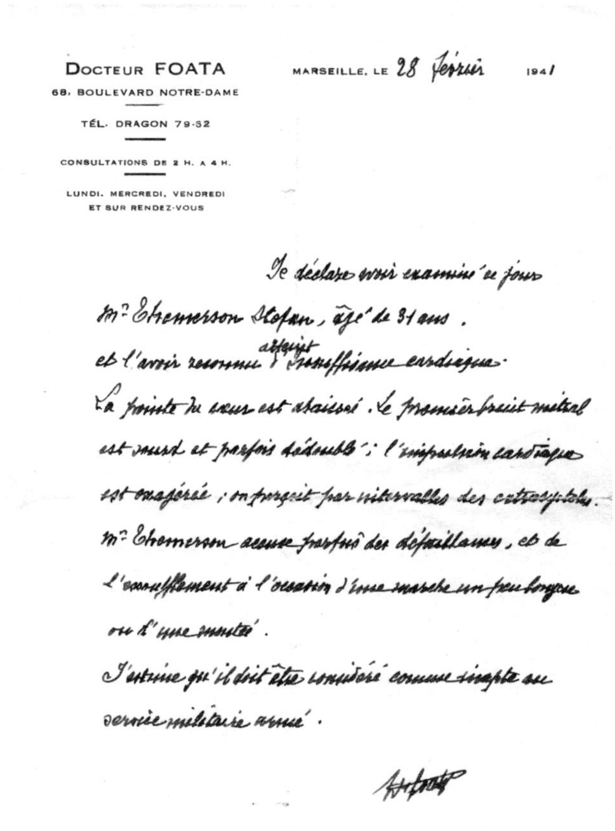

DOCTEUR FOATA
68, BOULEVARD NOTRE-DAME
TÉL. DRAGON 79-52
CONSULTATIONS DE 2 H. A 4 H.
LUNDI, MERCREDI, VENDREDI
ET SUR RENDEZ-VOUS

MARSEILLE, LE 28 février 1941

Je déclare avoir examiné ce jour
Mr Themerson Stefan, âgé de 31 ans.
et l'avoir reconnu atteint d'insuffisance cardiaque.
La pointe du cœur est abaissé. Le premier bruit mitral est sourd et parfois dédoublé; l'impulsion cardiaque est exagérée; on perçoit par intervalles des extrasystoles.
Mr Themerson accuse parfois des défaillances, et de l'essoufflement à l'occasion d'une marche un peu longue ou d'une montée.
J'estime qu'il doit être considéré comme inapte au service militaire armé.

[signature]

28 February 1941
Letter from Dr Foata in Marseille
(to whom it may concern)

I confirm having examined today Stefan Themerson 31-years old, and having recognised him to have a cardiac insufficiency. The tip of the heart is lowered. The first mitral sound is deaf and sometimes double. The cardiac impulse is exaggerated and from time to time one detects extra-systoles. Themerson sometimes shows excess of weakness and shortness of breath after a long walk or a climb.

I consider him to be unsuitable for armed military service.

Deciphered/translated by Michel Bronstein

21 Café au Brûleur de Loups in Marseille was popular with radicals and refugees.

28 February 1941

Concert in the atelier, with Léon. Bach's concertino (Herman and Léon with orchestra). Mozart serenade. Apart from that archival pieces from the epoch of Bach and Mozart. Conductor – Fendler, says that we spent New Year's Eve in 1938 together. Supper at Léon's.

Léon's remarks about the programme: That only great things matter, why search [for anything else]. Me: just the opposite – Warsaw [a place] of contrasts, after arriving in Paris one really values the daily bread of art.
Revue des Deux Mondes.

1 March **Diary entry**

English hospital
game of poker
Wysocki
Brûleur de Loups

Classicism (à propos Henri's remark yesterday that someone questioned whether Bach is a classic) is a question of definition. Marble was classical in Greek architecture, as reinforced concrete in modern architecture! Chopin a classic of Romanticism, as Bach is a classic of polyphony or Beethoven a classic of Classicism, programmed music of the Renaissance. In this sense classicism is modernism that has reached its thirtieth birthday. Classicism is what one fights against in order to create new classicism.

Goodbye, Mister Chips[22] – Oh, how I hate brats, they inspire such hope and afterwards grow into such swine.

English hospital
absorbed in poker
Wysocki
Brûleur de Loups
Englishman is leaving on Monday
idiotic cinema
loss of strength
supper at the Pension
Moszkowska is not there
to Chez Suzanne
nobody is there either
Vioudox

'Report' without chronology
To include here the sensation of being a detective

Time-table

2 March **Diary Entry**

51 rue Breteuil, Hicem, Marseille
1.30 Au Brûleur de Loups
Ford's address?

22 The film, *Goodbye, Mister Chips*, which was released in France in December 1939.

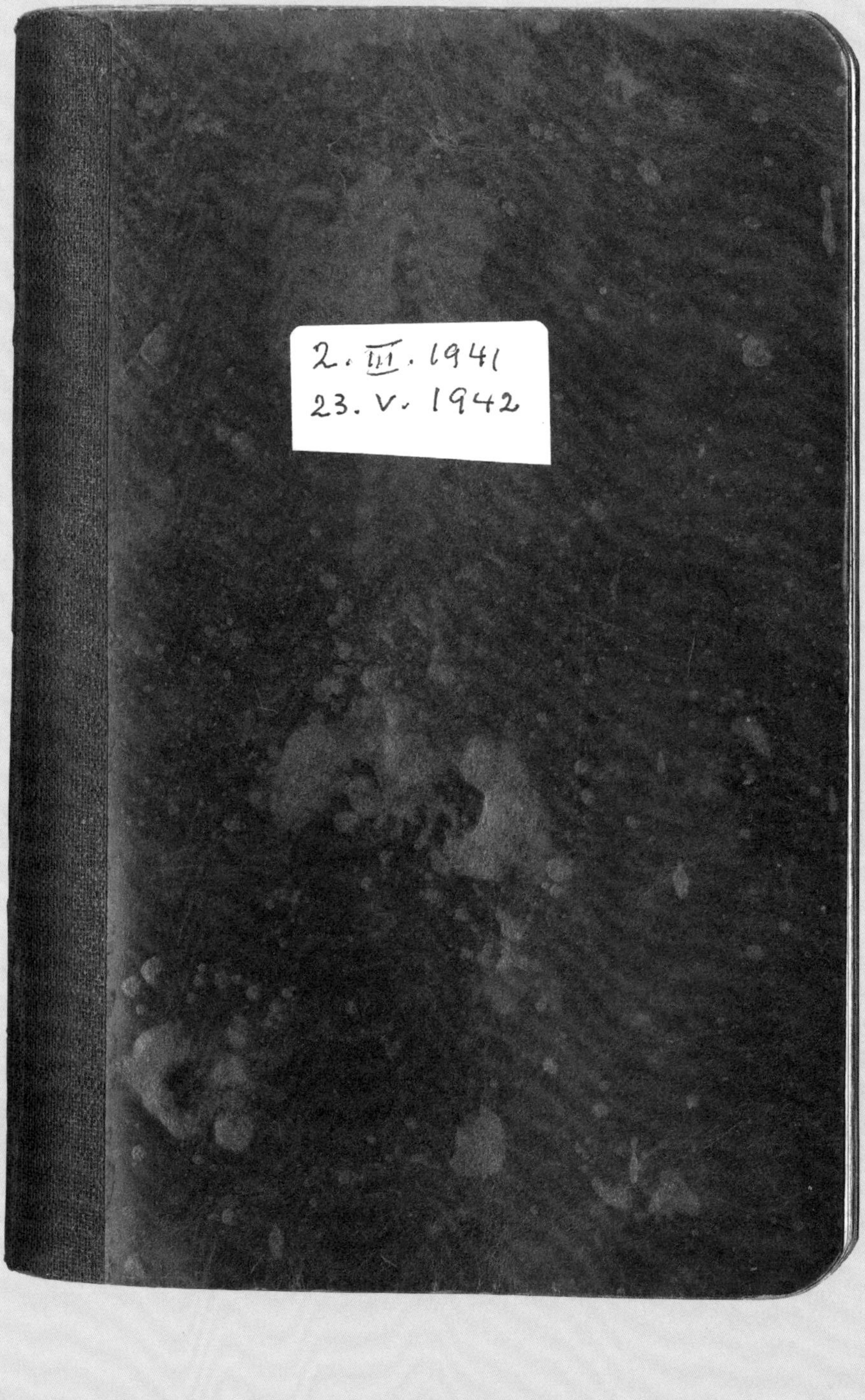
2. III. 1941
23. V. 1942

Dynowska's address (Teresa?)
3 – Léon – Corniche? ~~M Sauvage 2.30~~

From other end of the diary but on the same day

Rationalism
Objective and subjective truths
19th century – a century of high-minded rationalism (Introduction of Dr Olivier Chalgrin' to Laurent Pasquier in *Les Maîtres* by Georges Duhamel, (chapter 3):

> Avez-vous jamais réfléchi, mon ami, à ceci que Pasteur, ce vrai croyant, cette âme religieuse, a été l'un des plus puissants agents du rationalisme? … Je suis un homme du XIXe siècle et le XIXe siècle restera le siècle du rationalisme triomphant. On n'est jamais tout à fait raisonnable dans le triomphe et la raison elle-même n'a pas triomphé de façon modeste et mesurée… Le malheur est qu'un certain nombre de bons esprits, enivrés par le succès, ont pensé que la raison pouvait expliquer tout. Mon ami, voyez comme la conjoncture est délicate. Admettre dès le principe que la raison n'expliquera pas tout, c'est renoncer d'avance et c'est donner prise à la chimère, je le sais bien. Mais déclarer que la raison permet de tout expliquer, c'est créer une superstition nouvelle, c'est instaurer, par excès de présomption, une nouvelle forme d'ignorance et de barbarie… La connaissance rationnelle peut reconnaître sans honte qu'elle n'est pas la seule possible et qu'il y a d'autres voies, qui sont peut-être dangereuses mais qui conduisent quand même quelque part. Le rationalisme est assez fort aujourd'hui pour faire la paix. Vous m'entendez? Je souhaite, si vous voulez toute ma pensée, que le rationalisme ne se considère plus comme l'adversaire – né de la connaissance intuitive ou religieuse ou même mystique ou poétique. Ce serait une grande oeuvre pour le XXe siècle.

'I dream about things I don't know how to repeat,' said Sidorowicz, on the sofa in the salon of the Hôtel de la Poste. It was already after he had resigned from his post as secretary. Bureaucracy diminished a bit. 'I have abstract dreams, geometric forms, etc. It's very difficult to express certain things so that someone else will understand. I don't know whether it is altogether possible.'

Objective truths – Galileo
Subjective truths, which find their confirmation in experience, even though they contradict each other – Newton (corpuscular theory) and wave theory of light.
Subjective truths – 'private truths'
There are not as many of them as one would think.
Artists seek 'subjective' truths. They build these truths. Example: Greece created one subjective truth; modern painting created another.
Superficial difference: as if objective truths were absolute. Subjective ones – the creation of a man.

Either – or. Either man is a predetermined creation of nature and then his creations are also predetermined. Or – if art is a non-determined objective creation of man, then science is too. Rational objectivity is an instrument created by a man.

Objection: application of the same experimental conditions and the same scientific logic gives the same results. (Plus still experimental *crucis*). That means that a group of people, who are in agreement about a given type of thinking and enquiry, is ultimately in agreement with nature (i.e. with itself). Artists also find each other and create groups, clans of truths.

Afternoon with Léon. Walk on the Corniche. On foot to 'Suzanne'.

tel. Syngałowski
I'll write a letter to Teresa
English hospital
To Léon in the evening? The Moszkowskis?

Supper at Léon's. I give them 'Petit Nègre' to correct. Relatively few mistakes. We part very amicably.

3 March **Letter from Stefan to Franciszka**

My darling, this moment will be so distant when you get this letter and today's concerns will already be unimportant and will have passed – so what can one write about these days, when one lives the minute that has passed or the minute that is coming, but never that which is just here. Those just here, one pushes away into the unconscious, collecting them there just as profiteers hoard their dough in a *cache*, and this is responsible for getting old.

Sometimes for me life is sadder than sad, sometimes it seems completely normal, but I hold onto my sense of humour, and with that one can survive everything, to the very end.

Your drawing with the caption Memento Magnitudinis that I took with me, was left behind, so far away and I don't know who is looking at it, but I try to remember it all the time and everywhere.

Darling, that time of separation makes me so very much closer to you. When I read newspapers I don't think, I don't think at all, but my heart beats so hard with fear.

I am here still, I meet from time to time with Léon and Nadia, but I think that I shall return to my shelter – if waiting is all one can do, then there it would simply be more economical.

I kiss you darling so many, many times Stefan

Telegram from Stefan to Franciszka

CHÉRIE SUIS ENCORE MARSEILLE MAIS PENSE RETOURNER VOIRON RÉSPONDS ENCORE À NADIA EMBRASSE TENDREMENT BAISERS = THEMERSON

Draft of a letter from Franciszka to Mr Williams, Trading With The Enemy Branch[23], Treasury And Board Of Trade

Dear Sir

I learned yesterday in connection with my visiting your office that I am not allowed to request my friends in Lisbon to send any food parcels to my mother in Warsaw even of their own account. In order to prevent my friend Miss Z in Lisbon from forwarding any further parcels I wired her yesterday.

Yours faithfully

Franciszka receives the following letter from the Treasury and the Board of Trade

TRADING WITH THE ENEMY BRANCH
(Treasury and Board of Trade).

Telephone No.: HOLBORN 4300.

Telegraphic Address: "TRADENEMY, LONDON."

24, KINGSWAY, LONDON, W.C.2.

In any reply (which should be addressed to "THE CONTROLLER" at the address opposite) please add the letters H.K. to the address on the envelope placing them in the left-hand bottom corner.

The following reference should be quoted in any further communications :—T/E

PLEASE QUOTE IN YOUR REPLY Gen.21/921/1164

5th March 1941.

Madam,

The information furnished by you at your interview here on the 3rd March has now been carefully considered.

By the Trading with the Enemy Act, 1939, it is forbidden (without special permission which is not granted save in exceptional circumstances) to have any commercial, financial or other intercourse or dealings with or for the benefit of any person in enemy or enemy occupied territory and it is clear that, in asking friends in United States to send money to Lisbon to be expended in the despatch of parcels of food to your mother in Warsaw, you have infringed these provisions.

It is noted that you claim that you were unaware that arrangements of this kind were /prohibited

Mrs. Fr. Themerson,
1, Redcliffe,
262, Brompton Road,
S.W.5.

prohibited but it is, nevertheless, also to be observed that your friend, Miss U.Lubelska, with whom you have been living for some months, had already had some correspondence with this Branch on a similar subject, when these very provisions were explained to her, and, further, that you were aware that she had had correspondence with this Branch.

Having regard to all the circumstances, it is not proposed that any further action should be taken in this instance and it is not, therefore, necessary to consider further the real extent of your knowledge of the provisions of the Act, but it must be clearly understood that any further activities of this nature on your part will be regarded most seriously.

I am to ask you to be good enough to acknowledge receipt of this letter.

I am, Madam,
Your obedient Servant,

[signature]

23 German occupied Poland is enemy territory. 'Trading with the Enemy Act, 1939, renders it an offence to have any commercial, financial or other intercourse or dealing directly or indirectly with, or for the benefit, of a person in enemy territory'.

4 March 1941

Diary Entry

12.30 Léon. I pose for Nadia
Moszkowska
send letters to Blanche, Bobrowski, Michał, a telegram, Syngałowski

Jan Małęczyński, Polish office in Marseille

Pierre Brunet and Aldo Mieli
Histoire des Sciences (Payot) [1935]
Books: Huxley
Van Loon: *Histoire des Arts*[24]
Poesie 41
M. Louise Verrier *Les yeux et la vision* [Paris 1938]
S. Reinach *Grammaire Française*[25]
'Figaro' - Saturday issue (Lyon)
2.30 or 6.30 Bar au Sans Pareil, Ford
L'Echo des Etudiants, Montpellier[26]
Gulliver in English
Kopernik[27]

[Wojciech] Wasiutyński

Lunched at Léon's. Then I pose for Nadia: Léon was very moved and happy to have read 'Petit Nègre' yesterday. And I too. He said that it had cleansed him. Having lived for so long with the daily problems of getting food and visas, it's hard for me to believe that my clumsy French could touch anyone in this way.

Send a telegram to Franka.

Moszkowska – a terrible bore. 'I don't know whether to drink another cup of tea? I should wash my face, but should I do it before or afterwards? One will have to sit down. It was raining today, I didn't take my fur coat and I am wearing two woollen sweaters. Is it cold or is it just me that's cold?' Composer [Moritz] Moszkowski. Aryan/Asian origin from the Khazars.[28] etc.

Camille with Greta Garbo

5 March **Diary Entry**

Received a letter from Voiron

I didn't see anybody today and feel good about it.

[projects]
To start a card-index of types.
To visit a person as one visits a town. Not chronologically but according to topography.
To write as a Gulliver who visits a town that is somebody's whole life.

24 Hendrik Van Loon, *Histoire des Arts*, 1938; The Arts, 1937.
25 Probably Salomon Reinach, *Sidonie ou Le Français sans peine*, 1912 and reprints.
26 Magazine of L'Association Générale des Étudiants, Montpellier.
27 Copernicus.
28 A mediaeval khanate which adopted Judaism as a religion. It's been suggested that most European Jews are descended from them.

6 March 1941 **Diary Entry**

~~roh Nadia~~
Hotel [?]

Looking for a hotel. Changing the hotel. Nadelman – card from Lonia. His Fernande and some third person. Patrons, projects, it seems that they will set up a workshop – he in America, he will try as an inventor.

7 March **Diary Entry**

A letter from Michał Spisak – I write back
2 o'clock I pose for Nadia.
Post Office – a letter from Żmigrodzki.
5.30 to Henri at the hospital where he introduces me to the nurses – quel métier.
We go and walk to the centre to the priest (an Englishman?), the fellows have left.
The priest has no advice to give. We go back to Léon's.
For supper at Léon's
Conversations about the journey and America
At 9 pm Léon arrives. Léon talks about Henri Temerson, from his father's point of view
(his previous story was about his mother)

Léon's story:
'… quand mon père est venu à Paris il avait deux francs sur lui. Il avait cinq francs mais il a payé 3 francs to a barber et il ne lui en est resté que 2. Il n'avait pas de bagages. Il portait trois chemises, l'une sur l'autre et deux paires de caleçons longs. [In Poland he had trained as a tailor]. Le tailleur militaire. Mais il n'était même pas un bon tailleur. Parce que dans son pays il est resté à l'école jusqu'à 15 ou 16 ans. Et en même temps, il a travaillé chez un tailleur. Il n'a pas bien appris son métier. Mais, il m'a raconté tout cela. Il ne voulait pas vivre dans un ghetto, et il était le sixième fils dans sa famille, alors, quand il a vu que ses frères sont devenus des médecins etc – il est parti chercher la liberté. L'independance a été une obsession toute la vie. Il est venu à Paris sans rien et, quand même, il a réussi. Il avait son atelier, il s'est marié très jeune.'

Léon, at the age of 13 starts at the conservatorium – he earns. Henri – nothing. Father wants him to go into 'business'. He doesn't want to. Henri to school. The best pupil. A double baccalauréat. Father: that's enough. He has general education, now he must earn. Henri wants to study literature. Father says absolutely not. A compromise – medicine. Léon decides to pay for his education. Every day Henri gets up at 4 in the morning and works till midnight. Henri graduates in medicine and becomes an intern. He gets used to not earning. He doesn't realise how much it costs. Mother dies. Father crestfallen, never recovers. He works for himself and that's it. Léon gets married. He will maintain Henri for one more year, but that will be the end. Henri is astonished. He is jealous of the wife who is taking away his brother. He wanted afterwards to do 'internal sciences'. Career, honours, a car in the hospital, etc. But he can't understand that his brother doesn't owe him anything.

I return to the hotel.

8 March 1941

Following the telegram to Teresa Żarnower in Lisbon, of which we don't have the text, Franciszka writes a letter to her on 8 March of which she keeps a copy in case she has to show it later.

Dear Teresko

You received my telegram, didn't you?

It appears, as you may have guessed from my telegram, that I wasn't even permitted to know about parcels sent to my mother, even though I didn't pay for them. Don't send any more, darling. The same goes for letters. They are only allowed to receive letters via Cook's or the Red Cross.

Apart from that, there's nothing new. I continue to work in the Ministry. the work is rather wearing. By now I am completely fed up with compasses and I dream of a proper paintbrush and proper paints.

And how are things with you! What about the visa. At last, they sent Stefan an affidavit.

I'd so much like to receive a letter from you both from Lisbon.

Write, my dear, something about yourself, how you are and how life is treating you.

With warm embraces.

Franka

Parcels nevertheless continue to be sent. In November 1942, Franciszka will receive bills from the Ministry for sending 111 parcels to Warsaw.

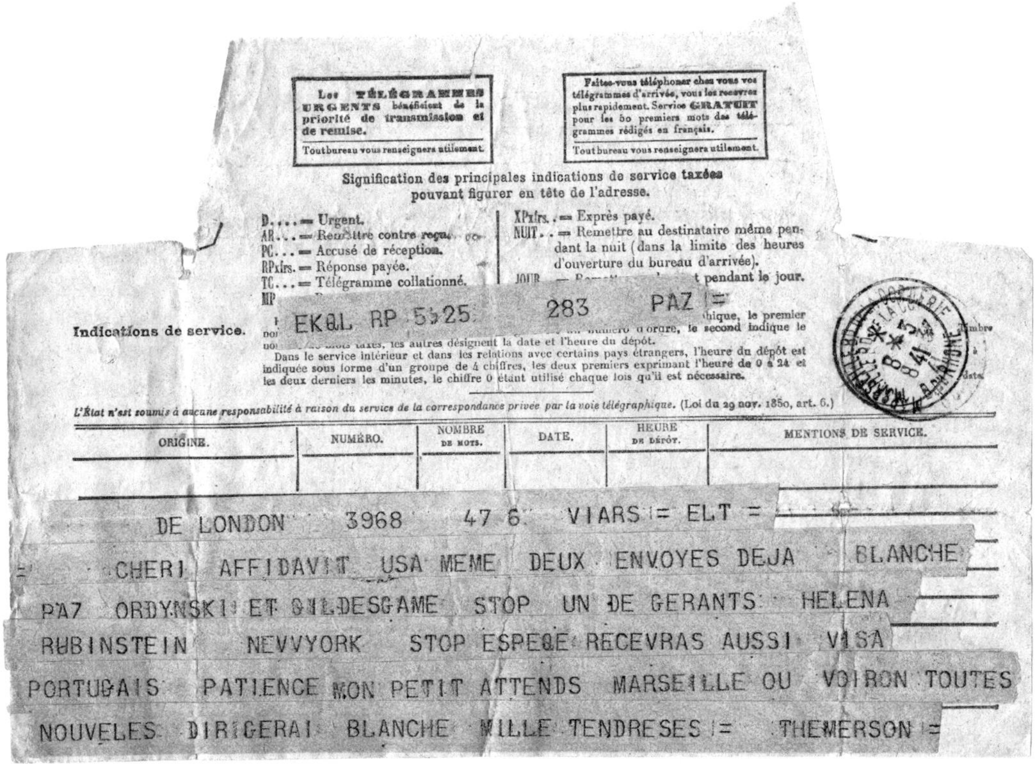

Indications de service. EKAL RP 5 25 283 PAZ =

ORIGINE.	NUMÉRO.	NOMBRE DE MOTS.	DATE.	HEURE DE DÉPÔT.	MENTIONS DE SERVICE.

DE LONDON 3968 47 6 VIARS = ELT =

= CHERI AFFIDAVIT USA MEME DEUX ENVOYES DEJA BLANCHE PAZ ORDYNSKI ET GILDESGAME STOP UN DE GERANTS HELENA RUBINSTEIN NEVVYORK STOP ESPEGE RECEVRAS AUSSI VISA PORTUGAIS PATIENCE MON PETIT ATTENDS MARSEILLE OU VOIRON TOUTES NOUVELES DIRIGERAI BLANCHE MILLE TENDRESES = THEMERSON =

Telegram from Franciszka to Stefan in Marseille

CHÉRI AFFIDAVIT USA MÊME DEUX ENVOYÉS DÉJÀ BLANCHE PAR ORDYŃSKI ET GILDESGAME STOP UN DES GÉRANTS HELENA RUBINSTEIN NEW YORK STOP ESPÈRE RECEVRAS AUSSI VISA PORTUGAIS PATIENCE MON PETIT ATTENDS MARSEILLE OU VOIRON TOUTES NOUVELLES DIRIGERAI BLANCHE MILLE TENDRESSES = THEMERSON

Letter from Franciszka to Stefan

Chéri, it is these last days that one has finally sent you the American affidavit. Perhaps two, since I asked two people at the same time. Leon [Grynblat] has cabled me that he has sent one for me too. I also hope to obtain for you the Portuguese transit visa. *Ah, mon petit, qu'on puisse enfin être ensemble.*

As far as lodging goes, would you like to live at Genek's? It's possible that you could work with him.

But perhaps you prefer to live with Ignacy, and that may be more sensible. What do you think?

As for Mira, I fear that I shall not be able to see her soon. It is in any case a question of months. But months pass, you see, mon petit.

The main thing is to have an American visa at last. When you receive it, please go and see monsieur Małęczyński at the Polish Office in Marseille. Maybe he will be able to give you all the help you need. *Mon petit chéri*, it is a very long time that I haven't had a word from you. To tell the truth I have only had one letter.

I hope to be able to arrange for you the ticket Lisbon–New York. Let me know if it is necessary to get the visa at once. *Je t'embrasse mon petit si tendrement*

Franka

Embrasse Blanche et Władek

Diary Entry

In Marseille
Henri in the morning
12–12.15 rue Dragon with Léon
19h Ford – *Sans Pareil* Ip.[?]
bath
with Henri at the hospital
lunch in rue Dragon
walk with Nadia and Léon on the Corniche
café at the seaside.
7pm *Sans Pareil* – Léon and the Ortamberts wait in front of the café with a telegram from Franka
Conversation with K. Ford
Cinema, English version – the problem of 'Hollywood' films
('Black Eyes'[29], Russian sentimental song, in the orchestra some 200 people, American orchestration)

9 March Diary Entry

2pm Nadia
Obrębski
pension Notre Dame

29 'Ochi chernye', Russian Gypsy song, mentioned frequently in *The Shop Around the Corner*, 1940 film.

Diary Entry

2.30 or 6.30 *Sans Pareil*
Obrębski – Prefecture – Consulate – sauf-conduit
9 pm Au Brûleur de Loups
Post Office
Obrębski, combatants (journey), cashed 115 francs
American Consulate (registration and visa), Polish Office
sauf-conduit
registered in the USA [American Consulate], Monday, 10 March 1941

11 March **Letter from Franciszka to Stefan**

My darling, look it's March already – and still, still you are not here.

Now, I am about to write a letter to you, a real letter to be sent by that dupe that promised so much – what will he accomplish? My little one.

I won't write any more – I shall, just do as I have been doing for a long time draw to you. Darling, how wonderful to be able to draw, – I kiss you so much. Fr

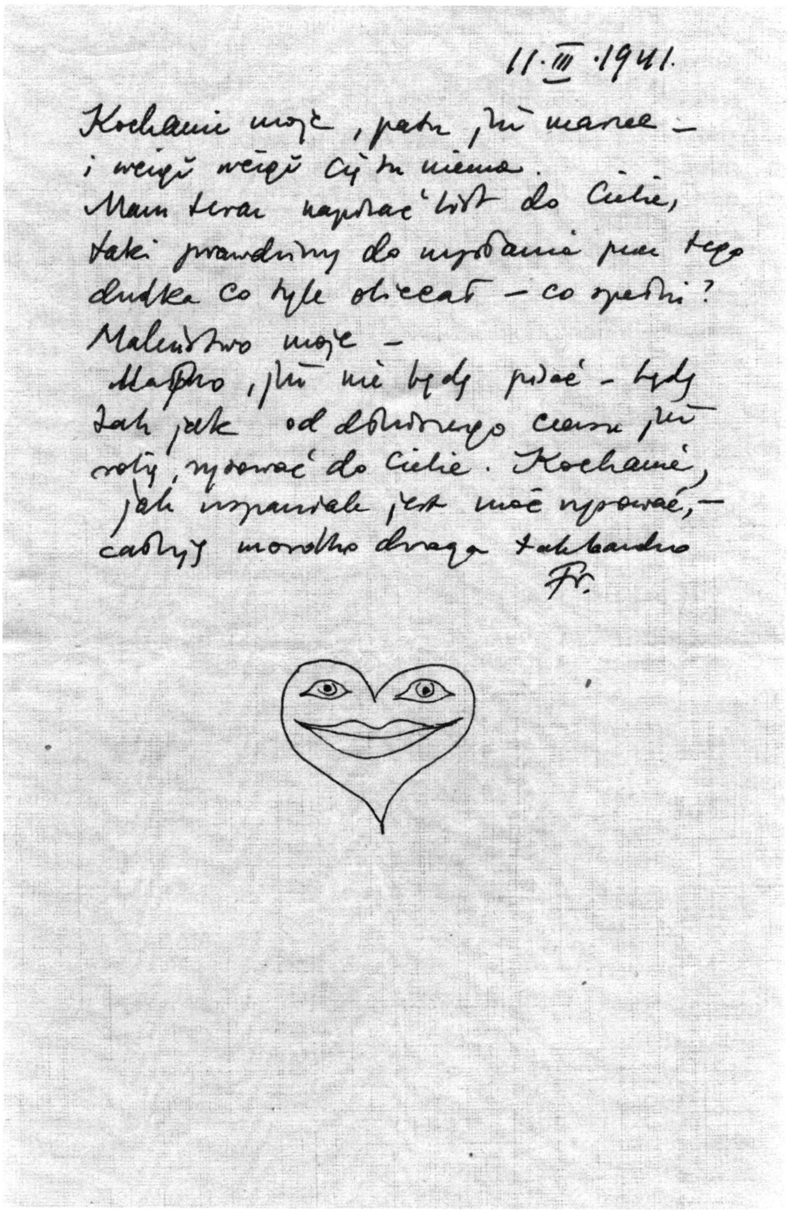

11·III·1941.

Kochanie moje, patrz, już marzec –
i wciąż wciąż Cię tu nie ma.
Mam teraz napisać list do Ciebie,
taki prawdziwy do wysłania przez tego
dudka co tyle obiecał – co zrobi?
Maleństwo moje –
[illegible], już nie będę pisać – będę
tak, jak od dłuższego czasu, już
robię, rysować do Ciebie. Kochanie,
jak wspaniale jest móc rysować, –
całuję mordkę drogą tak bardzo
Fr.

CROIX-ROUGE POLONAISE DE FRANCE

Délégué à MARSEILLE
103. Rue St-Jacques
TELEPHONE DRAGON 38-95

Nr.229.

Marsylia, dnia 10 marca 1941r.

150 frs

Do Pana Stefana Themersona,

Hôtel de la Poste
Voiron. (Isère)

Uprzejmie Pana proszę o podpisanie i zwrot załączonego przy niniejszym kwitu na zapomogę, jaką Pan pobrał w P.C.K. w Marsylii w dniu dzisiejszym, gdyż przez przeoczenie nie pokwitował Pan odbioru jej w odnośnej książce.

Z poważaniem
Delegat okręgowy P.C.K. w Marsylii
w/z.
Paweł Kopocz

1 załącznik

10 March 1941
Letter from Croix Rouge Polonaise de France in Marseille to Stefan

Requesting that Stefan signs a receipt for 150 frs grant-in-aid, which he had forgotten to do.

11 March Diary Entry

Léon Wednesday Tuesday 11
Ford 12.30 rue Dragon
Au Brûleur de Loups, 21h Théâtre d'Essai, rue Savante

Is Brochwicz in Grenoble?
(where is she?) – lieutenant – Ford

M and Mme André Monges and Mlle Marie Claire
58 bd de la Madeleine, Marseille
Hôtel St. Marie

6/7, 7/8, 8/9, 9/10, 10/11 paid 66 francs

'La Géline'

23 × 29 cm	117	frs
26 × 36 cm	142	frs
l'encre	7.25	frs

El. Ricord 8 bd Salvator, Marseille

Post Office (cards)
hotel
office?
12.30 rue Dragon (dedication)

A Marie-Claire [Monges]
Peut-être que TES trouvera le moyen de faire marcher le pont transbordeur et alors nous irons ensemble rejoindre Françoise qui a fait tous ces dessins pour toi.

11 March 1941

Write letters to:
Blanche, Wojciechowski, Franka – through Teresa Żarnower, Mira Złotowska, Aleksander Ford, receipt, Marie Claire Monges, Léon Temerson, someone in Lyon

'La Grande Dynamo Unipolaire'
(Palais de la Découverte) (*L'Illustration* I.III.41)[30]

> ...Des expériences particulièrement frappantes peuvent être réalisées en un point où la totalité du courant de 50000 ampères passe par une tige de cuivre rouge grosse comme le doigt produisant un champ de 20000 gauss: on constate, en particulier, *le changement de longueur d'onde de la lumière* (effet Zeeman).
> espère aff. rep. atens

12 March Diary Entry

Sleep at Spisak's. Stomach [empty]

Telegram from Stefan to Franciszka

CHÉRIE MERCI ATTENDRAI VOIRON AVEC PATIENCE STOP APRÈS RECEVOIR AFFIDAVIT ENCORE FORMALITÉS POUR PLUSIEURS SEMAINES C'EST SEULEMENT POUR TE REJOINDRE N'IMPORTE OÙ QUE JE VEUX PARTIR MAIS PENSES TU À TOI MÊME COMMENT VAS TU SUIS SOUVENT TRÈS INQUIET EMBRASSE SI FORT CHÉRI BAISERS = THEMERSON

13 March Diary Entry

Rent a room (next to Mainssieux)

14 March Telegram from Franciszka to Stefan

CHÉRI ESPÈRE AFFIDAVIT T'AIDERA REJOINDRE GENEK STOP ATTENDANT ESSAYE TRAVAILLER POUR TOI TOUT MON COEUR AVEC TOI SUIS PARFAITEMENT BIEN SOIS TRANQUILLE JE T'AIME MON PETIT TENDRESSES = THEMERSON

Diary Entry

On duty. Telegram from Franka. Letter from Blanche. Receipt to Marseille. Madzia [Turpin]'s story, who becomes convinced that she has a soloist's nature but neither the conditions, nor the means, and she wants to get rid of the piano.

On a separate piece of paper list of journals that Stefan would like to have.

– *Cinéma Suisse*
27 rue du Marché, Berne
– *Arts et Théâtre* 14.III
57 rue de Montchoisy, Genève
– *Ici et Ailleurs* 14 III
7 rue J.A. Gautier, Genève
– *Scène*
88 rue Carouge, Genève 14.III

30 An article by Pierre Devaux in *L'Illustration* 5112

– *Magazine*
1 av de la Harpe, Lausanne 15.III
– *Le Radio*
13 av de Beaulieu, Lausanne
– *Revue Suisse du Cinéma*
15 rue du Midi, Lausanne

Remangé et Liffran

Monsieur,
Je vous serais très obligé de vouloir bien m'envoyer un exemplaire spécimen de votre revue '… ' en vue d'un éventuel abonnement. En vous remerciant d'avance, je vous prie M d'agréer mes salutations distinguées.

Letter from Stefan to Franciszka

Darling Franek, I have just received almost simultaneously three of your letters – from November, January and February. Franeczko, I send you so many kisses.

I am once more here, this old wreck of a place but I have rented a room for myself, so I am not all the time in a crowd, I have my own table and an inkwell and I think that maybe I'll get down to something after all. For, apart from that, one just has to wait patiently and for a long time.

Here it's already real spring. I have already seen hyacinths and I must buy them – for you and simultaneously also as a present from you .

You ask about our acquaintances. The whole of August, September and half of October I spent together with Mietek B[ibrowski], [Ludwik] Lille, I lived for a time at Mme Clavel's; my cousin – Tema [Kaliszer], who was with us in the hotel before my departure, and her sister – showed themselves to be so exceptionally nice and helpful. I had also seen Zber and Horowicz. Edvard K. was also there, although I did not meet him once. Afterwards Chonchon [Sacha Bronstein] also arrived. I was embarrassed in the end to have to run away from them all, but since all the means by which I tried to learn something about you had failed, I decided to try my luck by myself.

And I recently met many acquaintances again. Léon and Nadia [Temerson] and the Ortamberts and Henri and wife (I saw them almost daily). They'll be going to America within a month. I also met there Schorov and Nadelman. He received a letter from Lonia [Janecka, née Nadelman], she writes that they are all working and father and she in their professions and earn quite well. She asks what has happened to Stefan Konorski. Sometimes, you know Franek, I was wondering whether we shouldn't realistically consider everything before even wanting to see Sewek again.[31]

In Grenoble are Danuta Seweryńska and Halina Lichtenberg. Bol Miciński is also there with wife, sister and daughter, as well as Paczkowski. Here, among others are [Michał] Spisak (composer) and [Władysław] Jahl, painter, with whom I am very close, and also Miss Rozenblat, with whom we were once long ago with Stefan in a Chinese restaurant.

I shall write to [Mieczysław] Wojciechowski now. Already many months ago I saw his name in the list of people searching for others looking for me, but here in the Red Cross they couldn't tell me anything.

About Zielenkiewicz(es) I have heard nothing.

31 Before even thinking of returning to Poland.

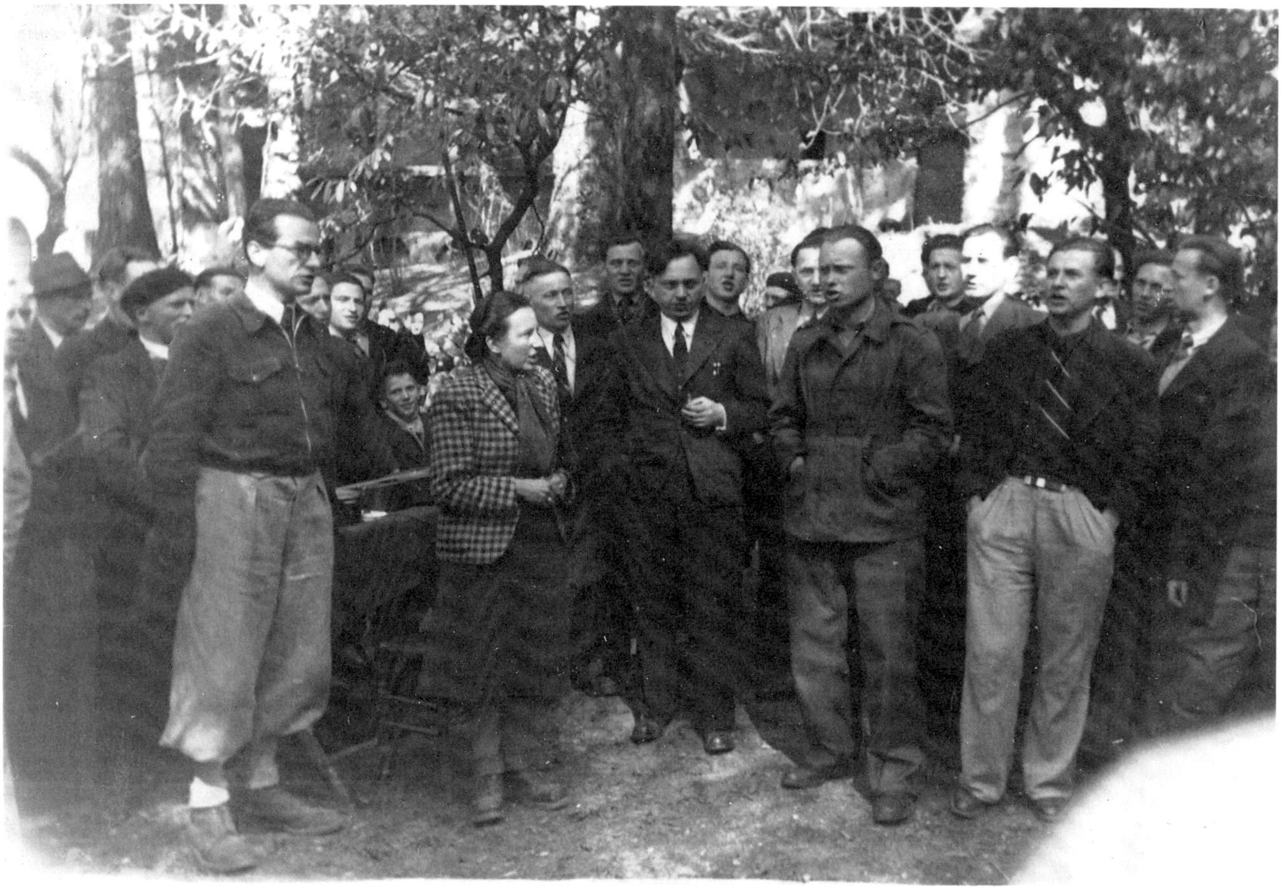

This photograph was found on the internet in a collection of photographs by Casimir Zdziarski. Stefan is on the left, 1941/42, Voiron

14 March 1941

However, could you find what has happened to Misiek? In May he was in Deux-Sèvres. His wife and children have no information about him so far.

My darling, I have just received your telegram. Thank you. Ah, I can imagine with what tremendous effort these affidavits were won! Franeczko.

I rented a room in town for myself and at last I am alone. I don't know if I'll do anything worthwhile, but I shall try to work. And wait. I kiss you my darling such a lot. Please write to me at length so that I may know how you live darling and what you are thinking.

Give a hug for me to all old and new friends, I so want all to go well for you, and for you to be happy despite it all. So often this depends only on ourselves.

And, we must not get frightened, mustn't magnify things that aren't anything to do with the individual but the result and the cause of great populations living together. These processes seem like physical phenomena. We get wet in the rain but we have no influence on its falling, even though to us it often seems otherwise. So many things are determined! What fantastic times for the sociologist, the economist, etc. For it is a matter of self interest and not of existence. Existence is that common denominator that a scientist extracts from these great populations. The single individual lives with self interests. Sometimes these don't have much in common with economics. And then a month of adventure is just a bit more boring than a week of loneliness. I embrace you passionately and kiss you – Stefan

16 March Diary Entry

Tourism is somewhat relative. Moving on something that doesn't move. Now, however, when all have reshuffled themselves throughout the world, one loses the taste for tourism.

There is probably an art in which the artist, like a camera with a film for taking infra-red or other pictures, discovers worlds that are unknown directly to the senses. He brings them into a visible spectrum, graspable time etc. Some astronomical, microscopic photographs have all the characteristics of a work of art. Man's contribution – the frame, trimming of the edges. Weren't such artists as van Gogh, Monticelli or Delacroix effectively cameras with photographic plates from outside the boundaries of the visible spectrum? Maybe these worlds are just inside them and maybe they are only a reflection – but so what? They exist.

Art as discovery of worlds.
Automatic art.

Great smarkata [32]

About Encyclopædias of the World

Greek: *en - dans, kuklos - cercle, paideia - enseignement; ensemble complet des connaissances.*

Definition of the encyclopædia in encyclopædias is imperfect, incomplete – nowhere does it say that it is a beautiful thing.

Everyone has his own private encyclopædia and they don't correspond to one another.

32 A girl wet behind the ears

Development of the encyclopædia, is rather the passage from one to the other. Because, all of them, equally well or equally badly, define the truth. Description of the ideal truth, or the truth of the future always defines, not itself, but the man who invented it, or the man who believes in it.

To a professor [who is a] fish seeking the truth, would our way of looking at the world be of a higher level? If that were the case, then her search for the truth should depend on changing herself, adapting herself to life in the air, to a warm-blooded brain. But somebody said that man is closer to absolute truth than fish. Man to his own truth and fish its own, and they can exist side by side. (Objective and subjective truths – 2 and 3 March.)

'A girl from a very, very ancient tribe took a handful of glowing ashes and threw them at the sky. And the sparks became stars.' – a fragment of a primordial encyclopædia. The Bible; *Don Quixote* and literature of chivalry; travel literature of the 17th century, Gothic art, French encyclopædia, encyclopædia of technology such as Meyer's encyclopædia[33]. Talent of the reader. Cinema, the press, radio as encyclopædias of our times – of our social and economic conditions, life's difficulties. If they held onto something with their hands, how could they 'talk'? [Meaning that gestures are necessary to accompany verbal communication.] (See also 26 March on encyclopædias.) To talk in the spirit of quiet, disinterested consideration. (An anecdote about an armless Jew who could not talk on the telephone.)[34] Reader's confidence in the printed word (Kokoszko, and own correspondence, etc). Violent acts planned over coffee in the Ziemiańska café. A filter for one's own sins, a sort of beam or a little sun [maybe stories in children's magazines] – a story about a Negro on a bicycle and a Jewish girl at the back of a crowd. Judgments based on feelings. (See below.) American advertising the same as propaganda, but at least price is shown at once.

> '... Inutile d'ouvrir la bouche avec cet air, enfin... abruti' – dit Voloquine – 'Le monde croit Han-Kéou communiste, tant mieux. Ça fait honneur à notre propagande. Ce n'est pas une raison pour que ce soit vrai' (*La Condition Humaine* by André Malraux)

Judgments and Feelings
Terminology – from convention, judgments from feelings.
Experience – theory of probability – a little inner machine to make calculations.
The truth of Plato's ideas, the truth of appearances, the truth of Galileo.

Progress visible within an epoch, but not between one epoch and another. It is clear in art, but also everywhere. The development of new science – it is still one epoch. Progress between the 20th century and the 19th century, but it does not make sense to talk about progress in relation to the primary concepts, etc.

Quotations from Geoffroy Atkinson's *Les Relations de Voyages du XVII siècle*[35]

About progress

> Il se peut bien que l'auteur n'emploie pas les termes "progrès", "amender", "améliorer" ou "remédier". Mais l'idée de progrès,

33 *Meyers Konversations-Lexikon*, German encyclopædia, editions from 1839.

34 [even if no-one could see him he could not speak without gesturing – or just that he couldn't hold the 'phone to his mouth and ear – in which case, why a Jew?] A similar anecdote: two Italians used to go for a walk together every day. They never spoke in the winter because it was too cold to take their hands out of their pockets.

35 *Les relations de voyages du XVII siècle et l'évolution des idées; contribution à l'étude de la formation de l'esprit XVIII* (1924) [*The extraordinary voyage in French literature before 1700*, Columbia University Press, 1920].

peut-être confuse et encore indistincte, existe déjà dans son esprit, et cela à cause de son expérience, à cause de *faits nouveaux*. Et ce qui est encore plus curieux, c'est que la première citation que nous avons donnée de l'idée de progrès ne traite pas des affaires morales…
(page 188)

… L'idée de perfectionner les hommes est une idée religieuse, et c'est de là qu'elle tire sa force.
(page 188)

Atkinson quotes: Pierre Bayle, *Pensées diverses sur la comète* (1683):

Que l'homme soit une créature raisonnable, tant qu'il vous plaira; il n'en est pas moins vrai, qu'il n'agit presque jamais conséquemment à ses Principes…
(page 192)

… notre vie détruit notre doctrine.
(page 193)

Sketch from nature

Haydn's quartet fills the air of this atelier. I can feel the warmth of the sun, there is a window in a niche just behind me. I rest my head on the window frame. 'This quartet is wonderful', says Szuki. He is sitting next to me, on my right, on a couch. On the left a poet, a bank clerk, an actress, two young men. Sunday, they have time and this is how they spend the afternoon, listening. 'Second bass!', shouts Mainssieux. I don't know what is outside the window, behind me – mountains, Voiron seen from the hillside, I shall not turn round, I feel the sky and space. Ta-ra-ram-tam! Oh, why Mainssieux, at the back a long wisp of hair, like a tassel fell from the bald patch onto his/your nape. Oh why is this wisp so disgusting. It's immoral. You substitute ethics for aesthetics and you are reminded of the dining-room in Płock, lunch – 'what is the difference between ethics and aesthetics?' you asked. What was there for lunch that day? – it occurs to you to wonder. 'C'est difficile', says the viola player? 'Ah, oui c'est difficile'. New quartet? 'Where did Haydn get it from?' asks Szuki. Two yellow curtains, like the blinkers of a cab-horse, screen the sides of the atelier. Behind the curtain on the right, Jahl with a paint box and a stretcher; behind the one on the left, half of Michał and the whole of Mlle Jourdans – the cello. Also behind the left one, a bit further, the two young ones; they probably finished smoking Balto cigarettes, because there is not a trail of smoke in the sun's ray, nor smoke. 'Deux premières petites reprises' commands Mainssieux 'Un…deux…'. Oh, he reminds me of a Chinaman with that wisp of hair; the Chinaman in *Manza*, that novel of my father's. A Chinaman painted by B[36]. Monsieur does not smoke opium, but I feel in him the yellow fluid from my own pipe. It is immoral. Because unaesthetic. The way he manipulates his bow is horrible. And why is there this asinine face, covered in paint, smiling from the very top of a huge mirror frame, hanging straight opposite, at the back of the room? Oh, how Mainssieux hurries and taps with his foot. Michał lights a cigarette. Mlle Jourdans gets up. A young man turns pages of the music score. The viola player turns to Jahl to have a look. 'Je reviens' says Mlle J. and also to Jahl – 'Oh, c'est bien.' 'Il y a un compartiment réservé' – says Mainssieux à propos our niche.

36 *Manza* with a reproduction of a painting by Stefan Bagieński

'Michał, get them to play a bit of Tchaikovsky', says Szuki. 'OK'.

Over the mirror van Gogh's chrysanthemums. They play Dvořák. But no, it isn't van Gogh. And these two on the wall on the right – portrait of a girl and a field are not van Goghs either. I don't want them to be!

Oh, how I should like to cut off Mainssieux's wisp of hair and stick it on this canvas in the gilded frame on the easel. Attach it to the red roof or the pink little cloud in the sky, or I'd like to cover with black this yellow road turning a corner at the crossing. And oh, this whole landscape is to be found in the squeak of his bow. 'Trois, quatre!'

Could one see all these sounds in some perceivable tempo; in a seeable visibility as they strike the wall, the gold frames and canvas. Yes, Monticelli is beautiful, the one on the left of the mirror and on the right. And authentic. And it reveals some normally invisible picture. And is true to itself. And you can neither add anything nor take anything away. 'Pardon!' says Mlle Jourdans. Oh, how this violin squeaks, how it falsifies the truth of the score. And Mainssieux's wisp of hair is swinging to and fro, to and fro. 'It irritates me to hell, this bohemia, this tziganerie, you know?' 'Damn it', says Szuki and goes to the table for cigarettes.

Why, why should the little Delacroix, covered with a red roof and a little pink cloud and the figure turning along the path under the cross be inundated in Mainssieux's inner musical discharge?

Oh, poor Michał, in front of me, half concealed by the yellow curtain – 'Vous avez tellement de belles choses', says Jahl, 'Mozart, Beethoven – pourquoi?' 'Jouons Tchaikovsky' says Michał 'si vous voulez'.

Oh, Michał, do something with your bow to produce pure sound that would exorcise the sham in which this atelier is immersed from floor to ceiling, from the left side with bookshelves full of alchemy and modern astrology and a dictionary of pastels – (200 frs, said Jahl). With a fake van Gogh and the gold frame, Michał on the right of the mirror reflecting the bald head of the bank clerk up to the yellow curtain, that covers sides of the atelier like the blinkers of a cab horse. Szuki rolled me a cigarette.

The sun has moved and I can see the shadow of my own head on the yellow curtain. The cigarette went out. And they play again. And I want to breathe, to breathe, to breathe! But why? You are not here. You are not here.

What happened to a little branch of the apple tree that I placed in a glass so that it will blossom as in the van Gogh? In a matchbox, it travelled for the winter to Marseille and here, the hotel chambermaid threw it away.

Oh, to close these yellow curtains, or to tear them down! Look it is growing, look how fast is growing M.'s wisp. It's taking root in his jacket, in his arched back. Pull it off, pull off this wisp and so rescue the soul of our hapless host.

Man as a fragment of nature
I am a bit of nature that other little bits of nature call Stefan Th.

If my intention here were to describe the world, it would be the intention of nature that wants to see what her image looks like, as seen by one of her fragments.

My toe sees me completely differently from my eye (fragment of my nose, or in the mirror) or by inner feeling. The two images different and perhaps even contradictory, are at the same time true.

Truth is not reality. Truth is a picture of reality (projected).

There is no precipice between me and the rest of nature, on the contrary, with each cell of my body I participate in her very self – everything I consist of was, is, and will be her after I die.

I don't have free will. Everything is decreed. Forces contained in me (that is me myself) compel, dictate. Sometimes, what I am compelled to do gives me pleasure, sometimes pain. It is not a reason to talk about real choice (what is pleasure and pain, etc?) I am writing these words because there exists a compulsion that dictates them to me.

I haven't the slightest reason to assume that behind this compulsion there are not forces that can be examined through physico-chemical means.

But what is the awareness of this compulsion (and those pleasures and pains)?

One could create a model of an ideal robot that would develop its own individuality by itself, a robot that would be taught (roulette, theory of probability, predictable traces that would erase themselves and the probability of such and not other connections would gradually increase with the robot's age). One could imagine self-construction of the whole centre of communications of individual subconscious in such a 'Man-Machine'. But consciousness alone would be left in our hands. Would that really be so? Wouldn't our hands be empty?

Relativism
Does nature have places that are less important and more important? (What does it mean 'important'?)

Denominations of political trends are denominations of something dictated by the existing form of a given developing philosophy.

Galileo – bodies fall at the same speed. Poet – pink bodies fall slower than the black ones. Why should Galileo's chronometer be absolute and our senses unequipped with a chronometer – 'illusory'. One is true in its context, as the other is true in its context. Two truths that can exist side by side, at the disposal of two observers. Since the times of Galileo, Europeans and then Americans started to build not only concepts, but also a world on the basis of the chronometer. If the result testified that Galileo was correct, this would seriously compromise him. Absolute truths are as human as truths that are 'illusory'. These and the others were created by man, who sometimes persuades himself of having made discoveries or revelations; he creates truths of nature in the same way that he creates symphonies, scores and staves. – And the one and the other can tell something about the world and about nature only inasmuch as their author is this nature's fragment.

If we are fragments of something for which we created the word: nature, then the old banality about 'forces lying dormant in man', will prove to be not without sense.

In London German air raids resume. Perhaps this is why there is no news from Franciszka until 25 March.

20 March Diary Entry

Yesterday 19th, Józef Żmigrodzki's nameday

Sketch from memory

Table in itself is neither bad nor good, neither decent nor obscene. When we sit at it – it is useful. When somebody blocks our door with a table – it is bad.

Man, in himself is neither bad nor good. A. is like this and B. is different. Oh, I prefer, I prefer A. But you prefer B. For X, A is good and B is bad. For Y, B is good, but A bad.

X and Y thread through everything of and not of this world, forming the red line of their judgment and pronouncing all things on the left to be good, all on the right to be bad. And the world covers itself with a net of demarcation lines, intersecting, entangled with one another, and everyone wants his own line to be absolute.

And it's strange, that those who are most persistent about their share of the world are those who have so-called social awareness. They fail to draw logical conclusions from their own premises – if it is true that everything, or even nearly everything is determined; if a given man is the result of processes and circumstances in which he lives, and which form him, then his opinions are not something absolute but the results of these processes, just as the production of a factory is the result of the whole economic life of a country, along with dirty tricks [totally unacceptable behaviour], etc. Do you, Wolf and Żmigrodzki, really need the awareness that the products of your intellect are something 'more' absolute? Do you really need to turn science into religion by seasoning it with beliefs? – The element that precludes the simultaneous existence of a truth other than ours. Truth is something personal. And two different individuals, formed by different circumstances cannot live by the same truth because it cannot, for both of them, correspond to reality. Nature – said [Sir James] Jeans – does not disclose its absolute truth; it only answers the question that man asks. – And people ask all sorts of questions and there cannot be just one answer.

Even in science there exist side by side apparently contradictory truths, but consistent with reality like the wave-particle duality. And one cannot choose one or the other, for what one theory explains the other does not.

Tides of probability
Ah, I don't mind that you think differently from me. You cannot think in the same way, neither can I, because we are two different characters in this performance, because we are two exhibits of this zoo. And even if you are a lion and I am a monkey, where is it written that a lion's truth is more perfect than a monkey's?

People and things that are all around are like physical phenomena, like rain, like temperature, like undulations, electrical activity, or a storm. We are elements of these phenomena and at the same time we are their product. We magnetise each other. But even if I am a little snow crystal in the shape of a star melting on the ground and you are the lightning pirouetting in the clouds, where is there a place for making hierarchies? And why should your electrical truth be more perfect than my biological mystery when I sink into the earth and a lily-of-the-valley will drink me up with its roots?

You want the poet to create a revolution. That he should do everything that belongs to heroes, to scientists, and that at which ministers fail. You want poetry to be the means of achieving a goal. To be the means of achieving a goal – that is the calamity of Polish poetry. And you say contemptuously: art for art's sake, without recognising what it really means; forgetting that one can talk about art just like engineers talk about a car, without worrying about who will drive it. No not art for art's sake; but equally not art for revolution. But a revolution for art.

You have something against the poet for writing lyrical verses. And you explain to him, smashing the already open door, that he himself is the product of his times. Change the times and in that way create a new poet. Because if you change only the man – you will lose the poet.

Michał about Erwin Wolff: he lines everybody up against the wall, but he won't shoot anyone.

Master is jealous about Madzia.

21 March Diary Entry

Grenoble

Sketch from nature
'Taverne des Dauphins' ORCHESTRE tous les jours, à partir de 15.30.
Clock like a huge daisy, with a number on every petal, shows 6.30. Outside the window, they are still walking about (not from the Marshal's reception, who was here day before yesterday).

No lending library
Museum
Found *Tricoti* and *Cochon*[37]

37 *Tout en Soie – Cochon aérodynamique* and *Tricoti Tricota* by May d'Alençon, illustrated by Franciszka, in the series 'Albums du Père Castor'. Paris, 1939. See overleaf

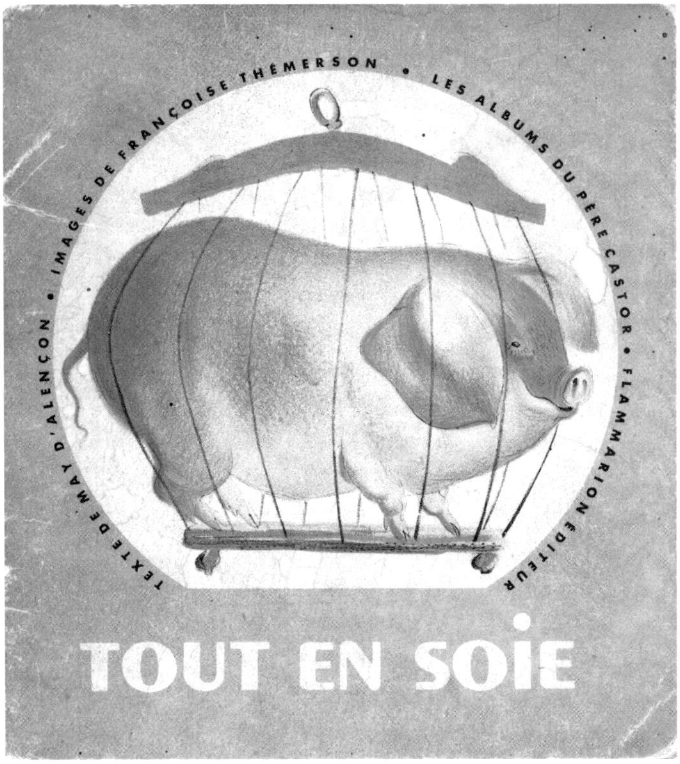

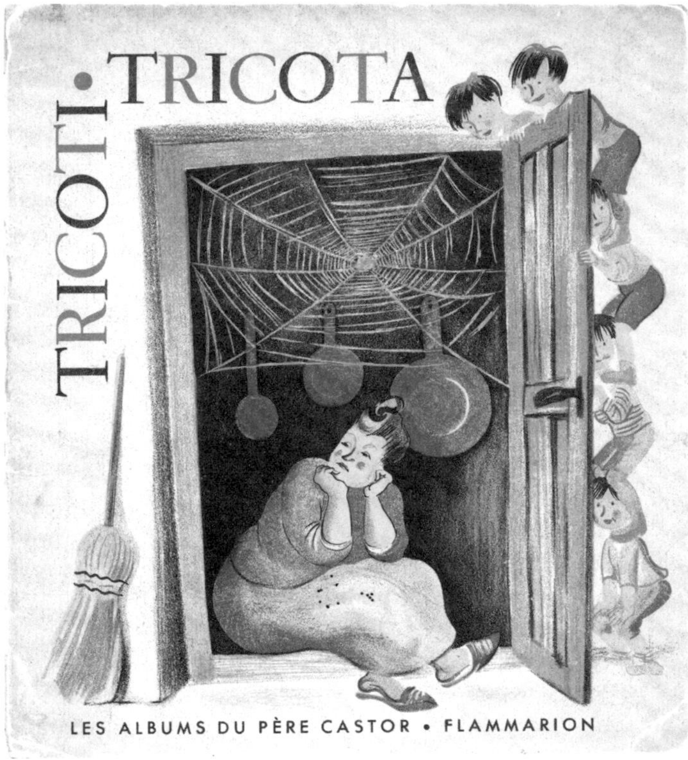

22 March **Diary Entry**

Voiron

<u>Sketch from nature</u>

Ah, wait a minute, till this wagon has gone by, with its iron wheels clattering on the pavement and the insistent ringing of the silver bells attached to the horses' necks that became elongated like the necks of giraffes to lift their ringing heads even up to the first floor, towards my window, to insinuate them inside, to look with interest around my room and to ring. The wagon, listen, is moving away, but in the window, still the ringing heads smile and sneer. Scent of the hyacinth. 'Et comment va votre plante?' asked Mainssieux today, drinking coffee at Vial's. 'Merci, elle va très bien'. I poured some water and my hyacinth drinks it through the hole at the bottom of the flowerpot.

I read *Sainte Jeanne*, Bernard Shaw

24 March **Diary Entry**

I finished 'Dno nieba' [Bottom of the sky] and read it to Jahl. He encourages me to publish it somehow.

<u>Michał about his grandfather</u>

84 years old. Lecher. He jumped off a tram after a woman and broke three fingers. White beard to the waist and white hair. Mother threw out the pomades. He boiled extract of chestnuts. And became a redhead. He subscribes to lonely hearts magazines. Writes letters, sends photographs of himself when young. Receives letters that they steam open. About spring, about birds and photographs of ladies.

24 March 1941

Once I managed to visit him. He was getting ready during the entire morning
– returned in the evening wretched.
An architect, squandered all his money on prostitutes.

Sent telegrams
Letter to Mira
I send a book to Marie Claire Monges

25 March **Telegram from Stefan to Franciszka**

CHÉRIE ATTENDS AVEC CONFIANCE MOMENT OÙ JE POURRAIS TE REJOINDRE ENFIN NOUS NOUS RENCONTRERONS PLUS VIEUX MAIS PAS MOINS HEUREUX VEUX TRAVAILLER POUR MOI MÊME HÉLAS C'EST PAS FACILE ET TOI SUIS TELLEMENT ASSOIFFÉ NOUVELLES DE TOI AMITIÉS À NOS AMIS EMBRASSE CHÉRIE = THEMERSON

Diary Entry

Conversations, books don't imprint [themselves] on my memory, just play on the keyboard of the brain cells and vanish. That's why I just don't remember. I know nothing, have nothing, apart from a recollection of the whole, memory of tastes, moods, but also truths.

Conversation with Lipski. Actors who can impose themselves on the audience are rare. They would sell their mother and father for a murmur from the audience.
I think that, in the theatre, houselights are turned off not to see the stage better but so that actors will not see the audience.

Lipski's story about his beginnings with Jaracz in 1922. He was with Hryniewicz. Escaped. He caught up with Jaracz in a taxi. 'Why are you trembling so much?', 'I am moved, Master – etc.' He invited Lipski to his place. Tea. 'Go on, tell me about yourself.' He talks about himself, that he wants to go on the stage – but for him it is a hazardous road (external circumstances?). Jaracz – that he will take care of him. The role in *Judas Iskariot* [38]. He overdoes it. He should speak with his own voice, 'naturally'. 'Yes, sir, but perhaps…' 'Go ahead! Get on with it! Stop in the middle of a sentence and be the part.'

'When you came to me for the first time – I was impressed by you. I was tremendously moved. You talked about yourself simply and expressively.
I thought you were worthwhile. If you could speak like that on the stage you would be better than me. But don't be so pleased, dear boy. It's not that easy.'

Divine Comedy [39]
Heaven with all its acknowledged saints and hell with 'wicked' sinners.

Gulliver or Sebastian in a strange city.

Time – 30 days per second. Voice equals light. This speed is not a process but a state (carousel). A mountain that is falling apart, all the time falling apart and all the time is – falling apart.

38 Tragedy by Karol Hubert Rostworowski.
39 Perhaps Stefan's idea for a film.

Galileo – when Gulliver went through the wall, etc. downstairs, a cloakroom with pink clothes so that the ones who enter should be lighter.

Gulliver visiting the earth – inversion in the mirror.

A stoker, whose work consists of thinking to make the locomotive move.

Musicians take forms into their hands, polish them, smooth them and arrange them into buildings one listens to.

A novel with the characters in the novel

Tartuffe (rehabilitation)
Scrooge (social scientific justifications)
Hamlet (a real man, not in bronze)
Don Quixote

Telegram from Stefan to Franciszka

CHÉRIE AFFIDAVITS PAS ENCORE ARRIVAIENT JE DEMANDE HICEM MARSEILLE PAYER VOYAGE NÉCESSAIRE POUR VISA AMÉRIQUE PORTUGAISE APRÈS SANS INVITATION PEUX PAS L'AVOIR AVANT N'AS TU PAS PRIS MON PASSEPORT MEGARDE TOUTES FORMALITÉS QUELQUES MOIS QUAND POURRAIS TE REVOIR CHÉRIE TENDRESSES BAISERS = THEMERSON

26 March **Diary Entry**

Children are the slaves of adults
The old – of the younger
Today those aged between 18 and 30 have the most to say. And individuals of this age forget that time passes.
(modern pedagogy – a free child – is connected with pedagogy).
this is one of the sections – freedom, slavery. There are more.

Encyclopædia itself is an element of the world (created by a man).
The world called primeval was also an element of the world but not the world, pictures of it were also created by a man.

> J'affirme que le XIXe siècle, et plus encore le XXe peuvent mettre le XVe siècle dans leur poche, en ce qui concerne leur capacité de croyance en merveilles et en miracles, en saints et en prophètes, en magiciens, et en monstres et en contes de fées de tous genres. La proportion du merveilleux par rapport aux récits immédiatement croyables est infiniment plus grande dans la dernière édition de l'Encyclopædia Britannica que dans la Bible.
> Shaw – Préface *Sainte Jeanne.*

João Brandão
sister, Nita Brandão Wikińska
João's father (Francisco?) worked in the Portuguese Consulate in Paris. The old Brandão left Paris for Portugal in June 1940. João was a Portuguese speaker in Paris, and moved south, presumably he left for Portugal. What happened to them and what's their address, via the radio/broadcasting station? João – quite well known as a singer. He sang in the Lisbon Radio-Club.
E. Wolf's address and where is M. Wikiński?
Must ask Teresa

Maksamin, Delegate of the Ministry of Welfare, visa section

27 March **Letter from Stefan to Franciszka**

My darling Franeczko, I kiss you so much and am still, still together with you. I wrote to you already that I rented myself a room, this is the most significant event in this my *patelin*, and at last I have somewhere to be alone with my own thoughts. I am working a bit, I am only writing poems – I am becoming so very 'lyricised', and all sorts of loose notes, from which one will be able to draw when thought, like wine will have matured. Next to me, a white hyacinth, for you and from you, fills the room with its scent. On the wall, two small pictures by Jahl, a painter with whom I have made friends here. I was recently in Grenoble, in a bookshop, and I found your Flammarion books. Now I have them on the table, the two books with your drawings. I would so much like to see you at last, although I know that it is going to take months at least.

I received your letters – from November and from 8 March. I wrote yesterday to Teresa [Żarnower]. Ah, darling, how much trouble you've had on my behalf! Here, I can only wait. Only after receiving the affidavits will the applications begin for an American visa (several weeks for sure), and then the Portuguese, the Spanish, and only then the exit visa. I can get it only thanks to the fact that I have never been in military service and because of my heart I am not fit for it now. Prepaid travel is necessary to get a Portuguese visa: But, darling, you can't have so much money. When I have the affidavits, I shall try in Marseille in Hicem and I hope that they will do it for me.

Having a Portuguese visa, perhaps it would be possible to go from Switzerland by air to Lisbon. And perhaps one could get a Portuguese visa on the basis of Genek's invitation or that of his friends. I know that in Lisbon there is a quota of 1000 visas for Poles, under the administration of Maksamin, former delegate of the Ministry of Welfare. I expect he is an acquaintance of Adam [Pragier]. I should like to meet Mira and Ignacy, but only in the event that you could do it too. Because my only reason for leaving here would be to be closer to you. Ah, darling, I don't know what could be sensible for you and what your wishes are. After my stay in Marseille I realised that I shall be sitting here still for long months to come, and time passes now both slowly and quickly simultaneously.

Darling, is your work very onerous? I so wish that you could arrange a quiet and pleasant life for yourself, despite everything and against everything.

How are all our friends, and what are they up to? Stefanja and Adam, Stefan (Lonia asked her brother, whom I met in Marseille, for his address), Genek. I asked in Grenoble about Wojciechowski – he left, already a long time ago, for Brazil, and is at the moment in Dakar. And what about Lindenfelds?

I haven't had any news from home for a very long time, since Hania [Kawa] stopped writing. I don't know if I can write to them direct.

Darling kiss you so much and I await your letter in which there would be a lot, a great deal about you. Love – Stefan

Léon and Nadia and the Ortamberts are going soon to New York.

Letter from Stefan to Franciszka – another version of the letter above

Darling, I got your two letters, one still from November and one from 8 March. So many long weeks, well, months, one will still have to wait patiently to get through all the formalities.

Chronologically, it looks like this – after getting the affidavits one has to try for the American visa. This takes a long time. Once you have it in your pocket you have to try to get a Portuguese one. For this one needs a prepaid passage to New York. (To pay for this, one can apply in Marseille to Hicem – that's several weeks.) However, it is possible that an invitation from Genek would be sufficient to get a Portuguese visa. In Lisbon there is a visa quota, under the management of Maksamin, a delegate of the Ministry of Welfare. Once one has a Portuguese visa, it is necessary to apply for a Spanish visa and at the same time for a French exit visa. This last one is the most difficult to get and I can count on it only thanks to the fact that I have never been in military service and that I am not fit for it because of my heart.

Having entry and exit visas one would have a chance of getting to New York direct. With a Swiss visa, one can go by air to Lisbon (that is rather expensive, 6000 French francs). At this moment one cannot do anything here – one has to wait for the affidavits. Naturally, I would like to see Ignacy but only together with you. Darling, I worry about you so often! I already wrote to you that after my return I rented for myself my own room and I am trying to work a bit. I kiss you darling so very many times. Stefan

Diary Entry

In Tunis the father of the bride must touch her forehead with each coin of her dowry.

28 March **Telegram from Franciszka to Stefan**

CHÉRI MERCI TIENS TOI MON PETIT JE VAIS PARFAITEMENT BIEN J'ESSAIE AUSSI TRAVAILLER POUR MOI OU PLUTÔT POUR TOI CHÉRI EMBRASSE LE PLUS TENDREMENT AMIS SALUENT = THEMERSON

Diary Entry

Piotrowski about confession. He will not go because he has double food rations. He had been turning it over in his mind for a long time and decided not to go (a lawyer). In the evening Budzyński's farewell.

29 March **Diary Entry**

Subject: Sebastian in a city where he is taken for somebody else. (Recognising a man by his apartment in Jacques-Callot. Sebastian is a policeman.)
Variation: (already thought of some time ago) Sebastian goes on a tour of a human being just like one tours a city.
Variation II an epic – journey through people like through cities. New Gulliver.

29 March 1941

Related theme: Sebastian's country. Dark objects fall faster than light ones.
Stealing the sunset. 11 Gulliver
Variation on a theme : novel about crime and nationalism
Diary: the simplest things in the style of the Bible
Fragment of variation on a theme: criminal fiction – Voiron
index

30 March

Vichy Government appoints a Commission to deal with Jewish Questions.

Diary Entry

Bread-sun is more of a metaphor.

Metaphor is something different from a simile. 'Love is like light'. With equal justification, one can say 'love is like night'. Neither one nor the other says anything about love; it is not a concept, it refers only to the momentary feelings of the author and nothing more. Whereas the metaphor 'light of love', 'blackness of love' – is a concept that with equal clarity can be used like the concepts: table, warmth, silence.

1. If you create *metaphors* in which the round loaf of the sun rolls golden out into the sky, why don't you write about a miraculous butcher who sits on the throne of the cathedral and hangs out bleeding meat on the gothic towers? Why don't you write about flocks of white clouds floating under his axe bearing blood from the wound of the red rose on the horizon? Why don't you write about crowds engrossed in prayer, who raise their eyes from down below to the skyline up here, draped with the beef-steaks of the sunset? If midday smells of a bakery, then the sunset smells of raw meat.

2. There are fewer and fewer things around not created by a man. Only this little bit of air you do not feel because you swim in it, only this little bit of sky which is a hole between roofs; and this is why the moisture of rain soaks through body and penetrates the bones – it is like a revelation and a caution.

3. Don't talk about a sun baked in a bakery unless you are also prepared to talk about that bleeding sunset of the butcher's. So little of the world has remained untouched. Don't let your metaphor take away those last surviving scraps.

Until recently Zeus was somebody else. Since my visit to Montpellier he is that man drinking wine.

31 March Letter from Franciszka to Stefan

Stefciu, my darling, a few days ago I received a telegram from you. Thank you darling. My pet, I feel that things are not well with you and that you're sad. Hold on child, after all we must, we must at last be together.

It is so very hard and endless.

Are you able, have you started to work a bit?

That is the only thing that can help us to endure all this.

I am drawing a bit recently and I miss you so terribly! To talk, to talk in some human way! To make sense of things. To sort things out, to clarify what's going on.

Here, one lives in such confusion of ideas, problems, sacrifices, personal interests and petty harassments, in such a crowd of good and bad idiots that we have to hold each other's hand firmly not to drown. Do you feel, darling, that I am always holding your hand?

Memento Magnitudinis! But, how difficult it is to keep great things in one's mind.

You know, sometimes, only the recollection of your words, or imagining how you will react to a given situation, allows me not to lose confidence in my own mind. Because sometimes I don't know if it's me that's so stupid, or if all those around me are idiots. It is not out of the question that both are true.

Darling, I don't know when you will get this letter, perhaps you will already be on your way. Oh, Stefan! I am so frightened of that journey for you!

You probably want to have some ordinary news about me and about how I live. You know, really, almost too well, – embarrassingly so! I am still living together with Genek [Cękalski] and Zośka Wojciechowska. Her husband left Marseille already in January for Rio and got stuck somewhere in Africa. I don't know if he dreamt about such travels when he was a small boy.

Genek, as usual, is working in a somewhat pseudo-artistic mess. Maybe you will lend support to his activities. He wanted me to work together with him but I preferred my regular boring work. Zośka is quite sensible and is one, among very few people here, with whom I can talk with a degree of understanding, at least on some subjects. Stefan [Konorski] is, as usual, 'a friend of the house', very loyal and warm.

Any other 'circles of friends', that is just about zero and abomination of sorts.

Stefanja is a complete idiot. The novel, of which you read the beginning, but which she re-lives here all the time, is a hysterical crime story and discussions with her result in a belly ache. Anyway, she has always been potentially stupid.

The rest are more or less educated in their professions. Their unpleasant characteristic is that they don't realise how deficient they are in good will. This whole milieu is truly a perfect school for cynicism.

Darling, do you know, that I have had from you only one single letter? Dear child, write, write! If you knew how much it means to me. After all I don't really know anything about you. Letters travel so slowly, but you see my pet, time passes and they arrive in the end.

I kiss you darling such a lot. Franka

Diary Entry

I copy for Żmigrodzki his manuscript about the organisations of mounted religious orders, that is about the Teutonic Knights and about Grunwald.[40]

strength in me heroism – in them brutality
in me pride – in them insolence
in me Polish wisdom – in them shiftiness and slyness

Private encyclopædia

40 Battle of Grunwald, 1410.

Stasio went to see his mother
Netzel visited Wandzia: the Rozenblats
They did some drinking too.
Patyna with a crazy look in his eyes came the following day to Netzel and hit him in the face.
So the judge of the supreme tribunal of the Polish Red Cross shelter in Voiron is coming, and there will be a trial.

Stupidity, naivety, law, papal court, patriotism, intrigues, plunder.
This is how the twentieth century socialist writes about fourteenth and fifteenth century feudalism. It is to science what the Bible is to physics.

Isn't there in Grenoble, Copernicus-Wasiutyński?
240 grams of bread per day

1 April Diary Entry

Tragedy isn't, as it would seem, the consequence of coincidences that appear like *deus ex machina* in the theatre. We shall always arrive at tragedy, whichever side/truth/idea we adopt, and as long as we are consistent, logical and fair in our thinking. Because the world is tragic. There is not a single truth for everything that exists and happens – perhaps with the exception only of observing it from the side – from the margins.

If you participate and are honest – you are tragic.

Tragedy is a more consistent and a more unequivocal resolution of a situation than holding onto what one believes.

Even a pacifist, who, only wishing for the victory of one of the sides, participates in war – is tragic.

A pacifist who remained a pacifist is illogical, he is an artlessly illogically thinking man (even though he may be an honest pacifist). A militarist participating in a war is a happy man.

2 April Diary Entry

I copy 'Płowce'[41] for Żmigrodzki.
One would need a Shaw for this subject.

Żmigrodzki tells an anecdote about a lecture by Prof. Florian Znaniecki, who came from Poznań to Kalisz. That the Church's role today = zero, but in the Middle Ages it was extraordinarily fruitful and all encompassing. 'Nothing induces me to confirm this apart from objective scientific truth, because I myself am a non-practising Catholic and don't go to confession.'

Headmistress of the school: 'And so… I thank you, Professor, for this lecture.'
A week later all the headmasters of all secondary schools went to confession.

41 Battle of Płowce between invading Teutonic Knights and King Władysław I, 1331, the victory was not conclusive.

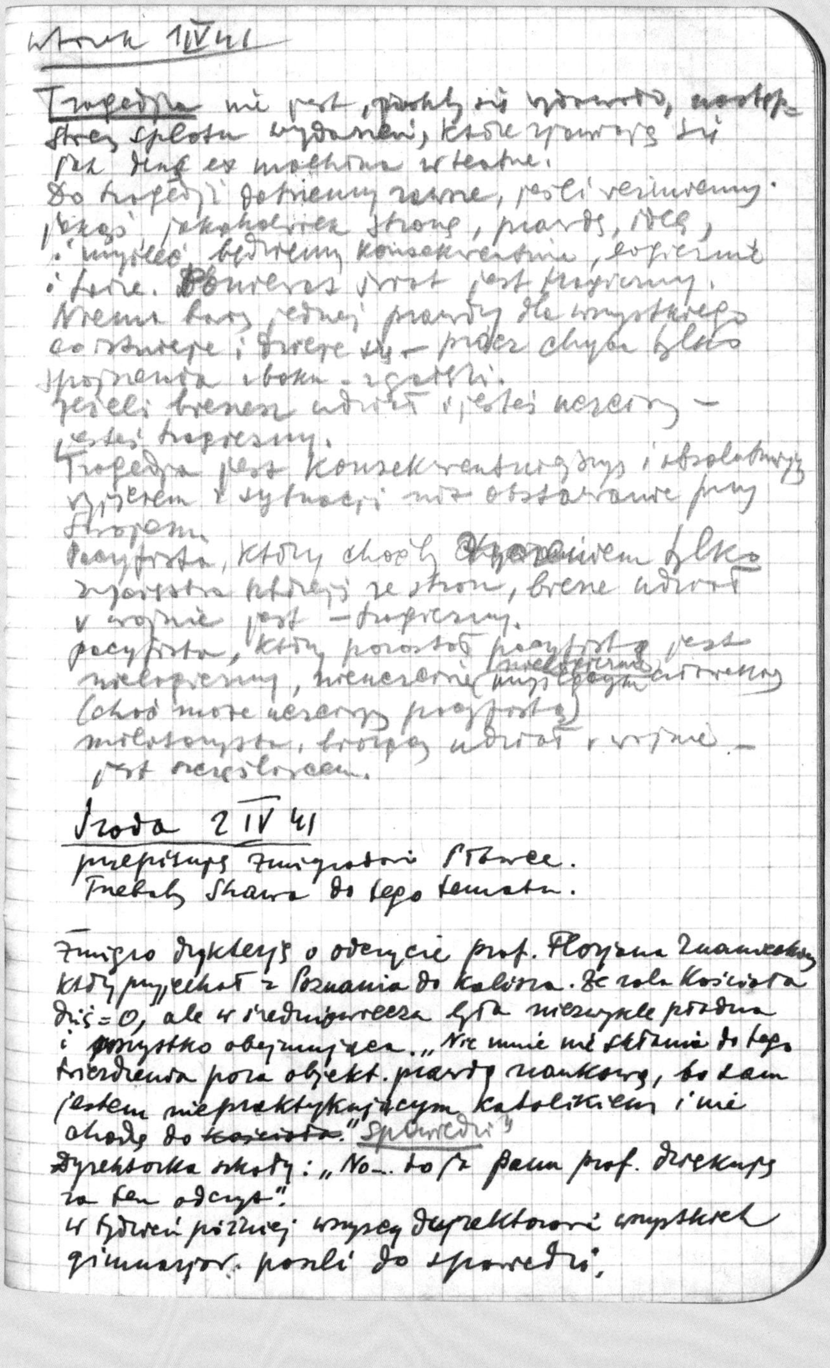

Wtorek 1 IV 41

Tragedia nie jest, jak by się wydawało, następstwem splotu wydarzeń, które [illegible] się jak deus ex machina w teatrze.
Do tragedii potrzebni jesteśmy sami, jeśli rezygnujemy. Wziąć jakąkolwiek stronę, prawdę, ideę, i myśleć będziemy konsekwentnie, [illegible] i [illegible]. Bohater sam jest tragiczny.
Niema tragedii jednej prawdy dla wszystkiego co istnieje i dzieje się — prócz chyba błota [illegible] [illegible].
Jeżeli bierzesz udział i jesteś uczciwy — jesteś tragiczny.
Tragedia jest konsekwentnym dążeniem i absolutnym wyborem w sytuacji nie [illegible] przy stronach.
Pacyfista, który chociażby [illegible] tylko [illegible] którejś ze stron, bierze udział w wojnie jest — tragiczny.
Pacyfista, który pozostał pacyfistą jest nietragiczny, niewczesny ([illegible]) (choć może uczciwy pacyfista) [illegible], bo [illegible] udział w wojnie — jest [illegible].

Środa 2 IV 41

przepisuję [illegible] [illegible].
Trzeba by Shawa do tego tematu.

[illegible] dyktuję o odczycie prof. Floriana Znanieckiego, który przyjechał z Poznania do Kalisza. Że rola Kościoła dziś = 0, ale w średniowieczu była niezwykle potężna i wszystko obejmująca. „Nic mnie nie skłania do tego twierdzenia poza objekt. prawdą naukową, bo sam jestem niepraktykującym katolikiem i nie chodzę do ~~kościoła~~." spowiedzi"
Dyrektorka szkoły: „No… to [illegible] pana prof. dziękuję za ten odczyt".
W tydzień później wszyscy dyrektorowie wszystkich gimnazjów poszli do spowiedzi.

Stefan's diary, 1–2 April 1941

laundry
4 pairs of socks
2 pairs of long socks
2 shirts
1 vest
3 pairs of pants
3 handkerchiefs

she-wolf of Romulus and Remus
the history of thought in biography
today in an imaginary world

7 April **Letter from Franciszka to Stefan**

Stefciu, my darling, I received both your letters from March. I am so happy, darling, that you took a separate room. I know how difficult it must have been for you to be with a bunch of others. Darling, when you were still with Lille, of course, I wrote to all those people that you were seeing. And to Kama [Clavel] and to Zber and to Sacha, and even to Irka Fürstenberg [cousin living in Belgium]. From her I have just received an answer, after half a year! That they are at the old address and that they don't know anything about the family. And, of course, to Hania [Kawa]. What worried me most was that you had not been in touch with her. Now you have the address of Złotkos [the Złotowskis], as a point of contact, should we get lost again. Who knows?

Mirka is at Marbury Hall Hotel, 164 West 74th Street in New York, and Ignacy in Minneapolis (Minnesota) College Inn Hotel, 1316 SE 4th Street. Write down these addresses, Stefciu, OK? Mira will probably join Ignacy. Mietek Wojciechowski, already in January, went to Rio, but didn't arrive, got stuck somewhere in Africa and is still there.

Did you get the affidavit?

I am so frightened now about a journey for you, darling. Don't go just on impulse: think many times before you make whatever decision. One has to have peace and quiet and self control, so much patience and understanding for so many things. I send you so many kisses Stefciu.

Thank you for 'petit poème'. Do you know that I have with me all the previous ones ? And our books and your poems. That was all I brought with me.

You want to know how I live and what I am thinking.

I live quite normally and simply. From 10 to 5 I am in the office: I treat it actually like this, as if at 10 I would go to bed and at 5 started to live.

I live, as you probably know, with Genek, his girlfriend Urszulka Lubelska and Zośka Wojciechowska. Together we talk, we worry and we drink. Sometimes we can't bear the sight of one another, sometimes we are happy together. We also have a guest sofa on which usually someone spends the night. For a time, Stefan [Konorski] lived here (now he lives not far), Jasiek Leyberg was here for some public holiday, Szczepan Baczyński and other friendly strangers. All of us are terrifyingly lonely – and the illusion of a home that one can pass onto someone else is 'valuable' and worth bothering one's head with. A head with which it is anyway so difficult to do any thinking. All that I have seen during the months of our separation – has not been insignificant: it was sometimes very difficult – and it doesn't allow me to shut myself off completely, and retreat within the shell of my own experiences. And this torments me because the only thing I can find within myself is cynicism; it really is not just an egocentric cynicism, but it is worthless in relation to reality and so gives me nothing. I try to work and I do this in a rather strange and, as far as possible, the most intuitive way I can. It is difficult for me to 'think out' the outlines in detail, I try to 'feel them out'. Ah darling how much I should like to be able to 'talk them out' with you.

You write about Sewek[42] [Chaykin]. And I sometimes feel instinctively and childishly that I'd like to be with him. But I know too much and I am sure that it would turn into the most boring adventure under the sun. Unless one would want to find some purpose or goal in it? But what for? Anyway, I'm not sure if we won't face this problem ourselves.

The only people I am really close to are Zośka, Stefan, Jasiek, Genek (you know what he is like), Hanka Poznańska. With her I had the best understanding, but she has gone to university. Other friends, Stefanja [Zahorska], Adam [Pragier], etc. are increasingly strangers to me. I can't bear their hypocrisy, their characters, and their future plans.

None of this is easy but it's interesting and afterwards I should really be quite grown-up. Darling, how much I should like to be able to embrace you. Remember me to friends.

I send you such passionate and tender kisses. Franka

8 April Diary Entry

Received an allocation refund 12 February to 13 March	240 francs
and for rent from 14 March to 14 April	+ 80 francs
	320 francs

Stefan continues to make list of subjects he might write about or include in his films, but the Sketches are preliminary notes for his long poem, *Croquis dans les ténèbres* [Sketches in Darkness].

Sketches from nature
Sketches in darkness
Synthetic sketches – literary sketches
Sketches from memory

Examples:
1. sketches in darkness (I Gucio)
2. synthetic sketch (Gucio himself)
3. sketch in darkness (fish)
4. sketch from memory (Bronisław Grab.)
5. sketch from nature (with a high forehead – editor's daughter, Jahl in the window, Karnecki in the bistro)

Today, here in Voiron, Comédiens Routiers. The same ones as in Paris under the Eiffel Tower on 14 July, the last 14 July. In the programme, portrait of the Marshal and under the aegis of Jeunesse.

In the second part, Molière's *Les précieuses ridicules*, the same as in August, at the Odéon. The same third row. Different neighbours. (Jahl, Konsul, Spisak)

42 Sewek is in Poland somewhere, outside the Warsaw ghetto for the time being, but in September 1941 he goes into the ghetto to be with his family.

I Sketch in darkness (rewritten)
'Gentlemen, it is the will of the nation'.
– What are you on about? Let him dress as he likes, we can listen (says Gucio in tone of gentle persuasion). Meanwhile that one stands on the rostrum of rough yellow wood, still smelling of resin, high [knee] boots on the planed wooden floor, white shirt on his chest.

Bright sun – and two accents of trees still below and the sun still in the sky, and the rest toned down as if through a gauze. Green lizard lives its own life in this landscape.

How many more things live their own life in this same landscape? … Yet one doesn't live one's own life in this landscape. And Sebastian [Sebastian is Stefan, of course] remembers a sentence that he wrote years ago in an unpublished novel.[43]

II Sketch in darkness
I appeal to the moon to rise differently, I beg the moon to rise differently. But it appears always in the same way, in the same way as in that watercolour I painted for Broniatowska in IVth or Vth form. What was it? A castle? Grażyna?[44] No, today one cannot stand romantic falsehood any longer. It's just another dishonesty if no-one will give you a tiny moment of pure lyricism.

O, moon, make your appearance without a castle. Enter the bare natural sky, in which there is no trace of man. Not his airplane, not his balloons, not his gods, not his pale and black angels.

Ah, Sebastek, where are you? Go about your own streets, what do you care? They want them to be recognised as important, these newspapers and radios, and bread and worries; you suffered your own lies and hungers and injustices, you have hardened yourself against it all so why should you care that it has proliferated all by itself?

In the damp mist that fills the streets, you can see fish swim above the road, between the walls of the buildings. Look, one of them fell through the window and it looks inquisitively around the flat with its bulging eyes. It circles around the clock, moving as fast as the second hand, it swims up to the vase of flowers – with what contempt she returns, with a flap of her tail once more into the street.

(Would she be closer to the truth, the truth of the world, if she saw through our eyes? If so, she should start the investigation with herself, she should adapt to life in the air and warm up the functions of her cold brain. And it's the same for man too, if he wishes to stand closer to the gate of truth. You have to begin, my friend, by changing yourself.)

And in the middle of the room stands Mlle X, wringing her hands. That's how happiness disappears, for which you wait your whole life. Oh no, happiness is not like a fish, happiness is not like anything else. But strangely, it disappears just like the fish.

Do you want the fish, swimming in the damp mist along the street, to understand you, you poor realist made of bricks? Mlle X sits down at the table and embroiders something on a circular embroidery frame.

Ah, I have to say everything on her behalf, like a historian who, 100 years after the war, knows everything better than the general, who either won or lost it.

What could Gucio do here to help? Ah, a certain mademoiselle would welcome him with the greatest pleasure. She doesn't herself realise how much

43 Stefan referred to this early novel on several occasions, but he had forgotten its title, and so far we haven't discovered what it is.

44 A character in a romantic poem by Adam Mickiewicz (1798–1855).

more she is worth – if only thanks to her being lost in thought, if only because of her hand-wringing, which represents the whole of nature.

How can Gucio approach her, through all those constructions of stone castles that contain her? Even if they are defending the right cause, they are artificial.

III Sketch in darkness

NB the servants in Molière's *Les précieuses ridicules* are from such an utterly different world, like those fishes, swimming into Mlle René's room.

The courtyard seen from so far above, a square of pavement in the centre of the field of vision, in the depths. Walls of houses, like the square walls of a well, but the light streams down over them, picking out the shadows of mouldings in the masonry, the hollows of the windows, the drain pipes. Down below, in the centre, by the well, Adam and Eve are simply there. And someone at the side talks with God who leans over the balcony of the top floor and looks down. Over the balcony an eye in a triangle and sunbeams painted yellow, and perhaps it is simply the act of looking that is painted with gold on the protruding rays of plaster. Oh, the same eye was once in the canonical square, above the green of the chestnuts, above the apartment of Mme Dunia, the dentist, who divorced her black Natan after 10 years. She packed his suitcases and food for the journey. But she had to divorce him because he gambled away all she had earned. And he himself did nothing. He will go to the capital, start working from scratch, and then he will take her to his place and they will remarry.

God looks down from the balcony, towards the well and suddenly a voice rings out, pleased with himself and even a little boastful!

'Elle est belle encore, hein?'

IV Sketch in darkness[45]

Calling for form.

'Come on, hand it over, Sebastek, Sebastek!'

And Sebastian is thinking, surprised, astonished: 'What do I have to hand over?

'Come on, hand it over, Sebastek!' … so much conviction in their voices, but Sebastek really doesn't know what they want.

The calm surface of the lake ripples and quivers – but no more than is necessary to show that it is alive. Above it, the sky, and much lighter clouds, like clouds in photographs taken through a yellow filter.

But on the bank, between the landing stage and the shore, in a dark gully, the olive-green water is a stagnant, motionless mass, here and there glinting when touched by light. It is only on the surface that things are reflected: the rotting boards of the landing stage, the stony shore, the sloping deck; but just scratch this surface picture and what will immediately appear – not to your eyes but to your nostrils and your mouth and your fingers – are the dark, humid, stinking depths where rats are swimming on their backs

And suddenly that ham actor Budzyński shows up. He goes and straddles the gully of stagnant water, he leans over it and looks into its depths, he smiles quite pleasantly, now and then glancing around him.

45 This is the first version of *Croquis dans les Ténèbres*

He's got very tanned recently, walking along mountain tracks, his naked head that he doesn't shave any more; and his short black hair is growing still very timidly, with twists and turns, and in little tufts, as if it didn't know that one day it would be allowed to lie flat, quietly and soberly, on either side of a parting.

He had a hole in his head, but they forgot to pour some oil through it. 'Is that why he shaves?' 'No, a different reason.'

Perhaps Budzyński thinks that Sebastian has hidden the something that they want from him in the water – A sunbeam perhaps, plucked, wrapped around a spool, and thrown into the bottom of the lake?

'Hand it over, Sebastek, we've had enough…'

'But what is it that you want? Tell me!'

They shut their ears, though. They can't imagine that he really doesn't know. They think that Sebastian is teasing them, and they demand once again: 'Hand it over!' Then Sebastian brings his hand up to the inside pocket of his jacket and he feels a handful of warm air in his palm. This is an unexpected discovery. He's afraid to look… he holds his hand under his jacket and with the tips of his fingers he senses the acute tiny trembling of a little yellow beak, and the tickling of the down. Then he grasps this handful of warmth more tightly, and brings it out of the darkness of his breast into the middle of the aerial landscape, suspended over the surface of the lake.

'Is this what you're talking about, friends?' They look at each other, themselves astonished. But there was so much candour in his question that they suddenly realise that he really didn't know what he had to hand over, what they were asking for. And, simultaneously, they realise that they themselves don't know what they want, either, or rather, that they can't imagine what form this 'thing' they are expecting should take. Is this little chick the form of their desires? Their hearts take fright, and they look Sebastian up and down as if he were a conjuror, and once again they don't know if perhaps he's still teasing them.

The little chick is in Sebastian's palm as if it were in a tiny nest, and they are afraid that the little bird might really be the form of their desires, they fear the quivering reality of the chick. Sebastian feels their agitation, and he hides the little bird in his breast.

A flag has been hoisted above the landing stage. It flutters in the wind with its gaily coloured zigzag, and it's the only clear spot in the milkiness that fills the air. In the middle of the lake there is a sailing dinghy with a mainsail the colour of a cloud hanging above it in the sky. Everything in nature seems held in stillness: the sail, and Sebastian, and the questions and answers.

But not everything in nature must keep its own form. The little chick, snug in the warmth inside his jacket, has melted into Sebastian's body. Sebastian holds out his arms, and, without a word, hugs his friends. And then as if they had learned something, as if they became wiser, they understood, that their demand for form – 'Go on give it to us Sebastek' – would have been shocking, if it weren't for the childish naivety.

9 April Diary Entry

<u>Sketch from nature</u>

Crack of the lighter, from which Imbirowicz struck a light, bounced off like a flea from Chrzanowski's monotonous voice. The cigarettes are as infectious as yawning. Old Jabłoński, sitting next to me, with a packet of 'Wiarusy'[46], shook

46 'Wiarusy' – the first Polish cigarettes to be sold in soft as well as in stiff wrapping.

his lighter which gave a screech – like a trickle [of liquid] spattering on a plate. Chrzanowski speaks in monotone, but he is certainly convinced about the excellence of his diction. Now and then he stresses syllables as if he was putting poles on a flat, rough road.

What a mixture of voice and smoke dissolved in the air, redolent still of soup and noodles. Because today Chrzanowski's lecture is not in the salon upstairs, but here in the dining room.

Behind walls, behind houses, mountains covered with snow, I can still picture their image in front of my eyes, glimpsed from the street. The wreath of snow, a thousand metres above our heads, already almost the efflorescent green, cooled the air – and this is why we are listening to those gathered here in the dining room that is warmer than the salon.

11 April Letter from Franciszka to Stefan

Stefciu, my darling, thank you. I received one more letter and so many poems. Darling! Suddenly I found you so near me. And I miss you even more. It is as if at any moment you'd come so that we'd be together. That fragment of a poem (from 2 August) is so beautiful.

And it tells me so much about you.

Darling, I don't know when this letter will reach you, so I am not writing about all the things that happen today, and in a week's time will be gone.

I also had letters from Mira [Złotowska]. But I don't want to go to her. I would only go if you could go there too. Darling, don't worry about me. There is absolutely no need.

I am living quietly and normally. I just wish that you could be with me. When I really can't cope, I write letters to you and throw them into a drawer. Just to be able to talk it all out, to lighten the burden of worrying problems, to have the illusion of talking to you. I can't always summon enough strength to resist writing to you and to draw!

I kiss you, darling, so very passionately and tenderly. Franka

14 April Diary Entry

Beethoven. (twilight. a rectangular window in the mansard – sky and branches. like a screen. One branch broken. Yesterday Michał told me that he has seen this branch break in the wind.)

At Michał's. Karnecki inebriated:
'... Prometheus: forgive me
'for lighting up the darkness.
'And NapoLéon (Apollo) replied:
'Not at all.'

'He is begging me. I implore him with a gesture, oh yes! Take pity...! and I'm clutching my knee – it hurts. Lifar was a lovely boy.

'At 12 the performance ends and Lifar comes and says let's go to the Negro cabaret. What is it called, the Negro district in New York?

'We arrived there, brother, everything was dead. At 4 am they did a cabaret especially for us, and then off we went – Niagara... and towns in Canada...

14 April 1941

Niagara, Toronto… and then Washington to Stokowski[47], Hollywood, Chicago, the biggest hotel in the world. Auditorium Hotel, I think. To the Turkish bath with Wladimir. We were drinking whisky.'

Darkness. Window. Broken branch. Michał, Żmigrodzki, Szuki.

Karnecki: 'And when I saw the first star! Look what a lovely star! Bonne chance! Ah, what a beautiful star. What a beautiful decoration, these branches and the star. Damn it! Let's drink more cognac, no?'

People without their own morality identify with the opinion of others around them. And the opinion of others is the outcome of needs and history, it is statistics.

16 April Letter from Franciszka to Stefan

Stefciu, my darling, I have just a moment ago received your telegram. That you still haven't got the affidavit. That formalities will take months. The affidavit should arrive any day, because I have already received mine. But afterwards? –
I am so frightened for you, my darling. So many times I have written this to you,

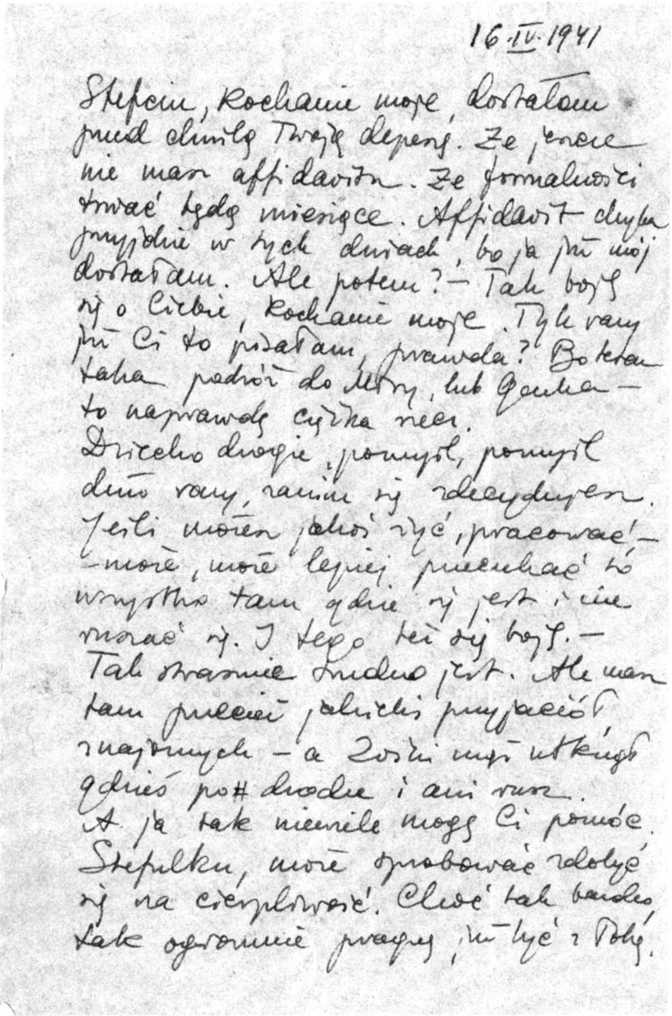

16.IV.1941

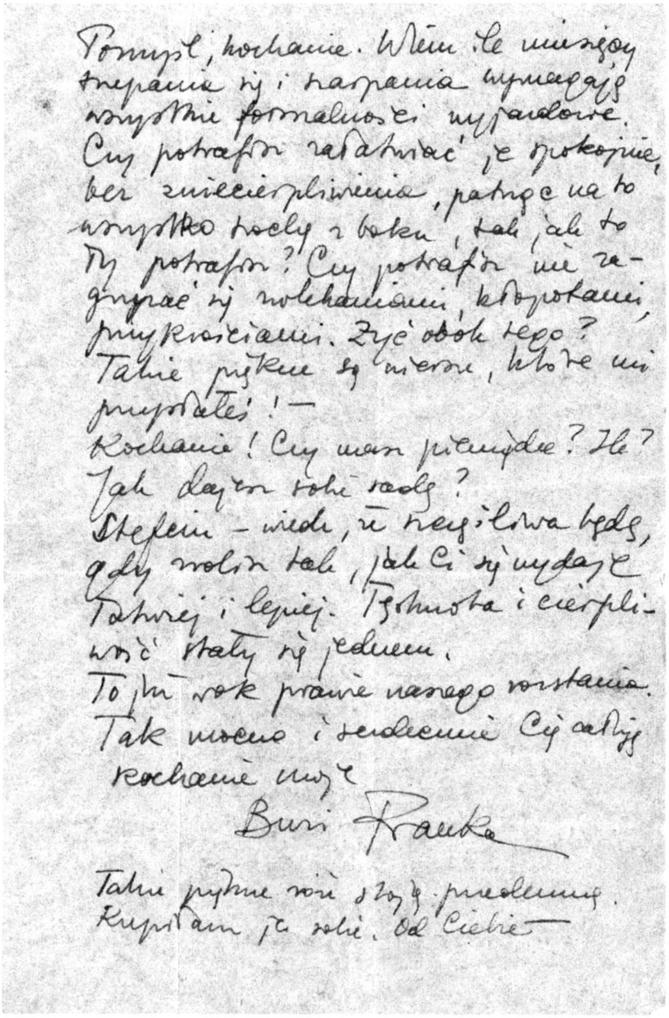

47 Leopold Stokowski (1882–1977), conductor

haven't I? Because now this sort of journey to Mira or to Genek – that is really a difficult thing.

Dear child, think, think many times, before you decide. If you can live somehow, work – perhaps, perhaps it is better to wait, to stay where one is through all of this where one is and not to move. But that frightens me too. It is so terribly difficult. And, after all, you have some friends there and acquaintances, – and don't forget Zośka's husband got stuck on the way and can't move. And I can do so little to help you. Stefulku, maybe one should try to summon patience. Although I want so much – so terribly – to be with you already, please think it over carefully, darling. Consider all that's involved, how many months, and such struggle from pillar to post, and all the formalities. Will you be able to cope without losing patience? Try to see it objectively, in the way that I know you can. Can you survive all the delays and worries and unpleasantness without getting upset by it all?

They are so beautiful those poems you sent me!

Darling! Do you have money? How much? How do you manage?

Stefciu – I want you to know that what will make me most happy is to do whatever you think is easier and better. Yearning and patience have become one. It is nearly a year since our separation. I kiss you so much and so tenderly my darling.

Love. Franka

Such beautiful roses are standing in front of me. I bought them for myself. From you.

18 April Diary Entry

I arrange Jahl's decorations in the theatre. Walk Lipski to the hospital. And no letters. (Jahl's story in Le Mans, and Szuki's and Michał's. And like a pillar under the second end of the constructed arch of a novel – a letter from his oldest daughter – that 'gothic madonna', whom he could not forgive for getting married, and he didn't talk to his son-in-law – a letter saying that she's getting divorced.)

19 April Letter From Franciszka To Stefan

Stefciu, my darling, today I received your letter of 27 March. It took 3 weeks. That is almost quick. I sent you a few letters recently so I suppose you know about my *cafards* [fits of depression]. I miss you madly darling, and it's hard that I can do so little to help you. Everything seems to fall apart in one's hands.

I suppose that you have already received the affidavit, is that true? I have already got mine from Max Wohl. Apparently they check very carefully the degree of 'kinship'. But I suppose the fact that he was a good friend of my father will be enough. Dear child, you ask if I want to be with Mira. At this minute I don't – but what can one know and decide today? Procedures involved in departure are long and difficult. But if, for whatever reasons, it would work it could be easier and better for you to go to live with Ignacy rather than with Adam [Pragier] and Stefanja [Zahorska] – then I shall stand on my head to do everything to be together with you. But this will still take a long, long time. We must, damn it, learn to accept this passing of time. It is necessary to come to terms with it inside oneself, and that's all there is to it. Can you imagine sometimes I, literally, pull myself by the hair just to keep my mind functioning. Darling, the ticket that you need to get a visa, I've been trying to get for a few weeks. There have already been interventions in the Lisbon Centre, and as soon as I have the address of Hicem, where you are applying, a telegram will be sent from here.

Darling, during the time that you will be waiting for the visa, will the Centre help you, so that the little money you have could be for the journey? These expeditions now take such a long time. I am trying [to make sure], that Genek's invitation would make it easier for you to get a visa. It's a long business. Genek is, after all, a complete impotent when it comes to matters that don't touch him directly. He is, as always, fortune's child. I shall also talk to Antoni [Słonimski]. Perhaps the PEN Club will help you. Because the idea that this visa quota is 'at the disposal' of M[aksamin] is a fairy tale that has gathered strength being passed from mouth to mouth. Would that it were so simple!

I assume that if you have a ticket, you will get the visa. Generally the route to America follows the trail of Ignacy and Mira, by way of Africa. And sometimes it's possible to get stuck on the way somewhere, just like Zośka's husband. I am frightened of that route, and it lasts for months. Of course, the best would be to go to Teresa directly by air. But how long does one have to wait for a place? I know that difficulties and problems will mount up for you and it is this that makes me sad. Keep going, darling. And don't lose your sense of humour – chin up. This is our best defence (humour not chin). By 'Our', I mean those crazy aesthetes, of course.

My darling – you ask about me. I wrote a lot to you already. I don't know if you got it. My life is a bit of this and a bit of that. My present work is terribly boring, but it doesn't annoy me too much. And a sense of humour saves me in critical situations. There's no shortage of material for that. I have been doing my own work for a while and have a whole pack of drawings, stumbling between surrealism and expressionism. I was working so 'directly' that I didn't have time to think about it. Only afterwards, in the cold light of day it alarmed me. Shall we always be 'followers'? [followers of the avant-garde], and 'nothing but'? My head is full of immediate anxieties. I fumble around with intractable problems. And I can't bear the intellectual superficiality à la Genek, even though he doesn't lack imagination and is pleasant to talk to. Stefanja [Zahorska] and Adam [Pragier], that is a separate chapter. Dangerous buffoons with phoney labels. Stefan is as he always was, friendly, warm – although he suffered a severe breakdown, and recently he received the news that his mother died in June, which he took very hard.

Do you have Lonia [Janecka]'s address? If so – write to her. With Stefan [Konorski] we talk about her very often and about Musia. I received today also by the same post a letter from Maryla. They are all well. Irka, Stef, Mother are living where they were before and work. Anka is also working. Write to them c/o Teresa.

Darling, write to me as often as possible. You cannot possibly imagine what a letter from you means. And poems! Darling, I have already written to you about them. I found all of you in them. Thank you. The first 'fragment of a poem' I know by heart. It is wonderful. I kiss you darling, so very much. Franka.

Remember me to Jahl.

20 April **Diary Entry**

On Saturday, a performance.

Jahl takes me aside at the theatre: have you bought a ticket for Szuki. 'I… I'll bash this son of a bitch in the face.' – Please tell him.

In the evening he waited in the street. But it didn't come to a brawl. Irony: the hotel was closed, he slept on the staircase in Chaumière, but again on Friday at breakfast he quarrelled with Karnecki. He rushed to the theatre to remove the decorations. Karnecki to the police station, to register. I sent Szuki to the theatre. I went there with Karnecki. And enjoyed a terrific performance.

Jahl doesn't talk to me again.

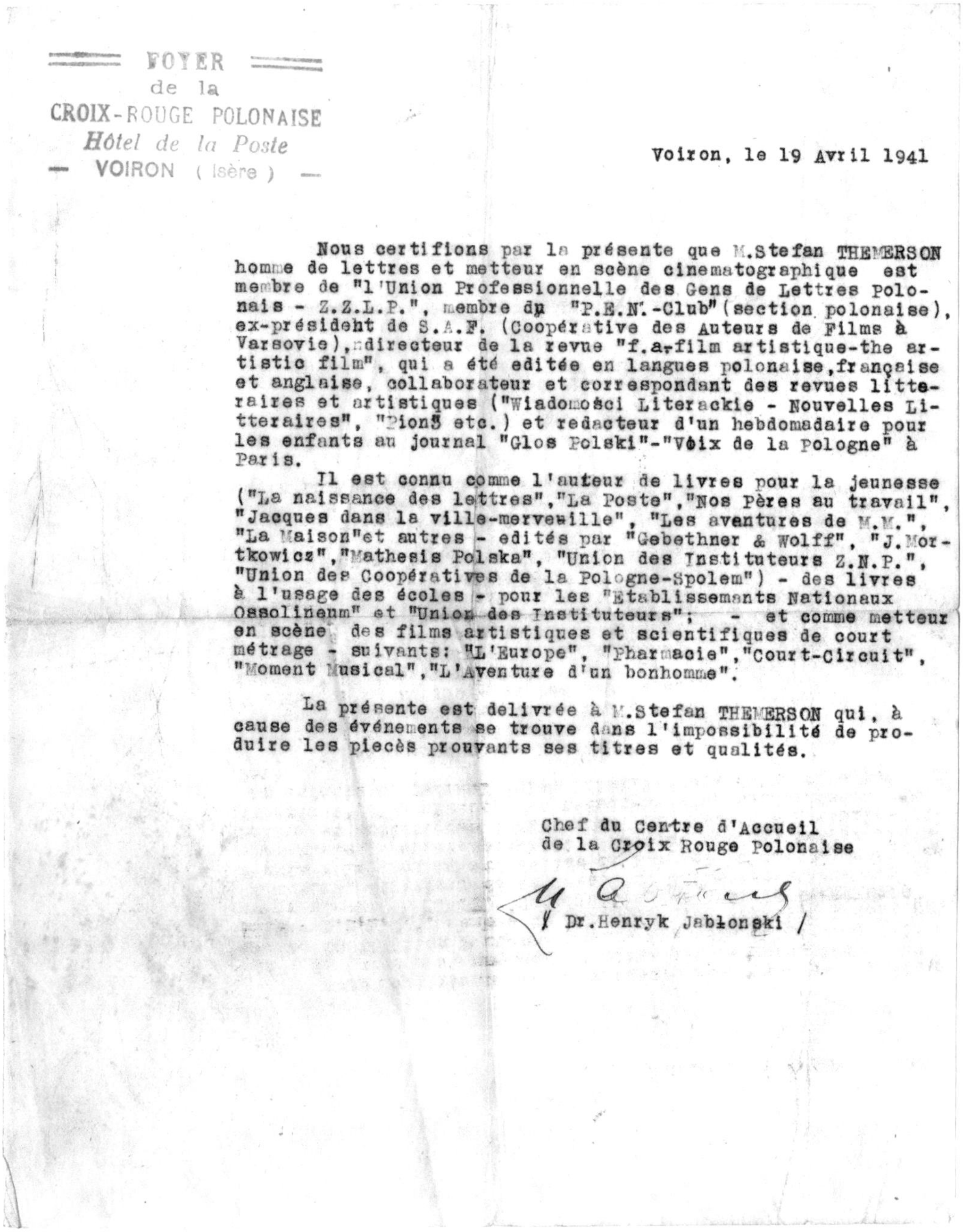

FOYER
de la
CROIX-ROUGE POLONAISE
Hôtel de la Poste
— VOIRON (Isère) —

Voiron, le 19 Avril 1941

Nous certifions par la présente que M.Stefan THEMERSON homme de lettres et metteur en scène cinematographique est membre de "l'Union Professionnelle des Gens de Lettres Polonais - Z.Z.L.P.", membre du "P.E.N.-Club" (section polonaise), ex-présidént de S.A.F. (Coopérative des Auteurs de Films à Varsovie), directeur de la revue "f.a.-film artistique-the artistic film", qui a été editée en langues polonaise, française et anglaise, collaborateur et correspondant des revues litteraires et artistiques ("Wiadomości Literackie - Nouvelles Litteraires", "Pion" etc.) et redacteur d'un hebdomadaire pour les enfants au journal "Glos Polski"-"Voix de la Pologne" à Paris.

Il est connu comme l'auteur de livres pour la jeunesse ("La naissance des lettres","La Poste","Nos Pères au travail", "Jacques dans la ville-merveille", "Les aventures de M.M.", "La Maison"et autres - edités par "Gebethner & Wolff", "J.Mortkowicz","Mathesis Polska", "Union des Instituteurs Z.N.P.", "Union des Coopératives de la Pologne-Spolem") - des livres à l'usage des écoles - pour les "Etablissements Nationaux Ossolineum" et "Union des Instituteurs"; - et comme metteur en scène des films artistiques et scientifiques de court métrage - suivants: "L'Europe", "Pharmacie","Court-Circuit", "Moment Musical","L'Aventure d'un bonhomme".

La présente est delivrée à M.Stefan THEMERSON qui, à cause des événements se trouve dans l'impossibilité de produire les piecès prouvants ses titres et qualités.

Chef du Centre d'Accueil
de la Croix Rouge Polonaise

/ Dr.Henryk Jabłoński /

19 April 1941
Certificate signed by
Dr Henryk Jabłoński

20 April 1941

By now Léon and Nadia Temerson are in Lisbon. They arrive in New York in May.

Letter from Stefan to Franciszka

Darling, what good news that you already have the affidavit. I would like you to leave as soon as possible, but on the other hand – I am frightened about your journey. I am sure that you know better than I do what you should do, what would be sensible in these chaotic times.

Darling, I ask you one thing (don't delay and don't hurry, although this has no significance), don't put off your departure because of me, if you think it's the right thing to do. If necessary we shall just wait until it's all over, and then we shall meet eventually, wherever we end up. I want so much for you not to be sad. Mira wrote to me about a new edition of *Tralaliński*[48] and about your new drawings. You know how much I should like to see them!

I kiss you so very much, darling – Stefan

Addition from Teresa Żarnower to the letter above, dated 24 May[49]

Dear Franka!

I sent on all the letters that I collected at the Post Office. Please forgive me for adding this note on the same sheet of paper. Just to save time. I am trying to get a ration-book for Stefan and for this purpose he sent me a photograph. I can assure you that he looks well and hasn't changed at all. Here things are really heating up, and I don't mean in the sense of climate. If my fate interests you, I, like the majority of our compatriots, am fearfully awaiting an American visa which in theory should only take two weeks but afterwards the formalities are likely to go on for another three. I shall probably go to Canada. I am going without a penny, I don't have cash to book any specific (individual) journey, so again it will most likely be some phantom ship, like that time from Angers to Lourdes… Too bad. Funding [body] obviously didn't consider me worthy of subvention, that (talent)..? etc. Clearly I haven't reached the age of common sense. But we'll see. Keep strong. My heartfelt kisses. I'll write before leaving. Teresa

21 April **Diary Entry**

(Lipska relates how [Bronisław] Mondszejn approached her)

'Are you sure that this is appendicitis?' 'Two doctors examined him'. 'That doesn't mean anything, it often happens that they cut open the abdomen and it turns out to be cancer'. Another time he tries to attract her attention from a distance, squinting at her from above his glasses: 'Do you know, these are such terrible pains that they would make someone who was dying want to climb the wall.' 'Do you advise me to go to hospital and take him home?' 'No, I am not saying that this is definitely so.' 'So, why are you telling it to me?' 'Because I know about medicine'.

Once Mondszejn told Jahl about rupture, that it causes twisting of the bowel, vomiting faeces and a most terrible death. – Since then, it seems, Jahl got to like Mondszejn.

Mondszejn tells Jahl's daughter that her father is crazy – he draws a chart of the normal and the mad.

48 *O Panu Tralalińskim* by Juljan Tuwim, Warsaw, first edition, Wydawnictwo J. Przeworskiego, 1938.

49 This is an indication how long letters take to reach their destination. Stefan's letter to Franciszka took over a month to get to Teresa Żarnower in Lisbon, who then forwarded it to London.

21 April 1941

Karnecki to Lipska – 'Bronisław won't have the operation on Saturday'. 'Why?' 'Because the doctor is going to the theatre.' 'What time is the performance?' 'At 8.30'. 'So he will have it later.' 'You don't know what it means to be a doctor. If the operation is not successful the doctor suffers because of the death of his patient. He wants to go to the theatre because he likes it, but above all, he likes dancing. A woman who works with him told me that the doctor will go to the theatre.' She meets him at 8. 'So, was there an operation?' Lipska is tired, doesn't want to talk about it and lies: 'No, it will be in two days.' 'You see, I told you?' 'I have just met this woman and she told me that he put off the operation and is going to the theatre.'

Piotrowicz (concerning his conversation with X about the Nowak family, she is eight months pregnant, two children, in a sunless room), 'and she told me that our children were born in sunny rooms and that it is harmful for them – living in rooms facing north, because they can die, but the Nowaks' children were born in northern rooms, so why should they take advantage of the war? – *and with a sense of humour* – and that appealed to me, she is right, isn't she?' [50]

Lay scripture

I do not know what was in the beginning. I do not know if there was any beginning and since if it is difficult to imagine the absence of a beginning how much more difficult it is to imagine the beginning.

23 April Diary Entry

affidavit (21 April – forms to Hicem)
(21 April – photographs to Teresa) [51]

24 April Telegram from Franciszka to Stefan

CHÉRI BESOIN D'ADDRESSE HICEM ESPÈRE RECEVRAI INVITATION THÉRÈSE GENEK PAR PENCLUB LONGUES FORMALITÉS STOP SI CELA DEVENAIT IMPOSSIBLE ET TU AURAIS RAISONNABLE POSSIBILITÉS PARTIR DIRECTEMENT NEW YORK FAIS-LE JE VIENDRAI APRÈS EMBRASSE TENDREMENT MON PETIT = THEMERSON

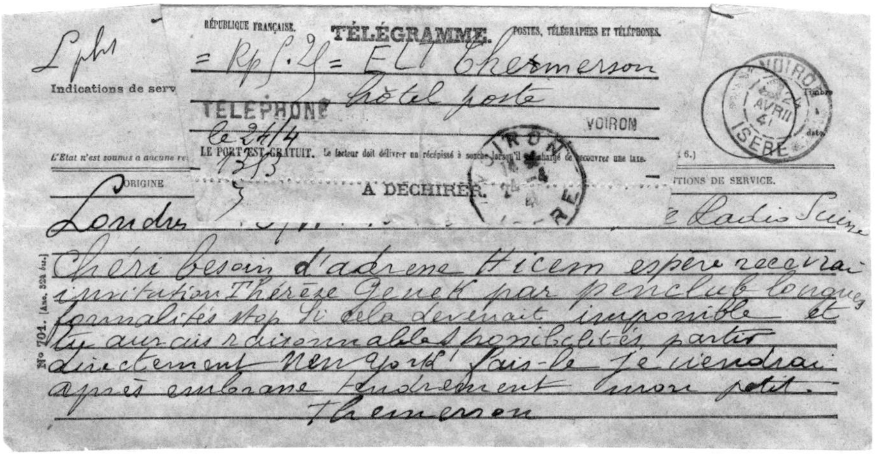

RÉPUBLIQUE FRANÇAISE. TÉLÉGRAMME. POSTES, TÉLÉGRAPHES ET TÉLÉPHONES.

Indications de serv

TELEPHONE

VOIRON

LE PORT EST GRATUIT.

A DÉCHIRER.

ORIGINE

Londres

Chéri besoin d'adresse Hicem espère recevrai invitation Thérèse Genek par penclub longues formalités stop si cela devenait impossible et tu aurais raisonnable possibilités partir directement New York fais-le je viendrai après embrasse tendrement mon petit.

Themerson

50 Stefan wrote a story in two parts under the title, 'The Investigation', which describes some of the events in the Hôtel de la Poste and its Annex, where some 120 Poles from all walks of life and professions find themselves living together in close proximity – a comparatively safe but socially difficult situation. These stories are at the end of the book.

51 Teresa refers to these in her letter of the 24 May, so it seems that the post between France and Portugal is working well.

Diary Entry

Order of the French authorities:
roll-call twice a day

deposit passport
the issue of sauf-conduit explained
not allowed to leave Voiron
there will be compulsory labour for those aged 18-50

Letter from Franciszka to Stefan

Stefciu, my darling,

Do you get any of my letters? I still don't have a reply. Only one letter and that so very long ago.

How are you, darling? Are you working a bit? And your health? I miss you so much, Stefciu! I thought that soon, soon we'll be together and again everything is so slow and time passes so stubbornly. Already April!

Did you already get the affidavit? Have you started visa applications?

Darling, how are you off for money? Please let me know by letter or by telegram. I have a certain amount that's all. I am so uneasy about how you are managing.

Do you have any close friends near you? This interim life of waiting and reminiscing and hope, stretches so mercilessly. Can you take everything in your stride and not torment yourself too much? I know that it's very difficult. It frightens me even to contemplate that labyrinth of formalities and worries that you must endure.

But what keeps me alive, only this, is that we shall meet in the end.

I had a letter from Mira. Apparently, she wrote to you twice. Did you get her letters? Józio [Wittlin], with his wife and Elżbietka, is also already in America and says that New York is Łódź with elephantiasis. Darling that's how words, sorrows and tenderness roam over the world. And there is so little, at the end, that's possible to write.

Recently, I did a bit of drawing for myself, but in reality for you or to you, darling.

Crawling out of me is some surrealist from under a black star. Perhaps I will manage to control it.

And what about you darling? – write!

Write to me to Freyd's address, the same as before. He gives me the letters immediately. I dream of a long, real letter from you, darling

I kiss you so very much and so tenderly, Franka

Just a moment ago I received two of your letters from March and 'Petit Nègre'. I kiss you darling, I am so happy and thank you for the hyacinth. Tomorrow I shall write more. bye! Fr.

30 April **Letter from Franciszka to Stefan**

My darling,

Your poems are the most beautiful letters that one can receive. Stefciu, you cannot even imagine, how much they give me and what they are to me. If I knew how to write this to you, I would probably also have to be able to write poems.

All geographical distances disappear. You are just here, so very near me. I am so very happy to have these poems, darling!

Have you managed to arrange something? What about Hicem? So many visa worries are beginning for you, as I write. What will happen when you will receive this letter? Can you get a Spanish visa?

Are you managing my darling? Remember, Stefciu, should you not be able to communicate with Genek, try to get straight to Mira.

Józio [Wittlin] with his wife and Elżbietka are there, and Al(eksander) Hertz, who is your devoted admirer for Marceljanek.

I will come as soon as I can get away from here. It will take time, but perhaps not so long now – darling! I kiss you and kiss you thousands of times. Franka

30 April – 1 May **Letter from Stefan to Franciszka**

My darling, for so long I haven't had a letter from you. I don't know what has happened to Teresa. Since six weeks she doesn't answer letters. I am trying to write to you direct, Franeczko, I think it will arrive.

I already know that I've got an affidavit. I am so happy that you also got yours. I should be calmer if you would make use of yours as soon as possible, if it makes good sense to set out on such a journey from there. It is all the same to me where I will go, just to meet you as soon as possible – darling.

My formalities here, and they are endless, must take time, it seems to me about two months, if everything goes well. Well, two months, today, that is almost like two centuries, and at the same time in a strange way – almost like two moments.

I received a letter from Hania, the first for a very long time. Written on the 14 of February. What emerges from it is that they all [family that is] are as well as is possible in these conditions. Maryla writes: – 'please forgive me that for so long I didn't give a sign of life. There are difficulties with sending letters. We managed to exchange the good flat for another with three rooms. Łucja, Maryla and Jasia are living at Śliska 7, m.10. One room I gave to my mother-in-law and brother-in-law. Another to Heniek with [wife] and Wandzia. We are managing. Jasia is learning in a group of pupils taking lessons privately, led by Maryla. Łucja also has a job, and on top of that Sewek doesn't forget us… If it were not for the fact that we so miss Sewek, Franka and Stefek – things would be bearable. From Franka we have frequent news through Lisbon. We were so happy to receive news from Stefanek, at last one could see his own handwriting. Please send them the news that we are all in good health, we think about him all the time and ask for frequent news. Stefan's whole family is in good health, Irka and Stefan work. Both our mothers add few words, Irka: ('– we are in good health and calm, – Anka is also in good health and works, we are in touch by telephone and letter'), Stefan [Miller] i Aneczka.'

My darling, I received also a letter from Mira, who writes wonderful things about your drawings and that there will be an English edition of *Tralaliński* with your drawings. I was so very glad, Franek, and want so very much to see them all.

Darling, I write so many things in my letters to you without order and sequence, but would really want just to cuddle up to you and sit for so long, so long – very quietly.

And this is the only real thing that I carry all the time in myself through the world without pretence, myths, childishness – and surrounded by people who don't have a grain of this most important of things: a sense of humour. In the end it doesn't disturb me at all (though bores me sometimes) because I am sitting here perched on my branch and have not the slightest wish for everyone else to climb onto it – it would break and again I would have to fly off somewhere else.

I send you goodnight kisses darling, it is late, I am going to bed. I wrote to you already that I rented my own room in town and the greatest treasure is that I have here – my own table, my own window, my own door, that I can lock with a key. Love, darling, Stefan

I have written to Leon Grynblat a letter thanking him for the affidavits. I was a bit taken aback by his helpfulness. Sonia Grynblat who sent me Hania's letter mentions that Pierre Gild. [Gildesgame] is in London. Remember me to him if there is an opportunity. What is happening to Mira and Ignacy – have they separated?

Darling, once more another big kiss – love. St

1 May Franeczko, dearest, today I received three letters at the same time: one from Teresa and two from you. Thank you Franek! Darling, don't worry about me. I manage very well and I don't get upset by things that do not depend on me, in the same way that I don't get upset by rain and the storm that is raging just now in the mountains. As for money I still have an awful lot, 7000 francs, Franeczko! I am so worried that you got into debt, darling. What I have is sure to be enough for a room and for the formalities and for the first stage of the journey.

Darling, please write me more about your drawings, I would so much like to see them. I so terribly miss looking at what you are doing, Franeczko.

Franek, to embrace you at last. Do you know, that soon it will be a year, a whole silly year?! (Did you get my poem 'Dno nieba' [Bottom of the Sky]? I send you the biggest kiss. Stefan.

Greet all our friends. What are they doing? How are they? Are Genek [Cękalski] and Stefan in London? And Stefanja and Adam? [From] Antoś [Słonimski] I heard once. Who else is there with you? I should like to get some news. Love Franek, bye. St.

Telegram from Franciszka to Stefan

MON PETIT REÇU LETTRES ET VERS J'EN SUIS HEUREUSE SONT MAGNIFIQUES MERCI STOP TÉLÉGRAMME APPUYANT ENVOYÉ DÉJÀ HICEM STOP TIENS MOI AU COURANT TES DEMANDES VISAS TOUTE MA TENDRESSE = THEMERSON

Diary Entry

Today I received three letters from Lisbon. Two from Franka.

Today is a holiday. Lilies-of-the-valley. I am reminded of Paris. But also the new Paris; because young boys were passing by, singing what the troops in Paris were singing.

1 May 1941

Now, to make up for this, an orchestra in the alleyway is showing off and screeching trumpets bend their way over the roofs and barge in here, through the window, into my room.

3 May

Using diplomatic means, the Polish Government-in-Exile informs the Allied and neutral governments about arrests and mass executions in Poland, deportations to Auschwitz and other camps, as well as the atrocities committed against the Jews.

Letter from Stefan to Franciszka

Darling, I am so pleased and cheerful. Yesterday I got three letters from Teresa and from you and today also three letters from March and April! And the telegram sent yesterday! The faster the post moves the closer you seem to be, darling. Yesterday I wrote a letter straight to you, the Post Office already accepts letters addressed directly and I suppose delivers them quickly. Did you get it?

Darling, do you realise how much I should like to see what you are doing? I miss looking, in the same way as I would lack bread. It isn't sentimentalism creeping out, it isn't romanticised tenderness, but a force simultaneously so abstract and so real as are the forces of gravity and hunger, or temperature and longing. One cannot grasp hold of the force of gravity, hunger, temperature, nostalgia, but bodies really do attract one another, the stomach really shrinks, atoms really whirl and the heart really beats. And all the time that which is abstract appears to be real, a realistic and naturalistic stone of Galileo or a bread roll, a warm stove, or kilometres to be covered, are the fragments of the interesting, though actually not so very interesting, fairy tale, in which one lives, but for which one neither bears any responsibility, nor collects royalties. It isn't even necessary to tell oneself: 'let's learn to swim'. It is as if the organism itself would demonstrate bankrupted Lamarcks and Darwins. It adapts, but does not attach any importance to the fact that it adapts, because it does not want to lend weight to that which is circumstantial – it simply accepts, just like it accepts that there is rain, wind, dew.

Darling, you see, I still can't write, I still can't bring to a conclusion the thread that I started. But, Franek, the truly genuine in what you do is so clear to me. I need so much to tear myself away in order to see all that you are doing.

Do you remember our journey [to Greece] four years ago? How much has changed along the road. Then, I was only worried about those Doric columns. But they endured and will endure once more. That which appears to be a problem on a scale measuring seconds, can look very different in a perspective of months and years. In the history of events we read that Roman soldiers conquered Greece, but in reality it was the Hellenic slaves who enlightened and conquered Rome. It's the same with the order of the Doric column; it can be repeated with the demise of the perspective of the Elysian Fields. But, it would take much patience, calm and wisdom to discover and reveal this from all those monotonous sculptures carved from coloured marble, with ivory eyes and bronze spears, like those that stand on the ground floor of the Louvre, documenting the transitional Hellenic influence on the city of seven hills. How much objective discipline it would take to discern such a development if the context were that of today, and one that touches us as directly as things do now. But I think the comparison is too flattering for this recent period, which leaves behind only a trail of regret, with perhaps just a grudging satisfaction that all the lies and false values of it all are exposed as illusions, and the shortsighted judgments of those who sanctioned such values are pricked like bubbles. *Ridiculus unus*. I would not envy either Sewek or Mira, wherever I'd go, I always take myself with me. And it is all the same to me where I am, as long as it is together with you. I kiss you, darling, as much as it's possible to kiss. Greet all our friends. And my best regards to Wojciechowska. It seems that her husband is going to leave quite soon. Mira's cousin [Adam Zandel] is with him, the one with whom we had once drunk champagne on Victor-Cousin.

I hug you, Franek, so very much. Stefan.

4 May Telegram from Stefan to Franciszka

REÇU LETTRES MERCI SI HEUREUX QUE TU TRAVAILLES POUR TOI VOUDRAIS TELLEMENT VOIR CHÉRIE REÇU LETTRE HANIA NOS FAMILLES VONT BIEN J'AI ASSEZ ARGENT TENONS NOUS CHÉRIE EMBRASSE SI TENDREMENT = THEMERSON

5 May Diary Entry

to the laundry:
1 pair long socks
5 pairs of socks
1 pair of pants
1 pair of shorts
5 handkerchiefs
2 shirts
1 pullover

Lay Scripture[52]

At the beginning was the atom of carbon. And there was a multitude of atoms, but it was the carbon atom that gave life its beginning.

But if in various versions of this scripture it will be written differently, do not seek the truth in the oldest, as has been done in the past, but in the newest.

Because the truths described here are not those that are revealed but those that are created by man.

And as man changes, so do the truths that are created by him.

And so these changes could be called advancement if the world is not to be demolished through stupidity or blindness, and if we do not turn back from the path of virtue and from the search for the truth that for centuries of centuries must be praised.

And if someone has a significant and logical right not to call these changes improvements, then he can call them something else.

And this one can have this right, and the other another right, and there is no need for them to fight each other.

And we know about the forty generations of ichthyosaur [unreadable] caused this.

But he had the stature of a great…

But the human eye did not exist then and nowhere in the world was there a picture such as we have today in reconstructions. Because there is no picture without the lens.

How did the world appear to the senses of the creatures that lived at the time?

52 These are early notes for the *The Lay Scripture, or a Draft for a Preface to a Textbook of Physics*. First published by Anthony Froshaug, London, 1947, in a limited edition of 120 copies.

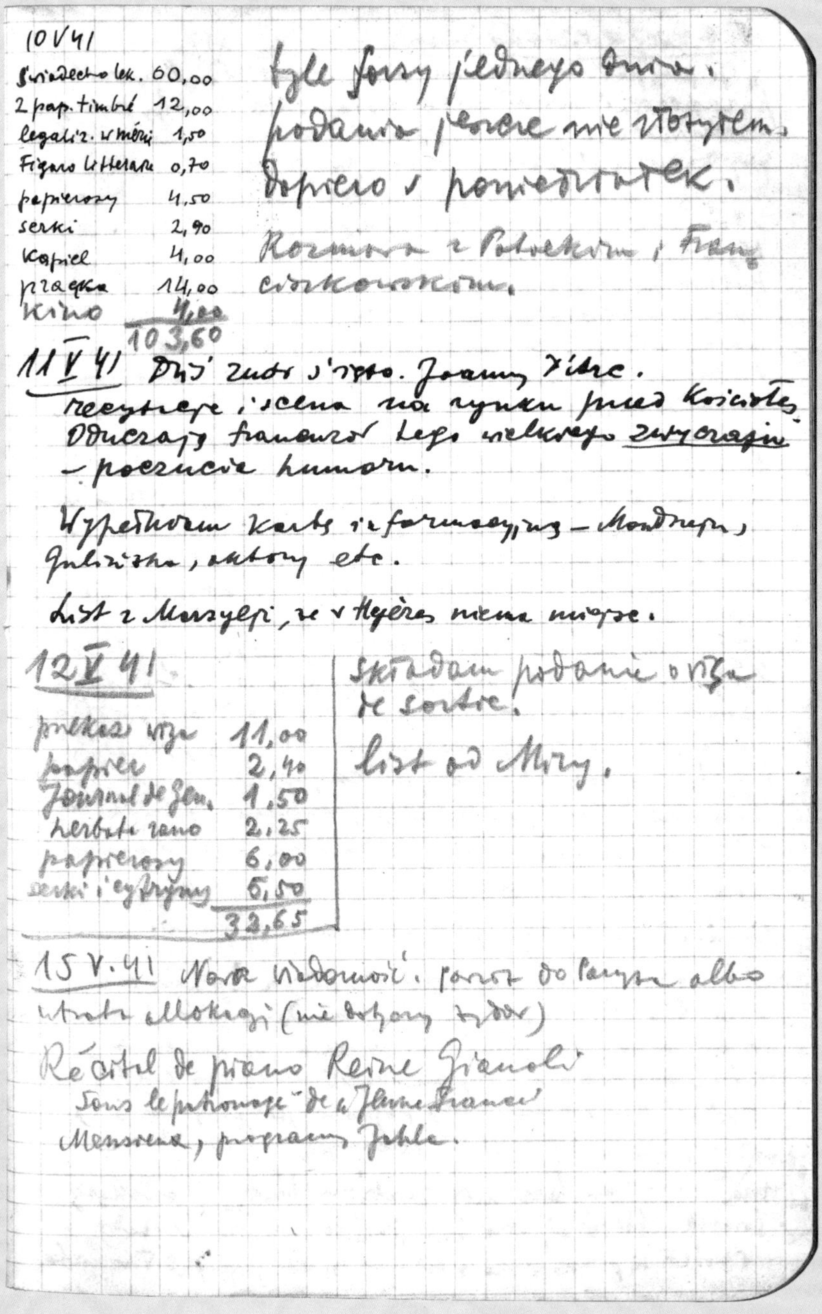

10 V 41

Świadectwo lek.	60,00
2 pap. timbré	12,00
legaliz. w mérie	1,50
Figaro Littéraire	0,70
papierosy	4,50
serki	2,90
Kąpiel	4,00
pralnia	14,00
kino	4,00
	103,60

Tyle forsy jednego dnia. podania jeszcze nie złożyłem. dopiero w poniedziałek.

Rozmowa z Polakiem i Fran[illegible].

11 V 41 Dziś znów święto. Joanny d'Arc. rekwizycje i scena na rynku przed kościołem. Odzwyczają francuzów tego wielkiego zwyczaju – poczucia humoru.

Wypełniam kartę informacyjną – [illegible], [illegible], [illegible] etc.

List z Marsylii, że w Hyères nie ma miejsca.

12 V 41

przekaz wiza	11,00
papier	2,40
Journal de Gen.	1,50
herbata rano	2,25
papierosy	6,00
serki i cytryny	5,50
	32,65

Składam podanie o wiza de sortie!

List od Miry.

15 V 41 Nowa wiadomość. powrót do Paryża albo utrata allokacji (nie dostanę żadnej)

Récital de piano Reine Gianoli
sous le patronage de la Flamme France
[illegible], program ładny.

Stefan's diary, 10–15 May 1941

10 May 1941

Diary Entry

doctor's certificate	60.00
2 stamped letter forms	12.00
Town Hall legal charges	1.50
Figaro Littéraire	70.00
cigarettes	4.50
little cheeses	2.90
bath	4.00
laundry	14.00
cinema	+ 4.00
	103.60

So much money in one day.
Haven't made the application yet. Only on Monday.
Conversation with Potocki and Franciszkowski.

11 May **Diary Entry**

Sunday. Today again a holiday, Jeanne d'Arc

Recitations and a stage in the market place in front of the church. They unteach the French that great custom – a sense of humour.
I'm completing a card with a questionnaire – Mondszejn, Gulińska, actors

Letter from Marseille, that there are no places in Hyères.[52]

12 May **Diary Entry**

visa transfer	11.00
paper	2.40
Journal de Genève	1.50
morning tea	2.25
cigarettes	6.00
little cheeses & lemons	+ 5.50
	32.65

Make an application for exit visa
Letter from Mira Złotowska

13 May **Telegram from Franciszka to Stefan**

CHÉRI SUIS PARFAITEMENT BIEN COMMENT VAS TU MILLE TENDRESSES = THEMERSON

15 May **Diary Entry**

New information. Return to Paris or lose allocation (this doesn't apply to Jews)

Récital de piano – Reine Gianoli
Sous le patronage de la Jeune France
Mainssieux, Jahl's programmes

52 Hyères, southernmost city in Provence, presumably where there is another Polish Red Cross Hostel to which Stefan wanted to go.

I

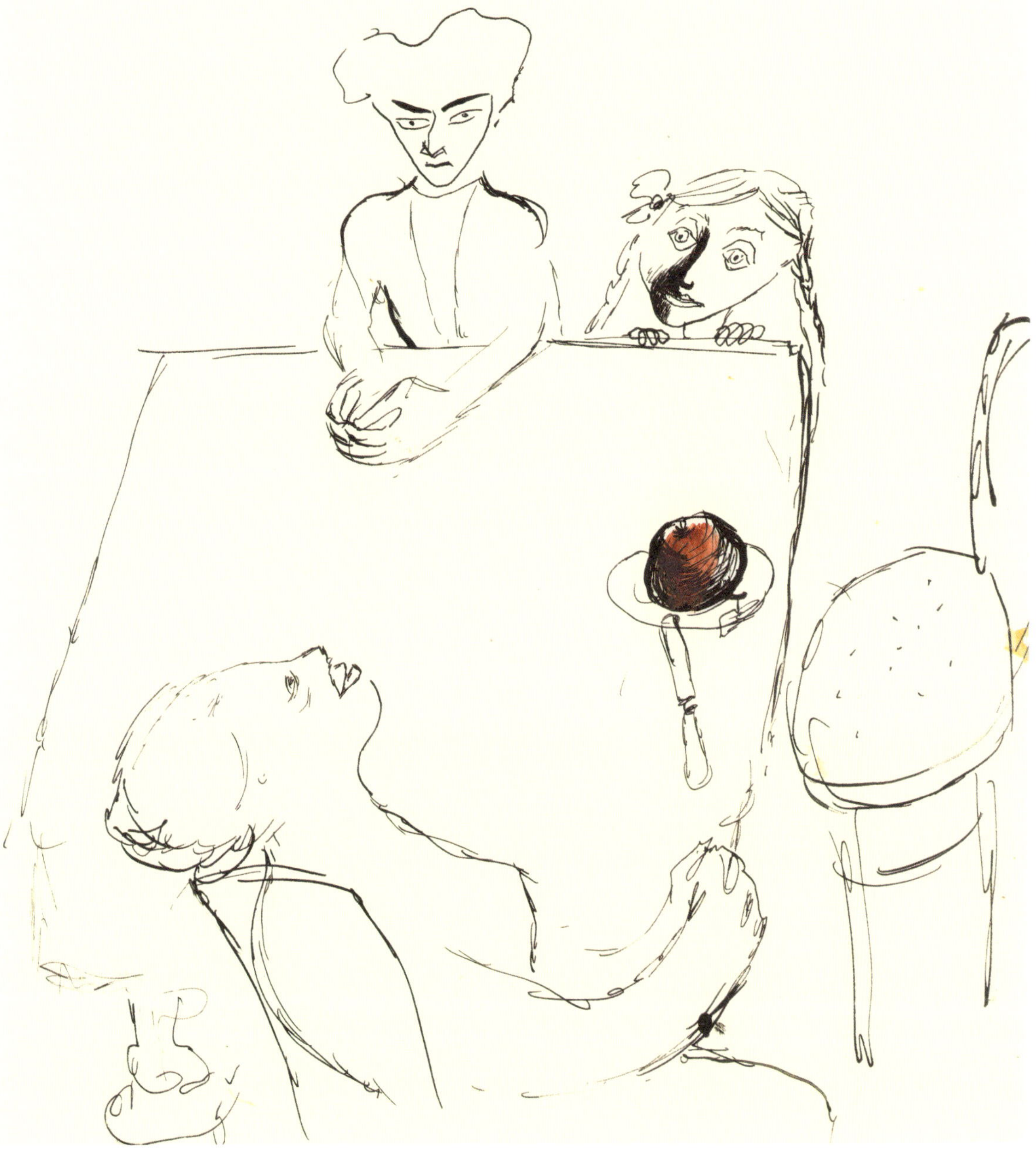

II

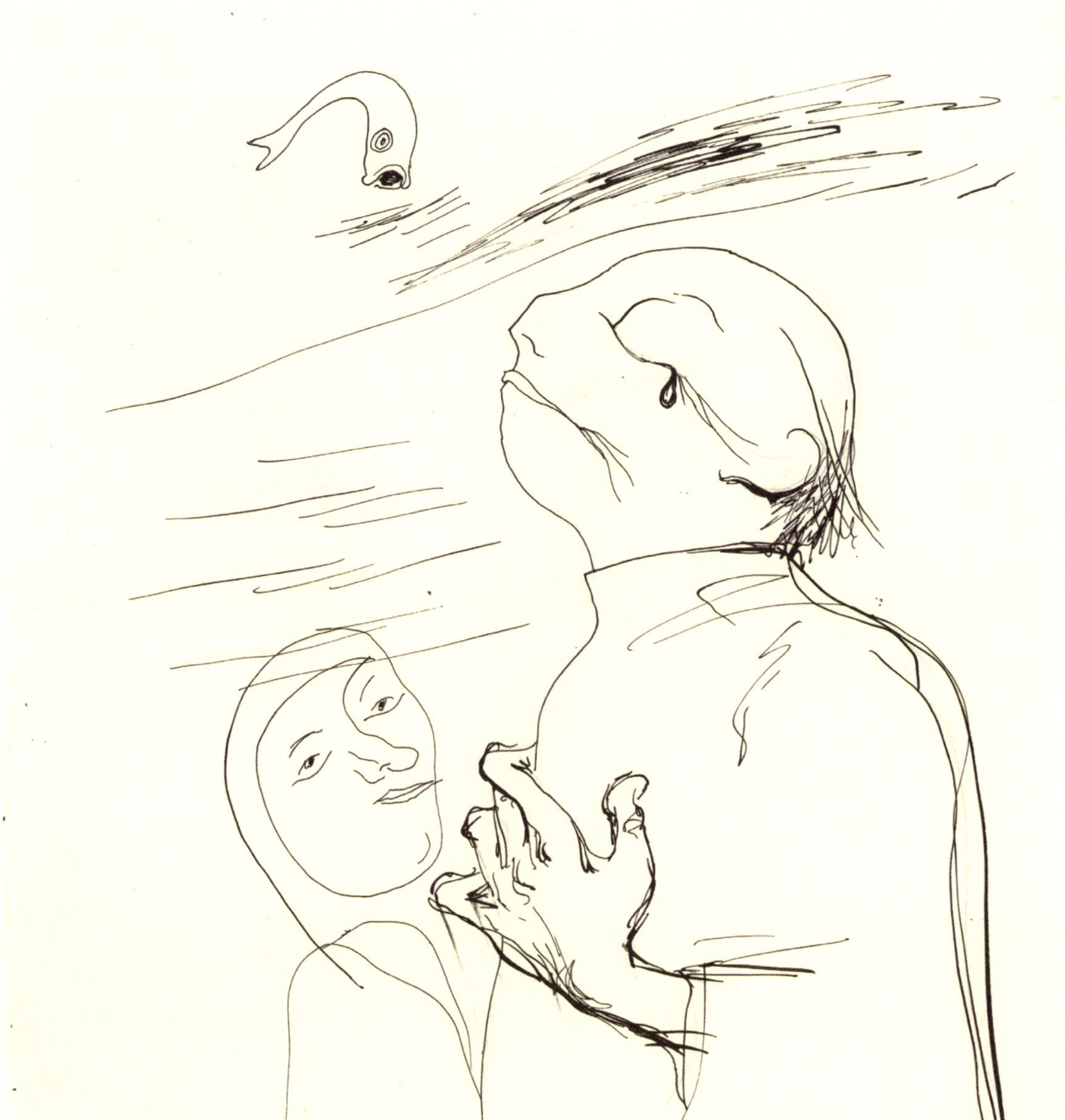

III

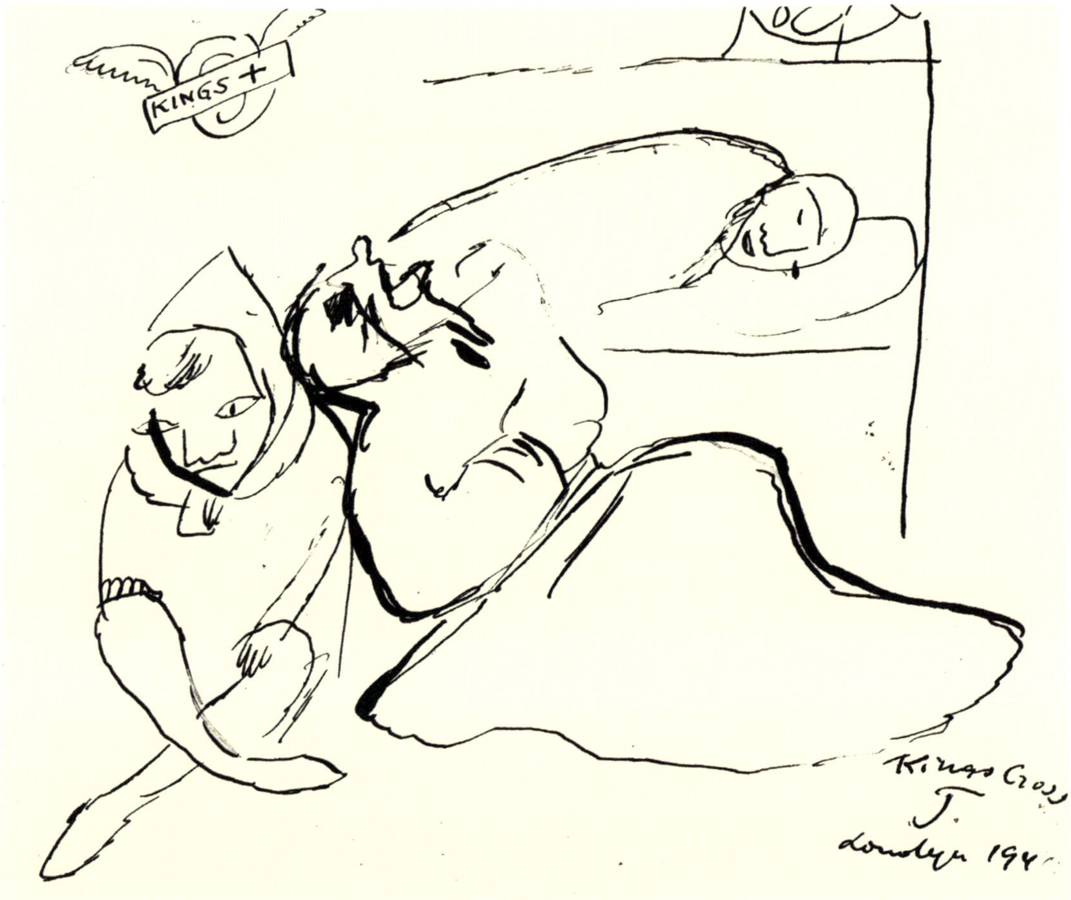

IV

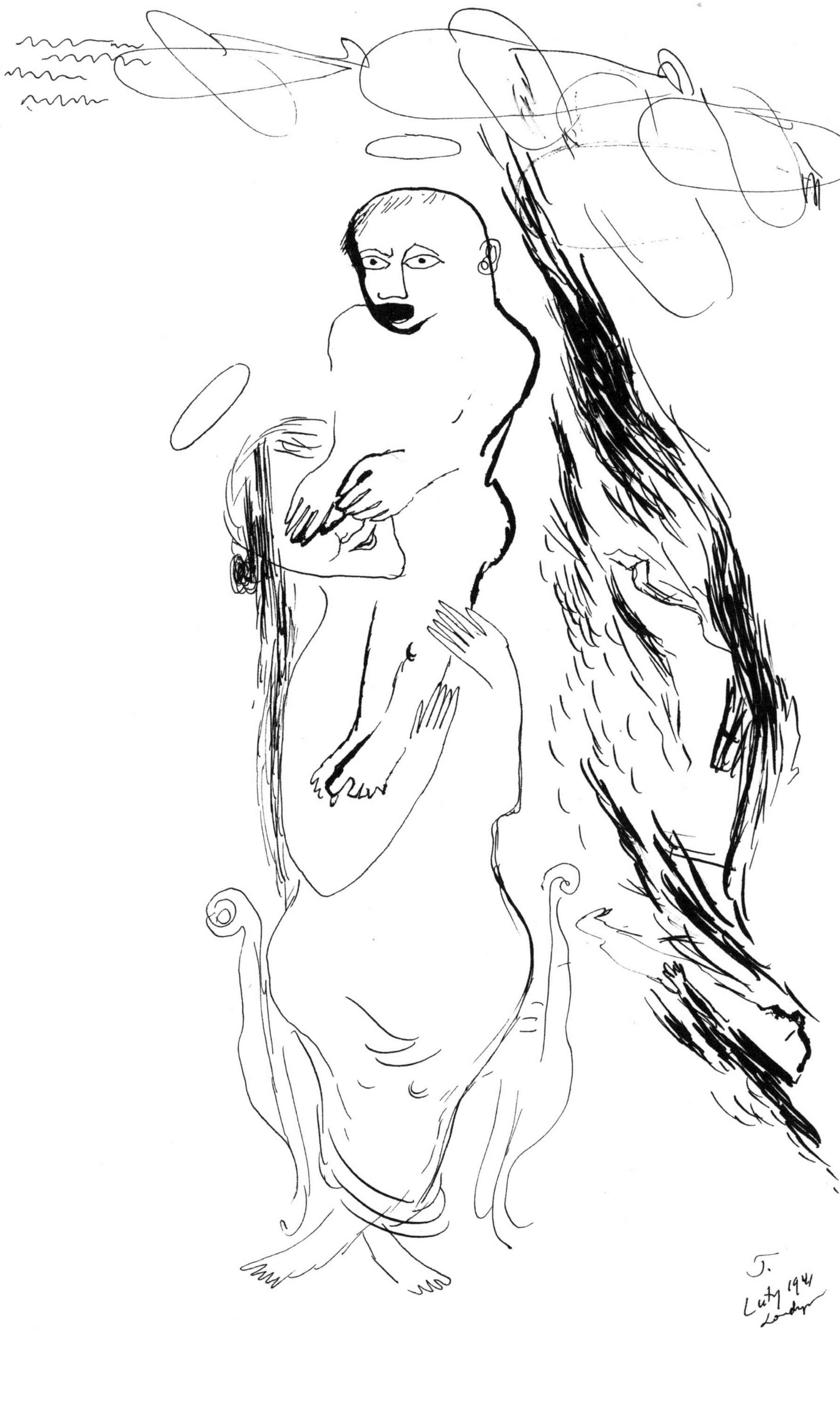

V

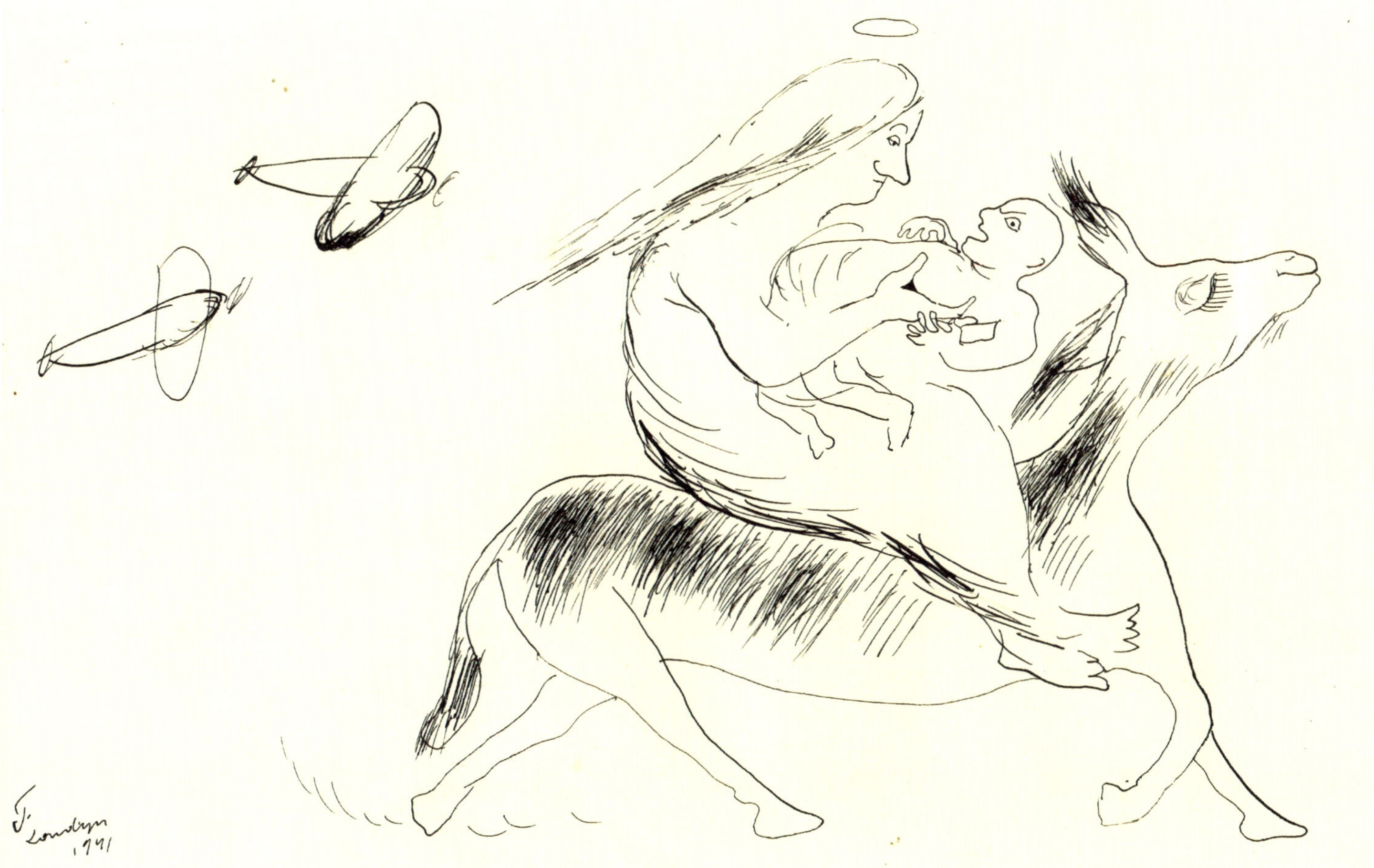
1941

VI

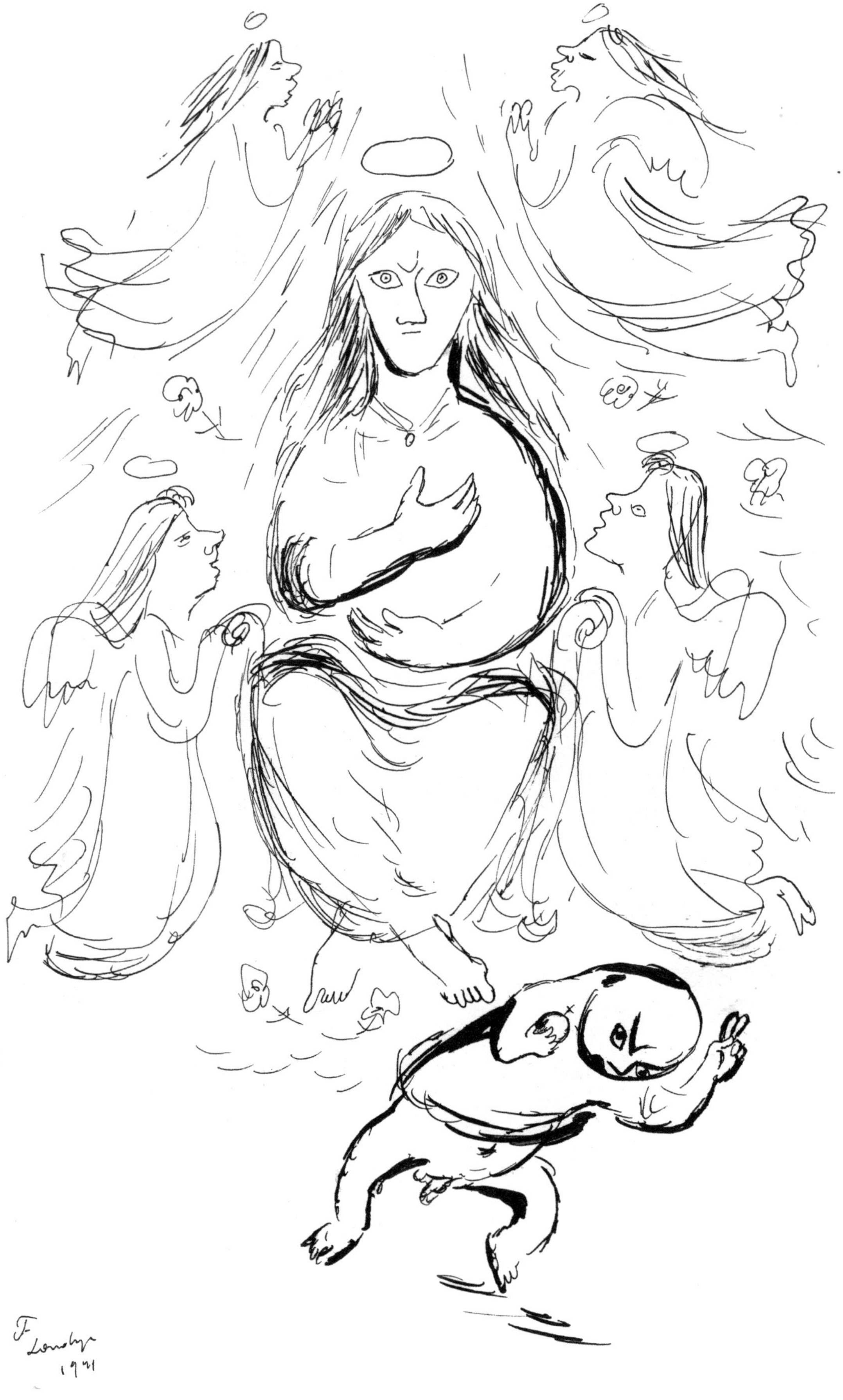

VII

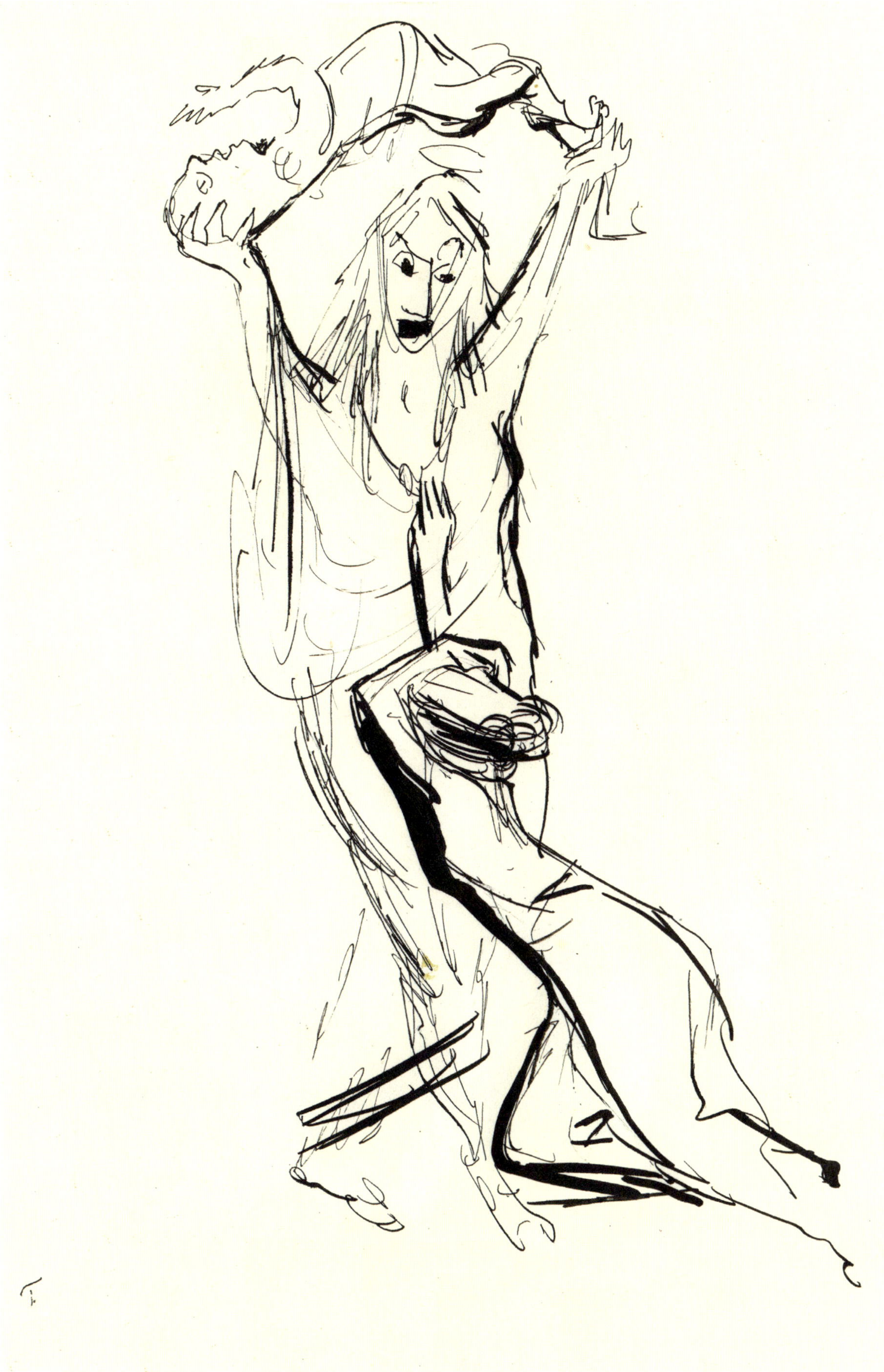

VIII

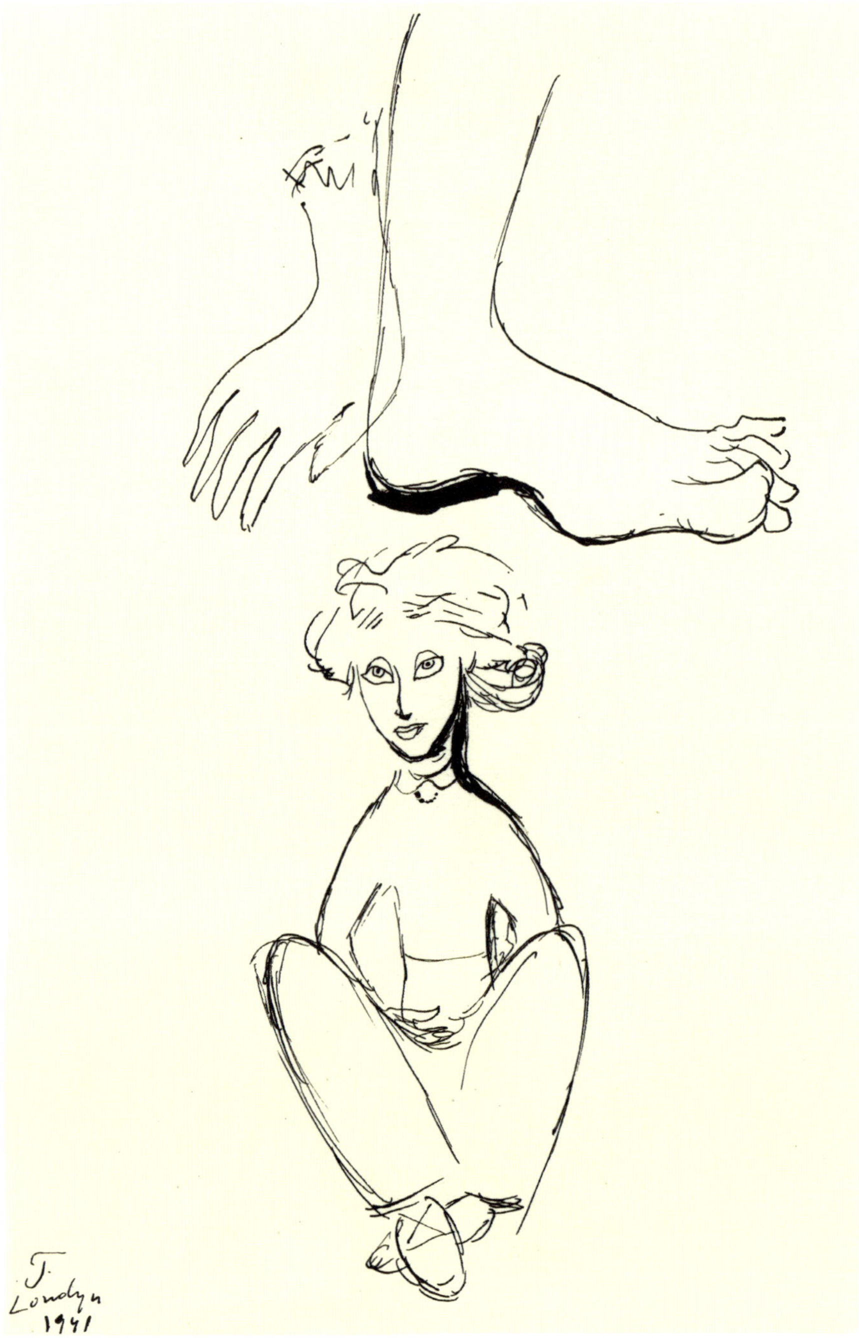

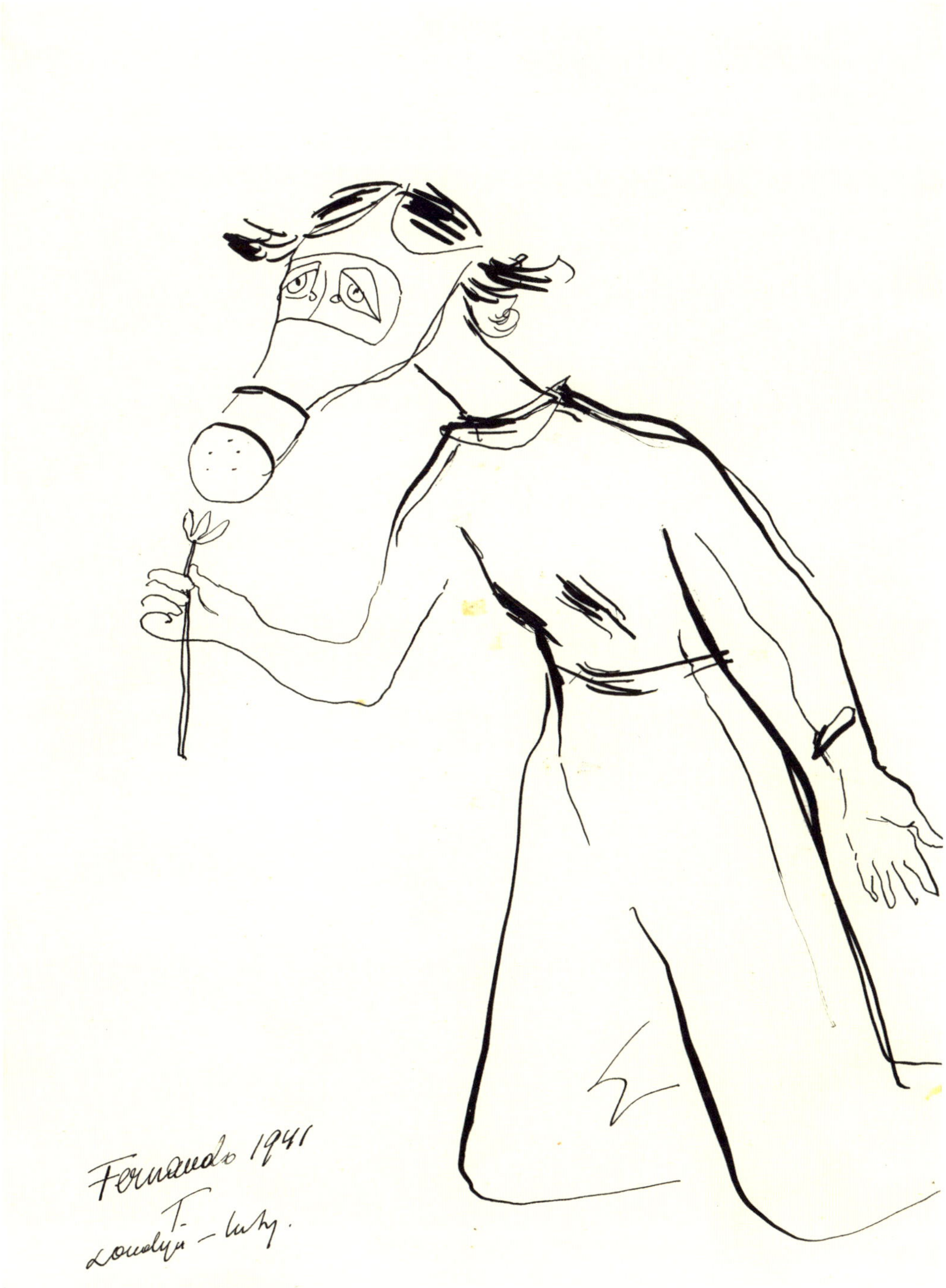
Fernando 1941
T.
Londyn – luty.

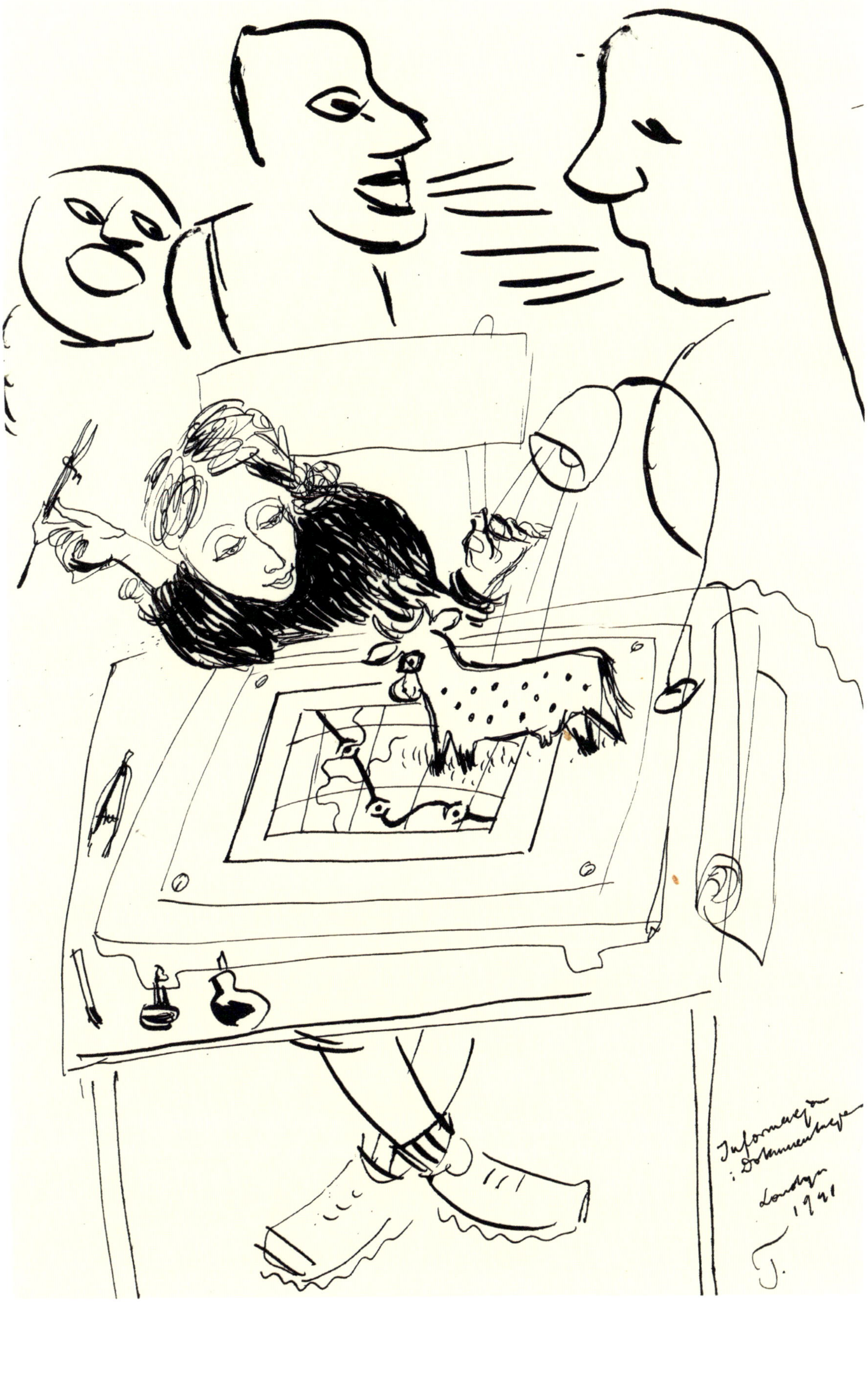
1941
J.

XI

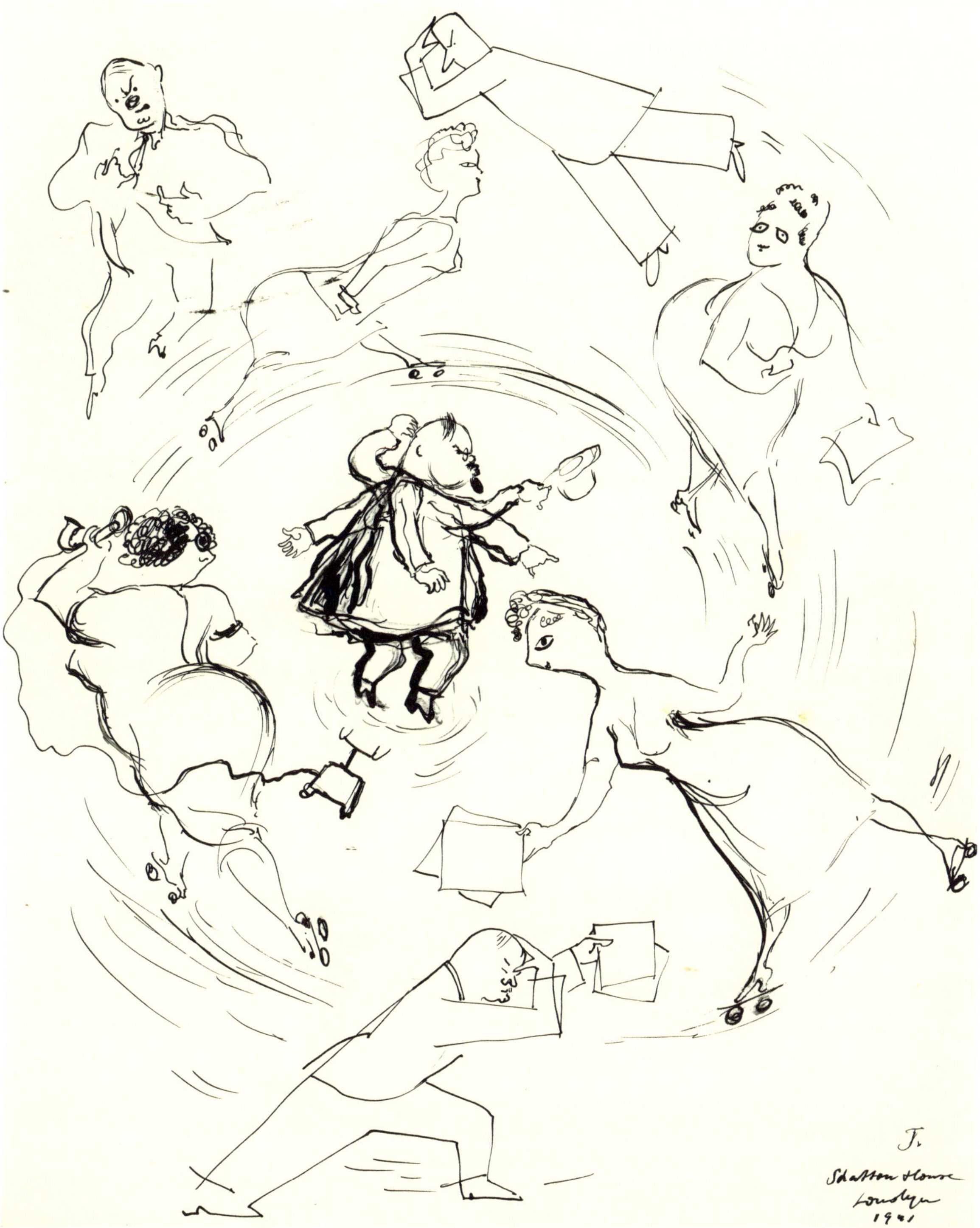
F.
Stratton House
Londyn
1941

XII

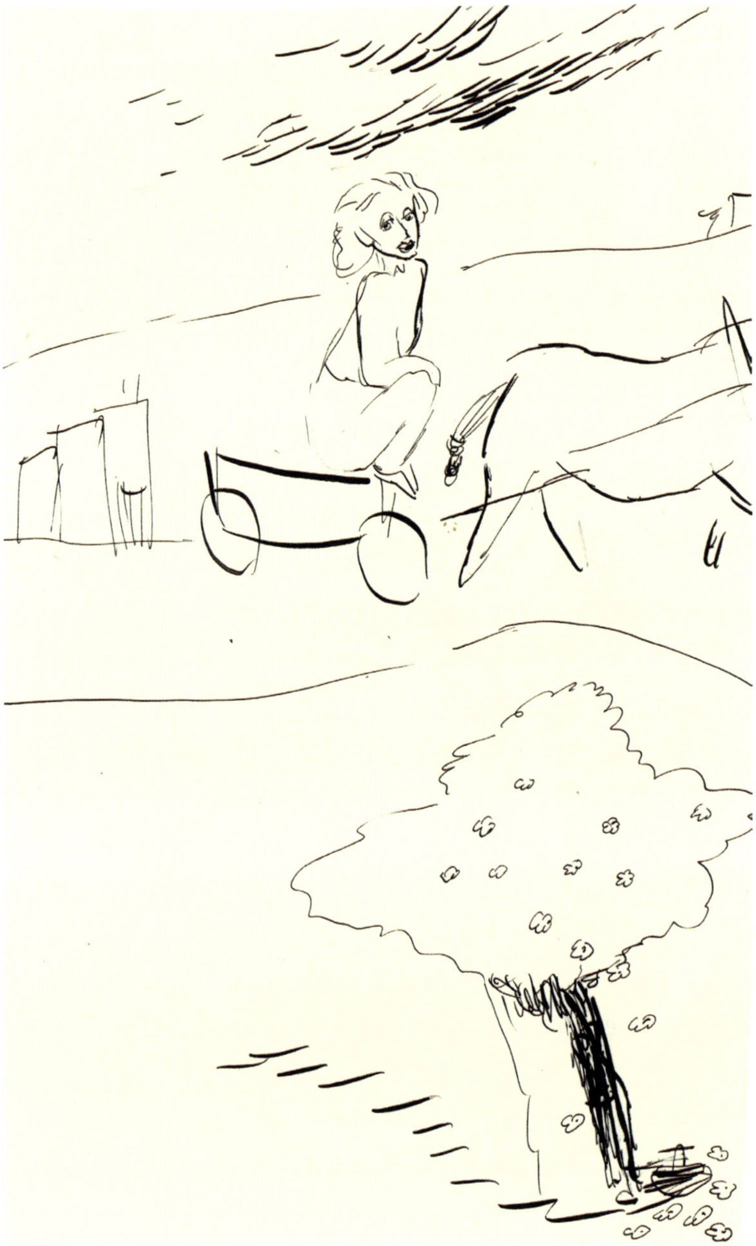

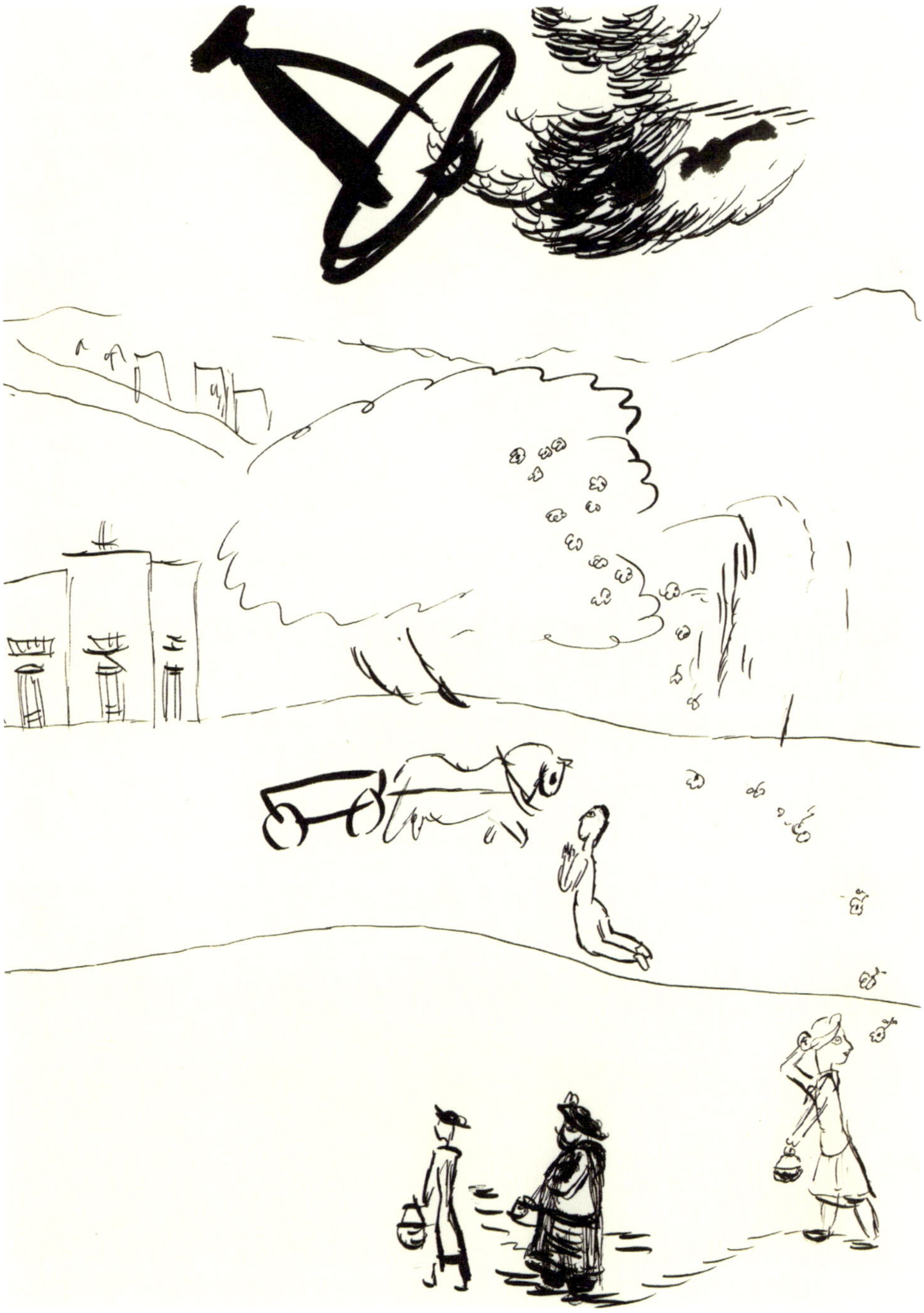

XIV

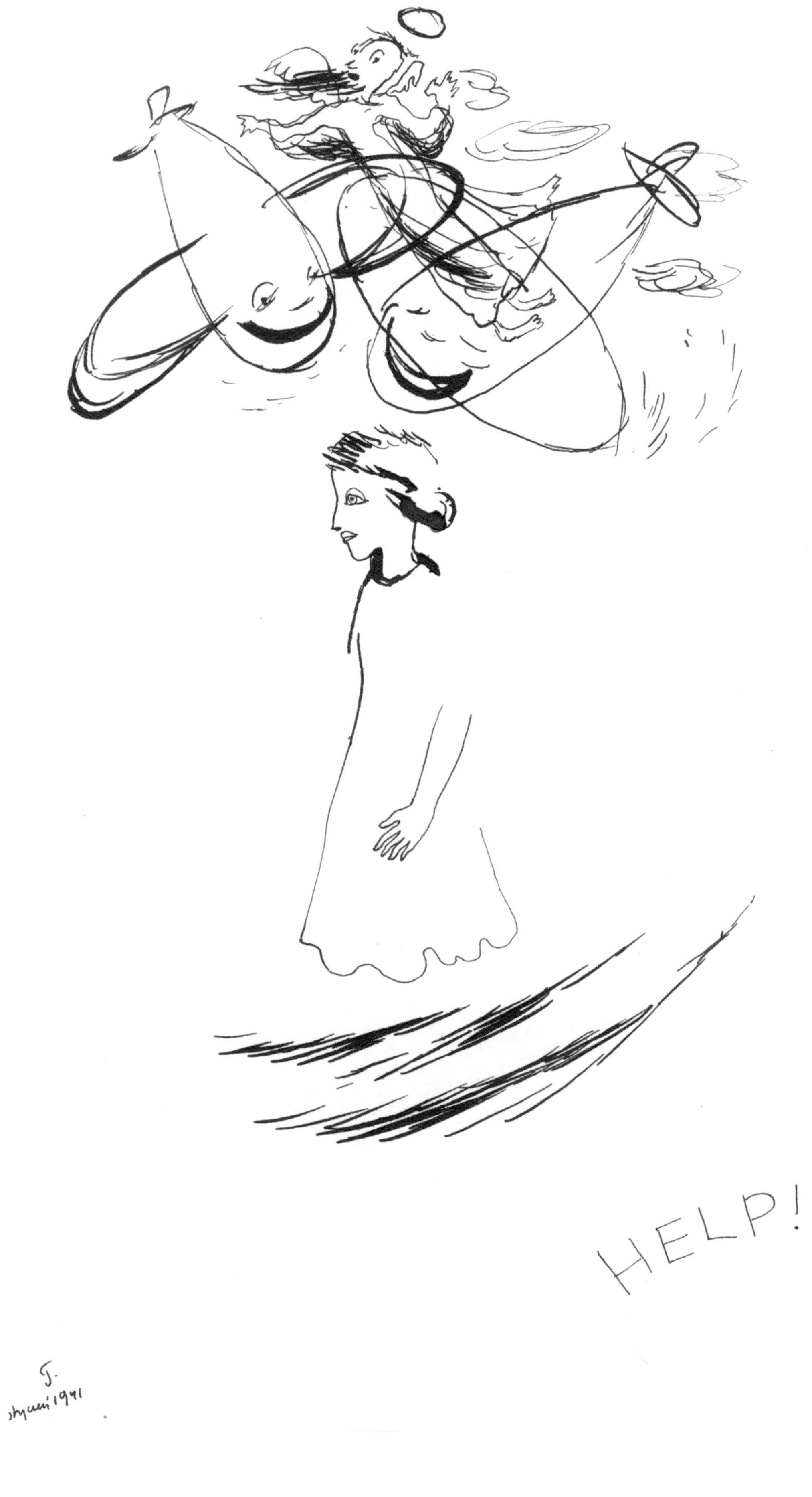

XV

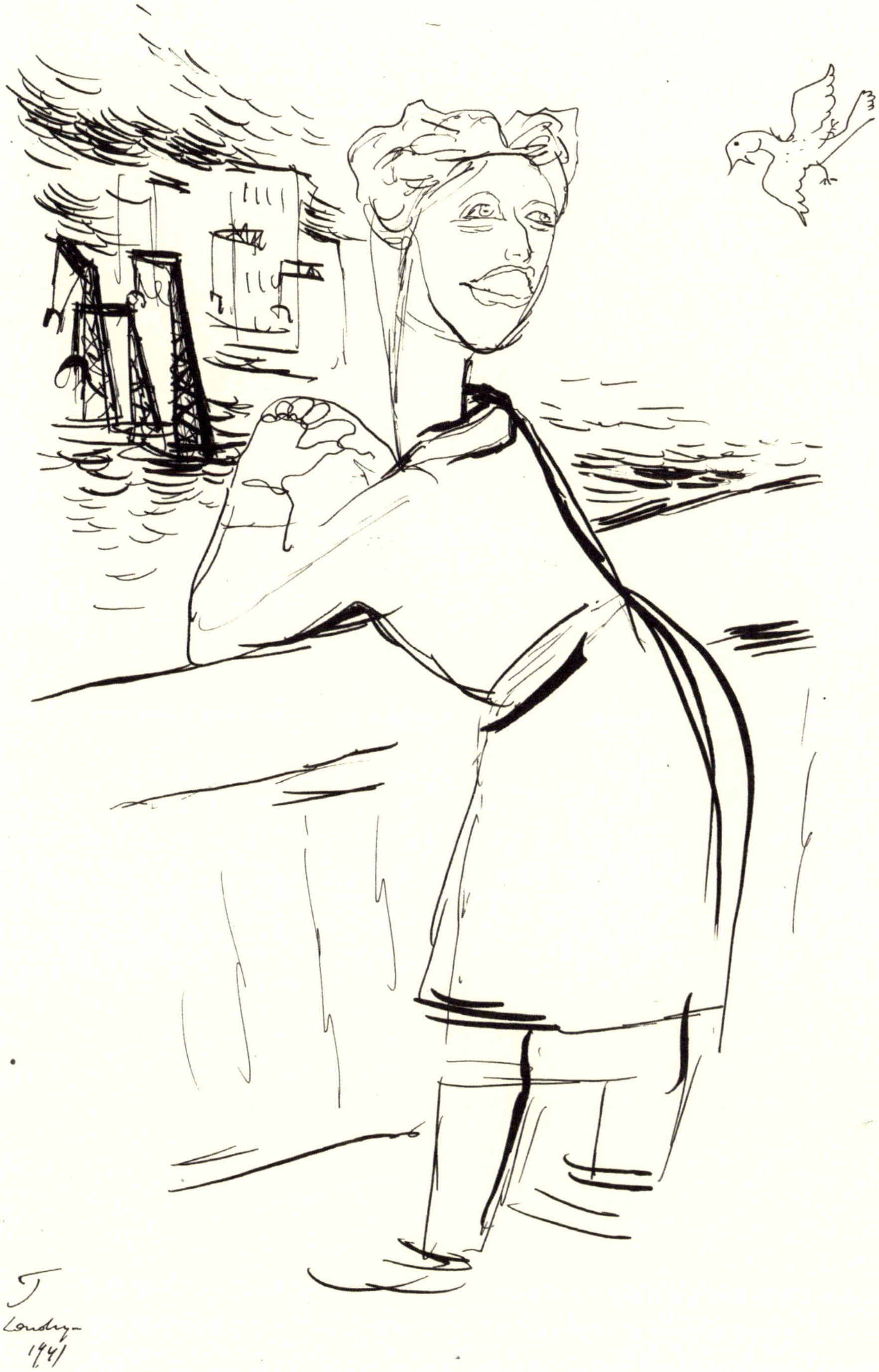

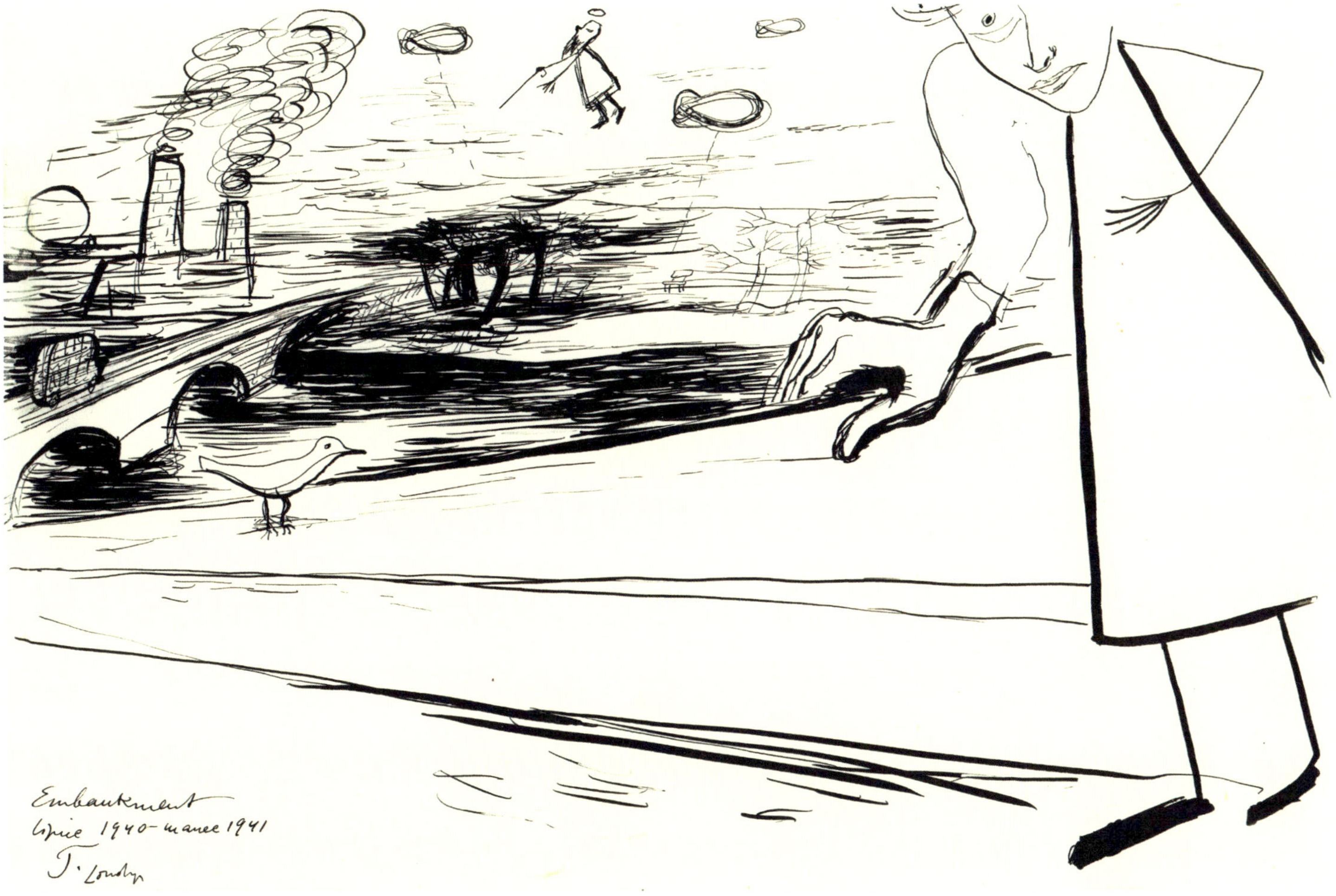
Embankment

XVII

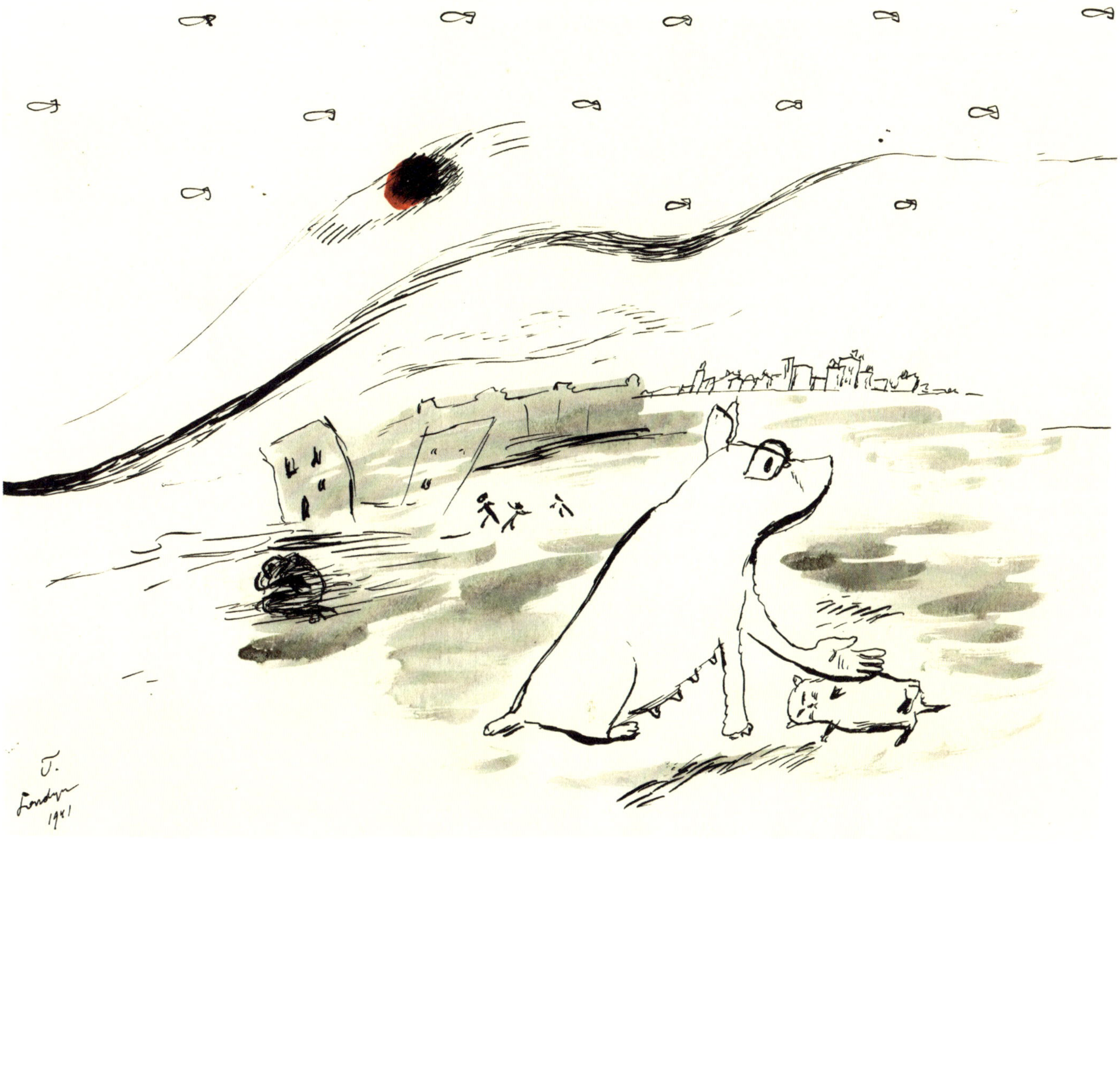
T.
London
1941

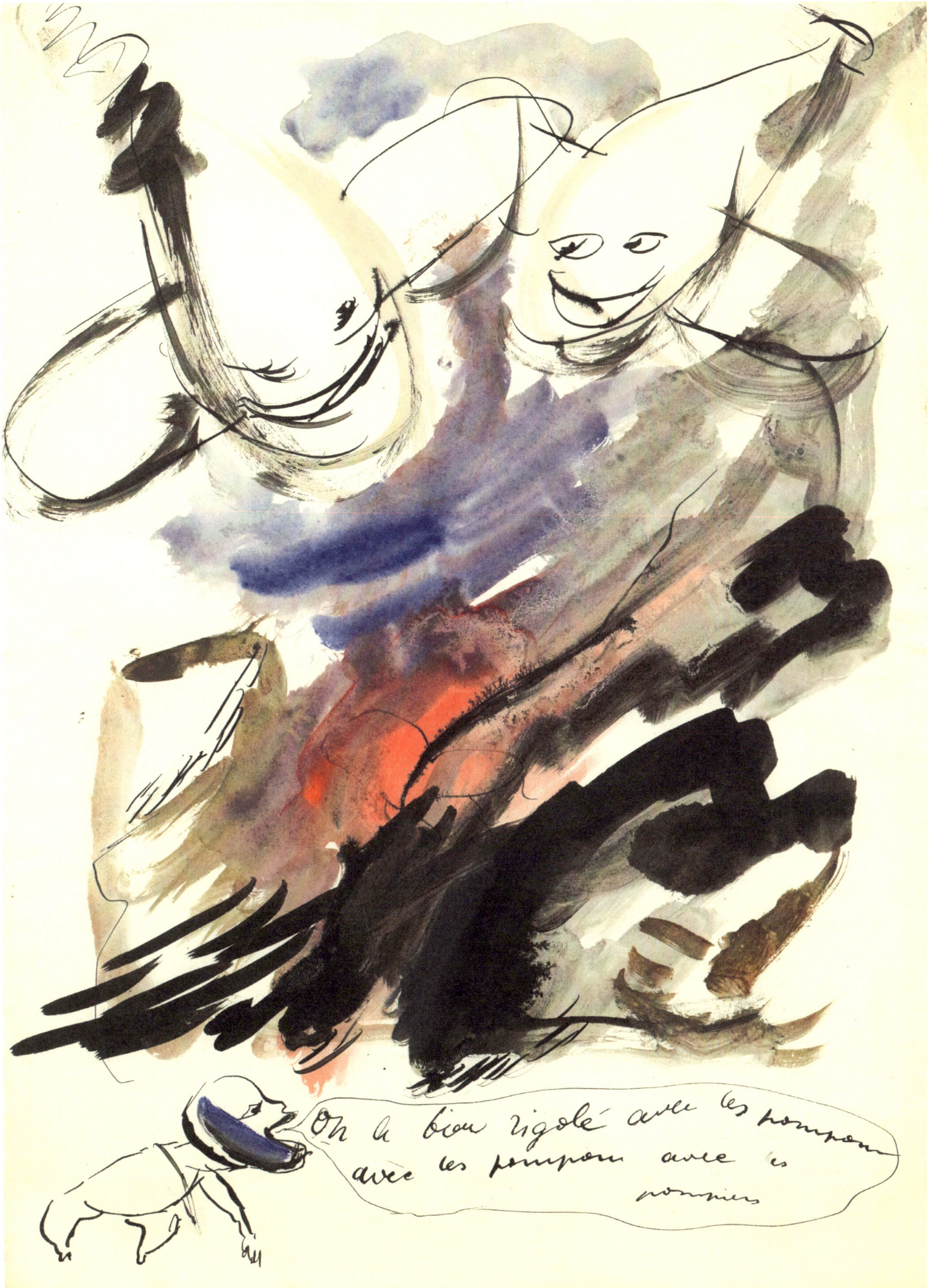
On a bien rigolé avec les pompon
avec les pompon avec les
pommiers

XIX

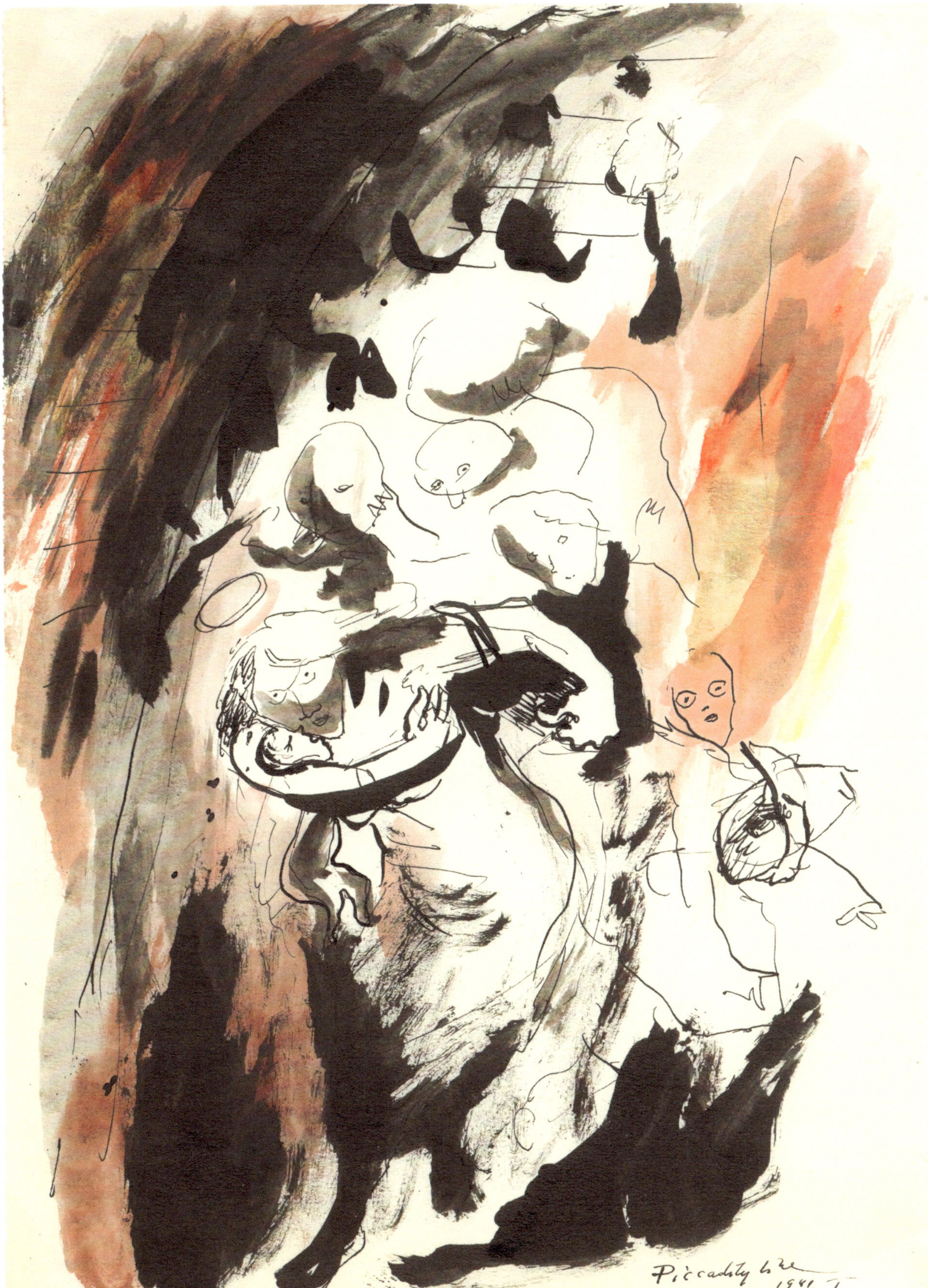
Piccadilly
1941 J.

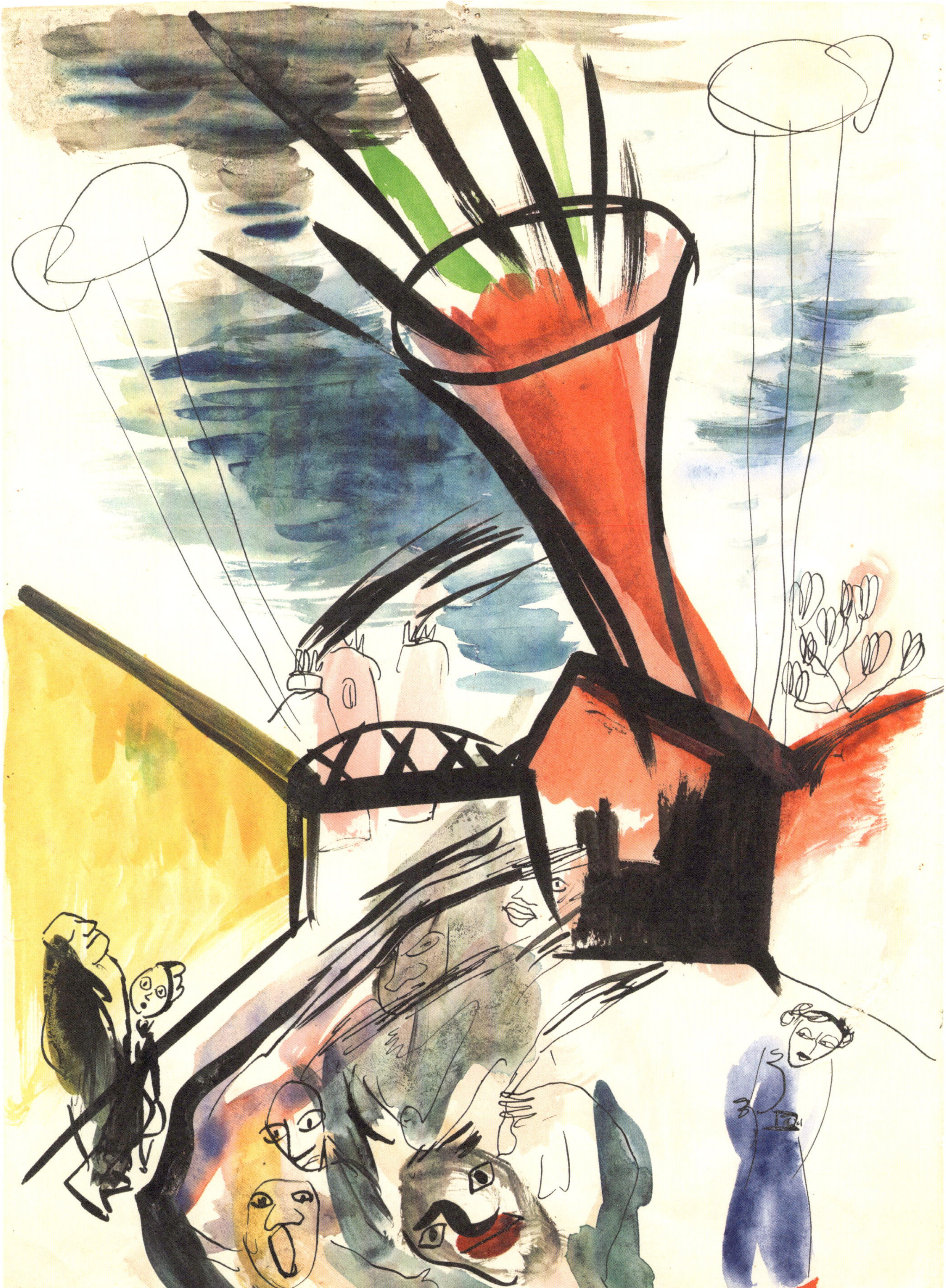

XXI

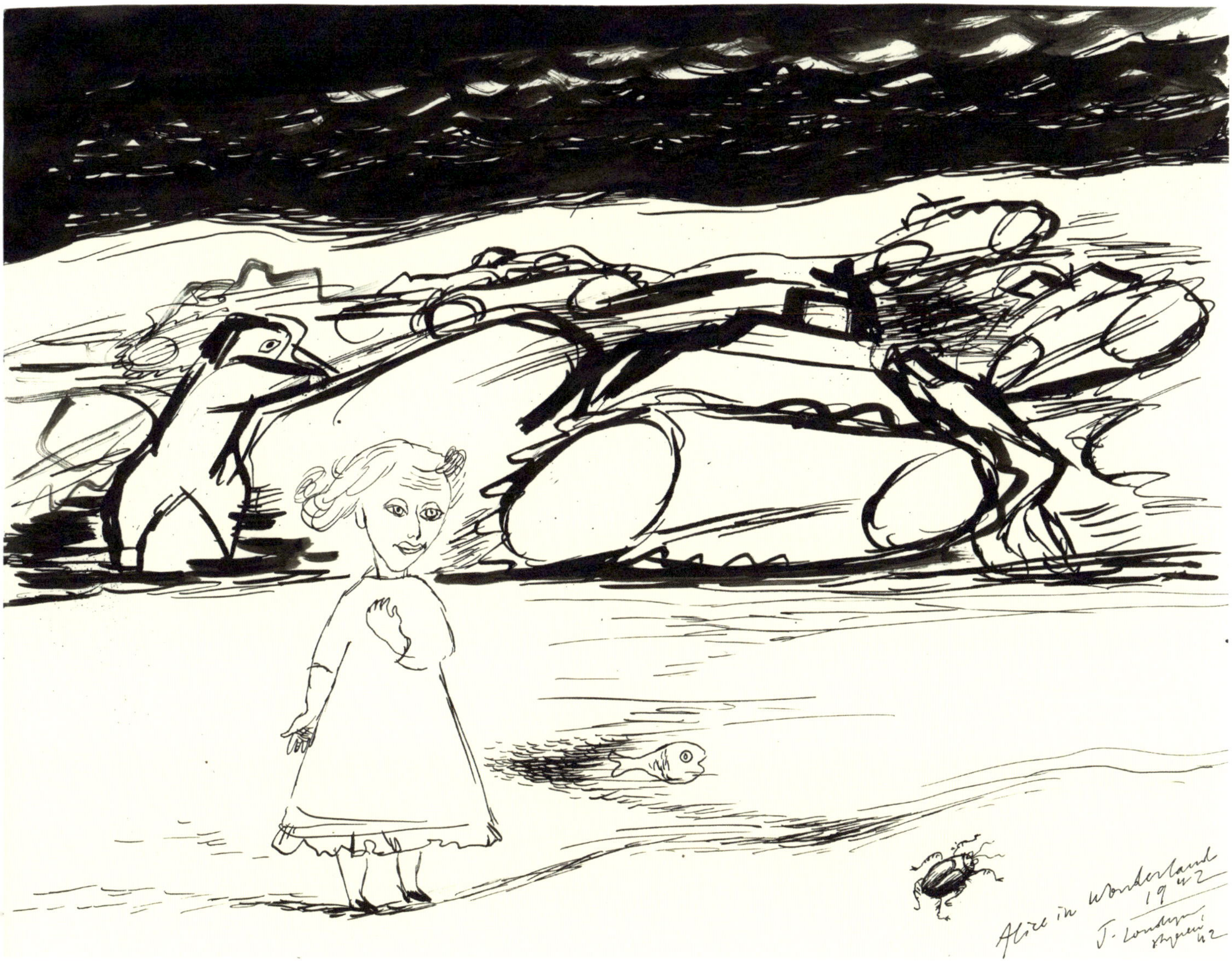
Alice in Wonderland
1942

I – *Distress, the artist's family*, 1941
II – *Escape I*, 25 June 1940
III – *Kings Cross tube shelter I*, 1940
IV – *Don't look*, February 1941
V – *Escape II*, 1941
VI – *Escape III*, 1941
VII – *Refusal*, 1941
VIII – *You can't help it, can you?*, 1941
IX – *Fernando* (self-portrait), February 1941
X – *Sentimental cartography. Information – Documentation* (self-portrait), 1941
XI – *Stratton House*, 1941
XII – *It's a long way I*, 1941
XIII – *It's a long way II*, 1941
XIV – *Help!*, 1941
XV – *Dialogue on Tower Bridge*, 1941
XVI – *Embankment*, July 1940 – March 1941
XVII – *Sirens*, 1941
XVIII – *On a bien rigolé avec les pompons avec les pompons avec les pompiers*, 1941
XIX – *Piccadilly Line*, 1941
XX – *Air raid*, 1941
XXI – *Alice in Wonderland*, January 1942

Croquis dans les ténèbres, part II[53]

'Je peux pas m'accoutumer à…' and fell silent. He sat down on the windowsill and glanced inside the room.

In this room there was a terrifying reality and he knew that he couldn't touch it, because the real fingers of an angel cannot grasp the void that is so sparsely filled with atoms, the fingers of angels are hard, and they can't get a hold on the void that is called matter.

In this room there was a woman, a woman lying on a bed, a woman covered with a blanket pulled right up to her closed eyes.

In this room there was a mirror in a gilt frame and this mirror reflected the woman on the bed.

In this room there was a table with a glass of water.

In this room the lamp was lit; had the woman forgotten to put it out? Had she been afraid to fall asleep in the dark?

It was not because of the light of the lamp that all of this existed, but because of his eyes.

Because in the room there was no image. They were only, in the angel's eyes, the images of the room, of the bed, of the woman, of the mirror, of the table, of the lamp. It may perhaps be difficult to imagine without light, but nowhere are there any images without eyes.

'It's too little: if I had different eyes,' said the angel, 'the world would look different to me. It would be different. Because the world is what I see.' And the angel, rather pleased with this profound philosophical thought, got down from the windowsill and went his way, along the street but high, high up above the road, as if he were walking along an invisible tram wire overhead.

But there weren't any trams in the town. The streets were empty, and the only living things were the houses, examining one another with their half-open windows.

And the angel sat down on the windowsills, and he kept glancing through the windows, and he shrank back in horror at the empty matter piling up in the rooms; often he clung convulsively to the window frames so as not to lose his balance, and he quickly retreated to the middle of the street, high up above the road, his head on the moonlit roofs.

But, attracted once again by the rectangular breach in the wall, he went back to it in order to look o u t s i d e f r o m t h e e x t e r i o r. And suddenly he found himself face to face with a man who was looking at the sky. The man was a poet, but he wasn't looking at the sky to find in the moon, as enigmatic as all nature, the inspiration to write a poem, a sentimental love poem. The sky was much more than that for him.

He looked out of the window and he knew that with his fingers, which were made of empty matter, he couldn't grasp – he could never get hold of – the hardness of the abstraction outside the window, which lives implacably outside matter.

The man sat down on the windowsill and suddenly shrank back, terrified by the hardness of his own thoughts – it is they that are 'abstraction'; he clung convulsively to the window frame because he was feeling giddy and he didn't want to lose his balance and fall down on the pavement below; he quickly retreated to the middle of his room, but soon went back to the window and again sat down on the sill.

53 This text is Barbara Wright's translation, 1995, of the French original, published in Stefan's *Collected Poems*, Gaberbocchus Press/De Harmonie, Amsterdam, 1997, pp. 21–24

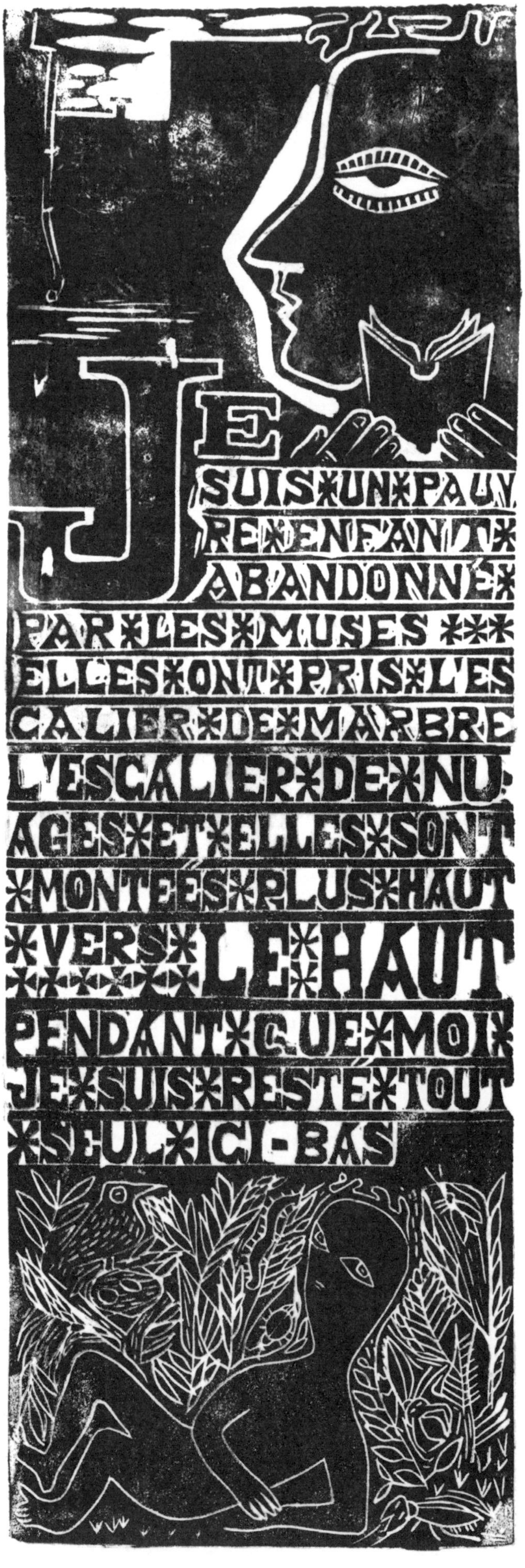

Stefan's linocut of his introduction, 'Petit Nègre écrit petit poème', to his 6-part poem *Croquis dans les ténèbres*, 1941

And then he found himself face to face with the angel, who was looking into the room. They stared at each other for a long, long time; they stared at each other in a friendly fashion.

It was the man who spoke first:

'Tell me', he began, 'what happens when someone has gone through the window? Is it true that he falls like a stone to the pavement, and that that's all?'

'Oh no,' replied the angel. 'That won't be all. At the same time you'll become quite real, you'll grow real wings, and all the angels will be able to touch you with their real, hard fingers… I assure you,' he added, in some embarrassment, 'it isn't particularly interesting.'

The man stared at the angel for a very long, long time, as if he wanted to read his eyes: was he speaking sincerely?

And then it was the angel who asked:

'And you, too – will you tell me what happens after you've gone through the window? Is it true that you become petrified, that you're transformed into winged stone, such as you see in the cemeteries of museums, and that that's all?'

'Oh no', replied the man. 'That won't be all. At the same time you'll become quite real. You'll become so real, as real as I am, that every man will be able to touch you with his fingers, and he *will* touch you, and there will even be too many of them who'll be touching you.'

The angel stared at the man for a very long, long time, as if he wanted to read his eyes: was he telling the truth?

Then the man pointed to the back of the room where a woman was lying on a bed, covered right up to her closed eyes.

The angel looked at the blanket and he noticed an enormous swelling where her big, pregnant belly was.

Somewhere up above, the clouds were gliding. The squall fell, trapped in the street below. The yellowish lamps were beginning to reveal twilight.

The lace curtain quivered, like the surface of a lake, and at that moment the window closed of its own accord.

For a very long, long time, they stared at each other through the transparent window pane, the man and the angel – who was no other than the man's thought.

And then they laid both their hands, the left and the right, on the surfaces of the window pane, and between their hands they pressed their warm lips on the cool glass, and they kissed the two sides of the same thing.

The clouds were racing each other beneath the moon and, on the earth, chasing their own sharp, shapeless shadows.

The man and the angel-his-thought turned away from the window, and each went his own way.

<u>Semi-automatic art</u>
Scientific photography and cinematography as a contribution to the theory of art.

Definition of art. Various definitions of art are possible, all sorts can be defended with equal justification even if they contradict one another. In defence – logic. But in selection – taste, which is the sum of inherited characteristics and experience of the individual.

Definition: discovering new worlds, not immediately accessible to our senses, is somewhat too wide to be worth taking into account. But what is it, to discover new worlds?

In this broad formulation it corresponds to the creating of new worlds. For everything here is presented as a possibility.

On one hand, there are all the future Shakespeares that can originate from the combination of our few dozen letters (of the alphabet); all future Bachs that will emerge from the combination of tones contained in our audible scale, all future Einsteins for whom our strange alphabet of symbols is enough to express their truths. (Painting?)

Tearing off pages of the calendar we approach these future masterpieces. But, if they were produced by some roulette wheel-cum-printer, or, as somebody proposed, by groups of monkeys typing on typewriters, we would never have enough time to select from practically unending numbers of samples, each of which creates for us an image of a new world. We produce future authors just like previous epochs produced contemporary ones. An author is a complicated instrument that is capable of choosing a short cut among all the possibilities that are presented.

(a walking stick – from the chronicle of the family Pasquier[54])

Letter from Franciszka to Stefan

Stefciu, my darling,

Already ten days that I've had nothing from you – look how spoilt I am, it seems to me that this is a long time – ten days... Thank you so much for your telegram (from 13 May) – I feel so close to you despite everything.

I keep on dreaming that you are arriving, just like that, as if for real. And in the morning I wake up again.

Are you working darling? I was going about completely drunk with your poems. You have here devoted admirers. I have to share them after all – it boils over.

Dearest, what about the visa? Does Hicem cover the cost of travel?

It's rather silly to ask questions with letters that take so long to travel. But suddenly it becomes obvious that after a few weeks nothing has changed. It is a year nearly since our separation. Darling – so much time. I would so much like to be together with you already, sweetheart!

Are you in contact with Blanche? Please stay in touch with her. Embrace her from me. As for Marceljanek – visa for him is being worked on. Genek [Cękalski] is making efforts in that direction – he will send it him, also probably a ticket c/o Teresa and her friends. So that he could start working with him soon. Genek is basically a good chap, it is only hard to get him started at the beginning. He would like me to work with him, because he very badly needs help, but they don't want to let me leave my slave labour. And I also prefer this sort of mechanical work because it doesn't demand putting any energy into it, except what I need to fight boredom 6 hours a day. But since I have the impetus to work for myself then, I have enough time – and that's what's most important.

54 Georges Duhamel, *La chronique des Pasquier*, ten novels covering family and social saga, *Les Maîtres*, 1933–45. See also page 129

Translation from the Polish.

MINISTRY OF JUSTICE
No. 76/1941/St.Cyw.
Ref. to No. 102/41/0

SUBSTITUTE DOCUMENT OF REGISTRATION.

On the basis of art. 1 of the Decree of the President of the Republic of Poland dated the 20th August, 1940, relating to substitute documents and amendments in the registers (Journal of Laws of the Republic of Poland No. 13, item 35), the Minister of Justice certifies the following :—

On the 22nd June 1931 a marriage was contracted between Franciszka Weinles, born on the 28th June 1907 at Warsaw, daughter of Jakób and Łucja, nee Kaufman in wedlock Weinles, and Stefan Temerson vel Themerson, born on the 25th January 1910 at Płock, son of Mieczysław and Salomea, nee Smulewicz, before the registrar of Non-Christian faith at Warsaw. Franciszka Weinles is of Jewish faith.

The authenticity of the above particulars is evidenced by the following proofs produced by the party :—

(1) Declarations deposed by the following persons in the capacity of witnesses :—

1. Witness, Ludwik Grodzicki, government official. Protocol of his declaration made on the 24th April 1941 before the Polish Consulate General in London /the original of the protocol is in the records of the Ministry/. 2/. Witness, Stefan Juliusz Konorski advocate. Protocol of his declaration made on the 24th April 1941 before the Polish Consulate General in London /the original of the protocol is in th records of the Ministry/.

(2) The following material proof :—

Verte:-

This document is issued in order to obtain the american visa.

Fee of 5s.0d. /five shillings/ has been collected by the Polish Consulate General in London. ~~The party is exempted from fees~~ (art. 9 of the Decree and Order of the Minister of Justice dated the 28th September, 1940, issued in agreement with the Minister of Foreign Affairs and the Minister of Finance relating to fees for the issue of substitute documents and amendments in the registers (Journal of Laws of the Republic of Poland No. 13, item 40).

London, the 5th May 1941.

By authorisation of the Minister of Justice.

Seal of the Ministry of Justice.

/-/
Director of the Department
Prof. Stefan Glaser

Extract from the Decree of the President of the Republic of Poland dated the 20th August, 1940, relating to substitute documents and amendments in the registers (Journal of Laws of the Republic of Poland No. 13, item 35) :—

"Art. 5.—In case of disclosure that the statements and produced evidence on the basis of which the substitute document of registration was issued are inconsistent with the real state of affairs, the Minister of Justice will rescind his decision, cancel the document and publish this fact in the second part of the Journal of Laws of the Republic of Poland."

No. 41/V/41.

The Polish Consulate General in London hereby certifies that the foregoing is a true and correct translation of the original produced to this Office.

London, the 6th May 1941
For Consul General:

L.S.

Harrison & Sons, Ltd., 44, St. Martin's Lane, W.C.2.

/Ficek/
Acting Secretary

5, 6 May 1941
Official English translation of the Polish of Substitute Document of Registration made for The Ministry of Justice

This document, which certifies that Franciszka and Stefan were married on 22 June 1931, was needed for Franciszka to make her application for an American visa. Stefan Konorski was one of the two witnesses.

15 May 1941

Recently I haven't been drawing – perhaps I had blown off enough steam – I only meander around town, it is warm at last and I reminisce about that other wonderful spring[55] – Darling!

You are curious what is happening with friends? Stefanja is permanently, still finishing the same novel of which you read the beginning. It gets worse all the time. Adam is buying ties and jackets. In reality I don't see them very much. I don't have the patience.

I had a letter from Józio W[ittlin]. He is in New York and complains as usual. From Ignacys [Złotowskis] I continue to receive letters. Remember, darling, if it would be easier for you to go to them, I shall come too, as soon as I can. I am making all the necessary efforts. Darling, I don't know how to express the tenderness I should like to send you. I kiss you and kiss you masses of times.
Franka

18 May Telegram from Stefan to Franciszka

J'AI FAIT DÉMARCHES VISAS SORTIE ET AMÉRICAIN STOP FAUT ATTENDRE PATIENCE CHÉRIE STOP AMITIÉS SINCÈRES POUR STEPHAN STOP SUIS PARFAITEMENT BIEN SOIS TRANQUILLE EMBRASSE LE PLUS TENDREMENT = THEMERSON

20 May Diary Entry

In the evening a reading by Chrzanowski and news about the dissolution of the Polish Red Cross.
Labour camps.

21 May Telegram to Schwarzbart from Hicem

CABLONS NEWYORK CONCERNANT FRAIS VOYAGE STEFAN THEMERSON = HICEM

Diary Entry

Wednesday, letter from Franka

Adults, that is those who not only know their rights and duties but also take them seriously.

To find out:
Hypatia, philosopher from Alexandria 370-414 AD massacred by Christians.

26 May Franciszka's draft of telegrams to Wittlin and Gildesgame

Ton intervention Schwarzbart Hicem Mira cabla Hicem New York concernant frais voyage America pour Stefan prière appuyez urgent.

28 May Letter from Stefan to Franciszka

My dearest darling,

Did you know that it is a year today, a whole round year! How much longer shall we have to endure our separation?

I don't know where I shall be when you get this letter I am waiting now from day to day for an answer, positive I hope, to my application for an exit visa.

55 The Themersons visited London in the spring of 1936. It is then that they met the artist, László Moholy-Nagy (1895–1946) painter, photographer, and advocate for the integration of technology and the arts and arranged screenings in Poland of English avant-garde films. The first issue of *f.a.* [art film] 1937, which they published, was about experimental film in England.

So long as I don't have that, it's difficult to do anything about the rest. I cannot leave now, not even to Grenoble, which is so near.

I received a card from Hania dated 12 May. She writes that all of them are in good health. Stefan [Miller] is still in Otwock. Hania is sending them 'small parcels' all the time, mainly sweets and soap. Sewek has arranged a modest professional office for himself. Hania herself has not left yet, she is extending her visa and doesn't know what to do next. About our family she adds: 'you know they are suffering more from the relatives of the young Hallerowa [Wandzia Haller][56] than from strangers'. I know them very well, and the others too, I am sure that this is no exaggeration.

It's already a long time since I've had a letter from you, darling, and it makes me sad. Has Teresa left yet? Because I've had no word from her either for a long time.

I had a letter dated 15 April from Mira. She says that she is trying to persuade you to go there. 'I have more correspondence with Franka than with anyone in the world, and more often than at any other time. When I think about her, I feel warmth in my heart. When I think of people that are the closest to me, I always think of you both first. You and Franka you will manage very well. There is a huge market. Apart from that, you are not toffee-nosed.' And she writes about your letters that they are 'just wonderful. So much humour'.

Darling, it's already half a year that I am sitting here and continue to think of it as temporary, as if I sit here for a moment on a branch preparing to fly off somewhere else. This branch is so unimportant that there is nothing to be said about it. I myself can't even see it. If Sebastian saw it, he would perhaps somehow write: 'hôtel de la poste-restante'.

Dearest, Franeczko, love

Give a hearty hug to Stefan for me. I wanted to write to him separately, but I can't do it and he would find it difficult to read. But I truly empathise with him.

Dearest darling, I kiss you so much – St

Diary Entry

It's a year today.

29 May **Diary Entry**

Application for a ration-card for a shirt in La Salle des Réunions

1 June **Letter from Franciszka to Stefan**

Stefciu, my dearest darling,

So many, many words come together and it is so difficult to write them down. It feels as if I could go on like this all the time, endlessly. All the time I feel the need to tell you something or ask you something. And simply to cuddle up to you, darling – I collect hours into days, and days into months, and every hour I want to be with you and during every moment, I miss you. There are so many thoughts, so many questions, so many feelings, to live through, to express, and to control. And when I feel fearful, I try to adopt your attitude towards me, it's the only one I can believe in. I am trying not to limit myself, not to give in to complexes, but it is getting too much for me. I've had enough of these mugs I'm surrounded by, and the mature adult control that I'd hoped to achieve during these immensely difficult, lonely months – it just cracks at the seams. I can't

56 Wandzia's parents, Heniek and Ludka Haller, relatives who share the flat with Franciszka's mother and sister in the Warsaw ghetto.

communicate with anyone, not even a bit, and find myself being rude to people. And the worst of this is that it doesn't lead to anything, it's like banging my head against doors that don't lead anywhere.

Today I spent a long time in the elevated company of our 'elite' – Stefanja, Adam, etc: probably why I am so gloomy. The boredom of that talk can't just be the result of my head-in-the-clouds 'lack of interest' in what was discussed. I didn't see a spark of life in any eyes. It was typical, like pouring from one empty saucepan into another, and all of that babble going on here drowns out my private thoughts about anything real and important.

But that's enough, you know it all well enough, and I expect your own experiences are much the same. I can't help complaining, if only to build up my stamina and renew my belief in the reality of magnitudinis.

It is so long now since I've had a letter from you – you can't realise all they mean for me. And poems.

I should so terribly like to be with you already, darling, – I've been thinking, that with Ignacy you'd have a better chance of some creative work than with Genek – what do you think? Do you know if Moholy is running that art college in Chicago? I want to contact him, but I am finding it difficult to write a letter to him. Perhaps there would be a chance of getting a grant?

I think about it a lot, but I suppose that external conditions will resolve these questions for us. Can one make any plans now?

It is already more than a year since I've seen you, darling. I don't know, if you will get this letter before 22 June [their wedding anniversary]. We are beginning to measure time in anniversaries. I kiss you darling so very tenderly and so much my darling.

I enclose in the envelope a photograph of me that Genek took. I kiss you once more, and write. Franka

Darling – the photograph hasn't been returned to me, so you must do without my mug. Masses of kisses. Fr. Oh Yes! I got the address of Moholy, he is in New York – Museum of Modern Art, Rockefeller Center.

7 June Letter from Stefan to Franciszka

My dearest darling,

I've been putting this letter off from day to day, because I would have liked to write after receiving the exit visa which I've been waiting for over a week. But I don't know why it isn't here yet. When you get this letter, darling, it will probably already be the 22nd – ten years, Franeczko, I thank you for them so much, so very much my very own little one.

Only recently I deluded myself that it is possible, after all, that at the end of June we shall be together somewhere in the world. But days turn into thousands and a fairy tale about patient waiting.

Ah, darling, chin up! And *sursum corda.* Do you remember? I kiss you so very much – raise a glass with your neighbours and drink to yourself and to me with this brandy of ours.

I've been working a lot during the last two weeks – maybe it will turn into a book, quasi philosophical essays, based on a broad canvas of social customs with a pinch of irony and constructed like a criminal thriller. I don't take the panic that exists here to heart too often. I do my own thing, or at least I try to, and I wait.

Darling, it is so long since I had any news of you – it's nearly a month since your last telegram, and in that time one letter only, an old one. Did you get my airmail letters sent direct?

Love, darling, I kiss you, kiss you so many times. Stefan

Diary Entry

Still no exit visa.
Today card from Teresa that in a week or ten days she will send it.[57]

I am still writing a book – crime/murder in the Hôtel Poste Restante

Louis Hourticq 'Monuments historiques' an article in *L'Illustration,* 31 May 1941

> … Auguste Comte: 'La société comprend plus de morts que de vivants'… Le vieux philosophe chagrin [Heraclitus] disait: 'Tout passe et l'on ne se baigne pas deux fois dans le même fleuve'. L'architecte pouvait répondre: 'Ce n'est jamais la même eau, mais ce sera toujours le même Nil tant qu'il reflétera les mêmes Pyramides.'

8 June **Letter from Franciszka to Stefan**

Stefciu, darling,

Today, I received two of your letters, one from April and one from 3 May. And yesterday a cable from Wittlin, whom I had asked to intervene with Hicem in New York (to whom your Hicem turned in this matter) about paying for the ticket. I am so happy that this has already been dealt with.

Darling, can you imagine what your letters mean to me! – I feel almost like Robinson Crusoe on a desert island, but it's actually worse than that here, because I'm surrounded by crowds all speaking some very alien language. It doesn't mean anything to me that it is Polish – I still can't communicate.

I try to say what I have to say in drawing. That's not easy either, but sometimes I do have the satisfaction of seeing that it immediately gets straight to the point instead of dissolving without a trace.

Anyway, there are only a few people to whom I show my drawings, preferably complete strangers rather than those who are supposed to think like us. Stefanja prattled on with so many idiocies that she stopped me working for two months. It wasn't easy for me to get over it immediately. After all, I had felt that I could trust her. Only a few people read your poems, but those that read them get a great deal from them. One could simply feel how they react confronting something real and alive.

You know – such moments of real emotion are worth a lot, and it is so beautiful when one can give them. This is a purely egoistic stand, even though superficially it sounds different.

I don't know what Mira wrote to you about *Tralaliński*[58]. A second edition really is going to appear, but someone else is doing the drawings. In the end I didn't pay any attention. There are so many considerations involved. I get on with my work anyway. Altogether, a nonsense.

57 What 'it' is, we don't know.
58 Franciszka had illustrated the original edition of Juljan Tuwim's *O Panu Tralalińskim* in Poland in 1938.

Recently Grydzewski asked me if I would illustrate a children's poem for him, that Councillor Leszek sent from overseas. Let him go to hell! I just wanted to weep – such a hideous doggerel. I refused, gave them a piece of my mind about it. I imagine they are furious, but these are the only advantages that my so-called work gives me. Afterwards it is quite difficult to keep on one's nose spectacles that focus and change one's perspective, because the crowd around is pushing and elbowing, driven by some shallow journalistic passion 'to know' what's happening today and what will happen tomorrow morning.

Perhaps it may be easier for us to retrench together. Making some universal division between those 'interested' and those 'not interested', that is to say egocentrics. But that would leave out a whole range of important and valuable points of view. Besides, I don't know how to and don't like talking about it anyway.

The letters from Ignacy, Mira and Józio are also rather strange. It is difficult to judge what it is really like for them over there. Anyway I would not know how to draw conclusions from that about what it might be like for us.

So, darling, my only thought is to be together with you – it doesn't matter where. Here, to all intents and purposes, work is assured, but if you decide (this means if you want to, or have to) to travel to Mira, I would come as soon I as I could. I delivered my affidavit to the American Consulate just in case.

Do you feel strong enough to work with Genek?

On the other hand, one doesn't know anything about Ignacy's situation.

Darling, I kiss you so very tenderly and passionately.

Love, Franka

Diary Entry

Sent letters to Mme Monges, Franka, Hania, and Mira.
Today news about Syria.[59]
For me, neither letters nor visa.
Until 2 am at Michał's and Szuki's – I talk about the structure of the atom, the mutability of concepts and the inflexibility of speed.

9 June **Telegram from Franciszka to Stefan**

CHÉRI REÇU NOUVELLES WITTLIN NEW YORK QUE TES FRAIS VOYAGE ARRANGÉS DÉJÀ PAR CENTRALE HICEM À NEW YORK. TOUTE MA TENDRESSE MON PETIT CHÉRI EMBRASSE = THEMERSON

Diary Entry

Today telegram from Franka – about a message from Wittlin that Hicem in New York will pay the cost of my journey.

From Grenoble	7.25	9.50	12.08	14.50	19.21	20.31	23.22
to Voiron	6.49	9.24	11.32	14.24	18.44	20.04	22.47
To Grenoble	7	9	12	16.45	18.20	19.35	21.10
from Voiron	7.44	9.28	12.44	17.16	19.04	20.14	21.42

Voiron is closing down in two weeks.
A place in Grand Hôtel

59 British and Free French forces invaded Vichy-controlled Syria on that day.

11 June 1941

Telegram from Maxamin in Lisbon to Freyd in London

LIVRET ENVOYÉ THEMERSON 4 JUIN = MAXAMIN

Franciszka's notes on the back of the above telegram

7 May 1941
Letter sent to the Home Office

28 June 1941
Wittlin – Est il possible malgré nouvel ordre intervenir sujet visa Stefan comme cas exceptionnel par PEN Club où n'importe comment. Seule possibilité de partir d'ici. Themerson

Other small notes

Zieliński
on Saturday 8 or 8.20 in Leicester Square, tomorrow Hicem
not at home, telephone 6 1126 Friday

Diary Entry

Letter from Franka
Letter from Seghers

12 June **Letter from Stefan to Franciszka**

My dearest darling, today I received your letter of 15 May. Thank you Franeczko. I am still here. Still without an exit visa. I continue to hope that it will come any day. Sometimes it seems that it will be any moment now, or very soon, and afterwards I watch the days change into weeks and weeks into snail-paced months. Do you remember the empty days from the *Magic Mountain*? What's different for the last two weeks is that I try to fill these voids by transforming them into a book, such as *Crime at the Hôtel de la Poste Restante*, or rather *des hommes restants*.[60] Although I must admit there are times when it feels as if I don't have the time to get down to writing. Darling, did you get my letter sent from here direct? When you get that letter I shall be in Voiron no longer, because this place is being wound up. I am trying for the South, to be closer to the Consulate, but I've been put down for Grenoble, at Grand Hôtel – the environment there, that's Bassano[61] – do you remember? I wanted very much to be in Grenoble during the winter because of the library (here there isn't a single one and I have to buy books), but now that the possibility of departure is becoming more concrete it no longer attracts me.

A strange thing happened. Published here, in collaboration with André Gide, is a bi-monthly magazine, *Poésie 41* which has a beautiful motto: *Et de sa blessure, fut la fleur vive*. I felt an empathy with them, for that elusive something that they have in common with our *f.a.* And I sent them 'Petit Nègre', just like that, just by itself, without a letter, after all I don't know how to write a letter in French without any mistakes. This is why I say that a strange thing happened. Can one write in a language that one doesn't know? That one doesn't hear? And just today I got an answer, which I am copying for you word for word:

60 For the story, which became 'The Investigation', see page 375

61 Here, Stefan refers to the 4-star hotel, Hôtel Bassano, near the Champs-Élysées.

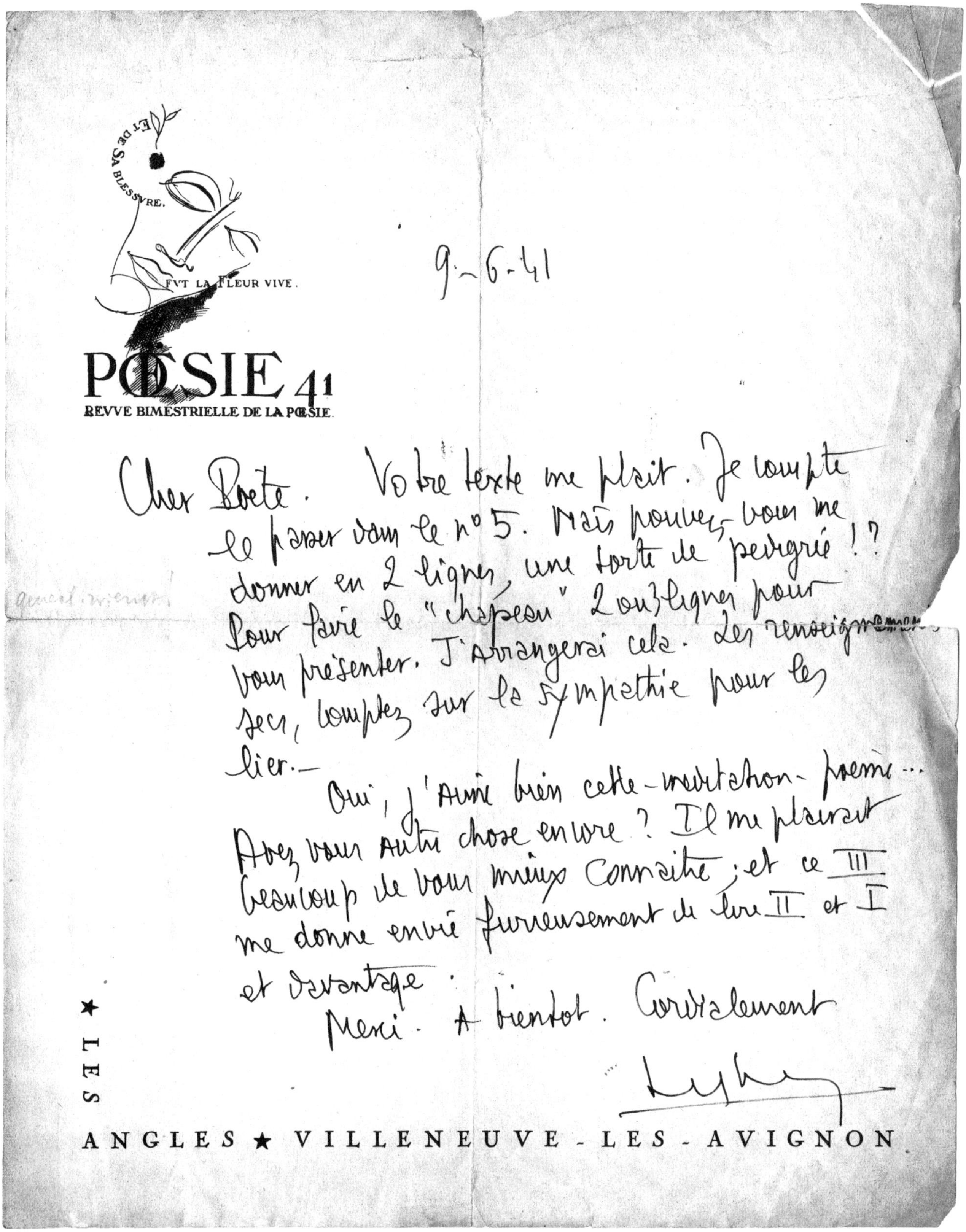

ET DE SA BLESSVRE.
FVT LA FLEUR VIVE.

POESIE 41
REVVE BIMESTRIELLE DE LA POESIE

9-6-41

Cher Poète. Votre texte me plait. Je compte le passer dans le n° 5. Mais pouvez-vous me donner en 2 lignes, une sorte de "pedigree"!? Pour faire le "chapeau" 2 ou 3 lignes pour vous présenter. J'arrangerai cela. Les renseignements secs, comptez sur la sympathie pour les lier.—

Oui, j'aime bien cette méditation-poème… Avez vous autre chose encore? Il me plairait beaucoup de vous mieux connaître; et ce III me donne envie furieusement de lire II et I et davantage.

Merci. A bientot. Cordialement

LES ★ ANGLES ★ VILLENEUVE-LES-AVIGNON

Letter from Pierre Seghers to Stefan, 9 June 1941

Cher Poète. Votre texte me plait. Je compte le passer dans le no.5. Mais pouvez-vous me donner en 2 lignes, une sorte de pedigrée? Pour faire le "chapeau" 2 ou 3 lignes pour vous présenter. J'arrangerai cela. Les renseignements secs comptez sur la sympathie pour les lier. – Oui, j'aime bien cette – *méditation-poème*… Avez-vous autre chose encore? Il me plairait beaucoup de vous mieux connaître; et ce numéro III me donne envie furieusement de lire no.II et no.I et davantage. Merci. A bientôt. Cordialement. Seghers

Under the title was the caption 'no. III', but I don't still have those two first ones, written in Paris. But that isn't what's important for me so much as the strange idea of something existing under the skin of poetry that is independent of words. One more reason why this letter gave me such pleasure, was that it proves again that against all the odds, there are everywhere people with whom one can share common melodies, even if they are being played on different instruments. You see, darling, how despite the smallness of this god-forsaken place, and despite everything that usually accompanies such insignificance, I don't give up and I persist all the time in this vast loneliness, which I won't even call difficult because I wouldn't even know how to define it.

Everywhere one bears oneself alone. In the end you must have the courage to admit this to yourself and to recognise it in others. Sometimes it seems to me that I am getting very old. It isn't true.

Once again I shall be young,
once again, before old age, I'll escape.
Once again I shall gorge on liberty,
once again I'll get drunk on freedom
before I drop dead.
You'll see me one day
romping in a field like a colt,
neighing out March and April,
kicking in the May spring,
and in my teeth I'll chew fragrant
blades of a green meadow and sky.[62]

Bo jeszcze raz będę młody
Bo jeszcze raz przed starością ucieknę
Bo jeszcze raz się nażrę swobody
Bo jeszcze raz się upije wolnością nim zdechnę
Bo jeszcze zobaczysz mnie kiedyś
pobiegnę po łące jak źrebak
zarżę marcem i kwietniem
zawierzgam majową wiosną
i w zębach zgryzę pachnące
źdźbła łąki zielonej i nieba.

Darling, you don't know how I miss you. I kiss you Franeczko so very much.

Today, I received a letter from Halina Lichtenberg from Marseille. She has got all the papers and the American visa, and she calculates that she will get her number in the Consulate only in August. And I, when?

Darling, I so very much want to see what you are doing. Isn't there a way?

I kiss you masses, masses of times, love Stefan.

Telegram from Stefan in Voiron to Franka

CHÉRIE ATTENDS TOUJOURS VISA SORTIE ET AUTRES SUIS TRÈS BIEN TRAVAILLE UN PEU ET TOI COMMENT VAS-TU EMBRASSE MON PETIT LE PLUS FORT POSSIBLE = THEMERSON

12, 13, 14 June **Diary Entry**

Finished second chapter[63]

62 'Fuga. Epod 2a (świt)'. Written in Polish, Voiron, November 1941. For the final version of this poem see *Dno nieba*, p.9, 1943; or *Wiersze Wybrane 1939–45*, p.91.

63 Of *Professor Mmaa's Lecture*.

Letter from Franciszka to Stefan

Stefciu, my darling, yesterday I sent a letter and today again. Darling I miss you so much. This month is full of dates, multiplied by memories of anniversaries before this year.

Last June, I spent the anniversary of our wedding day on the pier. Ah, dearest to be able to see you and to embrace you at last. How are you? What do you look like? Do you look after yourself? Can you look after yourself?

Darling, still, without a break I think about you.

Yes, – a lot has changed along the route of our journey since a few years ago. And we have, too. I have come to understand many things, but others I continue not to understand and probably never shall. I protect myself with cynicism against this impossibility to understand. But, luckily, things that are real and alive can penetrate, even through this cynicism.

What about you, darling? I am so very happy that you are working a bit. The poems that you sent are so close to me. Did I write to you that all those who read them are both moved and disturbed? It isn't easy to judge how much this means in this fossilised state and insane silence.

Darling, at this moment I don't work for myself. It actually isn't true, it's only just that I don't make 'surrealistic' drawings. But this was after all my last phase of work. For the moment I digest and re-digest, like a cow, quietly and without hurrying.

Oh, Stefciu, one thing that is urgent for me is to see and embrace you. Write a lot, darling. Letters travel very slowly, but a few words – even if they're one or two months old – are such a great pleasure for me.

I kiss you so tenderly and so much… Franka

Diary Entry

Performance without him.[64]

No. They played a lousy trick on Lipski, and that Mainssieux also a Jew, because he wrote unfavourably about Dygat.

Anti-Semitic decree is published by the Vichy government, after which the rights of Jews are limited.

16 June **Diary Entry**

Two letters from Franka

Jahl's case. That they will beat him up, because he is a Jew, because he boycotted Dygat.

For work. Doctor's certificate
Good relations with Jahl again.

18 June **Telegram from Franciszka to Stefan**

```
CHÉRI MILLE TENDRESSES POUR NOTRE ANNIVERSAIRE COMMENT VAS
TU MON PETIT STOP PRENDS CONTACT ZABIEŁŁO STOP AMIS GENEK
ME DEMANDAIENT AIDER FORMALITÉS VISAS STOP JE T'EMBRASSE
CHÉRI DE TOUT CŒUR  =  THEMERSON
```

64 Stefan doesn't explain but it must be Lipski.

Letter from Franciszka to Stefan

My dearest darling,

A moment ago your letter of 28 May arrived. Love, Stefciu. And I wrote to you that day. Did you get it?

Only today I learned about these new rules in connection with American visas. They don't want to give them to people who have relatives in occupied countries. And at the same time I received a letter from Teresa that they introduced it there already on 3 June, just at the time when her visa arrived. She writes that perhaps they will change it. I just don't know what to do, darling, at any rate I am cabling Józio [Wittlin]. Perhaps he will be able to intervene through the PEN Club, or something.

My sweetheart, so much has already been achieved, and yet seeing you darling, slips further away again.

At any rate Genek [Cękalski] is trying for a visa for you, only it takes so terribly long, oh darling!

But don't let's give up. You already told me that in a telegram once after all, Stefciu. Let's not give up. In the end, in the end, we shall meet after all. We must try very hard not to let this time of separation be as stupefying and fruitless as our daily conditions try to impose on us. Memento Magnitudinis. I am so happy with your poems, darling. I have read them so many times.

I gave to Antoni [Słonimski] 'Dno nieba', Fragment of the 1st poem: 'Mon pauvre ami' – he is the only person here in whose mind I have confidence. He liked your poems very much. He wants to publish them. He is going to publish a new literary journal and include them in it.[65]

My pet, I would so much like to know what you are doing now. And I have some drawings that I urgently want to show you. They are 'unposted letters' to you, really, not drawings.

Darling, remember that I so much want for you to be cheerful and that all should be well with you. Smile, Stefciu. The post is not regular. But, after all, I write letters to you all the time and often without pen and paper. I miss you so much, darling.

So, chin up.

You write that Mira is persuading us to go there.[66] At the beginning I rather didn't want to go, but now I should do so willingly. If only it were possible. It is not my capriciousness, only that the assembly of characters and concerns, about which I write to Mira, is a masterpiece of humour. And anyway with a tear – of sentiment or despair…

Apart from that there were situations where humour was the only way to survive. So you smile too, my darling.

Mira is anyhow a bit confused there. Recently she went to Minnesota, and she is probably cooking tinned peas for Ignacy just like in rue des Écoles.

Genek [Cękalski] is actually waiting with work for you darling.[67] There is an enormous amount to be done. But … do you want it? You know what that atmosphere's like, and I don't have the conscience to drag you into it. But to be together, really so close! – Darling!

Even so, if something else crops up to stand in the way and prolong our separation – darling – just stay cheerful. Think of yourself just as I think about you – so tenderly. I love you so much my sweetheart.

65 This will be the literary monthly, *Nowa Polska*.

66 To the United States.

67 Work at the Film Division of Polish Government-in-Exile

In two days, our wedding anniversary. I sent you a telegram, but what can one say in a telegram!

How difficult it is to wait for letters. They take a long time and are irregular. Our dialogue is broken, but it continues… I send you such long, warm kisses, my darling. Franka

21 June **Telegram from Stefan to Franciszka**

CHÉRIE TANT MEILLEURS SOUHAITS POUR TON ANNIVERSAIRE ET LE NÔTRE JE TE REMERCIE CHAQUE SECONDE DE CES DIX ANNÉES NE T ATTRISTE POINT CHÉRI IL FAUT PRENDRE TOUT SEREINEMENT COMMENT VAS TU SANTÉ ET MORAL VEUX TELLEMENT SAVOIR TES PENSÉES VIFS TRAVAUX ET SAIS SI PEU ÉCRIS ELLES SONT SI VIVIFIANTES TES LETTRES JE TRAVAILLE ET ATTENDS AVEC FOI VIVE MOMENT OÙ SERONS ENSEMBLE EMBRASSE SI FORT TANT BAISERS MON PETIT CHÉRIE TENONS NOUS

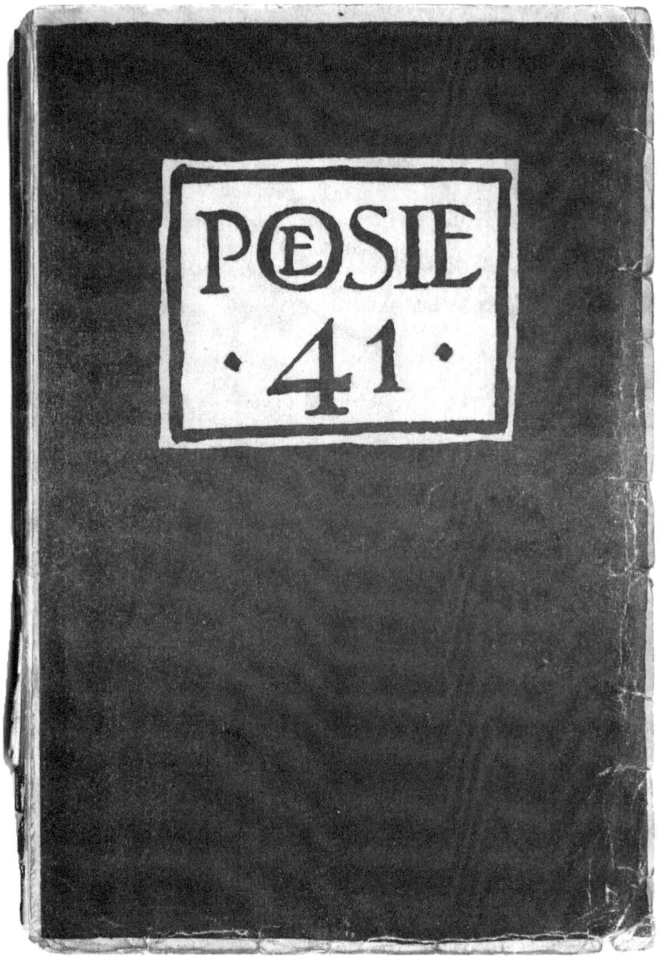

STEPHAN THÉMERSON, l'écrivain polonais qui fut en même temps le créateur du lyrisme « optique » appliqué au cinéma est dans un foyer de la Croix-Rouge, à Voiron. Tous les négatifs de ses films sont brûlés, ses manuscrits disparus: Il travaille à des traductions de poèmes et nous écrit à ce sujet : « *Ne croyez-vous pas que l'on peut trouver un moyen de présenter ces traductions comme des partitions qui ne sont pas lisibles pour le public mais qui suffisent pour un chef d'orchestre :*

1. *Violon : Texte original.*
2. *Violon : Commentaires sur les particularités de la langue.*
1. *Alto : Texte écrit phonétiquement.*
2. *Alto : Commentaires sur la phonétique.*

Percussion : Traduction mot à mot.
Piano : Traduction libre ».
Ce qui est, pour le moins, original !

In notes about the authors of the May/June issue of *Poésie 41*, Pierre Seghers contributes the above paragraph about Stefan.

21 June 1941
Telegram from Franciszka to Stefan

MON PETIT JE TE REMERCIE TELLEMENT POUR TÉLÉGRAMME SUIS HEUREUSE QUE TU TRAVAILLES NE PENSE QU'À TOI IL FAUT TANT DE PATIENCE JE PARCOURS NOS ANCIENNES PROMENADES ICI JE T'ÉCRIS SOUVENT À VRAI DIRE SANS CESSE EMBRASSE SI TENDREMENT CHÉRI = THEMERSON

26 June **Letter from Polish Embassy in London to the Ministry of Information and Documentation**

To whom it may concern
From the Embassy of the Polish Government in London

In connection with the letter from the Ministry of Information and Documentation of 30 April 1941, no.2275/4k, The Embassy wishes to inform you that as a consequence of steps undertaken, the British authorities have agreed to give a British entry visa to Stefan Themerson.

signed by II Secretary of the Embassy, M. Budny

28 June **Telegram from Józef Wittlin in New York to Stefan**

INTERVENTION A WASHINGTON POSSIBLE SEULEMENT SI CONSUL VOUS PERMETTRA VISA CONDITION WASHINGTON RETIRE RESTRICTION. WITTLIN

Telegram from Stefan to Franciszka

CHÉRIE MILLE TENDRESSES SUIS TRÈS BIEN ET OPTIMISTE STOP J'ATTENDS TOUJOURS VISA SORTIE ZABIEŁŁO PAS REPONDU VOULEZ VOUS TÉLÉGRAPHIER STOP JE TE SOUHAITE MON PETIT DE TOUT COEUR ET EMBRASSE SI TENDREMENT = THEMERSON

29 June **Diary Entry**

Wróblewski talks about his shop in Chmielna street. About Munia, who knew how to sell, and a shop assistant who was stealing. He hid four bananas in his jacket and took them with him when he was leaving. He had a mistress in Praga[68]. He had to sign that he left at his own request and without the possibility of making any claims.

30 June **Diary Entry**

3 mouchoirs
4 chemises
2 pantalons
6 chauss.

They steal from us time destined for life, as if there wasn't enough eternity beyond our days.

4 July **Cable from Wittlin to Franciszka**

FAISONS NÔTRE POSSIBLE LETTRE SUIT = WITTLIN YOLLES

68 A district in Warsaw.

THE AMERICAN CONSULATE GENERAL,

LONDON, W. 1.

Form B - July 1941.

BIOGRAPHICAL DATA CONCERNING

ALIEN VISA APPLICANT.

The information requested on this form should be inserted in the spaces provided below, by the person most familiar with the history and background of the alien desiring admission.

Separate forms should be used for each alien, except children under 18 years of age. Separate statements concerning such children are not required if their names are included in the form submitted on behalf of an accompanying parent or guardian.

Failure to fill in all of the spaces as clearly and fully as possible will cause needless correspondence and will delay the consideration of the case.

When all of the required information has been filled in by typewriter, the form must be subscribed and sworn to before a Notary Public or other person authorized to administer oaths.

Two letters of reference, preferably from reputable and responsible American citizens who know the person giving this data, must be attached herewith.

State of ______________________________ SS.

County of ______________________________

I, ______________________________________, being duly sworn, according to law, depose and say that I am a citizen or subject of ________________________ (Country), that my address is ______________________________________ that I have resided in ________________________ (Name of country), since ________________ (Date), and that I am interested in the alien whose name is given below who desires to come to the United States; and that I am able to give the following information regarding such alien in view of my familiarity with his (her) personal history:

July 1941
Blank form from the American Consulate

Biographical data concerning alien visa applicant consists of further five foolscap pages (not shown)

Letter from Franciszka to Stefan

My dearest darling, today I got your letter from 12 June.

Darling! do you know what your letters mean to me! The moments of reading them however many, many times are the only moments when I am really alive. And also when I am writing to you, or try to draw to you or for you. It does not mean that I don't draw from the deepest personal need – only that what is personal and deepest is indissolubly connected with you, darling. I dream about reading whatever you are writing now. The first chapter 'Petit Nègre' I have with me. I kiss you so much darling.

9 July I wrote this during last night, and this morning found your letter under the door. Your letter of 30 April. Darling!

The character of your writing on the envelope, simply under the door, on the floor, like before, like once upon a time. I sat down beside it and sat for five minutes before I opened it. Our black cat here, who thought that he knew my habits, sat opposite me and his ears stood up in amazement. Your letters are the most beautiful thing that I have seen in the world. Are you still in Voiron? I assume that they will forward your letters. If you move to the refuge in the vicinity, give my best regards to the Walfiszes. They are very nice people, and she is a very good friend of your cousin, Irka [Fürstenberg]. I was with them together in Angers and afterwards on the journey.

Darling, it is so good about *Poésie 41*. It had to be like that. You are after all a magician, the most genuine one. Look how I write to you in such a childish and stupid way! I should prefer to send you so much real, adult emotion. For some time now I haven't done any work for myself. That's because I have so much work in the office, it's hot, and during the evenings I only meander around the streets and parks and by the river. It's also that many things have to clarify inside me and this way of doing things helps me dispose of them immediately. But it's also because it takes me a long time to let off steam after the boredom and the monotony of the office. And I don't want to draw just from a mechanical need to do so. It's better to let the thought, the tension and the impulse to draw gather their own momentum. Only then will something come out. I try not to diffuse it in trifles, in isolated reactions to the strange or terrible things that happen, far or near.

It's terribly important for me that you are working, that's so necessary for life, like breathing. In that old letter from April you write about *Tralaliński*. It's nonsense. I have no idea where Mira dreamt this up. I haven't written to her about my work at all. It must be Stefan [Konorski], who is trying to see them and understand; he stands quietly nearby, friendly, with his charm of a nutcracker. He tries to find formulas for everything. He is resolving the world's situation, meets masses of people, is interested in everything. As always. Anyway he is in a terrible impasse, holds his chin up with both hands, but doesn't always succeed.

You ask about Ignacys. Recently, I have been worried about them. From the time that Mira went to Minneapolis to Ignacy, there was only one letter, probably already two months ago and after that nothing. I don't remember if I wrote to you that I met them in Bayonne. We wept from emotion, but I was frightened to persuade them to go with me. It was then quite risky. But I've so many times regretted that they're not here. It seems to me that they feel the lack of somebody with humour on whom they could depend. I have helped so many people here in all sorts of psychological and physical situations, but it hasn't been the nice people I feel closest to. Ignacy would surely be able to work here with the same Rockefeller grant. Mira too, probably. What absurdity! But we shall see.

Józio [Wittlin] wrote to me that he hasn't got your address, asked me to give you a hug. You can write to him c/o Yolles, 84 Boulevard New Rochelle, New York. He performed unheard of contortions in the cause of your passage to New York. It appeared that mine and my friends' cables were not enough, but he did it there and then and your Hicem has been informed. (It seems that Yolles, editor of *Nowy Świat*, who is Józio's guardian angel, paid something in advance.) Wittlin is crying all the time that he has no money to live there.

When it comes to Genek, he has already arranged a visa for Marceljanek [i.e. Stefan], with the help as well of Antoś [Antoni Słonimski]. Marcel [i.e. Stefan] is actually engaged to work and they are trying to get him a Lisbon transit visa. They even sent him a ticket there.

Darling, darling, I am so longing to be with you. To cuddle up in silence, as well as to talk, talk without end. That's right isn't it? Stefulku!

I've now got slightly more interesting things to do at work. (It's so amusing that Cękalski works in the room next door.) I am making a big colour book, a sort of illustration for a small annual. And when I sort out the colours, I make a maquette using real, coloured crayons. This immediately makes me feel more cheerful, even though basically it's still a waste of time.

From this Saturday I have two weeks vacation. I shall move about a bit and for a few days I shall go to the sea. Hanka Poznańska is there at the university and Jasio Leyberg is on duty in the hospital. I am on quite friendly terms with him so I shall have a school-type vacation, warming myself in the sun and talking with those two children. Oh, how much older I am. I feel as I were a designer working in a bigger range of dimensions. I had a long letter from Maryla. Husband and sister are helping her (Aneczka as well) but it all seems to be rather difficult. They are holding on bravely. Stefan and Irka are working. Our mothers are well. What's happening to them now? What about Sewek? What about Hania?

My darling, I have already written so much but still not enough. I kiss you, my dearest pet, so very tenderly. Franka

Stefan Konorski adds a few words:

Stefanku, a huge hug, I think that probably we shall meet reasonably soon. As soon as possible. Franka is a most super *mensch*. She did me a lot of good when I really needed it. But you, too, are almost essential for me. So as you can see – I long for you to be here for completely selfish reasons, but that's how it is. Yours, Stefan.

Telegram from Franciszka to Stefan

CHÉRI REÇU LETTRES JUIN ET AVRIL MERCI C'EST SEULEMENT EN LES RECEVANT SENS VIE RÉELLE MON PETIT BIEN AIMÉ STOP AI TÉLÉGRAPHIÉ WITTLIN SUJET NOUVELLES RESTRICTIONS VISAS AMÉRICAINS ESPÈRE REUSSIRA STOP INVITATION GENEK OBTENUE ADAM ZIELIŃSKI CAIXA 512 LISBONNE ARRANGERA J'ESPÈRE VISA PORTUGAIS STOP JE T'AIME = THEMERSON

Letter from Stefan to Franciszka

Franeczko, my dearest, – I received simultaneously two of your letters from the 8 and 20 June. And money from Blanka (2000). Darling, I have a lot of money and really there's nothing to spend it on – the journey recedes into the future, and what is there here? Thank you so much, Franek, but I know that it must be very difficult for you there and I much prefer that you organise a proper home for yourself – I am here all the time as if at a tram stop, waiting for a tram that doesn't want to arrive. Darling, I am so happy that you are drawing. Don't let anyone stop you, not even any Stefanjas, as none of them has sufficient awareness – moral if not aesthetic – to understand what you are doing. People develop opinions about others that suit themselves. It's very rare to find someone with sufficient disinterestedness to recognise and accept things as they are. And this is why when they judge, they don't illuminate the thing that they judge, but unmask themselves. Their opinions neither magnify, nor reduce what one makes. They merely magnify or reduce themselves. Darling, man is not at all as big or important as one had thought. One has to tolerate him but one should never let oneself be upset by him. And I would be broken here, and good for nothing, if I took my neighbours seriously in this the saddest of all zoological gardens. This is not egocentricity – who is more egocentric than those who live by appearances, who think that the moment during which they are alive is the most important of all moments past and future; than those whose 'interest' in what is happening in the world is of the same type as an interest in a frock that they are going to wear; than those who want to adjust events to conform to their economic or psychological interests.

Darling, I would so much like to see all that you are doing, and when I think that you have to sit so many hours every day in the office – it is enough to make me cry. Please look after yourself, Franek, I beg you. We know nothing yet of the next road and path we shall have to get through. How is your health, Franek, is there anything troubling you? I would do everything, without exception, everything, to be together with you anywhere. Darling, write me some more about your drawings.

You don't know how happy I am that you liked my poems. I should so much like to read them to you myself. And that is all that I can send you.

How are our friends and acquaintances. Do you have new ones?

How are Stefan and Genek?

Give my best regards to Antoni [Słonimski]. It seems to me that he is the only person from this whole band who is disinterested in his thinking, and one doesn't know why he still associates with them.

The hurrah of Leszek [Armatys] only acquires significance when you learn how he had in his time boasted that he had all his visas while he was still sitting quietly in his office.

Darling, have you had any news from home? I have no idea how they are. They depend a lot on help from Sewek. From Hania I've had no news for a long time.

Patience, my little one, I kiss you so much and so tenderly – Stefan

PS: Blanka [Blanche] is returning to her husband.[69] So don't continue to write to her address.

69 Going back to Paris

11 July 1941

Card from Hania Kawa to Stefan – in German

Dear Stef!

Yesterday, I received your friendly letter and was very happy, Matuś [Stefan's mother] will be enormously pleased by it. Your previous letter has reached us without any problems. I've heard nothing from Sewek for a long time. My niece, Marysia, is in the countryside and is expecting a baby around August 1-15. I don't travel, and my family stays here too. We are all in good health. Please write to us as often as you can because Maryla Ch[aykin] and all the others wait longingly for any word from you. I kiss you.

Your Hania

14 July **Diary Entry**

NB à propos Lipski, who truly believes. It is possible to be a true believer, even when it is just more comfortable.

It seems that political systems are not the best. That is why it is paradoxical to expect that the least educated will choose the best political system. It doesn't mean that the educated will choose a good one. If it is inconsistent with their personal material and psychological interests – the more they will fight against it.

Helena's story about her *pensionnat* for Catholic girls. Conversations about how people will look after the Resurrection, fashion from which year.
Chambermaid pregnant. The fiancé has fled.
Priest has long talks with the fiancé who marries the chambermaid.

Scenario for a ballet – treasurer, flower of the fern/the crock of gold.

Erwin's story about children who rescued the drunkard chauffeur who used to give them sweets.

Prophet in the shelters, sentenced in August for 25 days, for saying that Jahl will defend himself. Psychiatrists freed him. Now he says that in November a suicide and the end of the war. Everybody smells a rat!

Wiśniewski's story about Marysia in the manor house, where she worked as a cook for a countess. She got pregnant. She was going to church, an old beggar jumped out from a corner and raped her. She gave birth to a child. After a certain period of time it happens again. 'What's happening with you, Marysia?' 'I stuffed myself on noodles'. But it wasn't believable. 'Who?' 'I was going to church and a beggar from the corner etc.' 'What beggar, what did he look like?' 'He had a bag and a stick.' Police. No beggar. But people saw her visiting the steward, Kamieński. Countess to the steward: 'What's this all about, Kamieński?' 'I don't know anything about it, it isn't me'. They get Marysia to confess. Sobs. Countess: either he will marry or she will throw him out. He had a good job. He got married. Countess gave them a three-room apartment. A teacher for Marysia etc. An ideal wife and mother etc.

17 July **Diary Entry**

In Grenoble, exit visa
visit to Mme Paszkowska, Karnecki, Michał
ballet – Polish legends

Telegram from Stefan to Franciszka

CHÉRIE REÇU VISA SORTIE BEAUCOUP PATIENCE ENCORE MON PETIT MAINTENANT JE NE FAIS QU'ATTENDRE INVITATION GENEK VISAS DESTINATION ET TRANSIT STOP NOUVELLES RESTRICTIONS VISAS AMÉRICAINS SONT DURS J'AI ASSEZ ARGENT MERCI VAS TU BIEN CHÉRIE TRAVAILLES T'EMBRASSE SI TENDREMENT = THEMERSON

Diary Entry

à propos Mlle Dubouchet and the new housekeeper who also cleans all the rooms herself. Making herself, in reality, an old capitalist not interested in benefiting from material assets, but in the function of earning money.

(letter from Lyon that a Spanish visa is already there, but first I need a Portuguese one.)

24 July **Diary Entry**

Grenoble, Michał, René. Madzia [Turpin] was at the factory.
Two pianists – contrast and superficiality.

25 July **Telegram from Franciszka to Stefan**

MON PETIT CHÉRI J'ESSAYE T'ARRANGER DEUX GARANTS MORALES EXIGÉS POUR VISA AMÉRICAIN J'ENVOIE DÉTAILS NÉCESSAIRES À AMI WITTLIN PETER YOLLES ÉDITEUR NOWY ŚWIAT 374 SECOND AVENUE NEW YORK EMBRASSE LE PLUS TENDREMENT CHÉRI VAIS PARFAITEMENT BIEN BAISERS = THEMERSON

Diary Entry

Card from Mietek B[ibrowski]

26 July **Diary Entry**

duty in the kitchen. Exhibition in the Café. Bormat. René.
Sent 'Croquis dans les Ténèbres' to Seghers.

27 July **Letter from Franciszka to Stefan**

Dearest sweetheart Stefciu, I received your letter written specially for my birthday. Thank you darling. I bought myself a flower from you. I do it very often, to make things more pleasant

And to Genek [Cękalski] and to Stefan [Konorski] you can write to the same Post Office Box as to me. They both send their warmest greetings. Darling, what you are writing now interests me so much and I miss you enormously, Stefciu. I don't know how to write what I feel and wouldn't even know how to draw it. So I shall write about all these usual matters, visas etc., that are after all the means for us to be together again.

The American restrictions make things difficult and I know that till the end of July they did not make any exceptions. I enquired here at the Consulate and got a form, like the one that the two guarantors have to complete in New York and send to Washington. If they confirm, they then inform the relevant Consulate. You've probably secured all the necessary papers, haven't you? I sent all the necessary details in a 115-word telegram to Yolles who is looking after this for you.

He is a friend of Wittlin. He is some kind of big fish in the union of journalists and it was he who paid Hicem $50 on account for your ticket. Perhaps now, with those guarantors, it will work out for us. Oh, darling!

Have you been in touch with Dr Zieliński? Was Halina's American visa also stopped? Teresa's was.

And meanwhile so many things are happening in the world. And people react so strangely to every shock or turn of events. Recently Genek was performing somersaults here. He is a complete child. Ignacy writes that he can no longer bear to look at his test tubes and he is embarrassed to look in the mirror(!) It seems as if he wanted to escape to the other side of the world. Stefan is 'getting himself together' professionally and every few days says something different but with an equally determined expression. Only Wittlin remains strong and with common sense – he writes that he has had enough of these two hemispheres. Oh, darling, the only place I feel the authentic truth is in your letters and your poems. If I didn't feel I had that foothold in another world, I'd find it impossible to orientate myself in today's chaos.

I go about here in the same thicket as Alice in Wonderland, which I am just reading. But it doesn't matter, I prefer that to feeling any stupid sense of security.

Oh, Stefciu, I have already covered so much space with writing and literally about nothing. But it is so nice to talk to you for a while.

My vacation I am postponing all the time. I think that one day soon I shall go to get some fresh air. Bye, darling, I kiss you so very, very much.

Franka

Diary Entry

The 'community of interests' that exists among the Jews – retrieved (from outside the seat of cultural jargon) – is a community of a nature similar to that of the community of former comrades-in-arms, or an office community, but not any sort of a mythical community, as Zuzia[70] wants, and not a genetic one. Genetic characteristics signify diversity (perhaps the slanting eyes of a Chinaman exist also in the brain). This diversity is sometimes of no consequence at all, but at other times it can enrich, animate, lend colourful variety to all that springs from the cultural fulcrum in which it exists.

Story of the painter [Léon] Chaloin, a boxer, a gang stealing cars, among others that of doctor F[oata], who buys his picture from the exhibition.

Władek [Karnecki] in *Eugene Onegin* ballet in Antwerp, a wet towel rolled up in his pantalons and then two hundred letters from women.

Doctor's story about his women patients. You cannot screw them because they stop paying fees! One in Lvov – who after paying the first instalment became pregnant, although sterile for 5 years, she demanded repayment and on top of that he had to perform the abortion.

'Why the fuck do we need a knapsack, why the fuck do we need this belt, what the fuck do we need all this for when after all we won't be here.' Doctor's second song: 'And after all, and after all, and after all' etc. without end.

70 Jahl's daughter

27 July 1941

Erwin in Grand Guignol – a girl in the hands of a madman, he wants to take her soul away: his eyes are burning, he wakes up, a doctor brings him back to consciousness; today at the pharmacy mother of a girl who had pierced one of her eyes with something and then the other with a coat hanger.

28, 29 July **Diary Entry**

to Lyon
visit to the Polish office and the Ruszkowskis. Lunch with an engineer in the canteen. The engineer's room.

Portuguese Consulate. Mme Bobity moved away and I haven't got her address. Meeting with R. in the American Bar, Celesson Hôtel, rue des Archers, 20 francs. Bookshop. Puns: bock panaché (½ pint of shandy). No cigarettes. I sent Tema 400 francs. Return – letter from Bobrowski! and Tema. *Poesie 41*. Notes. Card from Hania.

Letter to Seghers.
Conversation with René at Monsieur Chaloin's exhibition. Jahl

1 August **Letter from Stefan to Franciszka**

Dearest darling, I received your letter from 9 July. Thank you Franeczko. I am so happy that you had a vacation. The day before yesterday, I went to Lyon to find out about my affairs. You know already that I have an exit visa and the promise of a Spanish transit visa, but I must still get a Portuguese visa.

Letters take so very long, but anyway all these matters untangle so slowly. It seems to me all the time that the things I might write about will actually have blown over before the letter arrives – and it seems that reality is even more sleepy than the snails that carry our letters. Each day is so similar to the next and all the time I am stuck here as if in one long day just like at a tram stop, dropping from time to time into a café for a beer, and then rushing out into the road and looking round to see if it's my tram coming. I am so tremendously old and so terribly childish, that sometimes it feels as if I should have a long white beard, and at other moments that I haven't changed at all since the time of my first memory, when at the age of three I ran away in Ciechocinek[71] to look once more at the fountain with Jaś and Małgosia, or that other time when I allowed myself to be caught by a dog catcher as I tread on his lasso to save a stray mongrel from capture. From the time of a thousand memories, which were all real experiences, of course, but in fact those of somebody else – since there is probably not a single cell left in my body that is the same.

And I don't regret these childhoods at all, nor my old age, ha! quite the contrary – especially when I look around me and see this terrible, neither hot nor cold but tepid, cloudy and completely nondescript adulthood. And who can blame me for paying attention to such trivia at a time when momentous events are happening all around us? It's very simple to see how disreputable the values are that have created all these momentous happenings. It's like Chekhov, both caricature and tragedy. We mustn't allow ourselves to be deafened by things that are overwhelming. Just as one shouldn't oppose or undervalue the small things. But don't think, however, that I am without feelings, which can boil up and cool

71 A small spa town on the Vistula River.

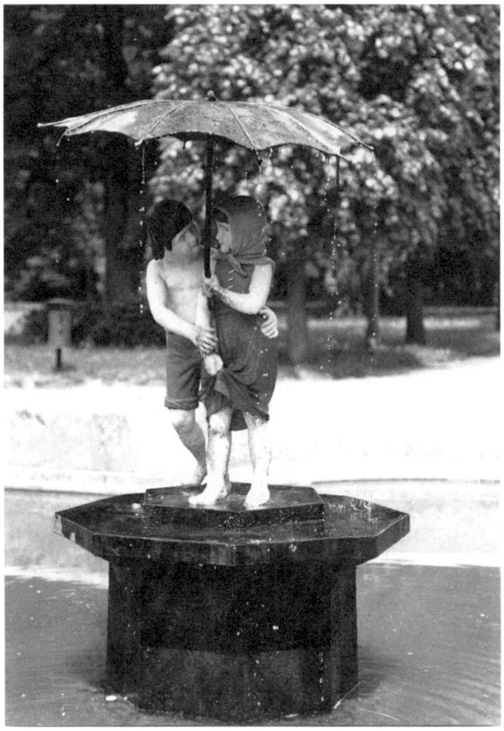

The fountain of Jaś and Małgosia in Ciechocinek Stefan refers to.

down. Darling, only exchanging a look and hugging you should I be able to tell you all the rest.

Yesterday I received a card from Hania, written 11 July. Only a few words, that she received my two letters, that she has had nothing from Sewek recently. That they are all well and await news. Do you have any more detailed information. Hania gives me some other, unreadable address and I don't know how to write to her.

I am very amused but also really pleased with my attempts to write in French.

Overcoming the old barriers of language, like the tower of Babel, is more difficult than many others things. And I am happy, first of all, that something within us can really strike a chord with other occupants of this biblical tower of entangled languages, and secondly that what is real, appears more valuable and speaks louder than spelling or grammatical mistakes, or than the music of fine words. Did you get my 'Croquis dans les ténèbres'? I also sent it to Seghers at *Poésie 41* and he writes back to me today:

> Cher poète – le VI de 'Croquis dans les ténèbres' me plait particulièrement. C'est très fort! C'est un très beau texte, avec cette prière si belle:
>
> > Un quignon beurré de liberté
> > une tranche de pain…
>
> Je pense pouvoir passer ce texte dans le No.6. Je vous tiendrai au courant.[72]

And he advises me to write to two other poetry magazines mentioning his name. But adds: *Réservez moi le VIe Croquis s.v.p.*

72 In the event, Stefan's 'Croquis dans les ténèbres' does not appear, Seghers mentions shortage of paper, but in *Poésie 41* No.4, Pierre Seghers includes a note about Stefan. See page 224. For his letter see page 220.

And he continues:

> Travaillez, mon cher ami et poète, gardez votre confiance:
> par l'amitié et par le temps, nous referons bien notre monde.

The ivory tower is collapsing. It isn't an earthquake that makes it collapse – it is greater than any seismographic events. I am sabotaging it from the inside. And thus, among these masses of monstrous, grown-up people they suddenly find here a living man. And that's a major event in this lonely world. Darling, such a lot of kisses and I would so much like to read your drawings! I do wish I still had your sheet of paper with your signature: Memento Magnitudinis – who found it, I wonder? Perhaps it meant something else to some unworthy person?

It was a year ago today that I was standing again on that Mickiewiczesque boulevard[73], without its characteristic noise and bustle but otherwise the same as ever. I abandoned it, alas, to settle down here – at this tram stop, and wait. Ah, darling, I feel that bitter and tart taste and the smell of waiting, like the chewed juniper berries. I kiss you, Franeczko, passionately and always. Stefan

Please hug Stefan [Konorski] and thank him for his note. Not once, not twice did I think of him in a more than friendly way. When are we all going to meet, all those of us who come together united by choice and not by chance? S.T.

In August, Hitler declares on the 'global extermination of all European Jews'. It will start to be implemented in France the following spring, which will lead to the loss of one third of the Jewish population in France.

Telegram from Zieliński in Lisbon to Stefan

LÉGATION DEMANDE VISA POUR VOUS RÉSULTAT INCERTAIN. ZIELIŃSKI

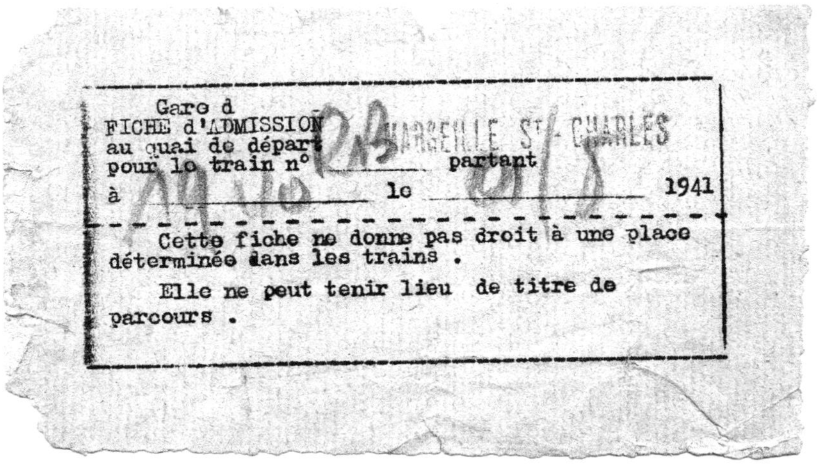

Gare d
FICHE d'ADMISSION
au quai de départ
pour le train n° partant
à le 1941

MARSEILLE ST-CHARLES

Cette fiche ne donne pas droit à une place déterminée dans les trains.

Elle ne peut tenir lieu de titre de parcours.

1 August 1941
Train ticket from Marseille St-Charles

73 Stefan alludes to the Epilogue of Mickiewicz's *Pan Tadeusz*:

> To think of such things in a Paris street,
> Where on my ears the city's noises beat
> With lies and curses, and with plans ill-fated,
> And fiendish quarrels and regrets belated.

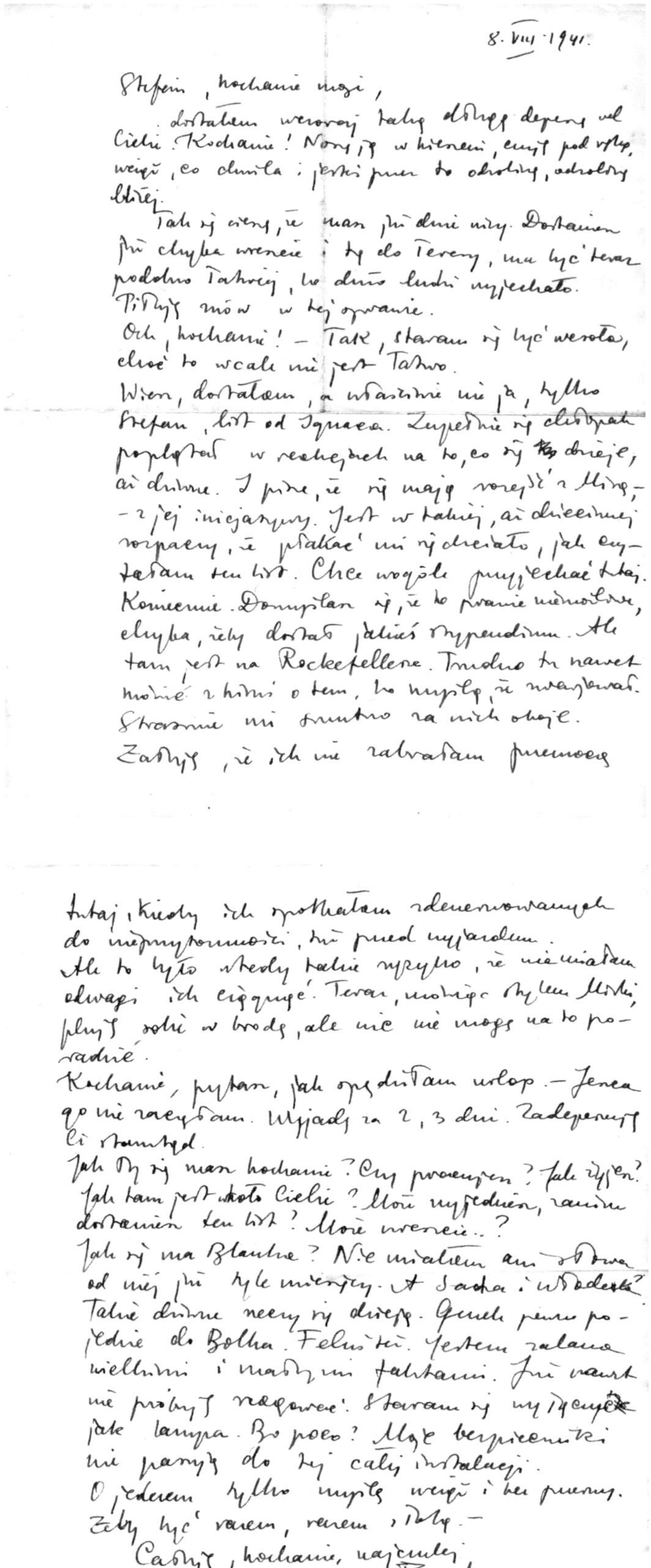

8. VIII. 1941.

Stefan, kochanie mój,

dostałam wczoraj taką długą depeszę od Ciebie. Kochanie! Noszę ją w kieszeni, czytam pod stołem, wciąż, co chwila i jestem przez to choć trochę, odrobinę bliżej.

Tak się cieszę, że masz już dni wolne. Dostaniesz już chyba wreszcie i tę do Teresy, ma być teraz podobno łatwiej, bo dużo ludzi wyjechało. Piszę Ci znów w tej sprawie.

Och, kochanie! – Tak, staram się być wesoła, chociaż to wcale nie jest łatwo.

Wiesz, dostałam, a właściwie nie ja, tylko Stefan, list od Ignaca. Zupełnie się chłopak poplątał w reakcjach na to, co się dzieje, aż dziwne. I pisze, że się mają rozejść z Mirą – z jej inicjatywy. Jest w takiej, aż dziecinnej rozpaczy, że płakać mi się chciało, jak czytałam ten list. Chce w ogóle przyjechać tutaj. Koniecznie. Domyślam się, że to prawie niemożliwe, chyba, żeby dostał jakieś stypendium. Ale tam jest na Rockefellera. Trudno tu nawet mówić z kimś o tem, bo myślą, że zwariował. Strasznie mi smutno za nich obojе.

Żałuję, że ich nie zabrałam przemocą tutaj, kiedy ich spotkałam zdenerwowanych do nieprzytomności, już przed wyjazdem. Ale to było wtedy takie szybko, że nie miałam odwagi ich ciągnąć. Teraz, mówiąc stylem Mirki, pluję sobie w brodę, ale nic nie mogę na to poradzić.

Kochanie, pytasz, jak spędziłam urlop. – Jeszcze go nie zaczęłam. Wyjadę za 2, 3 dni. Zadepeszuję Ci stamtąd.

Jak Ty się masz kochanie? Czy pracujesz? Jak żyjesz? Jak tam jest wkoło Ciebie? Może wyjedziesz, zanim dostaniesz ten list? Może wreszcie..?

Jak się ma Blanka? Nie miałam ani słowa od niej już tyle miesięcy. A Sacha i Władzia? Takie dziwne rzeczy się dzieją. Gdzieś pewnie pojedzie do Bolka. Felusia. Jestem zalana wielkimi i małymi faktami. Już nawet nie próbuję reagować. Staram się wyłączyć jak lampa. Bo poco? Moje bezpieczniki nie pasują do tej całej instalacji.

O jednem tylko myślę wciąż i bez przerwy. Żeby być razem, razem z Tobą. –

Całuję, kochanie, najczulej

Franka

Letter from Franciszka to Stefan, 8 August 1941

Diary Entry

parcel from Tema.
Find *Faust* and Einstein's theory of relativity.

5 August **Diary Entry**

letter from Wittlin with the address of Yolles.
telegram from Hicem.
letter from Teresa Żarnower
New ruling about recruitment for work and benefit payments

7 August **Telegram from Franciszka to Stefan**

INQUIÈTE CHÉRI EMBRASSE LE PLUS TENDREMENT THEMERSON

8 August **Telegram from Stefan to Franciszka**

CHÉRIE REÇU VISAS SORTIE ET ESPAGNOLE AU CONDITION PORTUGAL JE L'ATTENDS IMPATIENT RESULTAT INCERTAIN MAIS ESPÉRONS TOUJOURS SUIS TRÈS BIEN ET TOI AS TU BIEN PASSÉ VACANCES M'IMAGINE COMBIEN SOUCIS DOIS TU AVOIR MON PETIT SUIS HEUREUX QUE TU TRAVAILLES POUR TOI AUSSI TOUTES MES PENSÉES SONT AVEC TOI SANS CESSE SOIS GAIE MON PETIT CELA DOIT ÊTRE POSSIBLE TOUJOURS ET PARTOUT NOS FAMILLES VONT BIEN JE T'EMBRASSE SI TENDREMENT CHÉRIE = THEMERSON

Letter from Franciszka to Stefan

Stefciu, my darling, yesterday I received such a long telegram from you. Darling! I am carrying it in my pocket, I feel it under my hand, all the time, every moment, and because of it you are a tiny bit, a tiny bit closer.

I am so happy that you already have two visas. You will get surely in the end also the one to Teresa. It is supposed to be easier now that a lot of people have gone.

I continue to take care of things in this cause.

Oh, darling! – I am trying so hard to be cheerful, although it isn't at all easy.

You know, I, actually Stefan [Konorski] not me, had a letter from Ignacy. He's become very strange, completely knotted up in his reactions to what is happening. And he writes that he and Mira are separating – on her initiative. He is in such childish despair that I wanted to cry when I read that letter. He very much wants to come here. Desperately. As you can imagine, that's almost impossible unless he would get some kind of a grant. And there he has a grant from Rockefeller. It is difficult to talk to anyone else about it, because I think he's gone mad. I am terribly sad for them both. I regret that I didn't bring them here by force, when I met them in a very nervous state, just before departure. But then it was such a risk that I didn't have the courage to persuade them. Now, talking in Mira's style, I'm kicking myself, but there is nothing to be done.

Darling, you ask me how I spent my vacation – I haven't started it yet. I shall go in 2 or 3 days. I shall send you a telegram from there.

How are you darling? Are you working? How is your life? What is it like around you? Perhaps you will leave before you get this letter? Perhaps, at last..?

How is Blanka [Blanche]? I haven't had a word from her already for many months. And Sacha [Bronstein] and Władek [Vinaver]? Such strange things are happening. Genek will probably go to Bolek. Feluś also. I am flooded with facts, big and small. I don't even try to make sense of it all, just try to switch myself off like a lamp. What's the point of doing anything else? My fuses don't match this vast circuit. I only think about one thing all the time, without a pause: to be together, together with you.

I kiss you darling so very tenderly. Franka

9 August Diary Entry

Letter from Paszkowicz. She will arrive on Tuesday.

The case of Jahl and Zuzia – they went to Grenoble.

They locked up Lipski and threw away the key.
They shat on his doorstep and smeared the door.

S.S.L:4

4

PROTOKOŁ

Spisany przez przewodniczącego kompletu sędziowskiego, mgra Tadeusza Biernakiewicza w sprawie p. Władysława Jahla, żądającego przedstawienia zarzutów przeciw jego osobie, w związku z wrogim xxxxxxx nastrojem niektórych współmieszkańców schroniska P.C.K. w Voiron.

Dnia 16 lipca o godz. 14tej 30, zjawia się p. Józef DANIEC i zeznaje co następuje:

Na skutek wezwynia sądu shroniskowego w Voiron stwierdzam, że niechęć panująca w shronisku do p. Jahla wynikła z niezgoności poglądów na szereg istotnych spraw, drogich dla każdego Polaka, a lekceważonych lub poniżanych przez p. Jahla. Mogę przytoczyć pogląd p. Jahla na religję katolicką, który wygłosił w mojej obecności w czasie lekcji kowersacji języka francuskiego w miesiącu marcu b.r. w Voiron. Punktem wyjścia był wyraz ksiądz w języku francuskim. Obecni w czasie lekcji 4 wraz ze mną słuchacze/m.in. Patyna/w rozmowie podnosili różnicępanujące we Francji w obchodzeniu świąt katolickich w porównaniu z Polską. Przy tej sposobności p. Jahl w tonie lekceważenia spraw religji i duchowieństwa katolickiego tłumaczył nam, że we Francji ksiądz jest kapłanem tylko w czasie odprawiania nabożeństwa, a poza tym nie bierze na serio swoich funkcji duszpasterskich, czego najlepszym dowodem jest to, że jeden ze znajomych jego księży wyrazić się miał do p. Jahla, że "ma Świętą Hostię w d....."- przy czym p. Jahl całe słowo powtórzył. Byliśmy tak zaskoczeni i oburzeni tym, co powiedział p. Jahl, że nie byliśmy w stanie z oburzenia zareagować na słowa p. Jahla. W każdym razie stwierdzam, że cały ton i sposób wypowiedzenia swej opinii przez p. Jahla w sprawie religji i duchowieństwa katolickiego dały wyraźnie do poznania, że p. Jahl posiada poglądy społeczeństwa francuskiego na religją i że zamiarem wystąpienia p. Jahla była chęć podważenia zaufania do religji katolickiej i do jej duchowieństwa.

Stawiam wniosek by sąd schroniskowy wystąpił przeciw p. Jahlowi Wład. z oskarżeniem o sianie demoralizacji w postaci osłabiania wiary wśród mieszkańców schroniska.

Mgr. Biernakiewicz Daniec Józef.

One of seven court 'protocols' prepared by Judge Tadeusz Biernakiewicz from the hearing on 16 July 1941 at which the residents at the Hôtel de la Poste in Voiron are trying to get rid of Władysław Jahl. Here, Józef Daniec reports that Jahl's presence has created a hostile atmosphere as everyone is shocked by his crude jokes about the Catholic religion.

And of course, this is not the only reason for complaints about Jahl, see Stefan's defence of Jahl during his conversation with Żmigrodzki (facing page).

Piotrowicz's story about his childhood:
Erwin: why despite coming from landed gentry he is a real man.
P: when he was a kid, as the young master, he wanted to mount a stallion. The equerry did not allow it. He created a row with him. His father made him kiss the equerry's hand in front of everybody.

Erwin talks about violent death – and it brings to my mind the story of a young woman who wanted to throw herself from the third floor in Królewska street. Automatic reflexes.

M. who sold a painting to Dr F[oata]. After breaking the glass it transpired that it was cut out from *L'Illustration* and we have now a Jongkind dated 1937.

Conversation with Żmigrodzki. At Vial's. After lunch.

ż: And what's wrong with Jahl?

s: (exaggerating) Yesterday it was very bad. He had three attacks. Girowski was in Grenoble ('why not a Polish doctor?') and there were three French doctors. They confirmed that he has angina pectoris.

ż: What does that mean?

s: It means that he can live another fifty years or that the curtain can come down at any moment, before the end of the performance.

ż: And isn't there anything one can do?

s: He should live quietly, far from the idiots, who jerk the cord that holds up the curtain. He should have a pre-war diet and avoid stress. That's what he should do, in his condition. He was summoned today to present himself to Biernakiewicz. But he is in bed, of course, so he asked me to go in his place. I went there and read all these idiotic things he is accused of. Had he read them himself he would have died of a stroke either from laughter or from horror.

ż: So you went there today only as a substitute for him? Well, that makes things look different. I heard that you had undertaken advocacy. You know that I support you and that in your situation this would be rather unwise. I understand your intention, but I wouldn't want you to expose yourself to unpleasantness…

s: (as if he had not heard the last few sentences) I very much regret that I'm not a lawyer, by the way – you know, I should like to be a lawyer for a year, a priest for a year and a doctor for a year. Every self-respecting writer should undertake a 3-year education of this sort. But that's beside the point. I am sorry that I'm not a lawyer and am left instead with this rotten *esprit d'escalier*, because what could be more fine and worthy than to do just this to undertake the defence of a man who is surrounded by bad, conceited and self-seeking idiots? I regret that my role comes to an end with today's substitution. Besides, from no point of view do I see anything bad about appearing in his place today. Here, we sink into such terrible crankiness that we forget about ordinary, simple, human values. And if it wasn't Jahl who was accused, but, let's say, a swindler, thief, gangster, what if he were ill after a heart attack, and he asked you to represent him before a judge – would you refuse? Wouldn't you seize the chance? – not so much to perform 'a good deed' as to express your humanity? (a moment of embarrassed silence)

ż: You talk about thieves, swindlers and gangsters. In our circumstances here, what Jahl is accused of is much worse than a crime. Defending a gangster you remain innocent. But to defend Jahl is as if you agreed with him. 90% of opinion is against him.

s: Opinion?

ż: Yes. Don't ignore the public opinion here.

s: I don't ignore it, but I don't care about it. If anything, I care more for Jahl's opinion than that of the 90%. (silence)

ż: (starts on another tack) You get on well with Jahl. Now that he's ill and one feels sympathy for him, it's a pity that he should waste himself here... it could even be dangerous for him. Since it's a question of his welfare, couldn't you advise him to leave this place? To move to another shelter? Then this whole matter would be easier to suppress.

s: In other words, you want me to advise him to run away?

ż: Well, no ... I didn't think of it that way. Don't think that I am prompted by some kind of opportunism. God forbid! It's just that one shouldn't provoke them. You know that 90% are against him. One must consider majority opinion.

s: Even where justice is at stake?

ż: You take it all, so to say, objectively. But it is not after all a real court of justice.

s: Does Biernakiewicz know about your initiative to make Jahl leave?

ż: Look, the best proof that I'm concerned for Jahl's well-being is that these men from the tribunal said that even if he went away they were not sure whether they'd be able to withdraw the case against him.

s: It seems to me that they could certainly withdraw the case, because they could announce that Jahl left and in this way they would have a victory on their hands. And they're less concerned with justice than with victory. They started this dirty affair without realising whom they were dealing with. They thought they could repeat the case of Rudzik, who called his fellow-countrymen swine. They expelled him from the shelter, deprived him of social welfare. They succeeded with Rudzik, because there was nobody to take his side. Rudzik is a peasant, a member of the proletariat. He left his family back home, nobody took any interest either in the fact that Rudzik is an ordinary man, nobody considered with what bitterness Rudzik pronounced these words. The herd decided that he had committed a sacrilege and they sentenced him, and because Jahl defended him the headquarters immediately decided that Rudzik is a Jew and confirmed their verdict. Nobody spoke up for Rudzik. You are a member of the Polish Socialist Party but they also blackmailed you with patriotism and you didn't speak up for Rudzik either. But Jahl is not one of the proletariat. Jahl is a painter, quite a good painter. And he is known here and there in Western Europe. He is also known at headquarters and to the delegation. But these young upstarts think that if Jahl is sitting here modestly in Voiron, it means that he is abandoned and weak and that you can do what you like to him. But it has already turned out that Biernakiewicz himself did not get the gym teacher's job, because the headmaster, Zalewski, learnt that he, a judge, is taking part in this affair against Jahl. And it turns out that people speak up for Jahl. It seems that now these whippersnappers begin to realise that it would be more comfortable for them to withdraw from this whole rumpus. But I cannot advise Jahl to run away.

ż: My friend, I assure you that I am not an opportunist and I ask you not to suspect me of opportunism, but I also think you don't realise how dangerous is all this for Jahl.

s: You turned to me once before, in a similar case. When Karnecki got drunk and Bakalarski brought an action against him. On that occasion it was Karnecki whom you wanted me to persuade to leave. But you know, Karnecki is still here, and Bakalarski has gone.

ż: Yes, I admit, I just wanted to talk about it. Then something unforeseeable happened. It was the General. It turned out that the General got on well with Karnecki.

s: I hope that some unforeseeable event might occur now too. It could happen, for instance, that Jahl won't go away, but his accusers will be transferred to other shelters.

ż: I am not as much of an optimist as you… However, I would still advise that he leave, not for reasons of opportunism but for Jahl's own welfare.

s: If this is what you think why don't you simply drop in on him and tell him yourself. On the way to the second floor, you can stop at the first and take the opportunity to visit him. One even visits prisoners in prison. I can't be your messenger as you would wish, because I don't agree with you. But why don't you try yourself? It's possible that you will convince him… (a moment of silence).

ż: You see, because I share quarters with Biernakiewicz, my situation would be, how to say it … (a moment of silence) I know that Biernakiewicz didn't get the job for that reason. I also made an application but it was refused, I don't know why. But I fear that you overrate the progressiveness and radicalism of the people in Grenoble and underrate the power and possibilities of these people here.

s: You are mistaken in thinking that I suspect these Grenoble gentlemen of progressive and radical views. And why? They are simply a few of the most ordinary Europeans, and besides, not radicals but National Democrats. They would sign the verdict on Rudzik without qualms, but they won't support condemnation of Jahl. It's as clear as daylight. Nobody will support Rudzik. Even if your Socialist Party came to power. If a more radical party came to power these gentlemen have nothing to lose anyhow. But authorising the condemnation of Jahl could one day lead to retaliation. After all, it is funny to send an accusation that Jahl, a professional painter, violated 'our national Kossak sanctity' calling his painting shit – to Professor Z. who wrote a treatise about the influence of the Polishness of Jahl's paintings on Spanish painting. I don't want to exaggerate Jahl's importance, although I'd feel more inclined to do this from sheer cussedness and for the sake of contrast with this pack of hounds, wet behind the ears! They throw themselves on him with enough fury to make some sort of an involuntary hero. And, *nota bene*, should somebody one day think of writing Jahl's biography, this in itself might prove quite interesting, and these striplings could quite unexpectedly pass into history, as a gang of evil halfwits who were poisoning Jahl's life.[74]

ż: Well, yes, they themselves admit that this accusation about Jahl not liking Kossak's painting is ridiculous. But there are far more serious accusations. Do not charge me with opportunism, my friend, but…

s: All these accusations are of the same type, but this one appears more glaring because it is written naïvely and simply.

ż: You didn't let me finish. I already asked you not to reproach me with opportunism, but one has to consider the prevailing opinion here, of which ninety per cent is against Jahl.

s: Ninety per cent by doubling the vote of those who shout the loudest and halving that of those who remain quiet. It isn't the point that the *majority* is against him but that their position is easy; that they don't seek to find where lies the truth but only look who is for and who is against. This is why I said that they will make a hero of him. But it doesn't mean that we have to allow this tactic to pigeon-hole all of us. You talk of opinion! What has opinion to do with anything? As with Jahl in the case of Kossak, opinion can make you into an anti-patriot etc. if you were to say, for instance, that other national sacred cows like Miss Szpyrkówna or Miss Mniszkówna, who have entrapped the heart of majority opinion, that's shit. It's possible to try to live quietly, and outside these storms-in-a-teacup. One can give up fighting for justice, but one cannot be reconciled to this justice being replaced by the rough justice of public opinion .

ż: Yes, but you have to admit that Jahl talks too glibly.

s: Of course. But why is it that sometimes speaking out of turn is wrong and another time an act of moral courage? I value Jahl for his courage to say whatever comes to his head irrespective of opinion. Why doesn't one say that of Gajewski's talk? Gajewski is a pup and he doesn't realise that they pushed him out as a scapegoat and that he alone will be the one to suffer. And now tell me if the *Air Corps*, if it

74 What is all this about? To summarise: Jahl's outspoken criticism of a Polish painter was deemed unpatriotic, and 90% of the residents want him to be thrown out. He is called before the 'kangaroo' court of the Hôtel de la Poste. He cannot attend because he had a heart attack and is in bed. Stefan goes in his stead.

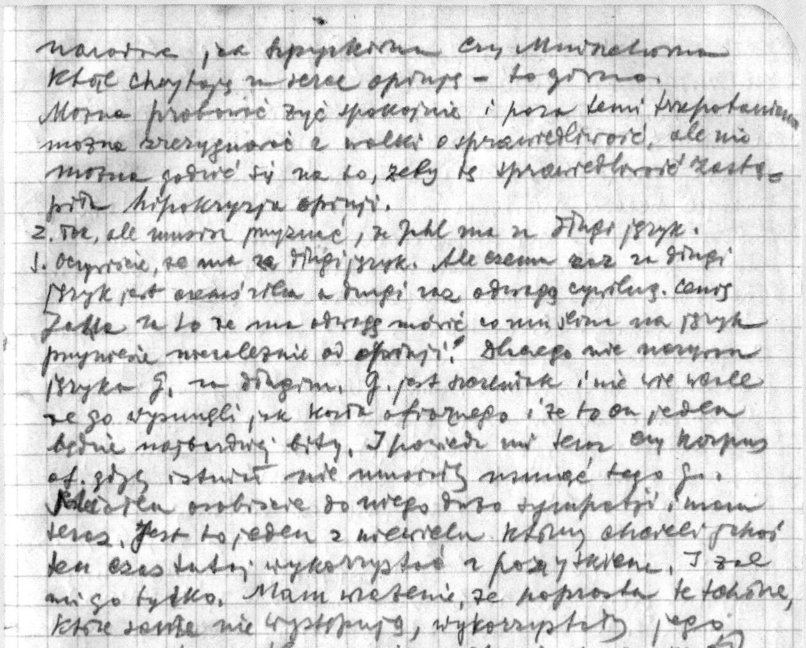

One of the pages in Stefan's diary containing the conversation with Żmigrodzki existed, should not have to get rid of this Gajewski? Personally, I had and continue to have a lot of sympathy for him. He is one of a few who wanted somehow to make some good use of the time spent here. And I feel sorry for him. It seems to me simply that these cowards, who won't step forward themselves, took advantage of the honesty of his thinking and pushed him out in front. But in the final analysis, what he did so naïvely, perhaps under their persuasion, is simply an ordinary denunciation. What else can one call it? He was going with Jahl's daughter to the swimming pool. To teach her to swim. On the way they talked about politics. And a month later the bloke accuses her of saying things he considers unpatriotic. General opinion shares his view. But opinion does not constitute justice.

ż: But the tribunal here is a matter of opinion. I don't look into and don't interfere in the matters of the tribunal, but I live with Biernakiewicz, so automatically I know what's going on. Keep it a secret, but I can promise you that all the members of the tribunal are –

s: – against Jahl.

ż: Yes. And they want to condemn him as soon as possible. This is why, not through opportunism, but knowing all this, I would advise Jahl to leave.

s: Could one enlist you as a witness?

ż: Me?

s: Yes, since in the circumstances one can't trust the impartiality of judges.

ż: But… but… but no, listen…

s: I know that witnesses can be called without their agreement.

ż: I… I know that your intentions are honest, but my situation would become similar to Gajewski's. It would be taking advantage of my sharing accommodation with Biernakiewicz. And it would be a denunciation, the same as Gajewski's.

s: With this tiny difference, that Gajewski's evidence is based on the views of a twenty-year-old adolescent, who changes her opinions weekly, but who nevertheless searches very honestly for some sort of truth; and that hers were words that didn't do anyone any harm and were to nobody's detriment. This tribunal, on the other hand, hatches a plot intended, by treacherous means, to trap an innocent man.

ż: You see, I am an army man…

s: So am I.

ż: But you only brushed up against the army, while I spend all my time now in these circles and you know what their attitude is. It would be difficult for me to extricate myself, especially because they have support in ONR[75], all of them…

75 Obóz Narodowo Radykalny (National Radical Camp), Polish extreme right anti-Semitic, anti-Communist, nationalist political party.

s: But the money that Jabłoński gets goes not to the Polish Socialist Party, but into the private hands of ex-quasi proletarians and disappears without a trace, here in the bar at Mme Vial.

ż: Don't blame the Polish Socialist Party, please. Jabłoński altogether seems to me to be strange. (a moment of silence)

s: (as if he were starting a new game, a new tug at the string) And, what about the union?

ż: What?

s: The patriotic union?

ż: You mean what we said here about Jahl and Erwin?

s: I don't know what you were planning, and I am talking about what happened in Grenoble.

ż: Has it already happened?

s: You didn't know about it?

ż: It concerns the National Democratic Party?

s: It concerns the union of non-ONR members. The first effect was that 'academic vows' organised on the model of Warsaw brawls were attended [under compulsion] by no more than thirty-five students.

ż: That's strange that I don't know anything about it. But who organises this?

s: I don't know.

ż: To whom could one turn?

s: I don't know. But you see the ONR is not the only possible organisation in exile. And this crowd of scoundrels that we have here, one cannot take as a symbol of public opinion. Listen, in such a case, as with Jahl for instance, if one side will predominate, the scale of indictment with the weight of opinion of a political party, what will happen if another party, for example, emerging now, will throw its weight on the side of the defence?

ż: Do you think that this is possible?

s: I think so. And in this case Jahl would really become an unintentional hero.

ż: One will have to find out about it.

ERWIN: Did you know that Ż[migrodzki] concealed from Biernakiewicz that he was in the Polish Socialist Party?

12 August 1941

Telegram from Adam Zieliński to Franciszka c/o Hanka Poznańska in Edinburgh

HAVE REPLIED NINTH STROŃSKI TWENTIETH YOU CAN DO NOTHING FOR YOU LEGATION ASKED VISA RESULT UNCERTAIN = ADAM ZIELIŃSKI

13 August **Telegram from Franciszka in Edinburgh to Stefan**

CHÉRI SUIS TRÈS BIEN VENUE ENFIN DEUX SEMAINES VACANCES AI FAIM PUISQUE PENSE À TOI TRÈS, TRÈS CHER PETIT ADRESSE CHEZ POZNAŃSKA 4 SCIENNES ROAD JE T'EMBRASSE LE PLUS TENDREMENT CHÉRI = THEMERSON

17 August **Letter from Franciszka to Stefan**

My dearest darling – I am on vacation. At last! Only now do I feel how nice it is to air oneself a bit after that office and – what is most important, after those people there. My vacation is somewhat extraordinary. You know that I went to Hanka [Poznańska]. We meandered a bit around town, which is anyway lovely, and we looked for a boarding house so we could find somewhere to lie down in the open air. All the hotels were booked up until the end of August and I was worried that I would spend my entire vacation sunbathing on Hanka's roof. But this is a strange country and we were without rhyme or reason 'invited' to a beautiful old house by the sea, by a nice old lady, whom we have never set eyes on till now. But here such things can happen. Hanka stayed with me throughout Saturday and Sunday. Today she returned to work and I am sitting in a garden full of roses, and there is the sound of the sea very close by. It is empty and fantastic. The house is more or less like Odette's, do you remember, and we celebrated each meal in just the same way. Anyway, here there live not only our charming grey-haired hostess, old and blind, but also a dog – beautifully preserved like his mistress – a cook, a chambermaid, a gardener and me. And all around are fields, and the sea.

Anka would have said that it is just like a film – in the morning comes the chambermaid announcing that the weather is beautiful (regardless of whether it rains or not – it's a ritual). After breakfast I go for a walk with the dog, and on the way meet an old man from the neighbouring farm who is also walking a dog. We tell each other that the weather is beautiful, again independently of rain – what a life! I twist my tongue twice more during the day, after lunch and after supper – usually also on the weather or some related subject. It's funny that I am writing you about all this, because you cannot even imagine what a tremendous rest this is for me. After all these continuous discussions about the war and social economy, after these quarrels, 'problems', 'postulates', when there wasn't a moment of time to think, or to think quite normally for oneself. And now for two whole weeks I can just look at the sea. I shan't go back to work until the 30th. Oh, if only you could be here, darling. The sea is grey and wonderful, every moment different. The beach is stony with lots of seaweed, some enormous, and sea shells, those real ones, like in Warsaw on the chest of drawers, huge and multicoloured.

The quiet is so complete that it is like a ringing all around. It's difficult to believe there are still such places in today's shattered times. If only I could send a bit of this peace to you there, silence and scented air – my darling.

Have you had any news from Hania perhaps, what is happening with Sewek? Could he have, and did he want to go to Bolek?[76] I would so much like

76 Bolesław Smulevich in Moscow.

to know what's happening with Lonia [Janecka]. So much is changing all the time all around. Genek gets letters from Janka from time to time. They are full of mystical reminiscences about topics as if from a young forest. Here spreads 'newtonianism' as confirmed by Jasio Leyberg in his hospital for the insane. It is all very difficult and boundlessly sad, but not because this is how people feel and think. These things might be thought beautiful and meaningful up to a point. But it's all a sort of psychotic hiding from reality – and it isn't creative. My hostess has just arrived and brought a blanket to cover my legs with, and a newspaper, and asked me if I am cold, if it is not too hot, if it is not too windy – she is spoiling me almost as much as her dog – and she brought me back to the reality of my vacation and the scent of roses all around.

Darling, I kiss you so very much. Franka

Hanka [Poznańska] and Jasiek [Leyberg] instructed me to send you their heartfelt regards. You know, Marysia Michałowska has arrived. She was with us all the time with Teresa [Żarnower], though I couldn't find out her address before leaving, but she is, it seems, somewhere in my neighbourhood.

Bye, darling, love Fr

28 August **Telegram from Franciszka to Stefan**

CHÉRI SUIS TRÈS BIEN RETOUR LONDRES STOP SAIS RIEN SUJET ARGENT REÇU WŁADEK SUIS HEUREUSE QUE TU N'AIES PAS BESOIN JE NE POURRAIS PAS T'AIDER CAUSE SÉVÈRES RESTRICTIONS DEVISES TENDRESSES = THEMERSON

29 August **Letter from Stefan to Franciszka**

My darling, I should prefer to send you only just thoughts, but there is no other means than words. Who could compose from letters a picture of all that I hide so jealously inside myself, for you? When will it be possible, instead of writing, or talking even, just to look at each from close to, and embrace?

Thank you for the letter, Franeczko, from a month ago.

I am horrified how much trouble you have on my behalf.

Here with American visas it is terribly difficult, impossible actually. Halina, who had everything ready, has also suffered a setback. Anyway, I don't want to go even further away from you. I am waiting for news from Lisbon, but will it come? And when?

Darling, at the end of June, Blanka received from Zabiełło 2,000 francs for me. That is a huge sum. Blanka has gone to Sacha, and Władek collects her correspondence. He writes to me: 'meanwhile arrived here in Blanka's name a money order for 7666 francs sent by Ortiz in Marseille. Is that from you?' I hope not, darling. That would be terrible. I don't want you to send me [money], I have more than enough, Franeczko and there is nothing that I need here. Don't be angry with me for writing like this.

I wanted to ask you how you spent your vacation, but before you get this letter you will be back in harness at the office and I won't be able to do anything to help you.

Have you received 'Croquis dans les ténèbres', my darling? I sent seven of them. The sixth will appear in No.6 of *Poésie 41*. Is Antoni [Słonimski] publishing those poems of mine that you mentioned?

My love, darling. I kiss you so very much and all the time.

Stefan

Letter from Franciszka to Stefan

My dearest darling,

I returned from holiday and today I go to the office. The date that is so difficult to forget, darling – how long, long and hard these two years have been [since the first day of the war]. I miss you so very much.

Look, I wrote these few words this morning, so as to start at least a little – and in the office waiting for me was a letter from you. Darling, a wonderful letter! It made me feel warm and pleasant. I am so happy that you are in contact with *Poésie 41*, but I still haven't received these 'Croquis dans les ténèbres'. It is sad because for so long I haven't had any of your poems. Darling. They are so close to me and so important and necessary, Stefciu. I would so much like at last to warm my cheek on your arm and to hug you so tight, so tight. In these strange and terrible times, when so many things have collapsed or torn themselves apart there is a continuum of experience that is hard to make sense of. Premature feelings of old age seem to merge into memories of childhood that you'd have thought were locked away in the past. And it's all so very real. Oh, darling!

Everything I do now seems completely unreal for me. My loneliness is so complete, as if I didn't live on 'my own' planet, not in 'my own times'.

There is a bit of friendliness and mutual attachment in my relations with Zosia Wojciechowska and Stefanja [Zahorska]. A bit of mutual trust with Genek. These substitutes for friendship allow me to take care of them or to accept their care – these are such valerian evenings[77] like at Anka's, do you remember? But here I haven't got even a tiny bit of a human being with whom I could or would wish to talk normally – in a human language, and not even in a borrowed language of this or that (even the wisest) newspaper.

And even these few nice people will each go their different ways very soon. Stefan to Bolek, Zocha to America. My stupid talking to the lamp about what is happening will stop. You write that one shouldn't undervalue the little things nor allow oneself to be deafened by those that are enormous. But is it not the most important thing to adjust everything to the capacity of one's own grasp? Magnify the small and painfully whittle down the huge.

Darling, by now the very small reserves of my sense of humour are depleted.

I had a letter from Maryla today. Everyone in good health, from Sewek they have not yet had any news. Who knows what is happening to him. Marysia Michałowska arrived here. She sends her best regards to you. She tells me that Jurek [Michałowski] has written a play. What do you think of that? I had a letter from Ignacy. Sad. I deduce from it, although it isn't clearly written, that Mira is living with Tempel. It seems to me that this is a bit macabre and silly. Ignacy definitely wants to come here. I don't know if he will succeed.

My darling, I kiss you so terribly much: my dearest sweetheart.

Franka

Ignacy Złotowski writes to Stefan, from the University of Minnesota, about his despair that Mira had left him, probably forever, and went to New York to start a new life. He will leave America one day, but first, to cheer himself up, he makes a tour around the country by car.

77 Pleasant evenings as if induced by the calming effect of valerian.

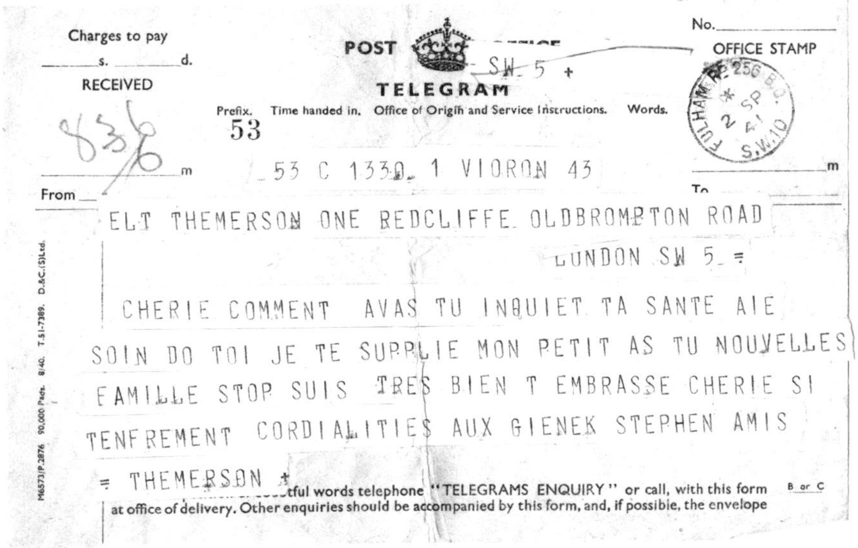
Charges to pay
s. d.
RECEIVED
POST OFFICE
TELEGRAM
No.
OFFICE STAMP
Prefix. Time handed in. Office of Origin and Service Instructions. Words.
53
53 C 1330 1 VIORON 43
From
To
ELT THEMERSON ONE REDCLIFFE OLDBROMPTON ROAD
LONDON SW 5 =
CHERIE COMMENT AVAS TU INQUIET TA SANTE AIE
SOIN DO TOI JE TE SUPPLIE MON PETIT AS TU NOUVELLES
FAMILLE STOP SUIS TRES BIEN T EMBRASSE CHERIE SI
TENFREMENT CORDIALITIES AUX GIENEK STEPHEN AMIS
= THEMERSON +
...tful words telephone "TELEGRAMS ENQUIRY" or call, with this form at office of delivery. Other enquiries should be accompanied by this form, and, if possible, the envelope

Telegram from Stefan to Franciszka

CHÉRIE COMMENT VAS TU INQUIET TA SANTÉ AIE SOIN DE TOI
JE TE SUPPLIE MON PETIT AS TU NOUVELLES FAMILLE STOP
SUIS TRÈS BIEN T'EMBRASSE CHÉRIE SI TENDREMENT CORDIALITÉS
AUX GENEK STEPHEN AMIS = THEMERSON

Telegram from Franciszka to Stefan

MON PETIT CHÉRI SUIS PARFAITEMENT BIEN AI NOUVELLES
FAMILLE BONNE SANTÉ AMIS SALUENT CORDIALEMENT JE
T'EMBRASSE MON PETIT LE PLUS TENDREMENT BAISERS
= THEMERSON

7 September **Diary Entry**

Supper at the Jourdans'. A bottle of wine for 24 frs.

In the garden with Erwin, view of the valley. Piotrowicz with Motosiński and the Jourdans return from mushrooming. To town for vodka. Jourdans shows his volume about Stendhal. A real apartment with furniture, books. I borrow Apollinaire's *Le Bestiaire* with Dufy's woodcuts, and Epictetus.

I look through interesting translations from Hindi and the Chinese.
In the Hindi translation the layout of the text is like prose, but the rhythm is broken with dashes – a lotus leaf. The text is so tranquil that one could read it perfectly well sitting in a chair on the lawn, but Mlle Jourdans feels obliged to return and sit next to me. Tomorrow at 9 am she has to walk with her cello eight kilometres to play at the wedding of Vicomte d'Orléans.

Back home Dr Girowski is plastered. I borrow from P. *La Vie des Jésus* – Mauriac.

9 September **Diary Entry**

Can I remember everything that happened today? There were no special incidents. But what does such a day look like? In the morning some sort of dreams that there is no way of remembering, especially when Madzia appears with coffee.

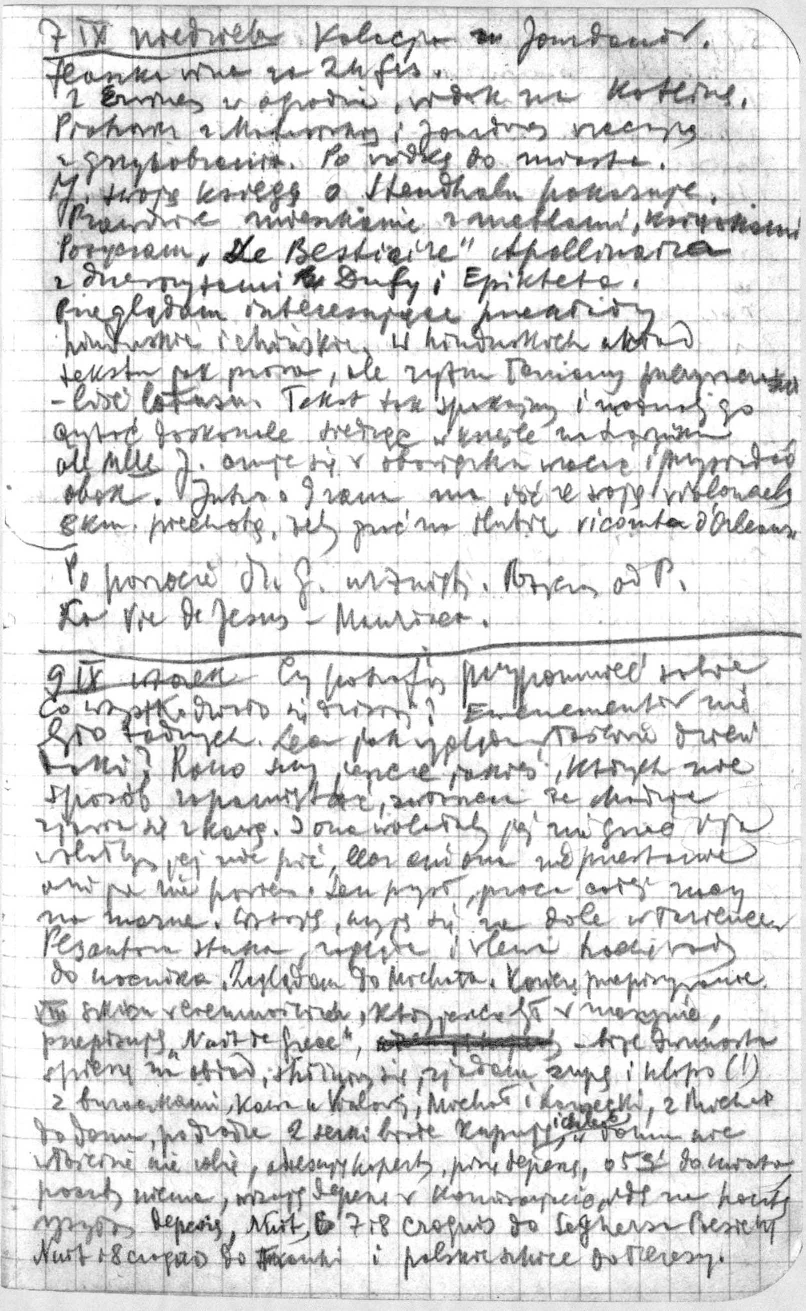

Stefan's diary, 7–9 September 1941

And she would prefer not to have to heat it up and I would prefer not to drink it, but neither will she stop nor will I say anything. The dream vanished, the whole night's work for nothing. I get up, wash downstairs in the bathroom. Pezantowa [i.e. Mme Pesanti] knocks, glances inside and pours some water into the chamber-pot. I look in on Michał. Complete retyping the 'Croquis dans les Ténèbres' VIII, which was still in the machine, retype 'Nuit de Grèce'[78] – strikes midday. I hurry to lunch, arrive late, eat soup and meat loaf! with beetroot, coffee at Mme Vial's, Michał and Karnecki, back home with Michał, on the way I buy two small white cheeses and bread. At home I don't really do anything, address envelopes, write a telegram, at 5 o'clock to town, there is no post. Have the telegram stamped at the police station, go to the Post Office, send the telegram, 'Nuit de Grèce', and 'Croquis' VII and VIII to Seghers, *Poèsie 41*. 'Nuit...' and 'Croquis' VIII to Franka, and Polish sketches to Teresa.

At the Post Office Lipski and Lipska stammering at the counter. To the laundry – they haven't found my shirt and 2 pairs of underpants. To the hotel. In front of the garage, Jahl. Inside, Erwin and the Jourdans at their machine for making briquettes from coal dust. Il fait augmenter la vitesse 80 per... Jabłoński also drops in. To the bakery for bread, supper. Milk with noodles and tomato salad. No letters. To the Bar Louis with Jahl. The lady cyclist chucked him even though she permitted him to go quite far, so he says. Zuzia comes. And afterwards Mlle Gauchet, who loves her grandfather. It transpires that she is a teacher. I don't go to Chrzanowski's live news bulletin. To Charavines[79]. Michał's three words. Madzia [asks him] to repair the machine [the cooker?]. At home. I decide to write down what actually happens during the day. I note down Sunday 7 September. Michał knocks. We go down. For two francs per head, a bottle of wine at Michał's. Talking nonsense. Michał is already stuttering and begins to be quarrelsome. It is already after 1 o'clock, I return home, lie down. I am just making a note of this. I have Epictetus next to me and a sketchbook and I'm just wondering what to do.

Je ne peux pas produire des pensées parce que je suis occupé à produire du gras.

In schools one is fed with information, one assimilates modes of thinking but one doesn't learn to think.

Arithmetic, algebra – thinking with quantities, but there is also thinking with qualities – Here logic is replaced by feelings; honesty is replaced by the interests of the individual, the group, idea etc.

11 September **Telegram from Stefan to Franciszka**

CHÉRIE RIEN NOUVEAU CHEZ MOI ATTENDS NOUVELLES THÉRÈSE SUIS TRÈS BIEN ET TOI TRAVAILLE TU POUR TOI MÊME MA SEULE PENSÉE TE VOIR PAS TRISTE ET HEUREUSE TANT SOIT PEU T'EMBRASSE MON PETIT LE PLUS TENDREMENT = THEMERSON

12 September **Telegram from Franciszka to Stefan**

CHÉRI TENONS NOS SOURIRES ET ESPÉRONS TOUJOURS MON PETIT BIEN AIMÉ COMME JE VOUDRAIS TE VOIR TOUTE MA TENDRESSE. THEMERSON 11 GREENCROFT GARDENS, LONDON NW6

78 The poem refers to the Themersons' visit to Greece. Having won *Wiadomości Literackie* competition in 1937 (announced in the issue of 18 July), they are given a ticket to Palestine. They exchange it for two tickets to Greece.

79 Charavines, a village on the lake Paladru to which Stefan sometimes refers as Charavignes.

Letter from Franciszka to Stefan

Darling, again for so long I haven't had a letter from you. It's actually only 10 days, but I would like them all the time, I miss you so much.

Today again I managed to make a further step towards getting the visa, perhaps at last… My darling pet.

I walk around this town and I just can't find a place for myself. All the time, all the time, I wait for you. So many things go round in circles in the head. To do something that would last, to avoid complete stupefaction, but nothing succeeds. Only the devil knows why. Anyway, since my vacation I have constantly a great deal of urgent work in the office. One job is hardly finished when a new one starts. And there is so much to laugh at in all this, so many pompous situations. Sometimes I feel like applauding. They are all born actors, but each has only one role that he plays to the ultimate absurdity (only in the characteristics of a type not in behaviour, God forbid) with such conviction that it could not come from the imagination of a comedian. It is a sad entertainment, especially against the painful background of the reality.

It is difficult to swallow all that, even though our throats have been stretched in such an ugly fashion.

I am so very, so terribly, happy that you are working. Darling. You just cannot imagine how much this means to me. If you send me something that you have written, please write on top for whom, because it could fall out of the letter and afterwards they don't know where to put it and to whom to pass it on.

I have moved, you already know about that. I am living in a boarding house. I want to be alone for a while, perhaps it will help me.

But I am not sad, darling. It is only that I miss you so much. I am all the time smiling at you, even though from such a long distance. And believe me, even though this letter sounds so stupid and perhaps sad, I am determined to retain a smiling mug and *ça va*!

I got today a letter from Wittlin. Write to him: Clarkstown Country Club – Nyack NY USA He also wants to come here. Ignacy too. It's funny, strange, but unwise. This only proves in the end that they are not happy there. Mira is working in New York in the editorial office of *Nowy Świat*, at Yolles. They have separated. So everyone has dispersed. I had recently a letter from Freyd from under the pole. Oh well!

My darling, I kiss you so much and so very tenderly. Franka

17 September **Diary Entry**

I went to bed and that's it!
If the photograph of me would spring to life, for me the new person would be completely indifferent and boring.

19 September **Diary Entry**

Now Luiza again; je resterai avec vous tout le temps.

I went to the doctor – Dusset-Bon, hypotension [low blood pressure]. Prescribed strychnine and phosphorus.

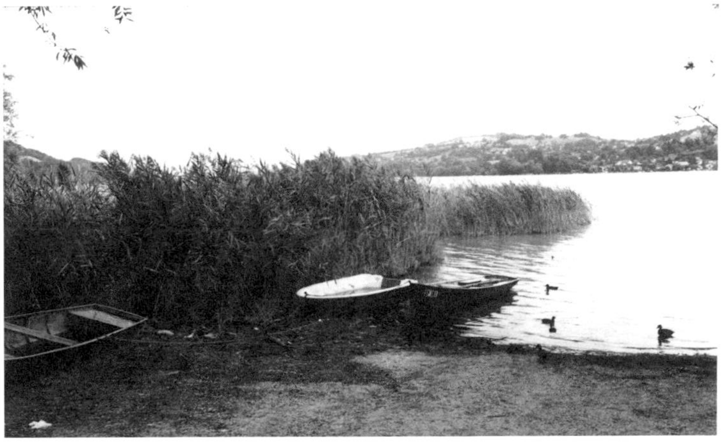

The lake Stefan refers to as lake Charavigne is actually Lac de Paladru in Charavines

20 September **Diary Entry**

No letters. I'm going to Charavigne. To get on a bus is not enough to get rid of familiar faces. Mme et Mlle Robert and all clerks from Société Générale are going to a déjeuner at Charavigne. We get off at the Hôtel de la Poste. And, good-bye. But a moment later Renée rushes up panting, catching breath with her little hunched lungs – says that she will show me Hôtel du Nord.

M Robert on a motorcycle. 'Écrivez-moi une petite carte "poste restante" à Grenoble'. It's impossible to find lodgings. 'Plus de provisions'. I walk and walk. About 20 km on both sides of the lake.

4 o'clock. The company from Société Générale drank their fill of champagne and vocalised to their hearts' content. They went. I ask there and get a room and board (45 frs).

At the open sluice-gate – boats.

Roaches eat mosquitos and crumbs extricated from my pocket which I throw to them.

Mother, son, daughter and little Françoise are in the water, swimming. Françoise! Françoise! they call.

And then they disappear, they leave, and again nothing.

Supper: clear soup with bread, potato purée with tomato sauce, escalope de veau from horsemeat, white cheese, grapes, 2 pieces of bread, quarter of wine.

The room turns out to be further. 3 minutes. Second floor, and a lavatory in the courtyard, and what with the actual need of bismuth... (A. Pétigny, Pharmacien, Ex-interne des Hôpitaux de Lyon-Chartreuse, Bismuth).

The layout of the hotel is clearly a problem because Stefan is suffering from diarrhoea, hence his need of bismuth.

In the evening I drop into the Hôtel de la Poste for a verbena infusion. 'Peintures Régionales à vendre'.

There is one painting that could hang in IPS (Instytut Polskiej Sztuki)[80], and at least half of them in Zachęta[81]. Provincial France is as musical visually, as provincial Italy is musical acoustically.

'C'est noir. Trop sombre. Pas de soleil probablement' à propos the painting. But almost never a word about the painted objects. Like the Italians who certainly pay no attention to the words of the song that is sung.

Mlle Gauchet talked about the need for the teaching of sport. That children are miserable. That they are very gâtés. As if she knew nothing about the slave labour of those under-age, twelve-year-old Madeleine on the farm in the Loire, from daybreak till late at night, hired out in exchange for the lease of a piece of land; here in the Café 10-12 year old girl, Marie, serves alcohol (despite Saturday, jour sans alcool) at a time when the countryside is already asleep, and this boy from the *Memoirs of the Emigrants*, who helped his father with bricklaying and was ruined physically by the age of 13 – children are serving in all the bars.

Generated inside us is a picture of reality far more real than the reality that is perceived. We allow ourselves to be coerced by leaves, petals, a lake, fragments, we allow ourselves to be blackmailed by the inhabitants of Voiron, of Charavignes, by Europe. We allow ourselves to be blackmailed by passers-by, neighbours and advisers, we allow ourselves to be blackmailed by words and sentences, but above all by the moments in which we live when a shattered glass can become something more than the Thirty Years' War. And today's war more than all wars that one can think of. Only the Church blackmails with the greatest promises.

Suddenly, the portrait of the Marshal fell to the floor. A tall fellow, drunk, with a badge on his beret stands to attention and salutes. A girl, strangely embarrassed by the sight of the portrait on the floor, calls out: 'Look, the Marshal has fallen!'

Erwin's story: When he was a little boy he tried to shoot carp in the neighbouring park with a flobert rifle. But he never achieved a direct hit. He would plunge a stick into the water to get some idea of the angle of refraction but even then he couldn't aim properly.

(It is lucky that God is also unable to orientate himself with light's refraction between the void and the air, and so hits the mark less often than people multiply.)

Erwin's second reminiscence:
A kindly priest at a class on religion: self-determination as a basis of ethics. Everyone has the choice whether to be good or bad.
Erwin: 'Then why is the number of crimes inversely proportional to the number of square meters of floor area per person?' (The temptation of St Anthony expressed in square metres!) The priest asked him privately to give his classes a miss. Erwin started going to classes on Catholic religion. There was an experienced Jesuit priest who didn't allow himself to be led up the garden path.

80 Institute of Polish Art.
81 Zachęta, National Art Gallery in Warsaw.

The Nowak family dropped like a meteor of Polish countryside, with bedbugs, pregnancy, etc.[82]

21 September **Letter from Franciszka to Stefan**

My dearest sweetheart,

Yesterday I received a letter from you, and the seventh 'Croquis' a few days ago, and today two letters – still wishing me happy birthday – thank you, my pet. Oh, Stefciu, you have no idea how your letters help me, – they act on me so directly and so much, so much truth, the same support that I am trying to build here for myself. Our common truth is always in them.

Darling, I know that you received from me a few sad letters during these last months. Somehow I could not cope. But now I am managing very well again. Perhaps it was simply physical fatigue. I didn't have the strength to work for myself/you after the office, but that's just what I need – like water to drink, you know?

Now, after the holiday I feel very well – I moved to a boarding house. I know, this is funny, darling, I like now what you have always liked. I am discovering masses of your habits in myself. Your habits, and I am happy with that. I am sitting alone, they give me food but don't bother me. Rented by the week. I have just created for myself something rather like a tram stop, I haven't yet fully recognised the obviousness of this provisorium, in which I am stuck, and it is better like that.

I look through the drawings that I was doing several months ago. You will like them darling. They are sometimes so analogous to your poems, you know? It could be perhaps the illustration that I never knew how to do for your poems 'for grown-ups'. Illustration, resulting from resonance – at such distance – just think!

My darling I don't know if even with a hug and a look I would be able to tell you what I feel and how much. My dearest creature!

The 'Croquis' are beautiful. The best is the sixth. Clean in line, full of suggestion but quiet in form. And the seventh too.

I have a strange feeling that there's a fragment of Poussin deep down in these poems somewhere, but it's hidden and you have to work to fish it out, like in the first ones. I don't know why but probably because it reminds me of consciously sifting through memories.

All the time I have the impression, just as once when I read *80 panów i 4 panie*[83], that it is almost easy for me to feel that text as if I were someone who doesn't know anything about you. Without that possibility of completing an impression with an entire scaffolding from the past, the reader can very easily follow a wrong route. I seem to recognise the tendency of going down the same route, in another language – is that right?

The words that you start working with all spring from associations in your mind, but for the reader unfamiliar with your poems they are pure form. That's why, I think, it's only when you stand back from the associations and deal 100% with the words as words that you are in your métier and everything holds together. I think it's really a matter of you feeling your way not blindly through memories of childhood but through *new* experiences (and when I talk of childhood, don't imagine that I'm thinking of the name Runia), I'm thinking of new intellectual experiences, which are less clogged up and less sentimental. They cover a far wider spectrum, and they call by name those things that with a childish intellect would

82 The Nowak family is the subject of Stefan's story 'The Investigation', p.375

83 *80 gentlemen and 4 ladies*, a story that must have been written by Stefan

suffocate in a cloud of metaphors, pictures and distant associations. It even seems to me that there are times when you create images to replace them. For example, *Mme Roumie avec ses seins et ses sandwiches* – does not belong in the world of your poetry so much as with things seen at a particular time and place. So it stands in for all those things that remain unexpressed and therefore unreadable. This is why poems such as 'Dno nieba' and 'Fragment poematu I' are so strong and excellent. There is no trace in them of fumbling in all that fluff. They are the result of a fresh intensive experience, a mature, 'articulated' experience. And the truth of that experience springs like a refreshing fountain from each poem.

I know these are very similar to the difficulties I face now in my drawing. And also on several occasions I managed to disgorge things that are completely direct. And it is this that I am struggling with, to control the 'building blocks'. Can you write more to me about that? This is like our conversation used to be – but with breaks of months in between – my treasure! And do you know what else I felt? That in these poems where I feel truth grasped by the mane ('Croquis' VI, 'Petit Nègre écrit un poème') – language is brilliantly controlled and completely illuminating – a bulb that signals that a current has been connected. My darling pet, I kiss you so tenderly and so much. Franka

Telegram from Stefan to Franciszka

CHÉRIE SUIS TRÈS BIEN PARS POUR UNE SEMAINE CAMPAGNE REPOSER CHERCHER SOLITUDE ÉCRIS MOI LE PLUS SOUVENT C'EST DANS TES LETTRES QUE JE LA RÉTROUVE J'EMBRASSE MON PETIT SI TENDREMENT = THEMERSON

Diary Entry

Petit déjeuner. Coffee with milk and saccharine. 2 pieces of dry bread.
Little lake. Country lane. People hurry. White gloves. Prayer books in their hands.
I follow them.

Where there is no theatre, cinema, concert hall, community centre, reading room, library, where there is nothing apart from a bistro, in all these places you can still find a 'Gothic' or a 'Romanesque' church, built from concrete.

Every Sunday the same performance, in the same setting, before the same audience, throwing 5 or 20 sous onto the tray – takes place. And that is why, perhaps, it persists, because the language is always the same.

On the columns Romanesque capitals, and on the arches decorative mouldings – reminiscent of folk motifs. With folk decorations it is the same as with folk songs. It's possible to find in them examples of unexpected charm, just like Michał with his 'a little pigeon fell from the stove, smashed his belly'. But the aggrandisement and the practising of these things are unbearable.

White-haired vicar is preaching: the Church is not responsible for the war. And in 1870 and in 1914 and now newspapers accused the Church of provoking the war. It is not true. So many people perished, and so many are in captivity, and this in spite of the Church. The Church preaches the fear of God. And all that happened just because there is no fear of God.

The girls sing in small voices and out of tune. The priest is saying Mass in an impeccable imitation of a sheep. But in the church technical excellence is not what matters. Everybody knows the construction, the course and the form of the performance, and they don't want a great spectacle that would demand their participation, they prefer this transposing of a familiar score with the aid of humming and going through the motions.

A voluminous and extraordinary chef, with his back decorated with the cross turned to the public. He leans over his table, obscuring it with his bulk, and prepares a mysterious dish.

Saecula saeculorum and *Dominus vobiscum*, he sings. And two of the cook's boys, covered in little red and white surplices, walk from left to right, and from right to left, genuflecting in the centre and carry utensils from one side to the other.

Sound of the bell impels the public to lower their heads, so that no eye would detect the secret recipe – in accordance with which bread and wine are transformed on this miraculous kitchen table into flesh and blood.

And afterwards for an apéritif to Hôtel de la Poste.

Breakfast that is lunch: radishes, yesterday's purée with olives, spinach, yesterday's horsemeat, grapes. Without grapes this is lunch and supper in Voiron.

I hire a boat and glide around the lake. In underpants, in the sun, legs in the water. Only where algae touch the surface with tops of their heads – only there, one can feel the depth. But these are the places that are the shallowest of course.

I am sitting on a sill, on a very high floor
and immerse my legs in bottomless water below
the sun's rays glittering on my once sore heels
as the boat rocks blindly on the waves.

There exist such moments, not simply as fragments
of larger moments – as is a second in an hour –
but those moments when all the clocks in the world
fall silent.

Beneath me, the lake's invisible depths
– neither bad nor good, neither ugly nor fair –
so long as they remain unseen and unsullied by doubt.

But somewhere there just must be a drop that's
untouched
unimportuned by glances, at liberty from humans
I tread on it gently, touch it from afar
lightly, like all the weekdays touch the day of rest.

Siedzę na parapecie wysokiego piętra
nogi zanurzam w wodą wypełnioną przepaść
słońce blaski układa na zgojonych piętach
i cicho się po falach kołacze łódź ślepa.

Istnieją takie chwile, które nie są tylko
fragmentem chwili większej i sekundą godziny
wszystkie zegary świata w takiej chwili milkną.

Pode mną niewidoczne jeziora głębiny
ani złe, ani dobre, brzydkie ani piękne
póki ich wzrok nie chwyci i myśl się nie zlęknie.

Bo gdzieś musi być przecież choć kropla nietknięta
od spojrzenia natręta, wolna od człowieka
Po niej depcę ostrożnie, dotykam z daleka
lekko, tak jak dotyka dzień powszedni swięta.[84]

84 This poem, composed on Lake Charavigne (Lac de Paladru, Charavines) in September 1941, was re-written later by Stefan and called 'Sonetino' and it appears here in that version. *Wiersze Wybrane 1939–1945, Wydawnictwo* Uniwersytetu Śląskiego, Katowice, 2003, p.81

Mountain lakes, surrounded by slopes – a strangely shaped porcelain dish with views of Switzerland around the edges, into which someone poured water coloured with washing-blue. But it can be like that and it can be different. If all that exists, it is thanks to the man who swims on the surface of this soup.

How does the world look in the dark? A nonsensical question. In darkness the world can sound, smell, warm or chill, touch, circle – but it cannot look. – Is that really so? Yes, it is. – If you close your eyes, the world for you will be in darkness, but someone who is standing next to you with his eyes open can describe it to you more or less. – Yes, but his description will refer to the world in the light. It will refer to his world and not mine. Just like a photographic negative in the dark night of the new moon can photograph the world in infra-red, or ultra-violet, or in the invisible beam of X-ray, and theoretically perhaps even in the light of cosmic or radio-waves. But these will always be pictures of the world in a specific light. 'From this one can conclude that the world in darkness corresponds to the world in which we close our eyes? – Yes.' Furthermore, one more observation: that the world in darkness cannot be either warm or cool, because rays that can heat can also photograph. Nor can it have sound, because one can invent an apparatus to photograph with the aid of sound waves. It can't touch and circulate sound because even this can, within certain approximations, be traced on film. – Well, now the words have become so complicated that I understand neither what you are saying nor what I wanted to say.

Don't take away my eyes, they are valuable, they saw the Parthenon. This alone is enough to preserve them after my death, just like one keeps the hearts of poets, the brains of scholars and the bodies of leaders.

Now I realise precisely that with premeditation I ate at one sitting almost a kilogram of foul bread (four days' ration), green pears and then drank the buttermilk brought by Madzia. So as to palpably get to feel one's own stomach, the centre of living body. For a week, it's giving me trouble, but besides the worries this brings, there is still the physical satisfaction of consciousness that one exists.

Fragments of conversations in this bar during supper:
'On passe à table, ça vous dérange pas?'
'Elle n'est pas prise cette chaise?'
'Manger les restes' 'Ça faisait mille francs par mois' – 'Soixante-quatre' (they play cards at the next table)
'Il a bien joué…' 'On pouvait rien faire sans sous' – 'c'est vrai ça' – 'On a l'habitude nous, comme ça!' – 'Bien, du canard …' 'Regardez pas le prix, après le canard on mangeait…' 'On était content' – 'Et mangeait sur un bout de pain comme ça, comme maintenant – Ça ne viendra pas – oh, c'est fruit – Ah, je sais pas – Oh! la la – Quel travail quand même – la guerre n'est pas finie – il faut mener la vie dure – deux et trois: cinq (that's cards near by): Allo! fais attention – pas grand-chose à acheter un mark vingt francs, un peu de beurre. Oui ils changent bien, sûrement ils faut pas envoyer la lettre avec l'adresse de la banque. Pas les regarder (mores) mais envoyer à ces familles. – Voilà, Monsieur. Merci, belle-fille?'

Little conversations after lunch at the Hôtel de la Poste:
'C'est pas un chien, c'est une catastrophe.'
'C'est un chien de chasse, qui chasse tout seul.'
'Elle a un petit caniche.' (that about a child sitting at the next table)
'A-t-elle des dents, elles commencent à pousser?'
'Non'! – On a trop mangé – ils sont partis pour longtemps? – Une semaine environ. Moi, j'ai si mal à l'estomac ? – Oh, je ne suis pas grand'.
They pass by roads
–'un cent frs croquant un bon, un bon, un bon
de cinq litres d'essence!'

Supper: clear soup with bread, slice of cold horsemeat from lunch with a gherkin, spinach from lunch, piece of white cheese.

Altercation with guests over wine. No wine.

Today, the first Sunday without newspapers. There is no radio either. From one of the windows a loudspeaker sang the Marseillaise. But what is happening to the world?

From next Sunday one will not be allowed to ride a bicycle on Sundays without permission.

In the sound of the steps of soldiers' boots the relation of the creaking of leather to the clatter of nails is the expression of weariness, apathy, the reluctance of the one marching.

Letter from Franciszka to Stefan

Stefciu, my darling,

Today I received your telegram, that you are going to the country for a week. Is that really only to rest and to seek solitude? I'd be happy to feel sure that's why you're going! But I am so worried about your health, darling. Very worried. I imagine how you live. Please don't economise and buy everything that you can to keep strong and well. After all, we never know what else awaits us, my dearest pet. Do you have any warm clothes? You know, I never write to you about this but I am so worried. Look after yourself my pet. I kiss you so tenderly.

I am starting to draw my own work again, it makes me feel so good; even though what drives me is sadness – like it is with you. There are so many things in common in our work, it's extraordinary.

And you are so close to me all the time, darling.

I wrote a long letter to you yesterday. Did you get it? I so much want to have an answer to it already and to write back again so we can chat together even though from afar. You ask about friends. They are well. They miss you. Freyd left to join Bolek, I wrote to you about that. Stefan also wanted to but it didn't work out. Genek has also stayed and perhaps once more we shall all go to drink vodka – at last – Darling!

Have you heard from Mira at all? Neither she, nor Ignacy has written recently. You probably know already that they have separated. She works at Yolles's in the editorial office of *Nowy Świat*, New York, 374 Second Avenue.

My dearest darling. I kiss you so very much and so very tenderly. – Franka

Telegram from Franciszka to Stefan

CHÉRI REÇU 3 LETTRES ET POÈMES SI HEUREUSE TIENS TA MAIN PETIT CHÉRI COMMENT VA SANTÉ AIE BON REPOS JE T'ÉCRIS PRESQUE TOUS LES JOURS MAMAN IRKA ANECZKA EMBRASSENT JE T'AIME TOUTE MA TENDRESSE = THEMERSON

Diary Entry

It's Monday, newspapers are on sale again. I buy a newspaper. No, I defend myself. It isn't obduracy, it isn't even the instinct for self-defence, that locks emotions up with a padlock. Stoicism, rather. Picture of the world is already dark enough and one doesn't need to smear it with these or other private emotions too.

Only those emotions which constitute an element of creative production have some value. And emotions of the recipient have value only when they improve or transform this human-factory.

(Lunch: lettuce, baked potatoes, meat, white cheese. It occurred to me to take my pulse: 52, 56, 62 (after cola), 58 (at 2, at 5, at 7 and at 10)

Telephone Voiron, letters from Franka and Teresa. A few words with Erwin (who has his own troubles – his son hasn't returned, and the school year has started) and again I feel I am useless.

~~Darling you remind me of my own words: 'one shouldn't undervalue small things nor allow oneself to be deafened by huge ones.' And you write: 'But isn't the most important thing to adjust all things to the capacity of one's own arms? Blow up the small and painfully cut down the huge?'~~

Władek [Karnecki]'s story: So you see Lifar was a kid then, I was the first to put his legs right. I was in charge of a lower course. Diaghilev made him. Talented fellow, that goes without saying, but Diaghilev made him. Look at his face, what a nose he has. But just touch that nose! There was a famous surgeon in Berlin. Diaghilev sent Lifar to him. This is why Lifar pants for breath just like I do, although he is younger, because he can't breathe solely through his nose and catches breath with his mouth. So, you understand, it happened like this once during dress rehearsal, I stand and look at the white gloves, because you know, fuck it, in the spotlights you can see me, and I can't see the bugger, so the conductor has white gloves so that I can see the look on his face. We begin. I had to do a pas-de-deux and now I had to catch my partner and lift her, turn round with her and put her down. But she, poor devil, having stage fright or something, was late, didn't let go, I catch her, she doesn't let herself go. I grab – here's the music, patatatatam pam pam – and as I grab her, she doesn't let go, lift her up by force – music patatatam – and as I lift her by force, so just on the beat what do I do but fart, prrram! I turn around with her and I tell you, that stink penetrates around even more – the company can't stop laughing. That Lifar was there too. They say well, it's Wladi… naturally. And Diaghilev asks who did it? That's me.

In Lourdes in a drunken state he was looking for the lavatory. Smash! into the second door on the right. At three in the morning! Opened the door and started to pee. And this was room of the Lipskis who were asleep.

23 September 1941

Diary Entry

Return to Voiron.

24 September **Diary Entry**

I'm in bed.

25 September **Letter from Franciszka to Stefan**

My darling,

All the time I am with my thoughts and heart with you. How are you Stefciu? Teresa wrote to me that you already received books from her. And also that you are on the list for visas. My darling!

How are you? How is your work going? You write that you can only send me so much. – Do you realise how much that is? Darling! When I feel sad, I read your poems, those that you sent me and those that you gave me before we left – and immediately I feel such comfort and tenderness that there's no longer room for sadness.

Today in the news – a photograph of Władek B[roniewski?] with whom we were drinking at Wróbel's once on New Year's Eve. And his poems. When I look at that emaciated face and I read the poems, I hear how simplistic his commentaries are, however well-intentioned. I hear from people who had seen him – what and how, and that he started doing the same work as Żyw. And what is said by all sorts of fools here and there, and what still awaits this poor soul. These are the hardest things about it all, how the most worthwhile people are thrown around in circles as if in a funfair, but again they get up and are once more full of strength. They manage to revive their own hundred-times-slaughtered ability to regenerate. That is impressive, and so painful.

How hard they had to struggle with themselves, those people there in Sewek's circle, to do whatever they wanted to do and how disgustingly their need of faith and enthusiasm was exploited, from all sides.

How much one has to think in order to grow up, and how much one has to see. It is difficult and sad, darling. Maybe we shall still be able to come out of it untouched, but with a wiser, mature view on things. Probably – I think so, yes. – Of course! Smile at me darling. I kiss you tenderly, so very tenderly. Franka

Diary Entry

They move me next door, I am to share a room with Karnecki.

26 September **Telegram from Zieliński in Lisbon to Stefan**

CHÉRI TOUT ARGENT LODEK POUR TOI STOP NE ME DEMANDE JAMAIS
CE SUJET TENDRESSES = FRANKA
VISA TOUJOURS SANS DÉCISION = ZIELIŃSKI

Diary Entry

Grenoble. I meet Danuta and her boys. Various projects.
Conversation with Strawiński (to Lens)
Conversation with Puget

novembre 3 – février, mars – juin

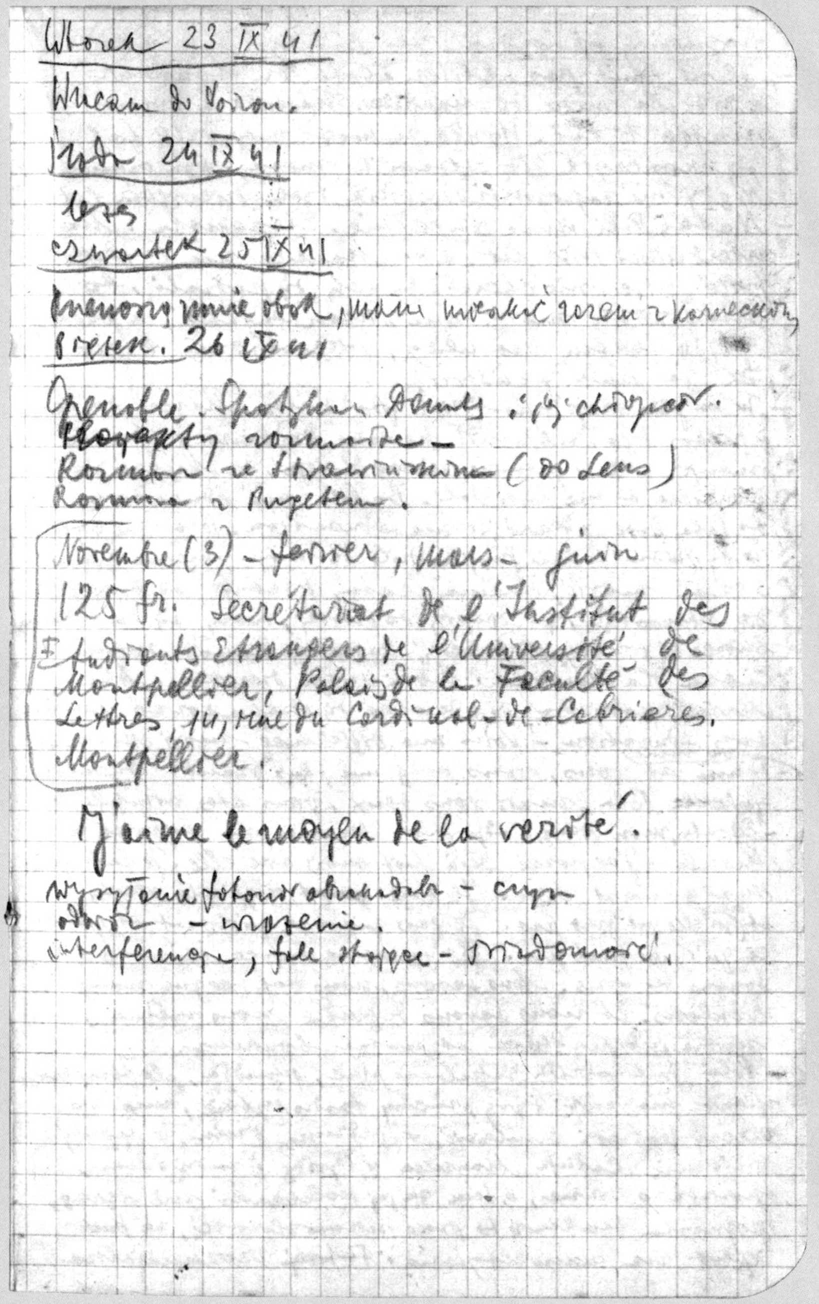

Wtorek 23 IX 41

Wracam do Voiron.

Środa 24 IX 41

[illegible]

czwartek 25 IX 41

[illegible] obok, [illegible] razem z [illegible]

Piątek. 26 IX 41

Grenoble. Spotykam [illegible] i [illegible].
Kontakty rozmaite –
Rozmowa ze [illegible] (80 lens)
Rozmowa z [illegible].

Novembre (3) – fevrier, mars – juin
125 fr. Secrétariat de l'Institut des
Etudiants Etrangers de l'Université de
Montpellier, Palais de la Faculté des
Lettres, 14, rue du Cardinal-de-Cabrières.
Montpellier.

J'aime le moyen de la verité.

wysyłanie fotonów [illegible] – [illegible]
[illegible] – wrażenie.
interferencje, fale stojące – [illegible].

Stefan's diary, 23–26 September 1941

125 frs. Secrétariat de l'Institut des Étudiants Étrangers de l'Université de Montpellier, Palais de la Faculté des Lettres, 14 rue du Cardinal-de-Cabrières, Montpellier

J'aime le moyen de la vérité.
The emission of photons abracadabra? – deed, action, feat
reception – impression
interference, vertical waves – consciousness

Fragments of stories by Pola Bobita:
'Il ne faut pas habiter à côté du bonheur' a dit la mère de Maurice. She ran away from home at the age of 18. When she was 27 she lost her husband. 8-year old son. She will never forget the happiness of those nine years. Pola's mother, completely different. Elegant. She is 45. But because Maurice is 35 she wouldn't want them to marry, because she would have to say to him 'mon enfant', but when they are together in the street, strangers take them for a married couple.

'Vous la gâtez trop', said Marcel half-jokingly to Maurice à propos that he went to wait for his wife in front of the office where she works. But basically because Marcel prefers Maurice, and he doesn't like Pola. Because Pola is educated, because Pola lets you know that she is educated. Pola doesn't want all sorts of people to visit her – she doesn't have anything to talk to them about; she doesn't have time; she works from nine to twelve and from two to six, she is studying for her exam, waking up in the night between three and six in the morning – she doesn't have time for Maurice and is protective about her happiness. But Marcel is suspicious of her, that she wants to isolate herself because of her education – voilà, une différence – says Marcel to me. Marcel is decent and simple and wants to be valued for what he is.

'Tema et vous, vous êtes mieux instruits que Pola, mais vous deux, vous êtes simples?' 'Écoute, mon vieux'. – Maurice responds to Marcel's first remark – 'J'ai passé déjà huit mois avec elle. Je la connais bien maintenant. Je sais ce qu'elle veut et ce qu'elle ne veut pas. Il n'y a aucune sphère où nous soyons rivales. Nous savons, nous deux, ce que nous voulons. Et nous savons nous défendre nous-mêmes, notre indépendance et notre bonheur.'

Pola had been suffering a bout of pneumonia, she got thinner, but continued to have a lively temperament, very quick movements, an enormous number of things can fit into her day, in one minute. She kisses Maurice on his bald head and talks about it, talks about the office, about the fact that her female colleagues don't believe, simply treat it as an impossibility that she is at a university. For them the boastfulness of such lies is more comprehensible than the truth of 'extravagance'.

'Savez-vous, T' – she says – 'pourquoi j'aime cet escalier – C'est plus difficile de monter par là, mais je monte toujours par là. Il y a toujours des chats sur cet escalier. Nous sommes montés une fois, mon mari et moi, il y avait un chat qui descendait lentement et si posément! Une fillette le suivait et l'attrapait.' "Il faut être sage, mon petit, il faut toujours être sage" – a-t-elle dit. Et elle est montée tout en haut. Et après deux jeunes filles descendaient, la main dans la main, et elles chantaient, elles chantaient si gaîment comme nous tandis que nous montions en haut – la fillette nourrissant son chat, elle lui donnait la soupe dans une assiette creuse. "Maintenant on est sage – a-t-elle dit – on est sage et on prend son déjeuner." Et au sommet de l'escalier en pierres il y a une rue. Savez-vous pourquoi j'aime cette rue? Il y habite un vieux monsieur, il ouvre sa fenêtre et il appelle, il appelle tout simplement: "venez!". Et les oiseaux viennent et ils mangent de sa main des morceaux de pain. Quand ils ont tout mangé il dit, tout simplement: "vous avez tout mangé alors, partez maintenant". Et ils s'envolent. Et encore plus haut il y a une ruelle, une ruelle tout ordinaire. Savez-vous, T, pourquoi j'aime cette ruelle? Parce que elle s'appelle rue des Projets. Elle est maintenant tout achevée, mais elle s'appelle toujours rue des Projets. Ça c'est magnifique, n'est-ce pas?'

We were still going uphill. From place Bellevue one could see the Rhône down below and roofs of the houses stuck together reminiscent of an ant hill on yet another ordinary day. Above them, a skyscraper soaked in the shapeless grey cloud that the town, like a magnet, pulled down towards itself, freeing the azure of the sky, which covered the hill of the Croix-Rousse like a dome. The square already breathed with the air of autumn. The green of the trees was interwoven with the crimson of creeping vine, which climbed high between the huge boughs and small branches, and dotted with the yellow leaves of the melancholy acacia.

27 September **Cable from Mira Złotowska to Franciszka**

CABLE NEW ADDRESS AND PASSPORT DETAILS STEPHAN STOP POSSIBILITY VISA ARGENTINE LOVE ZŁOTOWSKA 164 W 74 STREET

Telegram from Franciszka to Mira – undated, pencil draft only

STEFEK STILL VOIRON ISÈRE HÔTEL POSTE BORN JANUARY 25 1910 PŁOCK LACKING ONLY PORTUGUESE VISA TO JOIN WIFE – LETTER FOLLOWS LOVE THEMERSON 55 GREENCROFT GARDENS

29 September **Letter from Franciszka to Stefan** – unposted

My sweetheart, I write – probably just for myself, I miss you so much – so desperately miss you. And I am so anxious. I work all day and talk with people and smile while my heart shrivels up with worry – Darling, I am now sitting alone, it is evening, alone at this tram stop of mine, which I created parallel to yours – I took your letters in my hand, and your poems – and wept. My pet – it is so difficult to bear – and I would like to draw for you – and I can't. Why? I am so hopelessly sad – but no I'm not sad, because you wrote so many times that I shouldn't be, my pet. And I am ashamed too. Our nearest and dearest live in such torment. It's unbelievable. And you are alone, I know how alone you are and how difficult and hard it is. And how you endure it as far as your health is concerned. I can't, I really can't think about it – and I am frightened for you.

I would be so happy, if I could feel that you had friends there. If someone would take care of you, if you would smile because you feel good – that would make me so happy. It is too much and too hard to be alone for so long – my pet I love you – so much – and that is the only thing that I really feel.

What I am writing isn't what I usually think and I'm not all sure that I'll give it to you to read, but I must, must talk to you.

You know, all the time I feel that one will still be able to do so much and it will be so wonderful to work together again and that keeps me going – stops me from falling apart completely. My pet! – I kiss you so tenderly from afar. Probably you feel it, darling – my little one!

I can't analyse all this, until I can really begin to draw – my feelings of being so absorbed with myself change into something external, abstracted. I don't always know how to grasp that moment. But then, sometimes, I don't draw because it seems to me that I won't be able to bear it, that it will be too strong for me.

Everything is trembling inside me from thousands of muffled desires and longings.

My pet, when I think of the moment when I shall lean on your arm again – my paper is wet with tears, and my hand shakes. What an idiot I have turned into – I absolutely can't control myself. But I must. And so it goes on, on and on without end. And I want to keep my nerves in some sort of human state for you. Now I can't write any more, even this is too hard for me. I can't send it of course. I kiss you, kiss you my sweetheart. Franka

Already October!!! Again.

In October 1941 Zosia Wojciechowska goes to America

1 October **Telegram from Franciszka to Stefan**

CHÉRI COMMENT VAS TU MON PETIT INQUIÈTE TA SANTÉ JE VAIS TRÈS BIEN T'ENVOIE TOUTE MA TENDRESSE ET TANT DE BAISERS = THEMERSON

4 October **Letter from Franciszka to Stefan**

My dearest little one –

What can I write you, darling, when I am full of your words? I am moved, simply moved with the magic of your poems. I read 'Nuit de Grèce' aloud many, many times. It is impossible not to read it aloud – it sounds so beautiful. By some magical means you have controlled the rhythm and sound of these foreign words. How do you do it, my pet? So that it sings and still reverberates after you finish reading – and then you start again from the beginning. What can I say to you with words – when my words are so clumsy?

I live through your poems, darling. I should like everyone to read them – I feel that one shouldn't, absolutely should not hide them in these days, when every living seed is so precious.

I would prefer Antoni [Słonimski] rather than Gr[ydzewski], but Antoni is not publishing anything. The potential editors quarrelled with potential publishers, as well as each party among themselves, and a week ago he told me that he already lost hope of doing anything. A pity. Maybe I'll try with Gr… – but this is such a stupid paper[85] now, and apart from that one cannot approach him in a human, straightforward sort of way – I don't like them. When it comes down to it, is there anyone I like at all?

The only thing I know is that I love you. So very much.

The rest – lies and fog all around. And it's all so unimportant, hurtful, superfluous and tiresome.

But none of this means anything, darling. On the day that I receive your poems I feel so very happy.

85 *Wiadomości Polskie, Polityczne i Literackie*, published in London between July 1940 and February 1944

4 October 1941

Darling, don't be angry with me about Ortiz. It means so much to me – I can be a tiny, tiny bit calmer. After all one doesn't know yet how it will all turn out. It could be useful. It is a trifle after all. Really.

Mira cabled me that there are some possibilities of an Argentine visa for Marceljanek. Anyway only in order to go to Teresa. But perhaps it will work out earlier, because this again is likely to be endless.

My dear darling, all the time without a pause I am with you in heart and mind.

I kiss you so much, so tenderly, and so many times Franka

30 September – 4 October

Diary Entry

I am going to Lyon. Bobitzes. Come back.

I meet Ruszkowski, bank – in Lyon, he says that Kama arrived and is in the south. Conversation with Czesław while unloading sugar. Visits to the Consulates. Meeting with Marcel.

Friday – Marcel takes me to his place, we must spend one day together. He sleeps at his friend's. He works in leather. Supper. We will go there for a second one. It's bizarre I blurted out. I was thinking not about us, but about the situation. Marcel: 'Pourquoi c'est bizarre? Il travaille dur, il faut qu'il mange.'

Cinema. To the fifth floor to Marcel's friend. Concierge. So we turn back.
Till 1 am through well lit streets. Quietly upstairs. Three of us sleep in one bed.
Saturday morning – departure.
Voiron.

Letters from Franka, from Ignacy, from Władek.

Władzio K.[86] always stresses that he never lies. I ask him why… 'Because I don't like to.' I say: 'There must have been an occasion when you paid heavily for your lie.' And Władzio responded by telling me how when he was 11, he stole 10 crowns from his father. He bought himself 'gants glacés' – for 2 crowns. Pony-trap ride in the park, water with raspberry juice in a café, etc. But there were 2 crowns left in his coat pocket. The father found them and gave him such a beating that he fainted. (The shop assistant beat him, Władzio said, and immediately added, 'who lived with us'.)

Żmigrod's story: he invited me for a glass of liqueur, a farewell drink, he is leaving day after tomorrow, on Wednesday. 'I must say', says Józek, 'I am lucky, I must say'. Karnecki looks with indulgence and interest at this thin, bony figure, in the little room, the bits and pieces. 'You call it luck?' he asks. 'Yes'. 'Call it luck, if you will'. 'Well, that's very nice', says K, 'but there are other people who are more lucky than you, who made careers, who are somebodies now'. 'These are swine, blackguards, scoundrels.' 'Yes, I agree with you, you are right, but they are more lucky.' 'You see', says Józek, 'we are different in this respect. I mean something else by luck. Nothing ever came to me easily. When I finished school I had to battle to go to the university, I had to battle to finish my humanities degree. I have no exaggerated notion about myself, but forgive me, I shouldn't have been a school teacher in Kalisz. What I should have done was to join the BBWR[87]. But I didn't

86 i.e. Wladi Karnecki

87 Bezpartyjny Blok Współpracy z Rządem (Nonpartisan Bloc for Cooperation with the Government) cross-party organisation established in 1927 to support Józef Piłsudski.

want to do it. I was in the PPS [Polish Socialist Party]. And I couldn't become a candidate for the council, because I would lose my teaching job in the secondary school. I wasn't lucky. I always wanted to prove myself and I wanted to participate in the war. And I tell you, I was in such deep water, people next to me were dropping like flies, and I didn't have the slightest scratch. I call that luck, I haven't lost anything in this war. I had no fortune to lose. My sister, the only one who stayed there must suffer for sure. And I think, I am convinced, that after the war I shall have greater luck than before. I shall get credit for my war service, if need be, and it didn't cost me a single scratch.'

> Dorion, plus paisible, disait: 'Certes, les atomes qui s'associent pour composer cette femme présentent une combinaison agréable à l'oeil. Ce n'est qu'un jeu de la nature et ces atomes ne savent pas ce qu'ils font. Ils se sépareront un jour avec la même indifférence qu'ils se sont unis. Où sont maintenant les atomes qui formèrent Laïs ou Cléopatre?…' Anatole France (*Thaïs*)[88]

5 October Telegram from Stefan to Franciszka

MON PETIT CHÉRIE NE T'INQUIÈTE PAS SUIS PARFAITEMENT BIEN J'ATTENDS TOUJOURS VISA AVEC ESPOIR ET IMPATIENCE T'EMBRASSE SI CORDIALEMENT ENVOIE TANT BAISERS TENONS NOUS ENCORE MON PETIT = THEMERSON

7 October Letter from Stefan to Franciszka

My dearest darling, don't worry about me, Franek! My health is absolutely fine. I'm in control of myself and, apart from a quiet impatience, feel anæsthetised to it all. I await our reunion.

I don't allow anyone or anything to deprive me of this art of sobriety. To those blind fools, greedy for a slice of the cake; for jobs, positions, commendations, honours, hierarchies, etc. this must seem like 'living in the clouds'. I am aware of the different appearance that various realities can assume and of the concreteness of abstractions, which have an even greater sense of reality. One can touch a stone with one's hand and with one's eyes touch the stains on paper – but neither the stone nor the stains have in themselves meaning. Meaning can only be created through abstractions that defy touch, such as one calls 'gothic', or this or that sort of painting, etc. And man has no innate significance – meaning is only found in the abstraction of life created by man. And larger or smaller groups of people don't have any greater meaning in themselves any than any other parts of nature – their meaning is only created first in the biological evolution, and again in the fever of abstraction – of ideas and notions, and so on. The ability to fight nature or to live with nature (and it comes to the same) depends on conquering it with its own means, on breaking up the material rock with the aid of the material pickaxe, and on dematerialisation, or the transformation of matter (whose existence we only know about from 'hearsay' through our senses) into an abstraction, which we discover, feel and know immediately, within ourselves. The rebuilding of the always unreal matter into the always real abstraction. How much more real is longing than homeland, and hunger than lunch!

Don't be anxious, darling, about gaps in our correspondence. They have to happen from time to time. Not so long ago I was in the country. All of two days.

88 Livre I - *Le Lotus*.

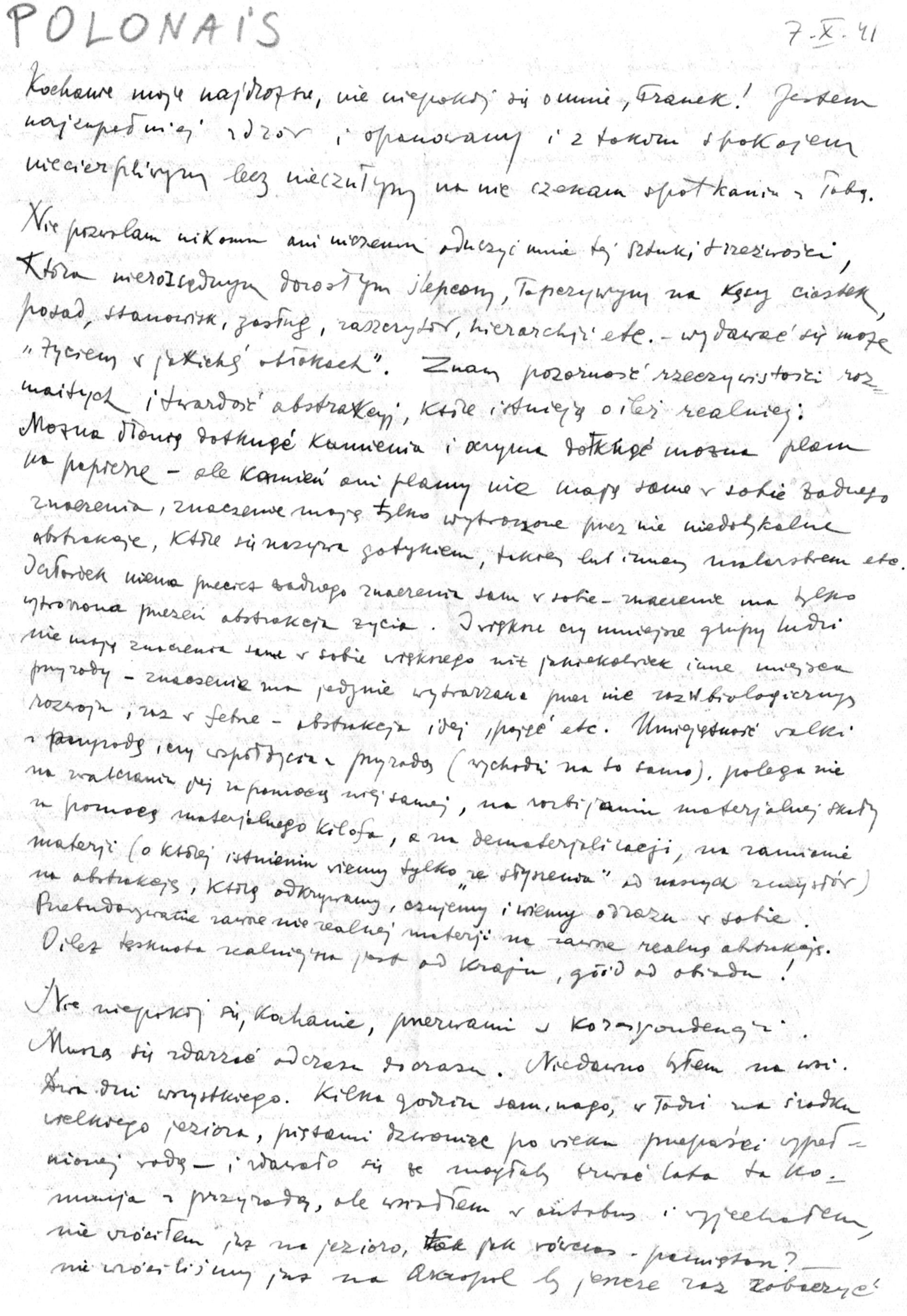

POLONAIS 7.X.41

Kochanie moje najdroższe, nie niepokój się o mnie, Franek! Jestem najzupełniej zdrów i opanowany i z takim spokojem niecierpliwym lecz niezłomnym na nie czekam spotkania z Tobą.

Nie pozwolam nikomu ani niczemu odebrać mnie tej sztuki, trzeźwości, która niezrozumiałym dorosłym ślepcom, łapczywym na kęsy ciastek, posad, stanowisk, zasług, zaszczytów, hierarchii etc. — wydawać się może „życiem w jakichś obłokach". Znam pozorność rzeczywistości rozmaitych i twardość abstrakcji, które istnieją o wiele realniej: Można dłonią dotknąć kamienia i oczyma dotknąć można plam na papierze — ale kamień ani plamy nie mają same w sobie żadnego znaczenia, znaczenie mają tylko wytworzone przez nie niedotykalne abstrakcje, które się nazywa gotykiem, takim lub innym malarstwem etc. Osobnik nie ma przecież żadnego znaczenia sam w sobie — znaczenie ma tylko wytworzona przezeń abstrakcja życia. I większe czy mniejsze grupy ludzi nie mają znaczenia same w sobie większego niż jakiekolwiek inne zjawiska przyrody — znaczenie ma jedynie wytwarzane przez nie rozw. biologicznych rozwoju, czy w sferze — abstrakcja idei, pojęć etc. Umiejętność walki z przyrodą, czy współżycia z przyrodą (wychodzi na to samo), polega nie na walczeniu jej za pomocą niej samej, na rozbijaniu materjalnej skały za pomocą materjalnego kilofa, a na dematerjalizacji, na zamianie materji (o której istnieniu wiemy tylko ze „słyszenia" od naszych zmysłów) na abstrakcję, którą odkrywamy, czujemy i wiemy obrazu w sobie. Przebudowywanie zawsze nie realnej materji na zawsze realną abstrakcję. O ileż tęsknota realniejsza jest od kraju, głód od obiadu!

Nie niepokój się, Kochanie, przerwami w korespondencji. Muszą się zdarzać od czasu do czasu. Niedawno byłem na wsi. Dwa dni wszystkiego. Kilka godzin sam, nago, w łodzi na środku wielkiego jeziora, palcami dotykając [illegible] po wierzchu przepaści wypełnionej wodą — i zdawało się że mogłaby trwać lata ta komunja z przyrodą, ale wsiadłem w autobus i wyjechałem, nie wróciłem już na jezioro, tak jak wówczas — pamiętasz? — nie wróciliśmy już na Akropol by jeszcze raz zobaczyć

First page of Stefan's letter to Franciszka, 7 October 1941

A few hours by myself, naked, in a boat in the middle of a huge lake, with my heels dangling on the surface of an abyss filled with water – and it seemed to me that it could last for years this communication with nature, but I got out and into the bus and I left I didn't return again to the lake, just like that time – do you remember? – we didn't go back to the Acropolis to see once more the silent and still truth of the Parthenon. You can't repeat things once they have realised themselves completely inside you. The world is built of causes and effects, each second is a fragment of a quarter of an hour, but there are moments perfect in themselves, indissoluble in the river of time. One can repeat, like screenings in a cinema, the illusion of the illusion of reality; but the moments themselves once completed are unrepeatable, because when a glass is filled to the brim it's impossible – and unnecessary – to add anything.

I spent a few days with Tema [Kaliszer]'s friends. I wrote to you about the treasures of friendship and humanity that she and her friends from Belleville revealed to me. These are the things that one cannot weigh, measure or count, but how concrete they are! How simple it would be to construct something out of the world with all its photons and nebulae, if there were no humans in it. And it is the greatest wonder: that matter can produce these concrete things by which we live and yet which may not be measured by centimetres, grams and seconds.

I received a long letter from Ignacy [Złotowski]. I despair on his behalf. He writes about 'flu-ridden scientific truths' and about his own 'adventurous projects'. All of us are awfully wise in quiet times, but who, blackmailed by the horror of events and falsification of slogans in times of catastrophe, is able to find courage to repeat, after Paul Valéry:

> Il n'est pas mauvais que certains hommes aient la force d'attacher plus de conséquence et de prix à la détermination d'une lointaine décimale ou de la position d'une virgule, qu'à la nouvelle la plus retentissente, à la catastrophe la plus considérable, ou à leur vie même.'[89]

This is not about 'blowing up small things and reducing big ones'! Things in themselves are neither big nor small, neither bitter nor salty. In the solidity of matter there is more emptiness between atoms, than in our universe between the stars.

That for us is the only scale of greatness. Taste and colour exist only in us. The Christians knew about it, and the Stoics knew about it. But I am neither concerned with Christianity and its God, Last Judgment and the reward after death, nor with the Stoics with their egoistic happiness for man-philosopher, although Christianity and the philosophy of the Stoics were the yeast of development of the European civilisation. I don't know what it is about. Perhaps it is about a sense of the aesthetic, that is the source of logic and mathematics, the basis of ethics and the sense of justice, the golden mean of art, the only criterion of truth. Slovenliness and egoism (both direct results of upbringing) are the greatest enemies of the aesthetic sensibility. We have deluded ourselves. We thought that everyone was irritated by the broken hand of a clock, the unnecessary leg of a table however beautiful, or a violin that hadn't been tuned. We didn't take seriously the fact that people really want to have their cake and eat it with cream on top. Bent over their plates, not only do they put on the blinkers of a cart horse – so as not to see the flattened noses pressed against the window of the café, so they can devote their life to this cake, not only their life but those of others – but they also

89 'Souvenir', *Mélange*, Gallimard, 1941, p.39

know how to treat seriously and with utmost solemnity the taste of the cream. Nomenclature originated from means and not from aims. Those that call themselves idealists are those who, in a romantic mist, fish for bits of matter. Materialists are those who want to build from matter its real abstractions – its ideas.

Some values are beyond comparison. Home, for instance, and *La Gioconda* cannot be compared with a barrister's speech or the diagram of a bird's flight. These values belong to different hierarchies. But, after all, there is no absolute hierarchy of hierarchies, if one is not a believer in one of the faiths of the Church or in civil ones. I am furious that a man like Ignacy wants to abandon his table, not because the table has crumbled to pieces from the inside but because of fire. In the name of solidarity he wants to extinguish the flames together with everyone else, although actually, in the name of solidarity, he should rescue that table of his, as he writes, of 'flu-ridden' truths. The art of solidarity is not only to know how to give but also to know how to take, even when a cataclysm warps the lenses of our eyes and it seems to us that what we have to gain is to be found more in some unknown absolute than what we have to give.

It is true. And yet I feel that in the demagogic speech that is calculated to blackmail the best people (those who don't think about themselves as the ultimate evolution), and in sayings that might sound like a slap in the face (such as 'to find your number, brother, you must look somewhere long after the decimal point, and then wait for others to discover for you your right to live') – in these things also there is a grain of truth. There are more truths than one. And when contradictory truths force their way into our minds, the curtain rises and a tragedy begins. There is nothing that can be done about it, because its existence is as real as the existence of other abstractions. And I don't know whether one should even try to 'do anything about it' because tragedy, too, is a value that one should not throw out of our trunk of European baggage.

Perhaps it is easier for me to write like this today, because even if I wanted to get rid of my own table – I couldn't do it.

Perhaps what I write has been influenced by my own recent life in this place, under a glass dome that cannot be broken out of, cloistered with people who wrap around themselves the coloured flags of their slogans, their own dreams about beefsteaks of old, sprinkled with vodka, about an old and trivial hierarchy of positions and injustices.

Sometimes, it seems to me, that despite my sins or merits, I am beyond the good and the bad, like a fragment of nature, like a stone, and that this state of inertia suspended in time is, after all, just a means of survival to reach the only reality that exists for me and for which I wait with such urgent longing.

Darling, when in the end my cheek will press yours, it will be possible to gulp down that reality!

Darling, I have so very much to tell you, so enormously much, but everything will find enough space in one moment, in one look, in an embrace and in a smile.

I kiss you, my dearest littlest one – so very much.

Stefan

19 October Telegram from Stefan to Franciszka

CHÉRIE REÇU TES LETTRES MERCI JE VAIS TRÈS BIEN ET
TOI INQUIÈTE TA SANTÉ TOUTES MES PENSÉES PRÈS DE TOI
MON PETIT QUAND TE REVERRAI JE T'EMBRASSE SI TENDREMENT
= THEMERSON

16 October 1941
Letter from the Polish Ministry of Foreign Affairs to the Ministry of Information and Documentation, both in London

With reference to the letter of the Ministry of Information and Documentation of 9 October 1941, no. 5809/41/Inf, the Ministry of Foreign Affairs advises that Spanish authorities granted already in July of this year a transit visa for Stefan Themerson. Currently, the Ministry of Foreign Affairs has once more requested the Legation of the Polish Republic in Lisbon with the aim of expediting the granting of a Portuguese transit visa.

W/UR
MINISTERSTWO
SPRAW ZAGRANICZNYCH
Nr.478/Th/I/41

Londyn, dnia 16 października 1941 r.

Ministerstwo ... L.Dz. 6221/41/Inf. Referenci ... p. Temersonowa ... Wpłynęło dnia

W związku z pismem Ministerstwa Informacji i Dokumentacji z dn.9.10.41 Nr.5809/41/Inf, Ministerstwo Spraw Zagranicznych komunikuje, że władze hiszpańskie udzieliły już w lipcu b.r. wizę tranzytową dla p.Stefana Themersona. Obecnie Ministerstwo Spraw Zagranicznych ponownie ponagliło Poselstwo R.P. w Lizbonie celem przyspieszenia uzyskania wizy tranzytowej portugalskiej.

ZA MINISTRA
/J.Marlewski/

Do
Ministerstwa Informacji
i Dokumentacji
w Londynie

z/a
OFFICE POLONAIS A MARSEILLE
BIURO POLSKIE W MARSYLII
2, Place Félix Baret
Tél. D. 43-61
Nr R.738/uch/r/The

Marsylia, dn. 20 października 1941

Biuro Polskie uprzejmie zawiadamia, iż zostało poinformowane przez Poselstwo RP. w Madrycie o przyznaniu Panu wizy tranzytowej hiszpańskiej, którą będzie Pan mógł ~~wykorzystać~~ podjąć w Marsylii po uzyskaniu tranzytowej wizy portugalskiej.

za Dyrektora Biura Polskiego
Jerzy Żołobnicki
Wicedyrektor Biura Polskiego

Pan Stefan Themerson
Hôtel de la Poste
Voiron (Isère)

20 October 1941
Letter from Office Polonais in Marseille to Stefan

The Polish Office kindly advises you that it has been informed by the Legation of the Polish Republic in Madrid that a transit visa for you has been granted and that you will be able to receive it in Marseille after you have been granted a Portuguese transit visa.

CONSULADO DE PORTUGAL

LYON

LYON, le 1er Novembre 1941.

Monsieur THEMERSON
Hôtel de la Poste
V O I R O N (Isère)

Monsieur,

Comme suite à votre télégramme d'hier, ce Consulat a l'honneur de vous informer que le Visa de transit Portugais ne peut être accordé qu'après une demande télégraphique qui sera faite par ce Consulat au Gouvernement Portugais.

Dans cette demande télégraphique, qui sera faite à vos frais, devront figurer les renseignements suivants :

1º - Pays de destination pour lequel on possède déjà soit le Passeport, soit le Visa du Consulat de ce pays, avec date de délivrance.

2º - Si entre le Portugal et le pays destinataire il n' existe pas de lignes directes et que le voyageur soit obligé de traverser d'autres pays avant d'atteindre le pays de destination, il est indispensable qu'il possède également les Visas de transit des pays traversés.

3º - Le passage réservé qui devra être communiqué à ce Consulat directement par les Agences établies à Lisbonne, qui indiqueront le nom du bateau et la date de son départ.

Aussitôt que toutes ces conditions seront remplies, ce Consulat pourra faire la demande télégraphique prévue ci-dessus.

CONSULADO DA REPUBLICA PORTUGUESA EM LYON

1 November 1941
Letter to Stefan from Consulado de Portugal in Lyon

20 October 1941

Telegram from Franciszka to Stefan

MON TRÈS CHER PETIT SUIS PARFAITEMENT BIEN SI HEUREUSE TU TRAVAILLES GARDES SOURIRE CHÉRI JE T'ENVOIE TOUT MON COEUR EMBRASSE LE PLUS TENDREMENT = THEMERSON

23 October **Letter from Stefan to Franka**

Darling, I am still here, and now it is nearly a year, acacia leaves have turned yellow, vine leaves are turning redder, mist has again closed in on the valley and it's raining. And still I defend myself against putting down roots in the reality of this place, which for me is little more than the illusion of appearances. You would think that the days would drag by slowly, that at daybreak the thought of twilight would be somewhere in a distant unknown, and that the only two signposts would be the times of the arrival of the post. But in practice, morning and evening almost touch, and whole weeks pass by, like trees outside the windows of a train, so quickly and fortunately without returning. Perhaps this comes from the motionless lying-in-wait that fills my time, when we spend these devalued days as fast as devalued coins! And it appears that in this still inactivity there is no time either for great sorrow or for great passion. There is only a great longing. It shields the ears from the ticking of the clock, continuing unchanged, completely filling everything with itself. So there's no room left anywhere for all the things, great and small, that are happening now unless you can think about them in a detached and objective way. But when you try to think like that, those things that are beyond our reach appear so remote that they may as well exist in the ancient past, or sometime in the future that Wells and Huxley have imagined.

My darling, I am so very happy that you are working. And I should love to see what you are doing. Your pictures exist but of course I don't have them here. Sometimes in my imagination your paintings stand in front of my eyes. But I clearly remember only those squares of houses in Mokotów[90], so very static, so very expressive; so boldly showing those huge and smooth walls. Darling, I am so glad to have spent those years together with painting, films and literature. I hug you so much sweetheart. Thanks to you I am happier than all those around me. I kiss you, so much. Stefan

30 October **Unsigned telegram from Lisbon to Stefan**

PRIER CONSULAT PORTUGAIS DEMANDER À VOS FRAIS TÉLÉGRAPHIQUEMENT SI POLICE INTERNATIONALE AUTORISE DÉLIVRANCE VISA.

2 November **Letter from Franciszka to Stefan** – written in Polish[91]

Stefciu, my dearest darling, it is nearly 18 months since we said goodbye at the railway station, and three days ago was the anniversary of your first telegram. My darling!

And another New Year is nearly here. I am frightened even to think about it. If, if only, it would work out for us to be together!

But don't worry, darling, – be cheerful, smile, Stefciu. It would be so much easier to bear our separation if I could feel sure you are well and that you've managed to organise your life in some reasonable way.

It's so difficult for me to imagine what it's like for you there, what you are doing, who you have to talk to. Please write to me about some of these ordinary

90 A suburb of Warsaw. We have no record of those paintings.

91 Sometimes the Themersons realise, or remember, that at the top of a letter one should announce in what language it is written.

silly details, even though I realise of course, that it's not easy. These are all such silly meaningless things. It's just that it makes it easier for me to imagine your life a bit, just a little bit.

Sometimes I even close my eyes and stretch out my hand to touch you, to work some magic – and bring you closer.

My darling, so perhaps one of these days I'll get some letters from you. I haven't had any post for a month.

Write and tell me what you are working on now, darling.

When, when shall we be able to get down to work together? It is so difficult for me to do anything alone, without your wise eyes near me. Oh, Stefciu!

I try to turn over in my mind sometimes, how and when and what sort of real work it will be possible to get down to. But it's difficult for me to breathe deeply enough. Everything is happening despite our will – so that sometimes I have to just keep on going, straight ahead, and despite my instincts without thinking. It just gets harder and harder to go on thinking all the time. It's too difficult. I bought for myself the collected works of the author of *Alice in Wonderland* and childishly I shut myself inside these extraordinary adventures of the last century, full both of momentum and of an old-fashioned world. Sometimes, I fortify myself like a child who pretends to be ill so as not to go to school. If I'm honest, it's perfectly true that I haven't done my homework. It is more and more difficult for me to find some serious engagement with people, at least one that's based on some common language. I seek it less and less. I treat people with 'indulgence'. There is nothing conceited in this 'indulgence'. Only helplessness.

Darling, Mira asked me for your passport details (number, place of issue and date of expiry, etc.). I didn't have these details. Her address is now, 164 West 74th Street, New York City. She wrote that perhaps she'll succeed in getting an Argentine visa for you. But as far as I know, to get a Portuguese one you would have to have a document to say that you have a place on the boat. I don't know if you would be able to arrange this yourself. But perhaps she could do it. If you think it would do any good, send her a telegram with the details she's asked for. Anyway maybe you would then get the Portuguese transit visa. I no longer know myself but I am writing these details for you so that you can orientate yourself with what possibilities there are. Oh, darling!

So much and with such warmth I think about you, sweetheart! I don't even know how to write this to you – there aren't enough words – there aren't enough letters. But I kiss you so tenderly, Stefciu. Love Franka

If you should meet Judge Walfisz and his wife in Grenoble, please give them my best wishes. His wife is a good friend of your cousin Irka [Fürstenberg]. I used to see them before I left.

I kiss you and kiss you. Franka

Franciszka does imagine some of the details of Stefan's environment. She draws them. There are trees, mountains and interiors and some of them turn out to be very accurate.

5 November 1941

Telegram from Stefan to Franciszka

CHÉRIE SUIS TRÈS BIEN ET TOI MON PETIT STOP J'ATTENDS TOUJOURS MON VISA QUI N'ARRIVE PAS IL FAUT TANT DE PATIENCE CHÉRIE T'EMBRASSE LE PLUS TENDREMENT POSSIBLE = THEMERSON

7 November

Letter from Stefan to Franciszka

My dearest darling,

I continue to wait, you understand? I continue to wait and that is all, absolutely all. Sometimes it seems to me that I am gaining some great wisdom in that process, but perhaps it is only the maturity of years, and I'd give up all the wisdoms in the world to bring the meeting with you a moment closer. All sorts of views about the world are possible and I know how to look at it from different points of view, without mixing up the perspectives, and without repudiating one's own desires and feelings when it's a matter of judgments and the mechanism of appearances, but the world doesn't allow this algebra of history to get mixed up with my private values. Of course always and everywhere there are sorrows and joys. But the daily sorrows and joys usually pass by the tram stop, where they have already been standing for a year, waiting. And they know neither how to 'reason', nor how to be really glad. Nothing can offer real peace when there is no possibility of movement. And it's only when something suddenly appears which suggests that the moment of leaving may be coming closer, that I realise how much static mental energy has collected in the still and quiet enclave that is inside me. I kiss you, darling, so much.

The formalities of my departure now look like this: the Portuguese Consulate in Lyon is waiting for confirmation that I have a visa for a destination, and a ticket. If that evidence arrives from Lisbon, the Consulate will send a telegram to Lisbon, and, after receiving permission from their authorities, will be able to present me with a visa. How long this procedure will take, I have no idea. Perhaps a few days, but it's also possible that, when you get this letter, things won't have moved at all.

Darling, I am so very glad that you are working. And I would so much like to see all that you are doing. You don't know how I miss not only your canvases and drawings but the sight of your easel and the smell of oil paint.

Sometimes it seems to me that you are very near, with a palette in your hand; sometimes it seems to me that I hear the scratch of the nib of your pen drawing living lines, alive with their own life on paper, my dearest darling.

Looking back now, I can picture so clearly the void[92] in which we worked together. To one side of it was the Parnassian *Wiadomości Literackie* usurping the right to approve or disapprove. On the other side, everyone else struggling for a bite of the cherry and the right to exist, judging everything by arbitrarily chosen criteria. Only secondary activities, like books for children or competitions announced by *Wiadomości Literackie* were accepted by our milieu. We both concealed everything else, but we should have worked openly, as we did with films, in order to educate friends – the audience along the way, without fear that our mistakes would be noticed and not expecting to produce a perfect masterpiece. One should leave traces along the way, even if one is searching in the dark, lest one ends up with one's own *Eureka*, in solitude, surrounded by impenetrable growth. Creativity demands courage.

92 Yes, it was a void in the sense that in the 1930s Poland there was no support for experimental film-makers. In all, there were only six, and the Themersons were the most prominent among them.

I bought myself Joyce's *Ulysses* in French. 900 solid pages of small print. What absorbing reading. The approach of a scientist in a wonderland, around which surge the sort of planets as all the volumes of Proust's *Remembrance of Things Past* and *Le Grand Meaulnes*. The courage to be free of scruples. Courage 'in the name of truth', alongside the knowledge that absolute truths don't exist.

Darling, who knows what the world will look like when the time comes to start work again? Creative work will depend on future conditions: some people will fight for the new content, the others will oppose it. They will want the glory of the past not to disappear. Everyone has his own truths, and everyone will always have his own truths, which he wishes to impose on others. Our private, biological truth = the passion for life and work must survive it all.

I kiss you Franeczko so much, so much my dearest darling.

Stefan

8 November **Telegram from Franciszka to Stefan**

CHÉRI REÇU TÉLÉGRAMME ET LETTRE SEPTEMBRE MERCI MON PETIT JE T'AIME TOUTES MES TENDRESSES EMBRASSE = THEMERSON

11 November **Telegram from Jolmission in Lisbon to Stefan**

MALGRÉ TOUS MES EFFORTS CONFIRMER GARANTIE VOTRE PASSAGE ULTÉRIEUR VISA VOUS A ÉTÉ REFUSÉ CAUSE MANQUE MOYEN TRANSPORT DESTINATION GRANDE BRETAGNE STOP EN EFFET PLACES AVION RETENUS POUR 6 MOIS STOP UNIQUE MOYEN POSSIBILITÉ CONSISTE OBTENIR LONDRES PRIORITÉ AVION AVEC GARANTIE DÉPART PORTUGAL PENDANT 30 JOURS. = JOLMISSION

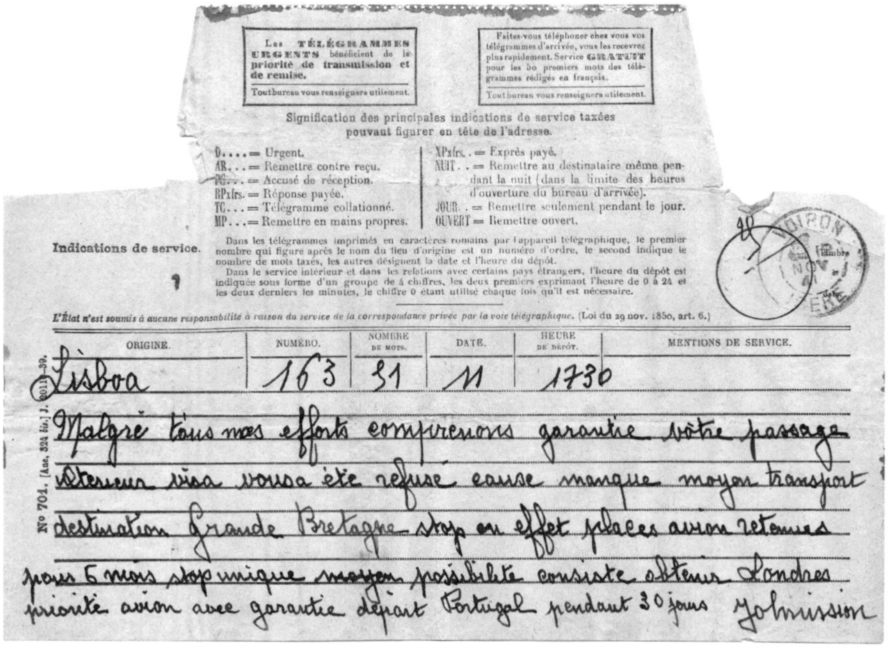

Les TÉLÉGRAMMES URGENTS bénéficient de la priorité de transmission et de remise.
Toutbureau vous renseignera utilement.

Faites-vous téléphoner chez vous vos télégrammes d'arrivée, vous les recevrez plus rapidement. Service GRATUIT pour les 50 premiers mots des télégrammes rédigés en français.
Tout bureau vous renseignera utilement.

Signification des principales indications de service taxées pouvant figurer en tête de l'adresse.

D.... = Urgent.
AR... = Remettre contre reçu.
PC... = Accusé de réception.
RPxfrs. = Réponse payée.
TC... = Télégramme collationné.
MP... = Remettre en mains propres.
XPxfrs. = Exprès payé.
NUIT.. = Remettre au destinataire même pendant la nuit (dans la limite des heures d'ouverture du bureau d'arrivée).
JOUR.. = Remettre seulement pendant le jour.
OUVERT = Remettre ouvert.

Indications de service.

Dans les télégrammes imprimés en caractères romains par l'appareil télégraphique, le premier nombre qui figure après le nom du lieu d'origine est un numéro d'ordre, le second indique le nombre de mots taxés, les autres désignent la date et l'heure du dépôt.
Dans le service intérieur et dans les relations avec certains pays étrangers, l'heure du dépôt est indiquée sous forme d'un groupe de 4 chiffres, les deux premiers exprimant l'heure de 0 à 24 et les deux derniers les minutes, le chiffre 0 étant utilisé chaque fois qu'il est nécessaire.

L'État n'est soumis à aucune responsabilité à raison du service de la correspondance privée par la voie télégraphique. (Loi du 29 nov. 1850, art. 6.)

No 701. [Anc. 324 bis.] J. 2011—39.

ORIGINE.	NUMÉRO.	NOMBRE DE MOTS.	DATE.	HEURE DE DÉPÔT.	MENTIONS DE SERVICE.
Lisboa	163	31	11	1730	

Malgré tous mes efforts comfirenons garantie vôtre passage ulterieur visa vousa ete refuse cause manque moyen transport destination Grande Bretagne stop en effet places avion retenues pour 6 mois stop unique moyen possibilite consiste obtenir Londres priorité avion avec garantie départ Portugal pendant 30 jours Jolmission

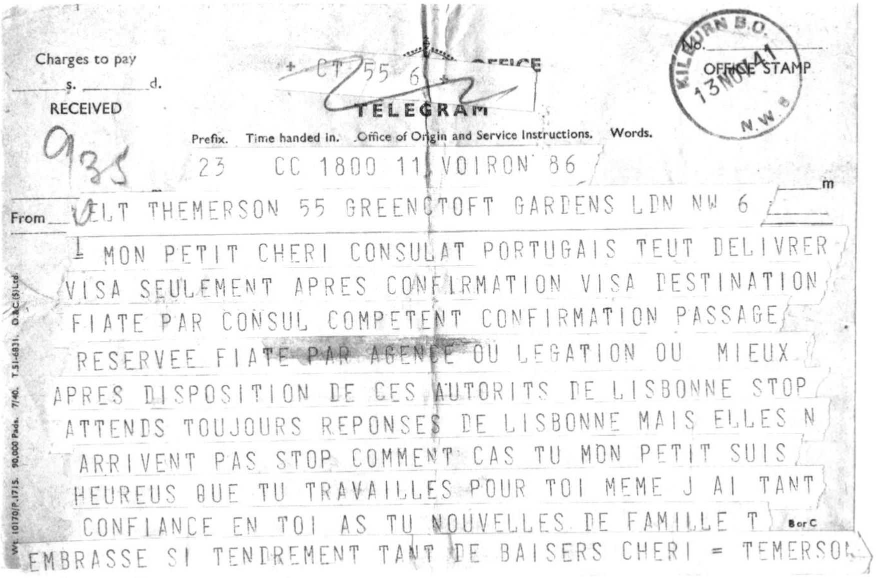

Charges to pay
s. d.
RECEIVED
TELEGRAM
KILBURN B.O. 13 NO 41 N.W.8 OFFICE STAMP
Prefix. Time handed in. Office of Origin and Service Instructions. Words.
23 CC 1800 11 VOIRON 86
From ELT THEMERSON 55 GREENCTOFT GARDENS LDN NW 6
MON PETIT CHERI CONSULAT PORTUGAIS TEUT DELIVRER
VISA SEULEMENT APRES CONFIRMATION VISA DESTINATION
FIATE PAR CONSUL COMPETENT CONFIRMATION PASSAGE
RESERVEE FIATE PAR AGENCE OU LEGATION OU MIEUX
APRES DISPOSITION DE CES AUTORITS DE LISBONNE STOP
ATTENDS TOUJOURS REPONSES DE LISBONNE MAIS ELLES N
ARRIVENT PAS STOP COMMENT CAS TU MON PETIT SUIS
HEUREUS QUE TU TRAVAILLES POUR TOI MEME J AI TANT
CONFIANCE EN TOI AS TU NOUVELLES DE FAMILLE T
EMBRASSE SI TENDREMENT TANT DE BAISERS CHERI = TEMERSON

Telegram from Stefan to Franciszka

MON PETIT CHÉRI CONSULAT PORTUGAIS VEUT DÉLIVRER VISA SEULEMENT APRÈS CONFIRMATION VISA DESTINATION FAITE PAR CONSUL COMPETENT CONFIRMATION PASSAGE RÉSERVÉ FAITE PAR AGENCE OU LÉGATION OU MIEUX APRÈS DISPOSITION DE CES AUTORITÉS DE LISBONNE STOP ATTENDS TOUJOURS RÉPONSES DE LISBONNE MAIS ELLES N'ARRIVENT PAS STOP COMMENT VAS TU MON PETIT SUIS HEUREUX QUE TU TRAVAILLES POUR TOI MÊME J'AI TANT CONFIANCE EN TOI AS TU NOUVELLES DE FAMILLE EMBRASSE SI TENDREMENT TANT DE BAISERS CHÉRI = TEMERSON

14 November **Telegram from Franciszka to Stefan**

CHÉRI NOTRE LÉGATION LISBONNE SOLLICITE DEPUIS LONGTEMPS VISA PASSAGE POUR DESTINATION PASSAGE PAYÉ GENEK STOP CEPENDANT CABLE À ZŁOTOWSKA 164 WEST 74TH STREET NEW YORK DONNANT NUMÉRO DATE ET LIEU DÉLIVRANT VALIDITÉ TON PASSEPORT POUR SOLLICITER ARGENTINE PEUT-ÊTRE SERA PLUS VITE STOP CROIS POSSIBLE ESSAYERAI OBTENIR POUR MARCELJANEK VISA CANADIEN ESPÉRONS CHÉRI TOUTES TENDRESSES = THEMERSON

Telegram from Stefan to Franciszka

CHÉRIE REÇU RÉPONSE LISBONNE VISA REFUSÉ CAUSE MANQUE MOYEN TRANSPORT PLACES AVION RETENUES POUR SIX MOIS STOP UNIQUE POSSIBILITÉ CONSISTE OBTENIR LONDRES PRIORITÉ AVION AVEC GARANTIE DÉPART PORTUGAL PENDANT TRENTE JOURS STOP T'EMBRASSE MON PETIT CHÉRIE = THEMERSON

16 November 1941

Letter from Franciszka to Stefan

Stefulku, my darling,

I have just received your two telegrams about the visa. Yes, I know, I've had all these difficulties and worries for a few months now. And they were only trying to determine the date of departure, but by ship because by air it is so terribly difficult. And I know that only if one has a reservation is it possible to receive a visa. It seems that they haven't succeeded since you have been refused for the time being.

I say 'for the time being' because in the end it must work out. From the beginning I wanted to try to get a *priorité*, but it is almost hopeless, and while there are some other ways to organise it differently, it wasn't possible even to consider these. Now, after your telegram, perhaps something can be done, but it is still a jungle. One has to learn about all the different ways and means, to know who and how and where one can arrange it, who can ask whom a favour and who can give orders to whom. I am already a fat encyclopædia about these matters, but this is a completely new volume. And, darling, it will again take months – unless, unless, suddenly something works out. Did you send a telegram to Mira, as I wrote to you? She asked me but I didn't know how to answer her. Do it, perhaps she will manage, as she wrote, to get you an Argentine visa, or maybe you could then, having had the letter certified in some agency, book a place on a ship and get a transit visa? Eventually, perhaps Mira will manage to arrange it through Hicem, or somehow. And then you will come here. What a matter-of-fact-letter, when it should sound so different.

Only tender words, thoughts full of endearments and so, so many things to talk about and so, so many things only to be silent about. Darling, darling –

It is already 16 November. Should I wish you a happy, and one such as you would wish, New Year? And now I'm thinking how sure I had been that we would already be together for this New Year's Eve.

I kiss you my dearest boy, so, so much and so tenderly, and endlessly. Franka

18 November **Telegram from Franciszka to Stefan**

MON PETIT ESSAIERAI OBTENIR PRIORITÉ AVION C'EST EXTRÊMEMENT DIFFICILE MAIS ESPÉRONS TOUJOURS TOUT MON COEUR AVEC TOI = THEMERSON

20 November **Letter from Franciszka to Stefan**

My darling little one,

I still haven't managed to get anywhere with that *priorité* for a flight. I talked to all sorts of people. I don't want to do it without thinking, because while it's easy to send out a letter even the most official one, it's even easier to get a refusal, and all the more so for a special application like this one.

It's such a very slim chance. If it weren't for that, I would have been trying long ago.

Darling, I doubt if I'll ever want to waste any of our precious time together to describe to you all the grotesque adventures that I've been through in my attempts to get the visa.

It would even be funny, if it weren't so sad that it takes so long – so endlessly long – one could laugh oneself silly.

My sweetheart, I long for you so much. With two hands I collect all those scattered threads of strange and marvellous things, I wrap myself in them and try to create here a part of our common world. But I am alone, and I don't add up to much on my own. But then always, when I feel really at the end of my tether, your letter or telegram arrives to help me. Sometimes it's just the sight of a mistiness moving across the sky, or old engraving on the wall, or, or I don't know what, some greeting from that real world that I'm missing so much. You know what I'm talking about darling, don't you?

And because it's all so strange for me, I sometimes wonder how can other people live now without this trust, in a distant but abstracted truth?

That's surely why they build up these paper barricades of ambition and vileness around themselves, so paltry, trivial and so painfully wounding.

My darling, this letter isn't sad, just serious. And I'm smiling at you without sadness, only with seriousness and very tenderly. And you smile too. And, my sweetheart, I so much hope that somehow life could be agreeable for you and that you might feel cheerful. Do you have any nice, friendly people there? Give them my heartfelt regards, if only because they are near you.

I kiss you my darling, so very tenderly. Franka

23 November **Letter from Franciszka to Stefan**

My darling little one, I must talk to you a bit, just to make myself conscious of how I am really responding to where I am and to what I am doing. I got lost somehow in silly everyday life. It is so very difficult for me to hold onto that strangeness of being, which is in its various forms the meaning of our life together, darling. It is so difficult for me 'to secure a place' in that abstracted continuity, however much I really believe in it. I can't work – I am not even talking about drawing – but my internal mechanism for transposing appearances doesn't always function.

I submit momentarily to this course of events, so as to keep in a reasonable physical shape. So that if you would come at last, my darling, you would not find a mere remnant of the human being that I was a few months ago. I am trying to maintain some sort of balance and often, for that reason, I don't make these risky expeditions into the metaphysical unknown. That feels absolutely beyond my strength. My sweetheart, when shall we go hand-in-hand to explore those ravaged terrains that are also so full of marvels?

What should I be doing here, really? What contacts should I look for? With whom should I talk? I am so terribly adult and so childish at the same time. But all my childish enthusiasm and hopes are locked deep down. And with the people around I talk like an older uncle. Actually, I don't talk but I look. And all the time I have to bend down, just to see something – and for what should one see it at all? And don't think that there is a trace of conceit in what I'm writing. It's only that they all crowd and mass together on one side of the scales and they seem to have no idea that another side even exists. And their entire attention is concentrated on the antics and vibrations of a brass plate on which they tread. Darling, who to look for, with whom to talk? I'm conscious all the time that small talk is not our world. That the only real sense of communicating with people is greeting through the written word or by some visual form that allows for its rediscovery somewhere, sometime, and for a genuine close response. What sincere and real friendship I feel for Carroll or Czukowski[93], how close to me is this or that painter or composer, even if they're unknown to me by name. I don't know

93 Korniej Czukowski [Korney Chukovsky] (1882-1969), Russian writer of stories for children published in Warsaw by J. Przeworski, translated by Władysław Broniewski, n.d.

if we could communicate with ordinary words. Are there really any means of communicating through conversation? What for?

It's so difficult for me now because I am not able to speak at all in this real language. So it is rather hard for me *to realise myself.* That's the best description – to realise oneself. The Polish equivalent is not sufficiently accurate, because 'awareness of things about oneself' can only be achieved through 'realisation'. Isn't that so? Bloody hell, I can't even put three words together.

What sort of a world shall we find ourselves in after the war, darling?

Dearest boy, how I miss you!

Imagine, my pet, I've tried for so long to create some sort of a warm home for you. To prepare everything and people, and the sky outside the window and ... and I myself don't even know what. But they fell apart, all these emergency friendships, these Blitz-created fragments of intimacy. I am only waiting for you so warmly and so impatiently. I've no idea what it all looks like around me – certainly not as I should wish. But I can't see, I only wait darling. As a symbol of our home I carry with me our El Greco. And next to it hangs our photograph, do you remember? Made in Arceuil in the studio.[94] I love you.

Telegram from Stefan to Franciszka

CHÉRIE REÇU TÉLÉGRAMMES MERCI VEUX PAS TE CAUSER ENNUIS MON PETIT ATTENDRAI TRANQUILLEMENT JE NE PENSE QUE À TOI AS TU NOUVELLES DE FAMILLES T'EMBRASSE SI TENDREMENT CHÉRIE = THEMERSON

Telegram from Teresa Żarnower in Lisbon to Stefan

DEMANDEZ AUTRE CONSULAT PORTUGAIS TÉLÉGRAPHIEZ POLICE INTERNATIONALE PERMISSION VISA ENTRÉE JE PARS 28 TÉLÉGRAPHIEZ NUMERO TÉLÉGRAMME LUIS NUNES RUA TOMAZ ANUNCIAÇÃO 69A = TERESA

24 November **Telegram from Franciszka to Stefan**

MON PETIT BIEN AIMÉ NE PARLE PAS D'ENNUIS TOUTE MA VIE ICI C'EST ESPOIR TE REVOIR EMBRASSER TRAVAILLES TU POUR TOI CHÉRI J'ATTENDS TES LETTRES NUITS ET JOURS FAMILLES BIEN ET T'EMBRASSENT TOUTE MA TENDRESSE CHÉRI = THEMERSON

26 November **Letter from Stefan to Franciszka**

My dearest darling,

Everything is already in these words and I stand hopeless in front of the rest of this piece of paper. Everything else, muses and detonations, they are already not mine but somebody else's, it is not what is inside me, but what is outside that one has to glance at, one way or another, from here or there, for it to exist.

Days and nights slip through the fingers and rinsing that red clod of earth that one holds onto greedily with clenched palms.

My darling little one.

I really have no idea how you live, what you think, and that too is important for me. How much I should like to see what you are doing, how much I crave for something by you. From a newspaper I cut out reproductions of drawings by

94 See page 6

Matisse and Dubuffet and hung them on the wall and I am so jealous that I can't have yours.

I kiss you Franeczko, so much. Stefan

What is happening with Konorski? Why not a word? And Genek? And everybody? I am also sending you 'Croquis dans les ténèbres' IX, actually a supplement for correction. I should like it to be how you would like it. I should like to be able to do it so that it would please you. S

27 November **Letter from Franciszka to Stefan**

My dearest darling,

Today, I received 'Croquis dans les ténèbres' in Polish. Thank you. There are so many beautiful, familiar, real things in them. And it is so nice to be at least a little with you, if only through these pages.

And yesterday I had a telegram from you, darling. Oh, don't say that you don't want to *causer ennuis*. My pet, after all it is everything that I live for, to see you at last, to embrace and again, again to be together.

What can they mean in comparison to this hope, these silly conversations with officials, telephone calls, forms? Only that none of this helps us much for the time being. The biggest 'fish' wait endlessly for this miserable *priorité* for the aeroplane. It's bound to take ages.

My darling love, how I should like to see you at last. Darling, you will probably get it before the New Year. I kiss you, my treasure, so much. Do you remember our last New Year together at Lapin à Gill?[95] The memory of that happiness is still so alive for me, that we are together. Already then, there were so many people separated. My sweetheart, smile, smile all the time. I think about you so very tenderly all the time. Love, darling. Franka

28 November **Letter from Eugeniusz Cękalski of the Polish Film Division to W. Henson of the Polish Ministry of Information**

Dear Henson:

I have spoken to you yesterday about Stefan Themerson, an eminent Polish film technician who is at the present time in unoccupied France: Hôtel de la Poste, Voiron, (Isère).

The Polish Ministry of Information want to employ him, and as you know the present shortage of film technicians makes it most necessary for us to secure his services.

The Polish Ministry of Information have been able to get the British visa for him (1 June 1941) as well as the French exit permit. The main difficulty is the Portuguese transit visa. The Portuguese authorities have informed Mr Themerson that the only possibility of obtaining this visa is to reserve a seat on a flight to England for him. They furthermore stressed that although a paid ticket is awaiting him in Lisbon, the priority and reservation of a seat in a plane have to be arranged from London. Immediately after this has been arranged the visa will be granted and sent to him 30 days before the date of the departure from Lisbon.

This is the only way of getting him out of France where, of course, the situation is most difficult.

I should be very grateful to you indeed if you could make some official steps to help us in this matter which is becoming rather urgent.

Yours sincerely, Film Officer

95 Le Lapin Agile, Cabaret in Montmartre frequented by artists

-:- UMOWA O PRACE -:-

Zawarta pomiędzy P. Adamem ROMEREM . . . .

. . Dyrektorem Biura Prezydialnego w Prezydium Rady Ministrów . .

działającym w imieniu Skarbu Państwa, a p. . . . .

. . . . Franciszką T H E M E R S O N O W A . . . .

na następujących warunkach:

1/ p Franciszka THEMERSONOWA . . . . przyjmuje od dnia 1-go grudnia . . . 1941r. . . . . . na czas nieokreślony obowiązki pracownika umysłowego w służbie państwowej.

2/ Pracownik, zawierający niniejszą umowę będzie pełnił obowiązki służbowe w: Ministerstwie Informacji i Dokumentacji . . . . w charakterze: pracownika pomocniczego / I.kat.pom./. . . . . . .

3/ W okresie pierwszych trzech miesięcy, licząc od daty, wymienionej w pkt.1/, uważa się umowę za zawartą na okres próbny.
Na poczet tego okresu zalicza się jednak czas, przebyty w służbie państwowej po dniu 30 września 1939r., a przed zawarciem niniejszej umowy.

4/ Pracownik, zawierający niniejszą umowę będzie otrzymywał tytułem wynagrodzenia miesięcznego kwotę Ł. 30.16.- /trzydzieści funtów szterl. i szesnaście szyl./ za każdy miesiąc kalendarzowy, oraz dodatek rodzinny według norm, ustalonych osobnymi przepisami.
Wynagrodzenie wypłacane będzie z góry.

5/ W razie podróży służbowych będą przysługiwały pracownikowi, zawierającemu niniejszą umowę, diety oraz zwrot kosztów podróży według norm ustalonych zarządzeniem Ministra Skarbu.

6/ W razie niemożności pełnienia obowiązków służbowych wskutek choroby lub nieszczęśliwego wypadku, a także w razie wykluczenia od zajęć przez władzę sanitarną, pracownik zawierający niniejszą umowę, zachowuje przez okres trzech miesięcy prawo do wynagrodzenia.

- 2 -

7/ Pracownikowi, zawierającemu niniejszą umowę przysługuje prawo do urlopu wypoczynkowego w wymiarze .x. 2 . . . tygodni rocznie.

8/ Pracownik, zawierający niniejszą umowę przyjmuje na siebie obowiązki takie same jak określone w art.21-27, art.28 ust.1 i 2, art.29, art.31 oraz art.32 ust. 1 i 3, Ustawy z dnia 17 lutego 1922 r. o państwowej służbie cywilnej / Dz.U.R.P. Nr.21 poz.164/ z późniejszymi zmianami, a ponadto zobowiązuje się stosować ściśle do wszelkich zarządzeń i instrukcji, wydanych przez władze przełożone.

9/ Rozwiązanie niniejszej umowy następuje:

a/ w okresie próbnym, to jest w ciągu pierwszych trzech miesięcy służby: - po uprzednim dwutygodniowym wypowiedzeniu, które powinno nastąpić na piśmie za dowodem doręczenia najpóźniej 1-go lub 16-go dnia miesiąca kalendarzowego,

b/ po zakończeniu okresu próbnego okres wypowiedzenia wynosić ma trzy miesiące kalendarzowe i kończyć się zawsze musi ostatniego dnia miesiąca kalendarzowego, wypowiedzenie nastąpić ma na piśmie za dowodem doręczenia, najpóźniej w ostatnim dniu miesiąca kalendarzowego, poprzedzającego okres wypowiedzenia,

c/ w razie wzajemnego porozumienia stron, zawierających niniejszą umowę,

d/ w przypadkach i na zasadach, przewidzianych w art. 28, 29, 31-33 i 36- 42 rozporządzenia Prezydenta Rzeczypospolitej z dnia 16 marca 1928r. o umowie o pracę pracowników umysłowych /Dz.U.R.P. Nr.35 poz.323/.

./.

- 3 -

10/ Po upływie trzech miesięcy niepełnienia obowiązków z powodu choroby lub nieszczęśliwego wypadku umowa może być uznana za rozwiązaną, o czym pracownika należy zawiadomić pisemnie:
W razie nierozwiązania niniejszej umowy, prawo do wynagrodzenia gaśnie a stosunek umowy trwa, przywrócenie prawa do wynagrodzenia następuje z dniem zgłoszenia się do pracy.

11/ W razie rozwiązania umowy niniejszej pracownik zawierający tę umowę obowiązany będzie zwrócić otrzymane zaliczki i uregulować zaciągnięte względem: Ministerstwa Informacji i Dokumentacji zobowiązania pieniężne i służbowe.

Londyn, dnia 1-go grudnia . . 1941r.

. . . .
/podpis pracownika zawierającego umowę/.

PREZYDJUM RADY MINISTRÓW

/podpis przedstawiciela Skarbu Państwa./

1 December 1941
Franciszka's employment contract with the Ministry of Information and Documentation as an assistant of first category, with a salary of £30.16 shillings per month, payable in advance, and 2 weeks holiday per year. There is also a 2-page document describing the responsibilities and duties of employees. (These Polish documents are not included.)

29 November 1941 **Letter from Stefan to Franciszka** – enclosing the typescript of 'Le Dieu de la Croix-Rousse'[96]

My darling, I am sending you this trifle, I know it's of no value. It's a month since I had a letter from you. Write darling, please.

I kiss you so very much my dear little one. Love – Stefan

30 November **Letter from Franciszka to Stefan**

My dearest darling,

How are you sweetheart? Will you get this letter for the New Year? I kiss you with such feeling and so tenderly, darling.

On 1 January 1940 I received your first letter here. It's nearly a year.

What are you doing, what are you feeling, what are you thinking? How did you survive that year? I know so little and so much at the same time – because of letters, because of poems, because – even telegrams told me so much.

Are you in correspondence with *Poésie 41*? Did they publish your 'Croquis'? Has the common cause, that should connect all the poets of the world, survived? Darling, how strange they sound such 19th century slogans. 19th century? No, simply eternal, aren't they?

It's very difficult to live in intellectual isolation. I can't find any human contact here, among our artists. It is the same snobbism, which served them as a screen in Ziemiańska[97], or it's just phoney opportunism, falseness that stands in the way, like a wall.

Is it easier to communicate with artists born here? Perhaps, but also here an enormous mountain separates us, the mountain of our misfortunes and our helplessness. How quietly they live, despite everything, by comparison with us uprooted from fragile flowerpots, and deprived of – I can't find a suitable word. That's another problem – deprived of what – ?

There are certainly many hands extended all around, seeking friendship, a kind word and understanding. But I can't bear the idea of joining hands with anyone if it is to reject, or negate, or condemn. As long as we are estranged from the only world that holds positive values for us, we shall be condemned to negativism. With a strong enough survival instinct, this negativism turns into cynicism and mockery, or – given a sense of humour – into laughter. But that's just tedious.

Memento Magnitudinis? That's all that one can catch hold of. And it's a lot. I love you my sweetheart, so much. I kiss you tenderly and endlessly. Franka

4 December **Letter from Franciszka to Stefan**

My darling little one, thank you for the long, wise, tender and longing letters. Yes, darling, and I too touch this daily reality only with the tips of careless fingers. What a strong, sole support you are for me, even though so far away, darling! And these truths that I wrestle with here are just what you are talking about, at the same time. It is so difficult to maintain this attitude in these times that roll over us, and with these memories and this hope that binds us so firmly and so tenderly over kilometres, over so many kilometres apart.

I want to do so many beautiful and interesting things for you – for you, because it is very difficult for me alone. But they are only fragments, small notes about my experiences, these drawings of mine now. I haven't solved it, I haven't understood enough to transform it completely, sincerely and seriously into lines, into patches of colour, into expression. But all this time spent burning in one's

96 'The God of the Croix-Rousse'. See page 369
97 Café in Warsaw where artists and writers used to meet

own fire cannot be without some result. So much more, I feel so much more mature now. With such seriousness, with such painful seriousness I talk to people who are so full of confidence and ambition of all sorts, impetus, everyday noisy enthusiasm. I am so calm and feel with such clarity your distant, understanding, helpful glance.

When I look at drawings that I was doing last winter, into which I put so much of myself – again I feel that I've have become still more serious since that time. Soon perhaps, when I start drawing more, shall I find the means to express what I have lived through and what I have gained? My darling, one day, in the end, will I be able to tell you all that I feel, so close to you, holding your hand? What happiness it is for me this awareness that you are there, so close to me and the only one, even though it's only the weak written word that wanders between us.

I kiss you, darling, so tenderly and such a lot. Will you get it for the New Year? Or for your birthday. Ah, darling, you know of course how much of my tenderness is there always with you.

I have made all possible application for *priorité* for the plane. There's a huge, huge number of people waiting, but in the end, after all, we shall be together, darling. So many big, warm, tender hugs. Love, Franka

5 December **Letter from Stefan to Franciszka**

My dearest darling, already Christmas and the New Year before you get this letter, Franeczko!

Darling, how long our letters are wandering. And it is so long since I had anything from you. Your last letter was from 4 October, from more than two months ago. Darling, did you get 'Sur la pelure de cette pomme' and the silly, tiny novelette 'Dieu de la Croix-Rousse'? I so regret that I can't do ordinary useful things, when I see that in themselves, these things on which I labour, sometimes are ordinary and useless.

I had news from Teresa. She was to leave a week ago. I thought that perhaps we would see each other before her departure, but it's too bad. I had news in November that all the places are booked for half a year. But I don't know if it means that if April is booked up, whether in March it would be possible, for me to leave. You can see what endless lengths of time I am already thinking in, darling.

I miss your letters so much, Franek. I would like to know so many things, those concrete, everyday, simple things, that one must preserve at all costs, from the other vacuous chatter (outpourings from the empty into the void) and that whole atmosphere created by people waiting for their Balzac – I can only guess at, with sadness. How do you cope with all that, darling?

My eyes are starved, and I long so much for what you are doing and I am so glad of every mention that you are working for yourself. I often place before my eyes your canvas that I hold in my memory, those square blocks of houses without windows, those ink drawings from the unfinished cycle, the coloured ones, and those drawings with lines as alive as arteries and synthesised like an algebraic equation, – and, with closed eyelids I look at them and could continue for hours.

What news of our friends? Genek, Stefan, Stefanja? From Ignacy I didn't get an answer to my long and silly letter which was an answer to his long sincere and desperate one. From Mira also nothing. Remember me to them all and embrace them for me. What about Sewek? From Hania not a word since a long,

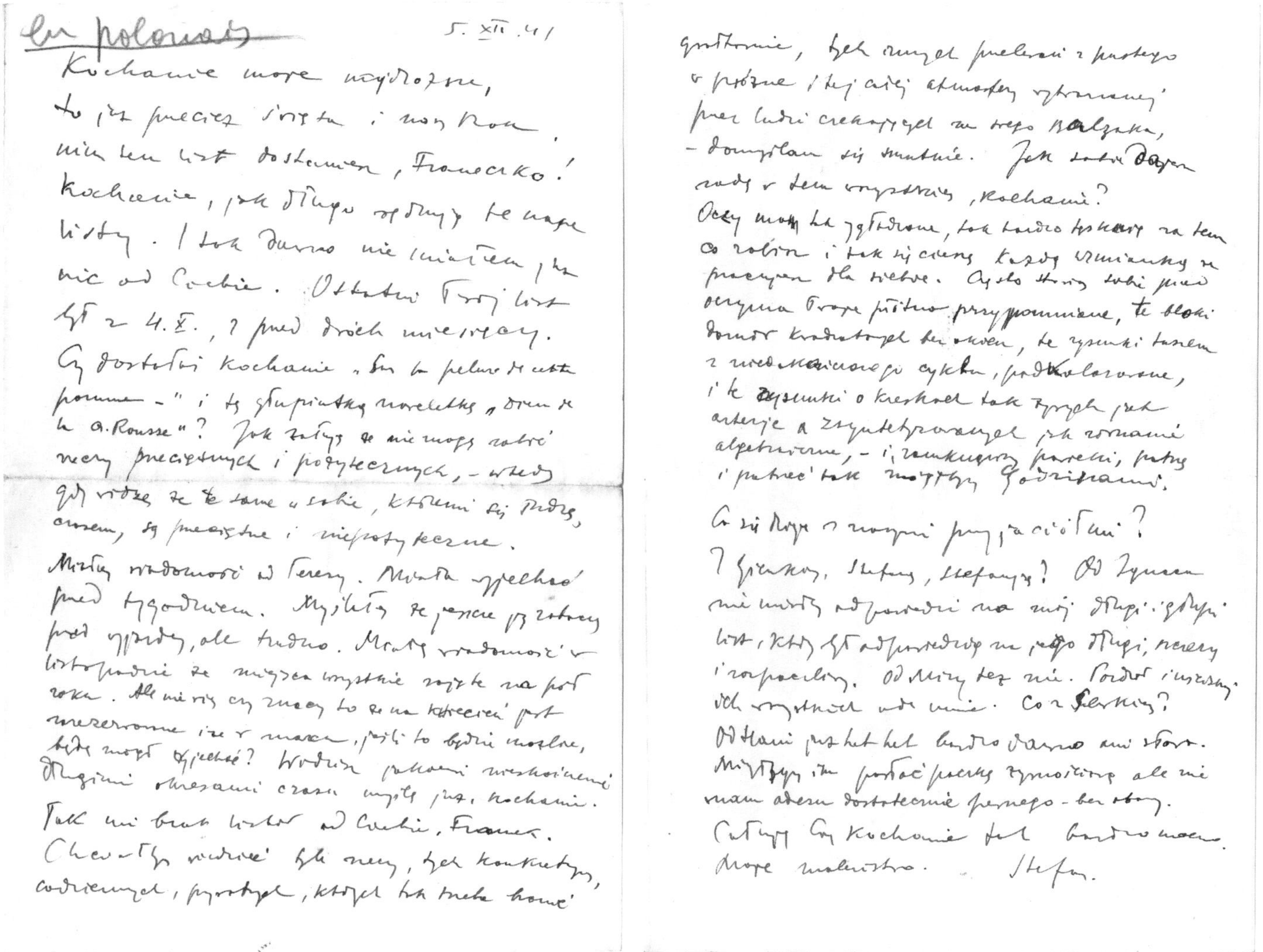

long time. I thought of sending them a food parcel but I don't have an address that is certain enough – without any misgivings.

I kiss you darling so much. My littlest one. Stefan

9 December **Telegram from Franciszka to Stefan**

MON PETIT REÇU LETTRE OCTOBRE JE T'EN REMERCIE SI TENDREMENT C'EST TOUTE NOTRE VÉRITÉ DONT JE SUIS TELLEMENT ASSOIFFÉE QUE LA FORCE TU ME DONNES AVEC TES SIMPLES MOTS ET TOI TRAVAILLES-TU CHÉRI STOP TOUTES DEMANDES POSSIBLES SUJET PRIORITÉ FAITES MAIS CELA SERA LONG PATIENCE CHÉRI SOIS GAI ET CONFIANT AS-TU TÉLÉGRAPHIÉ MIRA STOP AVEC TOUS VISAS PORTUGAL EXIGE DATE DÉPART FIXÉE STOP TENDRESSES CHÉRI JE T'AIME SI PROFONDEMENT = THEMERSON

Telegram from Stefan to Franciszka

MON PETIT CHÉRIE MERCI POUR TÉLÉGRAMME SOIS TRANQUILLE IL NE ME MANQUE QUE TES LETTRES OÙ JE RETROUVE NOTRE VIE NE T'ATTRISTE PAS MON PETIT T'EMBRASSE SI JOYEUSEMENT = THEMERSON

Diary Entry

For so long this notebook has been left untouched in the drawer of the little table. And what were these everyday things that happened? Teresa left. I bought a packet of cigarettes [Parisienne] Verte for 25 frs, yesterday I went to the cinema, in the interval, a fakir. I dictate to Luiza. I read *Ulysses*.

I listened to records of Bach and Stravinsky's *L'Histoire du Soldat*. There was Karnecki's spectacle and Centkowska's poems. Bibrowski talked to me today that one has to prepare for a year or two, and possibly for ending up in a camp, and do a book for children. I was in Lyon. I was in Grenoble. Baluk's death. A letter from Henio Polubiec. And that's it? There were cold spells. I bought a little electric cooker.

13 December **Letter from Franciszka to Stefan**

My darling little one,

Again I don't know if this letter will still reach you there, maybe, maybe you'll be able to leave. Today, I was told that *priorité* for the aeroplane is in the process of being done, and simultaneously I read about some possible difficulties with the departure. So today we still know nothing and it's so difficult to keep one's balance on this perpetual swing that has been going on for such, such a long time, suspended between hope and sadness.

I shall move before the holidays. I've always looked for a place where one could feel reasonably comfortable – where I wouldn't be pursued either by our immigrant packs, or by alien refugee mentality. A bit of solitude. I crave it for myself now anyway. Perhaps it will be easier there for me to work. I've rented two rooms. One day, I shall embrace you there, my darling.

We do not know what the world will be like when we're finally able to start all over again, but I can't believe that – after this period of immobile existence and gaining maturity – we would make false moves.

Our courage to 'create' as you call it, will surely find its proper course. And it will then reveal itself to be very close to what we had before. It seems to me that we had the right intuition even if not a conscious awareness. This time round, it might have become conscious knowledge. But I still understand so little, so often I feel completely lost in a confusion of things that goes from bad to worse. To extract a seed from all this and to 'grow it' into a real and full sentence in painting, or in words even, that sometimes seems to me almost impossible.

My little one, will you get this letter for your birthday? I send you all my tenderness, my darling.

And remember, if our correspondence were to be interrupted again, never forget my darling that my only thought is for you to be happy, and with every heartbeat I'm wishing that all will go well for you. Please think about yourself.

Are Tema's friends living near you? Might you go to live with them if your stay there were to be prolonged, despite everything?

I kiss you darling always and all the time. Franka

15 December **Letter from Stefan to Franciszka** – enclosing two poems: 'Sonetino' and 'Gra'

My darling, I have almost no news from you now. It will be 1942 by the time you get this letter. And how much time shall we still have to spend waiting? So much of it passes in inactivity. I am terrified by the fact that I haven't done anything at all that would be worthwhile. I kiss you, darling, as much as is possible. Have you heard anything new from family? How are our friends? I had a letter from Heniek Polubiec, from a prisoner-of-war camp in Switzerland. Zber is in the countryside? I so miss you, darling. Stefan

19 December **Letter from Stefan to Franciszka**

My dearest darling,

I am sending you this 'Fugue' even though I know that it is so terribly paltry and so terribly far from what I should really like to write, and give you. The year will end soon, darling, and a new one will start, but there is nothing I can do, no way I can make it more cheerful and easier for you, my dearest little one.

I'm afraid we'll still have a long wait ahead of us! I've tried all sorts of strategies but they were useless. Anyway, perhaps I should feel glad that they didn't work out, since not one of the friends or acquaintances who had better luck than me, is today somewhere where I'd want to be.

The best thing that I could organise would be to meet up with Janek [unidentified]. But then staying with him and waiting there would be just the same as waiting here, except again that I don't know what would happen to your letters.

Darling, I don't know why I'm writing such things. A year ago I only lived for them, they were all that mattered, and here I am still. I kiss you, darling, so very much. I don't like the thought that I'm waiting for someone else to pull my chestnuts out of the fire for me, but in reality – as you can imagine – there is neither fire nor chestnuts, only the futility of trying. And there is nothing to assure us about the future fate of those who try to penetrate this emptiness individually. That's what it looks like from here.

I kiss you, my darling, and I worry so much that there is nothing I can give you apart from this poem I'm sending, so very mean and paltry. Love, my dearest darling. Stefan

Telegram from Franciszka to Stefan

MON PETIT CHÉRI MES SOUHAITS LES PLUS TENDRES POUR NOËL ET NOUVELLE ANNÉE BAISERS, BAISERS = THEMERSON 36 LANSDOWNE CRESCENT W11

24 December **Telegram from Franciszka to Stefan**

MON PETIT GARDE SOURIRE CHÉRI NE T'ATTRISTE PAS MÊME SI TU NE REÇOIS PAS DE LETTRE ORGANISE TA VIE LE MIEUX POSSIBLE ET TRAVAILLE POUR TOI CHÉRI C'EST LE PLUS IMPORTANT JE LES ADORE TES VERS ET JE LES AI TOUJOURS SUR MOI NOUS NOUS RENCONTRERONS ENCORE PLUS VIEUX MON PETIT BIEN AIMÉ MAIS TOUJOURS SI HEUREUX JE T'EMBRASSE LE PLUS TENDREMENT = THEMERSON

27 December **Letter from Franciszka to Stefan**

Darling little one, will this letter get to you? – I don't know. After all, there are so many complications with the closing and opening of borders. But, perhaps. I'll send it, since I know after all what a letter means. It is the only real and close and dear thing – and one can read it all the time, so many, so many times. So here I am in a new flat. It's pleasant and quiet and I thought that by now we would be here together. One day, darling! The matter of the *priorité* for the aeroplane continues to be pursued. My sweetheart!

A lot of different people visit me, people I hardly know, acquaintances, friends, and they talk, talk for hours, arguing until they agree, boasting and blaming each other, gossiping. They solve problems, tell stories. And it is all noise, mumbling, the foggy background to my thinking, which is always and only the dream of seeing you again. The only thing I long for is to talk to you – to be with you. And among all the truths and lies that multiply, there is one truth, the truth of work, our work together. Although it might surprise us, this still keeps its constant, permanent value. And compared to that, the problems I wrestle with, problems of line or stain, or expression, seem very small fry. I am drawing some small things, sketches. I value the line in the same way that I value the word. I also talk very little, and when I have nothing to say – instead of talking, I draw. How much one grows up during these years. I really feel quite mature now. And I know this change is mutual, even though we're so far apart. My pet darling, I so wish it were a simple matter for you to be here. Your arrival, that seemed so imminent, might again be postponed indefinitely. Think about yourself, darling and be good to yourself. Every moment when you feel more comfortable and lighter at heart, you make me happier, darling. I kiss, kiss you darling with such big warm kisses
Franka

28 December **Telegram from Stefan to Franciszka**

CHÉRIE MERCI POUR TÉLÉGRAMMES COMMENT VAS TU AIE SOIN DE TA SANTÉ MON PETIT JE T'EN PRIE STOP SUIS TRÈS BIEN JE NE COMPTE PLUS SUR VISAS MAIS MALGRÉ TOUTES DIFFICULTÉS J'ESPÈRE TOUJOURS TE RETROUVER ENFIN STOP SALUE AMIS MEILLEURS VOEUX EMBRASSE SI TENDREMENT SOIS HEUREUSE GAIE ET TRANQUILLE CHÉRIE BAISERS = THEMERSON

Letter from W.L.M. Dunlop from the Foreign Office in London to Antoni Baliński – in English

Dear Monsieur Baliński,

With reference to my letter of 21 Dec. about the case of Monsieur Stefan Themerson, I write to say that the British Air Attaché in Lisbon has been requested to arrange for Monsieur Stefan Themerson to be granted an air passage to this country as soon as possible after his arrival in Lisbon.

Yours sincerely, W.L.M. Dunlop

30 December **Letter from Franciszka to Stefan**

My dearest darling,

I received your two letters from the end of November. Thank you, thank you, my most precious one – for the letters, and for 'Croquis' IX, and for 'Croix-Rousse'. Do you understand what they are for me? How I love every word? Darling, how elusive it is to hear the wind *que dans les tuyaux des orgues* and to recognise the serious and wise whiteness of the plate on which lies our green apple.

How difficult it is to live quietly and inactive with one's own – how can one say it? – sense of presentiment, when all around there's a confident crowd arguing with loud voices or with underlined words. When that's happening, how much I need then to rest my head on your shoulder, and to understand everything at once with my hand in yours. And to wander together over the land in which you're a magician.

From time to time I feel transported to such a place on Świętokrzyska[98] and return in my mind with a parcel of strange books, unexpected journals, avant-garde publications of another time, forgotten miracles. It's a quite an arbitrary dream – without any sense, without basis, the same randomness that characterises the people around me. But sometimes, suddenly, there is an intuitive word, a wise sentence, a beautiful poem, a strange drawing, with the scent of our *f.a.*, a familiar fragrance close to the heart. Pages composed with feeling, more or less successful as the case may be, but complete in their sincerity, full of search and longing. With all this in my head, I bury myself in the blanket and pillows on the settee and turn the pages. I taste it, put it away, come back again.

Sometimes I close my eyes and try to imagine how you are living. I comb through your poems, words, commas, for some trace of your life. The street down which you walk, the window that you open in the morning, the sky that you look at. I yearn for that street, for that window, for that sky. My sweetheart!

I write, write so very often and send a letter every few days. I can't understand why you receive letters so rarely. In reality, I write all the time, because I measure the time from letter to letter, the one received and the one written. And if I get worried about the letters, frightened that they might stop – the sadness I feel, full of tenderness and pain, for a moment stops the beating of my heart.

But one has to cope, my dearest little one. And the whole time I try not to let go, to keep my nerve and resilience of thought, for you, my darling, and for that moment at last of our meeting. Forgive these awkward and pompous-sounding words. There is nothing in them except enormous tenderness and enormous longing.

Darling, you cabled: *sois heureuse*… the happiest in the world! What else can one wish for in the New Year? Another New Year!

Perhaps this letter will reach you for your birthday, darling!

I wrote to you that I am already in a new flat. When I took it, I was sure that soon you would be there. It's funny, with cotton curtains with flowers and a large table to work. I haven't yet started to draw here.

And one can go out on the ordinary tiled roof, sit and look at the sky. One can see a lot of sky. Like on Czeczota[99].

Have you had something from our family? I had a long time ago a letter posted in September. That's all. Apparently Sewek was in the native town of Jalu Kurek[100].

Darling, keep strong and be cheerful and write. You simply don't realise how much magic and truth there is in what you do.

I kiss you, darling, so much, so tenderly and … without end! Franka

PS: Today is Genek's birthday. I've just been there and am adding this after my return. It was boring, as usual. There were all Genek's girls, chronologically from the last three years, with whom he 'used to sleep'. But I did manage to meet and get to know the man from here who is trying to get that *priorité*. I have his telephone number and I shall follow it up myself. Perhaps one will be able to do something else reasonably quickly, so that it won't be delayed… Love Fr.

98 Warsaw street with a bookshop
99 This is where the Themersons lived in Warsaw before leaving for Paris
100 Kraków

Telegram from Franciszka to Stefan

MON PETIT MERCI POUR TÉLÉGRAMME TOUTE MA TENDRESSE ET TOUTES MES PENSÉES JE TE LES ENVOIE TOUS LES JOURS GENEK PRÉPARE TOUJOURS PRIORITÉ AVION PEUT-ÊTRE MALGRÉ TOUT ON SYNCHRONISERA ENFIN TOUTES FORMALITÉS EMBRASSE MON PETIT SI TENDREMENT = THEMERSON 36 LANSDOWNE CRESCENT

Letter to the Ministry of Information & Documentation in London from the First Secretary of the Polish Embassy, Antoni Baliński, forwarded to Franciszka on 3 January 1942

In connection with the letter from the Ministry of Information and Documentation of 12th inst [i.e. December 1941] No.7665/41/Rż, the Embassy encloses a signed letter from the Foreign Office, regarding an aeroplane place reservation for Stefan Themerson.

per/pro the Ambassador: Antoni Baliński, 1st Secretary

1942

Stefan's diary and two notebooks used in 1942

Telegram from Franciszka to Stefan

MON PETIT CHÉRI SUIS SI HEUREUSE AS-TU REÇU TÉLÉGRAMME DE PEN CLUB SUJET PRIORITÉ AVION OBTENUE? STOP LES PLUS TENDRES BAISERS CHÉRI = THEMERSON

Telegram from Poznańska to Stefan

PRIORITÉ AVION DE LISBONNE ACCORDÉE PAR AUTORITÉS BRITANNIQUES STOP PRIÈRE SOLLICITER ENCORE UNE FOIS VISA PORTUGUAIS = POZNAŃSKA, PEN CLUB POLONAIS

5 January **Letter from Franciszka to Stefan**

My dearest little one, I'm really banking on it that you'll be leaving before this letter arrives, but what can one know? I still try to send you a bit of love for the journey.

Darling, this *priorité* suddenly worked, like a miracle, when it was so terribly difficult and it again looked as if we'd have to accept that our separation would last for years. Everybody here was amazed – all of them, or rather those who pretended to help get it for you. Darling, perhaps, this time it really will work out.

If there are any problems with the transits, do let me know immediately, won't you, my pet?

I am so emotional, darling, I can hardly write. How do you feel? What do you look like? It's taken so long that I don't know anything. Do you have enough money for the journey?

My darling, but if again something didn't work out, don't worry – I am so concerned that you will get this letter when you're in the middle of some disagreeable moment. That's why it is so terribly difficult to write.

I just want to kiss you my dearest little one so very tenderly. Franka

Letter from Stefan to Franciszka

My dearest darling, I received your letters, the one for the New Year and one for my birthday – thank you, darling, so very much. Also the telegram about *priorité*. I am approaching the consulate once again, at the same time I cabled Zieliński, because only in Lisbon can one arrange these formalities. Otherwise one will probably have to wait for a warmer spring. I didn't succeed last spring, maybe I will now. Who knows?

My darling, I am so glad that you are working, so very glad. Darling, despite our separation, despite the fact that I only *am* actually when I have your letters in front of me, and that apart from then I'm not here at all, despite this and really because of this, I am so much happier than all those around me.

I received a letter from Heniek Polubiec, from Switzerland, from an internment camp. He writes about fleeting youth, greying temples and balding head, about the sadness with which he looks at the threadbare collar of his uniform. His wife is in Lourdes, after an appendix operation. Tadek Melchinkowicz is a prisoner of war. Mietek works in the municipal council and his prospects are excellent. Staszek works at the spirit factory and is drunk around the clock.

Did you receive the poems I sent you recently? Among them the 'Fugue' which I know is not good but I was thinking about you so much when I wrote it.

I don't know, darling, if I will ever manage to do something really significant – even to me? Perhaps it doesn't matter? One needs at least a grain of some sort of ambition just to find a single purpose, but even that minimum seems beyond me at the moment.

My darling little one, I send you so very many kisses. Stefan

Do you have any news from home?

What is happening with our friends? Not a word about Stefan K[onorski]. And Genek what is he doing and how is he? I can't bring myself to write to them separately, but I send them warmest regards, hugs and wish them all the best. Stefan

Additional note from Judge Walfisz and his wife [dated 25 December 1941]

Dear Franka!
We are sitting with your husband in our house having coffee and talking about you. And so I take this opportunity to send our heartfelt wishes for the new year and a big kiss. Stefan wrote to you once to ask if you would be able to find my aunt. Her address is: 57 Wentworth Road, Golders Green, Mrs S. Freudenheim, and give her our regards. Maybe she could be helpful to you.

We are reasonably well, although we have sad news from home. You probably know that a few months ago I lost my only sister. So my parents are now alone. Perhaps my aunt could send them parcels, to Orla 11. This would help them and give great pleasure. Your husband looks well and dreams of seeing you. We are not making any plans, it's all too difficult, and apart from that our material situation is worse than miserable. We must try to survive this difficult period in these conditions.

Enormous hugs to you once more, my regards to our mutual friends.
Yours sincerely, L. Walfiszowa

My best regards, J. Walfisz

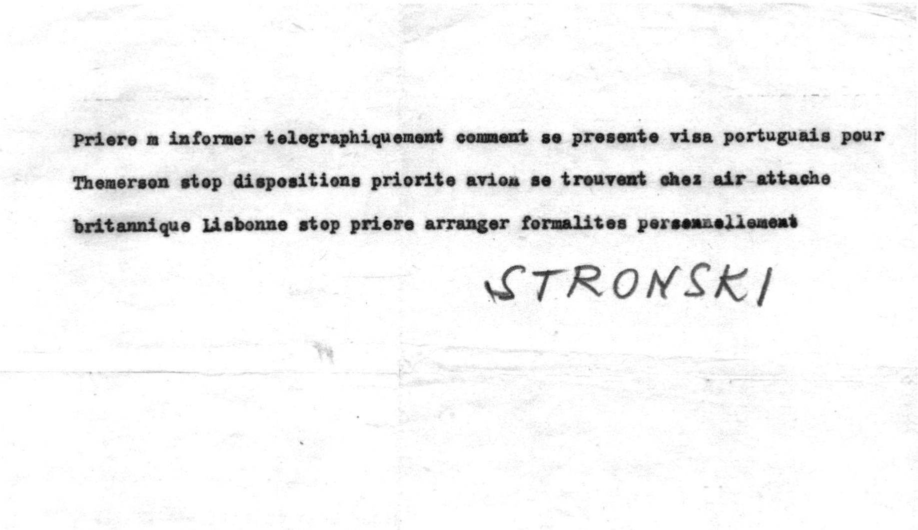

Priere m informer telegraphiquement comment se presente visa portuguais pour Themerson stop dispositions priorite avion se trouvent chez air attache britannique Lisbonne stop priere arranger formalites personnellement

STRONSKI

5 January
Carbon copy of typed text of a telegram written by Franciszka to Zieliński and signed Stroński

Prière m'informer télégraphiquement comment se présente visa portugais pour Themerson stop dispositions priorité avion se trouvent chez air attaché britannique Lisbonne stop prière arranger formalités personnellement = Stroński

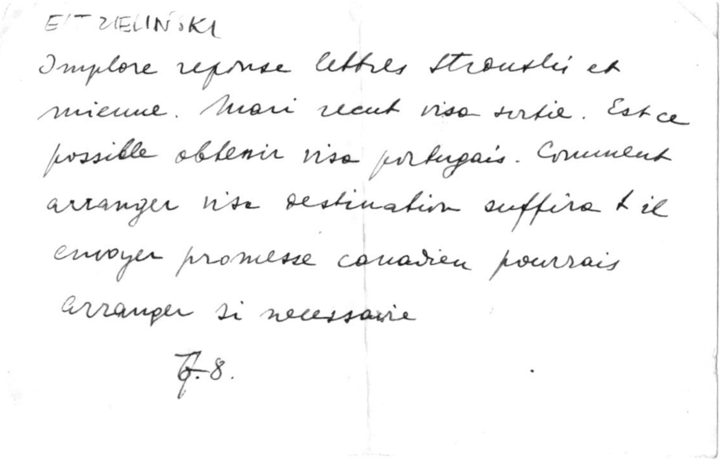

E/T ZIELIŃSKI
Implore réponse lettres Stronski et mienne. Mari recut visa sortie. Est ce possible obtenir visa portugais. Comment arranger visa destination suffira t il envoyer promesse canadien pourrais arranger si necessaire
F.8.

5 January 1942
Manuscript draft of a telegram from Franciszka to Adam Zieliński

Implore réponse lettres Stroński et mienne. Mari reçut visa sortie. Est ce possible obtenir visa portugais. Comment arranger visa destination suffira t'il envoyer promesse canadien pourrais arranger si nécessaire = [?]

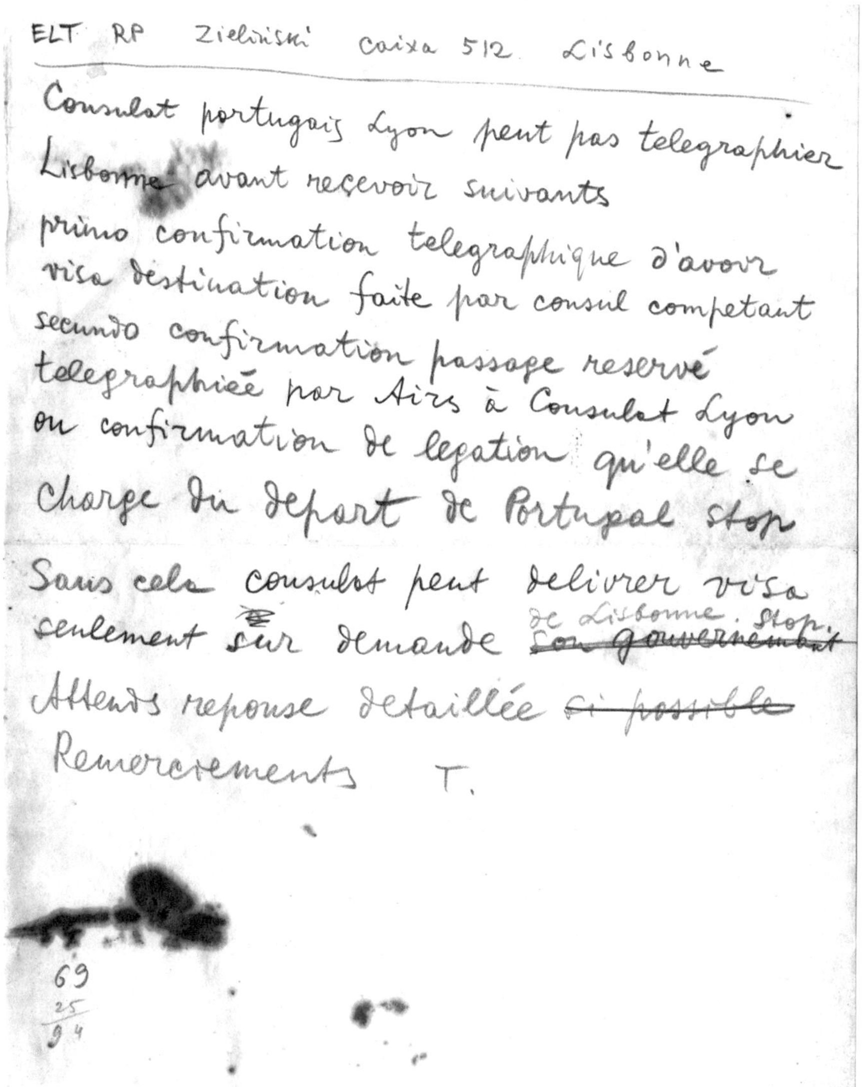

ELT RP Zielinski Caixa 512 Lisbonne
Consulat portugais Lyon peut pas telegraphier Lisbonne avant recevoir suivants
primo confirmation telegraphique d'avoir visa destination faite par consul competant
secundo confirmation passage reservé telegraphiée par Airs à Consulat Lyon
ou confirmation de legation qu'elle se charge du depart de Portugal stop
Sans cela consulat peut delivrer visa seulement sur demande de Lisbonne stop. ~~Son gouvernement~~
Attends reponse detaillée ~~si possible~~
Remerciements T.
69
25
94

5 January 1942
Another manuscript draft of Franciszka's telegram to Adam Zieliński

7 January 1942

Letter from Adam Zieliński in Lisbon to Franciszka

Dear Franciszka Themerson

I received your telegram and immediately contacted Zdziarski, who is in charge of this matter. The situation looks like this, the Portuguese authorities agreed to give visas to transit groups of 15 to 20 people; when every member of this group leaves Portugal, a new group can be granted visas. From this 'first' group several people have already left by air for England. A few are still waiting, since they don't have a paid-up air ticket, or one for a boat. And, there are some ladies, who, even though they have everything organised, are not in a hurry to leave France, and so they are blocking the following group. Nobody can influence this, because from here we cannot compel anyone to leave, and it is a basic principle that one cannot cancel these people's visas, because according to the Portuguese it would undermine the entire procedure. The formation of these 'groups' is done by a military evacuation office and I have no influence over that. Because of my insistence, anyway, your husband has found himself in the second 'group' – that's not too bad because there are several hundred candidates. But now there is nothing to do but to wait, because all the formalities have been dealt with, the formal promise has been made and as soon as the last person of the 'first' group leaves Portugal, the whole 'second' group will be given visas. This is how it was explained to me and it is what I am reporting to you.

In these circumstances, what could I have cabled to your husband? It isn't possible to explain all this in a telegram, and to send a telegram telling him to wait seems like mockery. This is why I thought that there would be no point in sending a telegram, and so I am taking advantage of a courier, who in a few days' time will be in London, to leave the sending of the telegram to you. When you send a telegram to your husband please ask the Post Office to arrange for a pre-paid reply and let me have the receipt. The sum is bound to be of use to your husband when he finally arrives here. When the visa is finally available, the Legation will advise your husband – as it does everyone – by telegram, so I don't have to ask Zdziarski for it specially.

According to Zdziarski's estimation, the matter should be resolved within a month, but of course neither he nor I can give a guarantee. Everything that could be done in Portugal has been done and apart from that, alas, I cannot give you any advice.

With the same courier you will find several letters from your husband that arrived here in the last few days.

Yours sincerely, Adam Zieliński

9 January **Telegram from Stefan to Franciszka**

MERCI CHÉRIE J AI RENOUVELE DEMANDE CONSULAT TÉLÉGRAPHIÉ ZIELIŃSKI PARCE QUE SANS CONFIRMATIONS OFFICIELLES CONCERNANT VISA DESTINATION ET PRIORITÉ SEULEMENT LISBONNE PEUT CONTINUER FORMALITÉS COMMENT VAS TU MON PETIT T EMBRASSE SI TENDREMENT = THEMERSON

10 January **Telegram from Franciszka to Stefan**

MON PETIT CHÉRI INQUIÈTE AS TU REÇU TÉLÉGRAMME POZNAŃSKA COMMENT VAS TU LES PLUS TENDRES BAISERS CHÉRI = THEMERSON

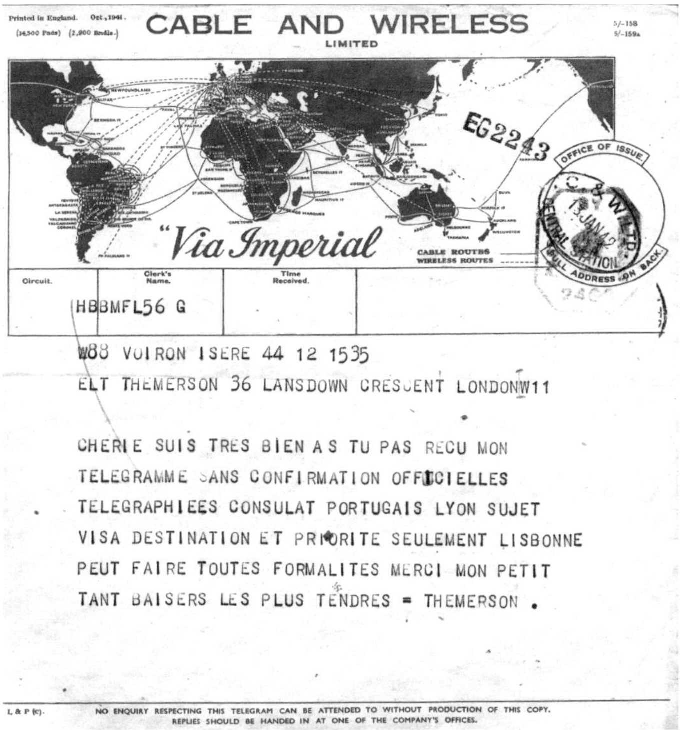
Printed in England. Oct., 1941. (34,500 Pads) (2,900 Bndls.)
CABLE AND WIRELESS
LIMITED
"Via Imperial"
CABLE ROUTES
WIRELESS ROUTES
EG2243
OFFICE OF ISSUE
FULL ADDRESS ON BACK
Circuit.	Clerk's Name.	Time Received.
HBBMFL56 G		

W83 VOIRON ISERE 44 12 1535
ELT THEMERSON 36 LANSDOWN CRESCENT LONDONW11

CHERIE SUIS TRES BIEN AS TU PAS RECU MON
TELEGRAMME SANS CONFIRMATION OFFICIELLES
TELEGRAPHIEES CONSULAT PORTUGAIS LYON SUJET
VISA DESTINATION ET PRIORITE SEULEMENT LISBONNE
PEUT FAIRE TOUTES FORMALITES MERCI MON PETIT
TANT BAISERS LES PLUS TENDRES = THEMERSON .

NO ENQUIRY RESPECTING THIS TELEGRAM CAN BE ATTENDED TO WITHOUT PRODUCTION OF THIS COPY.
REPLIES SHOULD BE HANDED IN AT ONE OF THE COMPANY'S OFFICES.

Telegram from Stefan to Franciszka

CHÉRIE SUIS TRÈS BIEN AS TU PAS REÇU MON TÉLÉGRAMME SANS CONFIRMATION OFFICIELLES TÉLÉGRAPHIÉES CONSULAT PORTUGAIS LYON SUJET VISA DESTINATION ET PRIORITÉ SEULEMENT LISBONNE PEUT FAIRE TOUTES FORMALITÉS MERCI MON PETIT TANT BAISERS LE PLUS TENDRES = THEMERSON

15 January **Letter from Franciszka to Stefan**

My dearest little one, Stefciu,

Maybe, maybe this letter will catch up with you en route. I still cling to these illusions, and all the time I allow myself to believe that at last, that now, that soon. So, so many times it has seemed to me that it's no longer possible to wait, but then had to wait. And afterwards again it is difficult to get back a grip of oneself, settle down, control oneself. I wrote to you several times, did you receive my last letters? – that I have moved. For the time being I live completely alone and every bit of wall, every fistful of air awaits you. I am happy here. On the wall are pinned-up drawings, as usual, and there are already some others in the drawer that I will pin up only when I can welcome you.

What funny autobiographical ferdydurki[1] I unloaded on paper. You know, a bit like a budding writer. I also catch something visceral, and sometimes with such naiveté, that after a while I can't even look at it. But now it is different. I am drawing a house and a window and a sky, and I look at it, and it's your house and window and the sky that you look at. I am drawing a road: the one along which you walk.

And the whole world is created. I pin it up around the walls and I travel through the world in which you live. It is always sky, trees and earth. After all, I don't know any more and this is anyway what is most important. And there are mountains and snow. There is white snow and sun through the pink mist here too.

My pet, how I long for you. Letters come so seldom. And every moment is, after all, so full of you. I kiss you so tenderly and so much. Franka

1 Bits of nonsense. An allusion to the title of a novel by Witold Gombrowicz.

Letter from Franciszka to Stefan

My darling, dearest pet,

Today I received your letter from the beginning of December, darling! so sad. My littlest one, I would give anything for things to be better for you and more cheerful. Don't say, darling, that you would like to do ordinary useful things. I understand this crisis, as I go through it myself often. But knowing that you are working for yourself there, and that you know, feel and understand, that you strive for the same truth as I do – it gives me so much strength, darling. And every confrontation with reality gives me greater strength and confidence to carry on – just in the sidelines, just quietly looking into oneself. You are right, darling, I should like to tell you all this quietly into your ear, to whisper, or to shout it loudly – so that you would feel, know, be sure that you are right, when you work, when you write poems. I shut myself in my poor, melodious, beautiful world with your beautiful poems. You mustn't lose confidence, I don't lose it even though they jabber, prattle and talk all around me; even though they make idiotic projects and plans, and talk nonsense. I am happy when I'm alone because then you are with me, even though so far away. And I like my drawings because you like them, because they are for you.

My little one, do you realise all you mean to me? Darling!

I spend a great deal of time at home nowadays. I see very few people, but anyway, I spend six hours each day among people in the office. And also it's lucky that I work with so many nice and intelligent people. At the moment I have some quite pleasant work, because one has to talk to the printers, making a maquette for an atlas and, of course, as you can imagine, very soon I shall send *Pan Tom*[2] for an estimate. Perhaps somehow I'll manage to print it. But I'll do this by myself without the fat Lindenfelds[3], just as before when we did it together. Talking with the printer also gives me pleasure, partly because we immediately reach an understanding even though the language, damn it, is foreign and the thing is complicated. But how I like colours, sheets of paper, pages; I feel as if I was in a warm bath. My dearest boy, it would be so marvellous if you were here already. To talk, talk, talk – and be silent!

You ask about friends – Stefanja is as usual; actually I don't have patience with her. She has just invited me for Sunday, but that's your birthday and so I probably won't go. Stefan is not too bad, but he is struggling quite a lot with the lack of direction in his life. He gets lost and meanders quite helplessly. He is anyway friendly and warm. We have become very close and a bottle of cognac which he got from the Złotowskis when he left Paris, is waiting for you. It is such a sentimental bottle of cognac! I haven't heard anything from Ignacy and Mira for a very long time, but Zośka Wojciechowska, who is in New York, writes that Ignacy has arrived there and that probably he and Mira will 'get married' again. I am very glad.

From Józio [Wittlin] I had as usual a complaining letter. Everywhere for you so many greetings and kisses! Genek [Cękalski] is preparing to travel to Bolek to take photographs. Oh my pet! My darling. One day we shall be together!

At this moment they are probably trying to do something about that visa. It is so difficult to do something from this distance. The final getting the *priorité* for the aeroplane is almost a miracle, but I managed because I was there on the spot and kept an eye on everybody: in the event I stood over Genek and in the

2 *Pan Tom buduje dom.* Published in 1950 by Gaberbocchus as *Mr Rouse Builds His House*

3 Henryk Lindenfeld, partner with Jakub Mortkowicz of the publishing company, G. Centnerszwer i S-ka, in Warsaw.

end he got it. After all, this should be enough to make us feel optimistic, darling. Oh, my pet!

I kiss you, kiss you so much, so tenderly and without stopping … Franka

22 January **Telegram from Franciszka to Stefan**

STEFULKU MON PETIT JE T'ENVOIE TOUS MES MEILLEURS ET PLUS TENDRES VOEUX POUR TON ANNIVERSAIRE TIENS TOI CHÉRI ET SOIS GAI COMME NOUS SOMMES HEUREUX AYANT L'UN L'AUTRE MÊME SI LOIN CHÉRI TRAVAILLES TU MON PETIT LES PLUS TENDRES BAISERS FRANKA CORDIALITÉS STEFAN GENEK = THEMERSON

24 January **Letter from Stefan to Franciszka**

My dearest darling,

It is already such a long time since I had news from you. Letters come in series, one after another, and afterwards nothing – it is so easy to get used to them and so hard to hear twice a day 'nothing, nothing for you'. But when I think what might have happened if still to this day we might have had no news of each other… When I now learn of the fates of some of my colleagues, my flesh creeps, and despite everything I am seized by a feeling of happiness that I know that you are there and that we are together despite these kilometres that commit us to separate lives. I wanted to try to escape again, but first of all it is cold here now, especially in the mountains, and the fresh news from you about the *priorité* gave a gleam of hope. And after all there'll be another spring soon.

And so I am sitting in this my little town. I bought myself a few cutting tools, and I've managed to get something very rare, some odd bits of lino and I am tinkering with it. Darling, I am wearing all of my pullovers, I wrap myself, like you do always, with a blanket and I sit for hours within my kingdom, and I remember what it was like helping you with the illustrations for *Marceljanek*[4] and I feel so good playing with this work. Despite the snow and frozen window panes, I feel such familiar warmth around me.

I haven't written anything recently. It's difficult to believe, and even harder to imagine, that anything will come from a train of thought containing two sparks, if when I try to catch a third, the first dissolves and fades away. It just shows me how limited is my ability to think clearly. Intuitively I feel some flickers of inspiration, but I need to put a sequence of them together before I can start writing.

Did you get a few poems sent in November or December and 'Fuga', a poem for you? It's bad, I know.

I kiss you so much darling.

Write to me about yourself, darling, as much as possible. You wrote to me so clearly and wisely that I should be good to myself – and you too darling, be good to yourself, I implore you, my sweetheart.

Do you have any news from home? Ever since Hania stopped writing I haven't heard anything, nor any address to which I could safely write. I am terribly anxious, especially now.

I kiss you darling so tenderly and so much. Stefan

What is happening with Stefan K[onorski] and Genek [Cękalski]? I haven't had an answer from Ignacy to my terribly long letter. Neither from Mira. Hugs for everyone

4 The Themersons' book for children, *Przygody Marceljanka Majster-Klepki*, Mortkowicz, Warsaw, 1938

Letter from Stefan to Franciszka

Darling,

Today I received your letter of 18 January. After just ten days! Darling, you want to know what it is like here, around me. But, truthfully I am not really here at all. There are swollen peaks on the snow-covered mountains around this valley that I have tumbled into, but whether they look like this or like that is of no interest to me. I am indifferent to what the café looks like where for 1.50 frs or 2 frs I drink coffee that is more or less bitter despite the saccharine, and even whether the people here are of one sort of another, and even – and this is harder to believe – whether there was this or that soup for lunch. All this is of no importance to me and doesn't affect me in the least, because I am simply not here. By trying not to generalise about facts and events that I witness only by chance, I reduce the risk of not seeing the truth which, as far as human communities are concerned, seems only to become tangible to me statistically, and therefore it requires a great number of different observations. By trying not to apply ready-made generalisations to people and events that surround me, I don't judge my fellow men and their deeds, and because of this my sympathies, which are lesser, greater, or none at all, are completely automatic. I feel two infinities, a huge one surrounding me ('Even the smallest puppy' – wrote Anatole France – 'is always at the centre of the universe'[5]) projected to the circle of the horizon, which, even with outstretched arms and finger tips, I cannot reach. The other, a tiny infinity, is inside me. I enclose it, I surround it, and I could swear that it is somewhere inside in the very centre of my breast, infinitely small, but in the infinite centre, which I can approach by contracting the cells of my body, by squeezing it from the thoughts or tears or smiles. I can approach, but cannot reach it. It is as if this holds a proof of the paradox of Achilles and the tortoise that he cannot catch up with. In between these two infinities there are events of a human scale that can be touched, compared to each other, and measured. For instance, by using such means one might be able to say that one forty-thousandth of a meridian is one meter, and to learn that the meridian is 40 thousand meters long, and to feel finally that one has understood something. Things on a human scale are also infinite, infinite in their ambiguity. The people here, living in such very testing conditions, daily subjected to identical tests, manifest their traits more vividly, but equally hide them even deeper. Sometimes, it seems to me, that I am like a naturalist changed into an ant and living in an ant-hill, or like a physicist changed into an electron and playing with photons. I sense the life of the ants, I sense the movement of electrons but, at the same time, I lose the ability to note down my observations, and draw conclusions that are even worse – theories. Perhaps one will need the perspective of time, with which to look backwards through our lorgnettes in order to bestow the title of 'descriptive work' upon a certain period of one's life. But already, one period has ended with such an abrupt crash that all chance of looking back through one's lorgnette was destroyed. Must one grow even older to be able to see one's own introspection from outside? 'Ornaments age faster than truths', said old Maeterlinck[6]. It could be put the other way round: 'that which survives in us, we call the truth'. In the great chaos of ornaments, polychromies and constructions, I am waiting with growing impatience for the paint to fade on the Parthenon. For the autumn wind that will blow away the yellowing ornaments, for the revelation of what from all this is the truth of the basic construction, and even though I know that for the maturity of old age one pays with one's life.

5 Also mentioned in ST's diary, 11 November 1940 (page 77)

6 Here Stefan paraphrases Maeterlinck's statement in his introduction to *La vie des termites*, 1926: '...embellishments are the first of all to fade...

My darling, you see, maybe this letter is both serious and silly (and this is the worst conjunction one can imagine) but it is not sad at all. Did you receive my 'Fugue', darling? I sent it already a long time ago, in the middle of December. It was specially for you.

Darling, I have money put aside for the journey and there is nothing, absolutely nothing that I need. I kiss you so passionately, my love. I find so many shared things in your letters and regardless of everything and despite everything, I am probably the happiest of all those poor people who have such a mixed-up hierarchy of values. I kiss you Franek, so lovingly. Stefan

Hugs for Stefan and Genek.

I have no news from Hania. Can I write to the family? At what address?

28 January **Letter to Michael Williams of the Air Ministry drafted by Franciszka**

We would like to make a request about bringing over from France the film-maker, Themerson, a member of our staff. In December 1941, on application from Interallied Ltd (Henson), Themerson was assigned priority for a plane seat, Lisbon-London, which is required by Portuguese authorities before one can obtain a Portuguese transit visa.

We have just heard from our representative in Lisbon that a certificate issued by the British Air Attaché in Lisbon, stating that Themerson will leave Lisbon 'as soon as possible', is insufficient for the Portuguese authorities. They demand either a precise date of departure (in which case they will issue the visa 30 days before that date) or eventual confirmation that Themerson will receive a seat on a plane at the latest within 30 days of his arrival in Lisbon.

The Polish Embassy in London turned to the Foreign Office in this matter several weeks ago, on the 18th inst. In reply to the question asked on the telephone, the answer was that a relevant document had already been sent to the Air Ministry.

Since this matter is of great importance to us, we turn to you to ask if a decision could be expedited.

4 February **Letter from Franciszka to Stefan**

My dearest darling, such an awful lot to say but I find it impossible to say anything. So many unfinished thoughts, which one can only express with silence or a handshake.

It's difficult to write. And everything that I draw seems to me to be so terribly naïve. Having grown up perhaps I should be wiser than I actually am. I can't solve, well, I don't even know how to begin dealing with the problems that surround me, crashing on top of me.

> Wide horizons become narrow because there's no way of knowing their breadth. Trying to put problems in order is impossible and meaningless.[7]

Sometimes, I feel like blowing on the thermometer and staying 'in bed', like a child before a school exam. But the exam follows me to bed.

I know that you too have such difficult days, even though you know how to look at things better than I do. And you wrote in one of the recent letters about 'doing useful things'. And about the honesty of Ignacy. But this is not the

7 An unidentified quotation

truth, Stefciu – and despite the feeling of nowhere-to-go that envelops me at the moment, I know for sure that it isn't true.

And how much more your lovely poem, 'On Lake Charavigne', gives me than any number of other words, spoken or written by other people.

Actually, in the end, I don't care at all what these people around me say – apart from facts, that this or that has happened, that yesterday this and today that. Only facts can be important, not commentary about them – because what's the point? Commentaries are lamps lit in full sunlight, torches with spent batteries and dirty bulbs. What for – when there's the sun? What is the use if they can't even be seen in the sunlight? What are these metaphors for anyway? I feel that I am as stupid as an old boot and persuade myself that all those around me are footwear too. This comparison turns out to be even more stupid.

Darling, darling, when shall I embrace you at last, at last.

I am trying at the moment to get the precise date of departure. *Priorité*, it seems, is not precise enough. Oh, darling! My little one, I so much want all to go well for you. Look after yourself for me! Darling, I kiss you, my sweetheart.
Franka

Telegram from Stefan to Franciszka

CHÉRIE SI POSSIBLE PRIÈRE CONFIRMER PAR AUTORITÉS VISA PRIORITÉ TÉLÉGRAPHIQUEMENT CONSULAT PORTUGAIS LYON STOP COMMENT VA TU EMBRASSE SI TENDREMENT = THEMERSON

Telegram from Franciszka to Stefan

MON PETIT REÇU INFORMATIONS LISBONNE CERTIFICAT DONNÉ PAR AIR ATTACHÉ QUE TU AS PRIORITÉ ET PARTIRA LE PLUS VITE POSSIBLE NE SUFFIT PAS EXIGE DATE DÉPART STOP JE DEMANDAI NOUVELLES INSTRUCTIONS POUR ATTACHÉ J'ESPÈRE RÉUSSIR STOP QUELLES AUTORITÉS SI PAS LISBONNE DOIS-JE TÉLÉGRAPHIER CONSULAT PORTUGAIS SUJET VISA STOP MON PETIT QUE JE T'AIME TENDRESSES = THEMERSON

5 February **Telegram from Polmission in Lisbon to Stefan**

POLICE EXPRIME ACCORD VOTRE VISA STOP PRIÈRE FAIRE TÉLÉGRAPHIER PAR CONSULAT PORTUGAIS DEMANDE FORMELLE AVEC RÉPONSE PAYÉE DÉPART ULTÉRIEUR AVION ASSURÉ = POLMISSION

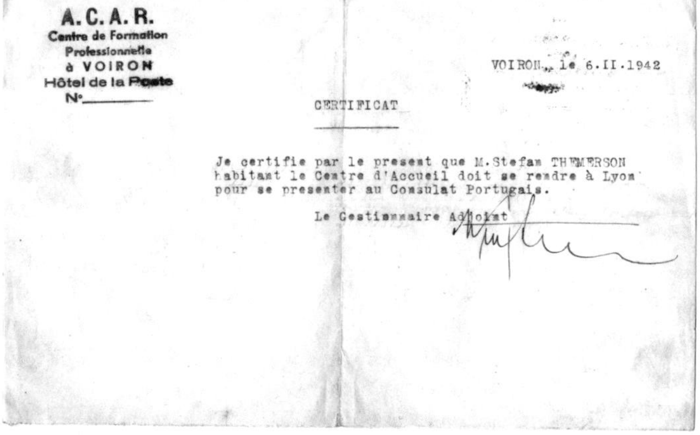

A.C.A.R.
Centre de Formation
Professionnelle
à VOIRON
Hôtel de la Poste
N°

VOIRON, le 6.II.1942

CERTIFICAT

Je certifie par le present que M. Stefan THEMERSON habitant le Centre d'Accueil doit se rendre à Lyon pour se presenter au Consulat Portugais.

Le Gestionnaire Adjoint

6 February 1942
Certificate from A.C.A.R. Centre de Formation Professionnelle à Voiron, Hôtel de la Poste

Je certifie par le présent que Stefan Themerson habitant le Centre d'Accueil doit se rendre à Lyon pour se présenter au Consulat Portugais.
Le Gestionnaire Adjoint

8 February 1942

Letter from Stefan to Franciszka

My dearest darling,
On Thursday I got a telegram from Lisbon and I took it with me to Lyon, but the Portuguese Consulate continues to refuse to send an enquiry to the head office. They demand in advance to be shown proof, even a telegram from the consulate of the country of destination about the visa, and from the travel agency about the matter of *priorité* and the travel. I don't know if I can get these things or if I can get them before this letter gets to you. And afterwards there will still be a lot of formalities, and will anything change in the meantime? It is winter now and it's difficult to even think about any initiative of one's own, especially since my experiences have been very unpleasant. But spring will be here soon, perhaps something will change then. A year ago I was in Marseille. Going there, determined, I never occurred to me that I would have to come back and that I would be here for another year. And afterwards, there was nothing for it but to be very glad to have returned.

Darling, I read through all your letters, from the first one still addressed to Zosia K. and to Blanche, that I got only in December or January – already over a year ago! – and telegrams, starting with the one in which you wrote that you are going to Toulouse, that misled me for so many months, and the one to Żyw which I only got in November and that first one to me personally. What a long, long stretch of time, darling!

9 February Franeczko, darling. The greater the gloom around us the more important it is to keep cheerful. It's difficult, but it is the only logical approach to life. And the greater the iniquity, cruelty and dogmatism the more necessary it is to preserve an inner sense of justice and that grain of a sense of humour that is rooted in us. The more that falls on one side of the scales, the less we have on the other. It seems to me the only logical, effective attitude to reality – at least under these conditions when an alternative, objective view, is inconceivable. It is difficult to achieve this in face of the terror of reality, but for that very reason one must. In other circumstances, even hatred and cruelty can be valuable emotions, like some inner secretions of energy that make the performance of certain actions possible. It is a hard enough thing to demand of a man the sort of strength necessary to do these things, without asking that he should do so with the objectivity of someone painting a still-life, for instance, or in the manner of a botanist or an engineer. It is only when certain concrete deeds must be performed that we need these passionate, inner secretions of our psyche. But when there is no such action to perform they are useless, and we choke on them helplessly. What are they then but a sign of impotence, of a weakness, which in a mood of confidence or chutzpah, would be called spirit or will power or a sense of reality.

This 'sense of reality' is something much greater than the ability to deal with everyday life, even when everyday life is not limited to matters of lunch or sleep, but embraces the so-called 'issues'. I am not just talking about sticking to the 'rigidity' of one's habits, views, principles, etc., but of throwing them onto the scales, even when they don't weigh more than the hole of a poor two-sous coin. And that is when the scales are inside us and not outside. Because our inner scales are not a mechanical reflection of weights and balances that exist in the world at large. It is the scale that weighs values! continued on page 321

I

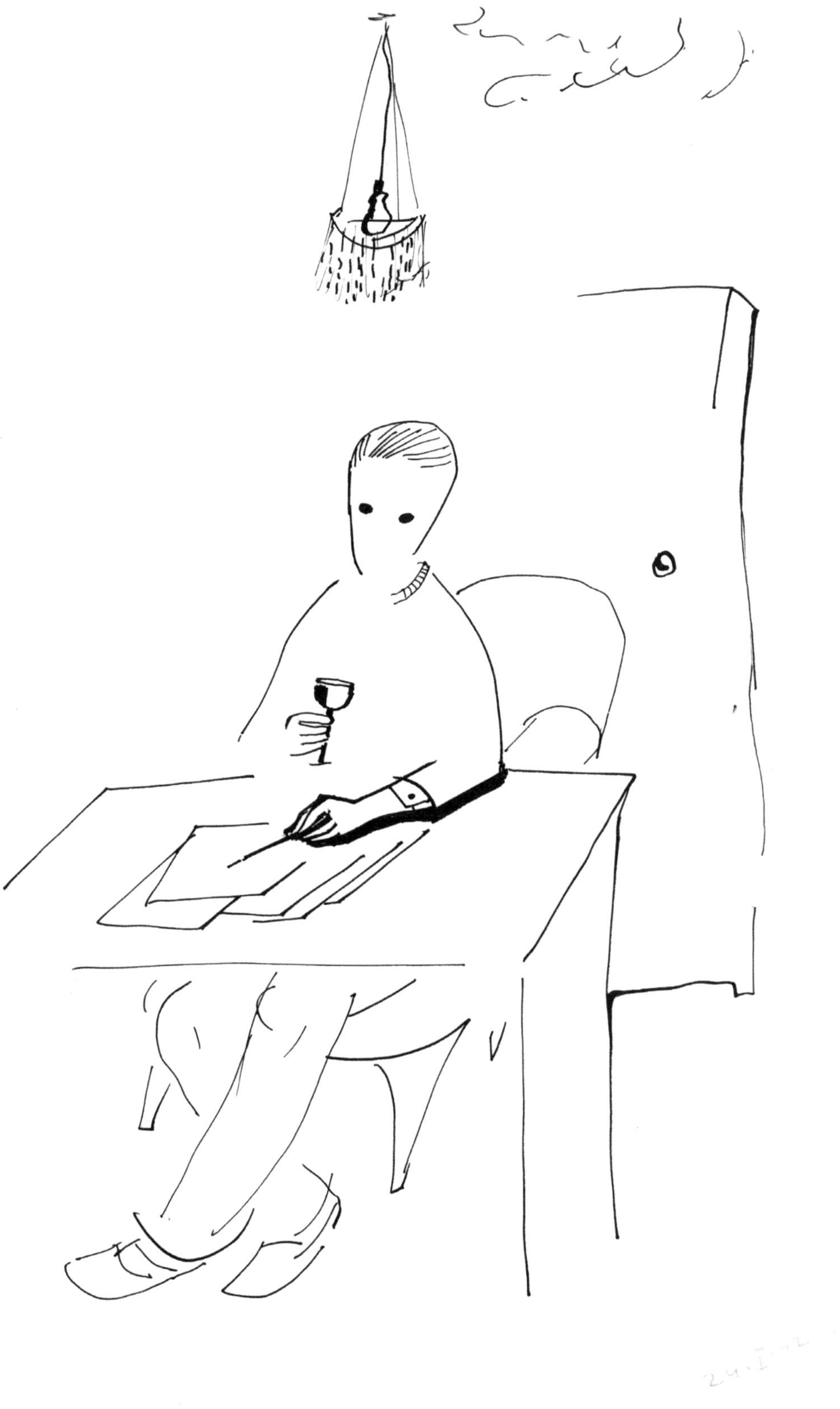

II

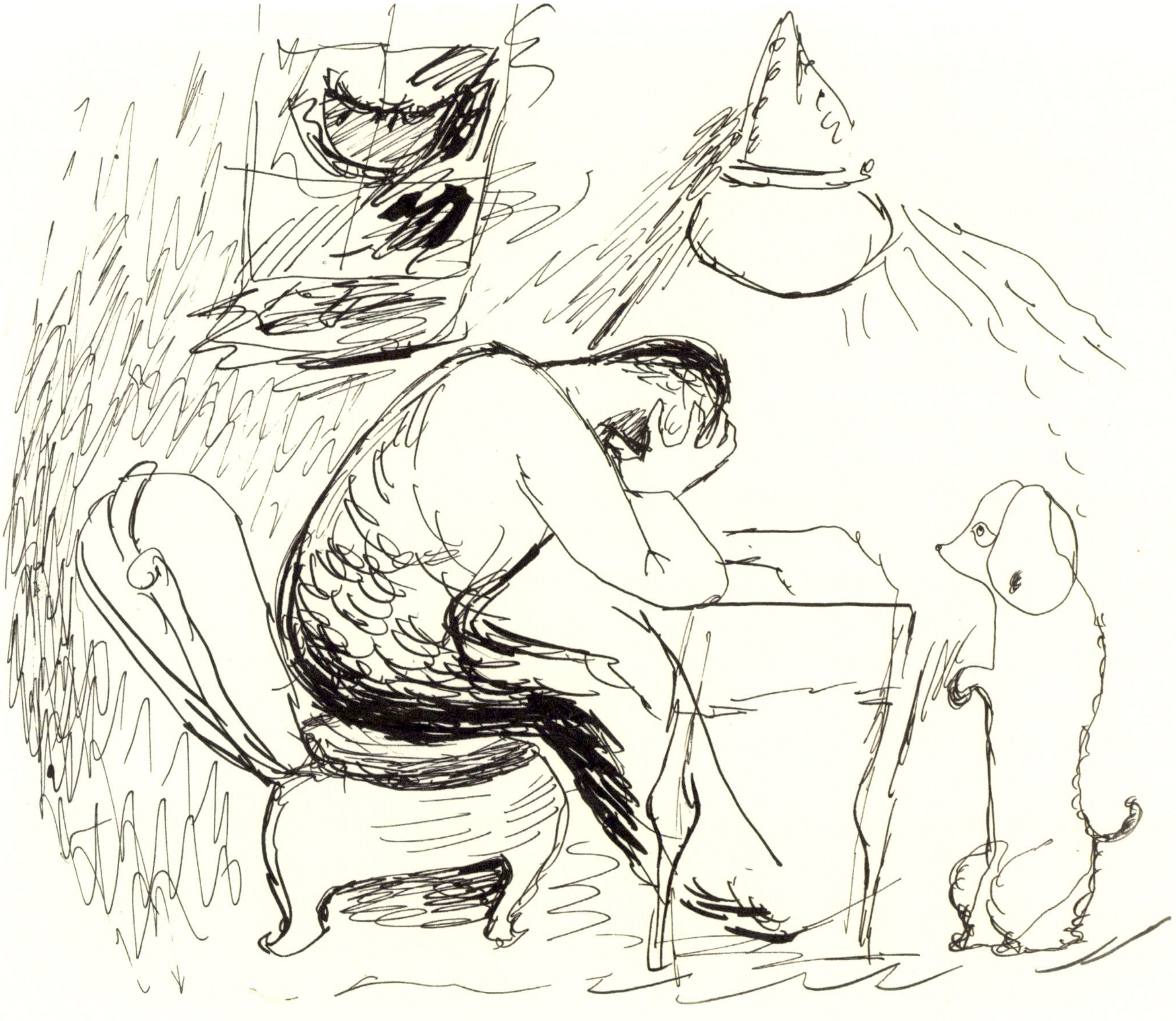

III

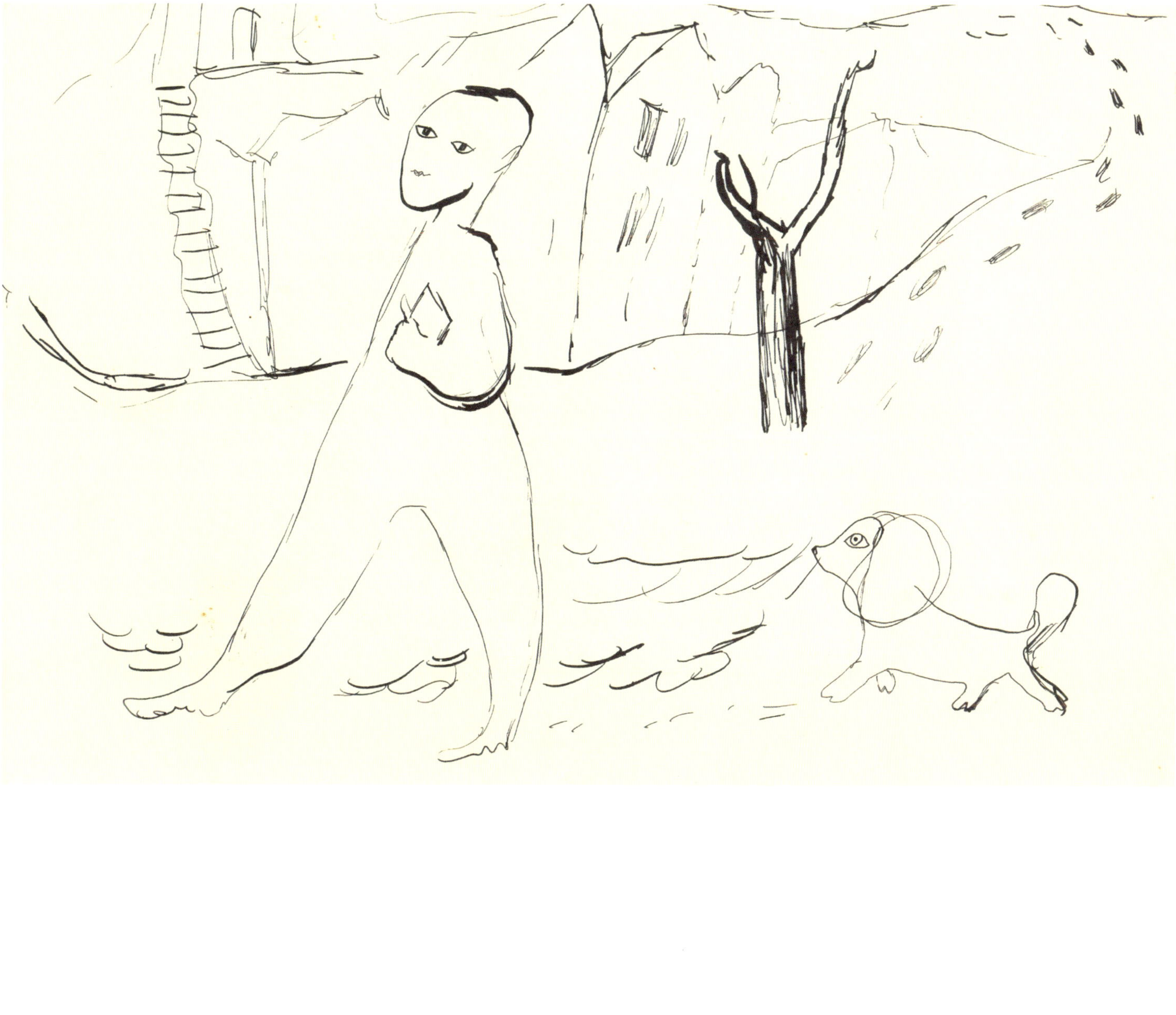

IV

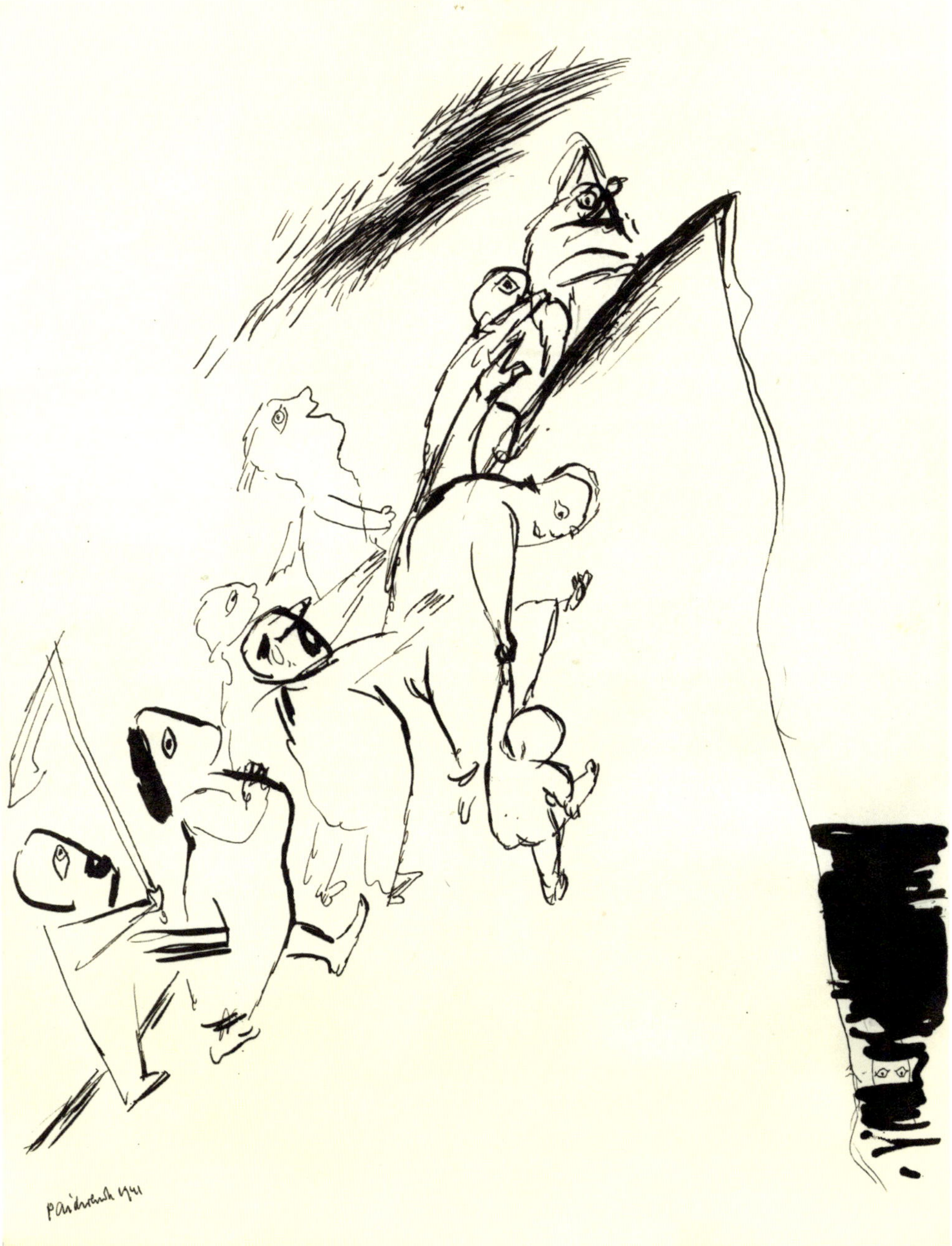

V

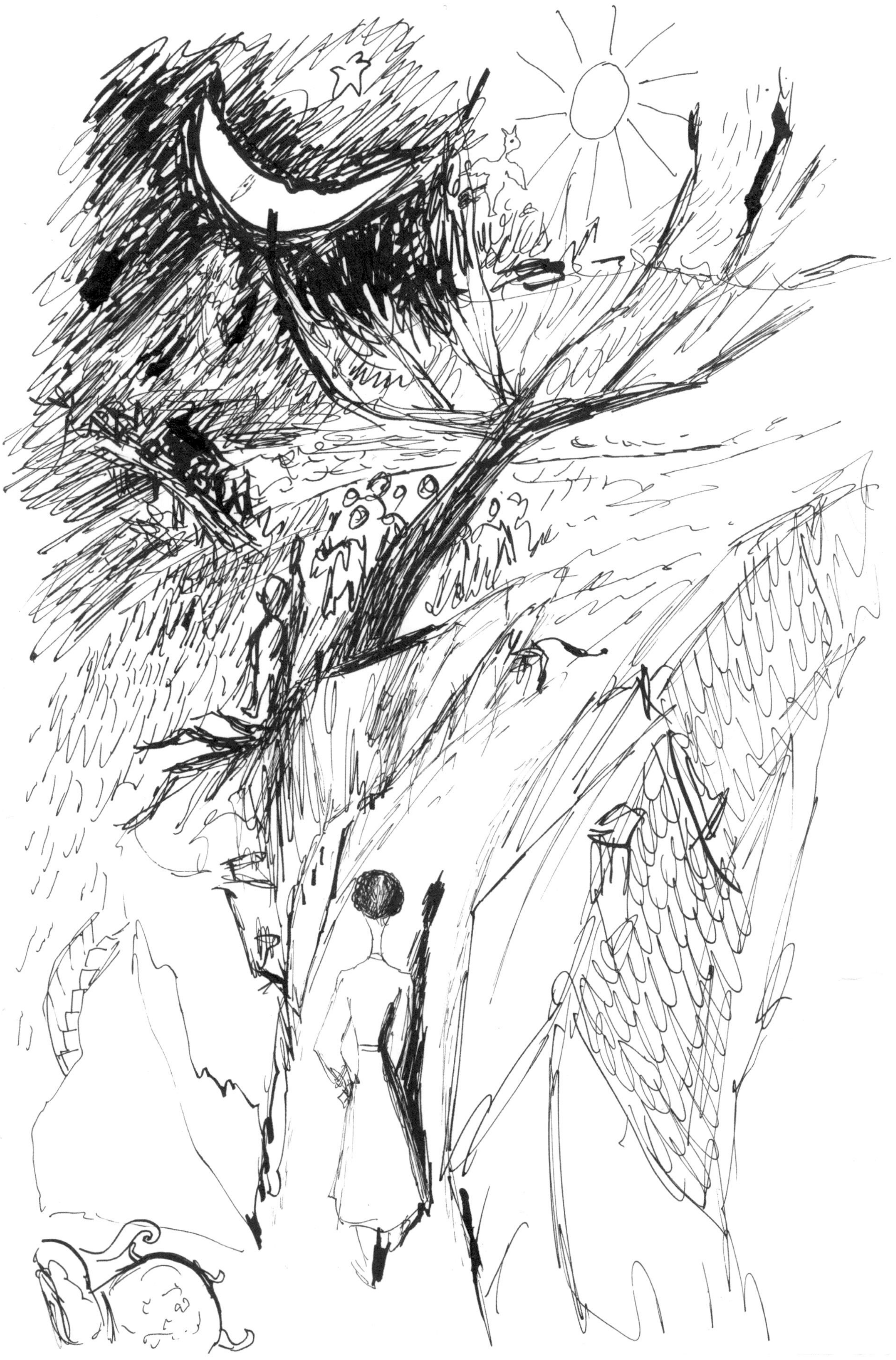

VI

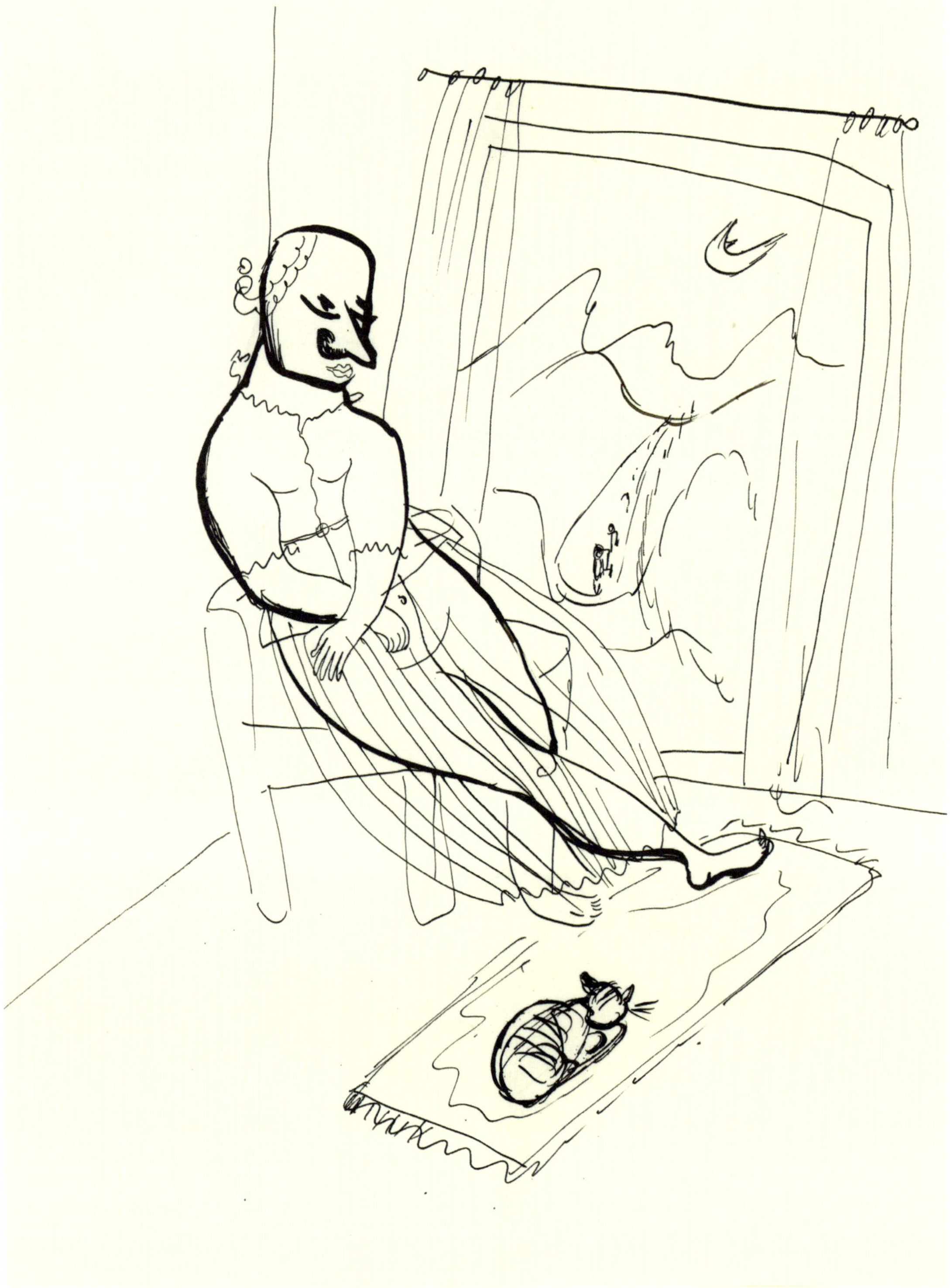

VII

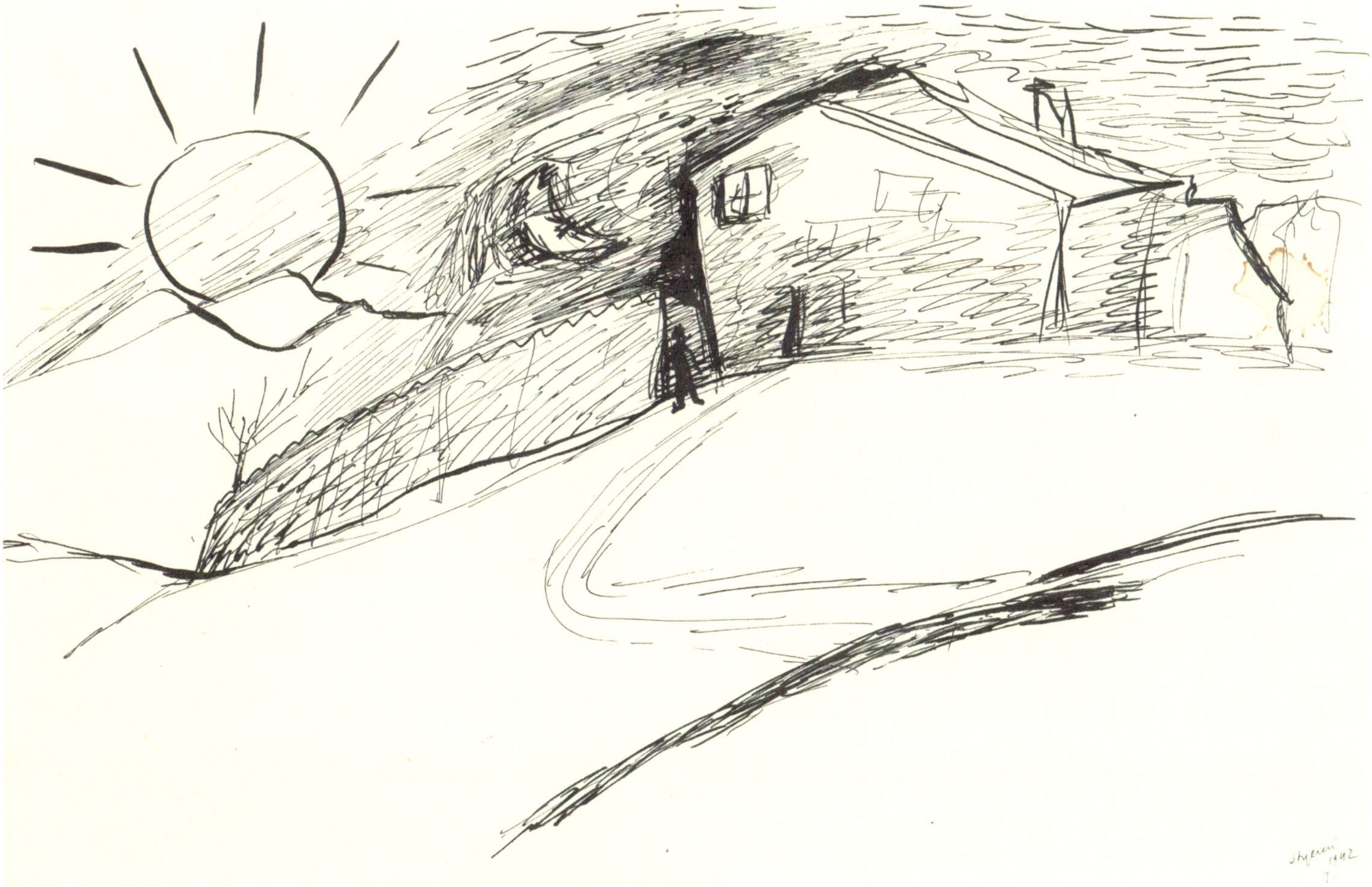

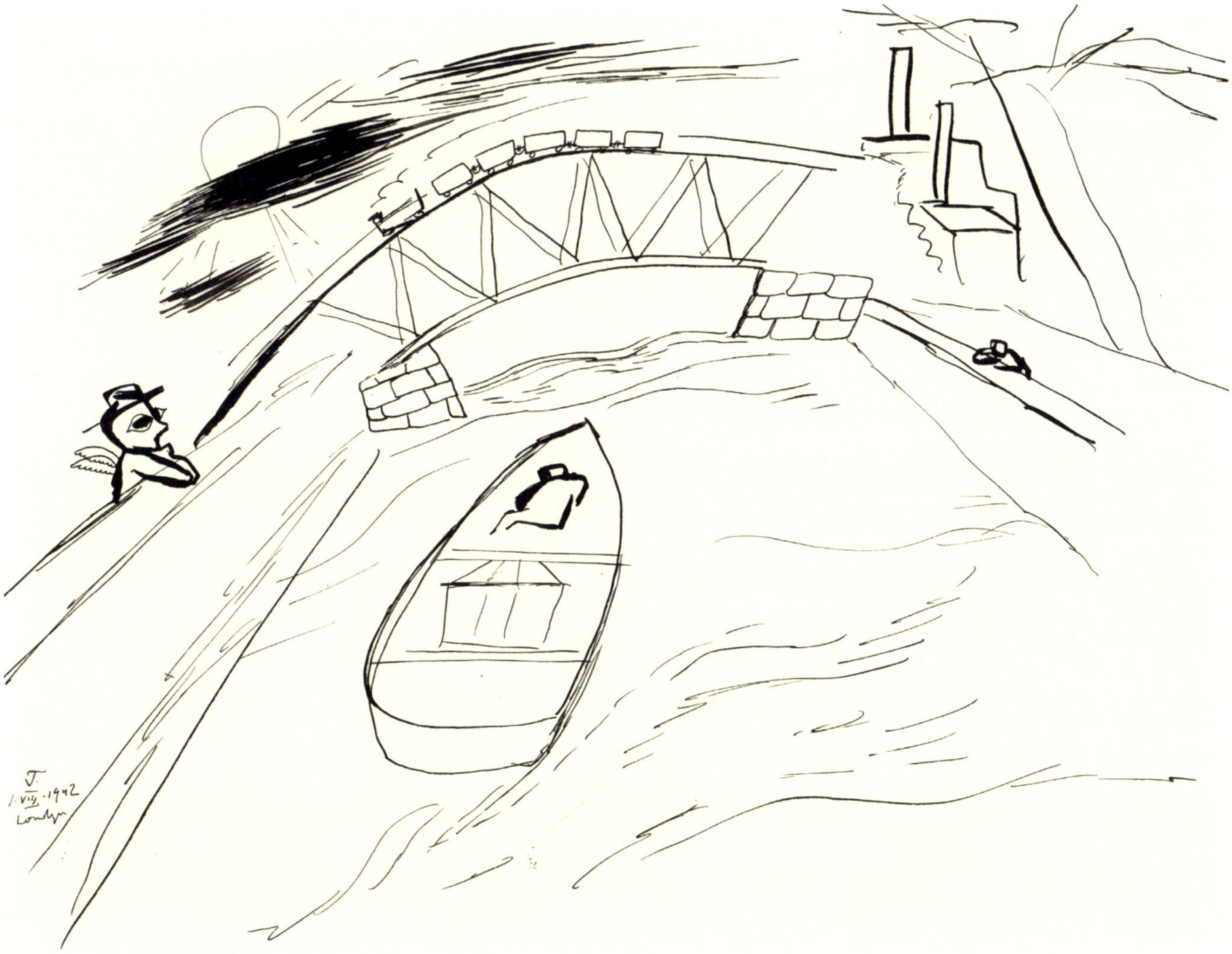
J.
1.VIII.1942
Londyn

IX

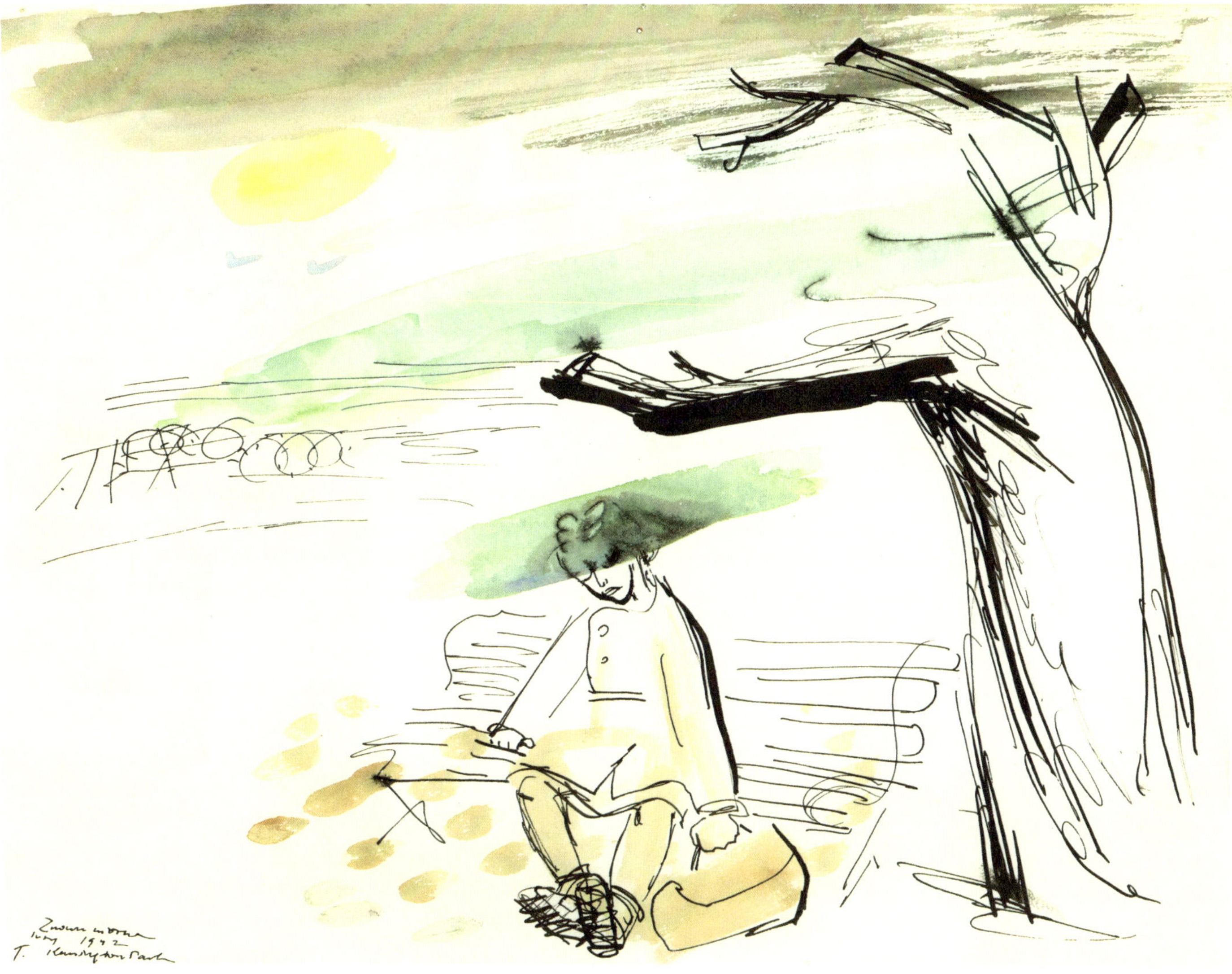

X

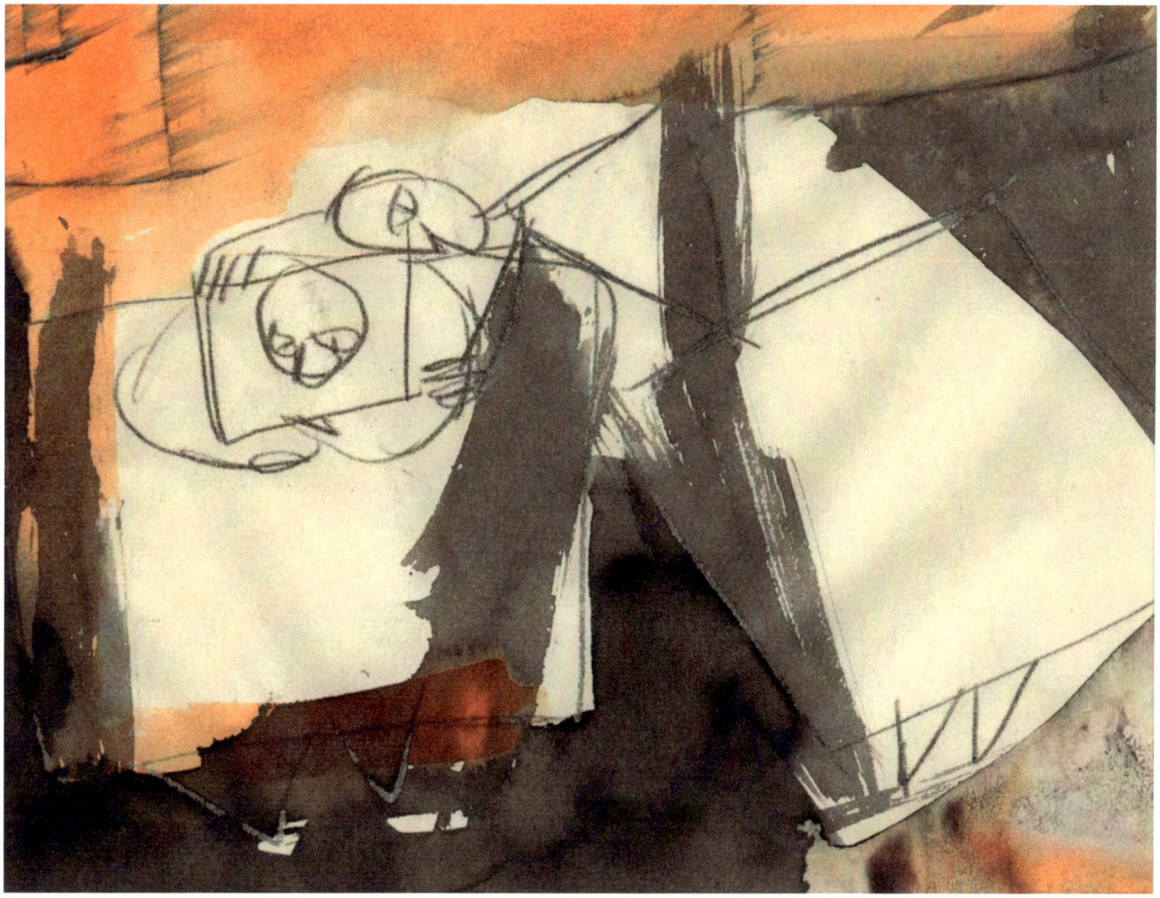

I – *Stefan at his table*, 24 January 1942
II – *Nuit de Ténèbres*, 1942
III – *On the track*, 1942
IV – *Stefan's escape I*, October 1941
V – *Stefan's escape II*, 1941
VI – *Waiting room*, 1941
VII – *Escape at sunrise*, January 1942
VIII – *Sous le pont Battersea coule la Seine*, 1942
IX – *Spring again, (Kensington Park)*, February 1942
X – *Consoling couple*, 1942

Epictetus[8] was owned by a fellow who apparently liked to experiment and wanted to examine the endurance of man's leg. When he tested one which belonged to Epictetus, the latter did not cry, but said calmly, take care because it will break. Later, he maintained that this, like the rest of life's experiences, did not affect his personal, inner independence, his freedom of thought. He was wrong, because they convinced him of his independence. But it could have happened differently. If one does not witness such a scene, one forgets the third actor: the broken leg of Epictetus. If one is a witness – one sees only this third actor: the breaking of the leg and one's first reflex is to defend him! And it seems to me that one should have defended Epictetus. But at the same time I know, and am able to say quite dispassionately and calmly, that it was the absence of such a reaction that ensured the survival of the real Epictetus up to our times.

The country in which I now live – doesn't it remind us of the leg of Epictetus?

Darling, we understand each other so well, that I know that you must know how happy I am that you are working, and how much I miss you and what you are doing.

Did you receive my 'Fuga', Franeczko, sent in the middle of December? I will send it once more. I kiss you darling so tenderly Stefan

Do you not have news from home?

Hugs for Stefan and Genek. Does Stefan [Konorski] have news of [his brother] Jurek? From Mira and Ignacy not a word. I am very glad that they are together. What about Teresa [Żarnower]? Hasn't Antoni S[łonimski] finished with that pack of conceited idiots, who unfortunately often have talent? In what way does 'their' independence differ from ours, if all is the same as before? S.

10 February **Telegram from Polmission in Lisbon to Stefan**

AVONS DÉPOSÉ POLICE LISBONNE CERTIFICATS BUREAU PASSEPORTS BRITANNIQUES CONCERNANT VISA ET ATTACHÉ AIR CONCERNANT VOTRE DÉPART PAR AVION STOP MAINTENANT POLICE EXIGE VOTRE DEMANDE FORMELLE QUI DOIT SE RÉFÉRER AUX DOCUMENTS DÉPOSÉES PAR CONSULAT POLOGNE = POLMISSION

Telegram from Franciszka to Stefan

CHÉRI RÉPONDS MOI CE TÉLÉGRAMME CITÉ PAR TOI ÉTAIT DE POLMISSION ET QUAND REÇU STOP ON M'INFORMA QUE TU DOIS FAIRE NORMALE DEMANDE VISA CONSULAT PORTUGAIS LYON ET PAYER SIMPLEMENT FRAIS DE TÉLÉGRAMME POUR LA TRANSMETTRE STOP PAS NÉCESSAIRE QUE CONSULAT FASSE AUTRE DEMANDE FORMELLE DE TA PART STOP SI ON TE REFUSE QUE JE NE CROIS PAS POSSIBLE PRIÈRE RÉPONDRE POLMISSION SANS AUTRES DÉTAILS QUE CONSULAT LYON DONNANT COMME CAUSE MANQUE CONFIRMATION OFFICIELLE VISA ET PRIORITÉ REFUSÉE ENVOYER TÉLÉGRAPHIQUEMENT DEMANDE STOP PRIÈRE DEMANDER EN MÊME TEMPS POLMISSION ARRANGER CHEZ AUTORITÉS PORTUGAISES LISBONNE INSTRUCTIONS VISA POUR CONSULAT LYON STOP IMPOSSIBLE ENVOYER VISA PRIORITÉ LYON ET MÊME SI C'ÉTAIT

8 Epictetus (AD55-135), Greek Stoic philosopher who stated that fate dictates external events which the individual cannot control and must accept, whereas he cannot ignore responsibility for his own actions.

POSSIBLE J'AURAIS SÉRIEUSES OBJECTIONS CONTRE STOP COMMENT TA SANTÉ CHÉRI PRENDS SOIN DE TOI JE T'EN PRIE TENDRESSES = THEMERSON

Draft of a letter from Stefan to Consulat Portugais in Lyon

Monsieur le Consul,

Étant en possession d'un visa pour la Grande Bretagne de destination britannique ainsi que d'une priorité d'avion, dont les certificats du Bureau des Passeports Britanniques concernant la possession du visa et l'attaché du British Air Ministry concernant priorité de mon départ par avion ont été déposées par le Consulat de Pologne à Lisbonne à la Police qui maintenant exige ma demande formelle afin de la référer aux documents déposés.

J'ai l'honneur de vous prier de bien vouloir faire transmettre ma présente demande de visa portugais à la police à Lisbonne par télégraphe.

Je possède le visa de sortie délivré par la Préfecture de l'Isère, le visa Espagnol m'est accordé par note du Ministère 176, juillet 17 je suis également en possession d'un certificat d'identité / Office Polonais à Lyon - N.00423/1-23553/41 et d'un Passeport valable pour tous les pays d'Europe et hors d'Europe, délivré par la Légation Polonaise à Lisbonne et valable jusqu'a 28.V.42 /N.1721/533/12/41

En vous remerciant à l'avance je vous prie d'agréer, Monsieur le Consul, l'expression de ma plus parfaite considération –

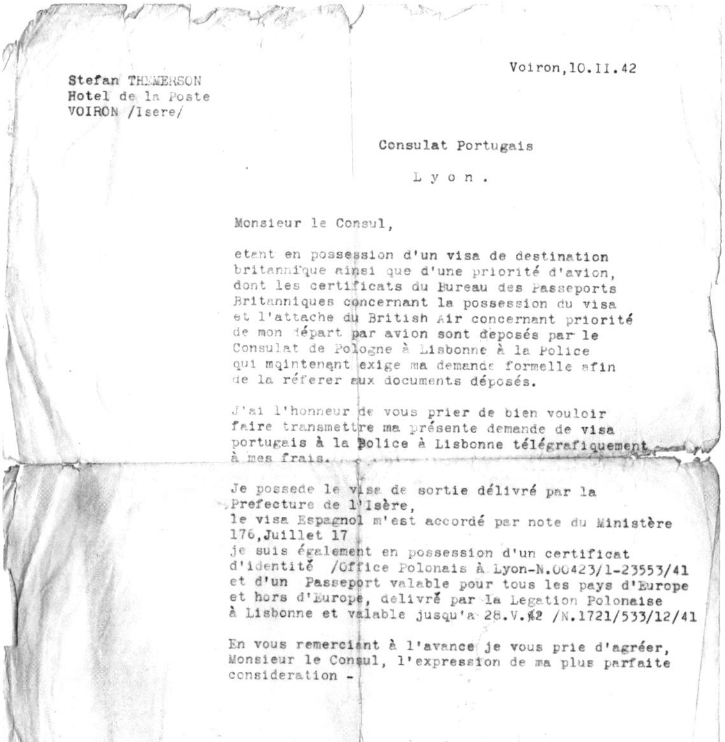

Stefan THEMERSON
Hotel de la Poste
VOIRON /Isere/

Voiron, 10.II.42

Consulat Portugais

L y o n .

Monsieur le Consul,

etant en possession d'un visa de destination britannique ainsi que d'une priorité d'avion, dont les certificats du Bureau des Passeports Britanniques concernant la possession du visa et l'attache du British Air concernant priorité de mon départ par avion sont deposés par le Consulat de Pologne à Lisbonne à la Police qui mqintenant exige ma demande formelle afin de la réferer aux documents déposés.

J'ai l'honneur de vous prier de bien vouloir faire transmettre ma présente demande de visa portugais à la Police à Lisbonne télégrafiquement à mes frais.

Je possede le visa de sortie délivré par la Prefecture de l'Isère,
le visa Espagnol m'est accordé par note du Ministère 176,Juillet 17
je suis également en possession d'un certificat d'identité /Office Polonais à Lyon-N.00423/1-23553/41 et d'un Passeport valable pour tous les pays d'Europe et hors d'Europe, delivré par la Legation Polonaise à Lisbonne et valable jusqu'a 28.V.42 /N.1721/533/12/41

En vous remerciant à l'avance je vous prie d'agréer, Monsieur le Consul, l'expression de ma plus parfaite consideration -

10 February 1942
Letter from Stefan to the Portuguese Consulate in Lyon

Letter from Stefan to Franciszka

My dearest darling, I received your letter of 4 February. Darling, think positively and be strong. It must be so very difficult for you, all of this, my sweetheart – and with so many worries about me still – certainly not pleasant ones. And one can't see an end to this whole game of playing grown-ups.

I think, in spite of everything, that I will still be here to receive an answer to this letter, darling.

I would so much like it, Franek, if you would describe what you are doing even a bit, although I know that it's not really possible. I miss so much everything that is yours and I am greedy for your work just as I am greedy for the truth.

I can see from your letter that you are sad and something in me freezes and petrifies. Darling, we must not allow ourselves to get so tired that we won't have the strength to smile.

Recently, I've been working quite a lot despite the poor conditions that somewhat diminish the value of what 'free time' means.

I have projects for three bigger things – books. The first is something like a philosophical diary arranged alphabetically. I haven't aged sufficiently to undertake the analysis of the traits of my character (*à la manière de Rousseau*), but I can already allow myself to confess my ideas, that is to say, not to limit myself to definitions of what I think about such things as infinity, soul, materialism, etc. (Such definitions would be no more interesting than any others. They are made for a purpose, and verifiable with the author, but not against reality.) My idea is rather to sketch a history of creating, bringing together notions that emerge from the process of thinking and facts that are connected with a given individual, which without doubt and despite everything, I am. It would be like primary material for the sociologist, collected critically and shamelessly, objectively and sincerely by the very object that is being studied.

The second project is a book, I won't say a novel, in the form of letters to an individual who, living in a certain milieu, plays an intimate role in its day-to-day activities. He is prodigal with his opinions and judgments, which are confused because they derive from self-interest imposed by daily life. He wants to see how this same incidental and vivid milieu is perceived by someone else. This book would consist of chapters each of which is devoted to a particular character and story of a different person. Objectivity coloured by the indulgence of thinking and by the way self-interest affects judgments imposed on others. But this wouldn't be reportage. The plot grows without chronological order, but is completed here and there from various angles through fragments, subsidiary details, which become the means for realising better the characteristics under discussion.

Finally, the third subject is *Professor Mmaa's Lecture*, i.e. a real scientific lecture in natural history about the species homo, 'delivered' by a common termite. This is inspired in some measure by Maeterlinck's *La vie des termites*. In parallel to this systematic lecture, the normal life of the termite colony continues, being a rather distorted mirror-image of our own reality. The element of humour, or satire, must be precisely the result of the objectivity and scientific precision of the description. That one is the furthest advanced. I am in the middle of Chapter IV. What worries me most is that probably I won't be able to send them to you. Perhaps, I might make a suitable précis.

Did you get my 'Fugue', darling? I sent it for the second time not so long ago.

Darling, I kiss you so very much. Write to me Franeczko as much as possible about yourself and about what you are doing. So that I can imagine it better. I would so much like to know about something that made you cheerful and content with yourself. I would so much like to know that you have some satisfactions and joys.

Love, my dearest little one. Did you have any news from home? Hugs for Stefan and Janek.

I kiss you, darling. Stefan

24 February **Telegram from Stefan to Franciszka**

CHÉRIE REÇU TA LETTRE SI TRISTE TENONS NOUS MON PETIT JE TRAVAILLE BEAUCOUP ET TOI T'EMBRASSE T'AIME = STEFAN THEMERSON

26 February **Letter from Stefan to Franciszka**

My dearest darling, I know so little about you and I am so very anxious. How are you, darling? Do you feel well, completely well? How I should like to see something in this new flat about which you wrote, my little one, darling.

27 February Darling, today I received your telegram. I am so happy that you are working, my little one. For two days I couldn't do anything, but now after receiving that telegram I got down to work once more. I am working on the 5th chapter of the book that I wrote to you about. I am so sad that I can't send it to you. It stops me and discourages me.

Franeczko, how is your life now? Certainly it is very difficult and certainly things must be very hard for you. Do you have a bit of time for yourself, apart from those terrible hours in the office, for work, for rest, for life? Here I am more than completely well, darling, and I don't need anything at all. I have money for the journey put aside, so that I won't have to ask anybody for anything, and apart from that I received now from Marcel as much as 4,000, which will last me for a very long time. So don't worry about me, darling, at all. I kiss you, darling so much, my little one. Stefan

Have you had any news from home? You don't tell me anything about this, and I have no news at all.

Hugs for Stefan. I should like to write him all sorts of things, but it is so difficult to lift up the pen; I think he will understand my fatigue and will forgive me. What about Ignacy and Mira? And Genek? Stefanja? St.

28 February **Letter from Stefan to Franciszka**

My darling, I am sending you the beginning of the book that I am writing now. Six pages: first chapter and the beginning of the second. I am already finishing the fifth, but I haven't copied it yet. I count on the intelligence of the censors, and think that you will accept it as an innocent attempt at satire – a look at oneself with an eye with which we look at termites in Maeterlinck's *La vie des termites*.

In order to see it, I thought it would be best to imagine how termites would see us – not real termites as imagined by us, whose level of thinking would have nothing in common with ours, but termites who are burdened with all our human characteristics.

I kiss you, darling, so very much, my dearest darling.

Love, Stefan

Letter from Franciszka to Stefan

My dearest sweetheart,

Again I am writing a letter while dreaming that you might be able to leave before it reaches you. After all that's perfectly possible, even if so uncertain. All the time I'm waiting for an answer about the final date of departure, I'm unsure whether I can make arrangements for that visa without it. I wait from day to day. All the time I am writing to and telephoning various people and it should, really should work out! You can bet there'll be some other formalities again. My dearest pet. Yes, darling, my burden is so much lighter than that of all those around me, because I have you and your letters and our common work, all that was and all that will be, and actually is there all the time, even if so remote physically. Because each of my thoughts can breathe, and each of your words forms my truth. Darling!

So difficult, so impossible to express in words what I feel. Each word is weak and silly and already a cliché. And when I'm drawing there are already times when I can't find the right line.

I got your beautiful poem from the Lake Charavigne and the 'Fuga'. Thank you, darling, thank you so very much.

'Twilight', 'Evening' and 'Night' are beautiful. And 'Dawn'. They have intense colour values, redolent of darkness and a serious quietude. I feel them with the ear, the eye and by touch.

The first part is too incisive, light, rugged. Why? I don't know – that's how I feel. From the words: 'our bodies will turn into the titles of chapters of history…' it is wonderful. What do you think about that? Write – even though I have to wait so long for an answer. I dream about talking with you. My pet!

I received your letter with a note from the Walfiszes. The house where her aunt lived is empty. I don't know if I'll manage to find her new address, but shall try to find out from acquaintances. I myself shall try to help her parents as well. Give them my sincere regards.

My dear darling, I kiss you so much. Franka

Telegram from Franciszka to Stefan

MERCI MON PETIT JE TRAVAILLE POUR MOI AUSSI STOP J'ATTENDS TOUJOURS RÉPONSE MA DEMANDE SUJET DATE EXACTE PRIORITÉ EMBRASSE CHÉRI SI TENDREMENT TOUT MON COEUR AVEC TOI THEMERSON

3 March **Telegram from Franciszka to Stefan**

MON PETIT REÇU PROMESSE DÉPART, TRENTE JOURS APRÈS ARRIVÉE LISBONNE STOP ESPÈRE SUFFIRA POUR VISA STOP J'AI TÉLÉGRAPHIÉ DÉJÀ POLMISSION STOP EMBRASSE LE PLUS TENDREMENT CHÉRI = THEMERSON

4 March **Letter from Franciszka to Stefan**

My dearest little one,

I received two letters from you of 24 and 28 January. Thank you darling so much. When I saw you like that, in all the pullovers, and with a blanket, bending over the linocut, it filled my heart with such warmth and tenderness. My pet, you could probably feel it all the way from here. So much feeling, tenderness as to a beloved child, and at the same time for myself I'd so much like to lean, just like a child, on your chest, my darling.

Yesterday, at last, I received a positive answer to the question of time limit for the *priorité*. It's probably better undated, because there are always some formalities with other authorities which can still take time. But with that, departure is guaranteed within 30 days of arriving in Lisbon.

My pet, I hope that this is finally all that is needed.

Stefan Konorski means to write to you all the time, and keeps on reassuring me that, finally, you will be here soon anyway. He is not in good shape himself. He constantly receives sad news about family or friends. And so we support each other, like the blind with the lame. For a long time, Genek was planning to go to Bolek, but he didn't get a visa – you see what difficulties there are! So he gave up the idea of leaving, and works as he always has done at a great pace, and in his own way, and in general he does things the right way. He's a good man, and in the end it was he who arranged everything to do with the *priorité*. I only had to keep on at him and to push where necessary.

I too have had no news of family for a long time, my pet. The last card from September, that Sewek is somewhere in the region of Naprawa [south of Kraków], with Michał [his brother]. That they are all well. That recently they – i.e. Maryla, Mother and Jasia – lived on parcels. It doesn't bear thinking about. Also a card came into my hands, which was written in November by my Mother, not to me but to the firm, asking for stock cubes and sardines. And since then, not a word. I also had a card from September from Aneczka. Your Mother, Irka and Stefan work as before. Maryla lives at Śliska 7. To Luciunia[9] you can write either directly, or to Caixa 572. Or, you can send it to me. Look at me, I'm still writing as if we were going to be separated forever, while really I believe that we'll be together soon.

Teresa is in Canada. At last!

Mira and Ignacy don't write to me, either. I think that they are buffeted by their love problems. Zośka [Wojciechowska] wrote that Ignacy was at Mira's for the New Year, and it seems that this prodigal couple will get together again.

Just look at me, darling, I'm writing you such silly things, and there's so much, so much I'd like to say, all sorts of warm, loving words.

I'm sending them to you my pet, in one enormous whispered and blazing assortment. You pick out whatever you want to read and perhaps somehow it will be more pleasant, my precious!

Are you looking after yourself, darling? Please do that for me! Take care of yourself Stefulku.

I kiss you, my dearest pet, an awful, awful lot! Franka

Yes, my darling pet, and I am the happiest of all here, because I have you.
F

5 March Letter from Zieliński in Lisbon to Franciszka

Dear Mrs Themerson

Just a few hurried words to let you know that the visa for your husband has been granted, if he will go to see the Portuguese Consul they will make an application. Our office has advised Mr Themerson by telegram.

Yours sincerely, Adam Zieliński

9 Łucja Weinles

6 March 1942

Letter from Stefan to Franciszka

My darling,

It's so long since I've had any letters from you. The last one was from 4 February, and so very sad.

Recently, I've been working quite a lot. I have just finished Chapter v of *Professor Mmaa's Lecture*, which I wrote to you about. I should so much like to read it to you. I sent you a few of the first pages, there is nothing in them yet, but did you get them? Are you getting my letters? And 'Fuga'? I sent it for the second time. You asked about *Poésie 42*. I have just received a letter from Pierre Seghers. He writes, inter alia; '*Je conserve naturellement vos textes. Et j'attends l'éclaircie dans la nuit du papier pour les passer*'.

I don't need any money at all, darling, for the journey, it's put aside. And recently I also received some from Marcel. Altogether, don't worry about me.

Darling, how are you? Do you have some time for yourself?

I kiss you, darling, all the time. Stefan

Hugs for Stefan and Genek and all.

Love, sweetheart, I would so much like to know that you are just a bit happy and content, darling. Stefan

10 March **Letter from Franciszka to Stefan**

My dearest little one,

Thank you, darling. I'd already got two of your letters from January a few days ago, and I have replied to them. But I am re-reading them all the time from the beginning just to be a tiny bit closer to you. My dearest!

You write about not judging those close to us. You are right, it certainly does not reduce the chance of seeing the truth. But how do we avoid making judgments when it becomes a lifeline at times? Because otherwise we lose balance and the ability to distinguish between humour and tragic pathos, between caricature and defenceless sadness, one feels compelled to discipline oneself to reject some things, and accept others.

When we are together, darling little one, perhaps I will be braver in letting myself confront this confusion of contradictions, perhaps I will find the courage to search for expression and sense through this crazy discord of emotions.

Now, at times, I stop as if on the edge of a precipice because I know that there is no hand that will help me, no words that will support me. Often, I have a strange feeling of wanting to throw myself, head first, into nonsense. But I stop because I am not sure of how to face that path, head first.

I stop myself and I wait. I bide my time. That's all. On other days I spend time with these or other friends on sad conversations about the way things are – or I simply go to the cinema.

About things at the centre of my life, our life, I don't talk to anyone now. Only sometimes, when I read your poems aloud to people. Because I feel sorry for people who haven't read them. Anyway, I try to be nice – so I am nice and they probably don't even notice just how faraway I am from them all. Precisely as far as from here to Voiron. My pet!

I love you Franka

10.III.1942

Maleństwo moje najdroższe,

dziękuję kochanie. Już parę dni temu dostałam dwa Twoje listy ze stycznia i odpisałam już na nie. Ale wciąż czytam je od początku żeby być choć odrobinę więcej z Tobą. Maleństwo moje!

Piszesz o niesądzeniu bliźnich. Masz rację, to napewno nie zmniejsza szans wyrażenia prawdy, ale jak ustrzec się przed sądzeniami gdy to staje się chwilami deską ratunku, bo brak równowagi i zatracenie poczucia granicy między humorem, a tragicznym patosem, między karykaturą, a beznadziejnym smutkiem zmusza do zdyscyplinowania samego siebie odrzuceniem rzeczy jednych, a uznaniem drugich.

Gdy będziemy razem, maleństwo kochane, może odważniej będę się puszczać w odmęty tych niemożliwości, może znajdę, może odważę się szukać wyrazu i sama pojmę zwariowaną dysharmonię odemnie.

Teraz chwilami zatrzymuję się, jak nad przepaścią, bo wiem, że niema ręki która mi pomoże, słowa które mnie podtrzyma.

Mam często dziwne uczucie chęci rzucenia się głową w nonsens.

Ale zatrzymuję się bo nie jestem pewna tej drogi głową naprzód.

Zatrzymuję się i czekam. Przeczekuję. — To wszystko. —

I mów wtedy spędzam czas z Żywi lub innymi przyjaciółmi na smutnych rozmowach lub aktualnych dowcipach, — lub poprostu idę do kina.

O rzeczach, które są mojem życiem, naszem życiem nie mogę mówić z nikim teraz. Czasem tylko czytam ludziom Twoje wiersze. Bo żal mi ludzi, którzy ich nie czytali.

Zresztą staram się być miła, — więc jestem miła i pewno nawet nie zauważają, jak daleko od nich wszystkich jestem. Dokładnie tak daleko, jak stąd do Voiron.

Maleńko!

Kocham Cię Franka

Letter from Franciszka to Stefan, 10 March 1942

Letter from Stefan to Franciszka

Darling, I still have no letters from you. Write, darling. I shall certainly still be here for a long time. Even if I get the Portuguese visa, there will still be quite a lot of formalities. The Spanish transit visas are already invalid. I will have to make a new application but only after receiving the Portuguese one. I will have to extend the exit visa that expired long ago, and how many things can change in the meantime!

12 March It's already nearly a month without letters from you, Franek. Either you don't write or they don't arrive? I only received a telegram. And I am increasingly worried by this silence, darling. Spring is already here, this time a real spring it seems, and perhaps the frosts won't return. And with spring again projects are born, but always there is the lingering possibility of never realising them, and so I get furious with myself – not with the world, because the world is as it is, but oneself could always be different. I've been working quite a lot, but somehow it came to a grinding halt recently, mainly because I can't send you what I am doing, so what's the point of forcing myself to overcome the thousands of obstacles in the way?

15 March Darling, I am writing and writing this letter and I can't finish it and put it in an envelope and send it. Still, I have no letters from you.

Are you painting? Are you drawing, darling? Do you have a bit of time for what is most important? I have so much of it – all of twenty-four hours rolling by through a void. The whole of last night I was looking at your paintings and I felt such crazy hunger in my eyes that I couldn't look at anything here. I was seized by anger that I didn't know how to make your life and your work easier before when I was with you.

It already frightens me just to repeat this anxious question – have you had any news from home?

I am still, still waiting for letters from you.

Hugs for Stefan. Oh, if he would like, without waiting for my letter, to write to me at length about everything that's possible to write about.

I kiss you, darling, so very much. Look after yourself, darling, that is all I ask!

Love, my littlest one. Stefan

Telegram from Franciszka to Stefan

MON PETIT COMMENT VAS TU J'ATTENDS DE NOUVEAU RÉPONSE DE LISBONNE CHÉRI JE T'ENVOIE SOURIRE LE PLUS TENDRE ET TOUTES MES PENSÉES T'AIME SOIS GAI PENSE À TOI-MÊME MON PETIT EMBRASSE DE TOUT COEUR = THEMERSON

18 March **Letter from Stefan to Franciszka**

Darling, yesterday I received your telegram. I replied immediately. Thank you, darling. But I still don't have letters from you. Why, darling? The last one was from 4 February, and it arrived relatively quickly, in the middle of February – and since then, not a word. But it was sad and bitter and I still feel its sadness and bitterness inside me. Anxiety rises between my hands and I feel I want to stifle it by force. I kiss you, darling, so much.

19 March My dearest little one, still no letters from you. I am sitting in a café, writing the 6th chapter of *Professor Mmaa's Lecture*. Small boys crawl under the tables looking for cigarette-ends for their fathers. But there are no more cigarette-ends on the

floor. Outside the windows, spring. Already, probably, a real one. Here, there are only four different positions for the hands on the clock – spring, summer, autumn and winter. Days, weeks, months seem not to exist.

'Sois Joyeux! Il faut être Joyeux, le devoir d'être joyeux. Je te le dis; moi qui passe un des moments les plus terribles et les plus désagréables de ma vie' – wrote a poet, compatriot of El Greco to his friend – Federico Garcia Lorca, in 1928.[10]

Write to me a lot, darling, about yourself. I miss your letters so much.

What is Stefan doing? How is he? And Genek? And all of them? Do you have news from Mira and Ignacy? What about Teresa?

I hug you my little one, love. Stefan

Telegram from Stefan to Franciszka

CHÉRIE MERCI SUIS BIEN IL NE ME MANQUE RIEN SAUF TES LETTRES QUE JE NE REÇOIS DEPUIS LONGTEMPS COMMENT VAS TU MON PETIT INQUIET TA SANTÉ TRAVAILLE FAMILLES ÉCRIS T'EMBRASSE LE PLUS TENDREMENT MILLE BAISERS = THEMERSON

20 March **Telegram from Franciszka to Stefan**

MON PETIT CHÉRI MERCI POUR TÉLÉGRAMME SUIS TRÈS BIEN TOUT MON COEUR AVEC TOI STOP REÇU LETTRE DE ZIELIŃSKI DATÉE 9 MARS QUE VISA PORTUGUAIS ACCORDÉ ET POLMISSION T'A TÉLÉGRAPHIÉ DE FAIRE DEMANDE CONSULAT STOP PAS NOUVELLES DE FAMILLES LONGTEMPS TENDRES BAISERS = THEMERSON

Letter from Franciszka to Stefan

My dearest darling,

I am seizing a free moment in the office to write at least a few words and send them immediately.

My little one, I received your letter of 8 February and the 'Fugue'. It's beautiful and thank you so much, darling. It is difficult for me to write more in this hubbub. Yesterday I also received a card from Zieliński, saying that the visa has been granted and you must just make an application at the Consulate.

I got in touch with him immediately, telling him that you have made the application already on 12 February (as you informed me in a telegram at the time). I think that he will check if the application was successful and will push things forward. Perhaps he will communicate with you. My dearest darling! I should like just to keep repeating these three words from the top of the page to the bottom. You write about last year's experiences and that it will be warmer soon.

Darling, be good to yourself and sensible. I am so worried about you, Stefulku!

I am in good state of mind, even though there has been no news from family for five months. The period of cynicism and resignation has passed for me. Everything takes so long that our innate instincts of fairness and balance, that we once treated like a leg to stand on, regenerate themselves. *À propos* leg, it's sad to be a leg of Epictetus, even the other one.

Excuse this chaotic letter but I am interrupted at every moment and it's difficult to collect one's thoughts. At last, I had a letter from Mira. Rather shattered but back with Ignacy.

Antoni didn't break with the band of idiots, but rather he replaced one with another.

10 The correspondent could be the Greek poet, Kostas Karyotakis , who comitted suicide that very year, in 1928, after leaving Paris.

I will write about it at greater length, quietly at home.

Bye, darling, I send you so many heartfelt tender kisses. Franka

25 March Letter from Franciszka to Stefan

My dearest darling,

A moment ago I received your letter of 20 March. Thank you, my little one. I escaped from the office and am sitting in a café and am writing so that I can send it immediately. Don't be anxious about me, Stefulku. I am well. Truly! And I smile with my whole heart. My letters are not sad, only I miss you a lot.

Yesterday, again there was a ray of hope. Ernest [Freyd] telephoned me to say that the visa will be there any day now. My pet, can you understand, how my heart jumped?

But I am frightened to be happy. So many times it has seemed so close.

I was terribly glad to receive those few words about your literary projects. Oh! How very much I should like to read them with you. Stefulku!

You ask what I am doing. Recently, I worked little, that means on a small scale – pen and ink on paper. But despite everything time isn't, must not be wasted, even though it is so very sad.

How are you holding up, darling? I am so anxious about your health. Is it warmer there already? Buy yourself a flower from me, treasure.

I kiss you, darling, endlessly with such tenderness. Love, darling. Franka

From our families I've had no news for a few months. Stefan and Genek send you warm hugs. Love Fr

Telegram from Stefan to Franciszka

CHÉRIE REÇU AUCUN TÉLÉGRAMME POLMISSION APRÈS MA DEMANDE VISA TÉLÉGRAPHIÉE PAR CONSULAT LYON À POLINTERNACION LISBONNE 11 FEVRIER NUMERO 161 STOP SUIS TOUJOURS SANS TES LETTRES ÉCRIS MOI MON PETIT CHÉRIE TEMBRASSE TENDREMENT = TEMERSON

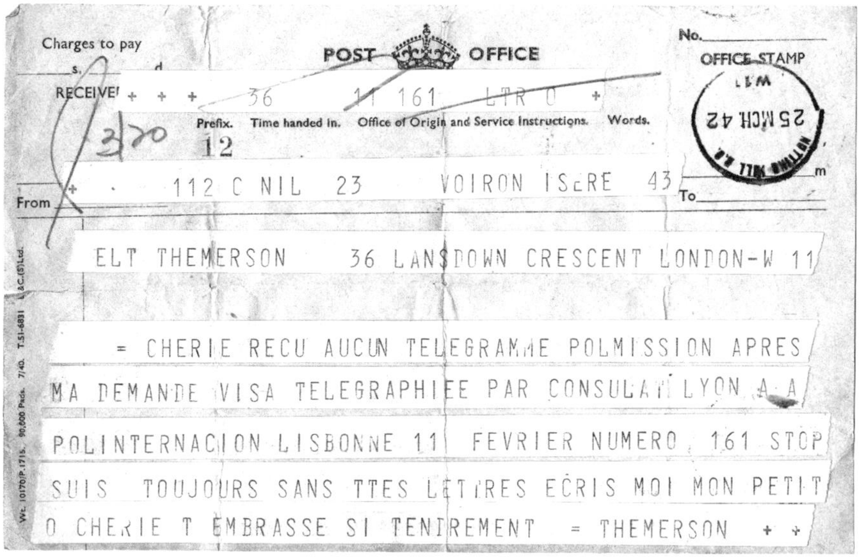

Charges to pay s. d.
POST OFFICE
No.
OFFICE STAMP
25 MCH 42
RECEIVED + + + 36 11 161 LTR 0 +
Prefix. Time handed in. Office of Origin and Service Instructions. Words.
12
3/20
From + . 112 C NIL 23 VOIRON ISERE 43
To
ELT THEMERSON 36 LANSDOWN CRESCENT LONDON-W 11
= CHERIE RECU AUCUN TELEGRAMME POLMISSION APRES
MA DEMANDE VISA TELEGRAPHIEE PAR CONSULAT LYON A A
POLINTERNACION LISBONNE 11 FEVRIER NUMERO 161 STOP
SUIS TOUJOURS SANS TTES LETTRES ECRIS MOI MON PETIT
O CHERIE T EMBRASSE SI TENDREMENT = THEMERSON + +

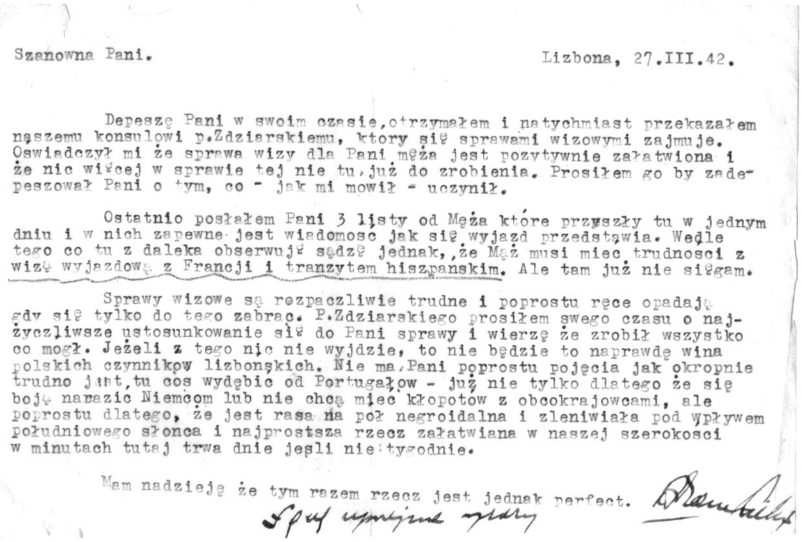

Szanowna Pani. Lizbona, 27.III.42.

Depeszę Pani w swoim czasie, otrzymałem i natychmiast przekazałem naszemu konsulowi p.Zdziarskiemu, ktory się sprawami wizowymi zajmuje. Oswiadczył mi że sprawa wizy dla Pani męża jest pozytywnie załatwiona i że nic więcej w sprawie tej nie tu, już do zrobienia. Prosiłem go by zadepeszował Pani o tym, co - jak mi mowił - uczynił.

Ostatnio posłałem Pani 3 listy od Męża które przyszły tu w jednym dniu i w nich zapewne jest wiadomosc jak się wyjazd przedstawia. Wedle tego co tu z daleka obserwuję sądzę jednak, że Mąż musi miec trudnosci z wizą wyjazdową z Francji i tranzytem hiszpanskim. Ale tam już nie sięgam.

Sprawy wizowe są rozpaczliwie trudne i poprostu ręce opadają gdy się tylko do tego zabrac. P.Zdziarskiego prosiłem swego czasu o najżyczliwsze ustosunkowanie się do Pani sprawy i wierzę że zrobił wszystko co mogł. Jeżeli z tego nic nie wyjdzie, to nie będzie to naprawdę wina polskich czynnikow lizbonskich. Nie ma Pani poprostu pojęcia jak okropnie trudno jest, tu cos wydębic od Portugałow - już nie tylko dlatego że się boją narazic Niemcom lub nie chcą miec kłopotow z obcokrajowcami, ale poprostu dlatego, że jest rasa na poł negroidalna i zleniwiała pod wpływem południowego słonca i najprostsza rzecz załatwiana w naszej szerokosci w minutach tutaj trwa dnie jesli nie tygodnie.

Mam nadzieję że tym razem rzecz jest jednak perfect.

Letter from Adam Zieliński in Lisbon to Franciszka

Dear Mrs Themerson,

I received your telegram some time ago and immediately passed it to our Consul, Zdziarski, who deals with visas. He declared that the matter of visa for your husband has been positively resolved and there is nothing more to be done about it at this end. I asked him to send you a telegram to that effect, and he told me that he had done it.

Recently, I sent you 3 letters from your husband that arrived here during a single day and in them is probably the news of his departure. According to what I observe from this far away, I think that your husband must have difficulties with the exit visa in France and the Spanish transit permit. But that's beyond the reach of what I can do.

Visa problems are desperately difficult and one is simply quite helpless whenever one has to deal with them. Some time ago I asked Zdziarski to be as helpful as he can be in your case, and I believe that he did everything possible. If it doesn't work out, it really will not be the fault of the Polish officials in Lisbon. You simply have no idea how terribly difficult it is to get anything out of the Portuguese – not only because they are frightened of offending the Germans or don't want to have anything to do with foreigners, but simply because they are a half negroid race and made lazy under the southern sun, and the simplest thing to be done that takes minutes at our latitude, here takes days if not weeks.

I hope that this time it will all work out perfectly.

With kindest regards, Adam Zieliński

29 March **Letter from Franciszka to Stefan**

My dearest little one,

Thank you for the letters, darling, it is difficult to express how much they mean to me, but you know that better than anyone.

How difficult it is to be brave enough to stand alone, independently, like you. How difficult it is to peel away the surrounding reality and events – that picture of an inevitable continuum, how difficult to focus careful thought on current events and not let oneself be overcome by those everyday things that muffle the critical faculties. And removing oneself even for a moment to a place far enough away, how difficult simply not to give up and bury one's nose in a pillow. A pity, it's all interesting after all, just so exhausting.

I don't even try to maintain a continuity in my thoughts, and I hold on to continuity of feelings with difficulty – so that one can, with time, decipher the series of my drawn notes. They're only notes – it's difficult to call these isolated expressions anything else; they have the value of reminiscences rather than statements. Not reminiscences of facts, but rather reminiscences of feelings. Facts, anyway, through their massive accumulation are subject to a desperate inflation. Anyway…

When, from time to time, I look at our books and think about our work together, and the strand of more or less conscious ideology that ran through it, I try to make up my mind how this strand should look today. Just that clear line, like a line one would give to a child (I so often feel myself to be a child), unsupported by the eloquence of philosophy, unprotected by the irrevocability of metaphysical feelings – but that has become a conviction. Could we raise a new generation of people? Could one inoculate them early enough? Couldn't one demand of each citizen a certificate of inoculation against smugness, hate and contempt, as one demands an inoculation certificate against smallpox?

And as a result of such upbringing couldn't there come about a community of, so-to-speak, 'benevolent' people? People (like Antoni and others here – this elite, these chosen few) who make idiotic declarations about human rights, based on nothing and leading to nothing, and write sentimental poems about Aleje Ujazdowskie[11] and the feelings of guilt.

All that comes out of this is a springboard for a band of rogues who hungrily devour the chestnuts roasted in their own fire. But if (as they devoutly believe) rogues will disappear, everything will lose its last modicum of sense.

Unfortunately (for them), the metaphysical elaboration of their arguments isn't real enough to overcome the objectivity of the individual. When a decorated armchair is not suitable for sitting on because it is uncomfortable, then neither is it beautiful enough to hang as a work of art on the wall. But we can breathe a sigh of relief, because at least it can be used to smash someone's head.

Unfortunately, it is most likely to smash the head of its creator – the carpenter – and the circle is closed.

Look, darling, I've written nothing but nonsense today. I hope you realise how much heartfelt tenderness I send you between the lines of text? You know. You must know.

Darling, how do you feel? Do you have money and the possibility of feeding yourself reasonably? Do you take some vitamin pills, Ovaltine, Phytin? I am so very anxious about you. Think about yourself, my darling, for me, won't you? I write to you so often, my pet, are you still without my letters?

I kiss you darling, kiss you so tenderly. Love Franka

Write, darling, to Aneczka, Pańska 48/66. It is terribly long since I had letters from anybody. I kiss you, kiss you. Fr.

31 March Darling, a moment ago I received a letter from Zieliński, and at the same time a telegram from our Consulate, that the visa has been granted. Darling!

Yesterday, I received 3 of your letters and the first chapter of *Prof. Mmaa*. It's excellent. Kiss kiss, Franka

11 A long avenue in the centre of Warsaw

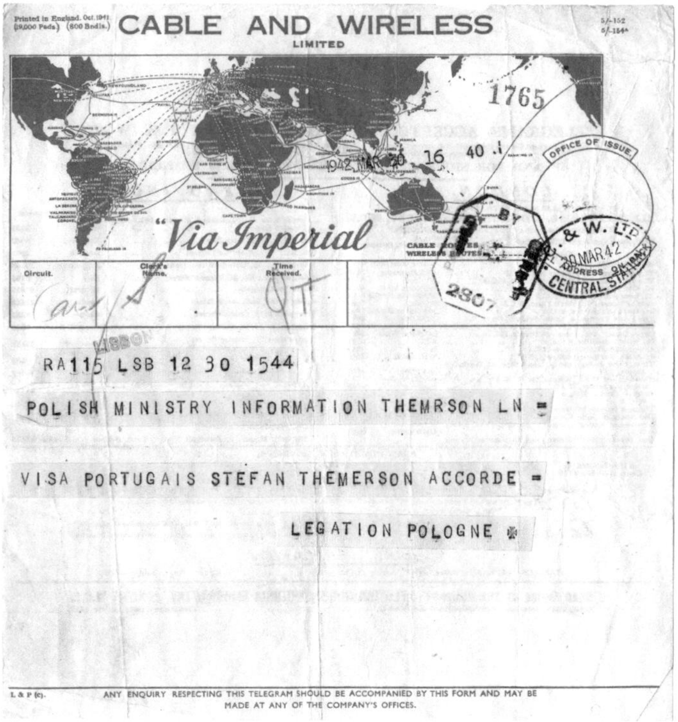
CABLE AND WIRELESS
LIMITED
"Via Imperial"
RA115 LSB 12 30 1544
POLISH MINISTRY INFORMATION THEMRSON LN =
VISA PORTUGAIS STEFAN THEMERSON ACCORDE =
LEGATION POLOGNE
ANY ENQUIRY RESPECTING THIS TELEGRAM SHOULD BE ACCOMPANIED BY THIS FORM AND MAY BE MADE AT ANY OF THE COMPANY'S OFFICES.

Telegram from Polish Legation in Lisbon to Polish Ministry of Information in London
VISA PORTUGAIS STEFAN THEMERSON ACCORDÉ = LEGATION POLOGNE

Letter from Stefan to Franciszka

Darling,

After such a long break, I received at last, one after another, three of your letters – from February and March. Thank you, darling. How are you managing, my little one? Are you painting? And is there anything around to look at, to listen to? Is anything happening around in which one can find support, and a foothold for one's work and an echo? You can't know how starved one's eye and ear can be, and I so much want you to take advantage of everything that's possible for both of us. All around me folds of mountains have settled down like malicious hunchbacks obscuring the world – but I suppose behind these humps changes must be taking place, through which one will have to pass and which one will have to get to know whatever they are like; with facts – and they are all facts – one doesn't argue with facts. It's no use arguing with people because they are either circumscribed by the time or the place in which they lived and live. They are – or we all are – it comes to the same thing. The melancholy barrier between me and the rest of our so-called *confrères* grows higher and higher. To co-exist with them, one has to agree with everything they want, down to the slightest detail. To follow one's own instinct, one has to do so despite them.

It would be so beautiful to be on the desert island of some Robinson Crusoe, where the only obstacles were those that one could conquer with one's own hands; where the only resistance was the resistance of a tree cut down and tied into a raft. Ah, if I'd been on a desert island for these 2 years, I would have cut down trees into a huge ark and sailed away.

I kiss you such a lot my little one. Stefan.

Darling, I am so glad that you find something you like in the 'Fugue' fragments. It is cyclic, or rather cyclotomic, like my life here, and this is why dawn and midday are white and sharp alternating with dusk and the blackness of night in the diurnal cycle. It is because these threads are different and disappear in the counterpoint of the cycle, that all this is called 'Fugue'. You ask about publishing. Of course, I should like to. But is there also a publisher who would want to publish it? And readers who would like to read it? You have to believe in the absolute of what you've done to push it before the public, and I know this is only relative. I've never had a mentor in any Skamander[12], Kwadryga[13], or other avant-gardes. And I think that my poor efforts are not strong enough in themselves either in quantity or quality, to survive in their own flowerpot.

I kiss you so very much, Franeczko, love Stefan

Hugs for Stefan and Genek.

Diary Entry

Nothing

In the same diary at the back:

Légation de la République de Pologne à Berne, Section Consulaire, Elfenstr. 20

2 April Telegram from Franciszka to Stefan

MON PETIT REÇU TÉLÉGRAMME DE LÉGATION POLONAISE QUE VISA PORTUGAIS DÉFINITIVEMENT ACCORDÉ STOP REÇU TES LETTRES TES VERS PROSE T'IMAGINES TU COMME J'EN SUIS HEUREUSE MON PETIT T'AIME T'EMBRASSE = THEMERSON

13 April Letter from Franciszka to Stefan

My dearest darling,

Lately, I've waited continuously, day after day for a letter from you, or a telegram. Already more than two weeks have passed. I waited so anxiously and stubbornly that I too for a whole ten days didn't send a letter. I write all the time, all the time, sometimes only a few words so that they will arrive quicker and more surely.

My pet, at last today I got a letter that is so sad and anxious, little one. I sent a telegram immediately – but how to fit into a telegram all this tenderness and pining. Sweetheart, be strong. Keep yourself strong in that magic seriousness and calm of yours, with your clarity of vision, and independence of judgment. Each few words of yours is for me a new source of strength and a pointer how to maintain the mind and heart in balance together, a friendly and loving hand – extended from so far away and, despite all that, so close.

Look after yourself, darling. Don't demand the impossible of yourself. You are as you are, and that is why you are so wonderful, darling. Allow yourself a bit of that indulgence that you have for the whole world. Little one, I don't have enough words, because words cannot be warm enough, and cannot be as warm as touch and as tender as a look. Well, they can when you write – but I don't know how.

I know that the visa formalities will still continue for some time. But can you organise your life in such a way that it can be at least reasonable and quiet? Buy yourself some beautiful book and a flower from me, darling.

12 Literary group in Poland (1916-39) initiated by Julian Tuwim, Antoni Słonimski and others. The name comes from a mythical river surrounding Troy.

13 The avant-garde literary group (1927-31), around the magazine *Kwadryga* in Warsaw.

I bought myself from you, *Ulysses* by Joyce in the original. I think I shall manage to read it even though it's difficult. Masses of words the meaning of which one must arrive at for oneself. I wonder how much will be gained by reading in its original language. But how much does one risk losing – like looking at a painting in a monochrome reproduction.

Little one, be good to yourself, please. My tender thoughts are with you through every passing moment. I kiss you, darling, endlessly. Franka

From our nearest I haven't had a word since a terribly long time. I am very anxious. I kiss you, little one Fr

Telegram from Franciszka to Stefan

RECU TA LETTRE SUIS TRISTE ET INQUIÈTE DE 19 MARS JE NE COMPRENDS PAS MANQUE LETTRES JE T'ÉCRIS TOUS LES QUELQUES JOURS STEFULKU REÇU TES VERS ET PROSES J'EN SUIS SI HEUREUSE TA PENSÉE SI CLAIRE ME DONNE TANT DE FORCE SOIS AUSSI CLAIR ET TRANQUILLE DANS TON COEUR CHÉRI GARDE TON BON SOURIRE JE TRAVAILLE AUSSI SEULEMENT POUR TOI TIENS TOI ET RAPPELLE-TOI QUE JE PENSE À TOI TOUTES LES MINUTES AVEC TOUTE MA TENDRESSE BAISERS = THEMERSON

Letter from Franciszka to Stefan

My dearest little one,

I sent one letter to you today, and tomorrow I will send this one. I am so worried that you still have no letters from me. I can't imagine why. Pet! I know how difficult it can be without letters, because I always wait so impatiently for yours. But there's nothing to be done about it. Anyway you must know, darling, that every minute is full of thoughts of you and of your distant presence. And whenever, at any time of day or night, you think of me, you always receive a loving response. Oh, how difficult it is to write such strange things. After all, we never said such things to each other. A look and a hug was enough. But when I cannot hug you and look into your wise, darling eyes, stupid powerless words burst like a crowd from my pen. But also I feel how very lucky I am to be able to write these words and to receive yours, which are so very comforting in return. My pet, don't worry about me. You know that I know how to look after myself. I am doing it for you too. When I have sometimes a great desire for some flowers, or a book, or paints, I buy them for myself from you. Darling, and you too spoil yourself a bit in my name. I am so worried about the state of your health. Write how you are.

I feel very well. The work in the office is even quite interesting. I no longer slog away over a drawing board. I have two draftsmen for that. Our room, among all the offices, is almost the only refuge where to find a sense of humour. Unfortunately there's no shortage of subjects in which to feed our humour. I am trying to maintain a borderline between laughter and despair – and every word from you helps me do so. There, I can always practise self control and a sense of detachment. A little of this, very little, I learnt from you, during the time of our wonderful life together. So often now, I think about the things that you would say, and in time I often find the word I need. And your eye is also a yardstick for me in my work – oh, pet, I love you.

I don't paint in oil at all, but I have acquired a special taste for black line and I have learned many things about drawing.

Pet, I hope that you will get this letter. It is so sad for me if you have no news. I sent a telegram to you today. Perhaps, you will be a little less sad tomorrow, when you get it – darling!

I kiss you and kiss you. Franka

Darling, from Maryla and from Irenka not a word for months. Love, Franka

14 April **Letter from Franciszka to Stefan**

My dearest darling, I must write just a few words because a day when I don't write to you, or don't have a letter from you, is not a real day.

Perhaps I will receive tomorrow or the day after an answer to the telegram. I didn't get any reply to the previous one. My darling!

My treasure, be cheerful and try to live in a way that won't make you feel bad. Look after yourself, please do this for me.

I am really in fine form, thanks to you, your letters and to that view of the world which I owe to you. Ah, you simply don't realise how far and how much it helps me. I've been reading a bit recently. From somewhere I got Baudelaire's *Les Fleurs du Mal* and I bought myself *Ulysses*. I feel the need to shut myself away a bit – from conventional life – and to mature. Doesn't this maturing imply old age? No, I don't believe that. I'm too young, sometimes too immature.

I kiss you, darling – but I shall carry on writing later. I've posted one letter already today. Love, Fr.

My pet, already evening. I am going to bed and will read *Ulysses*. Laborious struggle with the dictionary in which there aren't enough words, but it's worthwhile anyway. It is a special sort of pleasure of hunting words in this brushwood.

Darling, what are you reading? It is so sad for me when I read in your letters that you are struggling and that you are worried. Stefciu – be calm and quieten your anxiety, so that you can have a bit of peace and perhaps even some joy. You wrote once that you are so much luckier than so many others there. Yes, darling, I am probably the happiest here, because I have you, even so far away.

I see Stefanja very rarely. I am not really interested in these bits of private gossip and little intrigues. To keep up with our all friends and acquaintances one needs to forfeit a bit of one's precious free time. It's not worth it. Often, I prefer simply to look at the ceiling. Stefan was going to write to you today. He is not in a good state. His face has shrunk to the size of a fist and he is without any sort of foothold. Genek is a dreamer. From Mira I had a letter saying that she and Ignacy are together. Ignacy is silent. Teresa wrote to me from Canada. The usual nonsense.

Goodnight, darling, I kiss you so tenderly. Franka

15 April I received telegram, thank you, darling. Love Fr

Telegram from Stefan to Franciszka

CHÉRIE NE T'INQUIÈTE PAS SOIS GAIE MON PETIT REÇU TES LETTRES TÉLÉGRAMME MERCI STOP J'ATTENDS CONFIRMATION VISA ESPÈRE ARRIVERA BIENTÔT STOP SUIS TRÈS BIEN JE TRAVAILLE PLUS QUE JAMAIS ET NE PENSE QU'A TOI EMBRASSE SI TENDREMENT BAISERS = THEMERSON

18 April 1942

There is the first news that the Warsaw ghetto will be liquidated.

20 April **Letter from Franciszka to Stefan**

My darling,

How are you? This morning I managed to arrange for the visa to be sent to you by telegram. I don't understand why you still don't have it. Oh darling! I am so anxious about you.

It's already more than two weeks that I've had no letter from you. I'm waiting so impatiently again for even a few words. Did you get my letters from a few days ago and the letter from Stefan? Stefanja asked to send you a hug by letter, and so many friends you know, and friends you don't know, ask after you all the time.

Darling, I kiss you so much, so terribly much.

Love Franka

29 April **Telegram from Casimir Zdziarski in Lisbon to Franciszka at Polish Ministry of Information in London**

VISA STEFAN THEMERSON ACCORDÉ PAR POLICE EN PRINCIPE MAIS UTILISABLE SEULEMENT APRÈS DÉPART DU PORTUGAL PREMIER GROUPE STOP ESPÈRE POUVOIR TRANSMETTRE AUTORISATION DANS QUELQUES SEMAINES STOP POUVEZ ÊTRE SURE AFFAIRE SERA REGLÉ = CASIMIR ZDZIARSKI

Letter from Franciszka to Stefan

My dearest darling,

Yesterday I received your letter. From long ago, as far back as 19 March. And sad, even though you write – *'le devoir est d'être joyeux'*. Darling, days and nights are filled with thoughts of you.

Today at last I received an explanation why you still haven't got the visa. It has been granted, but the routine is to send it automatically only when the previous group leaves Lisbon. They hope that this will be in a few weeks.

My pet! I don't know if they will let you know at home. From what I hear, I doubt it. Probably you will have to enquire from time to time at the Consulate, don't you think? I'll try to arrange for our Consulate here to let you know when.

Darling, you ask me to write about myself. Actually, very little has been happening in my life recently. I simply stare at everything around me. And sunny days help me to do nothing. I fill all my free and stolen moments from work walking near the water. I am sharpening my eyesight, language and pencil on these stupidities around me. And I worry that I only see small things. Or, perhaps, I'm just a badly adjusted lorgnette.

I want to write to Maryla and Aneczka today. It is so difficult to write into the almost unknown. Still not a word, no news. At moments I simply have nobody to write to. And what can I write about myself, when I don't know, but feel in my bones, how black is the nightmare in which they will read it.

I help them as much as I can, but I know that during the summer it was really all that they had. But what then – nothingness, empty, not a word.

My dear darling, how I miss your warm tenderness, how I am waiting… can you imagine?

You ask after our friends. Stefan [Konorski] is managing somehow. Like everywhere, here too, he has masses of friends, half of whom are first class and half useless. Did you get a letter from him? He wrote to you recently. Mira and Ignacy 'got together' again and are, it seems, in the big world, according to what Zośka W[ojciechowska] writes. They don't give a sign of life. Teresa [Żarnower] is in Canada, and as always is making photomontages. Stefanja writes psychologically orientated elegies about Piotr-Adam and continues to struggle with menopause. Oh, pet, with great care, I preserve my sense of humour. Without it life would be difficult.

I love you pet, and kiss you with such great tenderness. Franka

5 May **Telegram from Stefan to Franciszka**

CHÉRIE INQUIET TA SANTÉ MON PETIT T'EMBRASSE SI TENDREMENT T'ÉCRIS TRÈS SOUVENT REÇOIS TU MES PROSES T'AIME MON PETIT STOP CONSULAT TOUJOURS SANS CONFIRMATION VISA MAIS J'ATTENDS AVEC PATIENCE CONFIANCE ET BON SOURIRE TANT BAISERS = THEMERSON

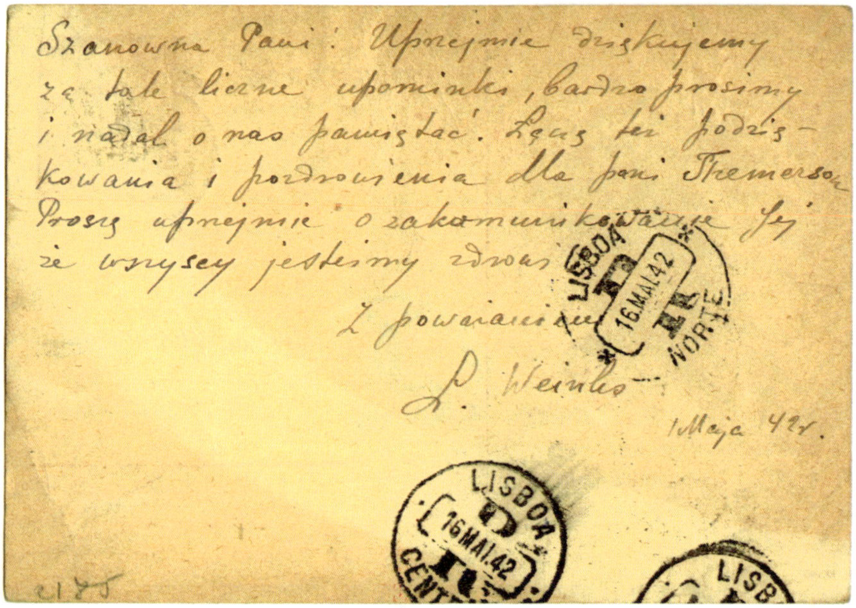

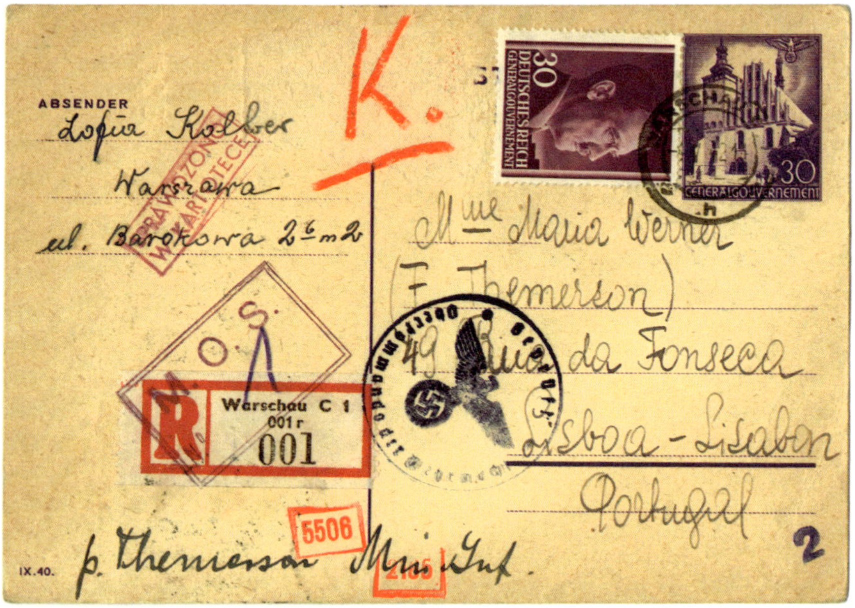

1 May 1942
Card from Sofia Kolber in Warsaw to Maria Werner in Lisbon. The post office would not accept a card from an address in the Warsaw ghetto.

Dear Madam, we thank you kindly for the numerous gifts, and ask you to be good enough to continue to remember us. Please convey my thanks and best wishes for Mrs Themerson and please be kind enough to let her know that we are all in good health. Yours faithfully, L. Weinles, 1 May 1942

The card is written and signed by Franciszka's mother and addressed by Maryla, her sister. Franciszka would recognise the handwriting.

5 May 1942

Letter from Franciszka to Stefan

My dearest darling,

I am just copying some texts to send them to the printers and am sneaking in a letter between two statistical tables. That is why I am typing.

I got your telegram, darling. I am so happy that you are working. I am waiting so hungrily for the following chapters.

A few days ago I learned, and you already know, if you got my previous letter, that the visa, even though it has been formally granted, can only be sent in a few weeks. My darling!

Yesterday I bought myself the singing angels of Della Francesca and pinned them to the wall. They give me a lot of pleasure.

They also showed for a week or two El Greco's *Christ driving the traders from the Temple.*[14] I went twice, and shall go again. Do you remember it?

The other day, Antoni [Słonimski] shouted in passing that he will publish, in the second issue, 'Fragment Poematu' or 'Sonetino'.[15] My pet.

I had a letter yesterday from Ignacy. For the next school year, he accepted a position in a women's college. Funny, don't you think? And he is so relieved that on the form that he had to fill in, they crossed out the blank space under menstruation. Because he already had doubts about himself. He has come to an understanding with Mira and from the autumn they're going to be together again. What a prodigal pair.

You ask about Stefan [Konorski]. I think that he wrote to you recently. He has as usual mornings, afternoons and evenings occupied with a cavalcade of old and new friends that he cares for. And each of his friends, especially the female ones, is convinced that he/she is the only one, and the rest are important business colleagues. And what is most amusing is that, due to his very complicated emotional mechanism, this is how it seems to him too. Funny fellow. Anyway, he is also, in his own way, decidedly unhappy.

Stefanja, as usual, allows herself to be 'kissed on the neck' between grand words, which is increasingly as grotesque from the point of view of the words, as from the point of view of the neck.

I'm frightfully full of mischief today, even though I'm actually in quite a gentle mood. Probably because I am writing in the office and it's difficult to concentrate. And the main function of the brain is simply to 'fertilise' my humorous garden, disposed to stupid jokes.

I kiss you, kiss you, kiss you, my pet, so very, very very much.

Love. Franka

6 May My darling, you see what stupidities I was writing, and how many different creatures crawl around one?

And I miss you so much. And I love you so terribly much, my little one.

Love, love. Franka

Telegram from Franciszka to Stefan

CHÉRI SUIS PARFAITEMENT BIEN SOIS GAI MON PETIT BIEN AIMÉ JE T'ENVOIE TANT D'AMOUR LE PLUS TENDRE CHÉRI BAISERS = THEMERSON

14 This is in the National Gallery. During World War II the paintings in the National Gallery were stored in a Welsh slate mine; however, a different painting was brought back and exhibited every month among contemporary art in the entrance hall.

15 Antoni Słonimski is the editor of *Nowa Polska* and that's where he plans to publish Stefan's poems.

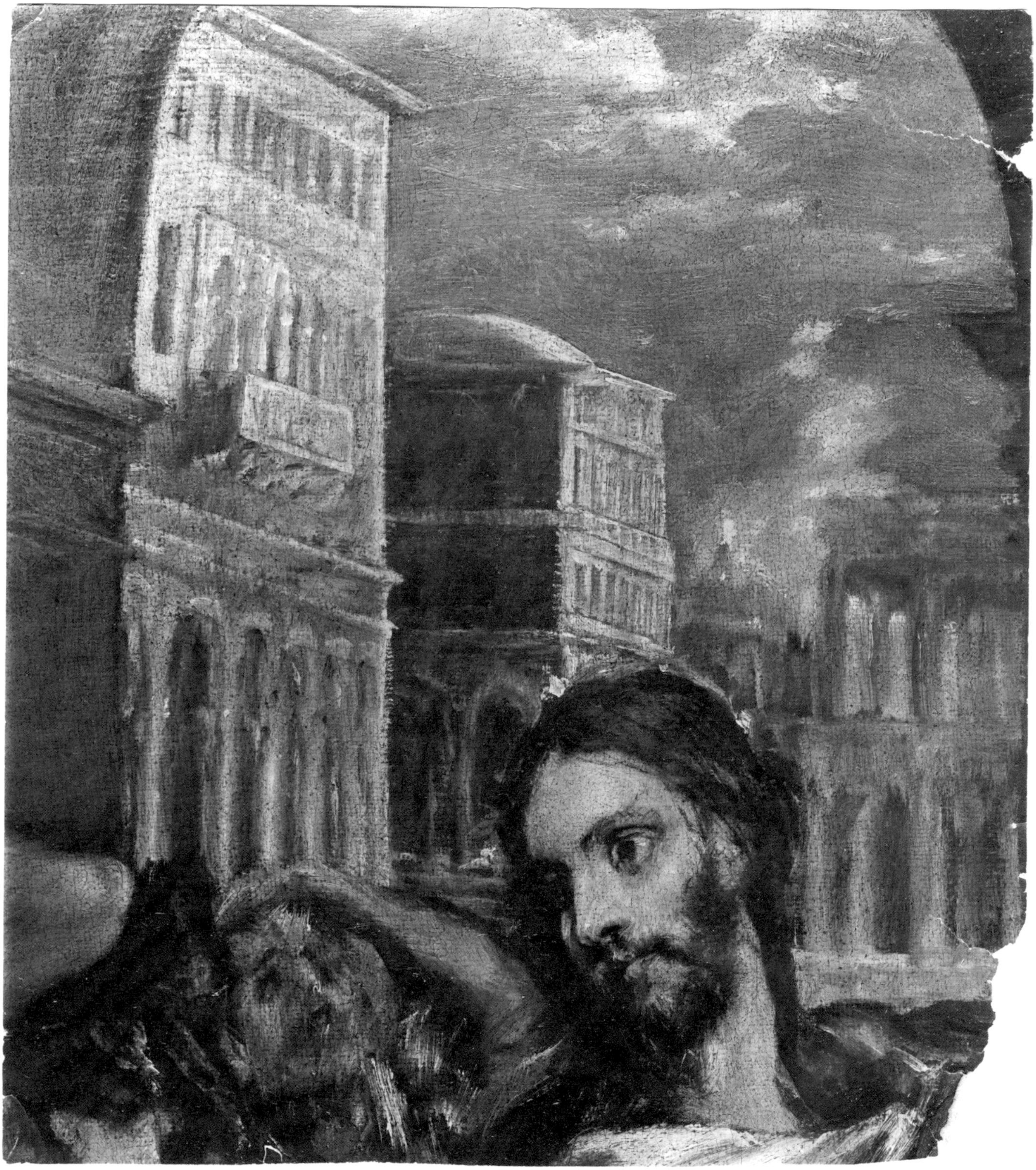

El Greco, *Christ driving the traders from the Temple*, (detail) c.1600

8 May 1942

Letter from Franciszka to Stefan

My dearest darling,

A big kiss. I received 3 chapters of prose, and they're very interesting. In places, absolutely fascinating. I shall write more about it. Now only a few words in a hurry, to send immediately.

My dearest little one! And so the whole day, in my thoughts, I am with you. I keep on wandering by the river somewhere and try to focus on something sensible. But it is very difficult for me. I wait so much to be together with you!

With everything that's around, it is so difficult to surround oneself with quiet thought, and not to fall into superficiality, exaggeration, lies. Sometimes it is almost impossible not to shut oneself away in a purely negative, uncreative place. But we shall find our own positive path, in due course.

My pet! Visa is supposed to be sent to you when the previous group leaves Lisbon. I think that you already know about it.

I hope that you won't have any more problems. How I should like to protect you from them. From our nearest ones still not a word. I am very worried. You didn't have anything either?

My little one, I send you so much tender love, darling.

Kiss, kiss Franka

Just this second they brought me a letter from you. You ask, *à propos* poems, if there are people that would want to read them. O God! Have you any idea how greedily people listen to them, those to whom I read them sometimes, and how many new friends, unknown to you, you have here? You don't know at all how wonderful you are. And among those hunchbacked mountains all around, you see more and do more than it is possible in this crowd and hubbub.

I kiss you. F.

Don't think, my littlest one that here are 'people', here are also only facts. Every person becomes a fact – just by existing, and functions in the simplest meaning of that word.

I adore you, my little one. Fr

11 May **Letter from Stefan to Franciszka**

My dearest darling,

I've had so little news from you recently. Two letters from the whole of April and that is all. You ask if I received a letter from Stefan [Konorski]. No, not a word. How are you, darling? It is so difficult to imagine here how you live. Is your work in the office very oppressive? Do you have a bit of time for yourself? Are you painting, drawing? Can you imagine with what an anxious cry I ask about the latter? Darling, my eyes long for everything that you do and I am terrified at the thought that they are stealing your time there, which belongs to painting, art, the only things that really exist!

I kiss you, darling, so much!

Are you receiving my *Prof. Mmaa's Lecture*? I write so often, two or three times a week. I should so like to know how you like it.

Love, Franeczko, I send you so many heartfelt kisses! My dearest little one!

Stefan

11 May 1942

Darling, a moment ago I received your letter from 13 April. Thank you! Thank you, Franeczko. It will soon be two years. I am so happy that you are well and that you draw. Kiss, kiss, darling. Stefan

12 May **Letter from Franciszka to Stefan**

My darling,

It is almost two years, pet! By the time you receive this letter, it will certainly be more than two years. My darling, thank you for every day of these two years, even though we have been so far from each other. But you gave me so much in your letters, and every moment of tender thought about you is so dear to me. Darling!

I was promised that they will send you this Portuguese visa in a few weeks. I asked Ziel[iński] to send you a telegram about it. And I quake at the thought that some formalities will still drag on. My sweetheart.

Listen, I have received already three whole chapters of this 'termite' saga. I like it tremendously. And I am terribly tempted to illustrate it. I only have to find a bit of time, go to the library, or a museum and find some encyclopædic material about termites. Wouldn't it be fun! Such half-encyclopædic drawings combined with human expressions and situations. The same combination as in the text – with an emphasis on playfulness where necessary, and elsewhere, where necessary, pathos. A little bit of journalistic humour, right? Do you remember that orator I drew in different poses? Such a synthesis transposed to termites could be terribly funny. You must write and tell me what you think about it. It will be a very amusing book. And it will be amusing to lead the reader by the hand according to the expression of the drawing. Sometimes to push him through the more difficult passages, sometimes to stop him at the most delicious ones. Write to me about that, won't you?

My darling, are you looking after yourself? It would be so much easier for me to bear this separation if I knew that someone there took care of you, that you have some friendly people around. Have you been receiving my letters more frequently recently? I write all the time. You probably had a letter from Stefan. Hugs from Genek. He was going to write to you, but he is overcome with sleepiness! And overworked at the same time. He had a letter from Lipiński from practically the other end of the world.[16] Szołowski died of typhus at Bolek's.[17] Others dispersed somewhere. About Aleksander [Ford] not a word. Staś Wohl works in film.

Mira's cousin, Zandel[18] is in Rio. Ignacy and Mira finally got together. Have you had a letter from him? He is again at his university. I don't know what is happening with our family. Still, not a word. Already about eight months.

My little one, I send you so much tender affection on this scrap of paper. Can you imagine? I kiss and kiss and kiss you, my darling. Franka

22 May **Letter from Franciszka to Stefan**

My darling,

I have already received four chapters of that saga. I await further ones. Do you know by any chance, where one can find encyclopædic drawings of a termite? I am terribly tempted to make such funny drawings. But I have no idea what the creature looks like. But I think that it should be very realistic, don't you agree? Write and tell me what you think about that. Pet, how I should like to talk to you already! They are terribly funny, some of our human characteristics when they are

16 Lipiński is in Persia.
17 Bolek is in Moscow.
18 Adam Zandel was also involved in exploring possibilities of obtaining a visa for Stefan to enable him to leave France.

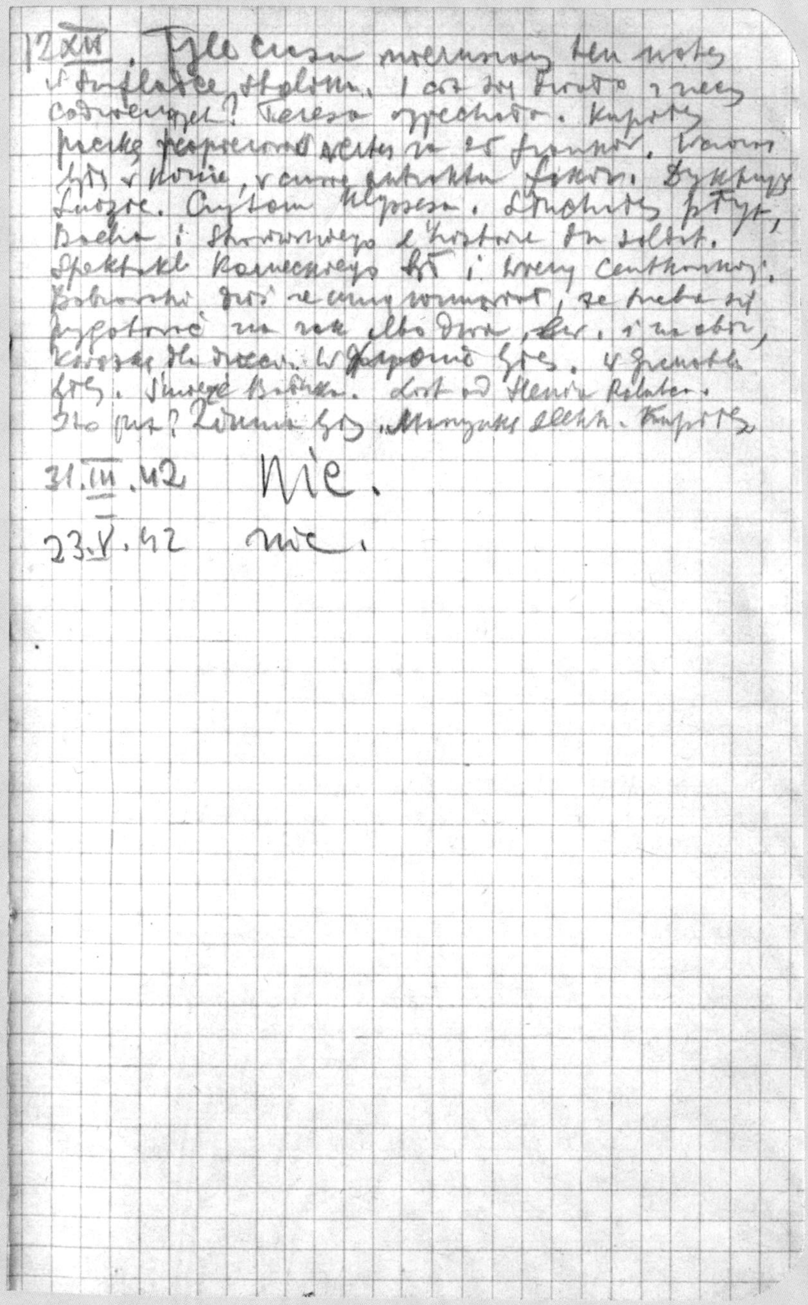

Stefan's diary, 12 December 1941, 31 March 1942, 23 May 1942

seen from a totally unexpected angle. I should like to be able to portray in the drawing the parallel of the termite and the human strangeness.

Oh, darling! So much love is contained in that exclamation mark. But anyway, you already know this, don't you?

I think that soon they should be sending you the visa. The previous group must leave Portugal. Anyway, it is only about 20 people altogether. Some of them have already gone, but it seems a few ladies still haven't deigned even to arrive in Lisbon. I think that somehow, in the end... They are supposed to send you a telegram when they grant the visa.

With me everything is just the same, but what does it mean actually 'the same'? I am waiting and pining, darling. I haven't been working very much recently. It's spring, warm and fragrant. One doesn't feel like doing anything.

My pet, I send you such tender, heartfelt kisses. Franka

23 May **Diary Entry**

Nothing

Letter from Stefan to Franciszka

My dearest darling,

It's Sunday today, so an empty day because there will be no post. I haven't had a letter from you for a long time, but I wait every day. From Stefan [Konorski], also not a word, despite the fact that you mentioned that he wrote to me.

I write three, sometimes four times a week, letters and fragments of my book. I know that you received the first chapter. But I sent you already six chapters and I still don't know if they arrived or how you like them. I have just finished the ninth, and am beginning the tenth, the last one of the first part.

Darling, I am so happy that your work in the office is easier and that you don't have to spoil your eyes working at the drawing-board. And, that you have time for drawing your own lines!

Darling, I kiss you, Franeczko, my dearest little one. Love Stefan

25 May Darling, today I received your letter from 5 May. Thank you, Franek. Love

What sort of work do you actually have in the office? Is it very boring and tiresome? I would so much like to know all about it. You don't know how happy I am about the singing angels of Della Francesca (the same that we saw at the National Gallery?)[19], and how I should like already to see yours, those you are drawing.

I am already writing the tenth chapter. And I worry because I assume that you haven't received any apart from the first one. Since I started work on *Professor Mmaa's Lecture* I haven't written any poems at all.

Hugs for all friends. It is nearly two years, Franeczko.

I send you so many warm kisses, my darling. Love Stefan

26 May **Telegram from Franciszka to Stefan**

MON PETIT ÇA FAIT DÉJÀ DEUX ANNÉES DEPUIS NOTRE DERNIER AU REVOIR QUE DE TENDRESSE QUE J'AI ACCUMULÉE POUR TOI MON PETIT BIEN AIMÉ SOIS GAI ET TIENS TOI ESPÉRONS CHÉRI REÇU NOUVELLES LISBONNE VISA PORTUGAIS SERA TRANSMIS AVEC PROCHAIN GROUPE BAISERS LES PLUS TENDRE = THEMERSON

19 Piero della Francesca, *The Nativity*, National Gallery, London. The Themersons saw it on their visit to London in 1936. This image was later used in the Themersons' film *The Eye & the Ear*. See overleaf.

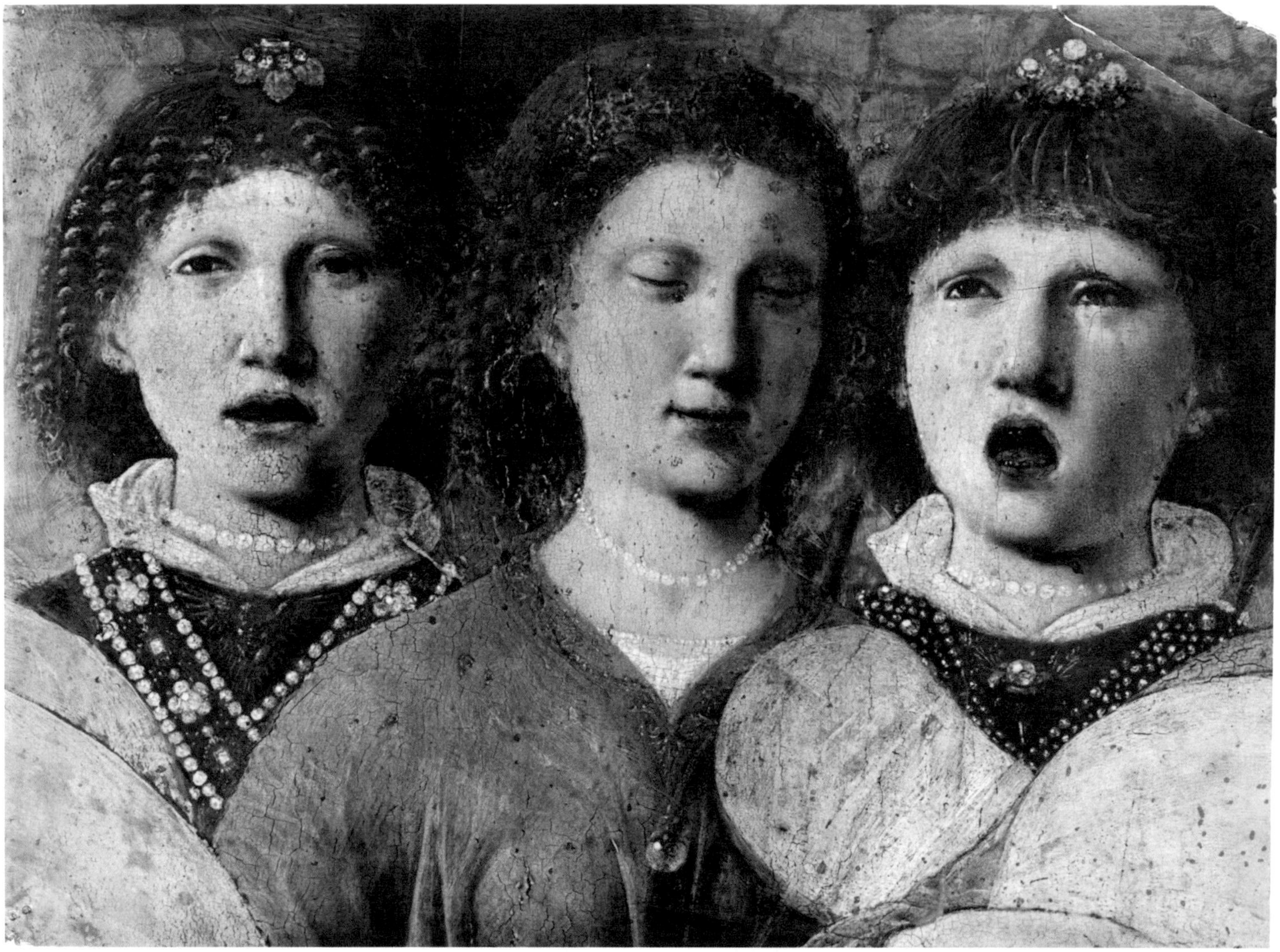

Piero Della Francesca, *Nativity*
(detail) 1470-1475

Letter from Franciszka to Stefan

My one and only darling,

How vividly the evening of two years ago hovers before my eyes. Sweetheart!

La Sainte-Chapelle reflected in the mirror, and pink clouds, and you so close.[20] So much time, so many days, so many hours.

Thank you thank you darling for all these wonderful letters. I know of course how very hard it must have been at times, but your letters were always so sunny, mild and wise. I have lived through them after all, and still do. And the poems… My sweetheart!

One day I'll be able to embrace you, darling!

I should like to write you so many things, everything that I feel. To send you that contraction of the heart and the smile directed to you from within these empty walls. But I lack the words. That's all.

Strange anniversary rituals buried deep in my brain call back for me so many things of long ago.

I should so much like to sit down with you, just like long ago, on that dusty little sofa at Anka's. What children we were then, Stefciu, happy children.

What about Aneczka, what about them all? It is so long since I had any word. I wrote just a few days ago to a former maid of the Chaykins. Perhaps that letter will get through and I'll get an answer. I don't have a word back in response to letters I send directly, nor to parcels, endless parcels.

Genek sometimes gets letters from Janka, but not often. He had a card from Lipiński, from somewhere in Persia, or some other distant part of the world. Karol Szołowski died from typhus at Bolek's. About the Fords and the Haltrechts, nothing. Staś [Wohl] is working. Wanda Jakubowska – no news, perhaps she stayed at home. Oh darling, I was looking at *Strachy*[21] one day, with that sentimental caption: [SAF] *Spółdzielnia Autorów Fimowych*[22]. I wept like an idiot. Anyway, they were all enormously moved. Grub, drink, or the abortion of the heroine? Was it really like that? And you know, I saw you. Do you remember that you were once at the filming and you had a walk-on part. My little one! Such a darling face with a pipe suddenly appeared. But let's not get sentimental. One still needs a lot of strength. Be strong treasure and know that I am always gay and happy when I think about you, however sad I might be.

I kiss you darling, kiss you so very much. Franka

Darling, even when you have the visa, there'll be other formalities to go through to get to Mira, or to somewhere else – advise Marceljanek or Zieleński by telegram, to let her know, so that she can try to organise it. Because, as we know, it's bound to be difficult.

Darling, perhaps you will get this letter for our wedding anniversary. Just think, eleven years. My sweetheart, once more I send masses and masses of extra love for that day. I kiss you Franka

28 May Darling, a moment ago I got the beginning of Chapter V, *Prof Mmaa*. It's wonderful – kisses, love, Fr

20 Franciszka refers to the reflection in their flat in Arcueil in Paris.

21 Film screenplay by Karol Szołowski, directed by Szołowski and Eugeniusz Cękalski made in Poland in 1938.

22 Spółdzielnia Autorów Filmowych (SAF), the Co-operative of Art Film Authors.

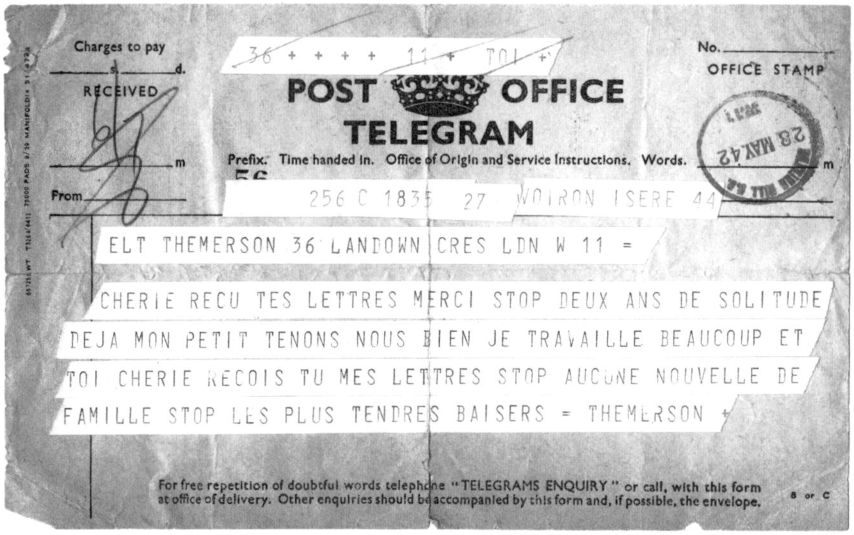
Charges to pay
RECEIVED
From
POST OFFICE TELEGRAM
Prefix. Time handed in. Office of Origin and Service Instructions. Words.
No.
OFFICE STAMP
28 MAY 42
256 C 1835 27 VOIRON ISERE 44
ELT THEMERSON 36 LANDOWN CRES LDN W 11 =
CHERIE RECU TES LETTRES MERCI STOP DEUX ANS DE SOLITUDE
DEJA MON PETIT TENONS NOUS BIEN JE TRAVAILLE BEAUCOUP ET
TOI CHERIE RECOIS TU MES LETTRES STOP AUCUNE NOUVELLE DE
FAMILLE STOP LES PLUS TENDRES BAISERS = THEMERSON +
For free repetition of doubtful words telephone "TELEGRAMS ENQUIRY" or call, with this form at office of delivery. Other enquiries should be accompanied by this form and, if possible, the envelope.

Telegram from Stefan to Franciszka

CHÉRIE REÇU TES LETTRES MERCI STOP DEUX ANS DE SOLITUDE DÉJÀ MON PETIT TENONS NOUS BIEN JE TRAVAILLE BEAUCOUP ET TOI CHÉRIE REÇOIS TU MES LETTRES STOP AUCUNE NOUVELLE DE FAMILLE STOP LES PLUS TENDRES BAISERS = THEMERSON

30 May **Letter from Stefan to Franciszka**

My darling, I am writing just a few words so that you can get them faster. I thought that on the 22nd[23] we would be together but I see that certainly it won't be possible.

Darling, buy yourself flowers and a present from me, please do. And for your birthday too.

And be cheerful, my little one, I will do the same, I promise.

Hugs for all the friends who will be together with you.

I kiss you, Franek, so very much. Love, darling – Stefan

2 June **Letter from Franciszka to Stefan**

My dearest sweetheart,

I feel so well, warm and happy when I sit down to write a letter to you, pet!

I don't actually sit down, because I am lying on a settee with a flowery cretonne cover, I hang my legs over the armrest of an armchair – it's hot and such a light azure blue evening looks in through the window. I would so much like to paint something for you and send it to you. But recently I haven't been drawing – it's not possible to send, anyway – and I should want to draw something so beautiful for you, but there's no way I can do that. Your poems are lying near me. I am always reading them when I feel like talking to you. I read the 'Fugue' probably for the hundredth time, and I have got to know so clearly how you spend the day. It's as if you were describing it to me in the minutest daily details. My pet!

I still haven't found a decent drawing of a termite, but on Thursday is Corpus Christi and I have a holiday from the office and the libraries are open so I shall look. I can't wait to start this work. I kiss you my darling.

I am trying to read a bit, sensibly, to develop my mind a bit and to achieve at the same time some sort of a spiritual discipline, so as not to depend on passing

23 The Themersons' wedding anniversary

fashions and feelings. I am reading Joyce and some old things that I found here – including Diderot. I try to keep with tested values, however difficult it is, even if it's only with the tip of my finger. There's such a lovely poem addressed to painters by Norwid[23], so I am sending it to you. It is called 'My psalm'.

Innumerable Marys (of these there are never enough!).
Fair Magdalens with luxuriant hair.
Circumspect Sophies and brilliant Theresas
And during days and nights I ask incessantly
That the world would finish with business once and for all...

This is my prayer – and errand,
for humankind to enter that space
which logically belonged to it since time immemorial
where there is no business of any sort
and where one doesn't do anything practical

And for this I ask these saints who wear
a comb made of light rays, and with a tear in the eye
and with Veronica of the Cloth
are carried on purple clouds...

Isn't it lovely? When suddenly something like this appears, it generates a feeling of pleasure and 'self confidence'. Because there's something that reaches across space and time that cannot be crossed in any other way.

Oh darling, I don't know why I was moved so much by this little thing. And I am sending it to you just as I would wish to send you all my feelings of love. And perhaps you will like it too?

I have come to a dead end with my drawing. All that I've done here so far was a quite personal, perhaps self-analytical (anyway uncontrolled and unthinking) autobiography. I should like to get out of this sphere, it doesn't really satisfy me – but that's not so easy. I have a positive 'need of a philosophy' and can't forgive myself for the enormity of the wind passing through my head.

My darling little one! You know, I got a few days ago a card from Maryla, Mother and Jasia! At last! From the end of April. Although it wasn't even written directly to me – just confirmation of receipt of a food parcel, addressed to the firm that sends them. I feel so relieved, darling. This is the first word since September! Is there nothing from Hania at all? I wrote recently to Aneczka. Perhaps she will reply this time. My darling, how are you? Oh dear, how I should like to see your little darling face!

I kiss you, Stefciu, so terribly much. Franka

Hugs from Stefan and Genek. Stefan is the same as always but not in good form. Genek gets thoroughly drunk from time to time. Oh, what a world!

Love Franka

24 Cyprian Kamil Norwid (1821–1883)
Polish Romantic poet

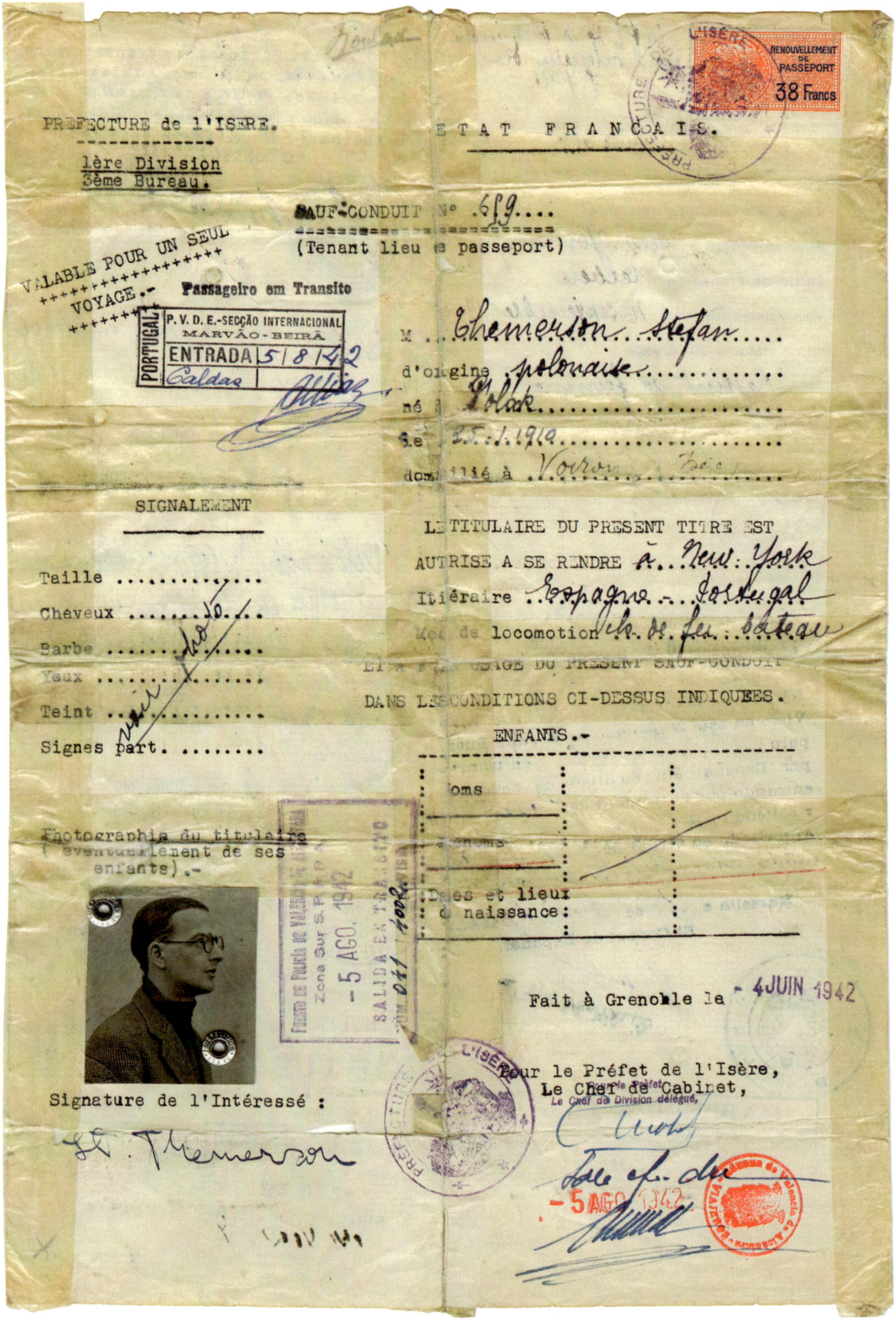

L'ISÈRE
RENOUVELLEMENT DE PASSEPORT
38 Francs

PREFECTURE de l'ISERE.

1ère Division
3ème Bureau.

ETAT FRANCAIS.

SAUF-CONDUIT N° 659....
(Tenant lieu de passeport)

VALABLE POUR UN SEUL VOYAGE.-

Passageiro em Transito
PORTUGAL
P. V. D. E.-SECÇÃO INTERNACIONAL
MARVÃO - BEIRÃ
ENTRADA 5/8/42
Caldas

M. Themerson Stefan....
d'origine polonaise............
né à Polak....................
le 25.1.1910..................
domicilié à Voiron Isère......

SIGNALEMENT

Taille ....
Cheveux ....
Barbe ....
Yeux ....
Teint ....
Signes part. ....

LE TITULAIRE DU PRESENT TITRE EST AUTRISE A SE RENDRE à New York
Itiéraire Espagne - Portugal
Mode de locomotion ch. de fer. bateau
ET A FAIRE USAGE DU PRESENT SAUF-CONDUIT DANS LES CONDITIONS CI-DESSUS INDIQUEES.

ENFANTS.-

Noms
Prénoms
Dates et lieux de naissance

Photographie du titulaire (éventuellement de ses enfants).-

Puesto de Policía de Valencia de Alcántara
Zona Sur S. P. P.
- 5 AGO. 1942
SALIDA EN TRANSITO

Fait à Grenoble le - 4JUIN 1942

Pour le Préfet de l'Isère,
Le Chef de Cabinet,
Pour le Préfet
Le Chef de Division délégué,

Signature de l'Intéressé :
St. Themerson

- 5 AGO 1942

4 June 1942
Stefan's sauf-conduit

issued in Grenoble, 4 June 1942,
valid for one journey before
5 August

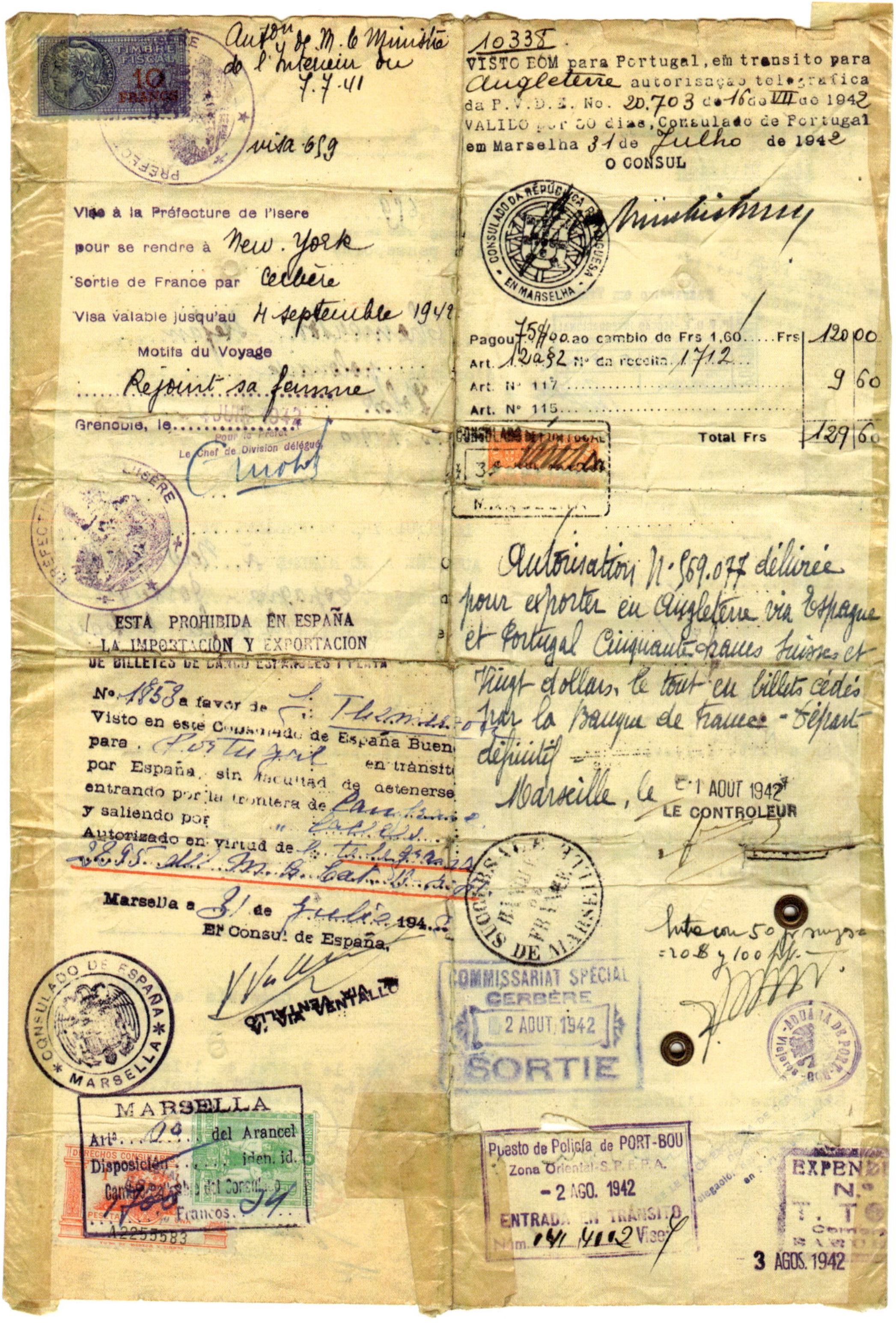

Timbre fiscal 10 francs

Autorisé de M. le Ministre de l'Intérieur du 7.7.41

visa 659

Visa à la Préfecture de l'Isère

pour se rendre à New York

Sortie de France par Cerbère

Visa valable jusqu'au 4 septembre 1942

Motifs du Voyage

Rejoint sa femme

Grenoble, le ....

Le Chef de Division délégué

Préfecture de l'Isère

ESTÁ PROHIBIDA EN ESPAÑA LA IMPORTACIÓN Y EXPORTACIÓN DE BILLETES DE BANCO ESPAÑOLES Y PLATA

No. 1858 a favor de

Visto en este Consulado de España Bueno para Portugal en tránsito por España, sin facultad de detenerse entrando por la frontera de Canfranc y saliendo por ...

Autorizado en virtud de

Marsella a 31 de julio 1942

El Consul de España

Consulado de España Marsella

V. VIA VENTALLO

MARSELLA

Artº 9º del Arancel

Disposición ... iden. id.

Cambio ... del Consulado

Francos ... 34

A2255583

10335

VISTO BOM para Portugal, em trânsito para Angleterre autorisação telegráfica da P.V.D.E. No. 20.703 de 16 de VII de 1942 VALIDO por 30 dias, Consulado de Portugal em Marselha 31 de Julho de 1942

O CONSUL

Consulado da República Portuguesa em Marselha

Pagou 75$00 ao cambio de Frs 1,60 ..... Frs	120 00
Art. 12 a 32 Nº da receita 1712	
Art. Nº 117	9 60
Art. Nº 115	
Total Frs	129 60

Autorisation N° 589.077 délivrée pour exporter en Angleterre via Espagne et Portugal Cinquante francs Suisses et Vingt dollars, le tout en billets cédés par la Banque de France - Départ définitif

Marseille, le 1 AOUT 1942

LE CONTROLEUR

Succursale de Marseille Banque de France

COMMISSARIAT SPÉCIAL CERBÈRE 2 AOUT 1942 SORTIE

Puesto de Policía de PORT-BOU Zona Oriental - S.P.F.P.A. - 2 AGO. 1942 ENTRADA EN TRÁNSITO

Aduana de Port-Bou

EXPEND... Nº

3 AGOS. 1942

5 June 1942

Letter from Kazimierz Zdziarski in Lisbon to Franciszka

Dear Mrs Themerson

This is to confirm the receipt of your letter of 15 May, received only two days ago, and I hasten to advise you that your husband is on a group list filed by me at the Police Station on 27 May, and for which I received basic agreement on 30 May. The question of the Portuguese visa is therefore completely settled and one has to assume that any time your husband will find himself here. As far as the French exit visa is concerned, I suppose that he could extend it. I don't have concrete information about that.

At any rate we haven't had any signs of alarm from your husband lately, so I rather believe that everything is alright.

Best regards, Kazimierz Zdziarski

7 June **Letter from Stefan to Franciszka**

My darling, I have just received your letter of 12 May. Thank you Franeczko. Do not worry about me at all, darling. I can't really complain to you or to myself either. On the contrary, I only need to think about the fate of others! But there are others still, close to me here, who on the face of it appear to be doing better. They have access to libraries, which they don't use, and eat butter, for which they don't need ration cards. But as Prof. Mmaa says 'for a decent termite it could be better to lose a volume from his library and to lose digested thorns of trichonymphae campanilae, than to lose one's self-respect'.

À propos Prof. Mmaa! Darling, you have read my thoughts so well. I should so much like you to illustrate this book of mine. I wanted to write to you about it so many times, but I feared that it would distract you from your own plans and projects and I know, and it makes me weep, that you are working in an office and don't have enough time for yourself and for your own work which should always come before everything else. Do you remember that Memento Magnitudinis, which you gave me for the journey and which got left somewhere in someone else's hands? I often wondered about it many times, and wondered if the person who found it saw something more in it, something more of that 'magnitudo' than the silhouettes of Parisian girls that you drew next to it.

My poems are smaller than me. My old prose, like 'The Bridge of St Louis' is also smaller than me. 'Prose poems', even smaller, because I grasp those pieces as if from outside. They shape themselves like something fully fledged, and I model it from the outside. I always know more than I am able to convey.

It is different with prose such as *Professor Mmaa's Lecture*. In that I start from the idea that I am smaller than what I am creating. I work on this prose, as if from the inside. I don't surround it, but am myself surrounded by its characters, events, situations. And I don't at all want to coerce the reader to accept my way of looking at things, because the material I'm presenting must conform not with me but with reality. And if it will be in accord with reality then it must be understandable from everywhere to which 'The Most Profound or The Most Shallow Being' has scattered the genus homo. I should like it to be a book like those books that are topical for their contemporaries – even journalistic, and which eventually become 'books for children'.

Recently, I bought myself *Gulliver's Travels*. It's a good thing I didn't do so earlier (or perhaps bad?) because Swift's perfection could have intimidated me and I'm not sure that I wouldn't have given up *Prof. Mmaa*. I don't mean the familiar travels to the Lilliputians and the giants [Brobdingnag], but the last one, *Voyage to the Country of the Horses* [Houyhnhnms]. I didn't know it at all, didn't even know it existed. It is simple and marvellous. I am sure that you would want to illustrate that. And this is why I regret that it was not me who wrote it. On the other hand, Swift's *Voyage to the Country of the Houyhnhnms* is now a book for children, and I don't know if *Prof. Mmaa* ever will be. *Pickwick Papers* is also now a book for children. And so are the figure of Don Quixote and some pages from Rabelais, but *Alice in Wonderland* may one day be a book for adults. I think that Shaw and Chesterton, whole volumes of Anatole France and Diderot's *Jacques le Fataliste* will be for children one day.

Darling, it may seem funny that I mention all these great works in connection with my *Prof. Mmaa*, but there's no conceit in that at all. I feel something liberating about all these ideas, and it is a way of thinking that is dear to me.

Darling, you have grasped just the right approach to these fantastic termites. Formal, encyclopædic correctness with a human expression. Playfulness never without a grain of pathos, and pathos never without a modicum of humour. Journalistic joke in 'scientific truth' – and 'scientific truth' in a loaded review sketch. Genuine, sincere lyricism in common vulgarity and a thorn of eternal absurdity in the most simple lyricism.

Darling, I've already sent you seven chapters. Did you get them all? I should love to see your drawings! They are inseparable, I am sure of it, from the written character of Prof. Mmaa, Nonobody and others, just as the drawings in Dickens are inseparable from Pickwick, Sam Weller and all the rest. And not only figures, characters, but also the environment, the atmosphere, the situations – and, what is most important, is that approach which, while being serious is not blind to the comic, and while laughing does not lose sight of the serious.

Darling, how wonderful it would be if we could still work together, even though so far from one another, like we used to.

Write to me, darling, more about all of that. I need letters from you so much.

I haven't written any poems for so long, not since I started *Prof. Mmaa*. Old age? Żuławski is said to have claimed, that he felt himself a poet most when he was writing *On the Silver Globe*[25].

Darling, the fragments I am sending you are not, of course, the final version. I am completely without resources here, a library and so on, and almost everything depends on memory. Perhaps, for the time being, this is better, because it makes it easier to catch the puppet quality of the subjects.

Franeczko, I've had no news from home. For so long now. Nor have I heard from either Ignacy or Stefan. Hug everyone from me, Genek and Stefan and Stefanja and all those whom I don't know but whom you like.

I kiss you, Franek, so very tenderly, my dearest little one,

Love, Stefan

Letter from Stefan to Franciszka

... I am sending you the end of the 8th chapter. You ask me what a termite looks like. I myself don't know. I haven't got a library here or anything. My only reference is a small Larousse and a pseudo-scientific fantasy of Maeterlinck. He has a bibliography at the end but it is not familiar to me. Once I had a good look at an ordinary ant and that's all. I am so glad that you want to illustrate this book. But do you really like it?

25 First part of a utopian trilogy by Jerzy Żuławski (1874–1915)

Letter from Franciszka to Stefan

My darling, I am writing in a hurry so as to send this immediately. Thank you, Stefciu, I've already received six whole chapters of this termite saga and I like it tremendously.

They've made their own assumptions about life so real that it's almost difficult not to believe. Clearly some tragedy is brewing, which in the parallel human world is called everyday life and social conditions. My pet, I must do illustrations for it, but I haven't yet grasped a suitable form. What do you think about it, darling?

I had a card from Mother dated 1 May. She writes that they are all in good health. I feel great relief though I can imagine how they suffer.

Pet, I don't know if you will get this letter still in Voiron. Yesterday I had a card from Zdziarski (our Consul in Lisbon) that you are on a list that was finally confirmed on 30 May.

Oh, darling! Have you got it yet and are the other formalities completed?

I have to finish, darling, so I only kiss you, kiss you so very much. Franka

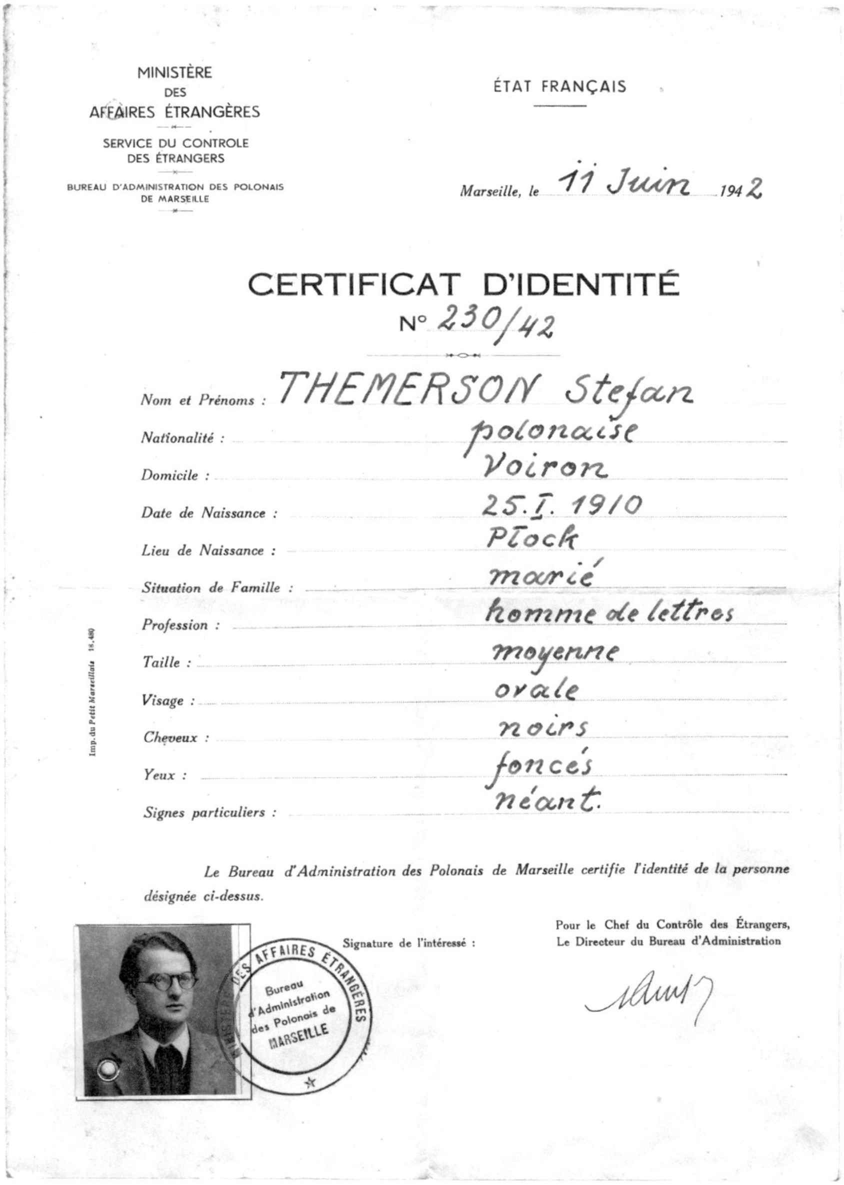

MINISTÈRE DES AFFAIRES ÉTRANGÈRES
SERVICE DU CONTROLE DES ÉTRANGERS
BUREAU D'ADMINISTRATION DES POLONAIS DE MARSEILLE

ÉTAT FRANÇAIS

Marseille, le 11 Juin 1942

CERTIFICAT D'IDENTITÉ
N° 230/42

Nom et Prénoms : THEMERSON Stefan
Nationalité : polonaise
Domicile : Voiron
Date de Naissance : 25.I. 1910
Lieu de Naissance : Płock
Situation de Famille : marié
Profession : homme de lettres
Taille : moyenne
Visage : ovale
Cheveux : noirs
Yeux : foncés
Signes particuliers : néant.

Le Bureau d'Administration des Polonais de Marseille certifie l'identité de la personne désignée ci-dessus.

Signature de l'intéressé :

Pour le Chef du Contrôle des Étrangers,
Le Directeur du Bureau d'Administration

AFFAIRES ÉTRANGÈRES Bureau d'Administration des Polonais de MARSEILLE

11 June 1942
Stefan's Certificat D'Identité

Marseille, from Ministère des Affaires Etrangères, Bureau d'Administration des Polonais de Marseille

14 June 1942 **Letter from Stefan to Franciszka**

Darling, I received your letter of 2 June. Very sad. Be strong, darling. Even if you live among all those lies, there is something much worse, I assure you, enormous by ordinary human pettiness. The ivory tower may have disintegrated, but only that tower of illusions – and one should not be sorry to have seen the truth, even though the truth appears mean and worthless.

Recently I received a letter from Seghers of *Poésie 41* about whom I wrote to you. Here is one sentence from his letter: *'Je vous envoie tous mes voeux de bon courage: le poète porte en lui des biens irréductibles, et c'est par ces biens que nous vivrons'.*

Look after yourself, Franek, I will write more tomorrow.

I kiss you so very much. Stefan

17 June **Letter from Stefan to Franciszka**

My darling,

I am writing all the time to you and you will probably receive several letters at once because I'd like it if at least one of them would arrive on the 28th[26]. I'm sending you, darling Franeczko, the very warmest birthday wishes. Not so long ago I thought that this time we would certainly be together. We still, still have to wait. And what I now most want is for you to arrange your life as well as possible during that time. Oh, those words, which can never convey the thought as well as an embrace or a look.

Darling, I so want your life to be good and joyful, I would cry if I didn't believe that you can live through all this with humour, it would really pain me to think of you being sad. Franeczko, still one day we'll shout *à nous la vie*, and we'll go down our own road together, away from it all, away from this world that's too-clever-by-half.

Smile, darling, and kiss kiss.

I have so much patience and hope.

I kiss you, my little sun – Stefan

18 June **Letter from Stefan to Franciszka**

My darling,

I would so much like it if you could receive this letter on the 28th. This is already the second time that we won't be together, darling.

How do you live, Franeczko? So little, I know so very little about you. And I wish so much that all would go well for you. Darling, I kiss you as much as it's possible to kiss.

Birthday wishes, my darling, and I wish you – my arms fall down with helplessness – everything you really want.

I wanted to write to Genek to buy you a flower, but I have neither his address nor Stefan's.

Darling, I kiss you and hug you so very much. And chin up and let your little face smile, my sweetest little one. I believe in you so much, and that you are strong and are not sad, not even a bit. Once more love – darling. Stefan

20 June **Telegram from Franciszka to Stefan**

MON PETIT REÇU TES LETTRES ET TOUTE PROSE MERCI J'EN SUIS SI HEUREUSE CHÉRI JE T'ENVOIE TOUTE MA TENDRESSE ET TANT DE BAISERS POUR NOTRE ANNIVERSAIRE FAMILLE BONNE SANTÉ EMBRASSE CHÉRI MILLIERS DE FOIS = THEMERSON

26 Franciszka's birthday

Letter from Stefan to Franciszka

My dearest darling,

I am sending you the final part of the 9th chapter of my book about my extraordinary termites. This is all that I have to send today. In the plan there are still two chapters to complete the first part. And the second part – quite different.

It is so difficult to write it without you. Letters travel a long time, and often don't arrive. One way or another I have to finish it. This is the only thing of any significance that I have done here. Apart from that, I wait. I wait. But I'm not counting the hours, days or years of this waiting – and this is the only dishonesty that I have practised on myself, not to count the passing of time.

Darling, I kiss you so very passionately!

You wrote to me about a holiday. How did you spend it, darling? Now, again work in the office inevitably takes up all of your time and I daren't even ask if you are painting. I feel so helpless. It's so difficult for me to elbow my way in… I still don't know how to, even though I would like to.

Love Franek. Masses of the most tender hearfelt kisses. Stefan

Hugs for Genek and Stefan (I wrote to him) and Stefanja. What is happening with Antoni? Best wishes to all.

21 June **Telegram from Stefan to Franciszka**

MON PETIT CHÉRIE T'ENVOIE TANT MEILLEURES TENDRESSES POUR NOTRE ANNIVERSAIRE MERCI POUR TOUT CHÉRIE SOIT GAIE HEUREUSE ET GARDE TON SOURIRE T'EMBRASSE DE TOUT MON COEUR T'AIME = THEMERSON

Letter from Franciszka to Stefan

My dearest little one

Thank you. I have just received your telegram and you probably already have mine. Do you know, I sent it exactly at the same time as you sent yours, my love! I send you such warm and tender kisses!

I have already received the beginning of the 8th chapter. It makes me so happy. And I recognise in it exactly your 'fairy tale for adults' quality. I had made that sort of association myself so clearly, even before you wrote to me about it. When action begins in this strange termitary world, it is funny how similar it is to our world – as when suddenly words are dropped into our human situations like 'little antennae', 'first left, second right, second left, third right', or things of this sort. When so often, during what sounds to us like poetic speech, the word 'thorax' jumps in or something else that jolts one back to one's senses – the whole situation becomes so like glossolalia of a Chaplin song emphasising gesture, pathos or nonsense, that any associations which had inhibited us disappear, and we laugh – suddenly becoming aware of so much more.

I am sorry that I still haven't managed to get enough materials to do the drawings.

Encyclopædic drawings are not adequate. I must definitely go to the library in the Museum of Natural History, and just now I don't have time during opening hours. I have masses of work in the office, and it's as if one job joins onto the next. This is because I'm involved in printing and drawing and proof-reading, and other related jobs. Anyway the result of all this gloom will be one modest statistical atlas. But apart from the concept, the whole job fills my head. It is not really tiring, because at least it is concrete work and not these ghastly discussions about nothing that go on throughout the endless chain of office units.

Apart from that all my free moments are spent trying to put together some ideas about these termites for illustrations. And for this, one needs a lot of time: to hit the nail on the head, to fit the drawings sensitively with the text – just as we always used to do. How I miss you my darling.

Goodnight, my sweetheart, I'll add more tomorrow before I send it. Love, love Fr.

22 June My little one, I put your telegram on the bedside table and woke up this morning in a 'holiday' mood. My darling, you are so close to me all the time at every moment, that sometimes it is difficult even to write letters, because I feel so much that you are next to me.

Probably at the beginning of July, I will take a week's holiday to get some fresh air into my head by the sea, and the second week that is due to me I will keep until you are here, dear pet. I kiss, kiss, kiss you littlest one. Franka

27 June **Telegram from Stefan in Marseille to Franciszka**

CHÉRIE T'ENVOIE MES SOUHAITS LES PLUS TENDRES POUR TON ANNVERSAIRE SOIS GAIE T'EMBRASSE DE TOUT MON COEUR TRAVAILLES TU POUR TOI STOP MERCI POUR NOUVELLES SUR FAMILLE CORDIALITÉS POUR NOS AMIS = THEMERSON

30 June **Letter from Franciszka to Stefan**

My darling,

Thank you. I received your birthday telegram. Darling! It was sent from Marseille. Have you got the visa already? I am so anxious and I wait so impatiently for you, dear pet. You'll probably have to run around to different visa offices again. All day I was feeling as if I were next to you. And I don't even know where and what to do now.

I received yesterday a few more pages of *Prof. Mmaa*. I like it enormously. The conversation with Nonobody after the march in the auditorium. This saga is already so long and I like it so very much. All the characters have developed such clearly delineated personalities. My ideas for illustrations are still weak, mainly because I still can't get the right books. But I've already caught the tone – and there will be a lot of pathos, the sort of defenceless pathos that has a lyrical spirit, like the figure of Mmaa himself. But humour just like that in the text must emerge of itself – funny, then it's a bit too real or a bit too sad.

Darling, I have a week's holiday from this Saturday, and I plan to go away, but I am waiting all the time, perhaps there will be another telegram from you. If I go, I will leave here a letter for you. Altogether I have a feeling that you might just arrive after all! Darling!

I don't know if you will get this letter, but I'm writing just in case you return to Voiron so that there would be some letters waiting for you there. I know how sad that is. And I want you to be cheerful and well. And I can't send you what I would like to – these drawings that I am doing for you – just as you were sending me what you were writing. You must know how much it means to me.
It's difficult for me to write, darling, I simply miss you too much.

I send you tenderest kisses, Stefciu. Love. Franka

1 July 1942

Letter from Franciszka to Stefan

My darling,

I sent you a letter today, but I'm writing again. How are you, darling? And where are you now? Will they find you in Voiron, these last letters of mine that so much wanted to express tenderness and longing? I am retyping that wonderful history of the termites, and it's very enjoyable. This balanced and penetrating view, with its analysis of the danger of sentimentality is like looking at the rather strange beings around me, and gives me a sense of peace; resignation too, and through that a lot of hope. It gives me perspective like that made possible by the clasp of a loving hand and the smile of dearest eyes. Darling!

Meanwhile, good night, it's so late already. Tomorrow I'll write some more.

3 July Stefulku, I am waiting all the time for a new telegram from you. The day after tomorrow I am going away for a week. By the sea – to get away from this work here. Genek is also going. We shall probably be talking, as usual, about Czeczota[26], Natalka with red hair, and Spółdzielnia Autorów Fimowych [SAF]. It's hard even to think about how good it was then, isn't it, my pet?

Naturally, I am leaving the landlady my address, so that she can send me your telegrams immediately. I wanted to wait, but that's too difficult for me since I've organised all the work in the office to enable me to get away for a week. My little one, all the time I am with you in all my thoughts. But perhaps tomorrow I'll have a telegram or a letter.

I love you, Stefciu and I feel it so intensely all the time.

I got for Maryla two pairs of shoes and a pullover and sweets for Janka [Jasia], and I am very happy about that.

Darling, I kiss you, kiss you so much and so tenderly. Franka

13 July **Telegram to Stefan from Legation Pologne in Lisbon**

AUTORISATION VISA TRANSMISE MARSEILLE STOP PRIÈRE S'ADRESSER BUREAU ADMINISTRATION POLONAIS MARSEILLE = LÉGATION POLOGNE

14 July **Telegram from Szumlakowski in Madrid to Stefan in Voiron**

VISA ACCORDÉ CONSULAT ESPAGNOL LYON NOTE MINISTÈRE 176 JUILLET 17 = SZUMLAKOWSKI

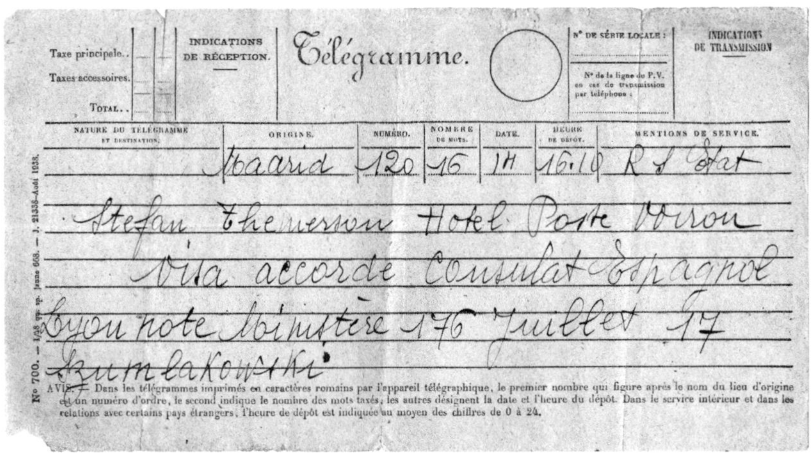
Télégramme.

Madrid 120 16 14 16.10

Stefan Themerson Hotel Poste Voiron

Visa accorde Consulat Espagnol

Lyon note Ministere 176 Juillet 17

Szumlakowski

27 Themersons' home before the war where their film magazine *f.a.* [art film] was produced.

14 July 1942

Telegram from Franciszka to Stefan

CHÉRI MERCI SUIS PARFAITEMENT BIEN STOP JE DEMANDE MÊME TEMPS NOUVELLES ZIELIŃSKI STOP T'AIME MON PETIT EMBRASSE = THEMERSON

20 July

Deportations begin from Śliska Street in the Warsaw ghetto. That is the street where Franciszka's mother, sister and niece had lived since 1940. By then only Maryla, Franciszka's sister and Sewek, her husband, remained, temporarily working in the German workshops. The others had left for Otwock some weeks before.

27 July **Telegram from Franciszka to Stefan**

MON PETIT REÇU NOUVELLES FAMILLE IRKA, STEFAN, MAMAN, ZOFIÓWKA BONNE SANTÉ COMMENT VAS TU CHÉRI EMBRASSE SI TENDREMENT BAISERS MON BIEN AIMÉ = THEMERSON

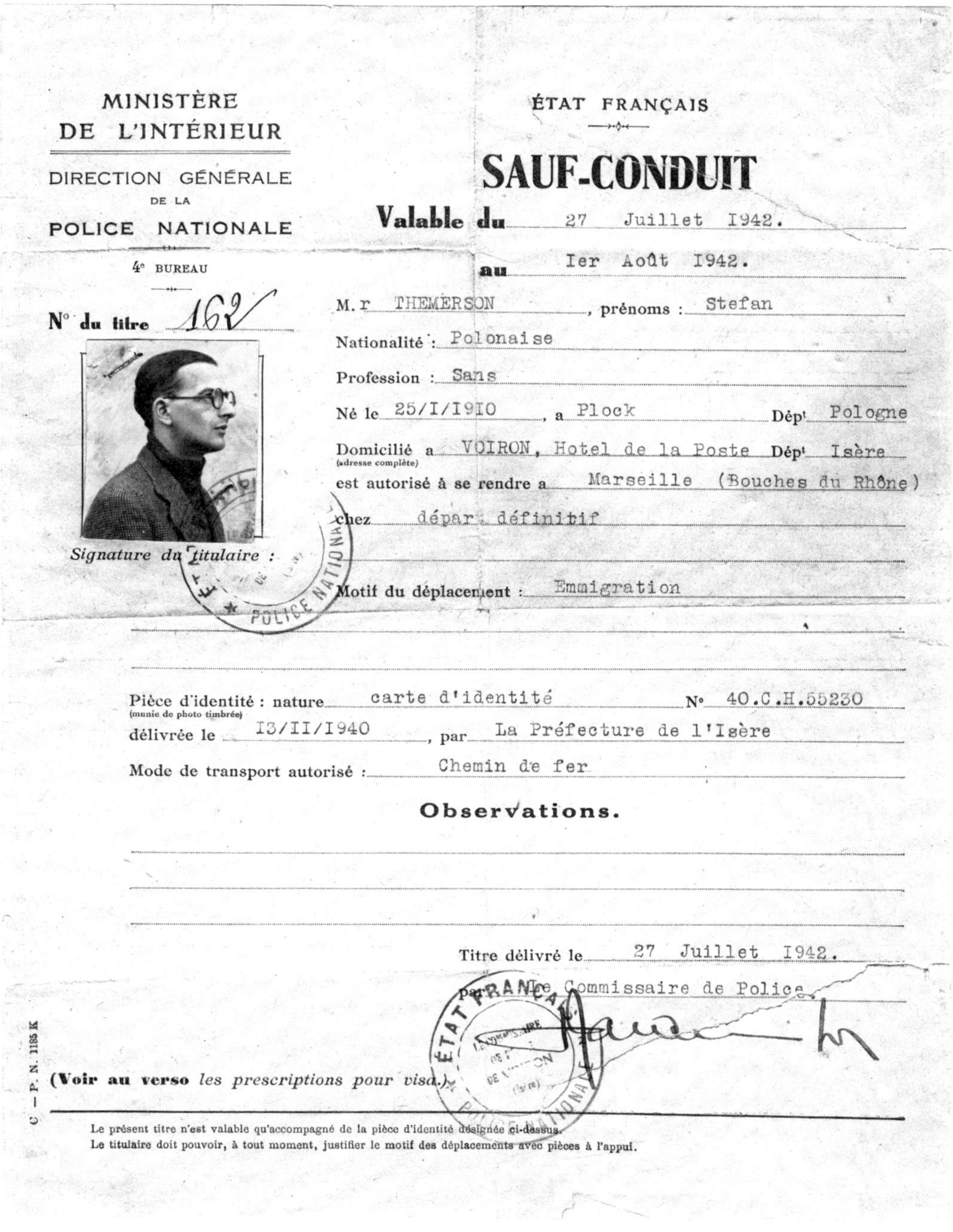

MINISTÈRE DE L'INTÉRIEUR

DIRECTION GÉNÉRALE DE LA POLICE NATIONALE

4e BUREAU

ÉTAT FRANÇAIS

SAUF-CONDUIT

N° du titre 162

Valable du 27 Juillet 1942.

au Ier Août 1942.

M. r THEMERSON, prénoms : Stefan

Nationalité : Polonaise

Profession : Sans

Né le 25/I/1910, a Plock Dépt Pologne

Domicilié a VOIRON, Hotel de la Poste Dépt Isère (adresse complète)

est autorisé à se rendre a Marseille (Bouches du Rhône)

chez départ définitif

Signature du titulaire :

Motif du déplacement : Emmigration

Pièce d'identité : nature carte d'identité N° 40.C.H.55230 (munie de photo timbrée)

délivrée le 13/II/1940, par La Préfecture de l'Isère

Mode de transport autorisé : Chemin de fer

Observations.

Titre délivré le 27 Juillet 1942.

par Le Commissaire de Police

(Voir au verso *les prescriptions pour visa.*)

C – P. N. 1185 K

Le présent titre n'est valable qu'accompagné de la pièce d'identité désignée ci-dessus.
Le titulaire doit pouvoir, à tout moment, justifier le motif des déplacements avec pièces à l'appui.

27 July 1942
Sauf-conduit from Ministère de l'Interieur, Direction Générale de la Police Nationale, no.162

Cable from Adam Zieliński in Lisbon to Franciszka Themerson in London

YOUR CABLE RECEIVED WITH DELAY STOP LEGATION POSSESSES DECLARATION PORTUGUESE AUTHORITIES THAT VISA FOR HUSBAND GRANTED STOP HUSBAND INFORMED STOP ALL DEPENDS ONLY HOW HE SETTLES AFFAIR IN MARSEILLE STOP CAN DO NOTHING MORE = ADAM ZIELIŃSKI

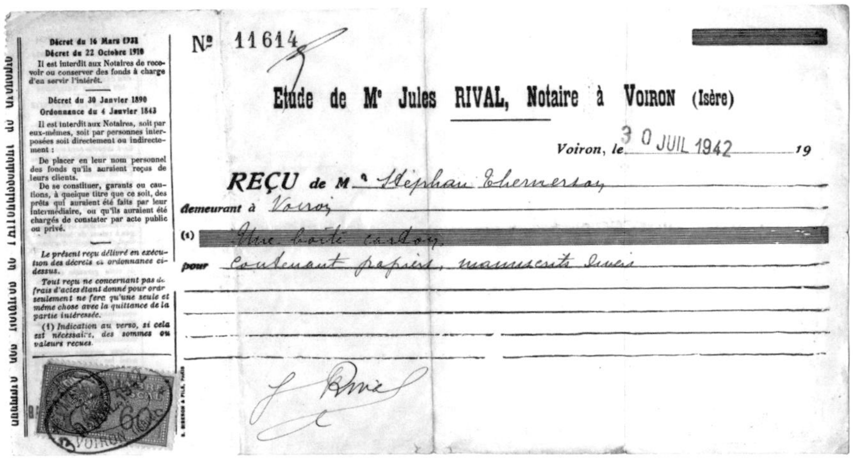

Décret du 16 Mars 193[illegible]
Décret du 22 Octobre 1910
Il est interdit aux Notaires de recevoir ou conserver des fonds à charge d'en servir l'intérêt.

Décret du 30 Janvier 1890
Ordonnance du 4 Janvier 1843
Il est interdit aux Notaires, soit par eux-mêmes, soit par personnes interposées soit directement ou indirectement :
De placer en leur nom personnel des fonds qu'ils auraient reçus de leurs clients.
De se constituer, garants ou cautions, à quelque titre que ce soit, des prêts qui auraient été faits par leur intermédiaire, ou qu'ils auraient été chargés de constater par acte public ou privé.

Le présent reçu délivré en exécution des décrets et ordonnance ci-dessus.
Tout reçu ne concernant pas de frais d'actes étant donné pour ordre seulement ne fera qu'une seule et même chose avec la quittance de la partie intéressée.
(1) Indication au verso, si cela est nécessaire, des sommes ou valeurs reçues.

N° 11614

Etude de Me Jules RIVAL, Notaire à Voiron (Isère)

Voiron, le 30 JUIL 1942

REÇU de M. Stéphan Themerson
demeurant à Voiron
(1) Une boîte carton
pour contenant papiers, manuscrits, livres

30 July 1942
Receipt No.11614 from Etude de Maître Jules Rival, Notaire à Voiron (Isère)

Reçu de M. Stéphan Themerson
Une boîte carton contenant papiers, manuscrits, livres

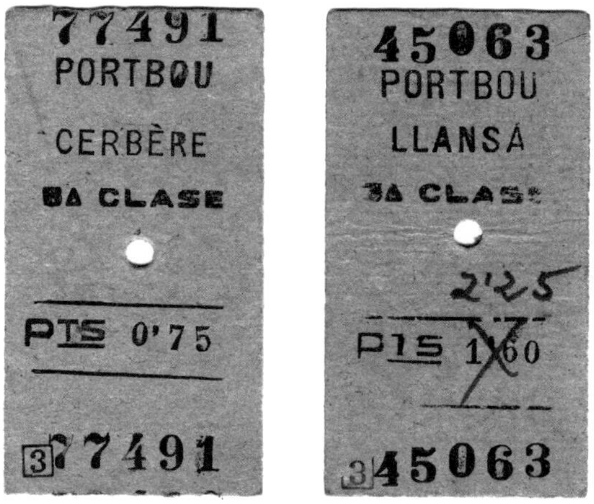

77491
PORTBOU
CERBÈRE
3A CLASE
PTS 0'75
3 77491

45063
PORTBOU
LLANSA
3A CLASE
2'25
PTS 1'60
3 45063

2-5 August 1942
Two railway tickets

2 August, Cerbère to Llansa, 5 August, Llansa onwards to Beira, Portugal

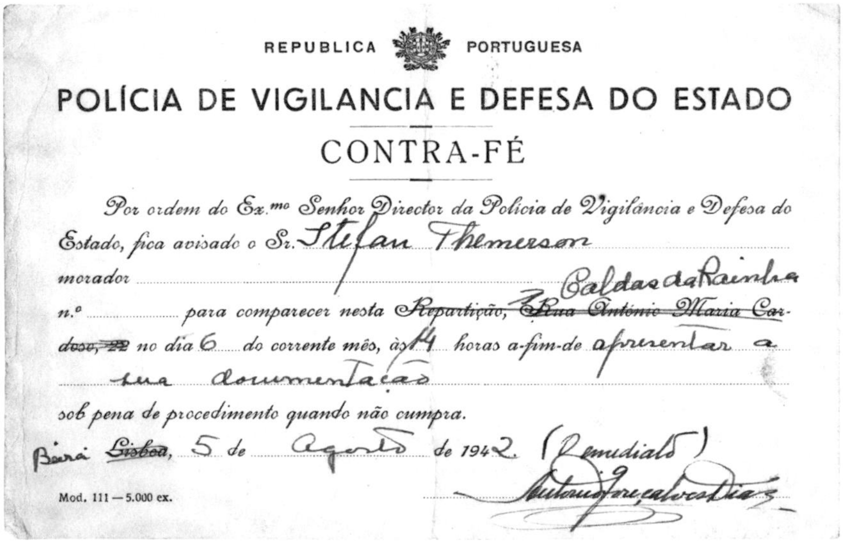

REPUBLICA PORTUGUESA

POLÍCIA DE VIGILANCIA E DEFESA DO ESTADO

CONTRA-FÉ

Por ordem do Ex.mo Senhor Director da Polícia de Vigilância e Defesa do Estado, fica avisado o Sr. Stefan Themerson
morador Caldas da Rainha
n.º ... para comparecer nesta ~~Repartição, Rua António Maria Cardoso, 22~~ *no dia* 6 *do corrente mês, às* 14 *horas a-fim-de* apresentar a sua documentação
sob pena de procedimento quando não cumpra.

Beira ~~Lisboa~~, 5 de Agosto de 1942 (Remediato)

Mod. 111 — 5.000 ex.

5 August 1942
Republica Portuguesa
Polícia de Vigilancia e Defesa do Estado

To complete official procedure Stefan is requested to present himself with his documents at 2pm on 6 August at the office at Caldas da Rainha

5 August 1942
Cable from Stefan in Lisbon to Franciszka in London
BIEN ARRIVÉ MILLE BAISERS = STEFAN THEMERSON

7 August Telegram from Franciszka to Stefan in Lisbon
CHÉRI SI HEUREUSE JE T'ATTENDS LETTRE SUIT MILLE TENDRESSES = THEMERSON

8 August Cable from Stefan in Lisbon to Franciszka
CHÉRIE MERCI ESPÈRE PARTIR FIN SEMAINE PROCHAINE T'EMBRASSE TOUT MON COEUR = THEMERSON PENSÃO VICTOR CORDON 19

9 August Telegram from Franciszka to Stefan in Lisbon
CHÉRI T'AIME T'ATTENDS AMIS EMBRASSENT MILLE TENDRESSES FRANKA THEMERSON

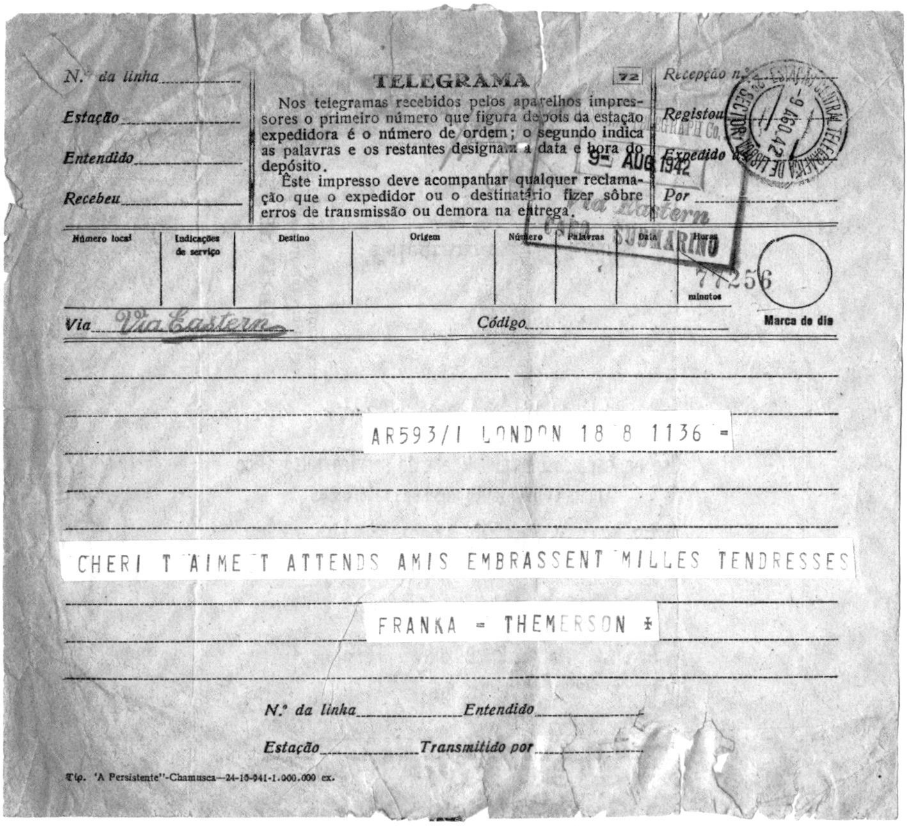
TELEGRAMA

N.º da linha
Estação
Entendido
Recebeu

Nos telegramas recebidos pelos aparelhos impressores o primeiro número que figura depois da estação expedidora é o número de ordem; o segundo indica as palavras e os restantes designam a data e hora do depósito.
Êste impresso deve acompanhar qualquer reclamação que o expedidor ou o destinatário fizer sôbre erros de transmissão ou demora na entrega.

Recepção n.º
Registou
Expedido
Por

9 AUG 1942
Via Eastern
Cabo Submarino

Número local	Indicações de serviço	Destino	Origem	Número	Palavras	Data	Horas minutos

Via Via Eastern
Código
Marca de dia

AR593/1 LONDON 18 8 1136 =

CHERI T AIME T ATTENDS AMIS EMBRASSENT MILLES TENDRESSES

FRANKA = THEMERSON +

N.º da linha Entendido
Estação Transmitido por

Tip. 'A Persistente'-Chamusca-24-10-941-1.000.000 ex.

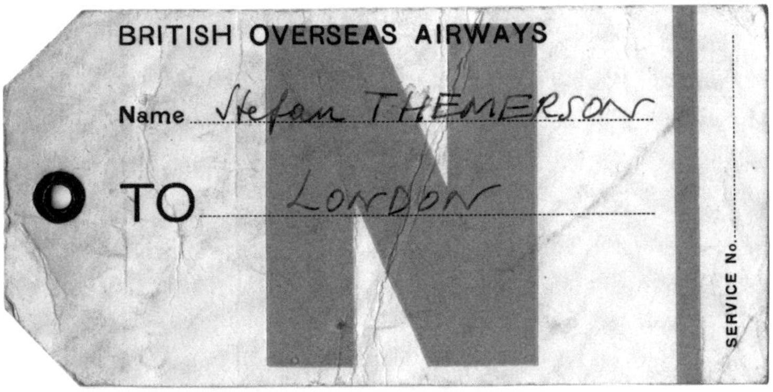

16 August 1942
British Overseas Airways luggage label

16 August 1942
Stefan arrives in England and soon after is sent to Scotland to rejoin the Polish Forces.

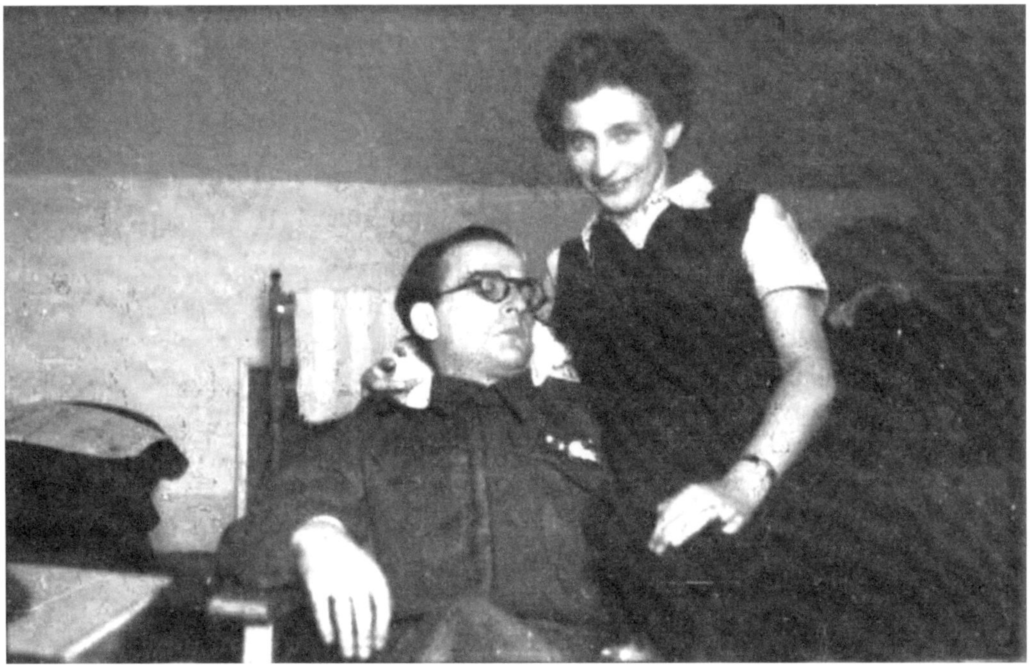

19 August
On 19 August 1942 begins the liquidation of the Otwock ghetto, which encompasses Zofiówka, the Psychiatric Hospital, where Stefan's and Franciszka's mothers are staying. Before that date, both of them, with other relatives, commit suicide. The two doctors, Stefan Miller and his wife, Irena, who had left earlier, were killed by 'guards' escorting them across the Polish border

14 September **Card from Stefan in Perth to Franciszka**

My dearest darling, a kiss to wake you up. This morning the plains in mild mist outside the window and it's nice.

The cold has gone completely. And the cough too.

I kiss you my littlest one and ? Be joyous, darling. St.

Letter from Stefan to Franciszka

My darling,

Today, I received two of your letters at the same time. Thank you, my little one. Unfortunately, with permits to leave it isn't so easy just to ask for something to be changed, etc. Anyway, on Monday I should already be leaving here. Tomorrow I'll drop in next door and go by bus to see Jordan and Fleszar. For a few hours. Apart from that I am very well. I wrote, on the other side, a half-sonnet. I am sad that I don't know how to master the art of metric verse, ending with a descending cadence, as if disconnected – but I have to send you everything after all, whether good or bad.

I also started, from the beginning, on chapter x of *Professor Mmaa's Lecture*. To tell the truth it's not easy to find a corner in which one can sit down and write, but I have to, even if that's not what I am here for. These are the two things that I really must write – two among many others.

I am so glad, darling, that you got a bit of money. I don't need anything at all. But you, Franek, don't be mean with yourself and look after my dearest little one.

Has Kamilka copied the manuscript? What does it look like now? Is she managing somehow? Most often, it seems that I am making a mountain out of a molehill. The truth is probably somewhere in between.

Make note, darling, that in Chapter III I should add a sentence about a man, who just like everyone else couldn't limit himself to a human size and looked for a god in a deterministic infinity either small (atoms) or enormous.

I kiss you my darling as much as possible.

On Monday, I will send you my new address.

Kisses! Stefan

Freedom of the 4 dimes

Oh centime with a hole, peseta, escudo
penny polished with sticky fingers,
Magic discs — you continually open gates
to new miracles in heaven and on earth.

Singly insufficient, but put together
you rise to the ceiling in a soaring column
and all the eyes around as if before an icon
sparkle as if suspended from my sad lips.

What shall I say? *Daily Express*? Or for another
whisky quite sensibly ask with due timidity,
swallowing this cruel liquid with too great an ease.

Oh you, a polished penny — freedom's key,
the whole of life between the cradle and the coffin,
to gain freedom must I learn how to use you?

Liberté de quat' sous

Dziurkowany centimie, peseto, escudos,
pensie wyszlifowany palcami lepkiemi,
Krążki czarowne! – wrota nowoczesnym cudom
otwieracie co chwila na niebie i ziemi.

Pojedynczo-mizerne, ustawione razem
wznosicie się pod sufit strzelistą kolumną
i wszystkie oczy wkoło, niby przed obrazem
rozbłyskują zawisłszy na mych wargach smutnych.

Co powiem ? Daily Express? Czy bardziej rozumną
prośbę o nowe whisky nieśmiało wymruczę,
połykając za łatwo płyn okrutnie trudny?

Wyszlifowany pensie, ty – wolności kluczem,
życie całe, pomiędzy kolebką i trumną –
Trzebaż abym tę wolność tobą otwierać się uczył?

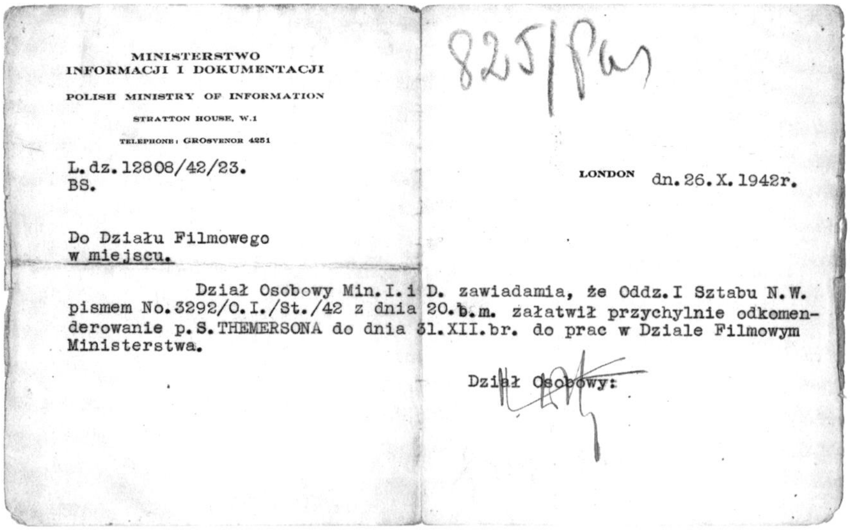

MINISTERSTWO
INFORMACJI I DOKUMENTACJI
POLISH MINISTRY OF INFORMATION
STRATTON HOUSE, W.1
TELEPHONE: GROSVENOR 4251

825/Par

L.dz.12808/42/23.
BS.

LONDON dn.26.X.1942r.

Do Działu Filmowego
w miejscu.

Dział Osobowy Min.I.i D. zawiadamia, że Oddz.I Sztabu N.W. pismem No.3292/O.I./St./42 z dnia 20.b.m. załatwił przychylnie odkomenderowanie p.S.THEMERSONA do dnia 31.XII.br. do prac w Dziale Filmowym Ministerstwa.

Dział Osobowy:

26 October 1942
Ministerstwo Informacji i Dokumentacji, Stratton House, London W1
Polish Ministry of Information to the Film Division of the Ministry

An official letter advising the Film Division that the Personnel Office of the Ministry of Information and Documentation has kindly agreed to the transfer of Stefan Themerson to work in the Film Division of the Ministry until 31 December 1942.

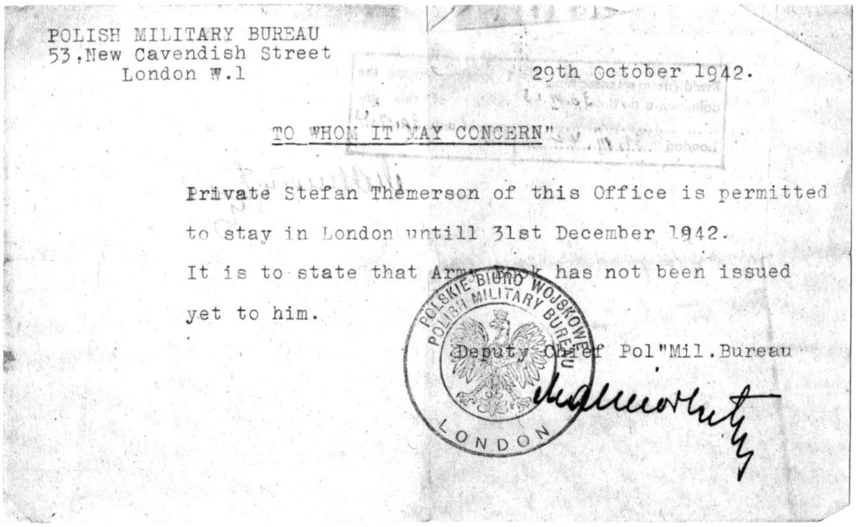

POLISH MILITARY BUREAU
53,New Cavendish Street
London W.1

29th October 1942.

TO WHOM IT MAY CONCERN"

Private Stefan Themerson of this Office is permitted to stay in London untill 31st December 1942.
It is to state that Army Book has not been issued yet to him.

Deputy Chief Pol"Mil.Bureau

29 October 1942
Polish Military Bureau, 53 New Cavendish Street, London W1
To whom it may concern

Private Stefan Themerson of this Office is permitted to stay in London until 31 December 1942. It is stated that the Army Book has not been issued yet to him.

Deputy Chief of the Polish Military Bureau

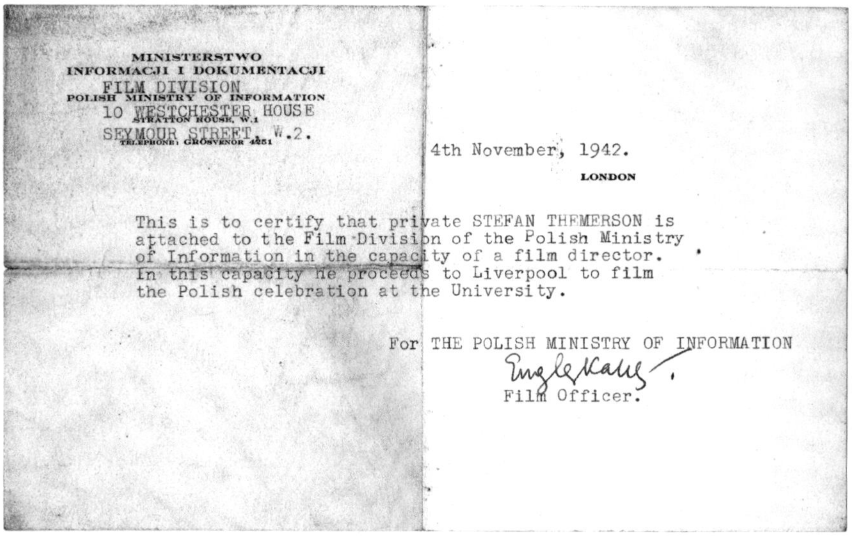

MINISTERSTWO
INFORMACJI I DOKUMENTACJI
POLISH MINISTRY OF INFORMATION
FILM DIVISION
10 WESTCHESTER HOUSE
SEYMOUR STREET, W.2.

4th November, 1942.
LONDON

This is to certify that private STEFAN THEMERSON is attached to the Film Division of the Polish Ministry of Information in the capacity of a film director. In this capacity he proceeds to Liverpool to film the Polish celebration at the University.

For THE POLISH MINISTRY OF INFORMATION
Film Officer.

4 November 1942
Polish Ministry of Information Film Division, 10 Westchester House, Seymour Street, London W2

This is to certify that Private Stefan Themerson is attached to the Film Division of the Polish Ministry of Information in the capacity of a film director. In this capacity he proceeds to Liverpool to film the Polish celebration at the University.

For The Polish Ministry of Information
Eugeniusz Cękalski, Film Officer

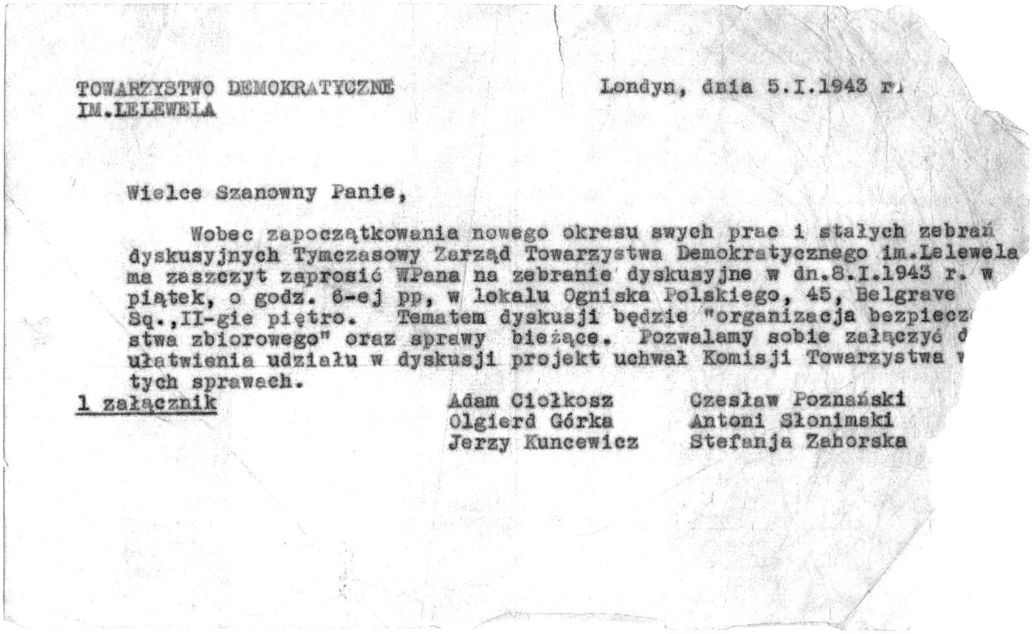

TOWARZYSTWO DEMOKRATYCZNE IM.LELEWELA　　Londyn, dnia 5.I.1943 r.

Wielce Szanowny Panie,

Wobec zapoczątkowania nowego okresu swych prac i stałych zebrań dyskusyjnych Tymczasowy Zarząd Towarzystwa Demokratycznego im.Lelewela ma zaszczyt zaprosić WPana na zebranie dyskusyjne w dn.8.I.1943 r. w piątek, o godz. 6-ej pp, w lokalu Ogniska Polskiego, 45, Belgrave Sq.,II-gie piętro. Tematem dyskusji będzie "organizacja bezpiecz stwa zbiorowego" oraz sprawy bieżące. Pozwalamy sobie załączyć d ułatwienia udziału w dyskusji projekt uchwał Komisji Towarzystwa w tych sprawach.

1 załącznik

Adam Ciołkosz　Czesław Poznański
Olgierd Górka　Antoni Słonimski
Jerzy Kuncewicz　Stefanja Zahorska

5 January 1943
Letter to Stefan from the Democratic Society named after Polish historian Joachim Lelewel (1786–1861)

Stefan is invited to a discussion on 8 January 1943 in Ognisko Polskie [Polish Hearth], 45 Belgrave Square. The theme of the discussion will be the organisation of social security and current affairs. The signatories are: Adam Ciołkosz, Olgierd Górka, Jerzy Kuncewicz, Czesław Poznański; Antoni Słonimski; Stefanja Zahorska

1943

28 January **Letter from I.St. Witkiewicz to Franciszka**

Parcels sent to Janina and Maria Chaykin and Łucja Weinles to Śliska 7, m.10 in Warsaw were returned, labelled 'unknown' for the three names. I shall ask the office to send once more one more parcel each with request for a receipt and forwarding to a new address if it is known where these ladies are currently.

1944

On 14 January 1944 Witkiewicz reports that he never received confirmation that the parcels he sent to Franciszka's family in Warsaw were received. The parcels were not returned. Quite naively he writes that perhaps the parcels were received but there was some difficulty with correspondence.

22 October **Letter from Franciszka in London to Nadia, Léon and Catherine Temerson in New York**

…We were so happy when Paris was liberated that we cabled you. I imagine what an excitement that was? How lovely it would be to meet at… for instance rue de Seine! Gosh! Do you think to return soon? We really don't know anything at all.

Feeling pretty well in the air. I don't think we could go to Poland after all that happened there. I don't know if we have anybody there to go to.

After all that, perhaps we are not quite the same enthusiastic people you knew in Paris. Certainly very much older. I really don't know how we could stand all that if we were not together now. That's a lot.

I just noticed that the words I am repeating over and over again in this letter are 'I don't know'. And those words paint the situation most accurately…

Having been temporarily relieved of his duties as a soldier, Stefan is engaged by the Film Division of the Polish Government-in-Exile as an operator and later as director.

His first commission is to produce a screenplay and to make a film about occupied Poland, based on photographs, diagrams and maps, to be called *Unfinished Journey*. This is in memory of General Sikorski. However, the film is eventually made by Genek Cękalski with screenplay by Ksawery Pruszyński and the commentary spoken by John Gielgud.

The first film made by the Themersons, *Calling Mr Smith*, was one of four anti-fascist films produced by the Film Division. The first screening of the programme took place on 5 October 1943 at the Gaumont British Private Theatre. There was no public showing and at the beginning of 1944, the British Board of Film Censors withheld a licence for the film unless the shot of a figure hanging from gallows was removed. The film remained uncut.

In August 1943, Franciszka resigns officially from her job with the Ministry of Information and Documentation because they cannot employ married couples. Even so, they continued to work together on the two films they made for the Film Division: *Calling Mr Smith* and *The Eye and the Ear*.

Stefan worked for the Film Division until it was disbanded in February 1945.

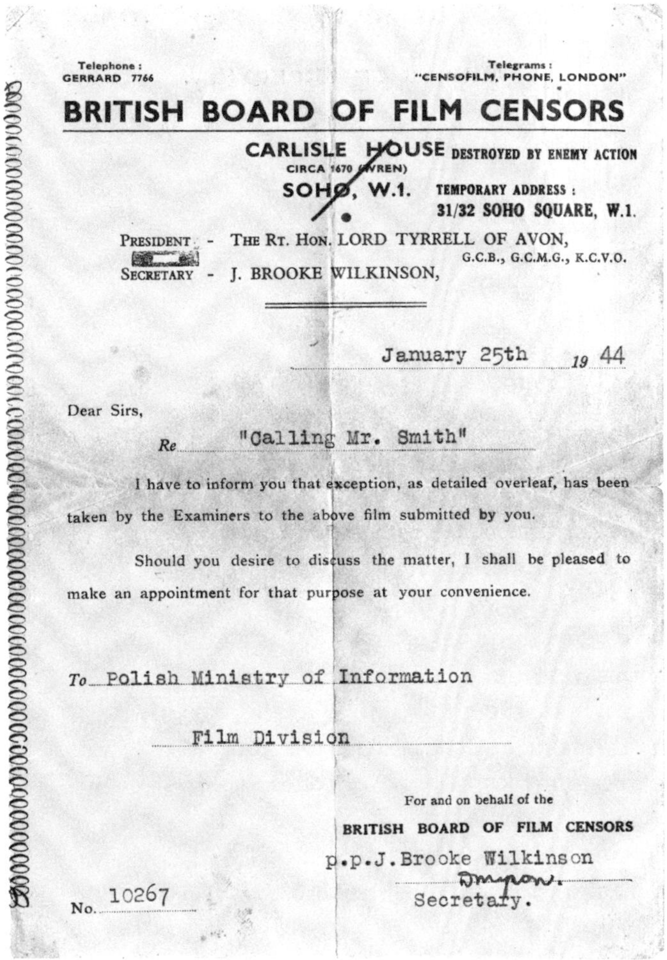

Telephone: GERRARD 7766
Telegrams: "CENSOFILM, PHONE, LONDON"

BRITISH BOARD OF FILM CENSORS

CARLISLE HOUSE DESTROYED BY ENEMY ACTION
CIRCA 1670 (WREN)
SOHO, W.1. TEMPORARY ADDRESS: 31/32 SOHO SQUARE, W.1.

PRESIDENT - THE RT. HON. LORD TYRRELL OF AVON, G.C.B., G.C.M.G., K.C.V.O.
SECRETARY - J. BROOKE WILKINSON,

January 25th 1944

Dear Sirs,

Re "Calling Mr. Smith"

I have to inform you that exception, as detailed overleaf, has been taken by the Examiners to the above film submitted by you.

Should you desire to discuss the matter, I shall be pleased to make an appointment for that purpose at your convenience.

To Polish Ministry of Information
Film Division

For and on behalf of the
BRITISH BOARD OF FILM CENSORS
p.p.J.Brooke Wilkinson
Secretary.

No. 10267

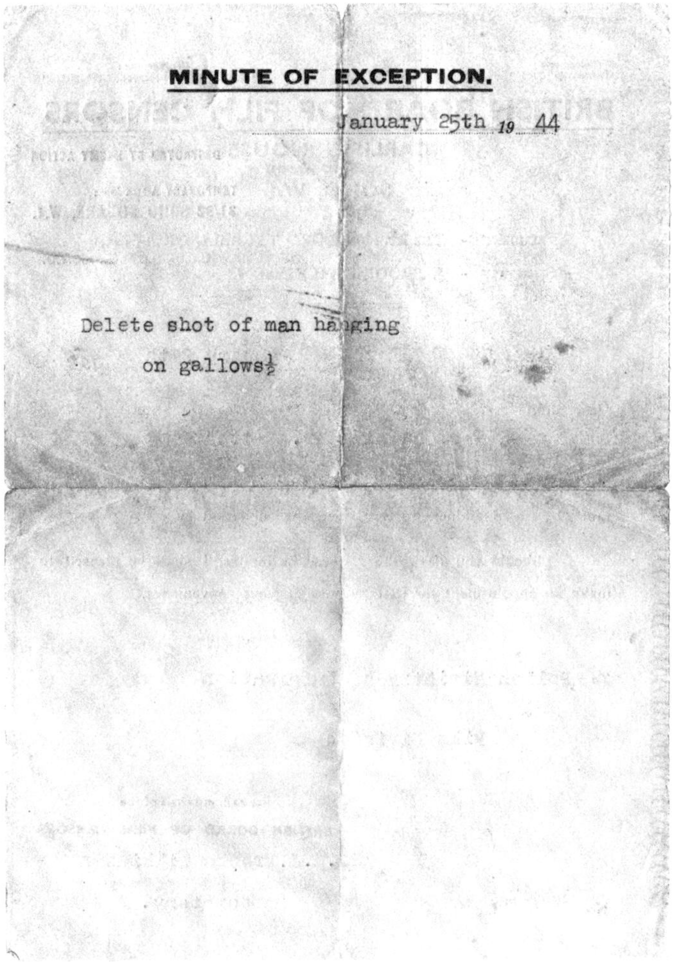

MINUTE OF EXCEPTION.

January 25th 1944

Delete shot of man hanging
on gallows½

25 January 1944
Document from the British Board of Film Censors refusing license for public showing for *Calling Mr. Smith* unless shot indiciated on the back is removed

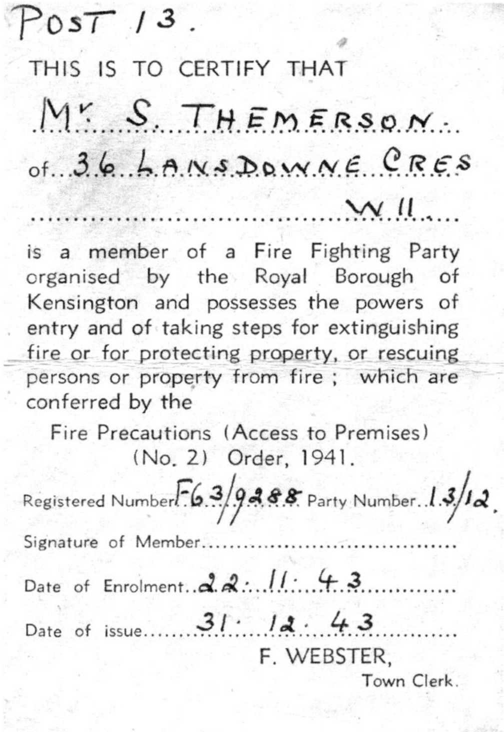

POST 13.

THIS IS TO CERTIFY THAT

Mr. S. THEMERSON

of 36 LANSDOWNE CRES

W 11

is a member of a Fire Fighting Party organised by the Royal Borough of Kensington and possesses the powers of entry and of taking steps for extinguishing fire or for protecting property, or rescuing persons or property from fire ; which are conferred by the

Fire Precautions (Access to Premises) (No. 2) Order, 1941.

Registered Number F63/9288 Party Number 13/12.

Signature of Member........................

Date of Enrolment 22. 11. 43

Date of issue 31. 12. 43

F. WEBSTER,
Town Clerk.

What else? Both Franciszka and Stefan enrol as wardens in the Fire Guard and attend training sessions in December 1943. They are on duty on Saturdays from dusk till midnight.

They publish two books privately in 1943. One is Franciszka's *Forty Drawings for Friends*, London 1940–42. These forty drawings are from the Unposted Letters. The tiny book, 13.5×11 cm, is published in an edition of 25 copies, printed by Lund Humphries. Introduction is provided by Stefan's poem 'To Christ lamenting in the Place de la Bourse':

We've eaten crumbs of peace, thrown down between two wars
We've drunk a swill of freedom leaking from cracked vessels

Oh my dear sir
how stately in your bowler hat
you are
Won't you join us
in sighing
"Aaah!"

"Aah!", for me
and for Franciszka, too
"Aah" for Mira, Ignacy, and Stefan,
and leave it at these few
lest we tire you with counting,
merciful Sire –

Jesus Christ, dear Sire,
beneath your bowler hat you cry.
Aah, brothers, let's go to a bar;
"Patron! pour moi: just a sigh"

Paris, May 1940

The other is Stefan's book, *Dno nieba* [Bottom of the Sky] which contains ten of his Polish poems, including 3 poems for children written in France. The book was printed in London by F. Mildner & Sons.

Stefan publishes his *Croquis dans les Ténèbres* with Franciszka's drawings in 1944 with Hachette, Continental Publishers & Distributors in London. This book is also printed by F. Mildner & Sons.

In July 1948 Stefan receives notice of his discharge from active service.

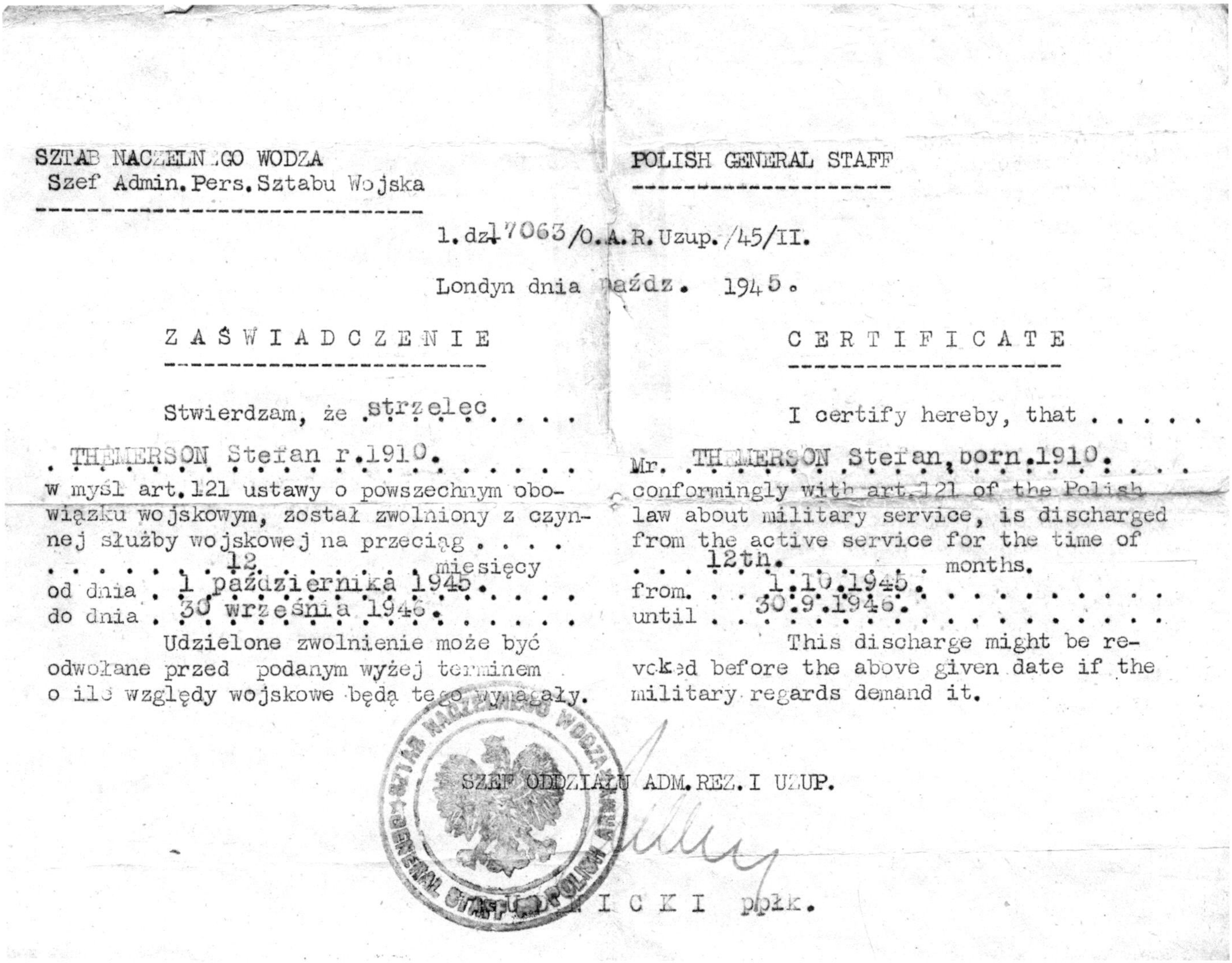

SZTAB NACZELNEGO WODZA
Szef Admin.Pers.Sztabu Wojska

POLISH GENERAL STAFF

1.dz.17063/O.A.R.Uzup./45/II.

Londyn dnia paźdz. 1945.

ZAŚWIADCZENIE

Stwierdzam, że strzelec . . . .
. THEMERSON Stefan r.1910. . . . .
w myśl art.121 ustawy o powszechnym obowiązku wojskowym, został zwolniony z czynnej służby wojskowej na przeciąg . . . . 12 . . . . miesięcy
od dnia . 1 października 1945. . . . .
do dnia . 30 września 1946. . . . .
Udzielone zwolnienie może być odwołane przed podanym wyżej terminem o ile względy wojskowe będą tego wymagały.

CERTIFICATE

I certify hereby, that . . . . .
Mr. . THEMERSON Stefan, born 1910. . . . .
conformingly with art.121 of the Polish law about military service, is discharged from the active service for the time of . . . 12th. . . . . months.
from. . . 1.10.1945. . . . .
until . . . 30.9.1946. . . . .
This discharge might be revoked before the above given date if the military regards demand it.

SZEF ODDZIAŁU ADM.REZ.I UZUP.

. . . I C K I ppłk.

Stefan Themerson

The God of the Croix-Rousse

‘Le Dieu de la Croix-Rousse’ starts with fragments of stories of Pola Bobita which Stefan recorded in his diary, 26 September 1941, pp.263–264. He sends it to Franciszka on 29 November 1941.

Translated from the French by Barbara Wright

The God of the Croix-Rousse

'We mustn't miss happiness,' Maurice's mother used to say. She knew very well what happiness was, and it was this knowledge that made her wise and good.

'If by any chance my mother-in-law ever upset me, I know I'd forgive her in advance because she's wise and good.' This is what Pauline used to say.

And in the old days, Maurice's mother used to say:

'I shall never forget the nine years of happiness I had.'

When she was fifteen, she fell in love and tried to run away from home. When she was eighteen, she married. When she was twenty-seven, she lost her husband. But she still had her eight year-old son, and she reserved all her love for him.

The Christians, in their search for eternal happiness, constructed a whole philosophy based on goodness. The Stoics, in their search for happiness on earth, invented a whole philosophy based on wisdom. Maurice's mother found her happiness by herself and in herself; to her it was like a great natural revelation, and it was what made her good and wise.

'We mustn't miss happiness,' Maurice's mother often said. It was still before the war when Maurice and Pauline were engaged, and when the question of the new household (where they would live, with whom, etc.,) was in the air, but being discretely avoided by everyone.

Pauline's mother was different, she was elegant, she didn't look her age – forty five – and she didn't find it easy to accept the situation where she would have to call Maurice her son, when he was already thirty-five and well on the way to becoming bald. Moreover, he wasn't 'Monsieur le Docteur,' he didn't have his own car, and it didn't look as if, once married, he would allow his mother-in-law to interfere in his life. But now that Maurice has escaped form his POW camp, now that he is married to Pauline in L. and the two mothers live on different sides of the demarcation line, these delicate questions have lost their topicality.

'You spoil her too much,' half seriously, half as a joke, Marcel said to Maurice, who had gone to meet his wife outside the office where she worked.

Marcel wasn't unkind. No. He was frank, outspoken, and he wanted people to appreciate his candour, his cordiality and his honesty, which he had acquired through the life he had led and not through any sort of education. And he was a little wary of Pauline, not because she was a university student but because he sometimes thought she considered her education to be something superior, and he didn't want people to think that an education could be more importamt than his own personal values which he had arrived at in the course of his hard and hard-working life. Pauline didn't want to invite a certain sort of people to her house; she had nothing to say to them, she hadn't the time, she worked at the office from nine to twelve and from two to six, she studied for her exam during the nights, waking up at three in the morning and reading her books in bed with Maurice asleep by her side. But the most important thing was that she didn't have enough time for her husband, and she would do anything to protect their happiness.

Marcel suspected her of wanting to drop her friends because of her education, and there was something of the innocence of the child who wants to revenge himself in him when he said to Maurice over lunch: 'You spoil her too much.'

'Is that true, Maurice? Is that true, my darling?' Pauline asked.

Maurice smiled.

'Listen, old man,' he said to Marcel. I've been with my wife for eight months and I know her well by this time. I know what she wants and what she doesn't want. I know what's necessary and what isn't necessary. We aren't rivals in anything: we aren't going to let ourselves become involved in the superficial trivialities of everyday life, in those silly little things that aren't really important. We both know what we want. And we know how to defend ourselves, our independence and our happiness.

A few months before, Pauline had had pneumonia. She had lost weight but she was still very lively, her movements as spontaneous as the lightning-flight of the bat, and her words left her mouth so rapidly that one had the impression that they were rushing to make the end of the phrase catch up with the beginning before it reached the ear of the listener. She kissed Maurice's bald head and went on talking at the same time, so that in the end, while her lips were still touching his bald patch she was already talking about her office and about the women and girls she worked with, who didn't want to believe the fact that Pauline was going to university and considered it quite simply an impossibility. They preferred to believe that she was lying, to make herself seem important; they would rather forgive her for lying than for having done something so incomprehensible.

The sun had conquered the light rain, and we were going home on foot.

'Do you know, Monsieur T', said Pauline, 'why I like these steps? It's more difficult to climb up this way, and yet I always take it. there are always some cats on this path. Once, my husband and I were climbing up it and a cat was slowly, and so seriously, coming down. A little girl was following it and she picked it up. "You must be good, pussy my love, you must always be a good pussycat," she said, and she carried it up to the top. After that, two girls came down the steps hand in hand, and they were singing so brightly.

'When we got to the top the little girl was feeding her cat, giving it some soup in a bowl. "You're a good pussy now," she said. "You're a good pussy and you're having your lunch."

'There's a road above these stone steps. Do you know why I like that road? An old man lives there who opens his window and quite simply calls: "Birds!" and the birds fly up and eat breadcrumbs out of his hand. When they've finished them he says quite simply. "Have you finished them? Then you can go!" And they fly away. And even higher up, there's an alleyway, a perfectly ordinary alleyway. Do you know why I like that alleyway? Because it's called Road Plan. It's completely finished now, but it's still called Road Plan. Isn't that magnificent.'

We were still going up. From the Place de Bellevue we could see the Rhône below us and the roots of the houses squeezed together covering up this hive of activity living its normal everyday life. Above the roofs the vague shape of a skyscraper could be seen in a greyish, amorphous haze that seemed to be attracted to the town as if towards a magnet that was trying to liberate the azure of the sky and to cover the slopes of the Croix-Rousse with its transparent dome. The greenery of the trees, here and there dotted with the little pale yellow leaves of the acacias, already saddened by the autumn, was entangled in the grip of the horrid purple vine climbing up its branches.

'And do you know why I like that statue?'

The statue was ugly. But that didn't matter. This wasn't the moment to discuss sculplture and art. I wanted to answer: 'I don't know why you like that statue, but I do know why you are happy,' but I didn't say anything. Because happy people don't like us to show that we recognise their happiness, that we know what it is. They can't believe that anyone could understand their happiness, which is unique, completely different from all the other happinesses in the world. And because they might suspect that we were jealous, it could spoil their joy.

In the poor houses in the Croix-Rousse, the weaving machines were falling silent. It was nearly dinner time.

'I've found some meal tickets for two hundred grammes of bread,' said Maurice. 'We'll buy them for tomorrow morning.'

And we went into a baker's shop which was full of the tepid, fragrant air of the sun. Standing behind the counter was a GOD. His shirtsleeves were tucked back, his skull was greyish with flour. He picked up a flûte of warm bread, cut it with a big knife and put it on the scales.

The God's bakery was full of people. But He – he glanced at Pauline and Maurice, and with a tiny little smile he threw another tiny little slice of bread on the scales.

And for a tiny little moment it seemed to me that this tiny little smile of the last Just God could still save the Ark of this world, which was already drowned by men's anger in the deluge of blood and hate.

But that evening they made the dove into soup.

'The Investigation' is a wartime story. It was first published in Polish in 1945 in London in *Nowa Polska*. Stefan Themerson wrote it in France sometime during 1941–42 when he was staying in the Red Cross Hostel for Polish Soldiers, referred to in the text as 'Hôtel de la Poste Restante'.

The story is about the life in the Hôtel and its annex, where some 120 Poles from all walks of life and professions find themselves living together in close proximity – a safe, but physically and socially difficult situation. There are conflicts and prejudices, hopes and despair. The characters in the story are real people whose names are changed. Stefan Themerson made a list of some the real people in the hostel with their pseudonyms in the story.

He also made a map of Voiron featuring the relevant locations mentioned in the story. It is included, redrawn by Nick Wadley (page 392).

After his arrival in London in the summer of 1942, Stefan rewrote both parts of 'The Investigation' in English. The first title he gave to this story in two parts was 'The Inquest', but he changed his mind and called it 'The Investigation'.

In these two parts of the story written by Stefan in Voiron, we encounter many of his cohabitants there. They are given different names, and here is the list. Real names on the left, pseudonyms on the right.

Baran — Owca
Budziszewski — Uspiszewski
Budkiewicz — Dudkiewicz
Erwin W. — Edwin Fuchs
Gostocki — Pizocki ?
Julinska Z. — Królinska Z.
Jahl Wł. — Krahl Wł.
Koch — Goch
Mannheim — Lorelei
Miarka Wł. — Cwiartka Wł.
Mirizinski — Bliski
Nalepa — Polepa
Pałasz Mich. — Szabla M.
Rozenblat M. — Lilienberg Lusia
Solestarska — Szczodropacka
Szeryng — Heryng
Wróblewski J. — Wróblewski J.

Bibliography

'Sledztwo' (short story). *Nowa Polska*, vol. IV, no.2, pp.128–37; vol.IV, no.6, 401–10, London, 1945.

'Sledztwo – abstrakcje i pluskwy'. *Literatura na emigracji*, Wydawnictwo Poligrafika, Łódź, 1946, pp.100–113

General Piesc i inne opowiadania, Warsaw, Czytelnik, 1980, pp.122–156

'Abstracties en wandluizen'. *Moderne Poolse Verhalen*. Amsterdam, Van Gennep, 1982, pp.17–29 (Dutch translation of extract by Gerard Rasch)

Performance

Adapted as an opera by Zbigniew Maciak, performed at the Teatr im. Stefana Jaracza, Łódź, March 1988, directed by Maciej Prus

Stefan Themerson

The Investigation

1 Abstractions & Bed-Bugs

To what event should one attribute the fact that the Nowak family was given the Sunny Room?

The fact that the Nowak family was given the sunny room should be attributed to two events. The first took place 32 years earlier, in 1910, some 1800 kilometres east-north-east. The second in 1920-21, at the same place.

What happened in 1910?

Piotr Januszewicz, aged 10, slapped the face of a stable-hand, Franciszek Laszcz, aged 68, married, six children: two sons, four married daughters, – because he, Laszcz, refused to allow him, Piotr Januszewicz, to mount the restive mare called Olga. He had also been forbidden to do this by his father, old squire Januszewicz, who, on hearing of Piotr's conduct, ordered him to kiss Laszcz's hand and to say: I apologise. Piotr kissed Laszcz's hand and said: I apologise.

What is the connection between that event and the question of allotting the sunny room to the Nowak family?

I do not know. I do know, however, that there must have been a connection, because Piotr Januszewicz told the story of this event directly after his talk with colonel Szczodropacki's wife, when he ran out of his office and came to Mme Vial's bistro for a drink.

What kind of a drink was it?

A badly distilled 'marc', harmful in Dr Lizocki's opinion because of the volatile essences it contained.

And what happened in 1920?

In 1920, a certain Antoni Wrona informed against Piotr Januszewicz to the Bolshevik authorities, whereupon Piotr Januszewicz spent two years in prison, where he learned cobbling.

What is the connection between that event and the decision to allot the sunny room to the Nowak family?

I don't know. I do know, however, that there must have been a connection, because Piotr Januszewicz told the story of this event after he had drunk the second glass of 'marc' at Mme Vial's.

Before he arrived at Mme Vial's, what was he talking about to colonel Szczodropacki's wife?

Colonel Szczodropacki's wife came to Piotr Januszewicz, the deputy chief of the refuge, and objected to the decision to allot the sunny room to the Nowak family, which, as she said, was unjust because the Nowaks were used to living in obscure sunless cottages and so there would be no harm done if they were given the room with the north light, while her little daughter, Xenia, was not used to it, and she was pale and anaemic.

Was Xenia Szczodropacka in fact pale and anaemic?
Yes, she was.

What did Piotr Januszewicz answer?
Piotr Januszewicz answered that Nowak's children were also pale and anaemic, that Nowak's wife was going to have a baby and that in a few days' time she would go to hospital, that altogether the Nowak family would not stay in the HÔTEL DE LA POSTE RESTANTE longer than two weeks, and that THEY WERE TO LIVE IN THE SUNNY ROOM.

And colonel Szczodropacki's wife?
Colonel Szczodropacki's wife turned and went away, to her room, on the first floor, and burst into tears. When her father, general Bliski, asked her "What's the matter?" She replied: "Januszewicz is a Bolshevik!"

And Piotr Januszewicz?
It has already been said that he went to Mme Vial's for a drink and related there the events of 1910 and 1920.

To whom did he relate them?
To Edwin Fuchs and to Dr Tadeusz Lizocki.

Did Edwin Fuchs also say that Januszewicz was a Bolshevik?
No, Edwin Fuchs considered himself a communist, and Piotr Januszewicz he considered a squire and an aristocrat.

Did Dr Lizocki say that Januszewicz was a Bolshevik?
No. Januszewicz was a Pole, and a Roman Catholic, and it was only all Jews whom Dr Lizocki considered to be Bolsheviks, and all Bolsheviks whom he considered to be Jews.

What did Dr Lizocki think about Edwin Fuchs?
He thought that Edwin Fuchs might, perhaps, be a communist, but he certainly was not a Bolshevik, because he was a Protestant.

What did Edwin Fuchs think about Dr Lizocki?
That he belonged to a social class which would disappear together with the historical epoch that was just passing away, but that he was a very fine chap, because he was a very fine chap, because he had served in the Narvik campaign and learned some things about life, though, perhaps, somehow differently from Edwin Fuchs, who had been in the international Brigade in Spain and had already been fighting fascism at the time when Dr Lizocki, content with living in the

previous historical epoch, had been giving gynæcological advice to society ladies of the city of Lvov.

Had Dr Lizocki been treating the society women only?
No. He was also a Health Insurance doctor.

So why did Edwin Fuchs put so much emphasis on those, society ladies'?
In order to simplify the picture of the world, and thus to facilitate his argument.

What did Mme Vial think about Edwin Fuchs, Piotr Januszewicz, and Dr Lizocki?
She wondered where they got the money for their drinks.

Where did they get it from?
Piotr Januszewicz had been a consul somewhere in Belgium or Holland before the war, and he had succeeded in running away before the invasion with his wallet in the back-pocket of his grey flannel trousers; Edwin Fuchs kept the accounts of the Refuge and what he got for that was just enough for the drink; Dr Lizocki practised as physician in the HÔTEL DE LA POSTE RESTANTE, and after all, earned enough to drink, enough to make him sing, 'What are our rucksacks for, /What for our tents, /If we shall be no more, /At all events!', alternately with the Horst-Wessel-Lied and the Internationale.

Did Dr Lizocki say anything about the Nowak family?
Yes, he said that he had examined the children, that the boy, aged five, was rachitic, the girl, aged four, had anaemia, and for that little one aged three he would prescribe a good portion of pork and cabbage; that Nowak's wife will be delivered of a child in two days' time; that in giving them the sunny room Januszewicz had done the best thing he could; that that very fact proved that Januszewicz came from a good family, that his father knew how to bring him up, and that if only our gentry were like him, those Jews-Bolsheviks would not be able to lead us by our noses.

What did Edwin Fuchs say?
Edwin Fuchs said that Januszewicz was a fine chap but that this would not solve any social problems.

What did Piotr Januszewicz say?
Januszewicz said that he had been filling out the Nowaks' form and noticed that the maiden name of Nowak's wife was Olszewska, so was that of his own mother.

Before Januszewicz had said that, did Dr Lizocki mumble something?
Yes, he did.

What was it?
He mumbled: 'Shit is going to solve your social problems!'

Is it known what the Nowaks were doing by that time?
They were sitting on their bundles in the HÔTEL DE LA POSTE RESTANTE corridor, waiting for the sunny room on the first floor to be free.

How long were they waiting there?
Their train arrived at 1.30 am. At 1.45 they were already in the hotel.

At what time did they enter their room?
At 5.30.

Did they go down to supper?
No. Nowak went down alone to the kitchen, and took up two pots, one with soup and the other with rutabaga.

The next morning, did they go down to the dining room for breakfast?
No. Nowak went down alone to the kitchen, and took their coffee upstairs.

At noon, did they go down to lunch?
No. Nowak went down alone to the kitchen and took up two pots, one with soup and the other with boiled vetch.

Did they ever go down to the dining room?
Never. Nowak always used to carry everything to their room upstairs.

Why?
I beg your pardon?

Why didn't they go down?
But there was a precipice all around the Nowak family! Had they gone down to the dining room the parquet would have split all round their table, the earth would have opened wide, and it is uncomfortable to sit at a table with small children, to eat rutabaga seasoned with small red tufts of gourd instead of fat, and all the time to have a precipice all around you. To be sure, both the dining rooms were fissured with precipices going along, across, aslant, zigzag, – but not one of them was as deep and impassable as the precipice which surrounded the Nowaks. A precipice divided colonel Szczodropacki's wife from a Brussels *maître de ballet*, but they could bridge it when playing cards; a precipice divided a former consul in USSR, Płycki, from the elementary school teacher, Szabla, but they were able to traverse it when discussing how to organise a choir; a precipice separated Edwin Fuchs from the one-time policeman Bujakowski, and the painter Krahl from the professional soldier, Sergeant Dantyszek, but they could jump over it during the English lessons given by Fuchs, and during the Spanish lessons given by Krahl; a precipice separated Polepa (the local leader of the 'Great Poland's Power' group) from the bleary-eyed Cudzik (who in the French coal-pits 'grew scabby with communism'), but it could be traversed by Polepa's scornful smile, and by Cudzik's hateful spitting in the other's direction; a precipice divided Lusia Lilienberg from Gustrzecki, but they could during their long walks at dusk, stretch out their arms over it and touch one another. There were some dozens precipices; all were, however, narrower and shallower than the precipice surrounding the Nowaks. All of them were precipices between memories, – between one person's memories and the other person's memories, – all of them were precipices between fictions – between abstractions that, in the panic of the exodus, had been carried out of that reality which had passed away, – which was no more. The precipice surrounding the Nowaks was a precipice between abstractions and the reality that survived.

Did anybody try to cross this precipice?
Yes.

Who?
The first person was Miss Zofia Krolińska. No later than the next morning she stopped Nowak on the staircase: 'How is your wife, Nowak?' He answered: 'God be praised, Lady, not so bad'. She drew nearer: 'You may have confidence in me, I can be trusted,' she said. 'I am a socialist, I belong to the Polish Socialist Party. I'm with the people, Nowak. But you had better be on your guard here in the Hôtel! A wide assortment of people is here, Nowak, you had better take my advice. There are National Democrats and people from the National Unity Movement; there are fascists and communists; Lutherans and Jews. The whole of Poland is here, Nowak! I tell you all this for your own good, Nowak.' 'Thank you, Ma'am,' answered Nowak and walked up two more steps. In both hands he carried cups filled with hot black coffee. She clutched at is sleeve. – 'With your permission, Ma'am', he said, 'the coffee is getting cold. And my wife isn't getting much warm food.' And leaving her on the stairs he climbed up to his sunny room.

Who else tried to cross the precipice?
Many people. Polepa, Płycki, Zenon, Lilienberg, Januszewicz.

What about Polepa?
At noon, when Nowak was coming back from the kitchen carrying the lunch, he was stopped by Polepa. 'How are things going, father?' asked Polepa. 'God be praised, Sir…' answered Nowak. 'So you see what has become of you, an old farmer!' said Polepa. 'Gadding about with your family, from one place to another, all round the world, instead of staying on your own land, ploughing and sowing! I hear you are going to work on some damned French farm?' he asked. 'That's right, Sir,' said Nowak. 'Were you driven away from Poland by Bolsheviks or by Germans?' asked Polepa. 'Neither, Sir. We emigrated before the war, Sir', said Nowak. 'The Jews,' said Polepa, 'the Jews had sucked all the blood out of you, and the Jews have remained in Poland, while you, a Pole, a true catholic, you had to go among those damned Frenchmen to find your bread. And when we used to tell you people: "Throttle the Jews!" you did not move, you were slow, heavy. Well, never mind! The Germans will now slaughter the Jews in Poland, then they and the Russians will annihilate each other, and then we shall come back and there will be Poland from the Baltic up to the Black Sea. The soil is rich there, and there is enough of it for all the Poles!' 'With your permission, Sir, the soup is getting g cold, and the best part of it for the children is the heat.' Leaving Polepa on the stairs, he went up into his room and closed the door behind him.

What about Płycki?
The former consul Płycki met Nowak one evening, in the corridor, at the door leading to the kitchen: 'And you, Nowak, let's hear what you have to say; are you hungry Nowak?' 'I'm used to it, Sir, by your favour, Sir.' 'You see, Nowak! We, the old generation, we are used to it. And look, Nowak, at the youth of today. They have organised a strike, went to school with breakfast, didn't come to lunch, and sent a complaint to the head-office. Instead of cutting wood somewhere in a camp, they are here, safe and sound, learning handicrafts in the French school, but are still

complaining.' 'They are saying that one of them fainted yesterday in the smithy, Sir, by your favour, sir.' 'Eh, Nowak, you listen too much to other people's conversations. You are not hungry yourself, Nowak, are you? And what a room you've got, a sunny room, in a genuine hotel, I am sure that you have never in your life been with your woman in such a place. And there is a bathroom, mind you. If the idea of taking a bath occurs to you, Nowak, you ask Januszewicz, he'll show you how to turn the water on.'

What about Miss Lilienberg?
'Do you like Chopin's 'Étude Révolutionnaire'? Come one day, will you? I'm in the annex, at Mme Fesanti, I've got a piano there, and I'll play it for you.' 'Thank you, miss, but I'm not young enough for dancing and singing.' 'It's not music for dancing, it's…' 'With your permission, miss, I can't leave my woman alone with the children, you know.' 'But that's not all it is – Have you seen any French farmers? It isn't rare to find a piano in their cottages. Every Sunday I walk seven kilometres into the country, to a peasant family that has a piano, and I play for them Chopin, and Beethoven, and Bach. People from the whole neighbourhood come together and listen. They do listen with genuine emotion, not like those snobs from the intelligentsia. They prepare a supper for me, and always give me a piece of butter or an egg when I leave.' 'With your permission, miss, but I'm not on my own, here. Where could I find a piece of butter or an egg?' 'What?! What do you says? What?! So you suppose that I play for them just to get supper?! You suppose that I walk seven kilometres there and back, that I play Chopin's Studies, Bach's Fugues, Beethoven's Sonatas, just to be given a piece of butter? My father, Old Lilienberg, had a textile factory in Lodz; 4,000 people were employed in it. And do you think that I left his drawing rooms, and carriages, and evening dresses – that I was arrested by the political police – that I escaped to France – that I drudged in an aeroplane factory, – in order to ruin my fingers and to play Chopin for French peasants in return for an egg?' 'Good Lord, forgive me miss, I didn't want to insult you, miss. It's only that I know how hard it is nowadays to find anything to eat'.

And what about Januszewicz?
Late in the evening, Januszewicz came into the Nowak's room bringing ration cards for meat and fats. 'I always have some snipped off ration cards in the office, but look here, father, you'd better not tell anyone that I gave them to you.' Nowak's wife: 'You are kindness itself, Sir. May the Virgin Mary repay you!' Januszewicz: 'That farm you are going to, how is it, father? Is the soil good?' Nowak: 'Haven't seen it yet, Sir. But, methinks, if she yields for others, she'll yield as well for me. That's how it is with the soil, sir, that she doesn't look who's tilling her, a Pole or even a Frenchman. What she does is to look how much sweat one puts into her.' Januszewicz: 'Let us hope for the best!' Nowak: 'I see you know something about farming, if I may say so, Sir.' Januszewicz: 'Well, my father had 4,000 hectares, you know, in Novogrodek voivoidship…' Nowak's wife: 'O my Lord Jesus and the Virgin Mary! Four thousand! And the son of such a squire to be a manager in a refuge!' 'Four thousand hectares!' repeated Nowak. 'A great squire!' he added with admiration. However, when Januszewicz left, Nowak locked the door behind him, turning the key very carefully.

Why is that word 'however' in the last sentence? Was there any connection between the 4,000 hectares and the locking of doors. If there hadn't been any 4,000 hectares, would Nowak not have locked his door? Did Nowak lock the door because Piotr Januszewicz's father had once been a lord with 4,000 hectares?

I don't know. Maybe.

If there is no more to it than 'Maybe', wouldn't it be better if the word 'however' had not been used in the sentence, and only the facts presented: 1. Januszewicz's words about his father; 2. Nowak's wife's exclamation; 3. Nowak's admiration; 4. Januszewicz leaving; 5. Nowak locking the door.

Maybe.

What are the words of the oath?

'I swear by God Almighty and by the Holy Trinity that I shall tell the truth, the whole truth, and nothing but the truth. So help me God.'

Isn't it true that the sentence without 'however' would correspond better with the exigencies of the oath than the sentence containing the word 'however'?

Maybe.

Did Nowak lock his door just that once?

No. He always used to lock it.

Were there any events in the Hôtel that would justify it?

Yes. Now and again petty thefts did occur.

The number 4,000 hectares produced by Januszewicz, and the number 4,000 workers, produced by Miss Lilienberg, are these figures accurate, or were they chosen in order to suggest a certain indirect thought?

They are not accurate, they are approximate.

Isn't it true then, that the sentence: 'My father, Old Lilienberg had a textile factory in Lodz: 4,000 people were employed in it' and the sentence: 'Well, my father had 4,000 hectares, you know, in Novogrodek voivoidship' would have been more in agreement with the exigencies of the oath, if there were no such an identical number as 4,000 in them?

Maybe.

When did Nowak's wife go to hospital?

On the fifth day after their arrival.

Did Nowak see her off?

Yes.

Did they go along the Grand' Rue, and then did they take the Serpentine, or did they turn left near the Quatre Chemins and take the footpath?

They went by the Grand' Rue and the Serpentine. It would have been too difficult for Nowak's wife to climb the footpath.

How long was Nowak in the hospital?
Till they had finished filling in the forms etc. Only when the nurses had taken his wife with them, did he go back.

What was the time?
5.15 pm

Did he go the same way?
No. He took the footpath.

Descending along the footpath, was it inevitable to pass near the police station?
That's right.

Did Nowak pass near the police station?
He did.

Didn't he go in, just for a moment?
No. He went straight to the Hôtel.

Had he seen anybody in the Hôtel that evening?
Yes. First he saw the cook who gave him supper for him and for the children. Then, in the drawing room, he saw almost everybody.

Why did he go to the drawing room?
That evening a conference was held there for all the inhabitants of the hotel.

What kind of conference was it?
A conference in honour of Polish Literature and Poetry.

A sample of what was said, please?
It was said that The Broad River of Polish Poetry was traversed by the Dark and Troubled Water of an Alien Stream whose Source was in the Marshes of the International, and not in the Pure Crystal of the Spirit of the Nation.

What was Nowak doing at the time?
He was standing at the end of the drawing room by the fireplace, under a life-size portrait of a certain Chevalier de Bachaumont, and, for want of tobacco, he kept in his mouth a small piece of wood, which he sucked as if it were a cigarette.

Another sample of what was said, please?
It was said that the Greatness of the True National Art consists in the fact that under the Writer's Iridescent Peacock Quill, sharp with Noble Pride and linked with Love, – what was yellow becomes Gold; what was white becomes Silver; what was livid becomes Heavenly Blue; what was the colour of mould changes into Greenness itself: and what was the redness of blood turns into heroic, sacred, and chivalrous Scarlet, Purple and Amaranth !

What was Nowak doing at the time?

He continued to stand at the end of the drawing room, by the fireplace, under the portrait of Chevalier de Bachaumont.

What would Nowak look like if one had made him up according to the colour prescription for the Greatness of Art just offered?

He would have a golden face, amaranthine lips, silvery shirt-collar, eyelids of heavenly blue.

How would the portrait of Chevalier de Bachaumont look if one had restored it according to the same prescription?

Just as it looked before.

How old were the speakers?

20 and 50.

How old was Nowak?

42.

Did Nowak go any more to the Hospital, and did he take the footpath from the Quatre Chemins?

Yes.

How many times?

Once a day, during the whole of his wife's stay in Hospital.

How long did she stay there?

A week. On the third day she was delivered of a child, a boy; on the seventh day she returned to the Hôtel.

Did Miss Krolińska's words: 'There are (in the Hôtel) National Democrats, and people from the National Unity Movement; there are fascists and communists, Lutherans and Jews. The whole of Poland is here, Nowak!' – correspond to the truth?

The first sentence did correspond to the truth. The second sentence did correspond to the truth only during the time when the Nowak family was staying in the Hôtel. It didn't before their appearance, and it didn't after they had vanished.

What does that mean: before their appearance, after they had vanished? Did they appear and vanish as ghosts do?

In a sense – yes, they did. And in another sense – no. They came normally by the railway train from the *département de la Drôme*, and left normally by the railway train, for a farm in Haute Savoie.

When?

The day after Nowak's wife came back from the Hospital.

Who took their room on the first floor?
When, after the Nowak family had departed, Szczodropacka wanted to take the room on the first floor, it turned out that there were bed-bugs there. They had been nestling in the crevices of the beds, behind the skirting-boards round the bottom of the walls, behind the bracket of the electrified Louis XV wall-candelabrum, behind the great Régence wardrobe, in the corner under the Empire wash-stand, behind the threadbare tapestry covering the Louis XVI chair *à médaillon*. Piotr Januszewicz took a tin, filled it with sulphur, put it in the middle of the room, lighted the sulphur, went out, and locked the door. Then he stuck long ribbons of paper all over the chinks and crevices of the door, and left the room thus for 24 hours. And it was only after these 24 hours, or – maybe – only when Szczodropacka and Xenia had taken the sunny room on the first floor, that the Nowak family was forgotten for good.

11 Another Fragment

'Who else used to go to the hospital at about the same time?'

'Lewicki had his appendix taken out. Though that was earlier.'

'Fuchs had also had an operation. Yet, that was later.'

'Uśpiszewski used to go to the hospital all the time, for injections and massage of his hand.'

'Was his right hand bad?'

'He could move his fingers only slightly. At the time, he still sat at the Jewish table, Miss Lilienberg cut up for him the food on his plate. Whenever there was anything to be cut at all.'

'And his left hand?'

'It was alright.'

'In a fight, would he be able to defend himself with his left hand? Could he, for instance, knock somebody down and grip his throat?'

'That would depend on the person's weight and strength.'

'What were his eyes like?'

'Light. Smiling.'

'Forehead?'

'A deep horizontal furrow between two thick folds.'

'Hair?'

'Fair. Tousled.'

'Height?'

'167 cm.'

'Was his hospital treatment bringing any result?'

'It was. He moved his fingers gradually better.'

'When walking to the hospital, was he taking the Grand' Rue and then the Serpentine up the hill, or was he turning to the left by Quatre Chemins and climbing the slope?'

'Now this way and then the other.'

'One day, at about that time, having climbed down the slope, did he drop in at the Police Station which was situated by the stream at Quatre Chemins?'

'Yes, he did.'

'What for?'

'To inform the police "commissaire" that some Jews are living in the Hôtel and at Mme Fesanti's Annex.'

'Had he seen the commisaire?'

'No. He had left a letter in the station office.'

'Was it written in French?'

'It was.'

'Without mistakes?'

'Yes.'

'Was Uśpiszewski's French fluent?'

'No. It was barely passable.'

'Who had written the letter for him?'

'Either his French girlfriend, or Polepa. Neither Owca nor Gałęczyński, Iwanow, Licki nor Ćwiartka, know French well enough. Unless it had been corrected by somebody from Lyon.'

'Who was Uśpiszewski's girlfriend?'

'A young girl, Mlle Marie, who worked in a grocer's shop near "Aux vius sans O", in the rue de Quatre Chemins.'

'Why is it that only the names of Polepa, Orca, Gałęzowski, Iwanow, Licki, and Ćwiatkowski have been put forward as a group?'

'Because they formed an ONR cell (National Radical Camp) and later an ONR, plus Samcja (Post-Piłsudski) cell. Uśpiszewski had joined them.'

'Who was the person from Lyon?'

'Once every week, on Saturdays, the person from Lyon used to come and participate in long discussions with Polepa and a few others.'

'Was the letter in a sealed envelope?'

'Yes. It was.'

'Was it addressed to the Commissaire?'

'It was addressed: 'Monsieur le Commissaire de Police à…'

'Whom did Uśpiszewski hand it to?'

'To the uniformed *agent de police*, François Fontaine, who was sitting at the desk'

'What did François Fontaine do?'

'He opened the envelope and read the letter.'

'And then?'

'He rubbed his neck, and holding the letter stretched his arm towards the plain-clothed *agent de police*, Bertrand Villeneuve.'

'What did Bertrand Villeneuve do?'

'He read the letter and said 'Ça commence…'

'And then?'

"What are you going to do with this?" he asked.'

'What was François Fontaine's answer?'

'I am going to pass it to the chief, *qu'il se débrouille!*'

'What exactly was written in the letter?'

'It advised the police officer that in the Hôtel itself and in Mme Fesanti's Annex there are nine Jews.'

'Was it signed with Uśpiszewski's name?'

'Yes, it was.'

'Was the information correct?'

'According to the Nuremberg criteria, there were twelve Jews in the hostel. According to the criteria of the French variation, the number was six. According to their affiliation to the Jewish religious community, the number was four. According to their belonging to the linguistic Hebrew or Yddish group, there were none.'

'How many people were there altogether in the hostel?'

'About 120.'

'What was the population of Poland, let's say, in 1938?'

'34,000,000'.

'How many of that number were classified as Jews?'

'3,000,000'.

'How did the *Commissaire de Police* react to Uśpiszewski's letter?'

'He asked the chief of the hostel for an explanation.'

'What did the chief of the hostel do?'

'The chief of the hostel declared in writing that according to the law in force in Poland, all the inhabitants of the hostel were Poles.'

'Did this declaration suffice for the police commissaire?'

'It did.'

'Did it suffice for Uśpiszewski?'

'No. He said that the police commissaire was a Jew. And that the chief of the hostel, the former consul Płycki, was a Jew.'

'Could one say of Uśpiszewski that he was a collaborator?'

'No.'

'Why not?'

'He fought the Germans in 1940 in France, and that's where he suffered the wound to his right arm. Besides, there should be no difficulty in imagining him fighting subsequently in the so-called "Mouvement de résistance.'

'In a French one?'

'No, the Polish one.'

'Against the Nazis?'

'Against the Germans. Therefore also against the Nazis, as long as they were Germans.'

'How old was Uśpiszewski at the time of writing the letter?'

'24.'

'How old was Rimbaud when writing his last poem?'

'19.'

'How old was Cervantes when *Don Quixote* was published.'

'1604- 1547 = 57'

'How old was Mozart when he published his first sonata?'

'7.'

'How old was Alexander Chodźko when he took over after Mickiewicz, the chair of Slavic Literature at the Collège de France?'

'54.'

'Is it so, that every day, in every place, some event must be happening?'

'It is.'

'What was happening in Italy, Spain and Portugal between the 5th and the 14th October 1582?'

'Nothing.'

'What was happening in France between the 10th and the 19th of December 1582?'

'Nothing.'

'What was happening in Germany and Holland between the 22nd and the 31st of December 1582?'

'Nothing.'

'What was happening in England between the 3rd and the 13th September 1752?'

'Nothing.'

'Why?'

'In 1582, in Italy, Spain and Portugal, there was then not a single day between the 5th day and the 14th day of October. The same year, there wasn't a single day between the 10th and the 19th of December in France. In Germany and Holland, there was not a single day between the 22nd and the 31st of December. In England, there was not a single day between the 3rd day and the 13th day of September 1752. By virtue of the bull of Gregory XIII of 24 February 1582, the day of the 5th October 1582 was renamed in Italy, Spain and Portugal, October 15th. By virtue of the edict of Henry III, 10th December 1582 became in France, the 20th of December. By virtue of the Act of 1750, the 2nd of September 1752 became in England, the 14th of September.

'How many days and when had those days been dropped from the calendar in Poland?'

'10. In 1586.'

'What is the accuracy of the Gregorian calendar?'

'One day in 4000 years.'

'How long is the life of a baobab?'

'5000 years.'

'What is a dream?'

'Dream is a marvellous invention. When reality is too nightmarish, one escapes into dream.'

'What is reality?'

'Reality is a marvellous invention. When dreams are nightmarish, one escapes into reality.'

'What is death?'

'Death is a marvellous invention. When both, dreams and reality are nightmarish, one escapes into death.'

'What is life?'

'Life is a marvellous invention. When death is nightmarish, all the cells of one's body cling to life.'

'What is a) metaphysics and b) physics?'

'Metaphysics and physics are marvellous inventions. When both life and death are nightmarish, the thoughts of the inhabitants of the Hôtel de la Poste Restante escape into a) metaphysics, or b) physics. In a), they consider in what kind of form the soul will dwell through eternity? In the form of its first young flowering which was man's proper due at the age of 14? Or in the wrinkled form which he assumed after 50? In the form in which he lies dying? Or in that one which thanks to the damage of a bullet might qualify him medically for a 90% invalidity pension? In b), they consider what might be the calorific nutritional value of the human sperm as a supplement to the monotonous diet of the Hôtel de la Poste Restante? Or, is the life of the baobab so much longer because physically, as an organism, it is less complicated?'

'Into what did Uśpiszewski escape? What did he do?'

'He joined Polepa's group.'

'What were Polepa's group promising him?'

'They were promising him a little Jewish shop near Zakroczym.'

'What did Uśpiszewski do before the war?'

'He worked in Co-operative Dairies.'

'Was his intention to return to work in the Co-operative once the war was over?'

'No.'

'Why not?'

'Because the Co-operative Dairies failed to save Poland.'

'Was it Polepa who had explained it to him?'

'No. It was Mlle Marie who worked in the grocery at Quatre Chemins.'

'What were Mlle Marie's plans for the future?'

'To become the proprietress of the grocery at Quatre Chemins.'

'What were Uśpiszewski's plans for the future?'

'To become the proprietor of the grocery near Zakroczym.'

'What would Mlle Marie's and Uśpiszewski's plans sound like in the language of La Fontaine?'

'Perrete, sur sa tête ayant un pot au lait,
Bien posé sur un coussinet,
Prétendait arriver sans encombre à la ville Zakroczym
Légère et court vêtue...'

'What was the name of the Jewish shop near Zakroczym in the language of Polepa?'

'Poland.'

'What was the 'pot au lait' Polepa himself carried on his head?'

'Power.'

'How did he plan to attain it?'

"...through conspiracy and by means of a 'national army' that was to be made ready."

'In France?'

'In France also.'

'Consisting of whom?'

'Of the Uśpiszewskis.'

'And to be prepared how?'

'By means of a duplicator hidden on the 2nd floor in Licki's room.'

'The title?'

'The Eagle on the Amaranths.'

'A sample of its style?'

"As the temporary allies of Russia today, and her potential enemies tomorrow – we must not help her to free herself from the German pincers. The plan is simple: to wait in readiness, fully-armed, till the German foes disable the soviet one, and, themselves worn out and exhausted will fall under the blows of the Anglo-saxons in the West and under ours in the East."

'Some more –?'

"Daydreams, stupid and criminal daydreams, are the political programmes of all those old parties and groups who think of an independent Poland of the future with Russia retaining her present frontiers. Only a Polish Empire could be sovereign. The minimum lands indispensable for life are those between Oder and Dniepr, and between the Baltic Sea and the Danube and the Black Sea."

'Some more –'.

"We have not yet fought the Jews and Moscow, yet here the Jews are being more successfully liquidated by the Germans than they could ever be by anyone else, and especially by us. Nevertheless, it may come to that that the Jews might not only last, but survive as a nation in Poland. How, therefore, should they be treated by us? Since we here are 90% Poles, there can only be one answer, as enemies!"

'And some more?'

"Freemasons have already declared that after the war ends with the victory of those nations with great Jewish and Masonic influences, Poland will not be a national state. For a National Poland, it will be necessary that Mussolini's Italy, and General Franco's Spain, get together and create an alliance of national states, capable of helping one another in their confrontations against countries governed by the Freemasons. Even a year or two after the Germans are pushed aside, the National Camp will be able to overthrow the government by force and take power into their own hands. And whoever has the power and is capable of holding onto it, will find himself in the position of the Piłsudski's Camp of 1918. Unless, the Polish working class, before it even has time to form itself, were to become infected with Marxism."

'Was the 'Eagle on the Amaranths' the only paper published in the Hôtel?'

'No.'

'What was the other?'

'The Poland we'll return to.'

'Was it printed on the same duplicator?'

'No.'

'Where was it printed?'

'A a French stationery shop. 9 frs. 50c. per page, for 500 copies.'

'Was it safe to do this?'

'The only dangerous element was that the same stationery shop supplied the hostel's office with writing materials. And it did happen once or twice that Ćwiartka, who worked in the office, popped in to the shop when the stencil and the copies were visible on the counter. Fortunately, he is shortsighted.'

'Who was connected with the "The Poland we'll return to"?'

'Dr Śliwkowski, Felicki…'

'Who was Felicki?'

'a) inmate in the hostel, b) a second lieutenant, c) tank driver (?) (in Poland, 1939, in France, 1940), d) member of the Sodality of the Blessed Virgin Mary, e) before the war, owner of a motor-coach company in the triangle Płock–Wrocławek–Sierpc, f) height, 182 cm; eyes: blue; parting on the left-hand side.'

'What was Edwin Fuch's opinion of him?'

"… Eh … I like him, he is a good sort, Francis!"

'What was Szczodropacka saying about him?'

'"Felicki is a handsome man."'

'What was General Bliski saying about him?'

'"Felicki should serve as an example for others to follow."'

'Did General Bliski know of Felicki's connection with "The Poland we'll return to"?'

'No.'

'Had he known, would his opinion of him be different?'

'Who knows?'

'What was 'The Poland' Felicki wanted to "return to"?'

'"Henry, for myself I want one thing only. When the war is over, I want to do the same thing I did before. I want to have in my hands that motor-coach business, in the triangle Płock – Włocławek – Sierpc. I love that job, dealing with drivers, luggage, passengers!"'

'"You mean you would like to have that motor-coach company back in your pocket?" said Dr Śliwkowski,'

'"You don't understand a thing." said Felicki'.

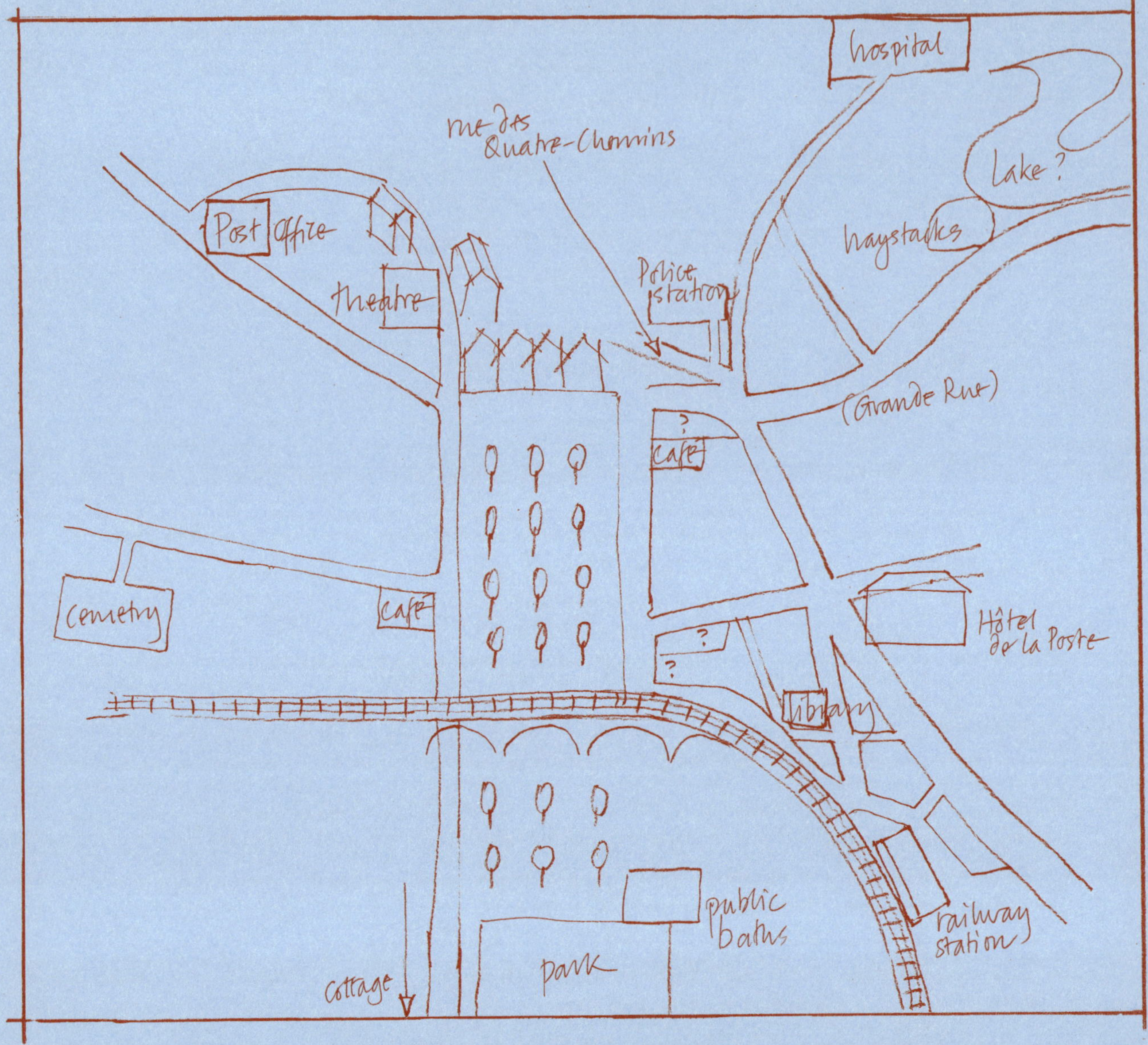

MAP OF VOIRON redrawn after a rough pencil sketch by Stefan, c. 1941. N.W.

There could scarcely be a starker contrast than that between the years of creative freedom of the 1930s – in which the Themersons followed their hunches, hand-in-hand, tripping relatively carefree through the improvised fields of the photogram, experimental film and imaginative books for children – and the dark uncertain years that followed. Almost from the moment they met in 1929/1930, their collaborations were the product of an extraordinarily sensitive creative dialogue in which they had felt immediately both complementary, and in tune with each other. The loss they experienced at their separation in 1940 was palpable. Their way of life was devastated almost overnight, and, like their whole European generation, they were cast onto shifting sands, a world in which nothing was reasonable, nothing remained stable long enough to be recognised. And they were each deprived of the one person with whom it might have felt possible to reason a way out of the chaos. For months they didn't know where, how, or even if the other was living. This is most painfully expressed in Franciszka's long unsent soliloquies, published here for the first time, confessing how lost she feels away from Stefan, and doubting that she'll ever be able to make any art again. Slowly, bit by bit, she claws her way back, recognising how much she has gained from their work together; how much she has discovered for herself about drawing ('I've acquired a special taste for the line'); how much more she has begun to understand, in her solitude, about the human condition. And in a mirror-image we may watch a similar measured reckoning in the words of Stefan's letters and diaries, as he too observes a world in disarray. At one moment, he wonders about what they may have done better during the 1930s – in the way they presented their films to the public, for instance – and at others, urgently remembers the smell of oil paint, the scratch of her pen on paper, and his need to see her at the easel again.

Re-united in London in 1942, they started to rebuild their creative lives, together and independently. Their Polish films had all disappeared during the war, as had any painting Franciszka made in Paris. So had almost all of their family. The sole survivor from their immediate family – Jasia, daughter of Franciszka's sister Maryla Chaykin – was discovered alive in Poland and brought to London to join them in 1946. (Her own remarkable account of war-time years in Warsaw, *Fifteen Journeys, Warsaw to London*, was published by Dalkey Archive Press in 2012.)

The Themersons collaborated on two more films, 1943–1945, for the Polish Film Division in London. And then, in 1948, they founded their Gaberbocchus Press. Over the next 30 years they published a string of titles (many first English editions), highly original in their design, that established the Press as a leading avant-garde imprint in Britain. When they worked together, there is still the same empathetic bond in their choice of subject matter and in the technical strategies they invent to realise it. Harmonious partnerships still came naturally, witness the elegant comic double-act, in word and image, of their *Semantic Divertissements* (1946–1962).

A — a young human being
who practises literary composition
forming a unity in itself
written in a metrical form
rhymed or unrhymed
good or bad
marked by high powers of imagination
& great beauty of language
after being persecuted by his parent (*D*)
who wanted him to become engaged in commercial transactions
those of buying-selling
commodities in bulk
or
quantity -
resigns his claim unto *D*'s inheritance
renders up all that had been his
does off all his garments
& restores them unto *D*.

C — his aunt
performs a swift
hasty act of using her eyesight
with the intention of seeing inside his lower
outer garment.

B — his uncle
who entertains
feelings of
charity &
kindness
towards *A*
turns the globular
bodies
comprising
his organ
of sight
towards the abode
of
a
certain
Sort-Of-R
egularity-
In-Nature.

D — his male parent
who extends some of his (*D*'s) muscles
in order to screen *A* with his palms
knuckles
fingers
& thumbs
& prevent the momentous
combination
of circum-
stances from
being seen by
the outside
world.

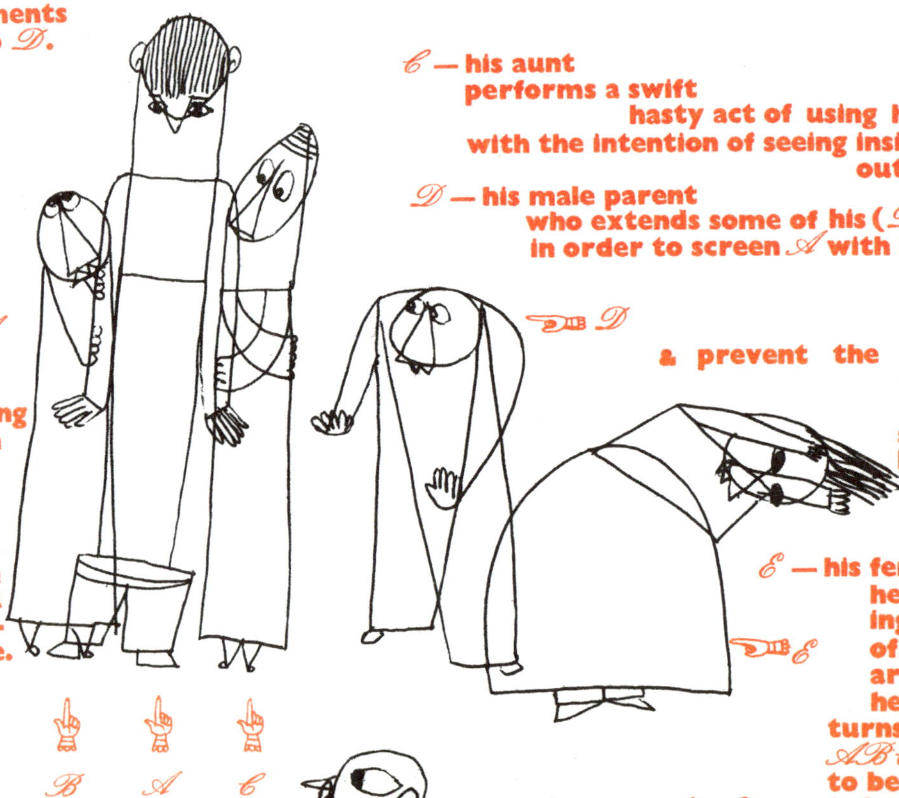

E — his female parent
her brain hav-
ing had enough
of stimuli
arriving from
her eyes
turns her back on
ABCD in order
to be undisturbed
in her entire
absence of hope.

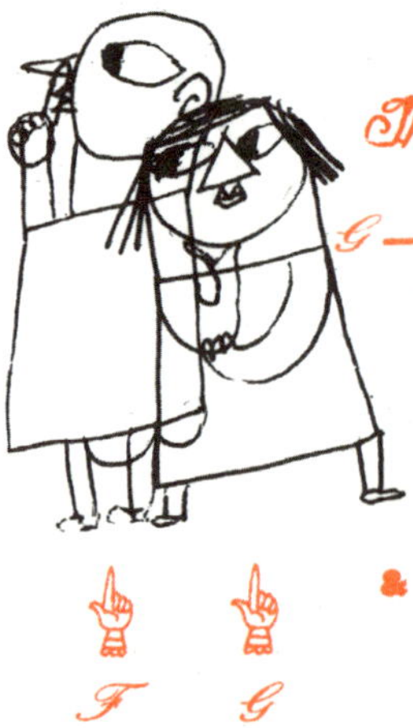

F — his younger brother
struck by the Mystery-Of-
Resigning-
Claims-Unto
-Inheritance
forms an abnormal
mental condition
which will lead him
to become a cardinal.

G — his younger sister
struck by the Mystery-Of
-Doing- Off-
Garments
forms an abnormal
mental condition
which will lead her
to study medicine
& to become a psycho-analyst.

When they work as individuals, a distinction between them became clearer after the war. Perhaps we recognise an independence in each of them that was hardened by their private struggles for survival during the wretched months of separation? It seems most visible in ways that relate to their medium. The increasing sophistication and finely-honed subtlety of Stefan's language contrasts with the emancipation of Franciszka's mature art, which in some later paintings and drawings verges on a primitive urgency and anger, and in others is touched with satire or farce. She also emerged in the 1960s as a highly original theatre designer (Jarry's *Ubu Roi*, Brecht, Aristophanes) and continued to grow in stature as a natural master-illustrator, and an inventive graphic designer. She designed most Gaberbocchus books – celebrated for their original, very different, always apposite appearances – and illustrated many of them.

Stefan wove abstractions, moving freely between media. While common concerns underlie much of his work – nine philosophical novels, an opera and a radio play, his many essays on ethics, aesthetics and language, his Semantic Poetry, his stories for children – it was a matter of principle to him to ignore boundaries and classifications. His writing is also alive with pictures of his ideas, often in words and sometimes literally, in diagrams and drawings.

Their last film in Poland, 1937, was a humoresque entitled *The Adventures of a Good Citizen*. It is the charmed fable of an everyman who overhears by chance that it is possible to walk backwards, and he proceeds to do just that. Carrying a wardrobe, he walks backwards out of the city, escaping from the conventional urban world into an increasingly lyrical nature, pursued all the way by demonstrators whose banners protest that 'Walking backwards is wrong!'. When the film was rediscovered around 1960, Stefan wrote to Poland wondering if it might still seem as subversive as it had in the 1930s. The individual freedom to do and say what you need to do and say, in whatever manner you wish to do and say it, is implicitly at the heart of all the Themersons stood for.

Their ethical position is most clearly encapsulated in Stefan's *The Chair of Decency*, delivered as the 1981 Huizinga Lecture, at Hooglandse Kerk in Leyden. In proposing that all universities should establish a Chair of Decency, he addresses the subject of Aims and Means. He argues that the blinkered pursuit of faiths and causes has deluded us into losing sight of the decent scale of human values with which we are born. Aims are cultural, he says, but the proper Means are biological.

Nick Wadley

St. Francis, page 9 of *Semantic Divertissements*, in which Stefan wrote the texts to Franciszka's drawings made with a biro pen in 1946. Gaberbocchus Press, London, 1962

Several names that appear in Stefan's diaries and in the correspondence cannot be identified at the time of going to press. They are nevertheless included in this list since they feature either in Stefan's diaries or in the correspondence.

Sometimes the Themersons refer to people by their first name and we never learn their surnames. If such a person appears in the text more than once, he or she is included here under the first name.

For the sake of consistency, dates and descriptions are given throughout, even in those entries that are familiar to English-speaking readers.

About names
Themerson – Stefan's father's surname was spelled in this way, with an 'h'. However, many of Stefan's relatives who have the same surname spell it Temerson, e.g. Léon Temerson, Stefan's cousin.

In letters written originally in Polish the correspondees are often addressed in a variety of diminutives, for instance:

Stefan	Stefek, Stefanek, Stefanku (vocative), Stefulek, Stefulku (vocative), Stefcio, Stefciu (vocative), Stef
Franciszka	Franka, Franeczka, Franeczko (vocative), Franuś, Franek
Zofia	Zośka, Zosia, Zocha
Irena	Irka, Irenka
Jan	Jaś, Jasiek, Janek
Eugeniusz	Genek (Cękalski)
Ignacy	Gienek (Złotowski)

Surnames for men and women have different endings:
the wife of Mr Lipski is Mrs Lipska.

Surnames ending in 'owa', mean Mrs:
Themersonowa (the wife of Themerson)

Surnames ending in 'ówna', mean Miss:
Weinlesówna (Miss Weinles),
Żarnowerówna (Miss Żarnower)

Since this Appendix also serves the purpose of an expanded list of contents of the book, it is divided under the following headings:

The Themersons – life before the war

World War II

Franciszka's family in Poland

Franciszka from France to England (chronology)

Franciszka's contacts in England

Franciszka's art & unposted letters

Franciszka, away from work

Franciszka's addresses in London

Stefan's family

Stefan joins Polish Army in France (chronology)

Stefan walks to Paris

Stefan in Paris

Stefan in Vichy France

Stefan is in Voiron from 10 November 1940, arrives in Lisbon 5 August 1942, stays at Pensão Serra, Rua Victor Cordon 192 and arrives in England c. 16 August.

Events

Places

People

Offices, officers & documents

Stefan's writings & projects

When one of Stefan's pieces – be it a poem, a short story, or a linocut – is reproduced in this book, the page(s) in which it appears are followed by a *. All other pages listed contain references to the work in question.

Poems

Prose

Other people's stories from Stefan's diaries

Art

Film

Literature

Music

People & places remembered

Etc – other things they write about

Other places

After 1942

Unposted Letters
Franciszka Themerson & Stefan Themerson

Published by Gaberbocchus & De Harmonie
Postbus 3547, 1001 AH Amsterdam
www.deharmonie.nl
www.gaberbocchus.nl

Edited by Jasia Reichardt
That part of the correspondence which was originally in Polish is now in English. Everything in French has remained in French. The only exceptions are a few of Stefan's Polish poems, and, of course, the scanned originals.

Drawings on bookmark are by Franciszka Themerson: drawing of Stefan and self-portrait drawing, both c. 1942

Designed by Pedro Cid Proença
Printed by Lecturis, Eindhoven, NL

ISBN 978-90-76168-76-0

De Harmonie-Amsterdam Gaberbocchus-London

Warmest thanks go to all those who have aided and abetted in the realisation of this large and complicated book.

The first person to undertake the difficult task of deciphering and translating the Themerson correspondence was Małgosia Sady. She couldn't have anticipated the extent of work that lay ahead. The process of making sense of this material continued over many years as the texts were typed checked and corrected and many visitors to the Themerson archive were asked to spare the time to examine the manuscripts with a magnifying glass. We are grateful to the writer, publisher and translator, Nina Karsov, familiar with aspects of Polish history, for tirelessly providing background information and checking the completed typescript, to Maja Żeglin for spending days on making scans of the letters and diaries. Anne Jenkins for copy editing. Pedro Cid Proença, who became interested in the Themersons at the RCA, for his attention to detail and inventing the sort of imaginative design of the book, that the Themersons themselves would have been proud of. To Jaco and Elisabeth Groot, who discovered the Themersons in 1965 and have ever since devoted energy and resources in support of Gaberbocchus Press, for their open-handed undertaking to publish this book. And finally, to Nick Wadley, who was an intimate friend of the Themersons and whose familiarity with their work has made an invaluable contribution to every aspect of the book.

Jasia Reichardt

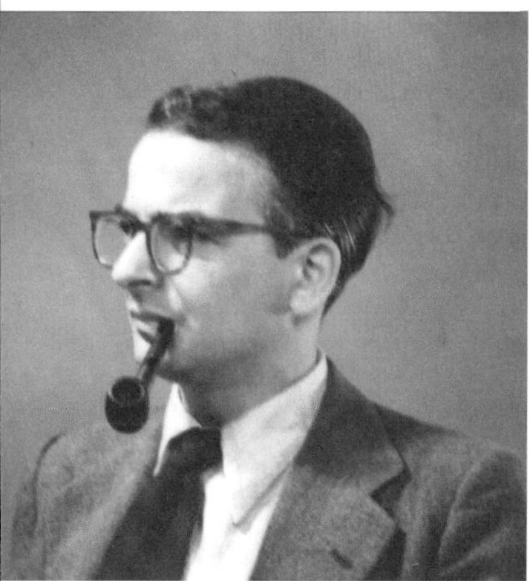